CAMBRIDGE LIBRAR

Books of enduring sch

CW01525359

Histor

The books reissued in this series include accou
movements by eye-witnesses and contemporaries, as well as landmark...
assembled significant source materials or developed new historiographical methods.
The series includes work in social, political and military history on a wide range of
periods and regions, giving modern scholars ready access to influential publications
of the past.

The British Navy

Sir Thomas Brassey (1836–1918), later Earl Brassey, was a politician with a
particular interest in maritime affairs. He was a keen sailor, and his wife's accounts
of their many voyages (also reissued in this series) were bestsellers. He subsequently
became a Lord of the Admiralty and Lord Warden of the Cinque Ports, and *Brassey's
Naval Annual* was for many years the authoritative survey of worldwide navies. This
five-volume survey of the state of the British Navy was published between 1882 and
1883. Brassey was much involved with questions of the modernisation and reform
of the Navy, at a time when international relations were marked by a maritime arms
race. The books provide much technical detail about the different types of ship and
weapons available to the Navy. Volume 1 surveys the development of armoured
ships and mastless ships.

Cambridge University Press has long been a pioneer in the reissuing of out-of-print titles from its own backlist, producing digital reprints of books that are still sought after by scholars and students but could not be reprinted economically using traditional technology. The Cambridge Library Collection extends this activity to a wider range of books which are still of importance to researchers and professionals, either for the source material they contain, or as landmarks in the history of their academic discipline.

Drawing from the world-renowned collections in the Cambridge University Library, and guided by the advice of experts in each subject area, Cambridge University Press is using state-of-the-art scanning machines in its own Printing House to capture the content of each book selected for inclusion. The files are processed to give a consistently clear, crisp image, and the books finished to the high quality standard for which the Press is recognised around the world. The latest print-on-demand technology ensures that the books will remain available indefinitely, and that orders for single or multiple copies can quickly be supplied.

The Cambridge Library Collection will bring back to life books of enduring scholarly value (including out-of-copyright works originally issued by other publishers) across a wide range of disciplines in the humanities and social sciences and in science and technology.

The British Navy

Its Strength, Resources, and Administration

VOLUME 1

THOMAS BRASSEY

CAMBRIDGE UNIVERSITY PRESS

Cambridge, New York, Melbourne, Madrid, Cape Town, Singapore,
São Paolo, Delhi, Dubai, Tokyo, Mexico City

Published in the United States of America by Cambridge University Press, New York

www.cambridge.org
Information on this title: www.cambridge.org/9781108024655

© in this compilation Cambridge University Press 2010

This edition first published 1882
This digitally printed version 2010

ISBN 978-1-108-02465-5 Paperback

THE BRITISH NAVY.

VOL. I.

AFTER E.W COOKE, R.A.

H.M.S. DEVASTATION.

HANHART IMP.

THE BRITISH NAVY:

ITS STRENGTH, RESOURCES, AND

ADMINISTRATION

BY

SIR THOMAS BRASSEY, K.C.B., M.P., M.A.

AUTHOR OF 'WORK AND WAGES'
'LECTURES ON THE LABOUR QUESTION' 'FOREIGN WORK AND ENGLISH WAGES'
AND 'BRITISH SEAMEN.'

VOLUME I.

PART I.

SHIPBUILDING FOR THE PURPOSES OF WAR.

Monstrum, horrendum, informe, ingens, cui lumen ademptum.

LONDON:

LONGMANS, GREEN, AND CO.

1882.

INTRODUCTION.

SOME EXPLANATION seems to be necessary of the unusual circumstance of the issue of a publication on naval affairs by a member of the Board of Admiralty. The present volumes were far advanced when the compiler had the honour of being invited to join that great department. He was equally reluctant to decline the invitation of the Prime Minister, and to abandon the work in which so much progress had been made. On reflection it appeared the wiser course to complete these volumes in the fitful intervals of leisure from official duty.

It is unnecessary to dwell on the labour and perseverance bestowed on the self-imposed task, which is now approaching its completion. I hail the prospect with a genuine sense of relief. As we reach the middle term of life, and

> Days decrease,
> And autumn grows, autumn in every thing,

it is natural to shrink from undertakings that can only be accomplished by continuous and protracted effort. Through twelve long years the work of this compilation has been going forward. It has been delayed by many interruptions, though interruptions have seldom come from keeping holiday. Those who have had personal experience of the House of Commons will best know how hard it is for a member of that over-worked assembly to keep the attention fixed continuously on a class of subjects, which can come but rarely under the review of Parliament. Frequent, yet uncertain attendances in the division lobby, the work of Committees and Royal Commissions, above all the feverish rush of the national life, as it makes itself felt near the centre and source of its pulsations, are disturbing causes, and difficult indeed it is to resist their influence.

Days and nights which should have been given to rest from other labours, to literary culture, and the kindly offices of friendship, have been devoted to the present work, and no small portion of it has been prepared under conditions far from favourable, in a scanty cabin, six feet square, rocked on the uneasy billows of the open ocean. I could not have persevered if I had not felt it my duty to bring to completion the enterprise on which I had embarked. The sea has been a passion with me from my boyhood ; but it has only been in later life, and by a chain of circumstances apparently fortuitous, that the disappointed memories of long vacations spent afloat, which should have been occupied with methodical study, have been partially soothed by the hope, in which I try to indulge, that my nautical experiences have been applied not altogether in vain to the service of my country.

Twenty years ago I was a candidate for the representation of Birkenhead. Rejected at Birkenhead I went to Devonport, from Devonport to Deal, from Deal to Hastings. Every electioneering speech that I have delivered has been spoken by the sea-shore, and has been largely occupied with maritime affairs. Having at last been elected by my present indulgent constituents, I soon found myself engaged on questions of the same class. The Naval Reserves, the abolition of the separate navigating line, the education and training of officers and seamen, the shipbuilding policy of the Navy, dockyard administration, the organisation of the Admiralty, the legislation relating to merchant shipping, marine insurance, the abolition of compulsory pilotage, the amelioration of the condition of merchant seamen, and other cognate subjects, have formed a circumscribed but congenial sphere of labour.

An economical and efficient administration of the Navy depends not only on the adoption of sound general principles, but on the skilful application of those principles to the details of a vast and complex system. The service, both in its naval and its civil departments, must be kept up to the mark by active and searching parliamentary criticism. Practical experience at sea is valuable, in so far as it enables those who have had it to follow the arguments and to enter into the views of the sea officers to whom the country looks for guidance. Even the voyages of an amateur are useful for the lessons they teach in hydrography and meteorology, and for the opportunities they give of acquiring a personal knowledge of the maritime resources of the country. Frequent cruises on the coasts of the United Kingdom would suggest to an observant yachtsman the policy of enrolling the fishermen as a second-class reserve, and would show the necessity of erecting drill batteries in those sea-ports whence the fisheries are carried on with the greatest activity. Voyages across the North Atlantic in small -vessels afford experience of the tempestuous weather that grain- and timber-laden ships must be prepared to encounter. After navigating in the contracted waters of the Sea of Marmora and the Gulf of Suez, the importance must be more keenly felt of a flotilla of vessels with superior evolutionary qualities. A knowledge of the estuaries and harbours of the eastern seaboard of North America would show the disadvantage of great draught of water to any squadron intended to operate on those coasts.

The present writer may be pardoned for referring to these details, in reviewing, for the first time and the last, his labours as an independent member in connection with naval and maritime affairs. Few men have entered the House of

Commons with a more slender share of what are usually described as parliamentary talents than the humble individual who writes the present introduction; and if, by devotion to special subjects, he has gained the confidence of the public, his experience may perhaps encourage others, conscious as he is of inability to influence public opinion on the greater questions of the day, but who may yet do excellent, nay indispensable, work by taking up a congenial subject outside the general line of politics. Unity and fixity of purpose, combined with patience and application, will slowly win the ear of the public and secure their grateful appreciation. The career of the leading statesman is more distinguished; the part of the orator is more brilliant; but statesmen and orators could not do their work without the aid of subordinates who are content to do the drudgery of special departments, forgotten it may be by the public except when a catastrophe occurs, but duly recognised by those who are responsible for the good government of the country.

We live in an active age. We are citizens of a wide empire, with manifold and complicated interests. The temptation is strong to dissipate our strength in the vain attempt to grapple with too many questions. Let us take to ourselves the wise admonition of Sir Cornewall Lewis: 'Men of encyclopædical minds are not always perspicuous or precise, still less often are they original or inventive.' 'Multum legere, non multa,' is a good maxim for all who desire to extend the bounds of a science, or to be sound practitioners in any art or profession.

Under our free popular constitution there is a place for every man who is resolved to do his duty—

Æquâ lege necessitas
Sortitur insignes et imos.

Shakspeare has compared the state of man in civil and political society to the diligent and well-regulated existence of the honey bees,

> Creatures that by a rule in nature teach
> The act of order to a peopled kingdom.

The compiler, in seeking for a parallel in the numerous orders and conditions established by those intelligent and industrious insects, passes rapidly down from the king, the officers, the magistrates, the merchants, the soldiers, the singing masons, and the civil citizens to

> The poor mechanic porters crowding in
> Their heavy burthens at the narrow gate.

Heavy, indeed, is the burthen of these six volumes, and narrow the circle of readers to whose libraries they will find admittance, but to all who devote themselves to the study of naval affairs, whether as administrators, as sea officers, or as owners of shipping, the present publication provides a collection of information such as it has not been attempted to bring together in any other work.

Passing from these general observations it may be convenient to explain the general scope and arrangement of the volumes included in the present compilation.

The first volume contains descriptions of the most important ironclads and unarmoured vessels, whether in the British or in foreign navies. Sir Edward J. Reed is the leading authority for the earlier types. A considerable quantity of matter has been translated from the excellent work entitled *Die Marine* by Captain von Littrow and Admiral Brommy. The majority of the plates are taken from this source and from a more recent work by Captain von Kronenfels, entitled *Das schwimmende Flotten-Material*. The valuable publications of Baron Grivel, Dislere, and Marchal have been freely used. From the *Navires Cuirassés* of Captain Tromp descriptions and some admirable drawings have been borrowed. Turning to the United States, Mr. King's *War Ships of Europe* has been, by his kind permission, almost incorporated into these volumes ; and much valuable matter has been taken from a work of similar design by

Lieutenant Very, U.S.N. For the vessels of the English Navy the descriptions have been chiefly taken from the able notices which have appeared at intervals in the *Times* and the professional newspapers, including the *Broad Arrow*, the *Army and Navy Gazette*, the *Engineer*, *Engineering*, and other journals. The papers and speeches read and delivered at the Royal United Service Institution have been a mine of wealth, as containing the criticisms and suggestions of some of the best officers of the Navy. To these selections from the writings of others the compiler has added a limited quantity of original matter. If it has no pretension as a literary performance, he ventures to believe that the present publication will be appreciated for its practical utility, as a comprehensive summary of all that has hitherto been published, whether in England or abroad, concerning the most important fighting vessels of modern times. It is intended to supply a want which must have been felt by many who have from time to time been occupied in naval investigations.

The second volume contains papers on armour, armament, torpedoes, torpedo-vessels, and other cognate subjects.

The third volume will, it is hoped, be found convenient and valuable as a collection of opinions on the main subjects of controversy with reference to our shipbuilding policy. The views of naval officers, naval architects, and persons in high administrative positions have been brought together, and it may be said with truth that the selection of matter has been made with strict impartiality, and a sincere desire to furnish to those interested in shipbuilding problems the means of forming a judgment for themselves.

The fourth and fifth volumes contain speeches delivered in Parliament, extra-Parliamentary utterances, and papers contributed to the *Contemporary Review*, and *Macmillan's Magazine*. The writer does not venture to value very highly this portion of his work. It is the accumulated result of assiduous toil and devotion to the great object of his public life—that of improving and perfecting the naval administration of his country.

The sixth and concluding volume is a reprint of a former work on merchant seamen. When Mr. Plimsoll commenced his crusade against the owners of unseaworthy ships, and proposed a rigid system of inspection by the Government, it was alleged that the loss of life was due not so much to defects in the ships as to deterioration in the quality of the seamen. As a member of the Royal Commission on Unseaworthy Ships, the compiler was deeply interested in this question; and subsequent investigations, while suggesting several remedial measures, convinced him that the British seaman of the present time was not so unworthy a successor of the great mariners of olden times as his numerous and not altogether disinterested detractors would have led the public to believe. The concluding chapter, in which the most recent efforts for the benefit of the seaman are sketched out, is from the pen of Mr. F. W. Haine, of the Board of Trade.

These volumes would have presented a certain homogeneity, which they do not now possess, and would at least have assumed a more literary character, if the numerous extracts from the Press and professional periodicals had been paraphrased and condensed by the present writer. It would not have been better writing, but it would have been his own writing. The attempt has not been made, because to have re-written so much would have demanded a large expenditure of time, and yielded no commensurate advantage from a practical point of view. The main object has been to supply correct information; and care has been taken to acknowledge freely the sources whence information has been derived. Our periodical literature on naval subjects is distinguished for the talent, the energy, and the knowledge with which it is conducted. The gratitude of the nation is due to those undesignated and unknown servants of the public, from whose valuable writings these volumes have been compiled;

and if we are much indebted to those who have served us with the pen, how much greater is our obligation to those who have borne the heavy responsibility of creating the fleets of modern days, and administering the affairs of the navy in a time of ceaseless and radical change !

Our earliest ironclads were produced under Sir Baldwin Walker, as Controller, from the designs of Mr. Oliver Lang and Mr. Scott Russell. Their work has been continued and perfected, under the directions of Sir Spencer Robinson and Sir Houston Stewart, by Sir Edward Reed and Mr. Barnaby. The nation will review the labours of those eminent naval architects in a generous temper of mind. It will make allowance for the exaggeration of minute criticisms, inspired by generous rivalry, and it will recognise and gratefully acknowledge the services rendered in the highest professional offices at the Admiralty. The distinguished naval officers who have held the appointment of Controller have had a different and perhaps a higher responsibility. It has been theirs to indicate to the Constructors the line of investigation which they ought to follow, and to formulate the conditions as to speed, armament, armour, and coal-endurance, required in our ships of war. The natural and the appropriate attitude of the naval mind on the subject of construction is neither critical nor inventive. It is the duty of our sea officers to accept without question the instruments of war which are placed in their charge, and to do their utmost to use them with effect. In the office of the Controller the position is reversed, and the lessons of experience should be used to discern and remedy defects, and to introduce into the Navy all the improvements which the progress of science affords. In the discharge of their heavy task, the successive Controllers of the Navy have been untrammelled by the prejudices and traditions derived from their service afloat. They have shown a large capacity for public affairs, and they have worked with a devotion and patriotism worthy of the noble service in which they have been reared. To such men the humble testimony of a Civil Lord of the Admiralty is of small value.

Their praise is hymned by loftier harps than mine,

It has been spoken in the parliamentary discourses of the ablest critics on naval questions in the French Chambers. It has been repeatedly recorded in the official documents of the United States navy. It has been testified to most conclusively in the imitation of our methods and principles in the designs and construction of foreign ships of war.

Having paid a well-merited tribute of praise to the sea officers and civilians in the service of the Admiralty, we must not be unmindful of the benefit we derive from the enterprise and ingenuity applied to naval construction in the private shipyards of the country. In these noble establishments we possess inexhaustible resources for the repair and construction of fleets.

It would be unjust not to render the honour which is their due to the distinguished statesmen who have filled the office of First Lord of the Admiralty. During my career in Parliament I have had an opportunity of forming a judgment of the policy which has been pursued ; and, claiming to be above the prejudices of political partisanship in dealing with naval affairs, I give my cordial testimony to the services which Messrs. Corry, Childers, Goschen, Ward Hunt, and W. H. Smith have in succession rendered to the British navy. It is my privilege to serve under a First Lord of the Admiralty who is worthy to follow a long line of strong and able administrators.

I have thought it my duty to avoid invidious comparisons of our fleets with the naval forces of other nations. Our position as a maritime power cannot be called in question by dispassionate minds. It rests on a broader foundation than the number of our armoured vessels. We are perfectly able to protect ourselves at sea, if we choose to do so. To the doleful imaginations of the author of *The Battle of Dorking* and the writers who have more recently addressed the British public in the same strain, we may oppose the more deliberate and the more favourable estimate of our strength formed by foreigners, who write *en connaissance de cause*. M. Xavier Raymond and Admiral Baron Grivel are writers of acknowledged authority on naval questions. Their views are the more favourable, because they look not so much to the fluctuating circumstances of the moment as to the elastic and permanent sources of naval strength.

In his *Essay on the Naval History of France and England from* 1815 *to* 1863, M. Xavier Raymond observes: 'Naval power depends upon three things, each of which is indispensable to the vitality, so to speak, of the navy. These three things are material wealth, an active and progressive industry, and lastly, a hardy and enterprising seafaring population The third element of strength can only exist where the merchant navy is flourishing and vigorous. Naval power, therefore, is a multiple of three sources of strength, and if any one of these is deficient the entire organisation becomes imperfect and feeble.

'What was accomplished by the Navy of Louis XIV. when he increased his naval armaments beyond his resources? Was the Emperor Napoleon, with his eighty line-of-battle ships, able to win a single victory over the fleets of England? Of what avail to Russia were her naval resources, in the creation of which so much pains had been bestowed? They melted away in the war of 1854–56 without firing a single shot.

'Setting aside the 80,000 men actually serving in the fleet, the Merchant Navy of England gives employment to at least 230,000 men in the foreign trade; and if the seafaring population were subjected to the regulations enforced under the French maritime inscription—the coasting trade, the fisheries, the boatmen, and the men employed in the ship-yards would supply a combined force of 700,000 to 800,000 men.

'This large seafaring population is not less remarkable for its physical qualities and its nautical skill, than the formidable numbers which can be brought into array. If the Admiralty may have made mistakes, we must not allow ourselves to suppose that the English have lost their intuitive genius in naval affairs. Their maritime enterprise is conducted at the present time with an energy and a talent worthy the traditions and the achievements of former days, and which may even be said to have taken a development in our own time on a grander scale than at any former period.

'Nautical enterprise is the peculiar and appropriate sphere of the English nation. It is the natural goal or aim, to which their highest and noblest efforts of patriotism are directed. The superiority which England has secured, in her financial resources, in her great facilities for shipbuilding, and in the numbers of her seafaring population, is in our judgment an element of small importance compared with the moral power which she has acquired, as the freest and the most united nation in the world.'

Baron Grivel, in his *Mission Militaire et Nouveau Programme de la Flotte*, writes in a similar vein :—'There are certain great truths which cannot be engraven too deeply on the memory. The first is that no human power, no effort of genius, however great, can suddenly undermine the bulwarks of a firmly established naval supremacy. Naval power is a plant of slow growth, and is rooted in the manners, in the occupations, in the geographical position of a nation. It is the ripe fruit of its wealth, its perseverance, its sustained wisdom, and its good and efficient system of government. The administration of the Navy is a work requiring forethought and sagacity, and above all, time is required to organise it on a stable and enduring plan.

'With these considerations in view, it cannot be denied that by her insular position, her numerous harbours, her deep and navigable rivers, Great Britain, from the earliest ages, was destined by the Creator to play that great part as a maritime power which we see her fill in every part of the globe. She is strong in the advantages of geographical position, and she is rich in inexhaustible mines of iron and coal. Her people are a proud race of men, endowed with rare vigour of mind and body, and her Government has known how to combine the powerful qualities of an aristocracy with a wise disposition to accept essential reforms. In this combination of natural advantages we must recognise something more than the mere result of chance. It is, indeed, a creation of Providence.'

On a general and dispassionate review of our position, we are led to the conclusion that the naval power of England, in all the vital elements of strength, is greater now than in any former age. Our maritime influence is commanding and universal : and it is gladly and generously acknowledged, because it has been used with magnanimity, and in the cause of Freedom.

OUTLINE

OF

THE PLAN OF THE BOOK.

———•◦•———

THE question as to the best design for each of the several classes of ships of war became the subject of serious discussion, as soon as it was admitted that steam propulsion had come to be a necessity of fighting navies. Up to that time the divisions of the floating material of fleets had remained practically unaltered for more than two centuries. The introduction of steam resulted in frequent departures—more or less wide—from old designs. The question has of late years been greatly complicated, and the difficulty of its solution has increased, as the practice of making use of defensive armour has extended, and the destructive effect of naval ordnance has been augmented. It is proposed in the present work to give an account of the different methods which naval architects have pursued in their more recent constructions, with the object of producing in each section of a fleet efficient and, as far as possible, perfect fighting ships. We shall pass in review the several types of vessel completed or laid down within the last few years by our own and foreign Governments, noting the advance that has been made from earlier plans. Having described the most important examples of armoured and unarmoured ships, it is intended to bring together the recorded opinions of the most eminent authorities, naval officers, and naval constructors, as to the qualities most to be desired in the several classes of ships. The evidence obtained will be summed up, so that it will be possible to decide to which side the balance of testimony in each case appears to incline. In order to accomplish the task which has been undertaken, it will be necessary to make this work consist to a great extent of figures and statements of fact. These will be taken from the writings of the highest professional authorities, and from published official or other authentic sources. The opinions which will be quoted will be chiefly those tendered by eminent witnesses under circumstances imposing a due sense of responsibility.

A review of recent naval construction will be best carried out by giving descriptions, more or less detailed, of the most important representatives of the various classes of ships to be found in our own and in foreign navies. An examination of the condition to which the latter have been brought will exhibit the influence that the existence of a particular type in a foreign fleet is likely to exert upon the efficiency of our own, and will serve to show the standard of strength at which the British Navy should be maintained. It will also enable us to trace the development of that remarkable process of transformation which has culminated in the mastless turret-ship and the mastless *barbette* ship, as the supreme embodiment of fighting power in the fleets of the present epoch.

The lines laid down in their work *Die Marine* by Vice-Admiral Rudolf Brommy and Captain Heinrich von Littrow will be in general followed. In the first part of the book an endeavour will be made to deal with the following subjects:— the classification of modern ships of war; the qualities to be desired in the several types, and the distinctive features of armoured and unarmoured vessels. Special chapters will be devoted to the earlier ironclads and floating batteries; the progress of armoured shipbuilding in France in the period 1861–73, and in England prior to 1868; English converted ships; Sir E. Reed's system; and to Italian, German, Russian, Austrian, and other armoured vessels built between 1861 and 1873. The monitors and early armoured craft for harbour defence, coast-service, and service in rivers, later examples of the same classes, special types, such as armoured cruisers and the Austrian ' bow-battery' ships, the later central battery ships, and seagoing turret and *barbette* ships, both mastless and masted, will be successively described. These descriptions will be followed by a chapter devoted to the unarmoured vessels of the chief navies of the world. A special section of the work will be occupied with the consideration of miscellaneous subjects, including armour and armour-experiments, guns and gunnery, torpedoes and torpedo-boats, and similar matters of naval interest. The strength and resources of the principal maritime Powers will be examined, and tables will be added containing details as to British and foreign ships and guns.

These subjects will complete the first two volumes. The remaining portion of the work will be occupied with an examination of the opinions on designs of ships of war expressed by British and foreign authorities, and with various other subjects of a naval character.

CONTENTS

OF

THE FIRST VOLUME.

———◦◦◦———

PART I.

ARMOURED AND UNARMOURED SHIPS.

———

HISTORICAL SKETCH.

	PAGE
Introduction of shell-guns	3
Crimean batteries. Batteries at Siege of Gibraltar	4
' La Gloire,' ' Invincible,' ' Normandie,' ' Couronne '	5
' Warrior,' ' Defence,' ' Resistance '	6
' Achilles ' ' Minatour,' Converted ships	7
' Magenta,' ' Solferino,' ' Océan,' ' Marengo,' 'Suffren,' ' Friedland '	7, 8
' Flandre ' type	8
Sir Edward Reed's designs	8
' Alexandra'	10
'Téméraire '	11
'Richelieu,' 'Colbert,' ' Trident'	12
French programme of 1872	12
' Redoutable '	13
' Dévastation,' ' Foudroyant '	14
' Kaiser,' 'Deutschland '	14
Coast-service ships	15
' Monarch,' 'Captain '	16
Coast-service monitors and rams	17
Committee on designs	19
' Devastation '	20
'Thunderer,' ' Dreadnought'	21
French coast-service vessels	21
German masted turret-ships	22
'Neptune'	22
French ' Alma ' class	23
Baron Grivel on barbette guns	24
Modifications in French programme of 1872	25
Belted cruisers	26
' Inflexible'	27
' Amiral Duperré '	28
Later French second-class ironclads	30
French floating batteries and rams	31
German coast-service vessels	32

CHAPTER I.

OUR NAVAL REQUIREMENTS IN WAR.

PAGE

Views of Admiral Jurien de la Graviere and Captain Colomb . . . 33
Objects of our naval policy 33
Views of authors of essays on development of our maritime power . . 33
Views of Sir Howard Douglas 34
Growth of the trade of the United Kingdom . . . , . . 34
Comparison of British and foreign tonnage 35
Dependence on foreign trade 35
Increase of our shipping trade . . . . . , . . 36

CHAPTER II.

CLASSIFICATION OF SHIPS OF WAR.

Recent naval construction reviewed 37
New British nomenclature 40
Sir George Elliott; essentials of a ship of war 41
Views of Señor Heriz 42

CHAPTER III.

EARLIEST IRONCLADS.

Kinburn batteries 43
Batteries démontables 44
The 'Gloire' 45

CHAPTER IV.

PROGRESS OF ARMOURED SHIPBUILDING IN FRANCE, 1861–73.

'Magenta' and 'Solferino' 48
'Belliqueuse' 49
'Alma' class 50
'Océan' 51
'Richelieu' 53
'Colbert' and 'Trident' 55

CHAPTER V.

EARLY ARMOURED CONSTRUCTION IN ENGLAND.

'Warrior' and 'Black Prince' 58
'Defence' and 'Resistance' 64
'Valiant' and 'Hector' 64
'Minotaur' 65
'Achilles' 69

CHAPTER VI.

CONVERTED SHIPS.

PAGE

Converted ships 76
'Lord Warden' 78
'Repulse' 79
Lord Clarence Paget: statements in Parliament 80

CHAPTER VII.

SIR E. J. REED'S SYSTEM; SHIPS BUILT FROM HIS DESIGNS.

Sir E. J. Reed's system 82
'Enterprise' 85
'Bellerophon' 86
'Pallas' 89
'Penelope' 91
'Viper' and 'Vixen' 92
'Waterwitch' 93
'Hercules' 94
'Audacious' class 100
'Triumph' 107
'Sultan' 108

CHAPTER VIII.

IRONCLADS BUILT FOR THE AUSTRIAN, GERMAN, ITALIAN, TURKISH, RUSSIAN, AND SPANISH NAVIES, 1862–73.

Turkish ironclads 111
Austrian ironclads 116
'König Wilhelm' 119
'Numancia' 121
'Vitoria' and 'Sagunto' 122
'Sevastopol,' 'Petropaulski,' 'Kreml' 123
'Pervenec,' 'Netronmenja' 124
Italian central-battery ships 125

CHAPTER IX.

MONITORS AND EARLIER ARMOURED VESSELS FOR COAST SERVICE.

First American monitors 129
Monitors for river service 131
'Dictator' and 'Puritan' 134
'Miantonomoh' 136
Enlarged monitors 140
'Rochambeau' 143
'Scorpion' and 'Wyvern' 146
'Rolf Krake' 146
'Affondatore' 147
Dutch turret-ships 148
'Huascar' 153
Brazilian ironclads 154

PAGE

Russian monitors 157
Russian seagoing turret-ships 158
'Royal Sovereign'. 160

CHAPTER X.

COAST-SERVICE VESSELS OF MORE RECENT TYPE, AND EARLIER MASTLESS IRONCLADS.

'Taureau' 165
'Bélier' class 165
'Arrogante' 167
'Tonnerre' 168
French second-class coast-defence vessels 172
'Terrible' 173
'Cerberus,' 'Magdala,' 'Abyssinia' 174
'Hotspur'. 174
'Glatton' 176
'Cyclops' 179
'Rupert' 181
'Belleisle' and 'Orion' 182
Popoffkas 184
'Livadia' 194
Brazilian armoured vessels for river service 204
Argentine monitors 207
Dutch armoured batteries 210
'Wespe' class 211
Armoured gunboats for the Rhine 217

CHAPTER XI.

ARMOURED CRUISERS.

'Hansa' 218
'Victorieuse' 219
'Duguesclin' 222
Belted cruisers: 'Minin' 226
'General-Admiral' 227
'Shannon'. 229
'Nelson' and 'Northampton' 236
'Almirante-Cochrane' and 'Blanco-Encalada' 252
Japanese ironclad cruisers 255
Austrian converted ironclads 258
'Vasco de Gama' 260
'King George' 262
Mr. Trevelyan: Navy estimates, 1881 263
'Impérieuse' and 'Warspite' 265

CHAPTER XII.

BOW-BATTERY SHIPS.

'Archduke Albert' 267
'Custozza'. 270

CHAPTER XIII.

CENTRAL BATTERY SHIPS.

		PAGE
'Alexandra'		273
'Téméraire'		283
'Kaiser' and 'Deutschland'		295
'Superb'		299
'Redoutable'		300
'Dévastation'		304
'Amiral Duperré'		308
'Amiral Baudin,' and 'Formidable'		315
'Tegethoff'		316
'Almirante Brown'		323

CHAPTER XIV.

MASTED TURRET-SHIPS.

'Monarch'		326
'Captain'		327
German masted turret-ships		329
'Neptune'		335

CHAPTER XV.

MASTLESS TURRET-SHIPS.

'Devastation': Mr. Barnaby		343
„ Sir Spencer Robinson		344
„ Mr. King's description		344
„ Remarks of M. Dislère		355
„ Sir Edward Reed		356
Dimensions of 'Devastation'		358
'Peter the Great'		360
'Thunderer'		364
Hydraulic loading gear		366
'Dreadnought'		373
Remarks of Mr. King		384
M. Dislère		386
'Inflexible'		387
Descriptions: Mr. Barnaby		388
„ Mr. King		390
Observation of *Nautical Magazine*		395
Experiments on armour: Colonel Inglis		395
Experiments at Shoeburyness, 1880		397
Turrets		398
Trials		401
Machinery		403
Rig		407
'Inflexible' and 'Duilio'		409
Criticisms of Sir Edward Reed		410
Enquiry by Committee		410
Observations on Report of Committee		426
M. Dislère on 'Inflexible'		428
Torpedo Appliances		428

PAGE

'Ajax' and 'Agamemnon' 430
'Colossus' and 'Majestic' 438
'Conqueror' 445
'Duilio' and 'Dandolo' 448

CHAPTER XVI.

MASTLESS *BARBETTE* SHIPS.

'Sachsen' class 455
'Italia' and 'Lepanto' 459
Remarks of M. Dislère 466
Description in *Standard* 467
Criticisms of Sir Edward Reed 468
'Helgoland' 469
'Collingwood'. 469
  Polyphemus' 472

CHAPTER XVII.

UNARMOURED CRUISERS AND SPECIAL VESSELS OF THE CHIEF NAVAL POWERS.

U.S. 'Wampanoag' 477
'Inconstant' 478
'Active' and 'Volage' 479
'Shah' 479
'Raleigh' 482
'Boadicea'. 486
'Bacchante' 488
'Euryalus' 491
'Iris' 491
'Mercury' 500
'Leander' class 505
'Rover' 506
C. and Gem classes 507
English sloops 511
Gun-vessels. 512
'Duquesne' and 'Tourville' 516
'Duguay-Trouin' 519
'Villars' 521
Third-class cruisers 422
Gun-vessels 523
German 'Leipzig' class 525
'Bismarck' class 528
German third-class vessels 529
Italian despatch-vessels 530
Russian clipper fleet 532
U.S. 'Trenton' 540
U.S. 'Vandalia' 542
Chinese Armstrong gunboats 547
Tables of Ships, British and Foreign 549

INDEX 607

LIST OF ILLUSTRATIONS

TO

THE FIRST VOLUME.

———◆———

'DEVASTATION.' By Ch. E. de Martino, after E. W. Cooke, R.A. *Frontispiece*

'WARRIOR.' After original sketches by Ch. E. de Martino . *To face page* 6

'AGINCOURT' . . . . ,, 65

'BELLEROPHON' . . . . ,, 88

'HERCULES' . . . . ,, 96

'IRON DUKE' . . . . ,, 104

'TONNERRE' (French) . . . . . . ,, 170

'GLATTON' . . . . ,, 176

'CYCLOPS' . . . . ,, 179

'BELLE ISLE' . . . . ,, 182

'NELSON'. . . . . ,, 236

'CUSTOZZA' (Austrian) . . . . . ,, 266

'ALEXANDRA' . . . . ,, 273

'TÉMÉRAIRE'. . . . . ,, 284

'KAISER' (German) . . . . . . ,, 295

'DÉVASTATION' (French) . . . . . ,, 306

'AMIRAL DUPERRÉ' (French) . . . . ,, 310

'PREUSSEN' (German) . . . . . ,, 328

'INFLEXIBLE' . . . . ,, 387

'DUILIO' (Italian) . . . . . . ,, 448

'SACHSEN' (German) . . . . . . ,, 455

'ITALIA' (Italian) . . . . . . ,, 459

'HELGOLAND' (Danish) . . . . . ,, 469

'COLLINGWOOD' . . . . . . ,, 470

Chinese Gun-vessel . . . . . . ,, 548

PLATE

I. 'Warrior'—'Minotaur'—'Bellerophon'—'Hercules'—
    'Penelope'—'Enterprise'—'Collingwood'   .   .

II. 'Sultan'—'Superb'—'Alexandra'—'Téméraire'   .   .

III. 'Téméraire's' guns—'Audacious'—'Shannon'—'Nelson'.

IV. 'Captain'—'Monarch'—'Neptune'—'Preussen'   .   .

V. 'Devastation'—'Dreadnought'   .   .   .   .

VI. 'Cyclops'—'Glatton'—'Hotspur'—'Rupert'.   .   .

VII. 'Inflexible'   .   .   .   .   .   .

VIII. 'Gloire'—'Magenta'—'Alma'—'Richelieu'—'Océan'

IX. 'Dévastation'—'Amiral Duperré'—'Duguesclin'.   .

X. 'Cerbère'—'König Wilhelm'—'Kaiser'   .   .   .

XI. Armoured Gunboat—Armoured River Gunboat—Angle port of
     H.M.S. 'Hercules'   .   .   .   .   .

XII. New Armoured Cruisers   .   .   .   .   .

XIII. 'Conqueror'   .   .   .   .   .   .

XIV. Italia and Duilio .   .   .   .   .   .

These plans to be bound together in numerical order at end of Volume I.

CORRIGENDA.

Page   5, line 12, *for* Etna *read* Erebus

  „   25, „   5 from bottom, *for* Montauban *read* Mont-calm

  „   29, „   1, *for* extend, *read* not extend

  „   85, „   4, *for* five wooden, *read* fine wooden

LIST OF AUTHORITIES

FOR

DESCRIPTIONS AND ILLUSTRATIONS.

NOTE.

Das Schw. is a contraction for *Das Schwimmende Flotten-Material* by Captain von Kronenfels.
La Marine for *La Marine à l'Exposition Universelle de* 1878.
Die Marine for the work published under that name by Littrow and Von Brommy.
The names of King, Very, Heriz, White, refer to their respective works on Naval Architecture.

CHAPTER III.

EARLIEST IRONCLADS.

Ships	Figures	Descriptions	Illustrations
Thunderbolt . . . ⎫ Erebus . . . ⎬ Terror . . . ⎭ Kinburn batteries .	1	*Die Marine*	
Palestro . . . ⎫ Arrogante . . . ⎬ Embuscade . . . ⎭	—	*Die Marine*	
Batteries démontables .	—	Heriz	
Gloire . . .	2, 3	Kronenfels . . .	*Das Schw.* Holley

CHAPTER IV.

PROGRESS OF ARMOURED SHIP BUILDING IN FRANCE, 1861–1873.

Ships	Figures	Descriptions	Illustrations
Normandie . . . ⎫ Invincible . . . ⎭	—	Dislère	
Magenta . . . ⎫ Solferino . . . ⎭	4	Dislère	Dislère
Provence, and nine sister ships . .		Dislère	
Belliqueuse . .	5	*Die Marine* . . .	*Die Marine*
Alma class . . .	6	Kronenfels . . .	*Die Marine*
Océan . . . ⎫ Marengo . . . ⎬ Suffren . . . ⎭	7, 8, 9, 10	*La Marine* . . .	*Das Schw.*

Ships	Figures	Descriptions	Illustrations
Friedland . . .	—	*La Marine*	
Richelieu . . .	11	*La Marine* . . .	*Das Schw.*
Trident . . .	12, 12a	*La Marine* . . .	Very
Colbert . . .	13	Kronenfels . . .	Very

CHAPTER V.

EARLY ARMOURED CONSTRUCTION IN ENGLAND.

Ships	Figures	Descriptions	Illustrations
Warrior . . . Black Prince . .}	14, 15	Scott Russell . . . Fairbairn . . . Barnaby . . . Elgar . . .	*Das Schw.* Fairbairn
Defence . . . Resistance . . .}	16	*Times* . . . Barnaby . . . Spencer Robinson .	*Das Schw.*
Hector . . . Valiant . . .}	17	*Times*	*Das Schw.*
Minotaur . . . Agincourt . . . Northumberland .}	18	*Times* . . . Rear-Admiral Scott .}	*Die Marine*
Achilles . . .	19	*Times*	*Das Schw.*

CHAPTER VI.

CONVERTED SHIPS.

Ships	Figures	Descriptions	Illustrations
Lord Clyde . .	20	—	*Das Schw.*
Royal Oak . . . Zealous . . . Prince Consort . . Ocean . . . Caledonia . . . Royal Alfred . . Repulse . . .}	21	Lord Clarence Paget . . *Times* . . . Scott Russell . .}	*Das Schw.*

CHAPTER VII.

SIR E. J. REED'S SYSTEM. SHIPS BUILT FROM HIS DESIGNS.

Ships	Figures	Descriptions	Illustrations
Bracket frame . . Construction .}	22	Fairbairn . . . Elgar . . .}	*Das Schw.*
Enterprise . . .	23	Reed	*Das Schw.*
Bellerophon . .	24	*Times* Scott	

Ships	Figures	Descriptions	Illustrations
Pallas . . .	25	*Times*	Very
Penelope . . .	26, 27	*Art Naval*	
Viper		*Times*	
Vixen	—		
Waterwitch . .	—	Chief Engineer King, U.S.N.	
Hercules . . .	28, 29	Captain Noel, R.N. . .	
		Die Marine . . .	
		Times	
		Art Naval	
		King, U.S.N. . . .	*Das Schw.*
		Barnaby	
		Reed . . .	
		Spencer Robinson . .	
		Armstrong . . .	
Audacious . . .	30, 31, 32	*Die Marine* . . .	
		King, U.S.N. . . .	
		Barnaby	*Das Schw.*
		Spencer Robinson . .	
		Rear-Admiral Scott . .	
Sultan . . .	33, 34	Barnaby	
		Rear-Admiral Scott . .	*Das Schw.*
		Times	

CHAPTER VIII.

AUSTRIAN, GERMAN, ITALIAN, TURKISH, RUSSIAN AND SPANISH ARMOURED SHIPS, 1862-73.

The descriptions of ships in this chapter are compiled from *Die Marine*, the Marine Almanac, published at Pola, the *Carnet de l'Officier de Marine*, and the works published by Chief Engineer King and Lieutenant Very of the United States Navy. All the illustrations, and a considerable portion of the descriptive matter, are taken from *Das Schwimmende Flotten-Material* by Captain von Kronenfels of the Austrian Navy.

CHAPTER IX.

MONITORS AND EARLIEST ARMOURED VESSELS FOR COAST SERVICE.

Ships	Figures	Descriptions	Illustrations
Monitor . . .	72, 73	Baron Grivel . .	*Das Schw.*
		Admiral Hamilton .	
		Admiral Touchard .	
		Die Marine . .	
		Scott Russell . .	
Roanoke . . .	74	—	*Das Schw.*
Colossus . . .	75, 76	—	*Das Schw.*
Camanche . .	77	Heriz	*Das Schw.*
Benton . .	78, 79, 80, 81. 82	Holley	Holley
		Admiral Hamilton .	
Dictator . . .	83	*Times*	*Das Schw.*
Miantonomoh .	84	Admiral Paris . .	*Das Schw.*
		Secretary U.S.N. 1878	
Kalamazoo . .	85	Admiral Paris . .	*Art Naval*

Ships	Figures	Descriptions	Illustrations
Puritan Terror Amphitrite Monadnock	—	Report of Secretary U.S.N. 1880	
Rochambeau	86, 87, 88, 89	Admiral Paris	*Art Naval*
Scorpion Wyvern	90	Admiral Paris Reed	*Das Schw.*
Arminius Rolf Krake	91, 92	Admiral Paris	*Das Schw.*
Affondatore	93	Heriz	*Das Schw.*
Prinz Hendrik	94	Admiral Paris	*Das Schw.*
King of the Nether- lands	95, 96	Kronenfels	*Das Schw.*
Schorpioen	97	Admiral Paris	*Das Schw.*
Stier	98	Kronenfels	*Das Schw.*
Buffel	99	Kronenfels	*Das Schw.*
Cerberus Heiligerlee Tijger Khokodil Bloedhound	100	Kronenfels	*Das Schw.*
Draak	—	Kronenfels	
Adder class	101	Kronenfels	*Das Schw.*
Huascar	102, 103	Admiral Paris	*Das Schw.*
Acahualpa Independencia Bahia	—	Admiral Paris	
Brazil	104	Admiral Paris	*Das Schw.*
Cabral Colombo	105, 106	Admiral Paris	*Art Naval*
Bronenosec	107, 108	Lieut. Juels, Swedish Navy	*Das Schw.*
Smerc	109, 110	Lieut. Juels	*Das Schw.*
Admiral Lazareff Admiral Spiridoff	110, 112	Pall Mall Gazette	*Das Schw.*
Admiral Spiridoff Admiral Schitchochoff	113, 114		
Royal Sovereign Prince Albert	— —	*Times* Admiral Paris	*Das Schw.*

CHAPTER X.

COAST-SERVICE VESSELS OF THE MORE RECENT TYPES, AND EARLIER MASTLESS
IRONCLADS.

Ships	Figures	Descriptions	Illustrations
Taureau Bélier Tigre Bouledogue Cerbère	116, 117	Baron Grivel	*Das Schw.*
Arrogante Implacable Opiniâtre	118	*Broad Arrow* *Pall Mall* *Carnet*	Lt. Very

Ships	Figures	Descriptions	Illustrations
Tempete . . . Tonnant . . . Vengeur . . .		*La Marine* Baron Grivel *Année Maritime* King Lebelin de Dionne	
Tonnerre . . . Fulminant . . . Furieux . . .	119, 120	*La Marine* . . . Baron Grivel . . . *Année Maritime* . . . King . . . Lebelin de Dionne . .	*Das Schw.*
Caiman . . . Terrible . . .		*Revue Maritime* Vice-Admiral Pothuau	
Cerberus . . . Magdala . . . Abyssinia . . .	121	Elgar	*Das Schw.*
Hotspur . . .	122, 123	Marchal	*Das Schw.*
Glatton . . .	124, 125	*Times* . . . Barnaby . . . Marchal . . .	*Das Schw.*
Cyclops . . . Gorgon . . . Hecate . . . Hydra . . .	126	*Times* . . . Barnaby . . . Marchal . . . Commmander Hayes, R.N. Commander Dawson, R.N. Admiral Ryder . . .	*Das Schw.*
Rupert . . .	127	*Times* . . .	*Das Schw.*
Belleisle . . . Orion . . .	128	*Times* . . . *Broad Arrow* . .	Admiralty
Popoffkas . . .	129, 130 132, 133	Goulaeff . . . Reed . . .	*Das Schw.*
	131	St. Petersburg *Vedomosti* . White . . . King, U.S.N. . . . *Broad Arrow* . . . *Army and Navy Gazette* . *Engineering* . . .	*Die Marine*
Livadia . . .	134, 135, 136, 137, 138, 139, 140	*Engineering* . . . Goulaeff . . . . Reed . . .	*Engineering*
Solimöes . . .	141, 141a, 142	*Die Marine* . . .	*Das Schw.*
La Plata . . . Los Andes . . .	143, 144	*La Marine* . . . *Army and Navy Gazette* .	*Das Schw.*
Gomm . . . Lindormen . . .	145	Kronenfels . . .	*Das Schw.*
Odin . . .	146, 147	Krononfels . . .	*Das Schw.*
Wespe . . . Viper . . . Biene . . . Mücke . . . Scorpion . . . Basilisk . . .	148, 149, 150, 151	*Die Marine* . . .	*Das Schw.*
Mosel . . . Rhein . . .	152, 153	Heriz	*Das Schw.*
Leitha . . . Maros . . .	154, 155	Heriz	*Das Schw.*

CHAPTER XI.

ARMOURED CRUISERS.

Ships	Figures	Descriptions	Illustrations
Hansa		*Die Marine*	*Das Schw.*
Victorieuse .		*La Marine*	
Triomphante	158, 159	Marchal .	*Das Schw.*
La Galissonniere		*Dislère*	
Duguesclin .	160, 161, 162	} *La Marine*	*Das Schw.*
Vauban			
Minin .	163, 164	*The Newcastle Chronicle* .	*Das Schw.*
		King	
General Admiral	165, 166, 167	*Dislère*	*Das Schw.*
Duke of Edinburgh		*Engineering*	
		Broad Arrow	
		Die Marine	
		Spencer Robinson	
Shannon	168, 169	*Dislère*	*Das Schw.*
		King	
		Noel	
		Broad Arrow	
		Die Marine	
		King	
Nelson	170, 171	*Dislère*	*Das Schw.*
Northampton		Barnaby	
		Broad Arrow	
		Times	
		Reed	
Almirante-Cochrane	172, 173	*Dislère*	*Das Schw.*
Blanco-Encalada		*Army and Navy Gazette*	
Foo-So	174, 175, 176	} *Engineering*	*Engineering*
Kon-go			
Hi-yei			
Don Juan .	177, 178 179	} *Die Marine*	*Das Schw.*
Kaiser Max			
Prinz Eugene			
Vasco de Gama .	181, 182	*Times*	*Das Schw.*
King George	183, 184	Kronenfels	*Das Schw.*
Impérieuse .		Mr. Trevelyan, M.P.	
Warspite .			

CHAPTER XII.

BOW BATTERY SHIPS.

Ships	Figures	Descriptions	Illustrations
Archduke Albert	185, 186, 187, 188	*Die Marine*	*Das Schw.*
		Marchal .	
Custozza	189	*Die Marine*	*Das Schw.*

CHAPTER XIII.

CENTRAL BATTERY SHIPS.

Ships	Figures	Descriptions	Illustrations
Alexandra . . .	190, 191 Sectional view	*Die Marine* . . . *Engineering* . . . King	*Das Schw.* Mr. King
Temeraire . . .	193, 194	*Dislère* . . . King . . . *Engineering* . . . *Times* . . .	*Das Schw.*
Kaiser . . . Deutschland . .	195, 196, 197	King . . . *Norddeutsch Zeitung* . . *Engineering* . . .	*Das Schw.*
Superb (Memdoohiyeh) Messudije . . .	198, 199	*Engineering* . . . *Broad Arrow* . . . *Iron*	*Das Schw.*
Redoutable . .		*La Marine* . . .	*Die Marine*
Dévastation . . Foudroyant . .	200, 201, 202	Bethmont . . . *La Marine* . . . Dislère . . . *Times* . . . *Daily News* . .	*Das Schw.*
Duperré . . . Baudin . . . Formidable . .	203, 204, 205	*La Marine* . . . Army and Navy Gazette .	*Das Schw.*
Tegethoff . . .	206, 207, 208	Dislère . . . King . . . Reed . . .	*Das Schw.*
Almirante Brown .	209, 210	Samuda	Samunda

CHAPTER XIV.

MASTED TURRET-SHIPS

Ships	Figures	Descriptions	Illustrations
Monarch . . .	211	Elgar . . . Dislère . . . Captains of Channel fleet .	*Das Schw.*
Captain . . .	212	Dislère . . . *Art Naval* . .	*Das Schw.*
Preussen . . . Friedrich der Grosse . Grosser Kurfürst .	213, 214, 215, 216, 217	*Die Marine* . . King . . . Engineering . . Dislère . . .	*Das Schw.*
Neptune . . .	218, 219	King . . . Dislère . . . *Times* . . .	*Das Schw.*

CHAPTER XV.

MASTLESS TURRET-SHIPS

Ships	Figures	Descriptions	Illustrations
Devastation	220, 221	Barnaby King Dislère Spencer Robinson *Times*	*Das Schw.*
Peter the Great	222, 223	*Revue Maritime* King *Die Marine* Dislère	*Das Schw.*
Thunderer	224, 225, 226, 227, 228, 229	King	*Das Schw.* King
Dreadnought	230, 231, 232, 234	King *Times* Barnaby Dislère	*Das Schw.* King
Inflexible	235, 236, 237, 238, 239, 240, 241	King Engineering *Times* Dislère	*Das Schw.* Admiralty Committee King
Ajax Agamemnon	242, 243, 244, 245	King *Times*	King
Colossus Majestic	246, 247	Rt. Hon. W. H. Smith *Times*	Admiralty
Conqueror	248, 249,	King	Admiralty
Duilio Dandolo	250. 251, 252	King	*Das Schw.*

CHAPTER XVI.

MASTLESS *BARBETTE* SHIPS.

Ships	Figures	Descriptions	Illustrations
Sachsen	253, 254, 255, 256	King *Revue Maritime*	*Das Schw.*
Italia Lepanto	257, 258, 259, 260, 261, 262	King Dislère *Standard* Barnaby Reed	King
Helgoland	264, 265	Danish Admiralty	Danish Admiralty
Collingwood	266, 267, 268	Barnaby	Admiralty
Polyphemus	269	*Iron*	*Iron*

CHAPTER XVII.

UNARMOURED CRUISERS.

Ships	Figures	Descriptions	Illustrations
Inconstant . . .	270, 278, 279, 280, 281	Reed . . . Scott . . .	Das Schw. Journal Institution of Naval Architects
Iris . . .	271, 272, 273, 274, 275, 276, 277	White . . . Times . . .	Das Schw. Journal United Service Institution
Medina . .	228, 283		Das Schw. Das Schw.
La Clocheterie . .	284	Dislère	Das Schw.
Duquesne . . .	285, 286, 287, 288, 289, 290	Dislère . . .	Das Schw. Very
Villars . . .	291, 292	Kronenfels . . .	Das Schw.
Eclaireur . . .	293, 294	Very . . .	Very
Lancier . . .	295, 266	Very . . .	Very
Crocodile . . .	297	Kronenfels . . .	Das Schw.
Leipzig . . .	298, 299	Kronenfels . . .	Das Schw.
Agostino Barbarigo .	300, 301, 302	Brin	Das Schw.
Asia	303, 304	King	King
Zabiaca . . .	305, 306	King	King
Trenton . . .	307, 308, 309	King	King
Chinese gunboats .	310, 311	Times	Armstrong

PART I.

ARMOURED AND UNARMOURED SHIPS

HISTORICAL SKETCH.

As a general introduction to the wide subject of Ship-building for the Purposes of War, the following historical sketch has been translated and condensed from the essay on armoured ships by Lieutenant T. H. A. Tromp, of the Dutch Artillery. It summarises the history of armour-clad construction in England, France, and Germany, and relates succinctly much that will be found described in fuller detail in subsequent chapters.

The invention of shell-guns, or rather of the practice of firing explosive projectiles from guns as well as from mortars, is usually attributed to the French General Paixhans, and the date assigned to it is 1819. The destructive efficiency of this description of firing against wooden ships is often said to have been first demonstrated by the Russians at Sinope on November 20, 1853, when a Turkish fleet, superior in numbers, but armed to a great extent with 24-pdr. smooth-bores, was destroyed by shells. General Paixhans' invention in reality consisted in showing that of two guns of a given weight, of which one had a large calibre and fired a hollow projectile with a bursting charge, and the other had a moderate calibre and fired a solid projectile of equal weight, the former would prove the more effective against wooden ships. There is reason to suppose that the same idea had occurred to other officers who had practical experience of the effect of artillery fire against wood-built hulls. Thirty years before Sinope an English naval officer, Captain Abney Hastings, had urged the use of explosive shells from guns of about the same size as the 68-pdrs., to be carried on vessels propelled by steam. A quarter of a century before the Russian victory he had on more than one occasion, during the Greek war of independence, practically shown in action how terribly efficient such a description of fire against ships of wood could be.[1] The massacre of the Turks at Sinope,

(marginal notes: Shell fire from guns. Sinope. Captain Abney Hastings.)

---

[1] The history of this gallant and prematurely cut-off naval officer, and the influence exerted by him on the development of naval tactics, are not

occurring at a moment when the public feeling of several powerful nations was strongly directed towards war, attracted special attention, and revealed very plainly to all that the shell-guns, with which Russia and most Western States had armed their fleets, had rendered the abandonment of wooden hulls inevitable.

Crimean batteries.

At the commencement of the Crimean war, Napoleon III. was not slow to apprehend that any attempt to attack either Cronstadt or Sebastopol with unarmoured ships was doomed to failure, and the more so because the channels in front of those towns were of small depth, and the heavy ships were obliged to remain a considerable distance from the shore. Ships of the ordinary type being unavailable, the Emperor caused floating batteries to be constructed with a moderate draught of water, and protected with iron armour capable of resisting both shot and shell.

Floating batteries at siege of Gibraltar.

The idea of armour protection was not original. It had been adopted by the Chevalier D'Arçon in the construction of ten floating batteries for the attack upon Gibraltar. These batteries were from 600 to 1,200 tons. Their wooden hulls were protected with bars of iron, and an outer covering or belt of cork. In the interstices sand had been placed, which was to be kept moist with salt water so as to prevent the ships taking fire from red-hot shot. The deck was housed in with a wooden roof of very solid construction, and covered over with thick 'green' hides. These batteries were armed with from ten to twenty-nine guns. At the attack upon Gibraltar of September 13, 1782, they were moored too close to one another, and one of the ships having caught fire from a red-hot shot, the conflagration extended to the other batteries, and raged with such fury that it soon became impossible to arrest its progress. D'Arçon, having entire confidence in the strength of the ships, had taken no precautions against the possibility of fire, and had even omitted to furnish the ships with boats. It is further to be observed that these floating batteries were not completely finished, so that the apparatus intended to moisten the sand worked badly, and in some cases failed altogether. Of the 5,260 men, who formed the crews, only 487 were saved. Five batteries blew up, and five others were burned to the water's edge.

English and French Crimean batteries.

It is not necessary to pursue the retrospective view of the subject. It will be admitted that it was the initiative taken by the Emperor Napoleon III. which brought about a complete revolution in modern naval construction for war. The French batteries, five in number, were commenced in September 1854; and in March 1855 the 'Tonnante' was launched at Brest, while the other batteries were launched in the month of July in the same year. They were all of the same dimensions, having a length of 172 feet, a breadth of 44 feet, and 9 feet draught of water.

The thickness of the armour was decided after experiment at Vincennes, it being finally determined to adopt 4½-inch plates on 17 inches of wood backing. The plans of these batteries were sent to the English Admiralty by the French Minister of Marine, M. Ducos, and, after considerable hesitation, it was resolved to build the 'Thunderbolt,' 'Etna,' and 'Terror,' three similar ships, for the attack on Cronstadt.

The proposed attack on Cronstadt having been abandoned, the three English vessels, and the French ships 'Dévastation,' 'Lave,' and 'Tonnante,' were despatched to the Black Sea. The French ironclads took part on October 17, 1855, in the bombardment of Kinburn, and rendered excellent service. The English vessels did not arrive until October 24.

In view of these successful results the *Conseil des Travaux de la Marine* determined to design ships which should combine with their protective armour satisfactory seagoing qualities. In process of time, as the competition between the gun and armour developed itself, the impracticability of constructing such vessels was recognised, and it was found necessary to design different classes of ships, each adapted for a special service. <sub-note>Experiments by *Conseil des Travaux de la Marine.*</sub-note>

Before elaborating a design, the *Conseil des Travaux de la Marine* determined to ascertain by experiment the best methods of constructing ironclads. Their investigations led to the adoption of 5-inch armour plates. The thickness of the plating and the methods of construction having been decided, a design was selected from those sent in by numerous competitors. That of the constructor Audenet was finally carried into execution in the building of the 'Couronne.'

In the meantime, the celebrated French constructor, Dupuy de Lôme, availing himself of the results of the experiments that had been made, had laid a proposal before the Government in November 1857, which was received with approval; and in March 1858 the first ironclad frigate, the 'Gloire,' was commenced at Toulon. <sub-note>'La Gloire.'</sub-note>

The construction of two other wooden armoured frigates, the 'Invincible' and the 'Normandie,' of the same type as the 'Gloire' and the 'Couronne,' was ordered. The latter ship differed from the <sub-note>'Invincible,' 'Normandie,' and 'Couronne.'</sub-note>

others not only in the materials employed but in the great strength of the deck, which afforded protection against the projectiles then in use. The 'Couronne' was especially constructed with the view of establishing a comparison between wooden vessels and those of iron. The four frigates were completely armoured above the water line with 5-inch plates resting on a 26-inch backing. The armament at that time consisted of thirty-six 5-ton guns mounted on a single battery extending along the whole length of the ship. The battery being only 6 ft. 3 in. above the water, it was often necessary to close the ports.

'Warrior.' England, where grave doubts had been felt as to the utility of armour, and the construction of armoured ships, such as France was then building, was regarded as a useless expense, was at last compelled to follow in the same direction. The 'Warrior' was ordered in June 1859, a few months before the completion of the 'Gloire.' This ship was constructed like the 'Gloire,' to keep out the projectiles of the 68-pdr. guns. It was thought in England as in France that for this purpose 4½-inch armour was sufficient.

The excess of nearly 132 feet in the length of the English ship, as compared with the 'Gloire,' made it difficult to handle her, notwithstanding that she had an advantage of two knots in speed. Everything having been sacrificed to combine the utmost speed with an adequate armour protection, the centre part only of the ship was protected over a length of 218 feet, whilst the bow and the stern were unprotected. The rudder and the steering apparatus were entirely exposed, whilst the stern was weakened by a large well for lifting the screw when under sail The stem was of the ordinary shape, but considerably strengthened at the water line, for the 'Defence' and 'Resistance.' purpose of ramming. The 'Defence' and the 'Resistance' were constructed after a similar type, but with the length reduced by 99 feet. Like the 'Warrior' and the 'Black Prince,' they were protected with 4½-inch armour on an 18-inch backing.

Rival efforts in France and England. In 1861 England was in the same relative position as France in 1859; but this condition of inferiority was of short duration. Construction was pushed on with great energy in the private yards and in the royal dockyards, the result being that in 1865 England was already possessed of thirty ironclads, and had reasserted her superiority at sea.

In 1861, following upon the four ships which we have just mentioned, England undertook the construction of not less than eleven ironclads, representing four different types. The list included the 'Achilles,' two ships of the 'Hector' type, five wood-built ships of the 'Caledonia,' and three of the 'Minotaur' type.

WARRIOR.

(After Original Sketches by Ch. E. de Martino.)

It was originally proposed to protect the 'Achilles' with armour 'Achilles.' similar to that of the 'Warrior;' but, during the construction, the disadvantage of the unprotected bow and stern was recognised, and it was resolved to extend the armour all round the ship at the water line, while the stem was modelled after the fashion of a swan's neck, and thus formed a ram. After the 'Achilles' came the 'Hector' and the 'Valiant.' These ships were completely protected above 'Hector.' water, and the armour amidships was carried below the water line.

In addition to these vessels, with the view of utilising the Converted ships. materials in store in the different yards, it was determined to convert into ironclad frigates a considerable number of wooden ships, including the 'Caledonia,' 'Royal Oak,' 'Ocean,' 'Prince Consort,' and 'Royal Alfred.' They were fairly protected with armour similar to that of the 'Warrior,' extending from below the water line to the upper deck. The 'Royal Alfred' alone was defended with 6-inch armour.

At the same date three large ships, constructed entirely of iron, 'Minotaur. were commenced. The armour of the 'Minotaur,' 'Agincourt,' and 'Northumberland' consisted of $5\frac{1}{2}$-inch plates, resting upon a 9-inch backing, with $1\frac{1}{2}$-inch skin plating. Although the thickness of the plating had been increased by one inch, the wood backing had been reduced; and it was afterwards discovered that the armour of these ships was not less penetrable than that of the 'Warrior.'

In all the preceding ships the armour is of the same thickness along the whole length of the ship. After the construction of the 'Minotaur' the thickness varied according to the greater or less importance of the protected parts; the boilers, the engines, and the magazines receiving additional protection. For this reason the thickness of the armour of the 'Minotaur' was diminished towards the bow to 3 inches, and at the stern to $2\frac{1}{2}$ inches.

In 1859, as it has already been stated, France had constructed 'Magenta' and 'Solferino.' two ships, the 'Magenta' and the 'Solferino,' of the same type. The armoured belt was of equal thickness along the whole length of the ship, but the depth was less than in the case of the 'Gloire.' Amidships the armour gave protection to a two-decked battery. By the greater elevation of the upper deck battery the inconveniences referred to in the case of the 'Gloire' were remedied. The great defects of these ships were that the armoured belt was much too narrow, and that they were entirely constructed of wood. Their armament consisted of fifty-two 5-ton guns. These were among the first ships fitted with the ram. The 'Magenta' was launched on July 22, 1866.

Shortly after the construction of these ships the *Conseil des*

Ten armoured frigates of 'Flandre' type.

Travaux was instructed to suggest improvements on the 'Gloire' type. Among the numerous propositions submitted to the *Conseil*, the most important was that of constructing ironclads of iron from the water line upwards, and increasing the armour from five to six inches. In 1862 ten frigates were commenced of the 'Gloire' type, but with thicker armour. They were named respectively 'Flandre,' 'Gauloise,' 'Guyenne,' 'Savoie,' 'Surveillante,' 'Provence,' 'Magnanime,' 'Valeureuse,' 'Héroïne,' and 'Revanche.'

'Océan,' 'Marengo,' 'Suffren,' 'Friedland.'

At this period little attention was directed to the modifications which were taking place in naval guns; but the introduction in 1864 into the French armaments of the $7\frac{3}{4}$ and $15\frac{1}{2}$-ton guns made the new fleet of ten ships obsolete even before it was completed. The last of the type was finished in 1867. It was, however, urged that by their uniformity of type these vessels possessed numerous advantages over the vessels of the English fleet of the same date, composed of types with widely different qualities. It was only in 1865, when the $15\frac{1}{2}$-ton guns had been approved, and the armour hitherto employed had become altogether inadequate, that the French determined to increase the thickness of their armour protection. The 'Océan' is protected at the water line with 8-inch plates, resting upon a $32\frac{1}{2}$-inch backing. The armament was mounted in a central battery, on the four corners of which are barbette turrets, projecting beyond the sides of the ship. The battery and the turrets are protected by $6\frac{1}{2}$-inch armour with $24\frac{1}{4}$ inches of backing. Even before the 'Océan' was launched on October 15, 1868, the armour had ceased to afford protection against the 23-ton guns which were then in use. The 'Marengo,' the 'Suffren,' and the 'Friedland' were constructed after the same type. The heavy armament of these ships consisted of four 23-ton guns in the battery, and four $15\frac{1}{2}$-ton guns in the barbette turrets. The 'Friedland' differs from the other ships in being constructed of iron, and having only two turrets, each of which is armed with a 23-ton gun.

Designs by Sir E. J. Reed, K.C.B.

The remarkable progress in gunnery, due to the employment of very heavy guns, led gradually to a complete change in the construction of ships. All the ships mentioned above were armed with numerous light guns. The new guns being heavier were fewer in number; and the increase in the calibre involved corresponding modifications in the armour, which it was necessary to construct of greatly increased thickness. The task of the naval architect was made easier by the reduction of the number of guns, inasmuch as they could be protected with a greatly reduced area of armour.

The exaggerated lengths of 383 feet in the 'Achilles' and

400 feet in the ' Minotaur ' had long been the subject of complaints in the English navy. The large spread of canvas was also disapproved on the ground that a considerable proportion of the weight of the spars and rigging could have been used to greater advantage in increasing the armour and the armament. It was further objected that the bow fire, as in all their predecessors, could only be obtained from unprotected guns. Having regard to the growing importance attached to the power of fighting in the end-on position, it was considered essential that these guns should be able to sustain a heavy fire.

These various considerations induced the English Admiralty, in imitation of the plan adopted in France in the case of the ' Magenta,' to place the guns in a central battery or *réduit*, and to diminish the number of pieces while augmenting their calibre, effective bow fire being secured by means of an armoured forecastle.

Sir E. J. Reed, appointed in 1862 to the office of Chief Constructor, undertook the construction of the ' Bellerophon ' in accordance with the new principles which had been adopted. The cellular system, then fully introduced for the first time, was intended to prevent the vessel from sinking, in case the outer skin received an injury. For the same reason the double bottom was divided into a certain number of divisions, communicating with the interior in such a manner that if one of these compartments had been submerged it would not have caused the loss of the ship. Attention was already being directed to the defence against the torpedo. ' Bellerophon.'

Shortly after the construction of the ' Bellerophon,' Sir E. Reed prepared a design for the ' Enterprise,' showing a considerable improvement in reference to bow fire. This improvement was effected by piercing the athwart-ship bulkheads of the battery with ports, and substituting moveable for fixed bulwarks. ' Enterprise.'

The same arrangement was adopted in the ' Pallas ' and the ' Penelope,' but a further improvement was introduced in the introduction of what are known as indented ports, which command a line of fire, forward and aft, within twenty degrees of the line of the keel, from completely protected guns. ' Pallas ' and ' Penelope.'

In the ' Hercules,' Sir E. Reed carried his system to a still further degree of perfection by cutting a port in the broadside. With the assistance of a revolving platform the guns in the angle of the battery can be trained to fire either on the broadside or nearly in line with the keel. The disadvantage of such a system is that, as in the case of the ' Hercules,' twelve ports were required for eight guns. Sir E. Reed remedied this defect in the ' Kaiser ' and the ' Hercules.'

'Deutschland,' which he constructed shortly afterwards for the German Government, by placing his guns in such a manner that they could be trained from the same port both to fire on the beam and in line with the keel. In the 'Hercules,' in order to obtain an all-round fire, a 9-inch 12-ton gun was placed under the forecastle and another under the poop, partly protected by armour. Thus, while the fire was principally obtained from the battery, Sir E. Reed had only secured the all-round fire from partially protected guns. He was, however, of opinion that an armoured battery at each extremity of the ship involved a disposition of weights which it was desirable to avoid. It tended to augment the pitching in a sea-way, causing the fire even with a moderate disturbance of the sea to be wild and inaccurate, especially from the stern. For this reason, when the 'Sultan' was designed, he removed the guns from the stern into an upper deck battery, placed at the after end of the central battery, and armed with two guns of the same calibre, which could be trained to fire both aft and on the beam. The battery in question was of unusual shape, projecting beyond the sides of the ship in such a manner that only a moderate tumble home was required in the upper works. With this arrangement the indented ports were no longer necessary, nor the embrasures in the athwart-ship bulkhead at the after end of the redoubt. The armament of the central batteries was the same as in the 'Hercules,' while the 12-ton guns, entirely unprotected, are mounted in the forecastle. In the 'Audacious' class he placed the heavy guns in two tiers in a central battery. The lower battery is completely protected and armed with six 12-ton guns, which can be trained on the broadside only. The upper battery projects so that its guns can be fired ahead and astern as well as abeam, the armament consisting of four 12-ton guns. In the vessels of this class two guns could be fired in line with the keel both ahead and astern.

In view of the greater importance which has been attached to the ram after the battle of Lissa, the English Admiralty decided to strengthen the ram and to give the ships a more formidable bow fire. The 'Alexandra,' originally named the 'Superb,' was commenced in 1873. Like the ships of the 'Audacious' type, the 'Alexandra' has a central battery with the guns mounted on two decks. The lower battery, however, is considerably longer than the upper battery, and in the forward part is constructed with indented ports armed with 18-ton guns, which can be fired within three degrees of the line of the keel.

The upper battery was the same as in the 'Audacious' class,

'Sultan.'

'Audacious.'

'Alexandra.'

except that the armament consisted of two 25-ton guns firing ahead, and two 18-ton guns firing in a line with the keel astern. The bow fire, therefore, was furnished by two 18-ton and two 25-ton guns, showing an important increase in the weight of metal as compared with the 'Audacious.' Considered, however, from another point of view, the 'Alexandra' was a still more formidable vessel, the thickness of the armour at the water line amidships being 12 inches, as compared with 8 inches in preceding vessels. Moreover, the armour belt was no longer of the same breadth for the whole length of the ship. Its lower edge was carried down at the stem to a depth of 12 feet below the water line, thus not only imparting additional strength to the stem, but protecting the vessel from a raking fire, which might have penetrated the hull below the armour. At a later date the same system of armour for the bow was introduced in almost all vessels. To protect the stern against a raking fire, a transverse bulkhead was constructed, plated with 6-inch armour, and extending to a depth of 6 feet below the water line.

The 'Téméraire' was commenced in the same year as the 'Alexandra,' but was constructed on a totally different plan. The lower-deck battery of the armoured citadel closely resembled that of the 'Alexandra.' For broadside fire there were on each side two 18-ton guns, and at each indented port a 25-ton gun, which could also be trained to fire on the broadside. In order to obtain an all-round fire, which was not possible from the central battery, barbette towers were placed forward and aft on the upper deck, armed and armoured in a different manner. The great disadvantage of such a system of construction is that the extremities of the vessel are heavily weighted, tending, as we have already shown, to increase the pitching movement. There is another objection, which might have been avoided. The armour of the towers is not carried down to the armoured deck, and hence a projectile penetrating below the armour might destroy the lower portion of the turret which contains the mechanical turning-gear and the turntable for the gun. The thickness of the armour at the midship section is 11 inches—less, therefore, than that of the 'Alexandra.' 'Témé-raire.'

The 'Téméraire' is the last central battery ship which has thus far been constructed for the English navy. In 1878 England bought from the Turkish Government several vessels, which were at that time building or nearly completed. The vessels referred to were the 'Memdouhyeh' (since named the 'Superb'), the 'Belleisle,' and the 'Orion.' The 'Superb' closely resembles the 'Hercules.' The 'Belleisle' and 'Orion' have a lofty central battery. 'Belleisle'
and
'Orion.'

A 25-ton gun is mounted in each corner of the battery, which can be fired either in line with the keel or on the broadside. These guns being raised to a considerable height, the topsides have not been constructed with the tumble-home which has been necessary in other ships. The thickness of the armour for the central battery, and that of the water line in the centre, is 12 inches.

In 1867 the German Government purchased the 'König Wilhelm.' At the same date the 'Kron-Prinz' was ordered in France and the 'Friedrich-Carl' in England.

'Richelieu,' 'Colbert,' and 'Trident.'

We now return to the development of the French navy—for which a fourth group of ships was commenced in 1868–69. They were plated with 9-inch armour, the resistance of which was considered equal to the 23-ton gun. These vessels were named respectively the 'Richelieu,' 'Colbert,' and 'Trident.' The 'Richelieu' is a ship of a type very similar to that of the preceding group, but with an addition of 33 feet to the length and 1,200 tons to the displacement. This increase of displacement is mainly due to the weight of the armament and armour. While the 'Suffren' has four 23-ton guns in the central battery, the 'Richelieu' has six guns of the same calibre, and a 15½-ton gun mounted on the forecastle. There are, therefore, in the central battery two 23-ton guns more than in the 'Suffren,' which has led to the necessity of increasing the length by nearly 39 feet. An advantage, however, was gained in another direction, inasmuch as it was possible to give increased protection to machinery and boilers. Compared with the preceding group, both the offensive and defensive power was considerably increased. On the other hand, there was a loss of one knot in speed. It was for this reason that some modifications were introduced into the two other ships of the same type. The two turrets in the after part of the central battery were dispensed with, and the armour was removed from the forward turrets. The armament of the latter was changed, by the substitution of 23-ton guns. In the stern an additional 15½-ton gun was introduced, firing in a line with the keel. With regard to speed, the 'Trident,' on the trials, steamed 14·47, and the 'Colbert' 14·75 knots. The hulls of these ships are constructed of wood, except the extremities forward and aft, in which the upper works, extending beyond the central battery, are of iron.

Programme of 1872.

After the Franco-German war a new programme was elaborated for the French navy, upon the completion of which the armoured fleet will consist of sixteen first-class ironclads, twelve second-class ironclads, and twenty coast-service vessels of the first and second classes. Several of the existing ironclads will be removed from the list as the construction of the new ships is advanced.

In regard to the general arrangement of the different types of ironclads, it was decided that for the future the hull and the deck armour should be of iron, chiefly because iron, in addition to its known advantages over wood, was better adapted for the construction, with the requisite solidity, of the numerous watertight bulkheads, which are always of iron.

Greater importance was attached to the strong construction of the bulkheads, in view of the injury which might be caused to the hull by a projectile, a ram, or a torpedo. It was deemed necessary to increase the armour on the deck, the more especially because in the English vessels the platform for guns had been raised as much as possible, and it was therefore requisite to provide against a very powerful plunging fire. It was decided at the same time to make use of steel, by which a considerable reduction of weight could be secured, and which might be turned to account in strengthening the armour and the armament.

Among the different designs prepared in accordance with these general principles, that of M. de Bussy, Director of Naval Construction, was adopted ; and in November 1872 the ' Redoubtable ' was commenced from his plans.

'Redoubtable.'

The hull and the internal fastenings were constructed of steel, and the outer plating of iron. Although of the same length, and having 6 feet 7 inches less beam than the ships of the ' Richelieu ' type, the draught of water was 3 feet 3 inches less, while the armour on the water line and on the central battery was considerably strengthened.

With regard to the general arrangements, the central battery, which is protected by curved transverse bulkheads, is placed amidships, and is armed with four 23-ton guns.[1] The ports are cut in these bulkheads, and the sides of the upper works of the ship fall inwards, so as to admit of direct fire ahead and astern in line with the keel. The guns on the broadside can be so trained as to obtain a converging fire. Above the casemate are two half-turrets, projecting beyond the sides of the ship, and armed with two 23-ton guns. They are protected against musketry but not against artillery fire. The remainder of the armament consists of a 23-ton gun under the forecastle deck, a gun of the same calibre astern, and a few 53-cwt. guns on the quarter deck and forecastle.

[1] The armament of most heavy armourclads in the French, as in other navies, is occasionally changed.

The 'Redoubtable' is protected at the water line amidships with 14-inch plates, and over the central battery with 10-inch plates. She is propelled by a single screw.

'Dévastation' and 'Foudroyant.'

In January 1876 the 'Dévastation' and the 'Foudroyant' were commenced. They are of the same type as the 'Redoubtable,' but have much more offensive and defensive power. Between 1872 and 1875 the necessity for a further increase in the strength of the armoured belt had made itself felt. These ships were to have a displacement of 800 tons more than the 'Redoubtable.' In order to prevent an excessive increase in the draught of water, the beam of 64 feet 6 inches of the 'Redoubtable' was increased to 69 feet 9 inches, while the increase in the depth of the hull was only one foot. At the same time steel was introduced as much as possible; the result being that, notwithstanding the increase in the dimensions, as given above, the weight of the hull was 110 tons less than that of the 'Redoubtable.' The thickness of the armour at the water line was increased from 14 to 15 inches. The belt at the water line was carried to a distance of 28 feet from the stern post, at which point it was closed by a transverse armoured bulkhead. A deck, armoured with 2-inch plates, was laid on a level with the lower edge of the armoured belt, closing in the unprotected after portion of the ship. The armament of the central battery was changed, and four steel, rifled, 47-ton guns were substituted. Having regard to the moderate draught of water, the vessel was fitted with the twin-screw, some doubt being felt as to whether the central screw would work as satisfactorily as in the case of the 'Redoubtable.'

In addition to the three ships last mentioned, three others were commenced, to which we shall hereafter refer.

'Kaiser' and 'Deutschland.'

In London, Mr. Samuda was constructing, from the plans of Mr. Reed, for the German Government, two ships—the 'Kaiser' and the 'Deutschland'—of a type closely resembling the 'Hercules.' They differ, however, from the 'Hercules' in the arrangement of the central battery, which is amidships in the last-named vessel, whereas in the German ships the battery is placed further forward. As the battery is of the same breadth as the ship at the midship section, the forward part has a certain overhang, which is so far an advantage, inasmuch as the topsides, forward of the indented ports, have only a very moderate tumble-home, and thus preserve their natural outline. A line of fire astern can be obtained through the foremost indented port, within fifteen degrees of the line of the keel.

A 10-ton gun has been mounted, in a small half-circular battery, as a stern-chaser. As it has already been observed, there is only one port for each gun on the central battery. The guns mounted at the indented ports can be fired both in line with the keel and also on the broadside, their fire converging at a distance of 276 feet, or about the length of the ship herself. The trials of these two ships have been satisfactory, a mean speed of 14½ knots being attained.

As regards the armour, these vessels were inferior to the 'Hercules.' They had this further disadvantage, that the engines were placed outside the battery, with no other protection than a steel deck of ⅝ of an inch in thickness.

Both the armour and armament becoming more and more colossal, it had long since been necessary to divide the armoured ships into several categories, it having been recognised as impossible to combine in one and the same ship all the qualities required. Heavily armoured ships intended for the line of battle must necessarily carry powerful guns. They must be able to traverse great distances, and must therefore have considerable stowage for coal. Great speed is required to enable them to meet the inevitable contingencies of an engagement. In a word, the class of ships which may be called battery ships must be furnished with very considerable offensive and defensive power.

Most of the ships already mentioned belong to this category. Their great size, however, and the enormous weight of their armour and armament, necessitate such displacements as render them unfit for coast defence. The vessels intended for coast service may be divided into offensive coast-service ships, and coast-service ships for local defence.

The offensive coast-service ships must be prepared for voyages of considerable extent, and must be of light draught, in order to bombard fortifications at close quarters, or to close in with the land when attacked by battle ships. Lastly, a great speed is indispensable, both to pursue the local coast-defence vessels, which are generally of moderate speed, or to attack, on the other hand, battle ships.

The local coast-service ships are employed for the defence of the coast to which they belong, and must be of still lighter draught than the last-named type. Being ordinarily small vessels, they have not only the advantage of a moderate draught of water, which enables them to navigate close to the land, but they are also more manageable than the larger battle ships, and can therefore always select the most favourable moment, whether for an attack or for retiring from an engagement into shallow water. In general their guns are few in number, and of heavy calibre. Great offensive power must, therefore, be combined with a very moderate draught of water, and with suffi-

Special types required.

Coast-service ships.

cient armour protection. These vessels, acting in combination with torpedoes, especially when employed in great numbers, are most dangerous adversaries to large and costly ships.

Of the two types already named the turret ships are the most important, and the engagement at Hampton Roads, between the 'Merrimac' and the 'Monitor,' in 1862, attracted the attention of Europe to vessels of this class.

'Scorpion' and 'Wyvern.'

In 1864 two small monitors, the 'Scorpion' and the 'Wyvern,' which had been constructed in England for the Confederates, were seized by the English authorities. They were subsequently purchased by the Government. Being the first constructed in England, they were inferior to the American ships, but the trials to which they were subjected gave fairly satisfactory results, and led to the construction of two larger turret ships, the 'Royal Sovereign' and the 'Prince Albert.'

The former was an old line-of-battle ship, which was cut down and fitted with four turrets, the three aftermost of which were each armed with a 9-ton gun, while the foremost turret was armed with

'Prince Albert.'

two guns of the same calibre. The 'Prince Albert' was constructed of iron, and was also fitted with four turrets, which were, however, armed each with 12-ton guns.

Designs by Captain Cowper Coles.

In 1865 Captain Cowper Coles, who had already constructed several turret ships for foreign nations, including the 'Prinz Hendrik' for Holland and the 'Rolf Krake' for Denmark, submitted to the British Admiralty a design for a seagoing ship. Captain Coles was vigorously supported by the newspapers, and the English Admiralty

The 'Monarch.'

finally decided to build the 'Monarch.'

After long discussions, Captain Cowper Coles, who had protested against the 'Monarch' as being considered to express his idea, at length succeeded in obtaining from the Admiralty authority to construct, in conjunction with Messrs. Laird, of Birkenhead, a ship which should entirely satisfy his own views.

The 'Captain.'

The 'Captain' was accordingly laid down, and was launched on March 29, 1869. On the upper deck, at a height of 8 feet above the water line, were two turrets, each armed with two heavy guns, the axes of which were 12 feet above the water line. The turrets were 120 feet apart, and had an internal diameter of 22 feet. Forward and aft a 6½-ton gun was mounted in addition, protected only by a light superstructure, which was considered necessary to improve the seagoing qualities of the ship. The 'Captain' was fully rigged, the lower masts being iron tripods on the Coles principle. The armour extended from 5 feet below to 8 feet above the water line. In the vicinity of the turrets it was 10 inches in thickness, elsewhere it was 7 inches, diminishing gradually towards the extremities. The thickness of the armour on the turret was $9\frac{1}{2}$ inches, and near the ports 10 inches. The deck was protected with $1\frac{1}{4}$-inch and with 1-inch plating over the whole length of the ship. The machinery was of 900 horse-power, giving motion to twin screws.

The principal points in which the 'Captain' differed from its predecessors were the following : the range of fire on both sides of the centre line of the ship was 21° greater than in the case of the 'Monarch,' in consequence of there being no armoured battery at the extremities, and also because the rigging was set up almost entirely from the flying deck. As there was no necessity to let down the bulwarks in action, or to remove the boats which were carried on the flying deck, the ship could be more expeditiously cleared for action   The thickness of the armour on the water line was increased from 7 to 8 inches. The improvements having been described, let us turn to the defects. Only one $6\frac{1}{2}$-ton gun was mounted in the bow, whereas the 'Monarch' had at first two guns of the same calibre, for which 12-ton guns were afterwards substituted. The bow fire was therefore more powerful in the 'Monarch.' Both under sail and steam the 'Captain' had less speed than the 'Monarch,' although her evolutionary qualities were superior. When launched, the 'Captain' drew 2 feet more water, and had a displacement of 869 tons in excess of that shown in the original design. It resulted from this, that the deck, instead of being 8 feet was only 6 feet above the water line. This limited freeboard, in comparison with the great spread of canvas, gave the ship a very small range of stability, and contributed to the terrible disaster on the night of September 6, 1870, when the 'Captain' capsized.

Sir E. Reed had placed the turrets of the 'Monarch' at a considerable height above the water line, while, on the other hand, the freeboard, differing in that respect from that of the 'Captain,' was very considerable. The loss of the 'Captain' led the Admiralty to decide to abandon the construction of fully-rigged seagoing armoured turret-ships. The advantages attaching to the turret system were, however, recognised, and the system was adopted for mastless ships. In the first instance, turret ships were constructed almost exclusively for coast service. *Coast-service monitors.*

These ships differed little from some of the American monitors. The freeboard, however, was not high, so that the surface to be protected was of less extent, the reduction of weight affording the means of increasing the thickness of the armour. The base of the turrets was protected by an armoured 'breastwork' to meet the contingency, which had frequently occurred during the American war, of a projectile falling on the deck and destroying the mechanism of the turrets. The working of the mechanical gear was, therefore, secured by the breastwork, which enclosed in addition the principal means of access to the interior of the ship. It presented this further advantage, that it admitted of the turrets being placed at a greater height above the water. The guns were also in some instances carried at a greater elevation than the armament of the broadside ships. A flying deck above the turret or turrets provided space for the crew, it being often impossible to make use of the upper deck of vessels of this type, even in a moderately rough sea.

Everything tending to circumscribe the range of fire from the turrets is removed from the deck in the turret ships lately constructed, even the boats being placed on the flying or hurricane deck. The relatively considerable elevation of the turrets renders it impossible to depress the guns sufficiently upon an enemy close alongside ; and as the working of heavy guns is always slow, a certain number of light guns, principally intended as a defence against torpedo boats, have been mounted on the hurricane decks.

'Cerberus' and 'Gorgon' types.

In addition to the three ships for the colonies—the 'Cerberus,' 'Magdala,' and 'Abyssinia'—the 'Glatton,' 'Cyclops,' 'Gorgon,' 'Hecate,' and 'Hydra,' all intended for coast defence, have been constructed on the same plan.

'Taureau.'

Following the example of the French constructors, who, in 1861, had laid down their first ram—the 'Taureau'—for coast defence, the 'Hotspur' was laid down in England in 1866.

'Hotspur.'

The 'Hotspur' was fitted with a fixed oval turret, probably because some fear was entertained as to the capability of the moveable turret to withstand the shock which might be produced by the blow of a ram. The turret was armed with one 25-ton gun, mounted on a turntable, and firing from four distinct ports of large dimensions. A revolving turret, armed with two guns, has recently been substituted for the fixed tower.

'Rupert.'

The 'Rupert,' constructed somewhat later for the same service, is a ram with an armoured breastwork, of somewhat larger dimensions than the 'Hotspur,' and having a revolving turret with two heavy guns. The light upper works are the same as those of the 'Hotspur,' and in addition a hurricane deck has been fitted abaft the turret.

Both vessels should be serviceable as offensive coast-service ships ; but their supply of coal is too small to allow of their undertaking lengthened passages. They seem to have good seagoing qualities.

During the Russo-Turkish war both these ships formed part of the fleet in the Sea of Marmora, and no complaints were made. Their draught of water, of 21 ft. 6 in. and 23 ft. 6 in. respectively, is too great to make them effective for coast defence.

Turning to the battle ships of the first class, the Admiralty, having regard to the increased range of the new guns, had ordered designs to be prepared for a mastless, armoured, seagoing turret ship. Convinced that the decisive combats, even for England, with her rich and numerous colonies, must certainly be fought in European waters, it was decided to construct three ships, which, both in their offensive and defensive power, would surpass all existing ships, and which should have such seagoing qualities, and carry such a supply of coals, as would enable them to keep the seas for an extended period.

In April 1869 the construction of the ' Devastation' was commenced. In the first instance, the armament was to consist of four 25-ton guns, with a coal supply of 1,700 tons. A few months later, the armament was changed to four 35-ton guns, causing an augmentation of the total weight of approximately 100 tons. But this increase of weight was compensated by an equivalent reduction in the supply of coal.

'Devastation.'

No change was made in the original design until the loss of the ' Captain,' in September 1870, gave rise to some doubts as to the safety of other armoured ships, but especially turret ships. With the view of removing these doubts, the English Government appointed a Commission to examine the plans of the ships in construction, including the ' Devastation.' This Commission, known as the Committee on Designs, composed of the ablest naval officers and the most eminent engineers, expressed an opinion that the ships of the ' Devastation ' type had more than sufficient stability against the rolling and heaving action of the sea, and specially recommended this type, while condemning the various types of armoured ships of older construction.

Committee on Designs.

The abandonment of sails was approved, as affording the means of increasing the armament and the supply of coal. It was pointed out, that the full rig entailed the disadvantage of the single screw, the double screw causing a great resistance to the effective use of canvas. The single screw, on the other hand, was objectionable, as being liable to be damaged, whether in action or in bad weather at sea, by the fall of masts and rigging.

A mastless twin-screw ship is, therefore, decidedly preferable to the existing types of fully masted ships ; and as the ' Monarch,'

'Hercules,' 'Sultan,' and other ships might possibly be compelled to decline battle with smaller and less costly ships, the Committee, being of opinion that their inferiority would be the direct and inevitable result of their being burthened with a full rig, reported that it was impossible to combine in the same ship great offensive and defensive power and a full spread of canvas; and they stated that it was their opinion that the Colonies beyond the seas and other important interests in various parts of the world would be more effectively protected by establishing at different points naval stations from which ships like the 'Devastation' could operate, than by building ships of such limited fighting power as the 'Monarch.'

Although this expression of opinion met with considerable opposition from naval officers, who adhered to the belief that the 'Monarch' and similar ships could rely upon their canvas to keep the seas for a lengthened period, and might consequently undertake extended ocean voyages, it nevertheless formed the groundwork upon which the English Admiralty determined to construct their policy for the future.

It is to be observed that ships of the 'Devastation' type carry such a large supply of coal as to be able to traverse a great distance, and in case it should be necessary to replenish the supply, a glance at the map of the world will show that England has excellent naval stations in every part of the globe.

'Devastation' as altered.

The Committee recommended certain modifications in the 'Devastation' which would have the effect of considerably increasing the stability of the ship and greatly improving the accommodation for the crew. The chief improvements were the following: The armoured redoubt or breastwork, as in the case of the 'Glatton,' did not extend to the full breadth of the ship, and hence the deck was carried to the same height amidships and at the extremities of the ship. It was accordingly determined to make no change in the armoured redoubt, but to carry up the sides of the ship, by means of an unarmoured superstructure, to the height of the upper deck of the armoured redoubt. This change is attended with some disadvantage with regard to the training of the guns at an enemy close alongside on the beam, but the accommodation for the crew is greatly improved. The armament was changed to four 35-ton guns. By these modifications the displacement was raised to 9,294 tons, being an increase of 200 tons, and the increased draught of water due to the displacement was 5 inches. The supply of coal was fixed at 1,350 tons, and was capable of being raised to 1,600 tons. With this supply a distance could be traversed at 10 knots in the one case of 4,876, and in the other of 5,572 knots. At 12 knots the distances were reduced to 3,109 and 3,553 knots. The distance from New York to Portsmouth is 3,075 miles.

The 'Thunderer' was constructed after the same type as the 'Devastation.' The elevation of the sides of the ship by means of an unarmoured superstructure, while, as we have already seen, it secured an improvement in the accommodation for the crew, involved not only some obstruction to the training of the guns, but also exposed the unarmoured part of the ship to speedy destruction at the first commencement of an engagement. If such an engagement were to take place in open waters, and with a disturbed sea, the ship, it was apprehended, might suffer a serious loss of stability as the water poured in through the openings pierced by projectiles in the unarmoured side. 'Thunderer.'

In the construction of the third ship, the 'Dreadnought'—formerly called the 'Fury'—it was decided to provide against such a contingency by making the armoured breastwork of the same width as the ship itself; in other words, by raising up the armoured side of the ship to a level with the upper deck of the armoured breastwork. The 'Dreadnought' was 35 feet longer than the 'Devastation,' while the armoured breastwork was 9 ft. 2 in. longer. The armoured belt was carried for the whole length of the ship at the same height above the water line. In the 'Devastation' the height diminishes considerably towards the bow. The lower edge of the armour is carried downwards in the vicinity of the stem both to strengthen it and, at the same time, to afford a more effective resistance to a raking fire. 'Dreadnought.'

In France, according to the programme of 1872, twenty ships had been proposed for coast service, one-half of which were to be constructed for offensive operations, and the other half for local defence. Thus, although divided into two categories, both the one and the other are constructed of the same type, differing only in the depth of the hull, the result being that the second type, that is to say the ships for local defence, draw less water and have a less displacement. Otherwise, or at least this is true of the earlier vessels of both types, they possess the same armament of heavy guns and the same armour. Speaking generally they bear a close resemblance to the 'Glatton' type. French coast-service vessels.

The following is a list of the vessels built, or building:—First class: 'Tonnerre,' 'Fulminant,' 'Furieux,' 'Terrible,' 'L'Indomptable,' 'Requin,' and 'Caïman.' Second class: 'Tempête,' 'Tonnant,' and 'Vengeur.'

The results obtained with the 'Tonnerre' type, as might have been expected, were not particularly satisfactory. In point of fact, while in England the changes which have been described were being introduced in the ' Devastation,' in France it had not been thought necessary to make the coast-service ships more seaworthy by raising the sides of the ship, like those of the ' Dreadnought,' to a level with the deck of the armoured redoubt. It is now apparently proposed to make the same additions to the ' Tonnerre ' which were made to the ' Devastation ' when the type was repeated in the construction of the ' Dreadnought.'

The Commission appointed by the Minister of Marine to present a report on the Exhibition in Paris in 1878, with reference to matters of naval architecture, has recently completed its task. The report has appeared in print under the title of ' The Navy at the Exhibition at Paris in 1878.' In this work a doubt has been expressed with reference to the possibility of making mastless turret ships good seagoing battle ships, on the ground that apart from their fighting qualities they do not possess, in a sufficient degree, the qualities of navigability, handiness, habitability, and perhaps, in certain cases, that absolute safety at sea, which are indispensable. This decision is diametrically opposed to the principle followed in recent years by the English navy. Practical experience thus far has not shown, at least conclusively, which of the two systems is the best.

' Preussen,'
' Friedrich
der Grosse,'
' Grosser
Kurfürst.'

In the meantime Germany had constructed three turret ships of precisely the same type as the ' Monarch,' but of somewhat smaller dimensions. These were the ' Preussen,' the ' Friedrich der Grosse,' and the ' Grosser Kurfürst.' Their armour at the water line is 6 inches thicker, while at the turrets it is 2 inches less than that of the ' Monarch.' Compared with that ship they have great advantages in regard to the range of fire of the guns.

' Indepen-
dencia.'

In the spring of 1878 England purchased from the Brazilian Government the turret ship ' Neptune,' formerly called the ' Independencia.' This vessel is an enlarged ' Monarch ; ' the length is 29 ft. 10 in. less, but the breadth is 5 ft. $3\frac{1}{4}$ in. greater, and the displacement is increased by 970 tons. The height of freeboard of the armoured redoubt or breastwork is, however, reduced from 14 in the ' Monarch,' to 11 feet in the ' Neptune ; ' but the greater beam seems, notwithstanding, to ensure for this fully-masted ship a sufficient stability. The armour is considerably heavier than that of the ' Monarch,' being 12 inches, as compared with 7 inches, and on the turrets 13 inches, as compared with 10 inches.

' Inflexi-
ble.'

During the construction of the ' Dreadnought ' Mr. Barnaby, who had succeeded Sir E. Reed as Chief Constructor, proposed to place the turrets from 9 to 11 feet outside the centre line of the ship, with a view of enabling three out of the four guns to be fired in a direct line with the keel ahead or astern. This proposal was at first rejected, but was adopted somewhat later in the 'Inflexible.'

Before passing on to a description of the principal features of this remarkable ship, we must retrace our steps by a few years to review some types of ships, in which the plan of a partial abandonment of armour was adopted.

As we have already seen, the armoured fleet had been divided into two principal sections, that is to say, seagoing ships and coast-service ships. In later years a third division had been added to the two former, namely, the armoured belted cruisers. With the view of giving more effectual protection to commerce it had been deemed necessary to construct ships capable of resisting the fire of unarmoured vessels and vessels with some slight protection. Great speed was indispensable both to capture a weaker ship and to escape from a more powerful enemy. In order to attain a certain maximum speed it was necessary that the armament should neither be too heavy nor too numerous; while, on the other hand, the armour was necessary to protect the ship against the armament carried by ordinary cruisers and small ironclads. It is obvious that ships of this type may also be employed in the line-of-battle at sea. In a naval engagement they would accordingly be placed in the second line; and, for this reason, we should reckon them amongst the second-class battle ships, as they are reckoned in France.

French 'Alma' class.

Formerly, small ironclads were appropriated to the same service, as being possessed of superior evolutionary qualities. The French, in 1863, laid down the 'Belliqueuse,' and the English the 'Enterprise' and the 'Pallas;' but it was in 1865, when the French constructed the 'Alma,' that the greatest development was given to ships of this type. The upper works of the 'Alma,' differing in this respect from preceding ships, were constructed of iron. A new system was for the first time introduced for securing a powerful fire both ahead and astern—a system which is still followed in the French navy, notwithstanding the numerous inconveniences which it entails. This system consists in placing above the central battery, or armoured redoubt, fixed turrets, whether full turrets or half turrets, which project somewhat from the sides of the ship, and in which guns are mounted *en barbette* on turntables. These barbette turrets were, in the first instance, armoured; in later ships they were protected only against musketry and machine guns, while, again, in the most recent ships they are protected with armour. It is true that a heavy gun in a projecting turret, with a considerable elevation above the water line, has decided advantages for a plunging fire, and can be fired with greater facility in a line with the keel ahead and astern, without the necessity of a tumble-home in the topsides of the ship ; but, with an arrangement such as that adopted by the French navy, neither the guns nor the guns' crews are protected. Moreover, it is impossible, at least in the ships constructed before 1872, to fire in a direct line with the keel without destroying, or at least very seriously injuring, the upper works of the ship.

Baron Grivel on barbette guns. Baron Grivel, in the 'Revue Maritime' of 1872, vol. ii., makes the following observations with reference to the 'Océan'—observations which appear of sufficient importance to be given in full : 'The fire of the guns placed in the turrets in a line with the keel, to which so much has been sacrificed both in the spread of the shrouds, the position of the boats, and the arrangement of the bulwarks, and last, not least, the light armament of the upper deck, appears to me a perfect chimera. The Commission appointed to carry out experiments were so much struck with the injury occasioned by the concussion from a 24 c/m., or $15\frac{1}{2}$-ton, gun that they determined that the guns should not be trained within 15° of the line of the keel. The shrouds and the boats at the davits had been covered up with wet canvas, and yet the force of the explosions was such that the greater number of the rivets near the upper deck were fractured, and two boats were so much injured as to be rendered unfit for use. Moreover. the fire of the foremost turret could not converge with that of the aftermost turret at close quarters without danger to the guns' crews. It would appear wise to fire the guns parallel with one another, or at least to attempt a converging fire only at a considerable distance. When firing within less than an angle of 45° with the keel line, the crews should be withdrawn from the extremities of the ship, on the side from which fire is being directed, and the men absolutely forbidden from passing near the bulwarks on that side of the ship.'

These remarks will suffice to show how much caution and care are indispensable in vessels of the 'Océan' type in working these guns *en barbette*. With the present projection of the turrets the extreme arc of training does not exceed a range of from 90° to 100°. Every effort should therefore be made to increase the projection of the turrets beyond the sides of the ship.

The depression of the guns is not quite sufficient for a plunging fire on the deck of an enemy at very close quarters. The means of elevating the guns, on the other hand, are remarkably good. The guns mounted in the turrets of the 'Océan' were the only guns which were able to reach the Prussian gunboats, anchored at a distance of 5,400 yards from the squadron at the head of the Bay of Witte, which the ships were unable to enter from their great draught of water. Their fire was so effective that at the sixth round these gunboats, including the famous 'Grille,' which had just given chase to the 'Jerome Napoleon,' disappeared into an inner channel communicating with that estuary.

We return to the general progress of armoured construction. For the new ships the turret system has been adhered to, but with every possible effort to diminish its disadvantages. The programme for the reconstruction of the fleet, adopted in 1872, contains the following proposals with reference to ships fitted with barbette towers: 'For the ironclad of the first class the upper battery will contain four 24 c/m., or 15½-ton guns in barbette turrets of 4·59 feet in height, and 19·68 feet internal diameter. Bow and stern chasers must be capable of being fired at point blank parallel with the keel. The fire of these bow and stern chase guns must not, in any case, interrupt the free circulation on the upper deck, and therefore the contraction of the upper works, both before and abaft the armoured redoubt, must be made as considerable as possible, having regard to the necessity for giving a sufficient spread to the rigging to secure a proper support for the masts. The conditions laid down will require that the line of flight of the projectiles from guns firing parallel with the keel shall pass at a distance of about 3 ft. 6 in. from the sides of the ship. One gun of 24 c/m., or 15½ tons, firing ahead under a forecastle, the after part of which is closed in, but not armoured, will complete the armament of the upper deck.' *Modifications in programme of 1872.*

In the first ships constructed in accordance with this programme, the 'Redoubtable' and the 'Dévastation,' the turrets are not armoured, while those of the latest ships, the 'Amiral Duperré' and the 'Duguesclin,' are protected. The sides of the ship have a greater tumble-home than in any preceding vessels, the result being that the upper deck is very narrow.

The 'Alma' is protected with 6-inch armour at the water line, and the armament consists of six guns of 19 c/m., or 7½ tons. After this type were constructed the 'Armide,' 'Atalante,' 'Jeanne d'Arc,' 'Montauban,' 'Thetis,' and 'Reine Blanche,' of which the greater number were completed in 1868. *The 'Armide,' &c.*

In 1869 the 'Victorieuse' was commenced. The displacement was 350 tons greater, and the engine was more powerful, giving a speed of 13 knots, as compared with 11·8 in the 'Alma.' The *'Victorieuse'* armament was altered in view of the introduction into the navy of the 24 c/m., or 15½-ton, gun. It is now composed of six 24 c/m., or 15½-ton, guns, one 19 c/m., or 7½-ton, and six 14 c/m., or 53-cwt. guns. The same armour is retained for the water line and the central battery, the increase in displacement having been appropriated almost entirely to the increase of the armament. The construction of this vessel was delayed by the war of 1870–71, and she was not launched till towards the close of 1875.

'Triomphante,' 'La Galissonnière.' The 'Triomphante,' which was launched in March 1877, is of precisely the same type; while the 'La Galissonnière' has somewhat less horse-power and a lighter armament, composed of six 24 c/m., or 15½-ton, guns, and four 40-pounders.

Russian belted cruisers. In 1872 the Russians had constructed the cruiser 'General Admiral,' partially armoured. The water line was protected with 6-inch plating, while six 9-ton guns were mounted in the centre of the ship in an armoured redoubt, or battery, projecting about 32 inches from the sides of the ship, and thus securing a range of fire ahead and astern. The armoured battery was protected with 4-inch plating; but it was only 30 inches in height, the guns firing *en barbette*. The armoured redoubt and water-line belt were not connected by an armoured side.

'Shannon.' Shortly afterwards Mr. Barnaby proposed to the English Admiralty to carry still further the abandonment of armour. In the 'Shannon,' constructed in accordance with this view, the water line is protected by an armoured belt, extending from the stern to within sixty feet of the stem, and terminating in an armoured transverse bulkhead. An armoured deck extends forward from the lower edge of the armoured belt. It is carried at first horizontally, but near the bow it descends to ten feet below the water line. The armoured belt is 8·98 feet in depth, of which 4 feet only are above the water line; the remainder of the ship is unarmoured, with the exception of the battery, the forward end of which is protected. The guns on the broadside are unprotected, and mounted at considerable distances apart, to mitigate the effect of shell. For the same reason the upper deck is not carried above the guns. It has, however, been proposed to divide the guns from one another by iron screens.

'Nelson' and 'Northampton.' The abandonment of armour in the bow suggested to Mr. Barnaby the idea of modifying the stern in the 'Nelson' and the 'Northampton' on the same principle. These ships exceed the 'Shannon' in displacement by 2,255 tons, an increase which is due to an increase in the armament from two 18-ton and seven 12-ton guns in the 'Shannon' to four 18-ton and eight 12-ton guns in the 'Nelson.'

Twin-screws admit of a division of the ship into two separate parts by means of a longitudinal bulkhead. The ship is further subdivided by numerous transverse bulkheads into ninety watertight compartments. The supply of coal is 600 tons, or double that of the 'Shannon,' and it can be increased, according to M. Marchal, to 1,100 tons.

In Italy the principle of the abandonment of armour had been applied to two turret ships, the 'Duilio' and the 'Dandolo,' and they had been protected in certain parts with 22-inch armour. Their armament was composed of four 35-ton guns, which was afterwards changed into four 100-ton guns. 'Duilio.'

The construction of these ships suggested the idea in England of preparing the design for the 'Inflexible.' In bringing forward this design Mr. Barnaby declared that England could not remain behind other nations, that it was therefore necessary to increase the thickness of the armour, which in the 'Dreadnought' was only 14 inches. It was not, however, mainly with this object that he proposed the construction of the new ship, it was still more with the view to improve the armament, which was to consist of guns of the heaviest calibre, for which if necessary other guns could be substituted of still greater power, if it were practicable to manufacture them. While the armament was the main object, he was able to protect the ship with 24-inch armour. To attain this object he placed, at a height of 6½ feet below the water line, a 3-inch armoured deck, extending over the whole length of the ship. In the centre of this deck an armoured redoubt or citadel is constructed, completely protected, 16 feet in height, 110 feet in length, and 75 feet in breadth. Above this citadel are two turrets, placed diagonally with reference to the centre line of the keel. The superstructure above the upper deck is constructed in such a manner as to admit of a direct fire from four guns ahead and two guns astern, the after-superstructure being wider than the forward-superstructure. 'Inflexible.'

It will be seen that the bow and the stern of the ship are protected not by armour, but by of a belt of cork about 8 feet in depth and 4 feet in width, and by the construction of numerous watertight compartments, which can be filled with fuel. It is supposed that this part of the ship may be riddled by projectiles without compromising the stability to a dangerous degree.

The inference which may be drawn from the details given is clear. The increased thickness of armour and the greater weight of armament involve a reduction in the area which can be protected, the only alternative being to have recourse to extraordinary dimensions, and an inevitable sacrifice of the seagoing and evolutionary

qualities of the ship. While reducing the protected area the armament was considerably diminished, consisting of a small number of
guns of very heavy calibre. Doubts were entertained by many
competent persons as to the success of the new type, and the English
Admiralty, which, after the loss of the 'Captain,' had appointed a
Committee on designs, once more directed a Committee to investigate
the seagoing qualities of the 'Inflexible' with reference to certain
contingencies of naval battle.

The relation between the length and the breadth of the 'Inflexible' has given rise to numerous discussions. The proportion of
length has become gradually less in the later ships. The direction
in which naval architects have been moving may be traced in the
following table.

Minotaur	.	.	.	.	6·73
Bellerophon	.	.	.	.	5·35
Hercules	.	.	.	.	5·50
Swiftsure	.	.	.	.	5·09
Devastation	.	.	.	.	4·58
Dreadnought	.	.	.	.	5·01

The Admiralty resolved to give to the 'Inflexible' the proportion of
4·26, the smallest which could be adopted having regard to the existing facilities of dock accommodation. Mr. Barnaby considered
the proportion of 4·5 as being the least which could be accepted
while giving to the ship the speed of 14 knots which had been fixed
when the design was prepared. In his judgment it could not be
made less, for otherwise the armour could not be extended sufficiently
below the water line to protect the vital parts of the ship, the
rolling movement tending to raise the side out of the water in
proportion as the beam was increased.

'Ajax,'
'Con-
queror,'
'Colossus.

After the 'Inflexible,' the 'Agamemnon' and the 'Ajax' were
laid down. They are of the same type but of smaller dimensions
than the former ship. The armament is the same as that of the
'Dreadnought,' though the armour is heavier. In the 'Colossus,'
'Conqueror,' and 'Majestic,' which have been lately commenced,
steel has been introduced as much as possible.

'Amiral
Duperré.'

While in England the armoured surface has been reduced to a
minimum, and the thickness of the armour has been increased to the
maximum, attention had also been directed in France to the partial
removal of armour. The French constructors hesitated, with wise
prudence, to incur the risk of a partial abandonment of armour, or at
least to remove the armour to the same extent as in the 'Nelson' and
the 'Inflexible' types. The armoured belt of the 'Dévastation' does

extend over the whole length of the ship, but the unarmoured length is only 27·88 feet, while that of the 'Shannon' is 59 feet, that of the 'Nelson' 98½ feet, and that of the 'Inflexible' 220 feet. In order to protect the water line with the maximum thickness of armour, the protection of the guns must be diminished; and this can be effected, in the opinion of the French constructors, by the abandonment of the armoured central battery. This battery, in their view, is ill adapted for carrying and working the heaviest guns, which, from their great length and complicated machinery, require a large space. It is for this reason that they mount their guns in armoured turrets, raised at a considerable elevation above the water line, the guns being mounted *en .barbette*, while the light guns are carried on the broadside in an unarmoured battery. Such is the fundamental idea of a seagoing battle ship of the first class, as represented in the ' Amiral Duperré,' which was laid down at Toulon in December 1876, and launched on September 11, 1879. The armour on the water line is of 22 inches, and the heavy armament consists of four 34 c/m., 46-ton, guns. It will be seen that both the offensive and the defensive power is increased in a great proportion in comparison with that of the ' Dévastation.' The 46-ton guns are placed in *barbette* turrets, two of which project from the sides of the ship, and afford a means of firing in line with the keel, while two other towers are placed in the centre line of the ship on the upper deck. The turrets are carried down to the armoured deck, which rests upon the armoured belt; they are entirely protected with 12-inch armour, and contain the machinery of the turntables and the communications with the magazines. They are, therefore, better arranged than those of the ' Téméraire.' There is another important modification. The funnels, and certain communications, giving access to the interior of the ship, are protected with circular 12-inch armour. This provision is looked upon as a matter of great importance, for if, in ships like the ' Shannon ' and the ' Nelson,' without a central battery, a projectile strikes somewhat above the water line and reaches the funnel, it will make an opening, by which the smoke may fill the battery and render it impossible to remain there. The range of fire from the turrets astern is interfered with as little as possible, the boats being placed upon a hurricane deck, which is carried above the turrets, and protects them from the fire of small arms and machine guns from the mastheads of an enemy's ship. A similar deck is carried transversely over the turrets in the forward part of the ship. The stern is fitted with iron falling bulwarks. In addition to the heavy guns, fourteen 14 c/m., 53-cwt., guns are mounted on the broadside. They are protected only by the light topsides of the ship. The hull is constructed almost entirely of steel. The 'Amiral Baudin' and the 'Formidable,' of a type similar to the 'Amiral Duperré,' have been laid down. They have 3 ft. 4 in. more beam, and 1,000 tons more displacement. Up to the present time we have no precise information with regard to these two ships. The heavy armament is to consist of three 100-ton guns, while 22-inch armour is retained for the water line, and the plating of the turrets has been increased from 12 to 16 inches. The thickness of the deck armour has also been increased.[1]

'Amiral Baudin' and the 'Formidable.'

About the same time a second class ironclad, the 'Duguesclin,' of the same type was commenced. The general arrangement of the ship is precisely the same as that of the 'Amiral Duperré.' The 'Duguesclin' is the first ship of the second class constructed in conformity with the revised plans of the programme of 1872. Comparing it with the former ships, the 'Victorieuse' and the 'Triomphante,' it will be found that the displacement is increased by 1,750 tons, and the armour from 6 to 10 inches. The armament, it is true, is reduced by two 24 c/m., or 15½-ton, guns, but it is placed much more advantageously. The hull is of steel. The 'Vauban,' the 'Turenne,' and the 'Bayard' are exactly of the same type as the 'Duguesclin,' except that the two latter are built of wood.

'Duguesclin.'

In Germany, a programme for the navy was elaborated in 1873. In this programme six armoured corvettes were proposed, as offensive coast-service ships, for the defence of the coast. Only one of these ships, the 'Hansa,' was completed. The 'Hansa' was commenced in November 1868, launched in October 1872, and only completed in the summer of 1875, having, therefore, occupied seven years in construction. This vessel has a casemate, like that of the 'Swiftsure,' consisting of two batteries, one above the other. From the lower deck battery a broadside fire can be obtained, while from the other, the upper deck battery, a line of fire can be obtained both towards the bow and the stern.

'Hansa.'

The first of the five other new ships was the 'Sachsen,' which was commenced in 1874 and completed at the beginning of 1878. In imitation of the English navy the armour is confined to the centre of the ship, and encloses a casemate like that of the 'Inflexible.' From the lower edge of the armoured belt, at a depth of 4·59 feet

'Sachsen' class.

[1] Four new ships of the type—the 'Hoche,' 'Magenta,' 'Marceau,' and 'Neptune,'—of less displacement but with thicker armour in places, appear on the list of ships of the French Navy for 1881. They have only just been begun, and their details are not yet settled.

below the water line, a 3-inch armoured deck is carried fore and aft, with no opening or hatchway whatever. The unarmoured part of the ship is provided, like that of the 'Inflexible,' with a belt of cork about 3 ft. 4 in. in depth and thickness. By means of a longitudinal bulkhead, and numerous transverse bulkheads, the ship is divided into 120 watertight compartments.

The armour at the water line consists of a double thickness of plating, viz., a 12-inch plate with 8 inches of teak backing, and a 6-inch plate, with 8 inches of teak backing, and two thicknesses of skin-plating. The deck of the central battery is protected with 2-inch plates. At the after end of the casemate is placed a square open battery, armed with four 26 c/m., or 18½-ton, guns at indented ports. These guns fire *en barbette*. Near the foremost end of the casemate is placed a turret of the same shape as those of the 'Téméraire,' and armed with one 30·5 c/m., 36-ton, gun, or two 18½-ton guns, which also fire *en barbette*, and can be trained in all directions.

Three other corvettes of the same type, the 'Baiern,' the 'Wurtemburg,' and the 'Baden,' have been already launched; while the last, provisionally named with the letter E, has been commenced.

We now turn to the coast-service vessels for local defence. In France four floating-batteries of the original 'Palestro' type had been constructed, in 1858, of a type very similar to the earlier 'Dévastation.' Those ships were soon found to be insufficient, and a new type was laid down from the plans of M. Lemoine. A casemate is constructed upon the deck in which the guns are mounted. The iron bulwarks forward and aft are fitted to let down. 'Palestro.'

The 'Arrogante,' the 'Implacable,' and the 'Opiniatre' were first constructed, and shortly after, with little difference in reference to type, the 'Embuscade,' the 'Imprenable,' the 'Protectrice,' and the 'Refuge,' the dimensions being somewhat greater. These seven ships still belong to the French fleet. They are protected with 5-inch armour in the 'Arrogante' type, and 6-inch armour in the 'Embuscade' type. In view of the increasing power of guns their armour was considered insufficient; and in 1863 a new type was proposed, protected at the water line with 6-inch armour. 'Arrogante.'

The 'Taureau' was the first ram constructed for coast defence. The armoured belt is only 2 ft. 3 in. above the water line, and it is protected with a 2-inch armoured deck. The top sides are of an extraordinary shape, like a half cylinder, which gives the general effect of a huge whale. In the bow of the ship, and resting on an armoured deck, there is a fixed turret protected with 5-inch armour. The 'Taureau' is fitted with a long projecting ram and twin-screws. 'Taureau.'

The 'Cerbère,' the 'Bélier,' the 'Bouledogue,' and the 'Tigre' were constructed on the same type, but fitted with a revolving turret, protected with 7-inch armour. The armour at the water line is increased from 6 to 9 inches, while the armament consists of two 24 c/m., or 15½-ton, guns. The hulls of all these ships are of wood, excepting the top sides, which are of iron. The three latter were only finished after the war of 1870–71.

With regard to the new ships projected in the programme of 1872 for coast defence, that is to say, the coast defence ships of the second class, they are very similar to those of the first class, though the draught of water is less. It may be presumed that the upper works of ships of this type will be changed, as in the case of the 'Tonnerre.'

'Glatton.' The English ships intended for local defence have been already described. In the first instance the 'Glatton' was intended both as a local coast-defence vessel and an offensive coast-service ship; but her nautical qualities are so inadequate that she is not adapted for offensive operations. For the local defence of the coast the English rely chiefly on unarmoured gunboats.

German coast-service vessels. In Germany seven monitors have been proposed for local coast defence. The southern coasts of the Baltic are easily defended by batteries and torpedoes, the greater number of the channels of approach being deep, but very narrow. It is otherwise on the coasts of the North Sea and Schleswig-Holstein, where the sandbanks are of vast extent, and require as the means of defence small ships with only a light draught of water. It is for this reason that it was determined, at a somewhat later date, to substitute for the monitors armoured gunboats, carrying one heavy gun, capable of penetrating the armour of a battle ship at a considerable distance. A more manageable and less costly type of vessel would be obtained, and for the sum appropriated to the construction of the monitors a larger number of gunboats could be built. The German navy had two little monitors, the 'Arminius' and the 'Prince Albert;' but the latter was condemned in 1878, while it is probable that the 'Arminius' will soon be unfit for service. Both were built in 1864. It was proposed to construct eighteen armoured gunboats, of which ten have been completed, of the 'Wespe' type.

CHAPTER I.

OUR NAVAL REQUIREMENTS IN WAR.

ADMIRAL JURIEN DE LA GRAVIÉRE has observed that we must first ask ourselves, 'What are the services we require from the navy?' before we can attempt to deal satisfactorily with the Navy Estimates. The Admiral unhesitatingly replies to this question, that the primary duty of a navy in war is 'to occupy the great ocean highways.' Admiral Jurien de la Graviére.

In an essay, which gained the prize of a gold medal given by the Royal United Service Institution, on 'Great Britain's Maritime Power,' Captain P. H. Colomb, R.N., summarised our naval requirements in war as follows : 'First, the shores of the British Isles must be preserved inviolate by a naval force close to them ; second, the cruisers of the enemy must be met and beaten at sea ; third, the enemy's fleets *may* be met at sea, and if so should be beaten ; fourth, some kind of naval force especially designed for attacking the territory of the enemy should be always kept in readiness.' Captain P. H. Colomb.

The views here expressed in outline as to the naval requirements of this country have been generally accepted by those who took part in the lengthened discussions to which Captain Colomb's essay has given rise. According to the most accredited authorities—details and minor points being left out of consideration—the naval policy of the country may be understood as requiring :—

1. Defence of our territory, in all parts of the world, from attack. Objects of our naval policy.

2. Maintenance of the lines of communication between the mother country and outlying bases of supply.

3. Protection of that portion of the wealth of the country which is employed in maritime trade.

4. Superiority of force to ensure either the shutting up of an enemy's fleets or their defeat when encountered.

Both Captain Colomb and the other officers, whose essays on the Development of our Maritime Power have been printed, have prac-

Authors of essays on the development of our maritime power.

tically formed very similar views of the naval requirements of the British Empire. The former 'looks upon the functions of the English navy as being confined to preventing damage being done to us by the enemy, and to promoting and covering attacks.' 'Blockade by sea' is explained to mean the cutting by a hostile power of our lines of supply, a disaster even more to be guarded against than invasion. The ships of a navy are divided by the same writer into 'Fleet ships,' armoured and carrying heavy guns, 'Frigates,' also armoured, and smaller classes not intended to take part in those great operations of warfare which it has long been the custom to style 'general engagements.'

Sir Howard Douglas ; 'Naval Warfare with Steam.' London, 1858, pp. xvi, xvii.

Other writers likewise divide the ships which are necessary for the naval defence of the empire into the classes of armour-clad fighting vessels and unarmoured cruisers, with further subdivisions, which, in this place, there is no need to specify. Sir Howard Douglas, writing twenty years ago, summed up the results of his examination of the naval requirements of the country as follows:—

'Great Britain, as an insular and colonial empire, can maintain that high position in the rank of nations which she has gained by the instrumentality of her navy, only by keeping that noble branch of her service, not merely in a state barely sufficient to protect herself against any one maritime power, but fully adequate to defeat any maritime coalition to which political circumstances may at any future time give rise. And it must always be borne in mind that, to enable the navy of Great Britain to act on equal terms with that of any continental nation, it ought by far to exceed the navy of such nation in number of ships of war of like force. Taking France as an example: while the naval power of that country will, in the event of a war, be chiefly collected in the two seas, on the shores of which her great arsenals are established, that of our country must be dispersed over the whole world with sufficient strength in every region to protect her numerous colonies and widely extended commerce.'

Growth of the maritime trade of the British Empire.

A few figures will show the growing importance of our ocean trade, the protection of which should be a main object of the strategic policy of the empire when engaged in war. It will not be necessary to note in minute detail the increase of the sums which represent the value of our exports and imports since the date of Sir Howard Douglas' remarks. Taking the year 1878, which may be accepted as neither exceptionally prosperous nor yet so unfavourable as 1879, we find that the total imports and exports of the United Kingdom amounted to 614,254,600*l*., or an average of 18*l*. 3*s*. 6*d*. per head of population. Imports of the value of 77,936,110*l.* were drawn from our possessions abroad, to which in return we exported 66,237,486*l.* of home produce. That the greater part of this trade was carried in ships flying the British flag, and especially depending upon the navy for protection in case of war, may be seen from the fact that during the year 1878 the total tonnage of foreign vessels, entered and cleared with cargoes only at ports in the United Kingdom, from and to foreign countries and British possessions was 12,602,758, whilst the British tonnage was 30,297,176. The registered shipping of the United Kingdom on December 31, 1879, showed a total of 25,884 sailing and steam vessels. To these should be added 12,201 vessels belonging to British possessions beyond the seas. The vessels built in the colonies in 1876 included 802 sailing vessels, with a combined tonnage of 149,778 tons, and 96 steam vessels with an aggregate capacity of 6,121 tons. These statistics will convey some idea of the magnitude of the interests involved in our maritime trade, and of the meaning of the phrase, so frequently used by writers on our naval requirements, ' protection of our commerce.' But their significance may be made even more apparent by comparing the total tonnage of the British colonial possessions only with that of the chief states of continental Europe. The tonnage of our colonial possessions in 1876 amounted to 1,701,245 tons, while the shipping of the German Empire, at the same date, measured 1,084,882 tons, that of France 1,028,228 tons, and that of Italy 1,127,154 tons. These figures show that the work of defending the colonial shipping alone would impose upon the navy a task little inferior in magnitude to that which would be imposed, in similar circumstances, on the navies of France and Germany combined. It is scarcely necessary to add that our colonial shipping, important as it is, forms but a part of that vast commerce which would claim protection from the British navy during war.

The nature of the cargoes carried by the ships which enter the ports of the British Isles, gives additional importance to this duty. To provide work for the large section of the population of Great Britain engaged in the manufacture of textile fabrics, there were imported during 1876 wool to the value of 23,637,809*l.*, and raw cotton to the value of 40,180,880*l.* Intimately as the prosperity of the country depends on the certain supply of these and similar substances, its very existence is more distinctly concerned in the safe conveyance of the vast quantities of articles which go to make up the food supply of its inhabitants. ' Your greatest commercial transactions,' says Captain J. C. Colomb, ' are based upon the precision and certainty of your steam communications. . . . upon these

Comparison of British and foreign mercantile tonnage.

Dependence on foreign trade.

water roads depends the sustenance of the people at home. . . . In the seven years ending with 1840 the import of wheat from foreign sources into this country amounted to 6,000,000 quarters. For the seven years ending with 1877, what do you think the grain imports to this country were ? 370,000,000 quarters. That is made doubly important by remembering that in England now, as compared with the England of twenty years ago, there are 800,000 acres less wheat grown ; and, to sum up shortly, in 1846 the import of corn and flour amounted to 17 lbs. per head of the population ; but in 1876, thirty years after, it amounted to 167 lbs. per head. In 1877 this quantity was further increased to 203 lbs. per head.'

The future development of our trade in food may be inferred from a retrospective view of its increase within the experience of the present generation. Our importations of food in 1840 were valued, in a return procured by Sir Stafford Northcote, at 27,599,431*l*. The corresponding value for 1878 was 149,759,829*l*. It is especially worthy of remark that the commercial depression, which had begun before the expiration of the period embraced in this review, had exercised no sensible influence in arresting the rapid progress of our importations of food.

Increase of our shipping trade.

In a summary compiled in the autumn of 1880 it was shown that our commerce grows faster than our population. Taking the imports and exports in 1879, a year of dull and declining trade, the ratio per inhabitant of the United Kingdom was 17*l*. 18*s*. 3*d*., against 17*l*. 4*s*. 6*d*. in 1869. The increase is not limited to the import trade. The exports of 1879 showed an increase of not less than 12,000,000*l*. sterling over those in 1869. Our merchant shipping, excluding colonial tonnage, shows an augmentation of 860,000 tons ; and the effective carrying power is almost doubled through the extensive substitution of steam for sailing vessels. The ratio of steam to sailing tonnage has advanced from 17 per cent. in 1869 to 38 per cent. in the latest returns. The carrying power of steamers may be computed as fourfold that of sailing ships. Our carrying power is now equal to 14,000,000 tons, as against 8,500,000 ten years ago ; and if we include colonial shipping, the total British tonnage would be equivalent to 19,500,000 tons, the total for all nations being a little over 40,000,000.

CHAPTER II.

CLASSIFICATION OF SHIPS OF WAR—ENUMERATION OF THE SEVERAL
QUALITIES NECESSARY IN FIGHTING SHIPS.

A REVIEW of recent naval construction will be made most complete *Recent naval construction reviewed.* by giving descriptions, more or less detailed, of the several classes of ships which are to be found in our own and foreign navies. These descriptions will be met with in the chapters on the various divisions of modern fighting fleets. They will exhibit the condition to which the navies of foreign powers have been brought, and will show at what standard of strength it will be prudent to maintain the British navy.

The subject of classification of ships of war is exhaustively *Classification of ships of war.* examined by the authors of 'Die Marine,' a book to which the writer of the present work is deeply indebted, and from which the greater part of this chapter is borrowed. Every large navy, they point out, at the present day includes armoured vessels for the line of battle and for coast service, unarmoured cruisers, gun-vessels, gunboats, torpedo vessels, despatch vessels, transports, training-ships, and various vessels for harbour service.

Modern ships of war may be divided most conveniently as follows :—

I. According to displacement— *Classification according to displacement;*
    1. Ocean-going ships.
    2. Vessels for coast service.

II. With reference to the material of which the ships are built, *according to material;* and the system of construction—
    1. Wooden ships:
        a. Built with wood frames, and a single outer planking of wood.
        b. Built on the diagonal system.

2. Iron ships:
    a. Built with transverse frames.
    b. Built with longitudinal frames.
3. Iron ships sheathed with wood.
4. Composite ships.
5. Steel ships.

according to defensive power;

III. According to their defensive power—

    1. Unarmoured ships.
    2. Armoured ships.

according to motive power;

IV. According to their motive power—

    1. Sailing ships:
        a. Full-rigged ships.
        b. Barques.
        c. Three-masted schooners.
        d. Brigs.
        e. Schooners (and brigantines).
    2. Steam ships:
        a. Paddle.
        b. Screw.
            1. Single screw.
            2. Twin screw.
        c. Hydraulic.

according to the service for which intended;

V. According to the service for which they are designed—

    1. Battle ships:
        a. For European waters.
        b. For ocean service.
        c. Second class line-of-battle ships.
    2. Cruisers:
        a. For the capture of cruisers.
        b. For the capture of fast steamers.
        c. For the protection of merchant ships and mercantile and consular ports.
    3. Coast service vessels:
        a. Offensive coast vessels (coast-attack vessels).
        b. Defensive coast vessels (coast-defence vessels).
    4. Transports:
        a. For conveyance of troops.
        b. For conveyance of stores.

5. Training ships :
    a. Seagoing.
    b. Not seagoing.
6. Harbour ships.

VI. According to the system on which the guns are mounted— according to system of armament.

Masted Ships and Vessels.

1. With batteries extending along the whole length of the ship :
    a. All guns mounted on the upper deck (flush-decked corvettes and gunboats).
    b. Carrying guns mounted between decks.
        a. With one tier of guns between decks.
        β. With two tiers of guns, of which one is between decks.
        γ. With three tiers of guns, of which two are between decks (two-deckers).
        δ. With four tiers of guns, of which three are between decks (three-deckers).
    (β, γ, δ, are the now obsolete ' ships of the line.')
2. Central battery ships :
    a. With no guns firing ahead or astern.
    b. With two guns firing in a line with the keel.
    c. With three guns firing in a line with the keel.
    d. With four guns firing in a line with the keel.
3. Turret ships.

Mastless Ships.

1. Without a central redoubt, or monitor :
    a. Single turret.
    b. Double turret.
    c. Three turrets.
    d. Four turrets.
2. With central redoubt, or breastwork monitors :
    a. Single turret.
    b. Double turret.
        a. Turrets in line with the keel.
        β. Turrets placed diagonally.
3. Circular vessels, or *Popoffkas.*
4. Having the guns mounted on the disappearing principle.
5. Barbette ships, such as the ' Sachsen ' or ' Collingwood ' type.

Special types, as the 'Polyphemus,' may perhaps deserve a division of their own in the classification.

Arbitrary use of the terms 'frigate' and 'corvette.'

The terms frigate and corvette, which before the introduction of heavy guns designated well-defined types, were nevertheless used quite arbitrarily. Ships with 'tween deck batteries were called frigates or 'decked' corvettes. Ships with open batteries were called 'flush' decked corvettes. It has now become difficult to establish a distinction between frigates and decked corvettes, inasmuch as we cannot even use the displacement as a basis of classification. Ships which would be designated in one navy decked corvettes, are called frigates in another. Thus the 'Leipzig,' a rapid cruiser of nearly 4,000 tons displacement, 4,800 indicated horse-power, and armed with twelve 17 c/m., or 6-ton, guns, which was launched from the Vulcan works, near Stettin, on September 13, 1875, was officially designated a decked corvette, while the smaller Austrian ship 'Radetzky' is officially termed a frigate. For the sake of brevity, the special distinctive terms 'decked' and 'flush decked' are now rarely used, and the term corvette alone is substituted both in writing and conversation. A ship of 4,000 tons displacement, with a covered battery and armed with twelve 6-ton guns, is classed with a vessel of 1,000 tons displacement, armed with four 15 c/m. or 4-ton guns, mounted on the uncovered upper deck. Both vessels are concisely described as corvettes.

Ironclads.

These remarks apply still more strongly to ironclad vessels. For example, ironclads with central batteries are called 'casemate ships' in the Austro-Hungarian navy, while in the German navy all ironclads of the first and second classes, whether battery or turret ships, are designated officially armoured frigates.

This chaos might easily be reduced to order if it were only agreed to call all armoured fighting ships armour-clads, all cruisers with covered batteries frigates, and to limit the term corvette to those ships only which are at present called flush-decked corvettes. This would correspond with the original classification into ships of the line, frigates, and corvettes. It would put an end to the present confusion, and a further advantage would be secured in the abbreviation of the distinctive terms. The new British nomenclature affords a basis for the unification of the terms now so variously used in different navies.

New British nomenclature.

In it ships of war are divided into *Armoured* and *Unarmoured*.

The Armoured classes are :—

1. Battle ships, or heavy seagoing armourclads.

2. Cruisers, or ' belted ' ships, and some of the early broadside ironclads.
3. Special ships, such as rams and torpedo vessels.
4. Coast service ships.

The Unarmoured classes comprise :—

1. Cruisers of the 1st, 2nd, and 3rd classes.
2. Sloops.
3. Gun-vessels.
4. Gunboats, for general and for special service.
5. Despatch vessels.
6. Unarmoured torpedo vessels and boats.

As it was impossible to unite all the qualities which are to be Specialisation of desired in a ship of war in a single vessel, it became necessary to types. divide the leading types into subdivisions, each specially adapted to the use of a particular arm, or to perform some special service. For the battle ships, designed for naval operations in European waters, great offensive and defensive powers, and evolutionary qualities are essential, while the highest seagoing qualities, including habitability at sea, are, in the opinion of some, less essential. For seagoing battle ships, offensive and defensive strength must be partially sacrificed, in order to secure unquestionable seaworthiness. For ocean-going battle ships canvas is a valuable auxiliary. In battle ships for European waters, masts and yards involve a useless sacrifice of fighting power.

In the year 1867 Admiral Sir George Elliott wrote a paper, in Admiral which he set forth the essential qualities of a ship of war in the follow- Elliott on ing order, the order being modified according to the special purpose the essentials of a for which the vessel was designed :— ship of war.

Line of Battle Ships (for ocean service).

1. Seaworthiness.
2. Handiness.
3. Armament.
4. Speed under steam.
5. Speed under sail.
6. Coal endurance.
7. Draught of water.

First Class Cruisers (Frigates).

1. Seaworthiness.
2. Speed under steam.

3. Armament.
4. Coal endurance.
5. Speed under sail.
6. Handiness.
7. Draught of water.

Second Class Cruisers (Corvettes).

1. Seaworthiness.
2. Speed under steam.
3. Coal endurance.
4. Draught of water.
5. Speed under sail
6. Handiness.
7. Armament.

Señor
Heriz.
'Memoria
sobre los
Barcos
acoraza-
dos,' Bar-
celona,
1875, p. 4.

'In ships of war,' says Señor Enrique Heriz, ' our aim is to combine military or fighting, and nautical or seagoing qualities.

The Fighting Qualities include :

Attack.	*Defence.*
Guns.	Armour.
Perforating power.	Material (iron).
Shell power.	Compartments.
Ram.	Double bottom.
Torpedo.	

The Seagoing Qualities include :

Draught of water.
Displacement.
Stability.
Speed.
Handiness.

Although it will be found that other qualities, not included in the list, must also be considered, yet the above summary furnishes us with a tolerably accurate enumeration of the points most deserving of attention in the ships of war of the present day.

CHAPTER III.

EARLIEST IRONCLADS.

It was observed in the Introduction, that the earliest representatives of the modern armourclad type were the floating batteries suggested by the Emperor of the French.

Fig. 1.

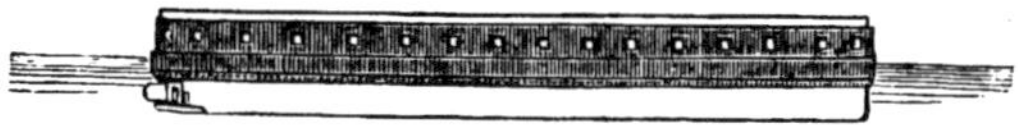

KINBURN BATTERIES.

These batteries were not protected in the mode which further experience has proved to be the most effective—that is to say, by massive rolled plates. The armour of these, the pioneers of the ironclad fleet, consisted only of built-up masses of thin plates, while the sides of the ships on which they were fixed were constructed with a considerable tumble home: it being assumed that the shot striking the plates at an angle would probably glance off without doing any serious damage. This theory was most satisfactorily verified at the bombardment of Kinburn; the floating batteries, constructed on the principles described, having been entirely uninjured by the Russian fire.

The action of Kinburn naturally directed the attention of the shipbuilders of this country to a system which had been found so effective for the protection of ships of war, and the Admiralty at once decided on building three floating batteries, the 'Thunderbolt,' 'Erebus,' and 'Terror.' These vessels, constituting the first instalment of the British ironclad fleet were built in the years 1855–56, and they were completed—to the credit, be it said, of the private ship-builders of England—in the short space of three months. In the interval, however, hostilities had been suspended, and happily no occasion has since arisen for a practical trial of these vessels in active naval operations.

The 'Thunderbolt,' 'Erebus' and 'Terror.'

Each of these floating batteries was of 2,000 tons burthen and 300 horse-power. The armament consisted of thirty heavy guns as calibres were reckoned in those days. Having been intended for an attack on Cronstadt, the only approaches to which were by shallow channels, rendered still more difficult by the artificial obstructions placed in the way of navigation by the Russians, these batteries were limited to a draught of 8 ft. 6 in. of water. With regard to the materials selected and the mode of construction, it may be mentioned that they were built of iron, and that their topsides were covered with teak 6 inches thick, extending from the gunwale to 2 feet below the water line. This teak was covered with iron plates 4 inches in thickness. The sides, like those of the French batteries, had a considerable tumble home.

The bombardment of Kinburn had shown that an effective attack could be made upon a fortress by employing vessels so armoured as not to be penetrable by the projectiles of the enemy, and able, owing to their light draught, to stand close in, and maintain a continuous fire on shore batteries. From that date the earlier wooden gunboats and bomb-vessels ceased to be admissible in modern warfare, and, as soon as the batteries returned from Kinburn to France, steps were taken to remedy all the defects which actual experience had disclosed. But trifling improvements were effected by these alterations, and the Kinburn batteries remained what they originally were, floating batteries, which have gradually disappeared from the navy list, without any further opportunity having presented itself of testing their efficiency. The progress in naval affairs was so rapid that after one day of brilliant service they were laid aside as useless.

The 'Palestro' type.

Towards the end of 1858 three new floating batteries of the 'Palestro'[1] type were laid down in France. They were somewhat smaller than the Kinburn batteries, and their armament was reduced in proportion. These vessels were far from successful.

The 'Arrogante.'

At the end of 1860 three batteries were constructed of the 'Arrogante' type, which will be described hereafter (see Part I, Chapter X.), and later four batteries of the 'Embuscade' type. The seven batteries last mentioned no longer appear in the list of the French coast-service vessels.

Batteries démontables.

This seems the appropriate opportunity for a brief reference to the 'batteries démontables,' a special type which is to be found only in the French service. These small craft were constructed to meet the exigencies of the Franco-Italian war.

[1] The earliest vessel of the name, not the one at present belonging to the Italian Navy.

Here it may be remarked that every protracted war will develop new requirements which must be met by the rapid construction of special types. The Crimean war produced the floating battery, the Civil war in America the monitor, and the Paraguayan war a new class of large, armoured, river gunboat. The recent hostilities in the East led to the construction for the Russian navy of a cloud of torpedo boats. Certain it is that the possession of superior facilities for creating a new and well-adapted *matériel* will be an immense advantage in the naval warfare of the future. At the present time the United Kingdom has the command of unrivalled resources in the private industrial establishments of the country. Each war produces a special type.

To return to the *batteries démontables* : on May 24, 1859, Napoleon III. telegraphed from his head-quarters at Alessandria to the Minister of Marine, asking if it were possible to improvise two floating batteries for river service mounting but one 12-pdr. gun forward, drawing 1 m. (3 ft. 3 in.) of water, having a *maximum* length of not more than 78 feet, and protected with armour to resist field guns. M. Dupuy de Lôme at once prepared a design in conformity with these conditions, giving to the batteries engines of 32 horse-power, capable of producing a speed of from 4 to 5 knots. He estimated that sixty days would be required to build them, and eight days to pack them up and put them together. Armour of 2 inches was considered sufficient to resist the Austrian projectile of 12 lbs. Five of these craft were ordered on May 31, from the well-known company, the Forges et Chantiers de la Méditerranée, the armament being changed to two rifled breech-loading 24-pdrs. On July 7 the first battery was built, taken to pieces, and put on board the 'Cacique' for transportation to Genoa ; the others followed in a short time. In thirty-seven days an iron vessel of 142 tons had been built and taken to pieces. Such is the early history of the French *batteries démontables*.

In 1867 attention was directed to the improvement of these little craft. Several having been put together under the direction of M. Dupont, it was ascertained that with eighty artificers and a working party of fifty men working effectively during 12½ hours a day, a battery of the 1864 design could be got ready for action in eight or nine days. A little later M. Brun, another member of the French staff of constructors, undertook to increase the speed of the batteries by improving the draught of the furnaces by mechanical means. With these alterations a speed of 6·5 and even seven knots could be attained.

From the close of the Crimean war the development of the ironclad fleet was entirely neglected by the Admiralty, until the success The 'Gloire.'

achieved by M. Dupuy de Lôme, the Director-General of Construction of the French Navy, in the production of the 'Gloire,' once more attracted the attention of our naval administration to the ironclad question.

M. de Lôme selected for conversion the 'Napoléon,' a two-decked

Fig. 2.

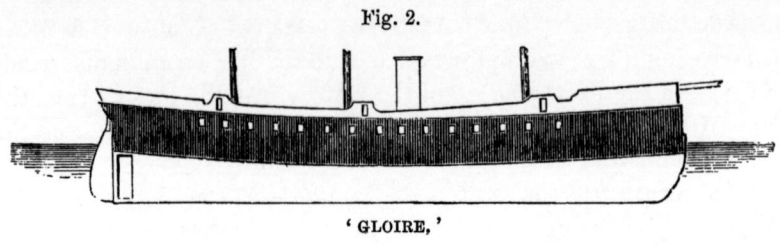

'GLOIRE,'

Fig. 3.

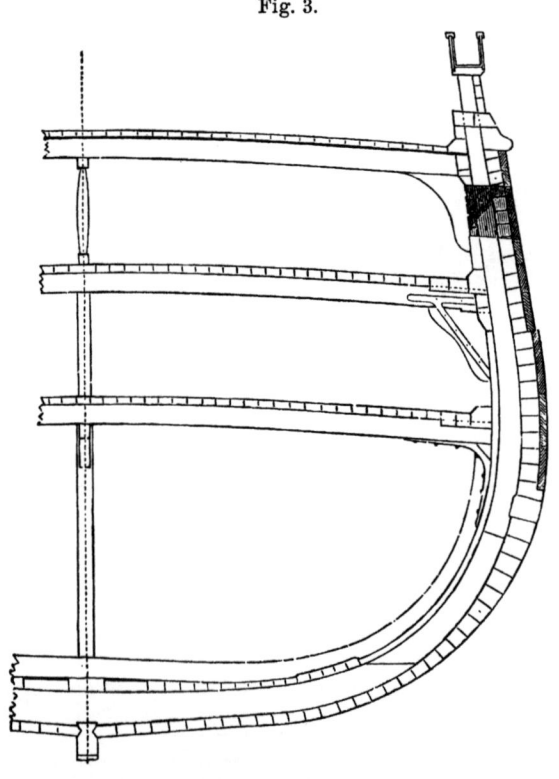

'GLOIRE': MIDSHIP SECTION.

91-gun ship, as being the finest vessel in the French navy in 1857. This model ship had engines of 900 horse-power, and her speed under steam was nearly 13 knots. The crew numbered 900 men. The displacement exceeded 5,000 tons, and the principal dimensions were : length 233 feet, breadth 55 feet, depth 25 feet. The lower ports were 6 feet above the water line.

M. Dupuy de Lôme commenced the process of conversion by removing the two upper decks. The vessel thus razèed was lengthened 23 feet, and armoured from stem to stern. In this manner was produced the celebrated 'Gloire.'

On trial this vessel proved sufficiently successful to induce the French authorities to follow up the principle without delay, by the construction of a large fleet of similar vessels, with such slight modifications only as experience proved to be desirable.

CHAPTER IV.

PROGRESS OF ARMOURED SHIPBUILDING IN FRANCE, 1861–73.

More important types adopted in the Navy of France. IN his work on the ironclad navies of the world M. Dislére has given an account of the progress of armoured ship construction in France, by following which we shall be able to consider closely the more important types adopted of late in the navy of that country.

'The construction of the "Gloire" having been finally approved, two other vessels of identical design, the "Invincible" and the "Normandie," were laid down at Toulon and Cherbourg. These three, *'Magenta' and 'Solferino.'* with the "Magenta" and "Solferino," laid down two years later,

Fig. 4.

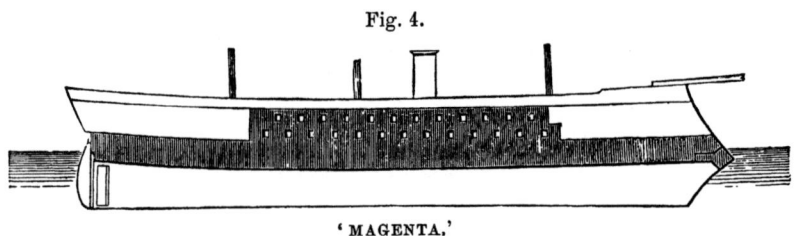

'MAGENTA.'

and the "Couronne" formed the first group of armourclads. The armour of 120 m/m. (4¾ inches) was capable of resisting rifled guns. The displacement, 5,650 tons, was kept within moderate limits.'

At the beginning of the year 1862 the utmost resources both of public and private shipbuilding yards were devoted to the construction of ironclads. France was ambitious of possessing an ironclad fleet which should rival that of England, and which should have the advantage of greater uniformity of type.

The 'Provence' class. The ten vessels of the 'Provence' or 'Flandre' class, laid down in 1862 from designs by M. Dupuy de Lôme, constitute the second group of sea-going ironclads (*navires d'escadre*). The displacement was very slightly augmented, but the protection was increased to 6 inches. It was determined to arm these ships with 16 c/m., or 5 ton, guns.

The 'Belliqueuse,' launched in 1863, was the first of a new class of ironclads of reduced dimensions, capable of cruising in distant seas and blockading an enemy's coast. This class was smaller and less costly than those of the 'Flandre' type. The principal dimensions of the 'Belliqueuse' are—

Length	230 feet
Beam, extreme	46 ft. 3 in.
Draught of water, mean	21 ft. 4 in.
Displacement	3,747 tons
Sail area	1,773 sq. yds.

The 'Belliqueuse' is a wooden ship, protected at the water-line and on the battery. As in the case of the 'Magenta' and 'Solferino,' the upper works at the extremities are unarmoured and built of wood, the bow and stern being exposed to destruction by shot and shell. At the date when the 'Belliqueuse' was built it was not believed to be practicable to combine wood and iron in a solid structure. It was for this reason that the hulls of the greater number of the French

Fig. 5.

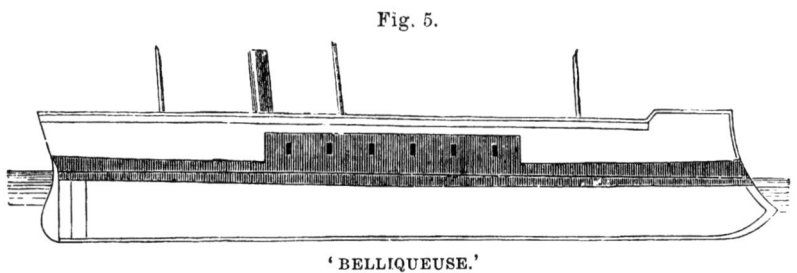

'BELLIQUEUSE.'

ironclads of that date were constructed of wood. The water-line is protected with 6-inch armour. A conning-tower, two storeys in height, stands between the mizen and main masts, the latter being forward of the funnel. The lower storey protects the steering gear. In the upper storey protection is provided for the captain and officer of the watch. The armament consists of four 19 c/m., or $7\frac{3}{4}$-ton, guns, and four 16 c/m., or 5-ton, guns in the battery, and four 14 c/m., or 46-pounders, on the upper deck. The engines are of 1,227 indicated horse-power, driving a single screw. The speed at the measured mile was 11·78 knots. The 'Belliqueuse' is barque-rigged.

In 1865 the French began building their new ironclads of the 'Alma' type, slightly modified from the design of the 'Belliqueuse.' It was determined to abandon the use of wood for the construction of the unarmoured upper works of these ships; and a new system of building was adopted, which seemed better calculated to bind together the upper works with the hull below the water-line. The difficult problem of 'bow fire' was solved by the introduction of fixed towers, projecting beyond the bulwarks and affording armoured protection to the greater part of the machinery for working the guns. The armour had a thickness of 6 inches at the water-line, a considerable weight for ships of moderate dimensions; although plates of this thickness gave no protection against the ordnance which was now being mounted on board ship. In England the 12-ton, or 9-inch, gun had ceased to represent the maximum of offensive power, and 18-ton guns were now proposed for the armament of the 'Hercules.' In Germany, at the great establishment of Krupp, the art of manufacturing guns of cast steel had reached a degree of perfection of which the French were destined, six years later, to acquire a painful experience. The 'Alma' was built at Lorient from the designs of M. Dupuy de Lôme, and launched in 1867. Seven ships were built from the same designs.

While the 'Alma' class were in progress, several cruising ironclads

Fig. 6.

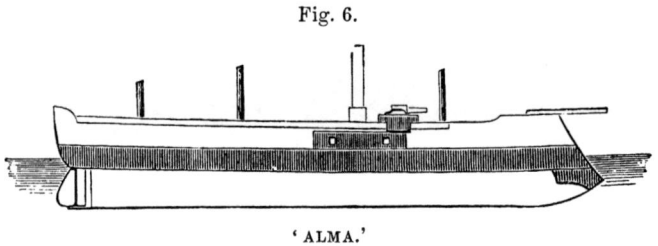

'ALMA.'

were constructed of the 'Belliqueuse' type. Their hulls were of wood, and they certainly were not formidable rivals of our own 'Hector.'

Introduction of heavy breech-loading ordnance into the French navy, 1867. In the year 1867 all the French ironclads were armed with guns of a new pattern. Ships of the 'Magenta' class received ten breech-loading 24 c/m., or 9½-inch, guns of 14 tons. The 'Flandre' class received four guns of the same calibre, and seven 19 c/m. (7½-inch) breech-loaders of 7¾ tons. At the same date the construction of 27 c/m. (10¾-inch) guns of 20 tons had been decided upon. In view of the changes in armament armour plates of 6 inches were no longer deemed sufficient.

The 'Océan,' 'Marengo,' and 'Suffren.' The 'Océan' and 'Marengo' were accordingly laid down. They were launched, the one in 1868 and the other in 1869. The 'Suffren,' the third vessel of the same group, was launched in 1870. The following details concerning this type, and the remarks on the policy of construction of which they are the embodiment, are taken from the recent French official publication, 'La Marine à l'Exposition Universelle de 1878.'

Figs. 7 and 8.

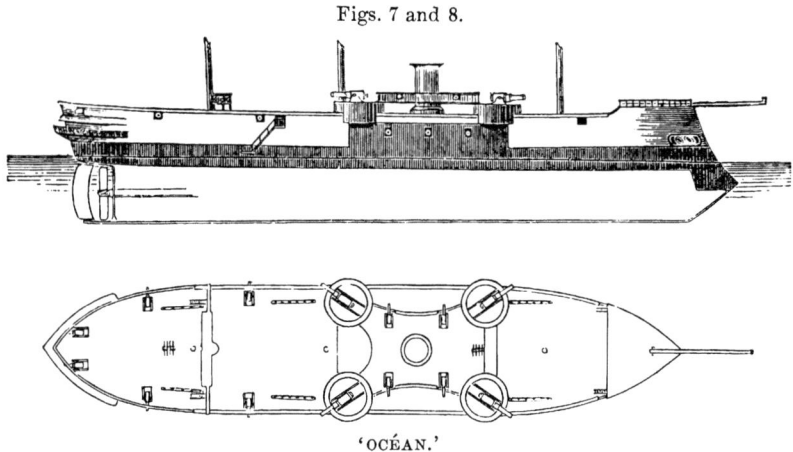

'OCÉAN.'

The 'Suffren' belongs to the 'Marengo' and 'Océan' class, designed in 1865 by M. Dupuy de Lôme. She represented a new

Fig. 9.

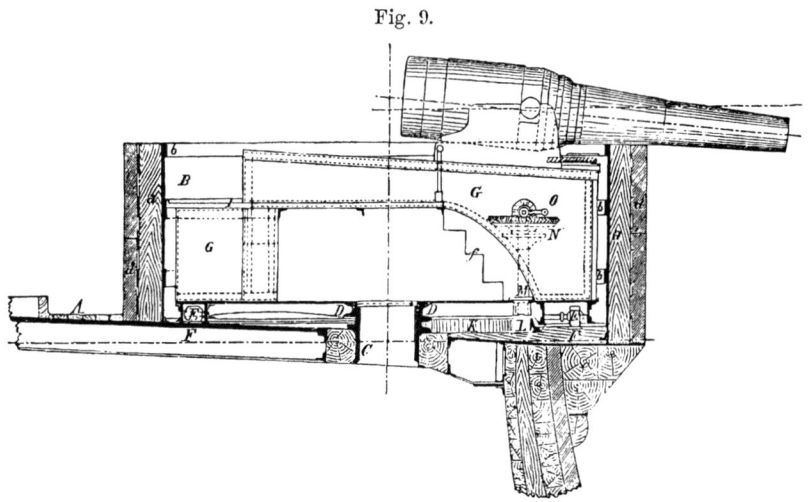

BARBETTE TURRET OF 'OCÉAN' CLASS.

A, upper deck; B, turret; *a a*, backing; *b b*, inner skin; *d*, armour; C, pivot, hollow for supply of ammunition; D, ring revolving on pivot; E E, rollers; G G, slide and carriage; I, platform for working the gun; K, toothed rack; L M N O, turning gear.

class in the armoured fleet, in addition to the four distinct types of the 'Gloire,' 'Couronne,' 'Magenta,' and 'Flandre,' which had successively appeared in the short interval from 1859 to 1861.

Armour.

In the 'Suffren' class the thickness of the armour was increased to 8·6 inches at the water-line, and 6·3 inches on the sides of the battery, which rendered necessary a displacement of 7,500 tons. This increase in the weight of armour was proposed with the object of resisting the 24 c/m. (9½-inch) gun, which was being introduced in the armament of ships, and was almost immediately followed by the 27 c/m. (10¾-inch) gun.

Fig. 10.

Iron was used in the construction of the unarmoured extremities of the upper works, whilst wood was retained for the remainder of the hull. The ram was definitively adopted. The speed was raised to 14 knots. After the abandonment of some intermediate combinations a new armament was supplied, composed of 27 c/m. (10¾-inch) guns of 20 tons, each placed in a *barbette* turret, with the addition of some light 12 c/m. (4¾-inch) guns. These modifications involved an addition to the displacement of 1,430 tons in the original design, and 1,760 tons in the eventual displacement of the ' Océan ' and ' Flandre.'

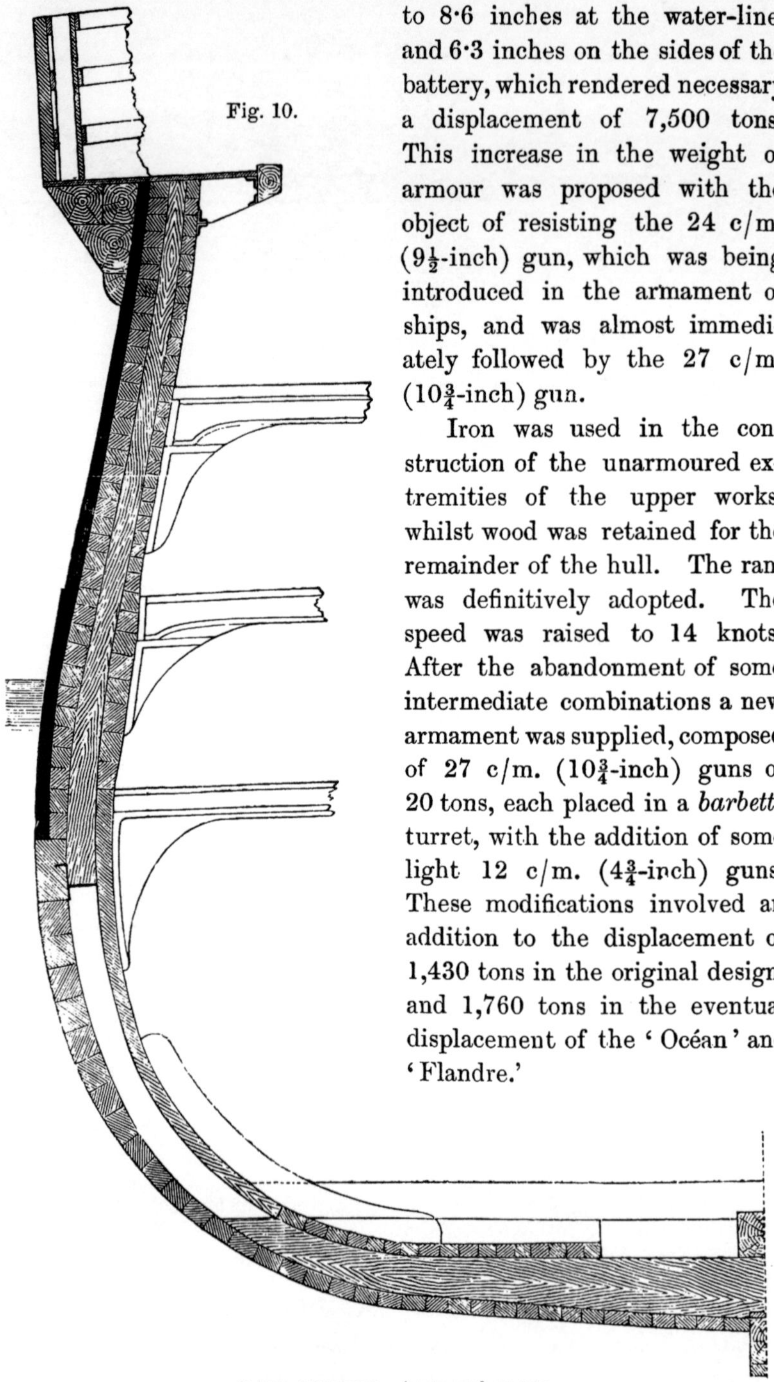

HALF SECTION : 'OCEAN' CLASS.

The principal details of the 'Suffren,' after completion and trial trips, may be given as follows:—

Length at the water-line . . .	282 ft. 6 in.
Beam	56 ft. 10 in.
Depth in hold	25 ft. 10 in.
Mean draught of water . .	27 ft. 2 in.
Displacement	7,604 tons
Immersed surface of midship section .	1,307·3 sq. ft.
Spread of canvas . . .	2,368 sq. yds.
Metacentric { with the bunkers full .	23·2 inches
height { with the bunkers empty	20·47 inches

The hull is of wood, except the upper works at the extremities of the ship, which are of iron. It is divided into several watertight compartments. The armour-plates have a thickness of 8 inches at the water-line, 6·3 inches on the battery, and 6 inches on the turrets. The crdnance is composed of four 27 c/m. (10¾-inch) guns in the battery, and four 24 c/m. (9·4-inch) guns in the *barbette* turrets.

The engines, built at Indret, are on the compound principle, having three horizontal cylinders, the middle being the high-pressure cylinder. During the turning trials the ship described a complete circle of 470 yards in 5 min. 58 sec. The 'Suffren' is fitted with steam steering-gear and powerful pumping arrangements in case of leaks.

The 'Suffren,' 'Marengo,' and 'Océan' are good seaboats, which in some respects may be attributed to the notable diminution of their metacentric height.

The 'Richelieu' may be taken as a prominent specimen of the armoured first-rate in existence in the French navy. She was designed by M. Dupuy de Lôme, and laid down in 1868.

The 'Richelieu' is intended to be an improvement on the 'Suffren' and 'Marengo' class. The most important difference consists in the elongation of the central portion by 32¾ feet, which involves an increase of 1,200 tons in the displacement, with a corresponding addition to the offensive power. In order to mount six 27 c/m. (10¾-inch) guns on the broadside, instead of four, it was necessary to extend the length of the battery from 66 ft. 6 in. to 100 ft. 9 in. By this addition to the central armoured battery protection is afforded to the engines as well as the boilers. A 24 c/m. (9·4-inch) gun, mounted on the upper deck under the topgallant forecastle, was added to the armament. The thickness of the armour at the water-line was increased by about ¾ of an inch, and the spread of canvas was augmented. In accordance with the opinion

The 'Richelieu.'

so generally prevailing in their favour, the 'Richelieu' was fitted with twin screws.

Like the 'Suffren' class already described, the hull of the 'Riche-lieu' is of wood, except the upper works at the extremities before and abaft the central battery, which are of iron. The watertight bulk-heads are increased in number, as compared with the preceding types in the French navy. The principal effective dimensions at the trial trips of the ship in 1875–76 in full seagoing trim are set forth in the following table :—

Total length of the hull at load water-line .	322 ft. 7 in.
Beam, extreme	57 ft. 10 in.
Mean load draught, when first commissioned	27 feet
Corresponding displacement . . .	8,790 tons
Immersed surface of midship section. .	1,330·02 sq. ft.
Spread of canvas . . .	2,756 sq. yds.
Metacentric ⎱ with bunkers filled .	24·7 inches
height ⎰ with empty bunkers .	20·47 inches

The armour has a thickness of 8·6 inches at the water-line, and 16 c/m. (6·3 inches) on the battery. The ordnance consists of six

Fig. 11.

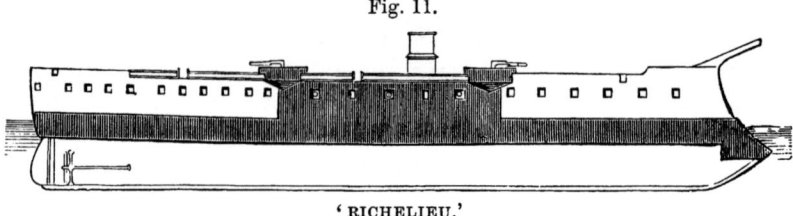

'RICHELIEU.'

27 c/m. or (10¾ inches) guns in the battery, which can be trained over an arc of 40° before and abaft the beam. Four 24 c/m., or 9·4 inches, guns are mounted *en barbette* in towers rising above the four corners of the battery. One 24 c/m., 9·4-inch, gun is mounted under the topgallant forecastle. These turrets protrude beyond the sides of the ship, sponson fashion, so that no tumble-home is required to give them an uninterrupted arc of fire. The guns, however, have no protection from plunging fire. They are worked on revolving platforms. A few light guns are distributed along the upper deck, one of which can be fired through a port under the topgallant fore-castle.

The 'Richelieu'[1] is a full-rigged ship. Each engine has three horizontal cylinders. The boilers have 32 furnaces, the grate surface

[1] This ship was partially destroyed by fire at Toulon, and was scuttled to prevent damage to the dockyard and other ships, at the end of 1880: it is intended to try and recover her. Her hull has been got afloat.

is 632·5 sq. ft. The engines are of 4,006 indicated horse-power, and, with a draught of water of 26 ft. 9 in., gave a speed of 13·11 knots. The coal supply is 650 tons. A special boiler is fitted for working the steam steering gear and the pumps. On her trial trip, the 'Richelieu' completed the circle of 498 yards in diameter in 6 m. 24 sec. The sides of the ship at the stern rise perpendicularly from the water-line. A hurricane deck, or large bridge, is fixed before the funnel, on a level with the top of the turret armour, and on it is a wooden pilot-house, which contains the wheel. Another wheel is in the usual place before the mizen mast, surmounted by a high central conning platform and chart-house. Arrangements are made for stowing the boats on deck when the ship is cleared for action, and the davits can be turned down out of the way of the fire of the guns. The rudder is of the curious double form lately introduced into the French service. A towing torpedo is carried outside, abaft the mizen rigging, hung from two outriggers by slip ropes; the tow-line being led forward on to the topgallant forecastle. The seagoing and fighting qualities have been considered satisfactory, but the 'Richelieu' design has not been repeated.

The 'Colbert' class, including the 'Trident' and 'Friedland,' was begun after M. Sabattier's proposals had been submitted in 1869. A fine model of the 'Colbert' was shown in the recent Exhibition in Paris. It represents the logical and successful development of M. Dupuy de Lôme's earlier conceptions of the class of heavy wooden masted ironclad ships. The 'Colbert' The 'Trident.'

In the 'Colbert' a further effort was made to gain fighting qualities by a gradual increase of dimensions. About 900 tons was added to the displacement of the ships of the 'Suffren' class as compared with the 'Richelieu,' in order to obtain the desired increase in the offensive and defensive qualities.

As in the other classes already described, the hull is of wood, except the foremost and after extremities of the upper works outside of the battery, which are of iron. Below the 'lower' deck these ships are divided into numerous watertight compartments by transverse and longitudinal bulkheads.

The following are the principal dimensions of the new design:—

Length at water-line .	317 ft. 9 in.
Beam .	56 ft. 6 in.
Depth in hold	25 ft. 4 in.
Mean draught of water	26 ft. 3 in.
Displacement .	8,314 tons
Immersed surface of midship section .	1,259 sq. ft.
Spread of canvas	2,545 sq. yds.

A wood sheathing ten inches thick having been added whilst the ship was building, with a view of carrying the copper sheathing up to the armour, the beam has been increased to a corresponding amount.

The armour is distributed, as in the case of the ' Victorieuse,' in a belt, protecting the central battery, and two *barbette* towers.[1] The armour has a thickness of 8·6 inches at the water line, and 6·3 inches on the battery. The armament consists of six 27 c/m. (10¾ inch) guns in the battery, and two other guns of the same calibre mounted on deck in elliptic half-turrets. Two 24 c/m. (9·4 inch) guns are mounted on the upper deck, one under the topgallant forecastle, and the other on the quarter deck. Lastly, four 14 c/m. (5¾ inch) guns are carried on the main deck outside the central battery. The *barbette* towers project sponson fashion from the ship's side abaft the foremast. The hammock-nettings and bulwarks are retired abaft them for some feet inside the ship's side, and the main and mizen lower rigging is set up inboard. By these arrangements a direct fire ahead and astern can be obtained from the towers. The contrivances for keeping the boats clear of the guns in action are not so complete as in other classes.

The vessels of the ' Colbert' class are full-rigged ships. They are fitted with a single screw. The engines have three horizontal cylinders, and an indicated power of 4,652 horses. At a mean draught of 26 ft. 2 in. a speed of 14·47 knots was realised at the measured mile. The grate surface is 632·5 sq. ft., and the coal supply 700 tons. Special engines are provided for the steering gear and pumps. The hull, though built of wood, is divided into several compartments by iron water-tight bulkheads. With an initial speed of 13 knots the ' Trident' completed a circle of 485 yards diameter in 6 m. 2 sec. The results of the trials of the ' Trident' and the ' Colbert' were considered satisfactory, especially as regards speed, which in the case of the ' Colbert' was maintained at 14·75 knots for more than an hour after three hours' steaming at full speed.

We add to the details already given from the most recent French authorities the following particulars from the admirable volume compiled by Chief Engineer King, U.S.N. Referring to the ' Richelieu,' ' Colbert,' ' Trident,' and ' Friedland,' he says, the former were launched in 1875, the other two upwards of a year ago. The first two were laid down in 1869, and having been six years in building, they were not so heavily armoured as later designed ships, but they are nevertheless formidable vessels, carrying on their main decks

[1] The difference in the distribution   ' Colbert' will appear from the drawings
of the armour of the ' Trident' and   on p. 57.

heavy rifled guns, besides guns of considerable power in the two side turrets and lighter guns under the armoured forecastle. Their speed on trial was about thirteen knots.   M. Dislére, in the official publication on the naval section of the recent Exhibition in Paris, gives the following general view of this group of armoured ships of the first rate.

Figs. 12 and 12 A.

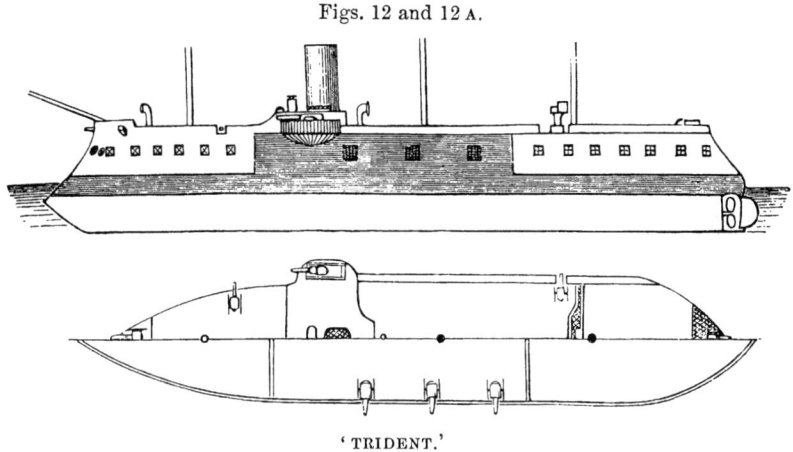

'TRIDENT.'

' The armourclads of the first group, the " Richelieu," " Suffren," and " Trident," appear to be good squadron ships, and realised without doubt, at the beginning of the period subsequent to 1867, a great advance, chiefly with respect to offensive power, beyond the designs

Fig. 13.

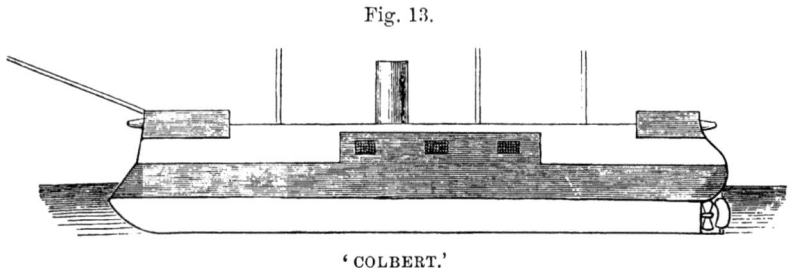

' COLBERT.'

of the preceding period.   They are the last representatives of the old ironclad fleet with wooden hulls and upper works partly of iron, having a mean displacement of 8,400 tons, heavily armed, but slightly protected by armour.'

CHAPTER V.

EARLY ARMOURED CONSTRUCTION IN ENGLAND.

Commencement of armoured construction in England.

THE simultaneous construction of the ' Gloire,' ' Normandie,' ' Invincible,' and ' Couronne ' was not at first regarded by the maritime Powers as the opening of a new era in ship-building for war. In England, especially, it was condemned as a visionary and costly experiment, in which France would dissipate several millions, with no other result than the addition to her fleet of a few floating batteries, which at best could only be stationed at important points to defend the coast. Public opinion, however, in England did not await the launching and the trials of the ' Gloire ' before a conviction was established that our own navy must possess the same novel but formidable types of fighting ships which had been introduced in the French navy. All the other maritime powers, whether willingly or unwillingly, were compelled to follow the same line.

Captain Cowper Coles.

Though the naval administration of this country had shown no disposition to commence the construction of ironclads, private individuals had devoted careful attention to the subject. A design for an ironclad ship of improved type had been submitted to the Admiralty so early as the year 1855, and Captain Cowper Coles had been employing his half-pay leisure, after the close of the Crimean war, in designing a cupola for the working of the heavy guns which were rapidly being introduced into the service.

Sir J. Pakington invites designs for the ' Warrior ' class.

Being compelled at last to follow in the line so confidently taken by the French Minister of Marine, the Admiralty of 1859, under Sir John Pakington as First Lord, with Mr. Corry as Secretary, called for designs for a ship of the ' Warrior ' class from six leading ship-building firms.

' Warrior ' and ' Black Prince.'

Drawings were prepared in compliance with this official invitation ; but the Chief Constructor of the Navy, thinking that some improvements were possible in every one of the designs submitted, prepared plans of his own, in consultation with Mr. Scott Russell, from which the 'Warrior,' the 'Black Prince,' and, with some slight modifications, the 'Achilles' were built.

In addition to an effective cuirass of armour plates, two points, says Mr. Scott Russell, were especially considered in these designs:

Fig. 14.

Fig. 15.

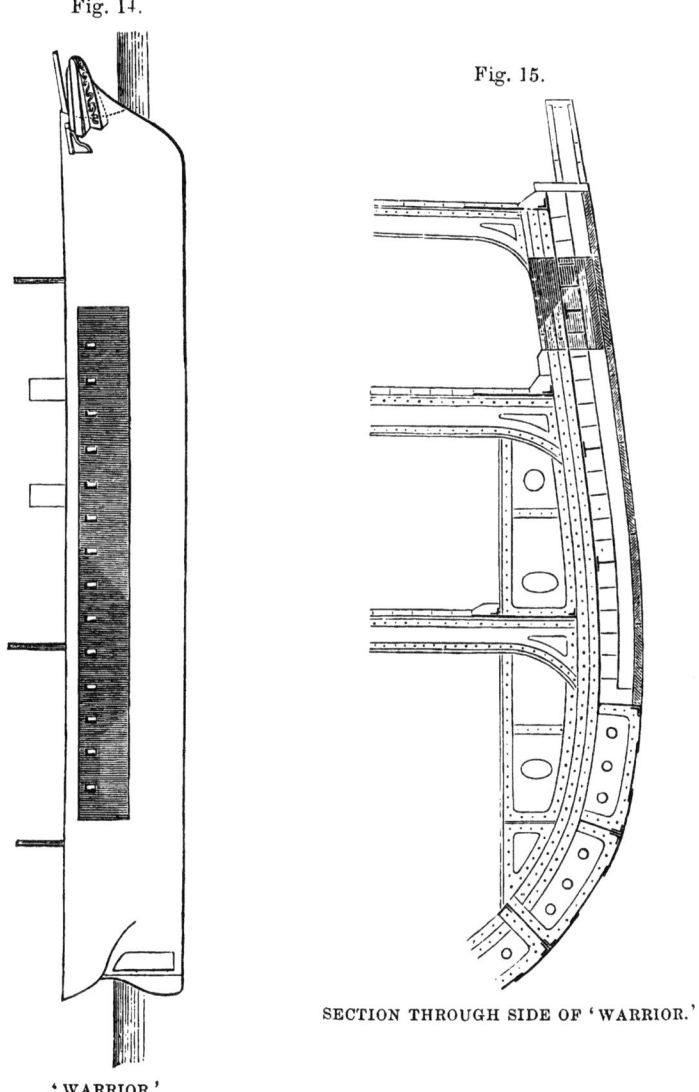

SECTION THROUGH SIDE OF 'WARRIOR.'

'WARRIOR.'

namely, high speed especially against strong winds and heavy seas, and stability of platform. The fine ends of these vessels, which it was impossible to protect with armour-plates, were subdivided by horizontal, transverse, and longitudinal bulkheads into numerous compartments.

The principal dimensions of the 'Warrior' and 'Black Prince' are as follows : length 380 feet, breadth 58 feet, displacement 9,210 tons.

Prior to the recent alterations, the number of guns protected by armour plates was twenty-six. The thickness of the armour-plates is $4\frac{1}{2}$ inches, with 18 inches of timber backing, and an inner skin behind the armour-plates $\frac{9}{16}$ths of an inch in thickness. The bows and stern are unprotected for about one-third the length of the ship. It was considered dangerous to overload with armour-plates the extremities of ships of such fine lines. The weight of this modified cuirass of armour-plates and backing is 1,300 tons.

Design of the 'Warrior.'

The process by which the design for the 'Warrior' was finally completed is described by Mr. Scott Russell in his work on 'Iron Ship-Building.'

Mr. Scott Russell on this class.

'It having been decided,' he says, 'that the "Warrior" class should carry an armament of forty guns on one deck, and that a space of 15 feet was required between the guns; this gave, as the necessary dimensions of the battery, a length of 300 feet, and a breadth of 50 feet. On this calculation the midship body was formed. Next, in order to attain the desired speed of 15 knots, some reduction was necessary in the midship body, while a bow was added 135 feet long, and fine lines were secured for the after body of the ship, by giving to the run a length of 90 feet. This gives as the dimensions of the "Warrior" class the figures already mentioned. Provision was made for carrying 900 tons of coal, or enough for five days' steaming at full power.'

Cost.

In a paper on 'Modern Ships of War,' read by Mr. Barnaby at the Royal United Service Institution on January 29, 1872, it is stated that 'The first seagoing ironclad, the "Warrior," cost, exclusive of ordnance and ordnance stores, about 376,000*l.*'

Special features of the 'Warrior.'

Mr. Elgar, the author of the introduction to 'Our Ships of War,' calls attention, in the following passage, to the leading characteristics of the 'Warrior,' and to the great advance upon all previous war ships which had been realised in the design, construction, and armament.

1. She was built entirely of iron, possessed far greater structural strength, and was much less liable to be destroyed by fire than a wood ship.

2. Such vital parts of the ship as the boiler and engine-rooms, magazines, shell-rooms and battery, were protected by armour-plating that could not be pierced, at a distance of 200 yards, by any gun that could then be brought against her at sea.

3. The whole of her armament consisted of the heaviest guns afloat.

4. Her speed under steam was over fourteen knots per hour, or nearly $1\frac{1}{2}$ knots more than the most favourable specimens among the latest line-of-battle ships and frigates.

5. She had a strong stem, of a ram form, under her light knee of head, which would enable her to sink any wood ship.

These several qualities indicate that an immense stride was made in naval construction when the 'Warrior' was built. She possessed the rudiments of the most desirable requirements of a war ship, and although she was far inferior in power to an ironclad of the present day, and had many defects which have been remedied in later years, she was as perfect as a first experiment could be expected to be, and indicated, in many ways, the direction which future improvement should take.

Two ships, the 'Warrior' and 'Black Prince,' were built from the same design. They were both ordered in 1859. The 'Warrior' was completed in October, 1861, and the 'Black Prince' in September, 1862.

Mr. Barnaby, in the paper already quoted, pointed out a grave defect in the design of the 'Warrior,' and in the smaller but similar ships, the 'Defence' and 'Resistance.' The steering gear was unprotected by armour. It was a source of weakness for which no thickness of armour in the middle of the ship could compensate.

Steering gear.

This was the special defect which led to the building of the 'Minotaur,' 'Agincourt,' and 'Northumberland.' In these ships the rudder-head and steering gear are enclosed by armour plating, and the whole length of the ship is protected by a belt of armour in the neighbourhood of the water-line.

The 'Warrior's' armour—we are again quoting from the introduction to 'Our Ships of War'—was of uniform thickness. It is now the custom to regulate the weight of armour according to the relative importance of the parts protected; the greatest thickness being worked along the water-line throughout the space occupied by the boilers, engines, and magazines, and in wake of the fighting deck.

Armour.

As the powers of the guns carried afloat increased, the thickness of the 'Warrior's' armour became altogether inadequate for efficient protection. This defect has been overcome in recent ships by the successful application of great ability and ingenuity to the reduction of the weight of the structural part of the hull, while preserving the strength unimpaired. By these modifications of form and structure weight has been saved, and the area protected by armour has been diminished. These improvements have made it possible to put a much greater proportion of weight into the form of armour, and consequently to employ a greater thickness. As an example of this we would compare the 'Warrior' with the broadside ironclad 'Sultan.' The 'Warrior' carries about 10 per cent. of her weight, or 975 tons, in the form of armour, while the 'Sultan' carries 16 per cent., or 1,481 tons. The 'Warrior' is partially protected with 4½-inch armour, while the 'Sultan' is protected by 9-inch and 8-inch plates over the vital parts. Her steering gear is protected, and the whole length of her side at the water-line. We shall see, however, further on that the modification of form to which we have alluded has had more to do with enabling greater thicknesses of armour to be carried than the saving of weight that has been effected in the structure of the ship.

The 'Warrior' could only fire from behind armour on the broadside. This is a great defect, not only on account of the small range that could be commanded by the guns, but because it involved presenting the side to the enemy in the most favourable manner for penetration. This defect has been remedied in recent ships by providing, in various ways, for bow and stern fire of more or less power. The 'Warrior' carried a large number of small guns in a long battery, which necessitated a great area of armoured side. Recent ships carry a few monster guns in turrets, or a small battery, and thus can be protected by thicker armour with the same weight, owing to the diminished area of the protected side. The armament, on the other hand, consists of more powerful guns with an enormous increase of penetrative power. The 'Warrior' was long, and had fine lines, for the purpose of securing great speed. This made her unmanageable and unhandy. Recent ships are much shorter in proportion, and still obtain greater speed by having increased engine-power.

An examination of the designs of the armour-clad vessels constructed within the last twenty years will show a tendency to concentrate the armour about certain parts of the hull—generally amidships and in the neighbourhood of the water-line—whilst its thickness has been increased.

The 'Warrior' marks the first stage in that long succession of ships which at present compose the armoured fleet of England. She was built, like the 'Gloire,' to carry the 68-pdr., the heaviest gun then in use, and to resist the projectiles of guns of that calibre. For this purpose armour of 4½ inches was then considered sufficient both in England and in France.

Designed as a match for the ' Gloire,' the ' Warrior,' in the opinion of the French constructors, was inferior alike in offensive and in defensive power. If a higher speed was attained, its advantages were neutralised by the loss of manœuvring qualities, an inevitable consequence of increased length ; while the armour had been so far reduced that it afforded only an imperfect protection to the central part of the ship. ' Warrior' and ' Gloire.'

Sir E. Reed observes that ' The first examples of real ironclads were " La Gloire " in France, and the " Warrior " in England, neither of which presented any great departures from the forms and appearances of ordinary ships, unless the sullen, low-browed graceless aspect of " La Gloire " entitles her to some distinction in this respect. Nor was the " Warrior " in any marked degree a ship of singular appearance, except in point of size. She was a long, fine, handsome-looking frigate, masted and rigged as usual, and formed with a bow and stern in no way differing from the bows and sterns of the most recent and beautiful wooden frigates. The " Warrior " and her sister ship, the " Black Prince," were, however, destined to be the only English ironclads embodying those forms and appearances which had come to be regarded as the most favoured traits of beauty in a ship. . . . All British ironclads are now built with sterns approaching the upright above water. . . . Like changes of style have materially affected the sterns of our ironclads and for very good reasons. The bow has been modified in order to dispense with the overhanging weight, to increase its fitness to cleave and surmount the waves, and to adapt it for ramming purposes. The stern has been modified in order to give protection to the rudder-head, to deflect raking shot, and to render it more fit to receive easily the blows of the following waves.'

The first advance in design in the several navies of the world may be briefly traced from Señor Heriz' work already quoted. In 1859 the ' Warrior ' and ' Black Prince,' ' Defence ' and ' Resistance ' were begun. The ' Hector ' and ' Valiant ' of 6,800 tons displacement and 800 nominal horse-power, the ' Achilles,' and, lastly, the ' Minotaur,' ' Agincourt,' and ' Northumberland ' were all commenced in 1861. These vessels are of iron. Seven are protected with $4\frac{1}{2}$-inch armour. The ' Minotaur ' class are protected with 5-inch plates, and provided, like the ' Bellerophon,' with bulkheads, or transverse armoured partitions, to give protection from end-on fire. Ironclads built in England. 1859-61.

The following more detailed descriptions are taken from the *Times* and other newspapers and periodicals, published at the date when the ships enumerated were under construction.

The
'Defence'
and
'Resist-
ance.'

The 'Defence' and 'Resistance,' like the 'Warrior' class, are of iron, and partly plated. The system of armour adopted was precisely similar to that of the 'Warrior.' Their principal dimensions are, length 280 feet, beam 54 feet, draught of water 24 feet, displacement 6,150 tons; and they have engines of 600 horse-power. They combined, in a modified sense, the merits and defects of the 'Warrior.'

The earlier armoured ships were thoroughly tried at sea. They were attached to the Channel fleet, and in company with wooden vessels of the old type made frequent experimental cruises.

Trials of
ironclads:
Channel
fleet.

In 1863 a squadron, consisting of the 'Revenge,' 73, bearing the flag of Rear-Admiral Smart, with the 'Warrior,' 'Black Prince,' the 'Resistance' and 'Defence' in company, proceeded to Lisbon and back. The general results of the cruize were considered most satisfactory; all the vessels proved to be good sea-boats, very weatherly under canvas, and fast under either sail or steam.

The chief trials took place under sail; the ironclads were not found to roll much more than the 'Revenge,' though 38 degrees was

Fig. 16.

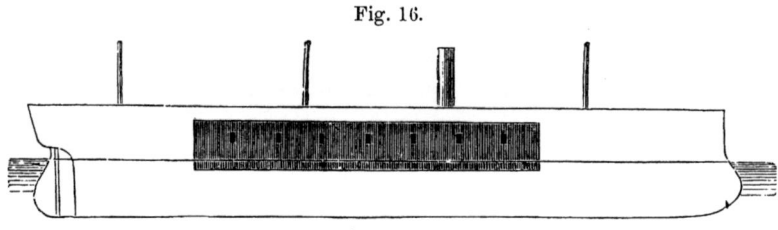

'DEFENCE' AND 'RESISTANCE.'

attained on one occasion in a heavy swell after a gale. The main deck guns were occasionally worked at sea, and practice at a target was once attempted when the ships were rolling as much as 18 degrees each way. The exercises under these circumstances were carried on under difficulties, but though divers minor accidents occurred, none of the guns were lost overboard, and all were at length secured after the morning's practice without any serious accident.

'Valiant.'

The following description of the 'Valiant' was published in the *Times* :—

'The length of this ship is 280 feet, breadth 56 feet, and depth 39 feet. While the lines are infinitely finer than those of broadbowed vessels like the "Defence," they are not to be compared in fineness to those of the "Warrior."

'On the other hand the bows, without having a regular beak to be used as a ram, are still sufficiently projecting beneath the water-line to enable her, if she had a chance of striking an enemy, to inflict

AGINCOURT.

fearful mischief without risking the safety of her own hull. The 'Valiant' is a sister ship to the 'Hector,' launched at the close of 1862. In the construction of the hull, the principle is the same as that of all the iron frigates. Within her armour of teak and 4½-inch iron plating the 'Valiant' is a perfect web of wrought-iron ribs and longitudinal girders. Like the iron frigates, she is plated from stem to stern in armour, the stern being almost as fine as the bow. By means of an additional plating of iron over her iron stern-post and rudder-head the safety of this essentially important feature is secured. About 80 feet from the bows in-board she is fitted with a semicircular shield, extending from one side of the vessel to the other, and rising from the main deck to the level of her bulwarks and spar decks. It is covered with 4½-inch armour-plates, and lined with teak in the same manner as the broadside. On the main deck it is closed, but on the upper it is pierced for two of the heaviest guns, to be used in chasing an enemy, or when bearing down to strike with the ram.' The 'Valiant' is fitted with engines of 800 horse-power. She was launched in 1863.

Fig. 17.

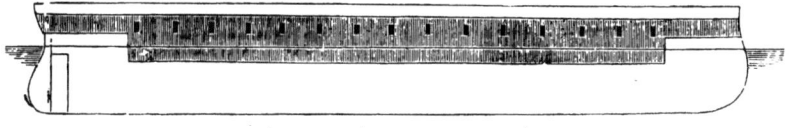

'HECTOR' AND 'VALIANT.'

The 'Hector' completed her official trials at Portsmouth in December 1864. The mean speed at full boiler power was 11·34, and at half boiler power 9·78 knots. *The 'Hector's' trial.*

The inferiority of the 'Gloire' to the 'Warrior' having been recognised, and the system of construction experimentally tried in the case of the 'Hector,' where the guns were protected while the extremities of the ship were undefended, having been abandoned, the plan of complete protection was adopted, and the colossal vessels of the 'Minotaur' type were designed. *The 'Minotaur.'*

The 'Minotaur' class were twenty feet longer and 600 tons larger than the 'Warrior,' and plated from stem to stern. They have engines of 1,350 horse-power, or 100 horse-power more than the 'Warrior's.' Three ships, the 'Northumberland,' the 'Minotaur,' and the 'Agincourt' were ordered to be built from the new designs.

The period from 1859 to 1861 has been called the 68-pdr. epoch. In one of their earlier reports, Sir J. Hay's committee on armour-plates expressed an opinion that 5½-inch iron and less backing afforded *Armour.*

a more effective protection than 4½-inch plate and more backing. In conformity with these views, the 'Northumberland,' 'Minotaur,' and 'Agincourt' were armoured with 5½-inch plates and 9-inch backing. This change in the protective armour was proved by subsequent experiments of the Iron Plate Committee to have been injudicious. The 'Warrior' target sustained the test of actual firing better than the target constructed on the pattern of the 'Minotaur' plating. Some sort of cushion, made of a comparatively yielding substance like timber, was found to be absolutely necessary, in order to diminish the jar produced by the impact of shot on a rigid mass of armour-plate.

The contracts for the 'Minotaur,' 'Agincourt,' and 'Northumberland' were entrusted by the Admiralty to the Thames Iron Works, Messrs. Laird, and the Millwall Iron Works, respectively.

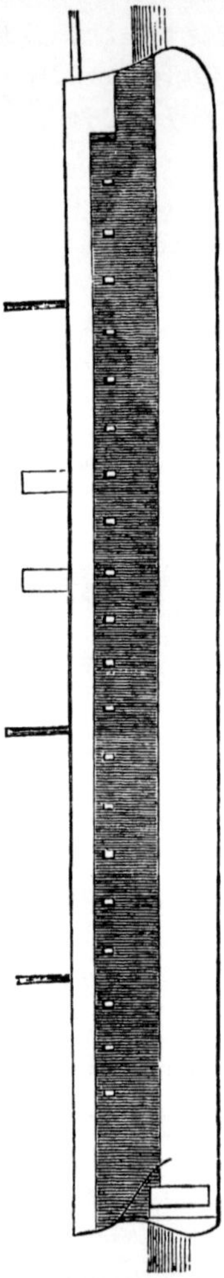

Description from the Times.

The '*Northumberland.*'

The following description is taken from the columns of the *Times* :—

'As compared with the " Warrior " the " Northumberland " class are longer, broader, and deeper, so as to make them of nearly 7,000 tons burthen,[1] and by this increase and a slightly flatter floor they obtain such an augmentation of displacement as enables them to carry armour-plating over all from end to end.'

When, however, the 'Achilles,' on trial at sea, was found, even with her increased dimensions, to be overburdened by the weight of armour-plating in her bows, it was determined in the case of the 'Northumberland' to remove a portion of plating at the bows above the water-line belt, and to adopt in that vessel a modification of Sir E. Reed's plan of a central armour-plated battery. A belt of armour was extended all round the ship at the water-line and the bow. This semicircular iron shield is continued down to the level of the main deck. It is plated with 5½-inch armour-plating and pierced with portholes, at which two guns of the heaviest calibre are placed, while the men working them are completely protected. By means of this shield sufficient protection is obtained to allow of the removal of the armour-plating above the water-line for a length of 30 feet from the bows.

Fig. 18.

'NORTHUMBER-
LAND.'

---

[1] 10,600 tons displacement.

The length of the 'Northumberland' class is 400 feet, the breadth 59 feet, and depth 41 ft. 6 in. The hull possesses massive strength, though the weight of material has been carefully economised.

The outer keel is replaced by an inner keelson, consisting of a huge wrought-iron girder 3 ft. $4\frac{1}{2}$ in. deep, which forms the backbone of the whole structure. To this the pointed ribs are riveted at alternate intervals of 1 ft. 11 in. and 2 ft. 4 in. These ribs vary in length from 10 feet long, by 3 feet deep, to 4 feet long, by 18 inches deep. They are made of wrought iron in these lengths to allow of their being riveted to the longitudinal ribs or beams, which run from end to end of the vessel, and which, by intersecting the rib, divide the whole bottom framework into a series of small cellular compartments of immense strength. Each pair of ribs forms a huge wrought-iron bow, 4 feet thick at the keel, and tapering off to 18 inches thick at the wales, where it is bent in, so as to form a ledge 15 inches deep, on which the teak backing and armour-plates rest 5 feet below the water-line.

The longitudinals form girders running from end to end of the ship, converging in the bow and stern, and binding together the whole frame of the ship. The beams, which carry the decks of the ship, are of wrought iron, and beneath the oak upper deck is an iron deck intended to keep out shell. The height from the floor of the lower deck beams is 21 feet, from the lower to main deck 9 ft. 2 in., from the main deck to upper deck 7 ft. 2 in. clear. Inside the backing, on which the armour is placed, is the skin of the ship, composed of wrought-iron plates. The backing is composed of 9 inches of solid teak-beams. The armour consists of $5\frac{1}{2}$-inch rolled plates, fastened through the backing to the inner skin along both sides of the ship.

The 'Northumberland' is fitted with longitudinal watertight compartments, or wing passages, extending from the floor to the main deck. They are 3 ft. 6 in. wide, and correspond in height to the height between the several decks. These wing passages are shut off from the body of the ship by wrought-iron bulkheads, and divided by transverse webs into watertight compartments, so that, in case of a shot entering, the leakage will be confined to the compartment which it has actually penetrated.

The bow of the 'Northumberland' is formed with a curve projecting at the water-line to a distance of $6\frac{1}{2}$ feet beyond the figurehead. The thickness of the armour-plating is gradually diminished from $5\frac{1}{2}$ inches abreast of the central battery to $4\frac{1}{2}$ inches at the stem and stern. The roundness of the stem and stern will, it is presumed, cause shots to glance off, so that 4½-inch armour is thought to afford sufficient protection. The inner and outer sternposts of the 'Northumberland' are gigantic forgings.

The stem is a single forging and weighs 31 tons. The ports of the 'Northumberland,' like those of the 'Warrior,' are 3 ft. 6 in. high and 20 inches wide.

Engines.   The engines, by Messrs. John Penn and Sons, are of 1,350 horse-power nominal. The bunkers are intended to hold about 1,400 tons of coal, or enough for ten days' steaming. The mean draught of water, when ready for sea, is 24 feet, being two feet less than the draught of an ordinary three-decker. The height of the port sills from the water is ten feet.

Rig.   In her rig the 'Northumberland' resembled her sister ships, the 'Minotaur' and 'Agincourt,' having, instead of the traditional three masts, five iron masts, three rigged with square yards, the two after-masts being fitted to carry fore and aft sails only.

The 'Achilles' was faster under sail than the five-masted 'Minotaur' by one knot an hour. This difference is due entirely to the masting. To alter the masts, it was originally estimated, would cost 12,000*l.* This operation has actually been carried out in the 'Northumberland,' which ship has been rigged as a barque. The alteration would appear to be fully justified in case the 'Northumberland' were employed in naval operations on active service. The saving of coal might be found an immense gain, when coal became difficult to obtain and could only be conveyed under convoy to the cruising fleets.

Armour.   In the 'Northumberland' and sister ships the weight of solid armour is no less than 1,660 tons, while the weight of the teak backing is 400 tons. These weights considerably exceeded the weight of the armour and backing of the 'Warrior,' the weight of that ship's armour being, according to Mr. Elgar, 975 tons, and that of her teak backing 350 tons.

The 'Minotaur' was launched in December 1863, and the 'Agincourt' was launched, or rather floated, in March 1865, from the graving dock in the building yard of Messrs. Laird Brothers, at Birkenhead. The 'Northumberland' was the last completed of the series.

'Agincourt's' steam-trial.   The 'Agincourt' was tried, as reported in the *Times*, with very satisfactory results, outside Plymouth breakwater. At this trial, which took place on December 13, 1865, with a draught of 23 ft. 4 in. forward, and 25 ft. 2 in. aft, she attained the mean speed at

full boiler power of 15·48 knots, and at half boiler power of 13·54 knots. The maximum indicated horse-power was 6,667, the nominal horse-power being 1,350 horses. Under full boiler power nothing could exceed the quiet manner in which this noble ship passed through the water at such enormous speed, while under half boiler power there was scarcely a ripple at the bows. The speed of the 'Minotaur' was 14·78 knots, a slightly inferior result to that attained in the 'Agincourt.' The 'Minotaur.'

While the 'Northumberland' class were entrusted to private shipbuilders, the 'Achilles,' a nearly sister ship, was being constructed at Chatham. The 'Achilles' was remarkable as the first iron ship built and fitted out in a Government dockyard, and the work, which was of unequalled excellence, was carried out by shipwrights whose previous experience had been limited to wooden shipbuilding. The following details have been extracted from the *Times* :— The 'Achilles.'

'Notwithstanding all that has been said to the contrary, the " Achilles " has been built in a shorter space of time than any of her sister ironclads. A great delay took place after the original order

Fig. 19.

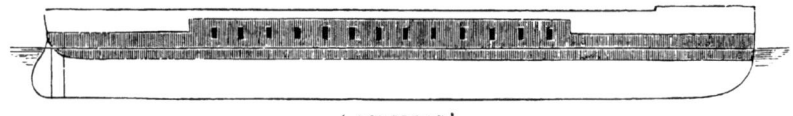

' ACHILLES.'

for building the vessel was received in Chatham in 1861. But this arose partly from the necessity of having to erect the necessary machinery for preparing the iron plates and other ironwork for a ship of the size of the " Achilles," the building of which was the first experiment in iron shipbuilding upon which the Admiralty had ever engaged. A further cause of delay was the defective character of some of the material supplied for the construction of the ship, which was insufficient to stand the tests of quality which were applied according to the Government regulations. Another cause of delay was the contemporaneous building of the " Royal Oak " ironclad frigate, which was completed at Chatham in eighteen months.'

The weight of the armour-plating of the 'Achilles' was 1,200 tons, exceeding by more than 200 tons the weight of the plating of the 'Warrior.' The 'Achilles' was the first iron vessel launched with the whole of her iron plates complete from stem to stern. The displacement is as nearly as possible 10,000 tons. The broadside plates of the 'Achilles,' 4½ inches in thickness, are of rolled iron from the Parkgate Works ; the thickness of these plates diminishes Armour plating.

gradually from stem to stern to a minimum thickness of $2\frac{1}{2}$ inches. The thin plating fixed to the extremities of the vessel was manufactured by Messrs. John Brown and Company. The armour plates are carried up to the floor of the weather deck for a length of 200 feet on each side. The battery thus protected is further enclosed by armour-plated bulkheads, running across the gun deck. Fore and aft of these bulkheads the armour-plates are carried as high as the floor of the main deck only.

Port sills.   The port sills of the 'Achilles' are closed with gun-metal lids, their dimensions being 3 ft. 8 in. by 1 ft. 11 in. They are embrasured on the inside, which enables the guns to be trained over an arc of 90°. At the load draught the port sills are 9 ft. 6 in. above the water.

Mode of construction.   In the mode of construction the 'Achilles' resembles the 'Minotaur' class. Being constructed with a two feet flatter section than the 'Warrior,' the machinery is two feet lower in the 'Achilles' than in the former vessel, in order to diminish the tendency to roll. The 'Achilles' has bilge keels similar to those on the 'Warrior.' In strength of material and perfection of workmanship, the 'Achilles' is at least equal to, if she does not surpass, every iron ship previously built, and the excellence of the workmanship reflects no small credit upon the officials at the Chatham yard, and upon the shipwrights, smiths, and other artificers employed upon the vessel. For a length of 220 feet the sides of the 'Achilles' are 3 ft. 1 in. in thickness, which is made up of 14-inch iron ribs, while the iron skin plates are $\frac{1}{2}$ inch in thickness, the skin being again covered by 18-inch teak backing and $4\frac{1}{2}$-inch iron armour-plates. All the between decks are exceedingly lofty, as is the case indeed with all the other ironclads.

Engines.   The engines are by Messrs. John Penn and Son, and are of 1,250 nominal horse-power. The screw was four-bladed. Stowage is provided for about 1,000 tons of coal, or sufficient for ten days' consumption. The 'Achilles,' at the light draught trial at Chatham, attained the very remarkable speed of 14·35 knots an hour, proving to be, at that time, the fastest vessel, after the 'Warrior,' in the Royal Navy. Improvements in her steering apparatus, and especially the absence of the screw-well, enabled this enormous ship, under steam, to answer her helm as easily as a cutter, and thus attain that quality of handiness so valuable in naval warfare, but in which unhappily, the 'Warrior' and the earlier ironclads are notably deficient. The 'Achilles' presents a fine, bold appearance; she has a good sheer, stands well out of the water, and has a very handsome bow.

It was reported in the *Times* of May 19, 1865, that the

'Achilles' is by no means a bad ship at sea. She lifts to a sea better than any other of the ironclads, and has a very steady deck for her gun platform, only rolling 14°, to 26° and 28° of the ' Black Prince.' This is the result of her flat floor, which gives her steadiness. She is quick and handy under sail, and nearly as fast as the other ships.

The progress in ironclad naval construction was such that the 'Minotaur' class, costly as they were, did not in the least degree fulfil the object with which they were designed, or justify the enormous outlay incurred in their construction. It was about this time that that remarkable development in the power of artillery began, the final issue of which it is at present impossible to foresee. While the 100-pounder Armstrong took the place of the 68-pounder on the broadside of ships, no addition was made to their armour protection. The ' Gloire ' was scarcely completed when the 68-pounder gun, with which she was armed, began to be regarded as obsolete, and armour of 4½ inches was no longer accepted as adequate. Some experiments at Shoeburyness in 1862 conclusively proved the tremendous powers of Armstrong's artillery, as developed in his 300-pounder rifled gun which, as a smooth bore, could fire a 150-lb. shot. Two shots fired in the course of the experiments in question with a 150-lb spherical shot and a charge of 50 lbs. of powder completely penetrated the hitherto invincible ' Warrior' target, and proved that our armour plates and backing encumbered our men-of-war with a heavy burden, but failed to keep out the shot of an enemy.

Increased power of guns: Armstrong 100-pounder and 300-pounder.

Experiments at Shoebury-ness, 1862.

Although obsolete in many essential particulars, the 'Minotaur' class may still be reckoned as valuable ships to the British navy. Various plans for remodelling these ships have been proposed. In an able lecture at the United Service Institution Admiral Scott dwelt at length on their condition and capabilities.

Admiral Scott on alteration of ' Minotaur.'

'The "Minotaur" class are well-built vessels, strong in the bottom, and showing,' he said, ' no signs of incipient decay. Their upper decks are firmly braced, and with local strengthening could easily carry four 38-ton guns, mounted on the same plan as the gun at Shoeburyness. On the main deck, so as not to add greatly to the total weight, a few powerful breech-loading 80-pounders, capable of piercing the thinner armour-plates, might be mounted. These, with some anti-torpedo 12- or 20-pounders, would render the "Minotaur" class powerful ocean cruisers. As their proposed main batteries would be on the upper deck, they might take in a very large supply of coal below. In war time the spacious decks of these vessels would be valuable for housing and lowering torpedo launches for an attack;

and this room would be equally valuable for working the Harvey and other torpedoes. As first-class troopships they would be unmatched, and just the vessels to fight their way with the troops.'

In 1875 the 'Minotaur' underwent a very extensive conversion. The details of the work carried out are given in the following extracts from the able reports of the resident correspondent of the *Times* at Portsmouth :—

'One of the largest, most difficult, and costly undertakings in the way of practical reconstruction is now drawing towards completion at Portsmouth dockyard. In 1861 three ships of the "Minotaur" class were ordered to be built, and seeing the important improvements which had been effected in naval gunnery, and the structural changes they have necessitated in the designs of our men-of-war, it was fortunate for the country that no more ships of the same type were constructed. They were plated with $5\frac{1}{2}$-inch armour, which was a slight advance upon that of the "Warrior," designed some two years or so before; but the extra inch gained in the thickness of the plating was to some extent counterbalanced by a material reduction in the backing. Substantially, the defensive power of the two classes of ships was the same; but the ships of the "Minotaur" type had this important advantage, that they were armoured throughout the whole of their length, so that the vital parts—such as the rudder-head, steering gear, and the watertight compartments—were efficiently protected against the penetrating force of the shot of the period. But, while the "Warrior" cost the country 356,990*l.*, the price of the "Minotaur" was 450,774*l.*, the engines in both instances being about the same. The gain, however, even at the time, was not proportionate to this important increase in the expense of construction, while at the present time the improved ships of the "Warrior" size would speedily place the five-masted leviathans *hors de combat*. The ships of the "Minotaur" class are 400 feet in length, and therefore unwieldy at sea, while the great difficulty which attends their steering unfits them for manœuvring in the narrow circles in which our modern men-of-war are required to pivot. The length of their broadsides and the great height of their freeboard would also render them tempting targets for an enemy's heavy guns. These defects, however, cannot now be remedied; but much is being done at Portsmouth at the present time to make the "Minotaur" a more dangerous antagonist by adding materially to her offensive power. She has been nine months under the hands of the shipwrights, and the total cost of her reconstruction and new equipment is estimated to amount to 50,000*l.*

'Launched at the end of 1863, the "Minotaur" is, of course, one of the most venerable of our ironclads, but during the thirteen or fourteen months she has been under the shipwrights' hands at Portsmouth, she has been practically converted into a new ship. Certain it is that she was never so formidable, either as regards attack or defence, as she is at the present time, and though she is of the inordinate length of 400 feet, which was at one time thought necessary to secure great speed under steam, her extraordinary nimbleness in steering renders her more versatile at sea than might have been expected from her size. The most important improvement which has been made in the "Minotaur" is in respect of her armament, which has been considerably increased in penetrating power, at the same time that the number of the guns has been reduced by about one-half. But while the Admiralty have declined to arm the "Minotaur" as heavily as the "Hercules," she will go to sea as formidable at least as the "Bellerophon." As a matter of fact her armament has undergone repeated fluctuations, and we venture to hope that she will some day carry the heaviest broadside guns in the service. As first designed she was to carry 58 Armstrong guns; then her armament was reduced to 26—viz., four 12-ton guns and twenty-two $6\frac{1}{2}$-ton guns; and in a few days hence she will proceed to sea with an armament consisting of seventeen 9-inch 12-ton guns, Fraser construction, for which new ports have had to be cut in the sides of the ship. With a powder charge of 43 lbs., these will carry a projectile 250 lbs. in weight, and will enable the "Minotaur" to pierce the "Warrior" at 2,000 yards, and a ship of her own thickness of armour and backing at 1,000 yards. But as the striking effect of a shot depends more upon its velocity than on its weight, it may be pointed out that in this particular up to a range of 1,700 yards, the 9-inch gun surpasses all the higher natures, the 10-inch 18-ton gun alone excepted, and that at shorter ranges it even excels that. The "Minotaur" carries two bow chasers for the sake of end-on fire, while a third gun is mounted upon a turntable under the poop, and commands a large arc of fire.

'It will thus be seen that the number of guns on each side of the main deck has been reduced from fourteen to seven, every alternate port having been altered to suit the heavier ordnance and to give increased room for the working of the guns, as well as additional space for elevating, depressing, and extreme training. This has been the slowest, most difficult, and most expensive part of the work, and it is understood that every port which has been operated upon has cost upwards of 250*l.* The whole has had to be performed by hand labour, and when it is stated that the $5\frac{1}{2}$-inch armour, the framework of the ship, and the 10-inch teak backing, have all had to be cut through by hammer and chisel after drilling, the exceeding difficulty of the task will be apparent. When, too, all this had been accomplished, the ports have had to be reframed in order not to weaken the ship in any way.'

These alterations have been criticised by Captain (now Admiral) Scott. In a speech at the United Service Institution, he said:

'Lately one of the " Minotaur " class had her main deck broadside ports enlarged at great expense merely to put 12-ton guns in them. For the same cost four 38-ton guns could have been mounted upon her *upper* deck, and thus have made her an efficient war vessel.'

The *Times* correspondent continues :—

'These alterations have necessitated others in the interior and cabin arrangements of the ship. The magazines and shell-rooms have had to be enlarged. The " Minotaur " has been provided with new boilers, one of Hirsch's four-bladed propellers, and new steam-steering gear. These, however, are what may be regarded as inevitable improvements. What is most noteworthy in the present outfit of the ship are the highly scientific adjuncts with which it has been furnished. For the first time a complete electrical apparatus for signalling and for detecting torpedoes has been fitted to a man-of-war. The induction machine is worked by the capstan engine on the lower deck, and although the circuit is complete from stem to stern, only one of Mr. Wilde's projectors has as yet been fitted. It is placed on a stand near the centre of the poop ; but it can be moved to the forecastle, where two stands have been erected for it, one on either bow. But the most important feature in the scientific furnishing of the " Minotaur " is the provision of a couple of rifle shields for the protection of the officer fighting the ship. For this purpose the fighting bridge has been removed from the neighbourhood of the main mast and brought 80 feet aft, and has been connected with the poop by a wing gangway on each quarter. The shields are rifle-proof structures, four feet broad and six feet high, placed at each end of the bridge, and project beyond the hammock netting about 18 inches. They are entered down a ladder from the bridge, and are provided with shutter outlooks. Each of these little compartments is, in its way, a scientific observatory, and materially tends to reduce the art of war to a mastery of mathematical methods on the part of the commanding officer.

'In the same way that the steam propeller has dispensed with the services of the sailing master, the scientific furniture of these structures will abolish the responsibility of individual gunners. Each shield is fitted with one of Elliot's directors, which is so nicely adjusted and graduated that the officer in command, when in sight of an enemy, will be enabled to ascertain from it the correct angle of elevation for range and the proper training for converged fire, before or abaft the beam. Having communicated his orders to the battery through voice tubes, and the guns being charged, he is provided in his retreat with the means of firing the whole broadside simultaneously by electrical contact. The arrangement has this disadvantage—that should the officer be wrong in his calculations, the whole of the battery would miss the target, whereas if each of the guns were individually sighted it is almost certain that some would hit the mark. In addition to steam trumpets the " Minotaur " has been supplied with the means of communicating in a fog by guns, in accordance with a code. There are seven watertight compartments in the double bottom, which, however, does not run throughout the ship, but is confined to the engine and boiler spaces ; but each of the three decks is protected by fifteen watertight bulkheads. These have all undergone a thorough examination, and various improvements have been introduced.'

The ' Minotaur,' after being twelve months in the hands of the dockyard officers at Portsmouth, was tried at the measured mile with the following results. The force of the wind at the trial was from five to six, and the direction east, the sea being smooth. The draught of water forward was 25 ft. 8 in., and aft 26 ft. 5 in. The nominal power of the ' Minotaur's ' engines is 1,350, and the horsepower developed at the trial was 6288·62. The load on the safety valve was 25 lbs., the pressure of steam in the boilers 25·16, the vacuum in the condensers 23·5 forward and 24 aft, and the mean pressure in the cylinders 25·175. The highest mean of revolutions per minute was 56·47, the mean per minute 55·74, and the mean per mile 238·83. The mean of the six runs on the mile at full boiler power was a speed of 14·065 knots. Four runs were also made on the mile at half-boiler power with the following results :—Pressure on the boilers 23·125, vacuum in condensers 25·87, and mean pressure in cylinders 16·125 ; highest mean per minute 46·71, mean per minute 45·62, and mean per mile 234·25. The mean of the runs at half-boiler power was 11·948. The engines were stopped from the time of moving telegraph in 35 seconds ; being stopped, they were started astern in 15 seconds, and, going astern, they were started ahead in 14 seconds. The temperature varied from 69° on deck to 130° in the middle stokehole.

Trial trip.

CHAPTER VI.

CONVERTED SHIPS.

Lord
Clarence
Paget,
1862. In 1862 in introducing the Navy estimates in the House of Commons it was stated by Lord Clarence Paget that we had in commission in the Channel fleet, and on the Mediterranean, North American, and distant stations, 149 men-of-war, nineteen of which were line-of-battle ships, while only two were ironclads. We had at that time fifteen ironclads built and building, of which eleven might be expected to be afloat in that very year. In 1863 he expected that the navy would possess twelve, and in 1864 fifteen ironclads. On the same occasion he announced the determination of the Admiralty to convert some of the most suitable wooden liners into ironclads. By

Fig. 20.

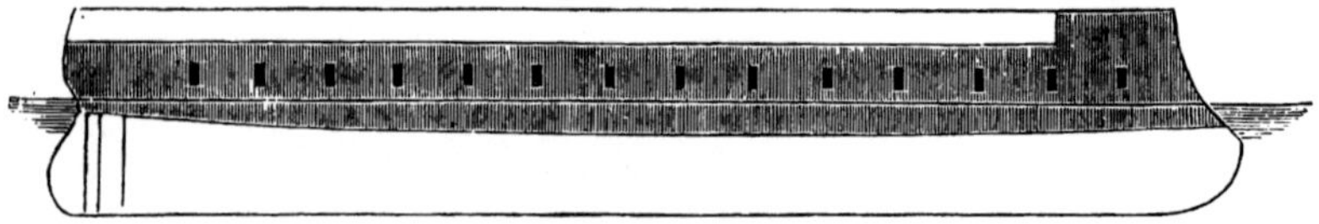

' LORD CLYDE.'

this means some portion at least of the national property in wooden ships, estimated by Captain Sherard Osborne as having cost at least 20,000,000*l.*, was to be rendered available for the new system of naval construction. This step was the more desirable in view of the progress made by France in the reconstruction of her navy. By means of this conversion we should possess an effective fleet of ironclads, at a much earlier date than would be possible if our armour-clad fleet were to consist entirely of new ships.

The vessels selected for conversion were the 'Zealous,' 'Repulse,' 'Prince Consort,' 'Ocean,' 'Caledonia,' 'Royal Alfred,' and 'Royal Oak.' Begun as line-of-battle ships, they were still on the stocks. They were now to be cut in two, lengthened, and plated all round with 4½-inch armour-plating, backed with thirty inches of teak. Four of these ships were of 800 nominal horse-power.

During the same epoch of activity the 'Lord Clyde' and 'Lord Warden' were built. They were of 8,000 tons displacement, 1,000 nominal, and 6,000 and 6,700 indicated horse-power respectively. They were fitted with rams, and had armour-protection all round, and thick skin-plating behind the armour. They attained a speed of 13·5 knots an hour.

'Lord Clyde.' 'Lord Warden.'

These nine vessels are of wood: the thickness of the armour in the first five is 4½ inches, in the two succeeding vessels 6 inches, and in the last two ships of the series 5½ inches. The 'Royal Oak' and the 'Prince Consort' were launched in 1862, and commissioned in 1863; the 'Ocean' and 'Caledonia' were launched in 1863. In the same year the 'Royal Alfred' was actually building at Portsmouth, and the 'Bellerophon,' the new iron ship designed by Sir E. Reed, the 'Lord Warden' and 'Lord Clyde' frigates, and 'Pallas' corvette, all of wood, were just commenced.

Progress of construction, 1862-36.

Fig. 21.

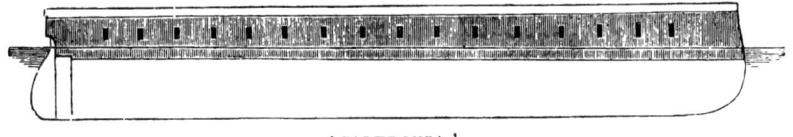

'CALEDONIA.'

The following general description of the converted ships is taken from Mr. Scott Russell's 'Naval Architecture.'

Scott Russell on converted ships. (Vol. I., p. 657.)

'The "Caledonia," the "Prince Consort," the "Ocean," the "Royal Oak," and the "Royal Alfred" are all about 273 feet long, 58 to 59 feet beam, and 4,000 tons. They carry their ports about 7 feet out of the water, and have been designed for a battery of 36 guns. They are plated with 4½-inch iron armour, having behind it 30 inches of oak side. The three first have engines of 1,000 horse-power, and the two last 800 horse-power, developing about four times their nominal power. They all draw from 26 to 27 feet of water aft, and 23 to 24 feet forward, and have a displacement of about 6,000 tons. The maximum speed of the class is from 12 to 13 knots.

The 'Caledonia' class.

The following details of the conversion of the iron-plated frigate 'Ocean' originally appeared in the *Times*:—

'The "Ocean" was a sister ship to the "Caledonia," and was intended to carry 91 guns. Her original dimensions were—length, 252 feet; breadth, 57 feet; depth in hold, 25 feet; burden in tons, 3,715. Her draught ready for sea was—forward 25 feet, aft

The 'Ocean.'

26 ft. 5 in. In June 1861, the Admiralty gave directions for her conversion into an iron-cased frigate of 34 guns of the following dimensions: length, 273 feet; breadth, 57 ft. 2 in.; depth in hold, 19 ft. 10 in. The burden was to be 4,045 tons, and the draught, when ready for sea, forward 24 ft. 7 in., aft 26 feet. The " Ocean " was accordingly cut in two amidships. The fore section was hauled up 20 feet, and five pairs of frames were inserted. The original framework of the stem and stern was taken down, and finer lines were given to the ship at either extremity.

' The thickness of the sides of the " Ocean " immediately below the armour-plating were made up of, outer 'plank, 12 inches; timbers, 14 inches; and inner plank, 6 inches; being a total thickness of 2 ft. 8 in. Thus the planking below the armour was flush with the facing of the plates. Where the armour-plating was fixed the outer plank was 8 inches thick, the inner 6 inches, and the timber 14 inches, which, with the $4\frac{1}{2}$-inch plates, made a total of 2 ft. $8\frac{1}{2}$ in. In the reconstruction 46 iron beams were introduced for sustaining the upper deck. Some of these weighed 22 cwt. each. The carpenters of the yard fitted the beams and the iron framework of the hatches in the engine-room. The work had been hitherto done by Government smiths, who were said to be excelled in it by the carpenters.

' In the converted ship the original upper deck was dispensed with ; and the new upper deck, which was flush fore and aft, was covered with iron plates $\frac{3}{8}$, $\frac{1}{2}$, and $\frac{5}{8}$-inch in thickness fastened to the iron beams. The plates were covered over with an oak deck, 4 inches thick. On each side of the upper deck amidships the " Ocean " was furnished with a round tower 7 feet high and about 5 feet in diameter, constructed of wood 12 inches thick, and plated outside with iron 4 inches thick. Access was obtained from below. The number of plates was 275. Of these, 168 of $4\frac{1}{2}$ inches were fixed amidships, while the remainder tapered from $4\frac{1}{2}$ inches to 3 inches in a distance of 40 feet towards the bow and stern. The weight of the armour-plates was estimated at 935 tons, and the cost from 35l. to 45l. per ton, exclusive of fastening. The bow of the " Ocean " below the water-line protruded 18 inches, or, in other words, the stem fell inboard like all the ships of her class, so that she might de prepared to act as a ram on an emergency.'

'Lord Warden.'
In the case of the ' Lord Warden,' a later conversion carried out from the design of Sir E. Reed, additional bow fire was obtained from four heavy guns firing ahead in line with the keel. With the view of correcting the tendency to plunge at sea, she had a long under-

water bow of the U form, projecting 10 to 12 feet beyond the stem. In the 'Lord Warden' and 'Lord Clyde' class 5½-inch plates are introduced over the guns, as well as at the sides of the batteries. At the water-line, in addition to the 5½-inch plates and 31½-inch backing, a 1½-inch plate is introduced between the backing and the sides of the vessels. The armour-plates weigh 1,300 tons. The 'Lord Warden' was intended to be armed with twenty guns, and measured 4,080 tons. Her original armament consisted of sixteen new pattern 9-ton 8-inch rifled guns, and four of the 100 lb. Armstrong, with the usual number of smaller guns for boat and field service. The engines were of 1,000 horse-power, by Messrs. Maudslay, Son, and Field.

The 'Repulse,' another of the converted ships, is still retained on the navy list; she has had two or three commissions, and is again fit for sea. This ship and the 'Lord Warden' are the last survivors of the class of modern line-of-battle ships converted into ironclads. The 'Repulse' was launched on April 25, 1868, and having seen some ten years' service she has required an extensive overhaul. A set of new boilers by various makers, and of various sizes and qualities, were supplied by the dockyard authorities of Devonport, but the repairs to the machinery have been undertaken by the original contractors, Messrs. John Penn and Sons, of Greenwich. The old crank-shaft, which was found to have been cracked, has been replaced by one which formerly did duty in the 'Donegal,' and new starting gear has been provided. The forward cylinder has been fitted with a new piston and trunk; new steam-pipes have also been supplied, while the expansion valves and gearing, the common condensers, and the moving parts of the engines have had all their defects made good. The pitch of the screw has been altered from 28 ft. to 26 ft., to meet the altered conditions in the boiler power, and the load upon the safety valves has, for a similar reason, been reduced from 30 lbs. to 20 lbs. to the square inch. Although it is not intended to introduce any alterations in or make any additions to the hull—a steam capstan excepted—beyond what are absolutely required to fit the ship for service, the necessities of torpedo warfare have greatly added to the cost of the refit. Arrangements are in progress for carrying the electric light on the ends of the bridge and on the poop, the current being produced by four of Siemens' machines, which will be driven by two independent sets of engines. The 'Repulse' will also be provided with twelve Whitehead torpedoes, 14 in. in diameter, which will be projected from four ports on the main deck—viz. two

The 'Repulse.'

Alterations.

---

¹ More correctly the 'Lord Warden' was built, not converted; but she and the 'Repulse' both belong to the wooden-armoured class.

before and two abaft the battery. Over the hammock berthing at
the waist a couple of Thorneycroft second-class torpedo boats will be
stowed upon crutches, and will be lowered into the water by means
of purchases from the mainyard, instead of by a special derrick or
davit provided for the purpose. Her armament of twelve 9-ton (8-inch)
guns will remain the same as before, but some addition will be made
to her torpedo guns, and she will, besides, be probably furnished
with Gatling or Nordenfeldt guns. At the six hours' trial of her
machinery after repairs the ' Repulse ' realised a speed of 11 knots,
the average revolutions per minute being $56\frac{1}{2}$, and the indicated
horse-power 2,734·98, which compared very favourably with the
results obtained under much more favourable circumstances eight
years ago. The cost of converting the ' Repulse ' into an improved
sea-going cruiser will be considerable, the estimated expenditure on
the hull alone being 20,000*l.* and on the torpedo gear 17,000*l*
more.

Lord
Clarence
Paget on
general
progress of
construc-
tion.
The general results of the earlier shipbuilding operations in the
armoured classes, which have been described in the preceding pages,
were summed up by Lord Clarence Paget. ' We have,' he said,
' seven ships of great speed ; but having a very great draught of
water, and therefore they cannot be docked out of this country.
This class consists of the " Warrior," the " Black Prince," the
" Achilles," the " Minotaur," the " Agincourt," the " Northumberland,"
and the " Bellerophon." The second class consists of vessels, possessing less speed, but also drawing less water, and their names are
the " Lord Clyde," the " Royal Oak," the " Prince Consort," the
" Ocean," the " Caledonia," the " Royal Alfred," and the " Lord
Warden." The third class consists of the " Zealous," the " Hector,'
the " Valiant," the " Defence," and the " Resistance," of still less
speed and draught. We have, therefore, a fleet of nineteen armour-
plated ships of the line. The next in order on the list are the
frigates, corvettes, and gunboats, that is to say, the " Favourite,"
the " Research," the " Enterprise," the " Pallas," the " Viper," the
" Vixen," and the " Waterwitch " ; and then we come to four ships,
which will do for coast defence, namely, the " Royal Sovereign," the
" Prince Albert," the " Scorpion," and the " Wyvern." These make
altogether a fleet of thirty armour-plated ships.'

Superior
strength of
iron hulls.
The British navy, though possessing no decided advantage
over the fleet of France in point of numbers, was constituted for the
most part of more durable ships. In the debates on the navy
estimates in 1863, it was stated by Sir John Pakington, that it was
reported that the ' Gloire,' the French wooden ironclad frigate, had

been seriously strained in cruising in the Mediterranean, while no vessel had ever been tried more severely than the ' Warrior ' in the Bay of Biscay, and stood the trial so well.   Lord Palmerston, in confirmation of these views, was able to point out that of our twenty-one ironclads eleven were of iron, while all the French ironclads, twenty-seven in number, were every one of them built of wood, except the ' Couronne.'

CHAPTER VII.

SIR E. J. REED'S SYSTEM—SHIPS BUILT FROM HIS DESIGNS.

Appointment of Sir E. Reed as Chief Constructor.

WE now return to the general history of the development of armoured construction. A new and remarkable impetus was given to naval architecture for war purposes by Sir E. J. Reed, who was appointed, by Sir John Pakington, to the important office of Chief Constructor of the Navy. A radical change was introduced in the

Fig. 22.

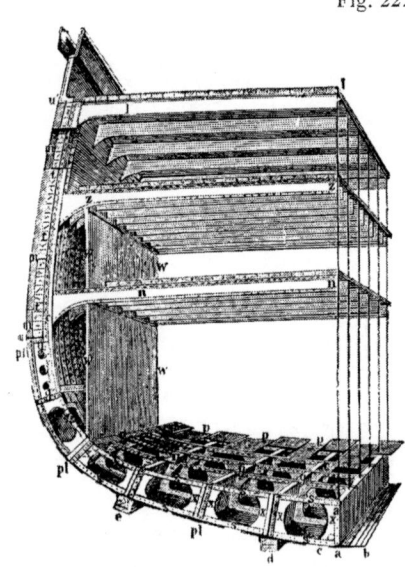

a, b, c, keel; *d, e,* bilge keels; *s, s', x,* frames; *g, g,* longitudinal girders; *p, l,* outer plate of double bottom; *p,* inner skin of double bottom; *w,* upright fore and aft bulkheads forming, with the ship's side, wing passages; *m,* armour; *t,* backing; *u, u',* extent of armour; *n,* lower deck; *z,* main deck; *l,* upper deck.

types of British ironclads, and our example was followed by the other maritime powers.

'Reed's System.'

The special features of Sir E. Reed's system of design were fully described by Mr. Fairbairn in his 'Treatise on Iron Shipbuilding.' Details of the plan of construction, known as the 'bracket-frame' system, are shown in the accompanying plate (Fig. 22), from the work of Captain von Kronenfels.

Sir Edward Reed provides for the concentration of a heavy Central battery. battery amidships. This battery is completely protected at the sides by armour-plating, and the armour is carried round the ship from stem to stern for a breadth of 5 ft. below and 5 ft. above the water-line. These batteries are protected from raking fire by armour-plated bulkheads athwartships, and the safety of the ship itself is secured by the application of armour-plating to every part where the penetration of an enemy's shot might prove a cause of very serious injury. When practicable two large guns are placed at the bow and stern, independent of the principal battery. These guns are protected by a shield of armour-plating round the bow and the stern.

With this improvement is also associated another, equally im- The U bow. portant, viz. the total change in the form of the vertical section of the bow : the new form of section being of the U shape, in opposition to the old V-shaped bow, to which the Admiralty have until now so pertinaciously clung. The slightest thought will convince anyone that when the bow of the ship is formed like a V it will cleave the water when the ship plunges, and thus tend to increase the violence of each plunge. A bow on the other hand formed like a U will be obviously the better by resisting the water in its descent, and thus diminishing the violence of the pitching motion. Another of the most marked features in Sir Edward Reed's ships is the increased length of the floor in proportion to the length of the ship. This is necessarily associated with an upright stern.

The ' Bellerophon,' ' Pallas,' and other ships of Sir E. Reed's designs have the buoyant bow of U form, which was not introduced into Her Majesty's Navy until these ships were laid down. This feature is not necessarily allied with great bluffness in the bow lines, it being quite practicable to fine the upper water-lines by means of the buoyancy gained with the full lines below, and thus to secure on the whole as small an average angle of entrance with the new form of bow as with the old.

A marked difference in the draught of water forward and aft was Difference in draught of water fore and aft. another novel feature in Sir E. Reed's system. Most of the ships of the navy had previously been designed to float on a nearly even keel, whereas in the ' Bellerophon ' the draught of water was five feet and that of the ' Pallas ' six feet greater aft than at the bow, a state of things unexampled in war shipbuilding. The objects aimed at in these innovations were highly desirable, the first being the deep immersion of large screw-propellers driven by powerful engines, and the second the power of turning the ship quickly on her keel under the action of the rudder.

Protection
of the
rudder.

In Sir Edward Reed's ships longitudinal keelsons and cellular construction were generally adopted. For every ship the armour was so distributed as to give protection not only along the water-line, but also round her rudder and rudder-head. Great credit seems to be due to Admiral Sir Spencer Robinson, the Controller of the Navy, for the improvements observable in Sir E. Reed's design in this important particular, by which the former vicious practice of exposing rudders to the shots of the enemy was entirely avoided.

Armour.

In addition to the general features of construction we have already mentioned, Sir E. Reed was of opinion that he ought to employ iron armour of some kind and to some extent in every class of fighting ship that would carry it, both large and small; that we should employ a few large guns where practicable in preference to many small ones, and give these large guns as great a range of fire as possible; that every vessel should be made strong enough to stand the shock of being used, on an emergency, as a ram against vessels of her own class.

Wood and
iron con-
struction.

When we want a ship to perform the service allotted to our sloops and corvettes in all quarters and corners of the globe, when we want a vessel to steam up and down rivers and in and out of harbours, and to feel her way over unexplored grounds, then Sir E. Reed pronounced himself in favour of building the hull of wood. On the other hand, if it was necessary that the ship should be driven at a 14-knot speed, he maintained that iron must be preferred as the best material. Small war vessels, if armour-plated, might be built of wood; but when high speed or large dimensions were required we should build of iron.

Free-board.

When built of wood the hull should be made solid throughout, in the wake of the armour. Sir E. Reed thought it essential that a ship should stand well out of the water, in order to make her, what is so much desired by all sailors, a good ship in bad weather at sea; and to enable her to be well ventilated, an object of much importance in hot and unhealthy climates.

Rig.

For cruising vessels he strongly insisted upon the necessity of a full spread of canvas. He endeavoured to secure, in every seagoing ship-of-war which he designed, such a distribution of weight that the hull should be sufficiently water-borne, as far as may be, at every part, and have no heavy overhanging portions to cause straining and leakage in a sea-way.

Distribu-
tion of
weight.

Sir Edward Reed contended that too little regard had been paid to that important feature in construction—the equal distribution of weight throughout a ship. As we had increased the speed of our ships and the size of our guns, the bow had been made finer below and fuller above the water-line to secure fore and aft fire, until we had rendered easy motion and high speed in rough waters impossible. When we attempted to drive our five wooden frigates at full speed, their burdened bows plunged into every wave, and the ship was thus brought almost to a standstill by every opposing sea.

The general result of these ideas is concisely and lucidly summarised by Mr. Elgar, the author of the introduction to ' Our Ships of War.'

General summary of Sir E. J. Reed's improvements.

'The type of ship advocated by Mr. Reed was one that would carry, behind armour, a small number of the heaviest guns that could be mounted on board ship, instead of a large number of small guns, and that would only have sufficient armour-plating for the protection of the vital parts of the ship, viz., the engines and boilers, the guns, the magazines, the rudder-head and steering apparatus, and the whole of the ship between wind and water. This was known as the belt and battery system, from the arrangement of the armour-plating, which formed a high battery in the middle of the ship, and a belt that extended throughout the whole length, and protected her from injury in the neighbourhood of the water-line. Captain Coles, as is well known, opposed the system of mounting guns on a broadside altogether, and advocated the placing of them in thickly armoured revolving circular turrets in the middle of the ship, and a reduction of the height of the armoured side of the ship out of water. Both of these plans met great wants and palliated grave defects that existed in the 15 ships of what, in a somewhat comprehensive sense, we may call the "Warrior" type. They left no vital points exposed to an enemy's fire, they involved a much less area over which armour-plating was required to be spread, and they gave powerful bow and stern fire. The advantage most appreciated at the time in connection with both plans was the great reduction rendered possible in the size of ironclad ships without any loss of offensive or defensive power. Mr. Reed's designs were looked upon most favourably at the Admiralty. They involved the least departure from existing types of ships and methods of naval warfare, and at the same time promised to effect all that could be desired in the way of improvement. Orders were given in 1862 for the conversion of the wooden ships " Enterprise," " Favourite," and " Research " upon his plans.'

In the case of the wooden corvette ' Enterprise,' the first vessel modified by Sir Edward Reed, the plating protects only the central battery and water-line. The four guns can be trained to fire at an angle of 20° with the line of keel, by being transported from the broadside

The 'Enterprise.'

ports to others which are under cover. The unarmoured ends are constructed of iron.

Sir E. Reed, in 'Our Ironclad Ships' remarks that 'the design of the "Enterprise" opened the way to the production of much smaller seagoing ironclads. This vessel was of less than 1,000 tons burden, and yet was armoured all round at the water-line, carried heavier guns than any other vessel of her date, and was of moderate draught of water.'

The 'Research' and 'Favourite.

The 'Research,' another of Sir E. Reed's early designs, is of 1,250

Fig. 23.

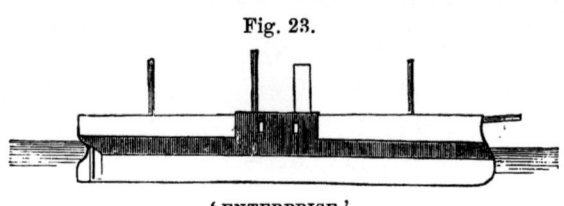

' ENTERPRISE.'

tons displacement; 200 nominal horse-power; and steams 10 knots an hour. The 'Favourite' has a draught of 21 ft. 6 in., and a displacement of 2,090 tons. With 400 nominal horse-power a speed of 11·85 knots an hour was attained at the measured mile. The ship carries a fuel supply of 350 tons. In the 'Research' and 'Favourite' the naval architect was disembarrassed of several limitations that fettered him in the 'Enterprise.' He avoided the iron upper works, and carried the armour up to the upper deck. These two ships, of 1,250

Fig. 24.

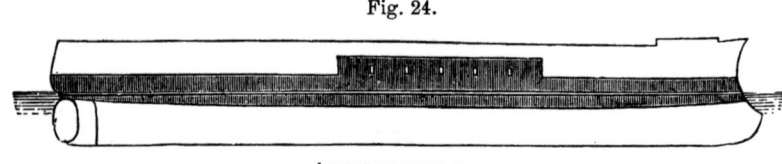

' BELLEROPHON.

and 2,090 tons respectively, were as completely plated with 4½-inch armour as the largest iron screw-ship then in existence.

The 'Bellerophon.'

The year 1863 is remarkable in the annals of ironclad construction for the laying down of the 'Bellerophon,' which represented in a more complete form the various ideas with which Sir E. Reed had inoculated the Admiralty. While retaining the central battery, we see, for the first time, the bow fire made a prominent feature. The 'Bellerophon' has her central battery so disposed that the guns mounted on it can be trained to fire at an angle of 45° with the line of keel. Two guns are also mounted in the bows, protected by an armour-plated bulkhead.

The necessity of preparing for fighting with the ram had become more and more evident, and every possible effort was accordingly made to give additional bow fire. The double bottom was a necessary consequence of the introduction of the torpedo. Each step in advance in offensive weapons called for increased means of protection from the naval architect. Iron plates 6 inches in thickness were used to resist 300-pounder guns, which at this period began to supersede the 100-pounder. Watertight compartments were introduced as a defence against the blow of a ram.

The following more detailed description of the 'Bellerophon' has been collected from notices which appeared in the *Times* and other periodicals during the construction and trial of the ship. *Description from the Times.*

'The "Bellerophon" is 300 feet long, with a beam of 56 feet, and a displacement of 7,551 tons. Though carrying the heaviest armament afloat, her draught is only 21 feet forward and 26 feet aft, being less than that of our ordinary two-deckers, while the height of her lowest ports from the water is $9\frac{1}{2}$ feet. The ship is 100 feet shorter, and was estimated to cost less, by 100,000*l.*, than the "Achilles," "Minotaur," or "Warrior," while, as a man-of war, she is far more effective than those vessels. Being relatively shorter, and fitted with a balanced rudder, the "Bellerophon" possessed a conspicuous superiority in the quality of handiness. The framing of the vessel was the same as that of the other iron frigates. Wherever steel could be used it was adopted, and Sir E. Reed estimated that by this method he saved in weight 200 or 300 tons. The armour of the "Bellerophon" is no less than six inches thick, and this rests on 16 inches of solid teak beams. The inner skin consists of two plates, each $\frac{3}{4}$-inch in thickness, with a layer of painted canvas between to deaden concussion. The "Bellerophon" is protected with armour of the thickness here described in the centre, for a length of 90 feet, and on the broadside, from five feet below the water-line to the level of the upper deck. This space contains the central battery, armed with ten 12-ton guns. Before and abaft the central battery the ship is protected by a belt of the same massive armour, which extends to the depth of five feet below the water-line all round. The armour-belt is carried to a height of six feet above the water-line. The stem is of the swan-shaped form. The engines are of 1,000 nominal, or 6,520 indicated, horse-power, from the manufactory of Messrs. Penn. The total weight of the machinery is 935 tons, and the quantity of coal which can be carried in the bunkers is 650 tons.

The "Bellerophon" is fitted with the Stanhope balanced rudder, which does away with the necessity for a heavy rudder-post. With this rudder the circle was completed in 4 min. 30 sec., and the half-circle in 1 min. 50 sec.'

Steam trials.

On her light draught trial, when the displacement was 5,630 tons, or less by at least one thousand tons than the true displacement when fully laden, the speed of the ' Bellerophon' was 13·645 knots. The speed would have exceeded 14 knots but for the adoption of a four-bladed screw, with which the engines could only make fifty revolutions a minute, as against seventy with a two-bladed screw.

In this trial occurred a remarkable phenomenon. The screw-propeller, while advancing with a speed of a little more than $12\frac{1}{4}$ knots, drove the vessel through the water at a rate of $13\frac{3}{4}$ knots an hour. Several explanations have been given of this circumstance. It has been said that the blades of the screw-propeller bend under the resistance of the water, and that they have a greater pitch when working than when at rest. But the assumption can hardly be sustained in view of the fact that the same phenomenon was observed in an equal degree when a stronger screw was used, and when the pliability of the blades of the propeller was thereby much diminished. The explanation is, that in vessels of high speed and full lines, like the ' Bellerophon,' a vacuum in the water in the region of the stern-post is caused by the onward progress of the vessel. This vacuum is filled up by particles of the water flowing, not in a direction from bow to stern, but at right angles to the course of the vessel. In some cases it has been shown that the vacuum at the stern is filled up by particles of water, which have a forward movement in the direction of the course of the ship. In this case the screw-propeller would necessarily have what is called a negative slip, proportionate to the rate at which the dead water in the wake of the ship was

The screw.

flowing in the direction of the course. The adoption of the four-bladed screw in place of a two-bladed Griffiths' screw is a serious obstruction to the speed of the ship under canvas. It is not to be expected that any amount of canvas would drive a vessel swiftly through the water, if held back by the drag of a screw having two large blades at right angles to the rudder-post.

At the trials of speed in seagoing trim a mean speed of 14·2 knots was realised with full boiler power, and 12·6 knots with half-boiler power. The displacement was 7,230 tons. These results may be compared with the speed attained in the case of certain other of the earlier ironclads :—

BELLEROPHON.

						Knots
Warrior	.	.	.	.	.	. 14·3
Black Prince	.	.	.	.	.	. 13·6
Achilles	.	.	.	.	.	. 14·3
Pallas	.	.	.	.	.	. 13·0
Defence	.	.	.	.	.	. 11·6
Hector	.	.	.	.	.	. 12·3
Scorpion	.	.	.	.	.	. 10·5

On her first steam trial the 'Bellerophon's' cleaver-shaped prow drove the water up as high as her hawse pipes, when going at full speed. An additional light iron head was therefore fixed to keep out the water.

The 'Bellerophon' was tried at sea, in a cruise extending over 32 days, with the Channel Squadron, under the orders of Admirals Yelverton and Warden. All the ships composing the squadron rolled heavily. The 'Wyvern,' being fitted as a turret-vessel, was unable to work her guns while rolling 22°. With a roll of 13° the 'Bellerophon' was just able to open her ports and fire her guns. The difficulty in working the guns arose, not from any failure in the gear, but from the quantity of water which came in through the ports. The 'Bellerophon' rolled less than the majority of the vessels. While the 'Caledonia' was rolling 35°, and the 'Pallas' 32°, the 'Achilles' did not roll more than 16°, and the 'Bellerophon' only 10°. *Trial at sea.*

The 'Bellerophon' is armed with three 6½-ton rifle guns, on the Woolwich pattern, outside her armour-plated gun battery. Two of these guns are mounted at the bow. In the midship battery are ten 12-ton guns, trained and worked, but not loaded, by machinery. *Armament.*

The armament of the 'Bellerophon' has been criticised by a high authority. In a lecture at the United Service Institution, Admiral Scott remarked :—'The "Bellerophon" is deficient in bow-fire, and should be supplied with two 18-ton guns, mounted in indented ports, *outside* the armour of her main deck, and at least two more 18-ton guns to replace 12-ton guns in her main deck battery *within* the armour. The two 6½-ton guns on the broadside of the upper deck should be done away with.' *Admiral Scott on the armament.*

The principles which Sir E. Reed had followed in the design of the 'Bellerophon' were generally adopted in the construction of other ships. The 'Pallas,' an enlarged and modified 'Enterprise,' was commenced at the end of 1863, and launched in March 1865. The remarkable feature in this ship is the arrangement for obtaining a direct gun-fire ahead and astern from ports in the angle of the battery. The range of fire from the indented ports is extended as *The 'Pallas.'*

much as possible by contracting the upper works before and abaft the battery.

The principal dimensions of the 'Pallas' are: length, 225 feet; beam, 50 feet; and tonnage, 2,372 tons. She is protected by 4½-inch armour.

The engines of this vessel, of 600 horse-power, by Messrs. Humphrey and Tennant, are among the earlier examples of the compound type, introduced into the Navy. They are described in a contemporary notice, as consisting of two cylinders of unequal area, the larger cylinder having an area four times greater than that of the smaller. The steam is admitted in the small cylinder at high pressure, and on the return stroke passes into the larger cylinder. Having surface condensers a much better vacuum is obtained than ordinarily, the benefit of which improvement is manifested over the whole surface of the large piston. By this means a comparatively large horse-power is obtained with a small consumption of fuel. The boilers are

Fig. 25.

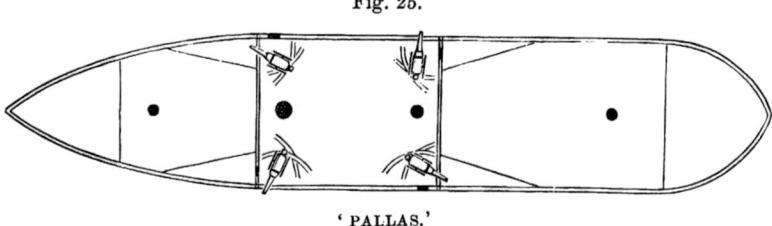

' PALLAS.'

supplied with superheaters, and every portion of the machinery is 'jacketed.'

The 'Pallas' is propelled by a single screw 19 feet in diameter. When the design was prepared by Sir E. Reed it was the general opinion that fast ironclad ships must be of large dimensions. The 'Defence' class of frigate, of 6,070 tons displacement, was the smallest previously designed for the Royal Navy; and her greatest speed was 11½ knots. The 'Pallas,' although less than two-thirds of the 'Defence's' tonnage, steamed 13·4 knots.

The hull of the 'Pallas' is of wood, solid oak frames being fitted throughout behind the armour. To enable the wooden frames of this ship to stand the enormous strains from the screw propeller in working at full power, the stern-post and dead wood have been connected with the sides of the ship by means of internal iron bulwarks and external brass castings, so as to bind the whole of the stern frame of the ship together in one rigid mass. The weight of the armour-plating is 580 tons, and the hull is protected from stem to stern up to the height of the main deck, and also over the whole extent of the central battery. The armament of the 'Pallas' consists of four 12-ton guns, two 64-pounders, and two 40-pounder Armstrongs. It has been previously stated that this battery is so contrived as to permit two of the most powerful guns to be fired almost right ahead or right astern. This arrangement has the great advantage of allowing the deck above the guns to be converted into a spar deck at a great height above the water. The fixed bulwarks rise no less than eighteen feet above the line of flotation. The ends have been loaded as little as possible, buoyancy at the bow and stern being of the greatest importance in a sea-way. Very superior seagoing qualities have thus been secured, while accommodation between decks is afforded to the officers and men to an extent unprecedented in small ironclad ships.

The 'Pallas' was consequently in every respect a sea-going ship,

Figs. 26 and 27.

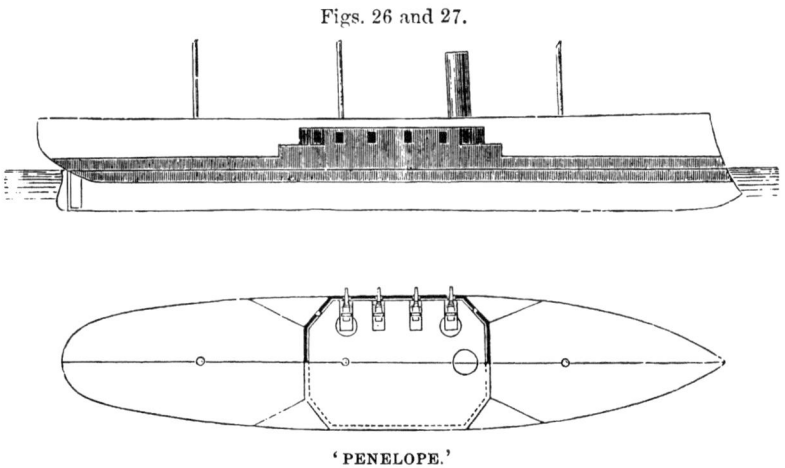

'PENELOPE.'

adapted for ocean service in any part of the world. She carried provisions for three months, 70 tons of shot and powder, and coal for steaming ten days continually at high speed. The under-water armour plating is sheathed with teak to prevent corrosion from the sea-water. The bow of the 'Pallas' projects ten feet below the water, and is armed with a formidable spur. Several minor improvements have been introduced in the internal economy of this vessel, including commodious washhouses and bathrooms for the crew.

The 'Penelope,' another second-class twin-screw ironclad, 'Penelope.' designed by Sir E. Reed at this period, and launched in 1867, has four angle ports in her battery; a draught of 16 ft. 9 in.; a displacement of 4,390 tons, and 600 nominal and 4,700 indicated horse-power. The speed realised at the measured mile was 12·8 knots. The 'Penelope' is built of iron with 6 in. plus 1½ inch armour.

'Viper,' 'Vixen.'

Among the other small ironclads built from his designs, it may be mentioned that the gunboats 'Viper' and 'Vixen' were launched in 1865 and 1866.

The 'Vixen.'

Suggestions having been laid before the Admiralty for combining the advantages of wood and iron in the same ship, this principle was adopted in the case of the 'Vixen,' a sloop constructed in Mr. Lungley's yard at Deptford. The frames of this vessel are of iron, while the external planking is of wood. It was hoped that by such a combination the general structural strength of an iron vessel would be combined with the superior local strength of the wooden ship, together with that freedom from fouling which can only be obtained by the use of copper sheathing. The 'Vixen' has a displacement of 1,228 tons; her length is 160 feet, beam 32 ft. 5 in., and depth of hold 13 ft. 7 in. Her engines, by Messrs. Maudslay and Field, are of about 740 indicated horse-power. She is fitted with twin screws.

On the occasion of the launching of the 'Vixen' the subjoined details were published in the *Times*:—'The armament consists of two 6½-ton guns. Stowage is provided for 97 tons of coal, which is equivalent to six days' consumption at full speed; for ten tons of water, which is equivalent to four weeks consumption, and for provisions for the crew for twelve weeks.'

The 'Water-witch.'

The 'Waterwitch' was built as an experimental vessel, to test the Ruthven system of propulsion by a turbine wheel, or what is known as the water-jet engine. She is built of iron; is 162 feet long, 32 feet broad, 13 ft. 9 in. deep; has a load displacement of 1,279 tons, and an indicated horse-power on the measured mile of 777. She has an excessively flat floor, is double-ended, and fitted with a rudder at each extremity. An armour-belt 4½ inches thick at the water-line extends round the hull, which rises at the middle of her length into a casemate rendered complete by athwartship

Mr. King in 'War Ships of Europe,' English edition.

bulkheads. The propelling instrument consists of a turbine wheel, or centrifugal pump, 14 ft. 6 in. in diameter, made of wrought and cast iron. This wheel revolves in a chamber 19 feet in diameter, in the centre of the hull, below the water-line; and the chamber is bored to a smooth surface inside, in order to reduce hydraulic friction to a minimum. The turbine has twelve radial blades or vanes, and weighs about 8 tons; it is put in motion by a set of three engines, arranged at angles of 120 degrees, the connecting-rods taking hold directly of a single crank rising vertically above the wheel-casing.[1] The engine cylinders are 38 inches in diameter, and the stroke of pistons 3 ft. 6 in., and they are supplied by steam from two ordinary box-boilers having six furnaces.

The wheel receives the water from a rectangular box, or tank, resting on the keelsons of the ship, and placed in free communication with the sea by means of a large nnmber of rectangular orifices in the bottom. From the wheel-casing perimeter at opposite sides, two copper pipes, about 27 inches by 25 inches internally, lead to the discharge-nozzles at the ship's side. These are 24 inches by 18 inches, and extend about 8 feet along the side of the hull just above the water-line, so that the engines have to raise the water through a very small height. A sluice-valve is arranged at each side in such a manner that the current from the turbine may be directed ahead or astern at pleasure by simply moving a lever, the engines revolving always in one direction. The water taken in through the bottom of the ship is expelled at both sides in the line of the keel, and the reaction of the fluid issuing at high speed imparts forward motion to the hull. The movement of the vessel ahead or astern is regulated by the direction of the escape of the water. If the water escapes aft, the movement will be ahead; if it escapes toward the bow, it will be astern.

The idea is exceedingly simple and very old. As far back as 1661, Toogood received a patent for propelling vessels by expelling water from their sterns. In 1730, Allen secured a patent for doing nearly the same thing; and the proposal was also made by Bernouilli eight years after. Indeed, the extreme simplicity of the system appears to have attracted many inventors, for down to the year 1857 it appears that upwards of fifty persons had either proposed or patented it in Europe, and many experiments had been tried from time to time. None of them, however, received much encouragement until Mr. Ruthven entered the field, and the success, such as it has been, which attended his exertions, seems to have been mainly due to his adoption of the centrifugal pump, with equable and enormous delivery, instead of the ordinary piston-pump commonly adopted by other inventors.

[1] As early as 1782, James Rumsey made a public experiment on the Potomac with a boat 80 feet long, propelled by a steam-engine working a vertical pump in the middle of the vessel, by which the water was drawn in at the bow and expelled through a horizontal tube at the stern; she went at the rate of four miles per hour. Benjamin Franklin and Oliver Evans suggested substantially the same mode of propulsion. Subsequently various applications of the principle were tried in the United States without success.—*King*; English edit.

Ruthven's first patent is dated in 1839. Under this, two small boats were built, and exhibited on a canal at Edinburgh. In 1849, another boat was built and exhibited on the Thames. In 1853, the 'Albert' was built on this principle in Prussia by Mr. Sydel, the engines and pump being furnished by the patentee. In 1865, the 'Nautilus' was built in England, embodying all Mr. Ruthven's improvements up to that date. With this little vessel several experiments were made in the presence of the Admiralty authorities, the results of which led to the construction of the 'Waterwitch.'

In consequence of the convenience of directing a vessel ahead or astern by the simple movement of a lever from the deck, this system of propulsion has been very fascinating to many officers; but unfortunately for this instrument of propulsion in common with the Hunter wheel, the Fowler wheel,[1] and all such submerged water-wheels in steam-vessels, an extraordinary power must be developed by the engines to obtain a small result; or, in other words, only a small amount of the power developed is utilised.

At the trial of the 'Waterwitch,' a vessel of only 1,279 tons displacement, of light draught and good lines, a power of 775 horses was developed with an average speed of $9\frac{1}{4}$ knots per hour.

Additional alterations and experiments were made in 1876 with a view to obtaining better results. These alterations consist in superseding the 140 small apertures through which the water is admitted, by one large aperture under the wheel and in the bottom of the ship, and in lengthening the nozzles at the sides through which the water makes its escape. The results obtained after these alterations were nearly the same as in previous trials. The speed of the vessel at sea has never exceeded five or six knots, and although ten years old, she has never been trusted out of sight of land.

The 'Hercules.' We now return to the ocean-going types. The 'Hercules,' launched at Chatham in 1867, was constructed from the design of Sir E. Reed. The main features of the type were described by Sir Spencer Robinson, in the discussion at the United Service Institution, on the essay by Commander Noel, which gained the prize offered by the Institution in 1876.

'The "Hercules" type is this—you protect the water-line of your ship by a belt; you protect the battery and the vital parts

---

[1] Fowler's steering-propeller is a submerged wheel revolving on a vertical shaft, with paddles which are feathered by an eccentric cam in such a manner that the paddles shall have a pushing and drawing action on the water while passing through the propelling arc, and present only their edges to the water while passing the dead points.—King.

of the engines and boilers by armour ; you protect your men and
guns over a limited space, because you cannot have sea-going qualities if you protect them over an unlimited space.   And that is the
type of ship represented in small ships by the "Iron Duke's" class,
and in large ships by the "Hercules" class ; and that is the type of
first-class ironclad which throughout the world at this day we shall
meet if ever we meet in hostility at sea.'

The principal dimensions of the 'Hercules' are as follows :—

Length .	.	.	.	.	.	325 feet
Beam .	.	.	.	.	.	59 feet
Displacement .	.	.	.	.	8,677 tons
Horse-power (nominal)		.	.	.	1,200
„ (indicated)		.	.	.	7,200

Figs. 28 and 29.

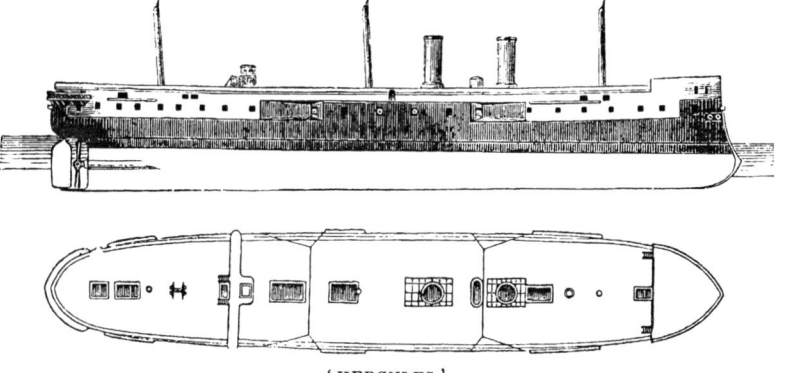

'HERCULES.'

The armament and armour of the 'Hercules' are fully described by   Mr. King.
Mr. King with much clearness and detail.   In this vessel 'an
improved fire was gained from the central battery, which consisted of 18-ton guns, by the expedient of recesses in the ship's
sides before and abaft the battery ; and advantage was taken of
the recesses to make four ports in the ends, or rather corners,
of the battery, from which four of the guns were able to fire
within a few degrees of the line of keel.   If required to fight
upon the broadside, these guns, which were mounted on turntables, were revolved to other ports.   The armament of this ship,
when put on board in 1870, was considered very powerful.   It
consisted of fourteen Woolwich rifled guns, of which eight were of
10-inches, two of 9-inches, and four of 7-inches calibre.   Her water-
line is defended by a belt of 9-inch armour, which was believed at
the time it was put on to be impenetrable at the thickest part by

any of the guns afloat in European waters. This defensive strength is, however, confined to the belt. The battery from which the largest guns are worked is protected by only 6 inches of armour; and experiment has shown that armour of that thickness with the ordinary backing can be penetrated at a distance of 1,000 yards and at an angle of inclination of 30° by the 9-inch rifled gun, and at close quarters by the 7-inch rifled gun, such as is carried by many armoured ships.[1] But the "Hercules" has other excellences; she is, for an armoured ship, a fair sailer, though represented to be awkward in tacking or wearing. She had a speed under steam on the measured mile of nearly $14\frac{3}{4}$ knots. She is said to be a very steady ship, and can, therefore, use her offensive powers under conditions of sea in which a less steady ship would be almost *hors de combat.*'

The 'Hercules' target.

The powers of resistance of the 'Hercules' target to the heaviest artillery at that date mounted on board ship were effectually tried in a course of experiments at Shoeburyness. On the first occasion an Armstrong 300-pounder $12\frac{1}{2}$-ton gun, loaded with a 300-lb. shot, and

---

[1] The 'Hercules' is much more efficiently protected than the text above indicates. In evidence of this we may quote the following passage from 'Our Ironclad Ships,' written in 1869 by Sir E. Reed, the designer of the 'Hercules':—
'The thickness of armour carried has, however, for the present, reached its maximum for sea-going broadside ships in the "Hercules," which has 9-inch armour at the water-line, 8-inch on the most important parts of the broadside, and 6-inch on the remainder. Outside the $1\frac{1}{2}$-inch skin-plating of this vessel, teak backing 12 and 10 inches thick is fitted, together with longitudinal girders of the usual character. This does not, however, constitute the whole of her protection, for from below the lower deck down to the lower edge of the armour the spaces known as the 'wing passages' are filled in solid with additional teak backing, and inside this there is an iron skin $\frac{3}{4}$ inch thick, supported by a set of vertical frames 7 inches deep. The total protection, therefore, of the most vital part of the ship in the region of the water-ine consists of the following thicknesses of iron and wood :—Out-side armour 9 inches; then 10-inch teak backing with longitudinal girders at intervals of about 2 feet, worked upon $1\frac{1}{2}$-inch skin-plating, supported by 10-inch vertical frames spaced 2 feet apart; the spaces between these frames are filled in solid with teak, and inside the frames there is a further thickness of about 19 or 20 inches of teak, the whole being bounded on the inside by $\frac{3}{4}$-inch iron plating, stiffened with 7-inch frames. The total thickness of iron (neglecting the girders and frames) is then $11\frac{1}{4}$ inches, and of this, 9 inches are in one thickness; the teak backing has a total thickness of about 40 inches. The trial at Shoeburyness of a target constructed to represent this part of the ship's side proved that it was virtually impenetrable to the 600-pounder gun; and perhaps no better idea of the increase of the resisting power of the sides of our ironclads can be obtained than that derived from a comparison of the 68-pounder gun which the "Warrior's" side was capable of resisting with the 600-pounder tried against the "Hercules" target.'

HERCULES.

at successive discharges with 45 lbs , 55 lbs., and 60 lbs. of powder, was directed against a target representing the exact construction of the broadside of the 'Hercules.' The target was not penetrated. In the second course of experiments, an Armstrong 600-pounder 22-ton gun was placed at a distance of 700 yards from the 'Hercules' target, and loaded with projectiles of from 575 lbs. to 585 lbs. in weight, with charges of 100 lbs. of powder. Except where two shots happened to strike on the same spot, the target remained still victorious. The lower half of the 'Hercules' target was faced with eight inches and the upper half with nine inches of iron. Both plates were supported by horizontal timbers, twelve inches in thickness, divided by four longitudinal plates. Inside the timbers was an iron skin of $2\frac{3}{4}$-inch plates. The whole was secured to the iron ribs representing the frames of the ship which are ten inches deep, and are filled in between with vertical timbers. Behind the ribs were two linings of horizontal timbers 18 inches deep, not bolted but confined by 7-inch iron ribs inside all. There was a $\frac{3}{4}$-inch iron skin within the innermost wood backing. It will be seen that the total thickness of this target was four feet.

Further and still more formidable tests were subsequently applied to the 'Hercules' target, the details of which are transcribed from the reports published in the *Times*. Seven rounds from Sir William Armstrong's 600-pounder gun having been fired against it, the following is a summary of the result :—

Round No. 1. With a steel rifle shot weighing 575 lbs., with a charge of 100 lbs. of powder, the initial velocity being 1,420 feet per second. The shot in this case buried itself completely in the target, breaking the rib of the ship, which was fixed immediately in the wake of the blow, and snapping off a considerable number of rivet-heads from the innermost skin.

In Round No. 2, the charge and weight of projectile were the same as in the case of the first round, and a similar effect was produced.

In Round No. 3, the gun was loaded with one of Sir William Palliser's chilled iron shot weighing 580 lbs., with a charge of 100 lbs. of powder. The shot struck the target close to the hole made by the shot fired in the preceding round. The inner skin and ribs of the target were torn asunder, and a great quantity of the pieces of the shot were forced through into the ship, producing all the destructive effect of langridge.

In Round No. 4, the shot, charge, and result, were the same as in the case of the third round.

Sir W. Palliser's chilled shot.

In Round No. 5, the third chilled Palliser shot was fired at the target, which struck the 5-inch plate a decisive blow, penetrating the target completely, and lodged in the backing, cracking the inner rib.

The gun used in these experiments is said to have shot remarkably well; the velocity of the heavy projectiles used, being from 1,420 to 1,460 feet per second, was very high. Both the gun and the powder, therefore, did their duty, and it appeared difficult to imagine how far more formidable artillery than that employed on these occasions could be adapted to practical service on board ship.

Letter from Sir W. Armstrong.

Upon this subject some remarks contained in a letter from Sir William Armstrong to the *Times* in the month of June, 1865, still possess considerable interest. The writer says that the whole range of the experiments at Shoeburyness has shown that, as the resistance of the target is increased, the weight of the charge of powder must also be increased, in nearly the same proportion, and that no variation in the bore of the gun or the weight of the projectile will supersede the necessity of such an increase of charge. Now a large charge naturally requires a large gun, not only as regards strength of iron to meet the great strain, but also as regards the capacity of the bore to give room for effective combustion of the powder and afford scope for the expansive action of the gas.

Mr. Barnaby. 'Hercules' and earlier ironclads.

The following comparison is drawn between the 'Hercules' and the earlier ironclads by Mr. Barnaby, in his paper on 'Our Modern Ships of War.'

'The ships of the "Minotaur" class, like the "Warrior," may be pierced by the 12-ton gun at 2,000 yards, but the next ship to be considered, the "Hercules," is impenetrable to this gun at all ranges; and also, along the belt amidships, to the 18-ton gun, at ranges beyond about 250 yards. Comparing her with the "Minatour," it may be said that for 100,000*l.* less money, or for the same cost as the "Warrior," a ship is produced throwing one-eighth more metal from the broadside than the "Minotaur;" having armour of more than double the resisting power, running at the same speed, and turning completely round in half the time. The drawback in this ship, as compared with her predecessors, is that whereas the "Minotaur" is propelled at full speed with 6,700 horse-power, the "Hercules" requires 8,500 horse-power to propel her at full speed. The speed is obtained in the former ships by fineness of proportion and form, and in the later ships by high engine-power. It is to be remembered that this increase in power at full speed does not represent a corresponding increase in the ordinary consumption of fuel, for in the first place the short ships are more manageable under sail, and require less steaming ; and secondly, the ordinary working speeds are very low. The indicated power at these low speeds, say at 5 knots, would be, in " Minotaur " 562, and in " Hercules " 798, *i.e.*, the difference would be only 236 indicated horse-power at 5 knots speed.'

The results of the trial of the ' Hercules ' under steam, in 1875, were thus described in the *Times* :—

Steam trial, 1875.

' The weather was somewhat hazy at starting, and the slight breeze from the south-west was only sufficient to ripple the water. Having rounded the Spit Buoy, the engines were put under a full force of steam, and continued at full speed for two hours and twenty-six minutes, in a run to the back of the Wight. The result was highly satisfactory, as will be seen from the following figures :—The draught forward was 23 ft. 0½ in., and aft 25 ft. 3 in. The pressure upon the boilers was 19 lbs. to the square inch; the pressure in the engine-room, 16½ lbs.; while the pressure upon the safety-valve was 20 lbs. The vacuum registered was 27 in. forward and the same number aft ; and the revolutions attained were 56·76. As the ' Hercules ' was not run at the measured mile, we can only arrive at an approximate indication of her speed through the water ; but so far as the log affords a means of judging, the speed attained was all that could have been desired, and more than could have been reasonably anticipated. The first throw gave 10·2, the second 11·6, and the third and best 12·9, or within a trifle of 13 knots an hour. It will be seen that as the engines warmed to their work a gradually accelerated momentum was obtained, and had the distance been prolonged it is probable that a rate of 14 knots would have been indicated. On the trial of her machinery at the measured mile, some six years ago, a speed of 15·91 was secured, but it must be remembered that her boilers were then new, whereas at the present time regard must be had to their comparatively worn condition. At the trial trip the I.H.P. was 7,187, while to-day it was only 4,975·80. At the trial trip again the number of revolutions per minute was 67·18, and the weight per square inch on the safety-valve 30 lbs. During the present trial the whole of the 40 furnaces were kept in full glow, and the temperature recorded was 102 degrees in the fore stokehole, 109 degrees in the after stokehole, and 89 degrees in the engine-room.'

On the capabilities of the ' Hercules ' under sail, Sir E. Reed, in ' Our Ironclad Ships ' makes the following observations : ' These recent ships, the " Hercules " and " Monarch," although so heavily burdened with thick armour and immense guns, have combined

The ' Hercules ' under sail.

therewith sail power enough to enable them to greatly economise
their fuel, which is the great object of their sails, and I feel certain
that it will be highly satisfactory to many readers of this work to
learn that the "Hercules" went through all the service performed
during the five weeks that the Admiralty flag floated over the
Channel Squadron, and returned to England with but one-half of her
coal consumed.'

Sir
Spencer
Robinson
on 'Her-
cules' and
'Achilles'
and French
ironclads.
In the discussion of Captain Noel's prize essay, which took place
at the United Service Institution in 1876, Sir Spencer Robinson
showed the changes and improvements of type, exhibited by the
'Hercules,' as compared with the earlier ironclads in our own service,
and the rival ships of the French navy.

'The first first-class ironclad this country possessed is a very
beautiful and powerful ship, the "Achilles." Let us compare the
"Achilles" with the "Hercules." The "Achilles" has a length of
380 feet, beam 58 ft. $3\frac{1}{2}$ in., draught of water 26 ft. 10 in., height
of port 8 ft. 8 in., displacement 9,094 tons. She carries 1,250 tons
of $4\frac{1}{2}$-inch armour-plating, and under that protection in her battery,
eighteen 7-inch and four 8-inch guns. Her speed is $14\frac{3}{10}$. The
"Hercules" has a length of 325 feet, beam $59\frac{1}{2}$ feet, mean draught
25 ft. 4 in., height of port 9 ft. 8 in., displacement 8,840 tons. She
carries 1,239 tons of 9, 8, and 6-inch armour, and mounts on her protected battery eight 10-inch guns and two 9-inch guns. Her speed
is $14\frac{9}{10}$ knots. But let us compare the "Hercules" with a first-class
French ship. The French first-class ironclad of that date is represented
by the "Friedland," the "Marengo," and others. The "Friedland" is
287 feet long, with a beam of 57 ft. 3 in., mean draught 26 ft. 6 in.,
height of port 9 feet, displacement 7,180, weight of armour 1,300
tons of 7, 8, 6, 2, and 4-inch armour. She carries in her protected
battery four guns of 10-inch calibre, and four $9\frac{1}{2}$-inch calibre guns in
towers *en barbette*. Her speed is 14 knots. I do not hesitate to say
that there is no comparison possible except an advantageous one to
the English type between the power of the two ships; that the
"Hercules," or that type of ship, could with great probability of
success, and with as much confidence as attends anything human,
engage a first-class French ironclad, and engage her with every prospect of being victorious.

'The "Sultan" is a little more powerful than the "Hercules," and
there is another French ship at sea, the "Richelieu," a little more
powerful than the "Friedland."'

The
'Auda-
cious' class.
The six ships of the 'Audacious' type were commenced in 1867.
It was a novel proceeding in English ironclad construction, where

hitherto each ship had, so to speak, represented a distinct type. According to the authors of ' Die Marine,' ' Sir E. Reed adopted for the "Audacious" very similar arrangements to those which he had devised for the "Pallas." By means of a considerable enlargement of the upper works, both forward and aft, it was possible to secure for the guns placed at the angles of the central battery direct fire ahead and astern. He also placed on the upper deck an armoured citadel, armed with guns nearly as powerful as

Fig. 30.

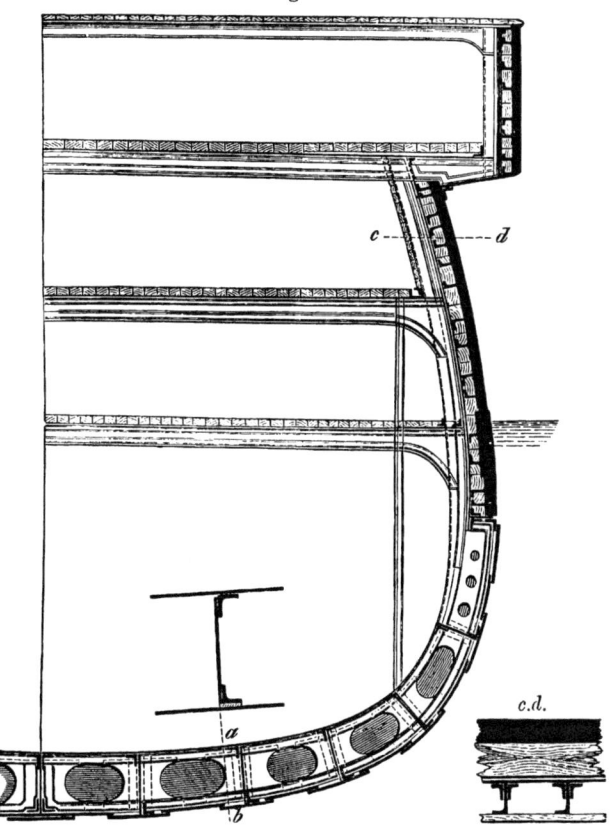

MIDSHIP SECTION—'AUDACIOUS' CLASS.

those carried in the battery below. With an armament of ten 12-ton guns, four could be so trained as to support an attack with the ram.

' These ships have therefore a double central battery ; the lower containing six guns with an arc of fire of 60°, and the upper four pieces, which are worked through the four angle ports of the battery, two ahead and two astern, the arc of fire being 90° These six vessels are of iron ; the thickness of armour in the first four is eight inches plus

$1\frac{1}{2}$ inch, and only 6 inches plus $1\frac{1}{2}$ inch in the last two.   The comparative smallness of the dimensions did not admit of an armoured protection equal to that of the " Hercules," and the water-line and central battery alone are armoured ; but notwithstanding that the armour is thus limited in area, ships of this type must be admitted to be very powerful and efficient.'

Mr. King
on designs
for 'Auda-
cious' class.
Mr. King, in his volume on 'The War Ships of Europe,' gives some important additional information as to the preliminary designs for the ships of this class.

'The loss of the " Vanguard " by sinking off the coast of Ireland, in September 1875, from the effects of an accidental blow of the ram of a sister vessel—the " Iron Duke "—drew public attention for a time to the comparatively easy manner in which one of these powerful and costly ships might be disposed of, as well as to this particular class of vessel.   The class consisted of six broadside vessels of similar

Figs. 31 and 32:

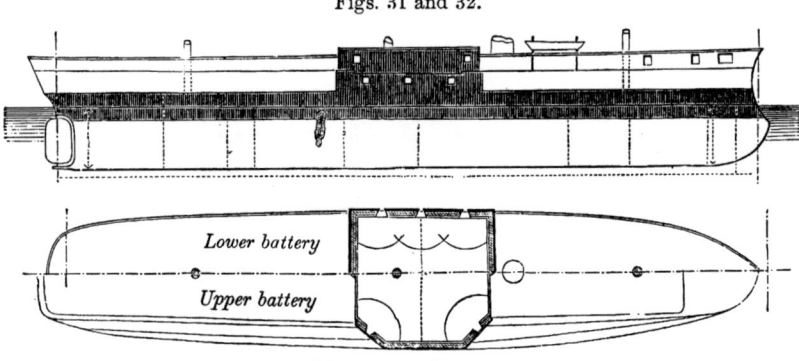

'AUDACIOUS' CLASS.

design, viz. the " Audacious," " Iron Duke," " Vanguard," " Invincible," " Triumph," and " Swiftsure."   The loss of the " Vanguard " leaves five.   They were all built for seagoing purposes, but the " Triumph " and " Swiftsure " were sheathed in wood and coppered. A brief outline of their history may serve to show how designs for ships of war have sometimes been decided upon by the Admiralty.

'In the year 1867, in the midst of the controversy between the advocates of the broadside and turret systems, the Board of Admiralty determined to invite the principal private shipbuilders of the kingdom to compete in designing either a turret or a broadside ship, at their option.   Certain conditions were imposed in either case: the displacement was fixed, the draught of water was to be $22\frac{1}{2}$ feet, and the speed $13\frac{1}{2}$ knots.   The armour-plating was to be at least 8 inches in thickness at the water-line, and 6 inches in other parts, except at the bow and stern ; and it was essential that an all-round fire should be obtained, or at least that some one gun behind armour-plates should command every point of the horizon.

'A prize was to be awarded to the successful competitor. Seven shipbuilding firms responded to the invitation, and sent in designs of various degrees of merit. The London Engineering Company proposed to build a broadside ship of 3,800 tons ; the Millwall Company, a compound of broadside and turret of nearly the same tonnage ; Messrs. Palmer and Co., a broadside ship with a movable upper deck battery ; and the Thames Company, a broadside ship ; while the firms of Messrs. Napier and Son, Messrs. Samuda, and Messrs. Laird each designed a turret ship, fulfilling the proposed conditions. The designs were referred to Sir E. Reed, then Chief Constructor of the Navy, with the result that the Controller of the Navy decided in favour of Sir E. Reed's ship over all the private designs, and expressed the opinion that the Admiralty designs of the " Audacious " class of broadside ships were superior to either.'

Six vessels of the ' Audacious ' class were thereupon ordered to be built, four of them being given out to be built in the yards of the disappointed shipbuilders.[1]

The improvements realised in the ' Audacious,' over the ships of the same class produced by the French constructors, are described in Mr. Barnaby's paper already referred to, read at the United Service Institution on January 29, 1872.

Mr. Barnaby on 'Audacious' class and French ironclads.

'The " Vanguard " class approaches nearest to the " Marengo " and " Océan " class in the French Navy. But in the French ships the guns in the upper battery are fought *en barbette*, and are dangerously exposed. Their armour also is so extended that, although they carry 1,280 tons of armour, as compared with 924 tons in the " Vanguard," and have 7·9 plates at the water-line, the average thickness of the iron to be penetrated in the French ships is less than in the " Vanguard." The French ships weigh about 900 tons more than the English, but half of this is in weight of hull, where it adds nothing to fighting efficiency. There is also good reason to believe that the French ships are inferior in speed to the ships of the " Vanguard " class, and that the present nominal superiority in weight of broadside thrown, does not represent real superiority. Even on the assumption

' Vanguard.'

---

[1] 'I have made it my business to consider how we can get most money's worth for our money, under all the possibilities of future European warfare on the seas. For this reason I have ex-

tolled, and I think justly, the " Vanguard " class for "rigged ironclads." ' —Mr. Barnaby, ' Modern Ships of War,' Journal, R. U. S. I. ; Jan. 29, 1872.

that the French 27 c/m. gun has 1,150 feet initial velocity,[1] which is believed to be greatly more than it has, and on the further assumption that the 24 c/m. guns in the upper battery are protected as fully as those of the "Vanguard," which they clearly are not, we should have the following comparative energy per inch of shot's circumference in a broadside of the protected guns in each ship:—

Vanguard	525
Marengo	430

It is to be remembered that of these French ships, "Océan," "Marengo," "Suffren," "Friedland," "Richelieu," "Colbert," and "Trident," only one is of iron.'

In the discussions on Commander Noel's prize essay, Sir Spencer Robinson made a similar comparison.

'Having shown you the difference between the second-class armour-plated ship, the type of which is so unreservedly condemned, and the former second-class ironclad, allow me to proceed to show you the comparison between this second-class ironclad and the French ships. The French, at the time this ship was built, had two classes of ships afloat—the one represented by the "Flandre," of which type there were ten—the "Surveillante," "Valeureuse," and a number whose names I do not recollect at this moment. They were first-class French ships; and bearing in mind what I have told you about the dimensions and thickness of the armour-plating and the armament of the second-class English ship, allow me to read you the dimensions, thickness of armour-plating, &c., of the French first-class armoured ship. The French first-class armoured ship of that day, as represented by the "Flandre," was 262 feet long, 55 ft. 9 in. beam, draught of water 25 ft. 3 in., height of port 7 ft. 8 in., displacement 5,711, carrying 980 tons of armour $4\frac{7}{10}$ inches thick, mounting 8 guns of 9·44 calibre, speed 14 knots. The ships I have described are first-class, and if you compare the power of the first-class French ship with the second-class English ship, I think nobody will say that there was any very great disadvantage in the English second-class ship if it had to encounter a French first-class ship. The second-class French ship was 230 feet long, beam 45 ft. 9 in., mean draught of water 19 ft. 6 in., height of port 6 ft. 6 in., displacement 3,400 tons; she carried 750 tons of

---

[1] The old pattern 27 c/m. gun of the French navy has a muzzle velocity of 1,416 feet a second for its armour-piercing projectile; the new pattern gun has a muzzle velocity of 1,542, and 1,656 has been realised with the heaviest gun of this calibre.

IRON DUKE.

armour-plate varying from 5·8 inches to 4 inches in thickness, and carried four 7-inch guns. The speed was 12 knots. With these figures before us, I am at a loss to find in what respects the " Iron Duke " failed in the object for which she was constructed. What was that object ? It was to fight on the sea any ship she might meet of her own size and construction, and to give the 450 men who embarked in that ship the means of fighting such an enemy as it might be their duty to engage, on fair and equal terms.'

Mr. Barnaby, in the same paper from which we have already quoted, gives a comparative table of the seven most characteristic ironclads which had been built up to that date for the British navy.

Mr. Barnaby's comparative table.

	Tonnage	Complete cost of Ship, and exclusive of Masts, Yards, Rigging, and Stores	Measure of Fighting Efficiency
		£	
Monarch	5,102	345,540	149·8
Hercules	5,234	360,147	113·4
Captain	4,272	330,000	83·3
Vanguard	3,774	255,000	83·0
Minotaur	6,621	430,000	61·1
Warrior	6,109	356,693	44·5
Defence	3,720	223,055	10·9

Commenting on these figures, he says, ' Before passing on to the unmasted ships, it may be as well to compare briefly the " Defence " and " Resistance," of 1861, with the " Vanguard," of 1871. The two classes cost practically the same for hull and engines; but on comparing them it will be seen that whereas, with a weight of hull of 3,730 tons, the " Resistance " class carries 607 tons of 4½-inch armour on 18 inches of wood, and a ⅝-inch iron skin ; the " Vanguard " class, with a weight of hull of 2,854 tons,[1] carries 924 tons of 8-inch and 6-inch armour on 12 inches of wood and on a 1¼-inch iron skin. In other words, with three-fourths of the weight of hull, there is an increase of more than one-half in the armour carried. While the ends of the former class with all the steering gear are unprotected, the latter class are completely protected throughout the hull, and the upper and lower batteries. The weight of the broadside thrown from protected guns is 1,250 lbs. for the former, and 640 lbs. for the latter. The speed of the two classes under steam is 13½ knots for the former, and 11¾ knots for the latter. The area of plain sail is 25,000 square feet in the " Vanguard " class, and 22,400 in the " Resistance " class. To these facts is to be added

[1] This weight includes the cement ballast.

the important consideration, that the former class has a double bottom throughout, and the latter for only a few feet on each side of the keel. It is to be observed further, in regard to handiness under steam, that the " Vanguard " class will turn completely round in $4\frac{1}{2}$ minutes, and that the " Resistance " class require 7 minutes to complete a circle.'

Sir Spencer Robinson and Commander Noel.

Commander Noel having expressed in his essay grave doubts as to the perfect success of the Audacious' type, elicited a warm vindication from Sir Spencer Robinson of the Admiralty designs. He said: 'Now I should like to ask every gentleman in the room what he meant by the word " failure." Is a ship a failure because you having aimed at one object, have realised that object, but have not aimed at another object, and have not realised that other object ? I should say certainly not. What is an ironclad, I may ask, designed for ? An ironclad is designed to fight such battles on the seas as we may be compelled to fight with weapons equal or superior to those that are brought against us. Allow me first of all to take you to the " Defence," which was the first of the second-class ironclads designed in England, and show you the difference between the " Defence " and the " Iron Duke." The length of the " Defence " is 280 feet, breadth 54 feet, mean draught of water 25 ft. 1 in., height of ports out of water 6 ft. 6 in. She was 6,070 tons displacement, carried 607 tons of $4\frac{1}{2}$-inch armour, mounted two 8-inch and eight 7-inch guns. Her speed was 11 6 knots, and her powers of action limited by 460 tons of coal. The " Iron Duke," designed as a second-class ironclad, was 280 feet long, 45 feet wide, her mean draught of water 22 feet, height of ports 8 ft. 1 in., displacement 6,034 ; she carried 924 tons of 8-inch, 6-inch, and $4\frac{1}{2}$-inch armour, ten 9-inch guns ; her speed was $13\frac{1}{2}$, and she carried 540 tons of coal.'

R.-Admira Scott.

Important modifications in the armament of the ' Audacious ' class have been suggested by Admiral Scott. The five ships of the ' Audacious ' class could, he said, ' be improved. They could mount six 18-ton guns, with shortened slides in their main-deck batteries, instead of six 12-ton guns, and be provided with two other 18-ton guns outside their armour, viz., one at the bow and the other at the stern, their upper decks being locally strengthened ; the ships would thus discharge five 18-ton guns on the broadside, and the danger of the bursting of a single shell, or of the vessel's catching fire, in the central battery, and thus stopping the firing of *all* her guns, be prevented. The armoured structure upon the upper deck, weighing about as much as that of the " Sultan," could then be swept away and the ballast replaced by cellular strengthening. This alteration would remove a weak superstructure, would save nearly 300 tons in weight, and would enable a much larger coal-supply to be carried. Both the " Sultan " and the " Audacious " class should be provided with suitable light upper-deck guns, mounted upon slides, 2 feet shorter than those now adopted.'

Admiral Ryder, whose flag has lately been flying in the ' Auda- *Admiral Ryder.* cious ' on the China station, has highly commended his ship for steadiness of platform in a sea-way.

In common with all the other types of ironclads in our navy, *Improvements in ' Triumph.'* alterations and improvements have from time to time been made in the several ships of the ' Audacious ' class. The ' Triumph ' has recently undergone a comprehensive overhaul and refit at Portsmouth. She has been furnished with an entirely new set of boilers from the Keyham yard, and her machinery has been thoroughly repaired and renovated by the contractors, Messrs. Maudslay, Sons, and Field. The old cylinders have been removed, and new cylinders and cylinder-covers have been fitted. The superheater, which is gradually being superseded in our men-of-war, has been removed, and a fresh-water donkey engine has been added to her complement of engines by Messrs. Brotherhood and Hardingham. The hull of the ship has also undergone important changes in order to bring her up to the requirements of modern warfare. She has been for the first time fitted with the Whitehead torpedo, two special ports having been cut in each bow and the usual racers and overhead gear provided for the carriages and the transport of the projectiles from below. The torpedo engine was manufactured at the Portsmouth yard. A Gatling gun has been placed on the foretop in addition to the one which she carried throughout her late commission in the Mediterranean in the main top ; and, as a further protection against the attacks of boats and small craft, she has been armed with four 20-pounder torpedo guns, which are mounted on the spar deck amidships. Shell gratings have been fitted in the wake of the boilers, in order to prevent fragments intruding into the stokeholes and disabling the machinery. The block compressors on the main deck have been removed, and new cable controllers have been fitted on the upper deck, the coal bunkers have received additional ventilation, and the steam steering-gear and the steam capstan have had all their defects made good. As the shell for the 12-ton guns has been lengthened to the extent of 2 inches, this alteration has necessitated important re-adjustments being made in the shellroom for the storing of the new projectiles. The other changes which have been effected mainly consist of the cabin re-arrangements, which were necessary to convert the 'Triumph' into an admiral's ship.

Contemporaneously with the breast-work monitors, 'Abyssinia,' 'Cerberus,' and 'Magdala,' which were mastless vessels, two new ships, the · Swiftsure' and 'Triumph,' of the 'Audacious' type were laid down by the Admiralty. The 'Sultan,' designed as an improvement on the 'Hercules,' was also commenced. The 'Abyssinia' was launched in 1868, the two other turret vessels in the following year. The 'Swiftsure' and 'Triumph' were completed in 1871 and 1873 respectively; the 'Sultan' in 1871.

Mr. Bar-
naby's
description
of 'Sul-
tan's'
plan.

The 'Sultan' is of the same general dimensions as, and much resembles the 'Hercules,' with the addition of an upper-deck battery. Eight 18-ton guns are mounted on the lower gun-deck, two of less weight in the upper-deck battery, and two on the same deck forward,

Figs. 33 and 34.

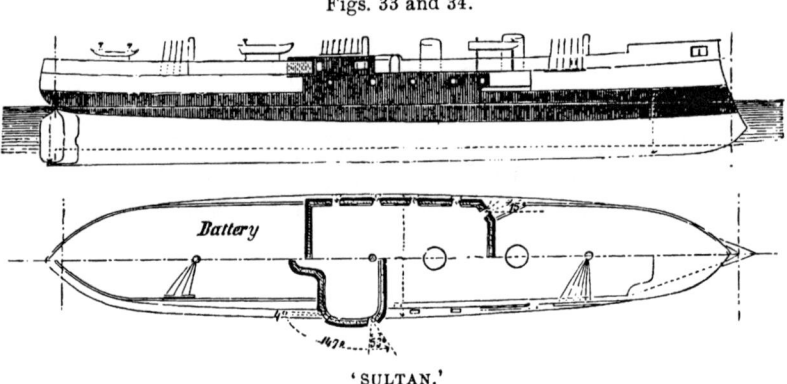

'SULTAN.'

but they do not command an all-round fire. The most important novelties in the plans for the 'Sultan' are thus described by Mr. Barnaby :—

' The " Sultan " has the same bottom and the same thickness of armour (viz., 9 inches) as the " Hercules." But the arrangement of the main-deck is altered. In the " Sultan," the main deck battery is lengthened twelve feet, and the after-embrasures and ports in it are abandoned as compared with the " Hercules." The armoured gun at the after end of the main deck is also given up, and the after-fire is obtained from an armoured battery upon the upper deck, firing in a line with the keel. The armoured bow-fire is also changed, the single 12½-ton gun on the main deck of the "Hercules" being replaced by two 12½-ton guns on the upper deck. While, therefore, the " Hercules " has ten protected guns, eight of 18 tons, and two of 12½ tons, together with four unprotected 6½-ton guns, the "Sultan" has 12 protected guns, viz.: eight of 18 tons, and four of 12½ tons, and no unprotected guns, except of small calibre. The weight of broadside thrown by the "Hercules" from the guns named, is 1,818 lbs., while in the "Sultan" it is 1,965 lbs.'

We find some important suggestions for an improved 'Sultan' in Part II. of Admiral Scott's paper, 'On the Maritime Defence of England,' read at the United Service Institution, June 30, 1876.

' The "Sultan," at the time she was equipped, was considered as one of the finest, and is certainly one of the best-built vessels in the world. Commencing with her bottom, the 600 tons of scrap-iron and cement placed there is now so much dead weight, and therefore a source of weakness, and must tend to strain the structure where it is comparatively light, viz., between the armour and the bottom, on the vessel's receiving any shock from ramming or being rammed. This dead weight, which if the vessel took the ground would risk her destruction, could be advantageously replaced by a cellular arrangement, carried out somewhat as Mr. Boold suggests. The cost of putting in 500 tons of such strengthening, he estimated at 20,000*l.* : but our own highly skilled constructors would, I believe, give equal strength by putting in less material, and at less than half this cost. To balance the removal of the dead weight from the bottom, and the carrying up of the cellular structure above the water-line, the cumbersome top-armoured structure, weighing, if I mistake not, 300 tons, should be removed, so as to leave a clear deck and an open view fore and aft for efficiently handling the ship. With this structure I would sweep away its two 12-ton guns and turntables, which would be in the way of working the sails, and utilise the turntables for the two 12-ton bow guns (which are now arranged to fire ahead only), so that they would each work two ports, and thus command a fire from ahead to abaft the beam. In the stern, abaft the armour, another 18-ton gun, sweeping round the stern and crossing fire with the bow guns, could be easily mounted on the main deck on each side. This, with the necessary strengthening, would weigh upwards of 80 tons. The result of the change would be a saving of nearly 500 tons in weight and a much stronger and better arranged ship, together with a fifth 18-ton gun for broadside fire.'

The ' Sultan ' has recently undergone a thorough overhaul. The additions to her fighting power are described as follows by the *Times* correspondent :—

' In the case of the " Sultan " it has been determined to provide her with a couple of Mr. Wilde's electric lights for the purpose of

Admiral Scott's suggestions.

Recent
additions
to the
' Sultan's '
fighting
power.

detecting night attacks, and to arm her with six Nordenfelt guns on the gunwale, and a brace of Gatlings which will be mounted in the tops. It is also intended to fit nine 20-pounder torpedo guns on the upper deck, and on the deck above the upper battery, for the purpose of repelling torpedo boats; and additional magazines have been erected for the storing of outrigger torpedoes and their gear. Two torpedo boats will also be mounted above the upper deck. The " Sultan " will carry twelve of the improved Whitehead torpedoes, and as this is a novelty so far as she is concerned, the alterations and additions which have had to be made are very great. Five ports have had to be cut through her 9-inch armour on the main deck, and racers, carriages, and transporting trolleys have had to be provided. Then an engine-room, store-room, and magazine have had to be built for the torpedoes, and the space and accommodation which have thus had to be found for additional fittings have rendered necessary further changes to be carried out in other parts of the ship. The ventilation, always defective, has been improved by means of supplementary cowls and fans, and the weight of her projectiles has been increased. The repairs to the machinery are completed, and at the subsequent six hours' continuous steaming the engines developed 7,736·11 horse-power, and a speed of close upon 15 knots was obtained.'

CHAPTER VIII.

IRONCLADS BUILT FOR THE AUSTRIAN, GERMAN, ITALIAN, TURKISH, RUSSIAN, AND SPANISH NAVIES, 1862–73.

No ironclads were launched in 1860, but many were in progress, and Armoured vessels of the new type were now considered necessary even in the ship building for fleets of maritime powers of the second rank. maritime powers of the second rank.

Austria had extended her shipbuilding yards considerably, and five ironclads had been laid down. The union of the various states of their peninsula under a single government had encouraged the aspirations of the Italian people to take a high place among the maritime powers, and the greatest efforts were directed to the formation of a powerful navy. The building resources of the country, when found insufficient for the work of quickly reconstructing the *matériel* of the fleet, were supplemented by assigning a portion of the programme to be executed to contractors in foreign countries. Two ships had been ordered in France in 1860, and others were Number of building in England and America. Holland, Denmark, Sweden and ironclads in different Turkey had also determined to introduce ironclads into their navies. fleets in 1867. At the end of the year the American navy included 52 ironclads built and building. In the same year the Spanish Government ordered five ironclads, and the Russians one ship of the same type. At the end of 1867 the naval powers had already developed the new type of man-of-war to such a point that their fighting fleets were composed exclusively of ironclads. England had 28 ironclads afloat, France 17, Italy 15, Austria seven, Spain six, and the remaining European powers together had eleven ships of the kind.

We shall now proceed to describe the shipbuilding operations of the several states in more minute detail.

We have already stated that the Ottoman Government had Turkish directed its attention to the construction of ironclads. Indeed, ironclads. among naval powers of the second rank, they may be regarded as the

pioneers in the construction of armoured vessels. All the Turkish armour-clads are built of iron. Among the older ironclads of Turkey the
'Osmanieh,' 'Orkanieh,' and 'Mahmoudieh' were the most powerful.

The 'Os-
manieh,'
'Orkanieh,'
and 'Mah-
moudieh.'
There is a considerable discrepancy between the descriptions of
these vessels given by Admiral Paris in his Report on the Exhibition
of 1867, and those more recently published. The Austrian 'Marine
Almanach,' the French 'Carnet de l'Officier de Marine,' Chief
Engineer King's 'War Ships and Navies of the World,' Lieutenant
Very's 'Navies of the World,' and Captain von Kronenfels' 'Das
Schwimmende Flotten Material,' all published in 1880, are in sub-
stantial agreement concerning these armourclads; and the following
details are taken from them. They were built and had their engines
manufactured in Great Britain. Their principal dimensions are:

Length, extreme	. 305 feet
Beam	. 56 feet
Draught of water, forward . .	. 24 ft. 9 in.
„ aft . . .	. 26 ft. 10 in.
Displacement ·	. 6,400 tons
Indicated horse-power . . .	. 4,500
Speed	. 12 to 13·5 knots

Mr. King gives their armament as one 12-ton, and fifteen 6½-ton
muzzle-loading rifled guns of the British pattern. The number of
guns given by Captain von Kronenfels differs from this, as he allows
them ten old pattern smooth-bore 36 pdrs., fourteen 6½-ton, and two
12-ton muzzle-loading rifled guns. The sides are armoured throughout with plating 5½ inches thick on the water-line, and 4¾ inches on
the battery.

The 'Hüfz-
i-rahman'
and 'Luft-
i-dschelil.'
The 'Hüfz-i-rahman' (Divine Protection) and 'Luft-i-dschelil'
(Sublime Grace) were built at Bordeaux and launched in 1868. The
'Luft-i-dschelil' was destroyed by the enemy during the late war.
The dimensions are:

Length	. 211 ft. 6 in.
Beam	. 41 ft. 6 in.
Draught of water . . .	. 19 ft. 6 in.
Displacement	. 2,500 tons

The water-line, two turrets, and forecastle are armoured. The
thickest armour on the belt is 5½ inches, on the turrets five inches.
The fore turret carries two 9-inch Armstrongs, and the after and
smaller turret two 7-inch guns. There is one lighter gun mounted
behind the armour of the forecastle. The turrets are worked by
hand power, and require 24 men to turn them. The nominal horse-
power is 200; there is one screw, and the speed at the trial was
twelve knots. The rig is that of a barque with tripod masts.

The 'Avni-illah' (God's Help) and ' Imim-i-zafer ' (Aid to Victory)
were built in England and launched in 1868.
Their dimensions are the following :—

Length	238 ft. 6 in.
Beam	35 ft. 4 in.
Draught of water . . .	16 ft. 6 in.
Displacement	2,380 tons
Horse-power (nominal) . ,	400
Speed	12·5 knots

Figs. 35 and 36.

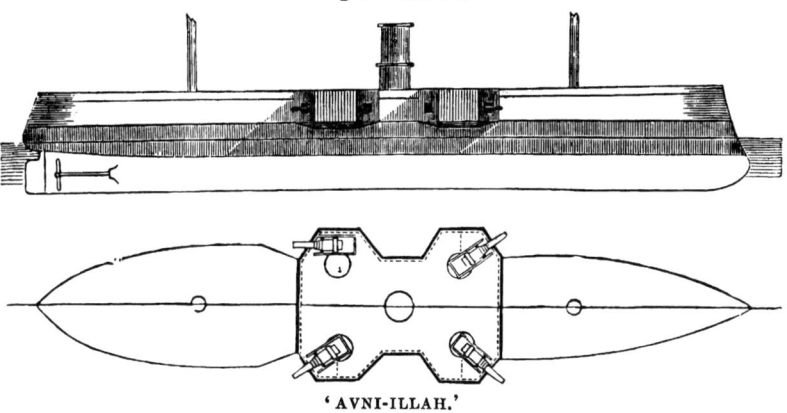

' AVNI-ILLAH.'

They have two overhanging octagonal batteries on the same deck.
Four of the eight ports allow of an angle of training of 100°, two
others of an angle of 95°, and two of an angle of 89°. Ahead the
line of fire can be brought parallel to the keel, and astern within 10° of
it. Each of the ports admits of fire right abeam. The armament is
composed of four 8-inch Armstrong guns. The ports are 6½ feet
above the water. The armour on the battery is five inches thick, on
the water-line amidships it is six inches, and elsewhere five inches.
The engines drive two screws, are of 400 nominal horse-power, and
give a speed of 12·5 knots.

The 'Assar-i-schefket' (Sign of Might), and 'Nedschm i-schefket'
(Star of Might) are sister ships, and are very like the 'Idschlalijé'
(Majestic). The two former were built at La Seyne, and launched
in 1869; the last-named was launched at San Rocco, near Trieste, in
1870. The dimensions are given below.

	' Assar-i-schefket '	'Idschlalijé'	
Length between perpendiculars .	203 feet	208 ft. 6 in.	The 'Idschlalijé.'
Greatest beam to outside armour	40 ft. 9 in.	41 ft. 9 in	
Draught of water, forward .	12 ft. 6 in.	14 ft. 9 in.	
,, aft . .	16 ft. 5 in.	17 ft. 6 in.	
Displacement . . .	2,046 tons	2,228 tons	
Coal supply . . .	250 tons	180 tons	

The battery in all three ships is armed with four 9-inch Armstrong guns. In the after end of the battery the 'Idschlalijé' carries a 7-inch, the other ships a 9-inch gun each. The battery armour in

Figs. 37 and 38.

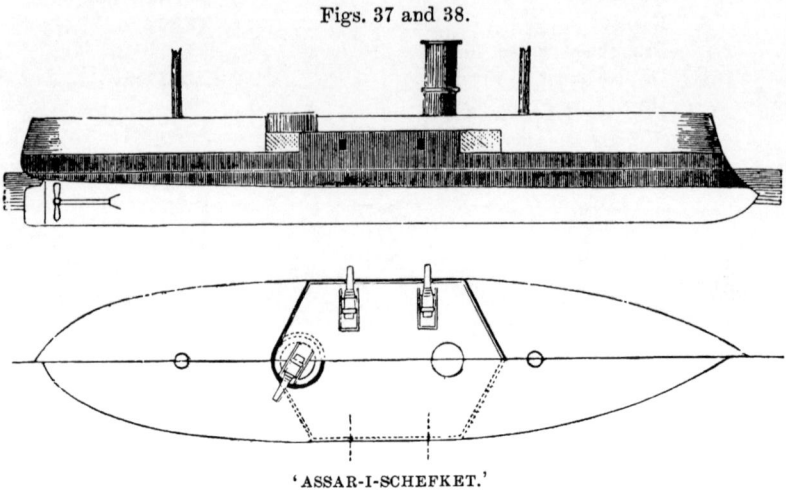

'ASSAR-I-SCHEFKET.'

all is $5\frac{1}{2}$ inches thick; the thickest belt armour on the 'Idschlalijé' is $5\frac{3}{4}$ inches, in the other ships $4\frac{1}{2}$ inches. The vessels are brig-rigged, and have a speed under steam of 11·3 knots.

The 'Feth-i-bulend' (Great Causer of Conquest) and 'Muka-

The 'Feth-i-bulend' and 'Muka-demme-i-hair.'

Figs. 39 and 40.

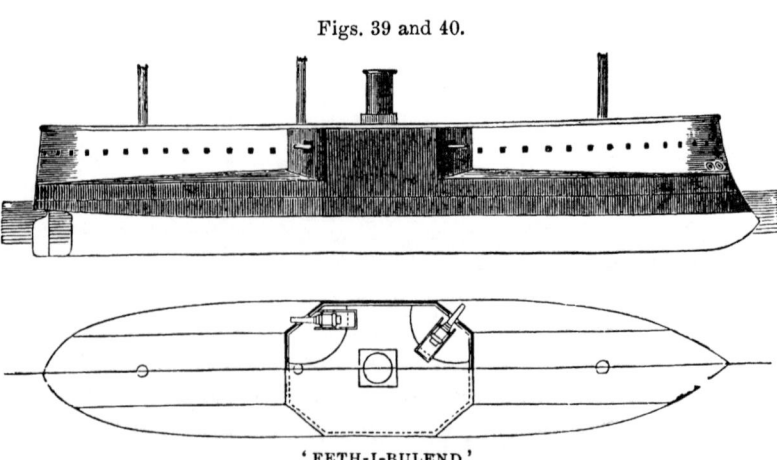

'FETH-I-BULEND.'

demme-i-hair' (Vanguard of Luck) are sister ships. The first was built at Blackwall in 1869; the second at the dockyard at Constantinople in 1872. Their principal dimensions are :—

Length between the perpendiculars	.	.	235 feet
Extreme beam .	.	.	42 feet
Draught of water, forward	.	.	17 ft. 6 in.
„ aft .	.	.	18 feet
Displacement .	.	.	2,760 tons

These ships are built on the cellular system. The armour amid-ships on the water-line is nine inches thick on a teak backing of ten inches, and diminishes towards the extremities. The battery armour is six inches in thickness. At the corners, where they are cut off, are four ports, in each of which is a 9-inch Armstrong gun, which can be fired from right abeam to within 5° of the keel line. The 'Feth-i-bulend's' engines, by Humphreys and Tennant, drive a single screw, and work up to 3,250 horse-power. The speed is 13·5 knots. The 'Mukademme-i-hair's' engines were made in the dockyard at Constantinople, and work up to 3,200 indicated horse-power, giving a speed of 12·5 knots.

Figs. 41 and 42.

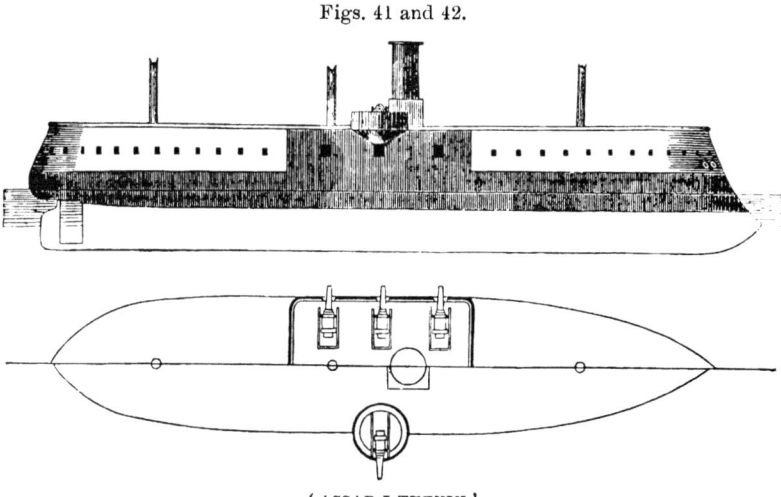

'ASSAR-I-TEFVIK.'

The 'Assar-i-tefvik' (Sign of Divine Assistance) was built at La Seyne, and launched in 1868. The principal dimensions are :— The 'Assar-i-tefvik.

Length between the perpendiculars	.	.	275 feet
Beam, extreme .	.	.	50 feet
Draught of water, forward .	.	.	20 ft. 4 in.
„ aft	.	.	22 ft. 6 in.
Displacement .	.	.	5,687 tons

The water-line is protected with 8-inch armour with a 9-inch backing. The central battery is armoured with 6-inch plates, and in it six 9-inch 12-ton Armstrong guns are mounted on the broadside.

I 2

Above the battery are two circular fixed turrets overhanging the ship's side, each being armed with an ' over-bank ' 9-inch Armstrong gun on a revolving carriage with a central pivot. The turrets are protected with 5-inch armour, and the conning-bridge forms an iron roof which will be a valuable defence against the deadly fire of machine-guns. The engines have three cylinders, high and low pressure, and work up to 3,560 horse-power. There is one screw, and the speed is 13·3 knots.

Figs. 43 and 44.

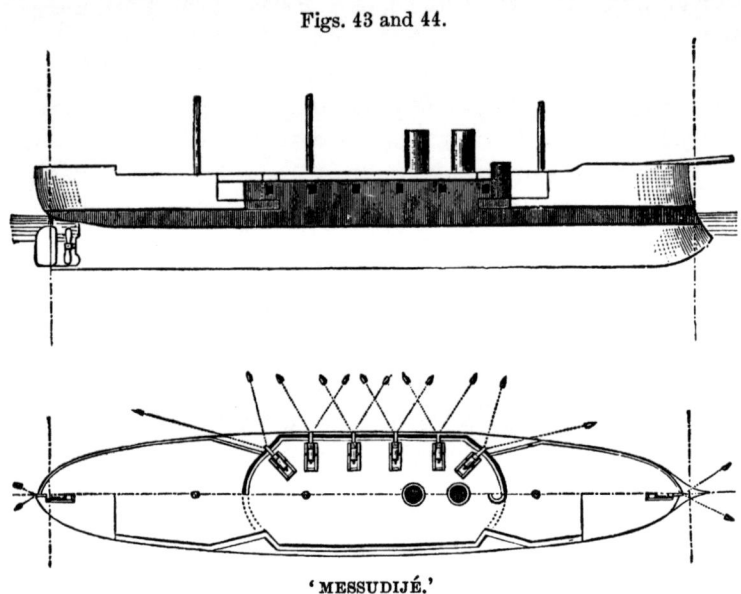

' MESSUDIJÉ.'

The 'Messudije.'

The 'Messudijé' (Fortunate), built at the Thames Iron Works, and launched in 1875, is a sister ship of the English 'Superb.' She carries twelve 10-inch, and three 7-inch Armstrong guns. The indicated horse-power is 7,910, and the speed 13·1 knots.

Austrian ironclads.

It was not until 1872 that any sea-going iron-built armourclads were actually afloat under the Austrian flag. The wooden frigates 'Ferdinand Max' and 'Habsburg' were launched in 1865.

The 'Ferdinand Max' and 'Habsburg.'

These vessels are alike, and were built from the designs of Herr Romako, the Chief Constructor of the Austrian navy, under the superintendence of Constructors Soyka and Pegan. The 'Ferdinand Max' was launched at the yard of the San Marco Company, near Trieste, on May 24, and the 'Habsburg' from the San Rocco Company's works, near Muggia, on June 25, 1865. In design, they somewhat resemble the 'Gloire. The following figures are taken from Captain von Kronenfels :—

Length between the perpendiculars .	262 feet
Beam, extreme	52 feet
Proportion of length to beam . .	5·11 to 1
Depth in hold	23 ft. 6 in.
Draught of water, forward . .	20 ft. 9 in.
„ aft . . .	25 ft. 6 in.
Displacement	5,140 tons
Immersed surface of midship section .	944·19 square feet

Fig. 45.

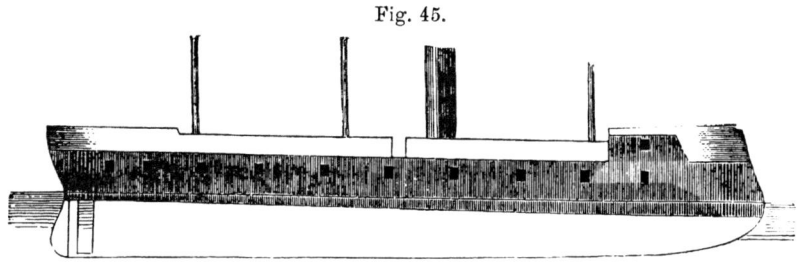

'FERDINAND MAX.'

The armament was originally intended to consist of thirty-two 48-pounder smooth-bores. At Lissa, in 1866, the 'Ferdinand Max' was armed with sixteen 48-pounder smooth-bores, and the 'Habsburg' with fifteen 48-pounders and one rifled 24-pounder. The armament was afterwards changed to fourteen 21 c/m. or 8¼-inch Krupp steel breech-loaders, and fourteen 7-inch Armstrong muzzle-loaders have now been substituted. The ships are completely protected on the broadside, the armour gradually tapering from a maximum thickness on the water-line of 5 inches on a 26-inch backing. The engines indicate 3,000 horse-power, and work a single Griffiths' screw, giving a speed of 10·3 knots. With full power the 'coal endurance' is 770 miles. Originally both ships were barque-rigged; they are now three-masted schooners, square-rigged forward.

Fig. 46.

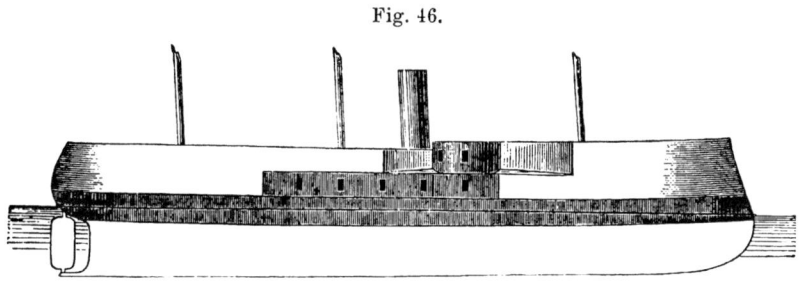

'LISSA.'

In 1869, the central battery wooden ship 'Lissa' was launched.

The unarmoured ends of these ships are of iron.   The draught of
water is 26 feet, and the displacement 6,000 tons.   The thickness of

Fig. 47.

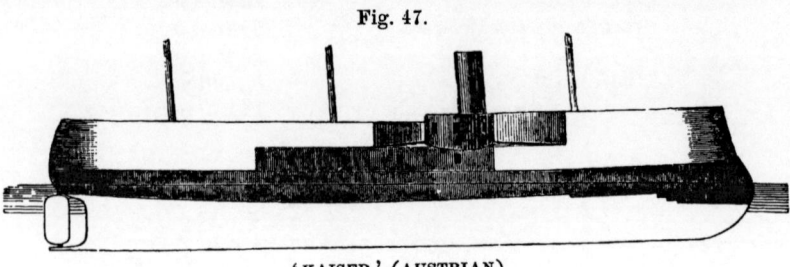

'KAISER' (AUSTRIAN).

the armour is $6\frac{1}{4}$ inches, the indicated power is 3,600 horses, and the
speed 13 knots.

Fig. 48.

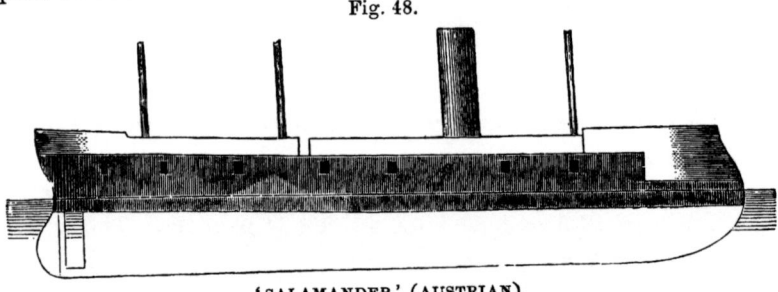

'SALAMANDER' (AUSTRIAN).

In 1872 the wooden line-of-battle ship 'Kaiser' was converted
into an ironclad of the 'Lissa' type.   The smaller class of armoured
corvettes is represented by a solitary example, the 'Salamander,'
built of wood.

In 1867, the iron armoured ship 'Friedrich Karl' was launched in

Figs. 49 and 49A.

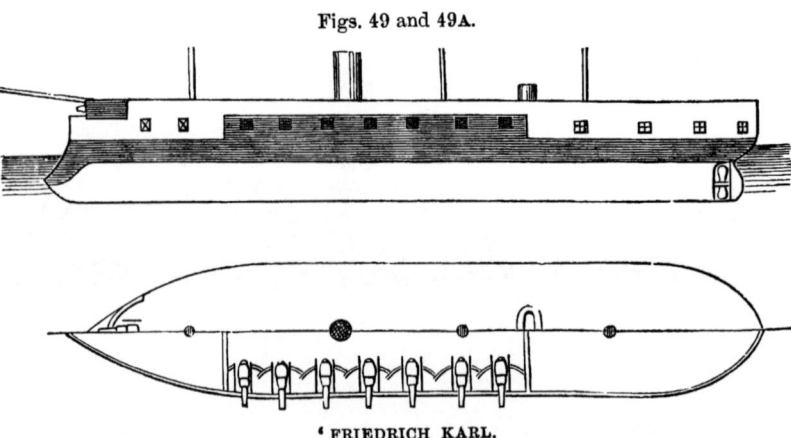

'FRIEDRICH KARL.'

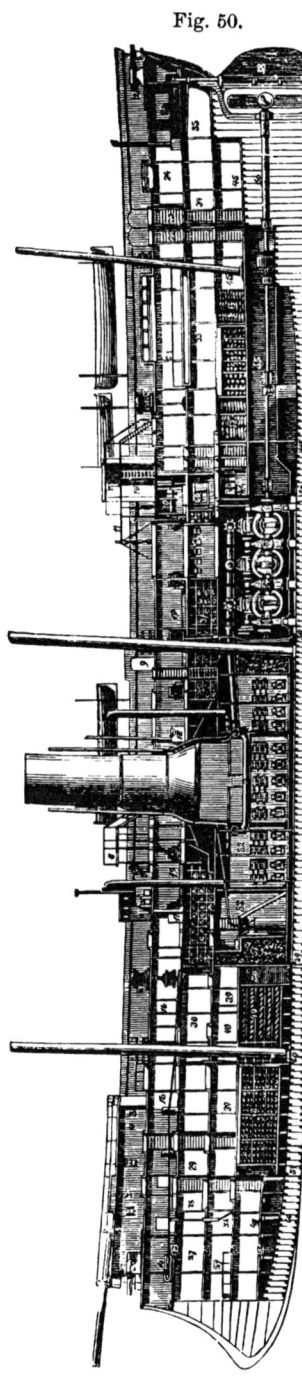

Fig. 50.

'FRIEDRICH KARL.'

France, and the 'Kron Prinz' in England. Both these ships had been ordered for the North German navy. North German ironclads 'Friedrich Karl' and 'Kron Prinz.'

They carried 16 guns, and were protected with 5-inch armour. The displacement of the former ship was 5,912 tons,[1] the indicated horse-power 3,500, and the speed 13·5 knots. The displacement of the 'Kron Prinz' was 5,480 tons, the indicated horse-power 4,800, and the speed 14·25 knots.

The great development of power in a ship of the central battery type which had been exhibited in the design of the 'Hercules,' naturally led to the construction of similar vessels for other navies. For Turkey a new ship was ordered in England, in which an effort was made to combine all the improvements that had thus far been realised. This vessel was purchased for the German navy, and received the name of the 'König Wilhelm.' The 'König Wilhelm

The 'König Wilhelm,' which was launched in 1868, is an iron ship. The armament consists of 23 guns, viz. eighteen 24 c/m., or 9·4-in., guns of 15·5 tons, and five 21 c/m., or 8·33-in., guns of 9·79 tons. An athwartship armoured bulkhead forward protects two guns under cover. Both these guns can be fired in a direct line with the keel, or from a port pierced in the bows, which admits of the gun being trained so as to fire on the broadside. The after-transverse armoured bulkhead affords a similar protection to two guns, which can be fired at an angle of 15° with the keel.

[1] These figures are from the official German Navy List; they differ, to some extent, from those given in the best unofficial books.

Figs. 51, 52, and 53.

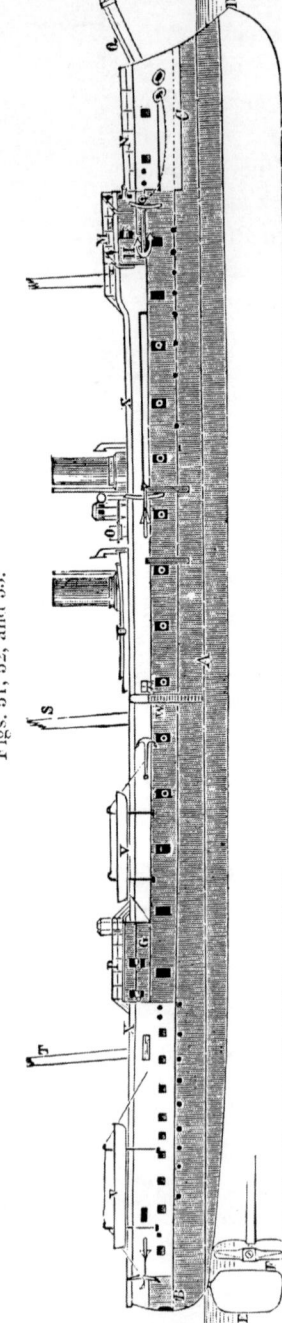

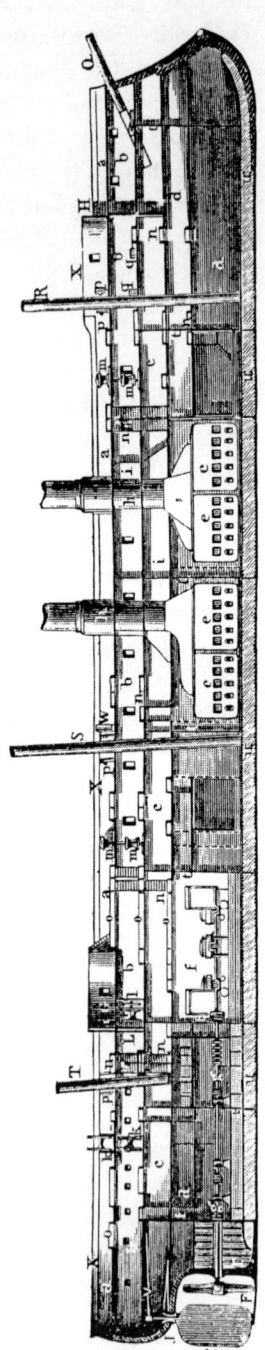

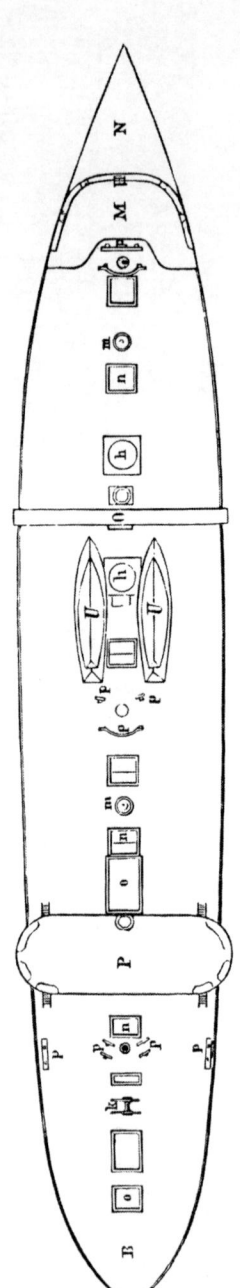

'KÖNIG WILHELM.'

A, Hull; B, C, Armour at extremities; D, Ram; E, Balanced rudder; F, Screw; G, Quarter-deck battery; H, Thwart-ship armoured bulkhead; O, P, Bridges; R, S, T, Masts. a, Upper deck; b, Main deck; c, Lower deck; d, Hold; e, e, Boilers; f, Engines; h, Funnels; t, Watertight bulkheads; n, Double bottom; r, Tiller.

The displacement of the ' König Wilhelm ' is 9,603 tons ; the thickness of the armour eight inches, the machinery is of 8,000 indicated horse-power, and the speed at the measured mile 14·7 knots. Though presenting no original features, this vessel combined all the most recent improvements, and was one of the most powerful afloat at the date when she was launched.

It has been stated that the construction of iron armoured ships, when the vessels of this type were first introduced, was prosecuted with considerable vigour by the Spanish Government. The ' Numancia ' was one of their finest armoured frigates. This ship was launched by the Forges et Chantiers Company at La Seyne in 1864. The principal dimensions [1] are : Length, 315 feet ; beam, 56 ft. 10 in. ; draught of water, 27 ft. 4 in. ; displacement, 7,420 tons. The bunkers are capable of containing 1,000 tons of coal, sufficient for nine days' steaming at full speed. The entire armament, consisting of 40 guns, is mounted

Spanish
ironclads :
The 'Nu-
mancia.'

Fig. 54.

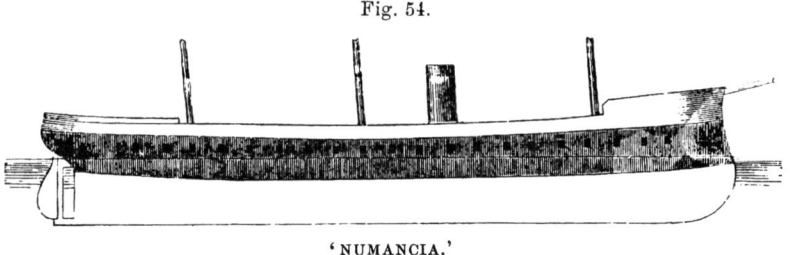

' NUMANCIA.'

on the main deck. The price of the ship was 315,800*l.* The thickness of armour on the water-line is 5¼ inches, tapering to 4 inches near the ends of the ship. On the sides, in the wake of the main deck, the armour is 4¾ inches thick. The backing varies from 14 to 17½ inches. The nominal horse-power of the ' Numancia ' is 1,000 ; 3,708 has been indicated, and a speed of 12·94 knots realised.

The ' Vitoria ' in some respects resembles the ' Numancia '; she The
' Vitoria.'

---

[1] Von Kronenfels' dimensions differ from these. He gives—

Length between perpendiculars	313 feet
Breadth at the water-line	52 feet
Draught of water, aft	26 feet 7 inches
Displacement	7,165 tons
Indicated horse-power	3,708
Speed	12·94 knots
Armour on water-line	5 inches
„ on battery	4¾ inches
„ at extremities	4 inches

was built by the Thames Iron Shipbuilding Works Company, and was launched in November, 1865.   Her principal dimensions are :—

Length	316 ft. 4 in.
Beam	57 feet
Draught of water, aft	27 ft. 8 in.
Displacement	7,100 tons

The thickest armour on the water-line is 5½ inches.   The armament originally consisted of four 9-inch and three 8-inch Armstrong guns,

Fig. 55.

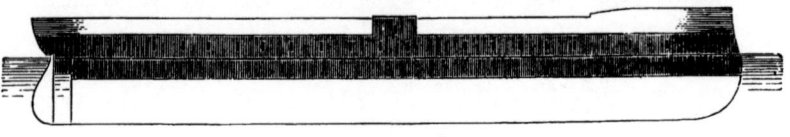

' VITORIA. '

besides fourteen 16 c/m. Spanish rifled muzzle-loaders.   The engines are by Penn and Sons ; the indicated horse-power was 4,500, and the speed 12·5 knots.

The 'Zaragoza' and 'Sagunto' are wooden ironclads, the former launched in 1867 and the latter in 1869.   Their principal dimen-sions are :—

The 'Zaragoza,' 'Sagunto,' and 'Mendez Nunez.'

	'Zaragoza'	'Sagunto'
Length . . .	270 feet	279 ft. 6 in.
Beam	54 ft. 6 in.	54 feet
Draught of water, aft .	25 ft. 3 in.	26 feet
Displacement, tons .	5,400	6,300
Speed, knots . . .	10·9	12·5

Fig. 56.

' SAGUNTO.'

The thickest water-line armour of the 'Zaragoza' is 4¾, of the 'Sagunto' 6 inches.   The 'Mendez Nunez' was a wooden frigate which was converted into an ironclad in 1869.   Her displacement is 3,250 tons.

Russian ironclads: 'Sevasto-pol' and 'Petro-paulski.'

We now turn to the shipbuilding operations of the Russian navy. In 1861 the wooden ships 'Sevastopol' and 'Petropaulski,' which were at that date in progress, were ordered to be armoured with 4½-inch plates.   The first of these, the oldest ironclad in the Russian navy, was launched at Cronstadt on August 24, 1864. The displacement of the first-named vessel is 6,275 tons, and the armament consists of eighteen 8-inch guns. The displacement of the latter

Figs. 57 and 58.

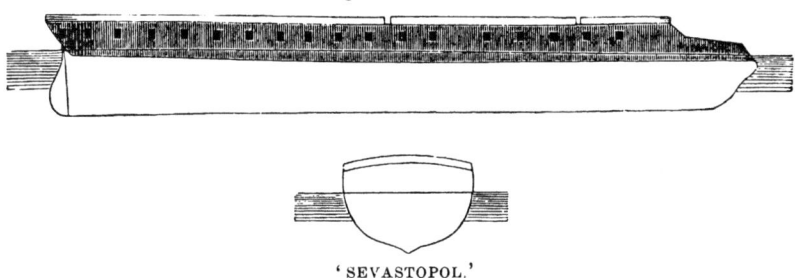

' SEVASTOPOL.'

ship is 6,175 tons, the armament consisting of twenty 8-inch guns. The ' Sevastopol ' nearly equals the British ironclads ' Black Prince ' and ' Warrior ' in her dimensions, and exceeds those of the French

Figs. 59 and 60.

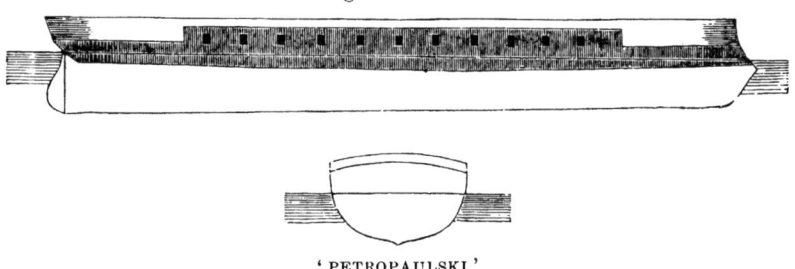

' PETROPAULSKI.'

' Gloire ' and ' Normandie.' Her plates are $4\frac{1}{2}$ inches thick, fastened to a double coating of teak, from six to nine inches thick. Her engines have a nominal force of 800 horse-power, and she has latterly been armed with steel guns of the greatest calibre.

Fig. 61.

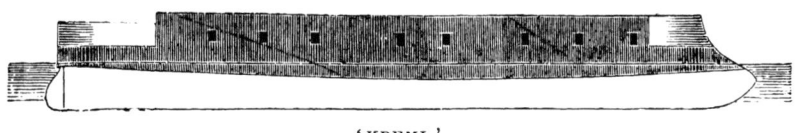

' KREML.'

In these ships the battery extends nearly fore and aft. An athwartship bulkhead is constructed at the fore end, which is pierced for two guns. The draught of water is, forward 23 ft. 11 in.; aft,

25 ft. 11 in.   They are propelled by engines of 800 nominal horse-power.[1]

 The 'Pervenec,' 'Netronmenja,' and 'Kreml' were launched in 1864–5.   The 'Pervenec' is an iron vessel of 3,277 tons, carrying fourteen 8-inch guns.   The 'Netronmenja' is of 3,870 tons, with sixteen 8-inch guns; and the 'Kreml' is of 3,412 tons, with twelve

Figs. 62 and 63.

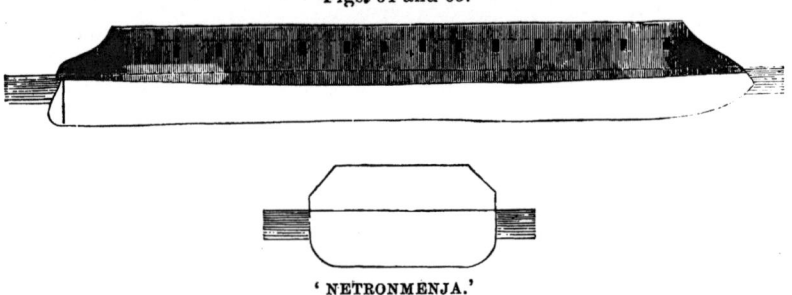

'PERVENEC.'

8-inch guns.   The armour of these vessels consists of plates varying in thickness from 4½ inches to 6 inches.

Figs. 64 and 65.

'NETRONMENJA.'

The central battery ship 'Knjaz-Pojarski' was launched in the autumn of 1867.   This ship was built of iron, the principal dimensions being—length, 280 feet; beam, 49 feet; draught of water, 21 ft. 6 in.; displacement, 4,566 tons.   The armour is 4½ inches in thickness, and extends the entire length of the vessel, from a depth of five feet below to six feet above the water-line, on a backing of 18 inches of teak.   Her armament is placed in a central battery, occupying about 80 feet of her length, of the 'box' character.   She carries eight 300-pounder steel B.L. guns. The engines are of 2,835 indicated horse-power; the speed of the ship is 10·21 knots.

We pass on to some of the earlier ships which are still included in the Italian Navy List.

Figs. 66 and 67.

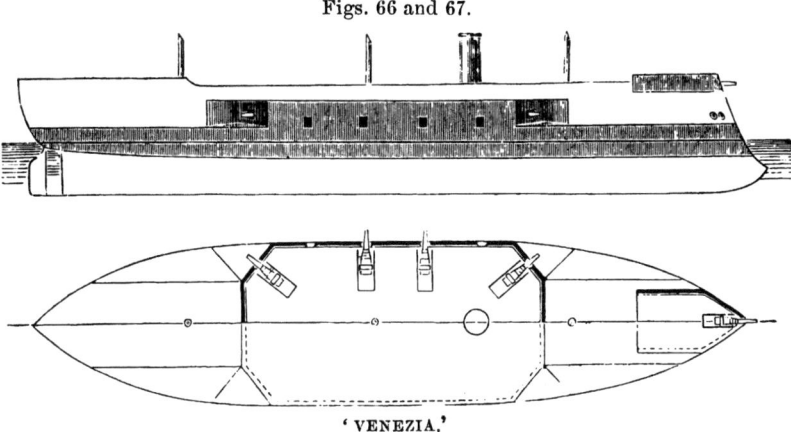

' VENEZIA.'

The 'Roma' and 'Venezia' are wooden ships with central batteries. Their draught is 24 ft. 7 in., and displacement 5,800 tons. They are protected with 4¾-inch armour. They have 900 nominal and 3,670 indicated horse-power, and a speed of

Figs. 68 and 69.

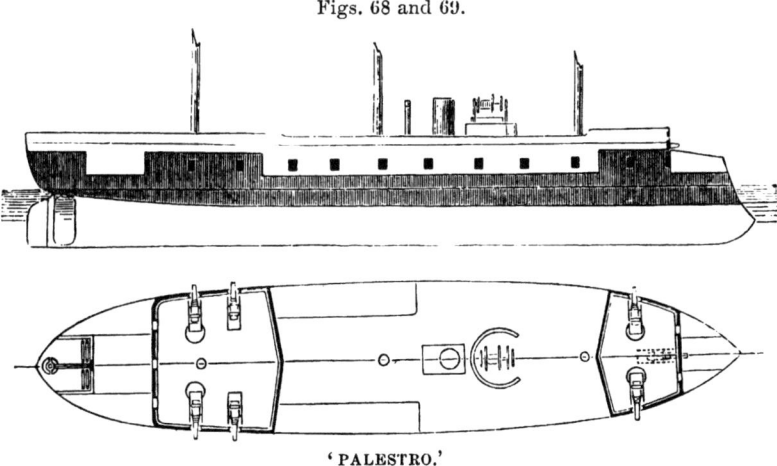

' PALESTRO.'

13 knots an hour. The 'Palestro,' launched in 1871, and 'Principe-Amadeo,' launched in 1872, are of iron, with central batteries. Their draught of water is 26 ft. 6 in. They have a displacement of 6,160 tons, and are protected by armour 8½ inches thick on the

The 'For-
midabile,'
'Terribile,'
and 'Conte
Verde.'

water-line, six inches on the batteries, and four inches on the athwartship bulkheads. They have a nominal power of 900 horses, and
their speed was ten knots an hour.[1] In 1861 two iron corvettes,
the ' Formidabile ' and 'Terribile,' were begun. Their principal dimensions are—draught of water, 18 feet; displacement, 2,700 tons;
nominal horse-power, 400 (indicated 1,200). The corvette 'Conte
Verde' is of 600 nominal horse-power, and displaces 4,100 tons.

The 'An-
cona,'
'Castelfi-
dardo,'
'Maria
Pia,' and
'San Mar-
tino.'

In 1863 and 1864 were launched the four iron corvettes, 'Ancona,'
'Castelfidardo,' 'Regina Maria Pia,' and 'San Martino.' Their
draught of water is 21½ feet; their displacement, 4,300 tons. They
are armoured with 4¾-inch plates, and are propelled by machinery of

Figs. 70 and 71.

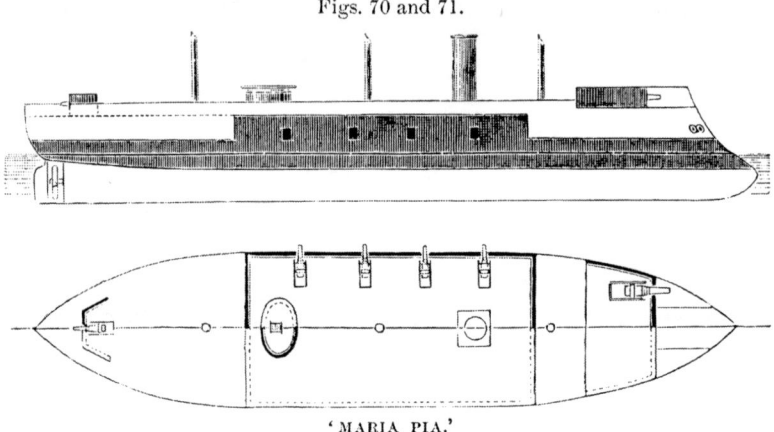

'MARIA PIA.'

700 nominal horse-power. The indicated horse-power and speed
of these ships are :—

	I. H. P.	Speed
Maria Pia	2,924	12·96
San Martino	2,924	12·00
Ancona	2,548	13·74
Castelfidardo	2,125	12·00

The
'Varese.'

The twin-screw central battery corvette, or gun-boat, ' Varese,'
built in 1865, carries four guns mounted at indented ports. Two
guns may be fired ahead and two astern. The draught of water is
4 mètres (13 ft. 1 in.), and the displacement 2,000 tons. The
nominal power is 300 horses.

Resuming the general narrative of the progress of armoured ship-

[1] Improvements having been introduced; the 'Palestro' is reported to have
had, on her trial trip on March 30, 1875,
3,496 indicated horse-power, and a speed
of 12·9 knots.

building, we find that in England the 'Hercules' and 'Monarch,' the ships of the 'Audacious' type, the 'Captain,' and the first breastwork monitors were launched in 1868–69. The 'Océan,' the 'Marengo,' and the rams of the 'Cérbère' type were completed in France about the same date. In the English dockyards the large turret-ships of the 'Devastation' type, and in the French yards the ironclads of the 'Richelieu' type, were commenced. Several other foreign navies were being increased by armoured vessels of different classes.

Summary of progress of armoured construction.

CHAPTER IX.

MONITORS AND EARLIER ARMOURED VESSELS FOR COAST SERVICE.

The ' Merrimac.'

THE outbreak of the civil war in America led to the construction of armoured ships with feverish energy. The Confederate vessel ' Merrimac ' was the first ironclad which took part in a naval engagement. The incidents of the duel between this vessel and the ' Monitor,' the first Federal ironclad, are well known, and need not be narrated

Monitors.

here. The vessels of the ' Monitor ' type were far more formidable for coast service than any armoured vessels which could be found at that date in European waters. Baron Grivel, in his volume entitled ' La Guerre Maritime,' remarks that it was reserved for the American people, under the impulse of the war with the States which had seceded from the Union, to take the initiative in creating, under the

Fig. 72.

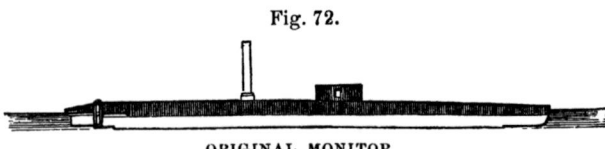

ORIGINAL MONITOR.

designation of ' Monitor,' the true type of harbour defence ship. With that rapidity of decision which has ever been a characteristic trait of the American genius, Congress, on August 3, 1861, voted supplies for the construction of armoured harbour defence vessels. On August 7 competitive designs were asked for, and on September 16, the proposals of Mr. Ericsson were accepted.

Mr. Ericsson's plans adopted.

It would appear that Mr. Ericsson had submitted a similar design to the Emperor Napoleon in September 1854, and Admiral Hamilton remarks that it is fortunate for us that the design was not offered to and accepted by the Russians, or our fleets in the Baltic and the Black Sea might have come to the same untimely end as the ' Congress ' and ' Cumberland ' frigates, when assailed by the guns and ram of the ' Merrimac.'

For a sum of 52,000*l*. Mr. Ericsson undertook to construct in the space of a hundred days an armoured shot-proof harbour defence vessel, having a displacement of 1,200 tons, drawing ten feet of water, and capable of steaming nine knots an hour. He kept his word. The original 'Monitor' was completed in four months, and arrived in Hampton Roads on March 8, 1862, just in time to prevent the 'Merrimac' from completing her work of destruction on the wooden fleet lying off Hampton Roads. These details are taken from a paper

Fig. 73.

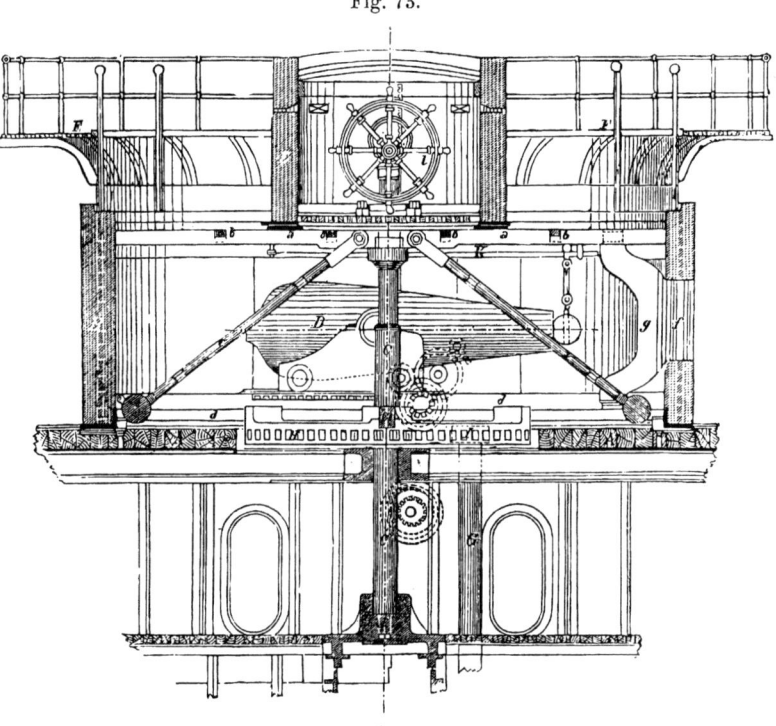

ERICSSON'S TURRET.

A, Deck; B, Turret; *a*, Upper beams; *c*, Lower beams; C, Turret spindle; D, Gun; E, Pilot-house; F, Bridge; G, Turret-turning shaft.

by Admiral Hamilton, on the naval operations of the civil war in the United States, read at the United Service Institution on May 24, 1878. *Admiral Hamilton.*

The main features of the 'Monitor' are thus described by Baron Grivel. The 'Monitor' is a flat-bottomed vessel, armoured on the sides and on the deck, which is almost on a level with the water. One or two revolving iron turrets rise above the armoured deck. The revolving arrangements of the turrets are very similar to the turn- *Baron Grivel.*

tables on which heavy locomotives, weighing sixty tons, are pivoted
upon the railways. The armour of the turrets is $10\frac{1}{2}$ inches, the armour
of the deck and the combings from 2 to $2\frac{3}{4}$ inches in thickness. Two
15-in. or 22-ton smooth-bore guns, firing heavy projectiles of 440 lbs.
with charges of from 35 lbs. to 60 lbs. of powder, are mounted in each

Fig. 74.

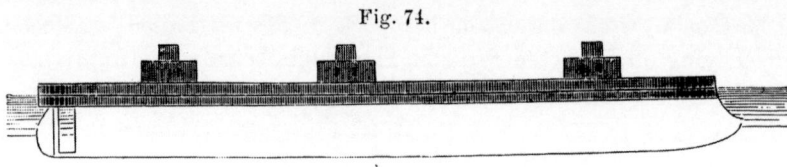

AMERICAN MONITOR 'ROANOKE.'

turret of the 'Monitor.' The type devised by Mr. Ericsson possesses
the two essential qualities which Vice-Admiral Touchard demands in
armoured coast defence vessels, that is to say, the maximum of in-
vulnerability and the maximum power of armament.

Figs. 75 and 76.

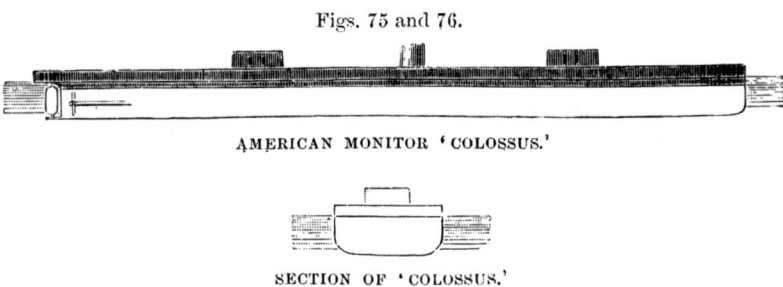

AMERICAN MONITOR 'COLOSSUS.'

SECTION OF 'COLOSSUS.'

Having adopted the 'Monitor' as the best type of fighting vessel,
the work of construction was prosecuted with the characteristic
vigour of the American people. A concise narrative of their shipbuilding operations has been brought together in the work of Señor
Heriz.

Fig. 77.

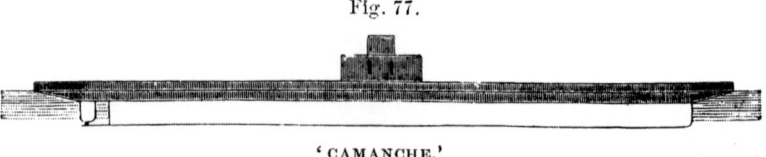

'CAMANCHE.'

Señor
Heriz.
Narrative
of ship-
building
operations
of United
States.
From 1862 until the end of the War of Secession, a multitude of
armoured vessels were built. The wooden frigate 'Roanoke' was converted into an ironclad, with three turrets and two guns in each.
The displacement is 6,300 tons, the thickness of armour at the water-
line is $5\frac{1}{2}$ inches, and on the turrets 11 inches, in an equal number

of 1-in. plates. The speed was only five knots. The 'Camanche, 'Catskill,' 'Jason,' 'Lehigh,' 'Montauk,' 'Nahant,' 'Nantucket,' and 'Passaic' were all similar to the original 'Monitor,' but somewhat larger.

The principal dimensions of these vessels were:—Draught of water, ten feet; freeboard, one foot; displacement, 1,650 tons; thickness of armour at the water-line, five inches in five layers; thickness of armour on the turrets, eleven inches in eleven layers; and one inch armour in two layers on the deck. They had an indicated power of 400 horses; their speed was seven knots; and they were built of iron.

Next came the following vessels of iron with a revolving turret containing two guns: the 'Ajax,' 'Canonicus,' 'Mahopac,' 'Manhattan,' 'Saugus,' and 'Wyandotte.' Their draught of water was 11 ft. 6 in.; height of freeboard, 1 ft. 3 in.; displacement, 1,800 tons; armour at the water-line, five inches in five layers, and two armour stringers of $6\frac{1}{2}$ inches × 4 inches; armour on the turret, eleven inches in eleven layers; indicated horse-power, 1,000; speed seven knots. *Two-gun single-turreted American Monitors.*

The success attained in the earlier vessels of the type led to the rapid multiplication of monitors for naval operations on the coasts of the United States. Screw vessels were found ill-adapted for the tortuous and narrow channels of the rivers which intersected the Southern Confederacy. Being unable to go straight astern, they exposed their whole broadsides in the act of turning or, if necessary, retreating. Accordingly for this special service side-wheel steamers were introduced, and thirty-four were built, having both ends alike, and adapted, like the steamers on the Upper Thames, for going either way. These vessels drew only eight feet of water, and were heavily armed. The accompanying plans of the armoured river paddle steamer 'Benton' are taken from Mr. Holley's work entitled *Ordnance and Armour*. They will furnish some idea of the ingenuity displayed by both sides in the War of Secession in improving the *matériel* of war both for sea and for river service. *Vessels for river service.*

Mr. Eads, of St. Louis, undertook to build seven ships supplied with engines and boilers, and ready to receive their crews and armaments within sixty-five days from signing the contract. The first vessel of the series was completed on October 12, 1861, forty-five days after the keel was laid; the next ten days later, and the remainder within the assigned time. These vessels, though only drawing six feet of water, carried thirteen heavy smooth-bore guns of 11-in. or 9-in. calibre, three being mounted to fire right ahead, and two astern. Admiral Hamilton justly remarks that, when we consider that this was *Mr. Eads.*

done on the Upper Mississippi, where an armed vessel had never been seen prior to the war, and that, when the contract was signed, the

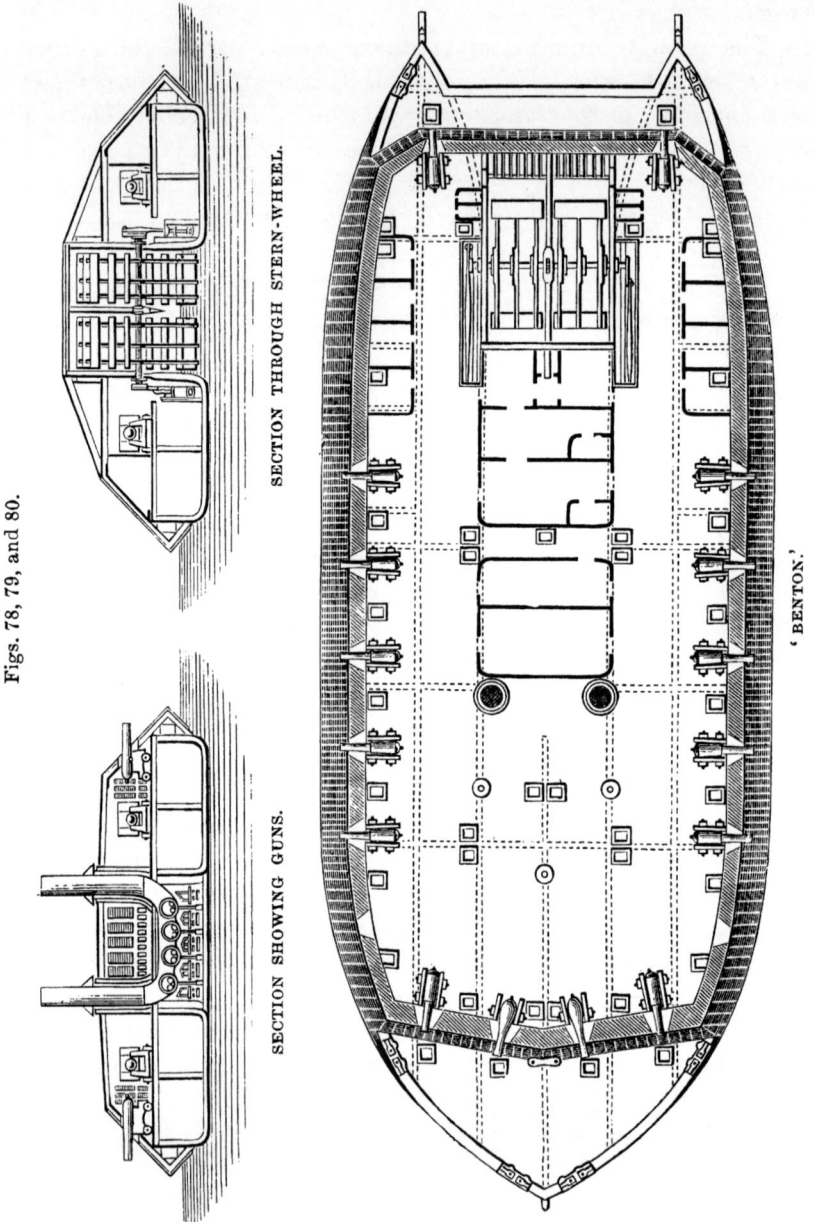

Figs. 78, 79, and 80.

SECTION THROUGH STERN-WHEEL.

SECTION SHOWING GUNS.

'BENTON.'

timber to construct them had to be cut, the engines to be built, and the rollers and machinery to roll the iron plates to be constructed, we may marvel at the boldness with which a private individual undertook the responsibility of such a task. His success shows what can be effected by a free people fighting for what they consider a just cause.

Figs. 81 and 82.

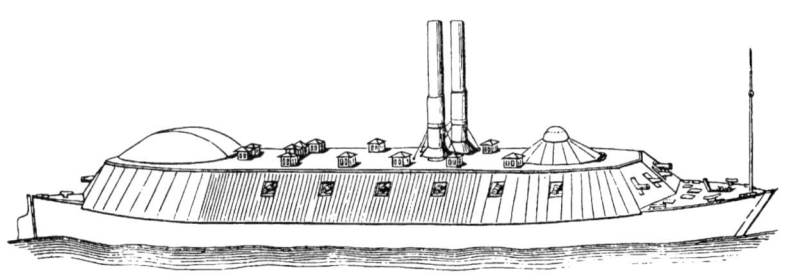

'BENTON' (FORE AND AFT SECTION).

'BENTON' (BROADSIDE).

Mr. Eads continued his remarkable efforts until the termination of the war. In April, 1862, he prepared plans for eight light draught ironclads, some drawing $5\frac{1}{2}$ feet, others $4\frac{1}{2}$ feet, with a turret armoured with 8-in. plates. He even contrived to build a vessel of the light draught of $3\frac{1}{2}$ feet, with a turret armoured with 6-in. plating. Most of the vessels he constructed drew less water, and had more speed than was contracted for. His labours were thus summarised by Admiral Hamilton, from whom the foregoing details have been obtained. 'In less than a year, Mr. Eads built fourteen armoured vessels, four mortar boats, and converted seven transports into 'tinclads,' as musket-proof craft were called—all vessels that may be considered perfect successes for the work they were built to perform. The American Government knew what they wanted, threw overboard all old ideas when found unsuccessful, and availed themselves of the undoubted inventive genius of the country and its resources, put their best men forward, and succeeded; and although their innovations were, in many respects, apparently startling, they were, in reality, well considered beforehand.

In 1862, a larger type of monitor was designed and built by Ericsson. The principal dimensions of the 'Dictator' or 'Puritan' class Larger monitors.

were : Length on the deck, 314 feet ; overhang astern, 31 feet ; overhang forward, 13 feet, which gives a length between perpendiculars of 269 ft. 10 in.   The draught of water was 20 ft. 1 in. ; and the freeboard only one foot.   The large monitors were propelled by engines of nearly 1,000 horse-power.

Mr. Scott Russell.   Mr. Scott Russell, in his treatise on *Naval Architecture,* states that they were protected with 7-in. armour, with 21 inches of wood backing. They carried smooth-bore guns, weighing over twenty tons, and having a bore of thirteen inches, and a charge of 80 lbs. of powder.

The comparative dimensions of the earlier types of monitors are given by Mr. Scott Russell in the subjoined table :—

	First Monitor	Second Monitor	Third Monitor.
Length on load water-line .	225 ft. 6 in.	222 ft. 6 in.	341 feet
Draught of water . . .	6 feet	12 feet	20 feet
Thickness of armour plates .	3½ inches	—	7 inches
Depth of armour below load water-line	1 ft. 8 in.	2 feet	4 feet

The most recent information relating to these ships is appended herewith from the columns of the *Times* :—

Fig. 83.

' DICTATOR.'

Times. *Large sea-going monitors.*   ' The American monitors " Dictator " and " Puritan " were certainly the progenitors of our " Devastation " type.   One of the best authorities both as regards what was actually accomplished with the monitors and the points in which they failed, has recently stated that in the design of the " Dictator " and " Puritan " Mr. Ericsson aimed at high speed, great coal-carrying power, and general capabilities for service at sea.   The shallow draught, which had been compulsorily adopted in the American monitors of the earliest type designed expressly for coast service, was given up, and a single screw was given to the larger monitors instead of the twin screws previously used.   The principal dimensions of the " Dictator " were: Length, 320 feet ; breadth, for armoured band, fifty feet ; for breadth of hull, forty-two feet.   The " Puritan " was designed with an extra thirty feet of length.   The draught of water of both vessels was

21 feet. A screw of large diameter was used, and their engines were to develop about 5,000 horse-power, giving an estimated speed of sixteen knots per hour. The coal supply with each was not to be less than 1,000 tons. Both in speed and in coal-carrying power the " Dictator " and her consort were therefore intended to be far in advance of any war ship of their date—1862–63—and were also to be superior in guns and armour.

'The " Dictator " has been completed, and carries two 15-inch smooth-bore guns in a turret; the walls of the turret, which have a total thickness of fifteen inches, being made up of hoops of laminated armour in 1-in. thicknesses, with circular bars of greater thickness between. The turret has no wood backing. On the sides of the " Dictator " the armoured belt has an overhang of about four feet beyond the hull proper. The armour consists of six 1-in. iron plates, bolted on to 42 inches of wood backing, detached iron bars being let into the wood backing at intervals. It has often been asserted that the " Dictator " has ten or eleven inches of side armour, but this is an absurd over-estimate of its strength. The total depth of the armoured band covering the sides of the " Dictator " is six feet. Thus, with a two-feet freeboard, the band only extends four feet under water.

'The intentions of the designers of these, the first mastless sea-going ironclads, were far from being realised in some essential particulars. The " Dictator " has proved to be much heavier in the water than was intended, and is said to have one-third less freeboard than was assigned to her. She can only carry one-half her intended coal supply, and steamed only nine knots on her trial, and her engines have never developed the anticipated power, or secured the looked-for speed of sixteen knots. The boilers have been modified, so that they can never do the work they were originally designed for, and the vessel herself is now said to have been taken from the list of those intended for long voyages, although she has been in commission, and is said to have behaved well in heavy weather. Compared with the two American monitors our " Devastation " is, therefore, a great and very creditable success, surpassing so far upon the trials yet made with her all the anticipations of her designers, in her speed, carrying power, and stability. . . . The " Puritan " yet remains unfinished.'

The following is from a German authority:—' In consequence of some recently discovered miscalculations the building of the already far-advanced first-class monitor " Puritan " had to be temporarily suspended. According to the accounts given the load displacement of the design amounted to 5,975 tons, that of the whole hull to the upper deck 7,075 tons. A fresh calculation of the weights lately undertaken for the ship when equipped produces 7,070 tons. Therefore, in order to insure the flotation, considerable reductions in the weights of the armour-plates, turrets, and guns were necessary. A special commission was charged with an inquiry into the history of this ship's construction.'

Double-tur-reted moni-tors.

At the termination of the war it was determined to build four sea-going double-turreted ships, without overhang at the end or the sides. The names of these vessels were 'Miantonomoh,' 'Monad-nock,' 'Terror,' and 'Amphitrite.' Though intended for sea-going purposes, they are practically coast-service vessels.

Their principal dimensions are: draught of water, fourteen feet; freeboard, two feet; displacement, 4,000, 3,600, 3,600, and 2,800 tons respectively. They are armoured on the water-line with laminated armour six inches in thickness. The armour on the turrets consists of twelve layers of 1-inch plating. They were driven by twin screws at a speed of $6\frac{1}{2}$ knots an hour. The hulls were of wood. Admiral Paris observes (*Art Naval*, p. 260) that the 'Miantonomoh' differs

Fig. 84.

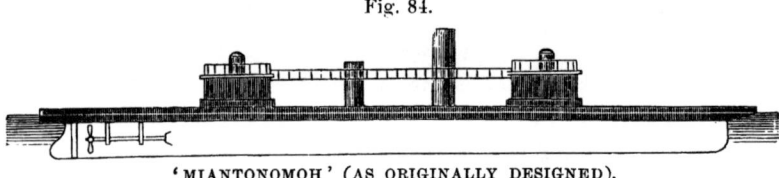

'MIANTONOMOH' (AS ORIGINALLY DESIGNED).

from the 'Dictator' in having two turrets, between which a flying deck is erected, affording space for walking, and also furnishing means for the supply of fresh air to the interior of the vessel. Vessels of this type are not fitted as rams, and do not steam so fast as the 'Dictator.'

These vessels exhibit in their framework and general construction a remarkable combination of iron and wood. Great difficulties must have been surmounted in order to secure the necessary rigidity in a flat-bottomed vessel of such length and beam, and carrying such heavy weights very unequally distributed in the form of turrets and armour-plating. The outer planking of the vessel is of considerable thickness, and the framework is strengthened from end to end by iron latticework and stanchions, very much after the fashion of a wooden trelliswork bridge.

Construc-tion of wooden monitors; the 'Kal-amazoo.'

The following section of the 'Kalamazoo,' a wooden monitor, will give an accurate idea of the method of construction adopted in the case of the larger sea-going vessels.

Fig. 85. THE 'MIANTONOMOH.' 137

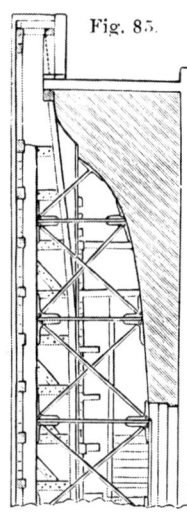

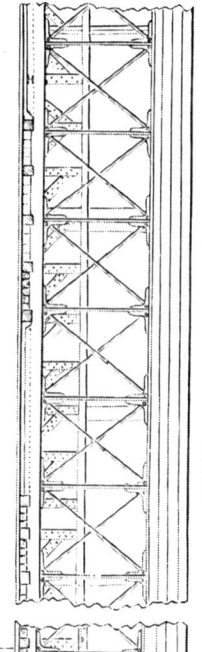

SECTION OF 'KALAMAZOO,' SHOWING FRAMING.

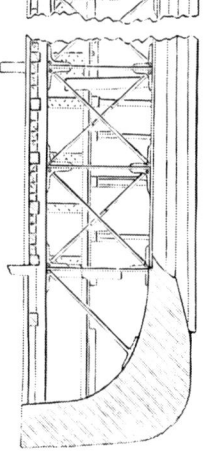

The armour extends along the whole length of the vessel in a belt 6 ft. 9 in. in depth, and $6\frac{1}{2}$ inches in thickness in seven layers. The turrets, two in number, are constructed of ten armour-plates ten inches in thickness. Each tower contains two heavy guns.

The 'Miantonomoh' is a twin-screw vessel, having originally machinery of 800 nominal horse-power. At full speed, with a consumption of forty tons of coal per day, the highest speed ever reached was nine knots, the mean speed of the voyage across the Atlantic being seven knots. The 'Miantonomoh' made the passage from St. John's, Newfoundland, to Queenstown in 10 days 18 hours. It is said that seas were encountered in which an ordinary frigate would have been unable to open her ports, while in the case of the 'Miantonomoh,' although the deck was covered with water to the depth of 4 feet with the wind ahead, the sea was so broken by the turret that it was possible to fire in a line with the keel. In a seaway, whether going ahead or with the engines stopped, it was always possible to fire to leeward, and the rolling was described as very moderate. With a following sea, the waves were divided in the same manner as when a head sea was encountered, but to windward the ports were constantly submerged. The captain reported that, instead of behaving as an ordinary vessel, the monitor allows the water to flow freely over the deck—thus imposing a heavy weight on the weather side, and causing the vessel to roll to windward. As the sea had to ascend an inclined deck, the greater part of the water rolled off on the weather side.

The guns being mounted in a central position were more easily worked than in an ordinary ship. The greatest angle of inclination observed in a heavy sea in the month of June was 7° to windward, and 4° to leeward, while the 'Ashuelot' and the 'Augusta,' two remarkably steady vessels, were rolling, the latter 18°, and the former 25°.

The 'Miantonomoh.'

It has been the policy of the Naval Administration of the United States to expend large sums in rebuilding worn-out vessels rather than in the construction of new designs.

The following detailed account of what may be called the rebuilding of the ' Miantonomoh,' has lately been published:—

' The " Miantonomoh " in course of time became antiquated, and at last it was resolved by the United States Government that she should be entirely renovated. This resulted in the building of a new " Miantonomoh," in which was to be worked up as much as possible of the old ship; but changes have been made from time to time, and very little of the original " Miantonomoh " is to be found in her namesake, and although called a third-rate, she is now, or will be very shortly, the most formidable ship of war possessed by the United States.

' The dimensions of the " Miantonomoh " are as follows :—

Length between perpendiculars	250 feet
Length on water-line	259 feet
Length over all	262 feet
Breadth of beam behind the armour	50 feet
Beam over armour	55 ft. 2 in.
Depth of hold	14 feet
Displacement at load draught	3,825 tons
Depth from base-line to top of armour	10 ft. 4 in.
Height of armour shelf above base-line	8 ft. 10 in.
Height of deck above water, amidships	2 ft. 6 in.
Area of midship section	716·5 square feet
Thickness of side armour, amidships	7 inches
Thickness of side armour, ends	5 inches
Thickness of wood backing	20½, 22½, 24½ in.
Thickness of deck armour	2 inches
Weight of side armour, solid plates	350 tons
Weight of turrets—two—with glacis	391 tons
Weight of armoured funnel	40 tons
Weight of armoured ventilator	25 tons
Weight of pilot-house	52·23 tons
Weight of engines and all dependencies	571·709 tons
Weight of boiler, water and dependencies, ex-bunkers	619·512 tons
Weight of coal contained in bunkers	300 tons
Number of turrets	2
Diameter of, outside	22 ft. 9 in.
Diameter of, inside	21 ft. 1 in.
Thickness of turrets	10 inches
Height of turrets above deck	9 feet
Number of guns, *kind undetermined*	4
Height of battery above deck	7 feet
Diameter of armoured funnel	10 feet

[1] *The Engineer*, April 16, 1880.

Height of armoured funnel . . . 9 feet
Thickness of armoured funnel . . . 10 inches
Diameter of armoured pilot-house . . 7 ft. 10 in.
Height of armoured pilot-house . . 6 ft. 4 in.
Thickness of armoured pilot-house . . 10 inches
Area of balanced rudder . . . 74 square feet

'The armour of the "Miantonomoh" was originally of the laminated kind, the United States possessing when she was built no facilities for rolling heavy plates. Her side armour was composed of five separate plates, each $\frac{15}{16}$-in. thick, secured by bolts and making up a total thickness of $4\frac{9}{16}$ inches. This was carried on a backing of oak, forming part of the side of the ship, which was built of wood. Laminated armour has been rejected, and the new ship is protected by solid rolled plates seven inches thick amidships and five inches thick fore and aft, the 'midship plates being eleven feet long and 2 ft. 6 in. wide. These plates are secured on an oak backing $24\frac{1}{2}$ inches thick, and are fixed with bolts $2\frac{3}{4}$ inches in diameter; wing passages the whole length of the ship permit access to be obtained to the nuts of these bolts. The turrets were originally armed with ten plates, each $1\frac{5}{16}$ inch thick. These are now to be replaced by solid plates about nine inches thick. It was originally intended to cover the vessel with oak planking and copper sheathing, but this part of the design has not been carried out.

'Her armour is carried on a shelf all round. The wrought-iron ram and its fastenings extend well forward of a collision bulkhead. The ram forging has been constructed of selected material of the very best quality, and is fastened to the hull with bracing as strongly as iron plating, etc., can be secured together. The rudder is only partly balanced, and is to be connected not only with the ordinary hand-steering arrangements, but also with steam cylinder steering engines. All the turret-turning gear of the original "Miantonomoh" has been put on board her successor, but it is so defective that it has been considerably modified to make it efficient.

'There are nine main watertight bulkheads, dividing the vessel into separate compartments, while the inner and outer hulls, or rather space between them, is divided by solid frames into twenty-two compartments, which are connected with three large wrecking steam-pumps of the Blake pattern, having cylinders of 16 inches and 16 inches respectively for the steam and water, and a capacity for the discharge of 1,000 gallons per minute for each pump. These pumps are, in addition to the engine steam-pumps and bilge injections, connected with the condenser circulating pumps.

'In the matter of the ventilation of this vessel, the improvement over the original "Miantonomoh" will be a great step forward. The first vessel had turret blowers only, distributing the air throughout the vessel by means of ordinary revolving fans, and with this air all the smoke from the turrets when in action, and there were no means of exhausting the foul air from the sleeping quarters of either officers or crew. In the new ship a totally different arrangement has been adopted. The ventilation will be effected by two centrifugal blowers. These fans are each seven feet in diameter by three feet in width, intended for about 500 revolutions per minute, and with a capacity for 20,000 cubic feet of air from each blower.'

The
' Terror'
rebuilt.

A similar reconstruction is being carried out in the case of the double-turreted monitor ' Terror,' another of the larger class of monitors. The hull was formerly of wood with heavy iron plating, but all the timbers are to be removed, a double-skinned hull of iron is to be substituted, and new engines are to be provided.

The
' Colossus '
' Massachu-
setts,'
' Oregon.'
Señor
Heriz, pp.
39–41.

The ' Colossus ' (see figs. 75, 76), ' Massachusetts,' and ' Oregon,' should also be included in the larger class of monitors in the fleet of the United States. They have two turrets and no overhang ; their draught of water is 17 feet, and displacement 6,000 tons. They are protected at the water-line by six inches of armour in two layers, with three longitudinal bars eight inches by eight inches. The turrets, as in the case of the ' Dictator,' are protected by 15 inches of armour in three layers ; and the deck has three inches of armour in two layers. These vessels are propelled by twin screws. Their hulls are built of wood.

The Secretary of the Navy, on May 11, 1880, communicated to the Speaker of the House of Representatives, in compliance with an Act of Congress, the reports of the Boards appointed to examine the ironclads ' Amphitrite,' ' Terror,' ' Monadnock,' and ' Puritan.

' The Board on the "Monadnock," at Mare Island, have determined that it is to the interest of the Government to complete that vessel according to the existing plans, models, and agreements with the following modifications : To substitute compound armour for that now used, to lower the turret armour from the inside structure, which will allow the guns the required depression and the base of the turret the protection of the outside glacis rim ; to fit a composite ring inside the turret to relieve the spindle from any sudden or heavy strain. They approve of the turret system and of compound engines with twin screws. The vessel has sufficient displacement to carry the weights which are to be placed on board, and if completed with the compound armour and such improvements' in detail as experience in the construction of the more advanced vessel, the " Monadnock," has shown to be desirable, she will be a valuable war vessel. The weights of proposed armour are:—

	Lbs.
Side armour	780,320
Turrets and base rings . . .	537,842
Pilot-houses	127,866
Smoke pipe	56,608
Ventilator	27,262
Total weight in pounds . .	1,529,898
Equal to	678 tons.

'The cost of compound armour without increase of weight or thickness is for the material, at 15 c. per lb., or £45,896, and for labour, 8 c. per lb., or £24,458; a total of £70,375. Deducting the expense of putting rolled iron armour on sides as per agreement, estimated at 17 c. per lb. for labour and materials, £26,531; leaves the net cost of modifications, £43,844.

'The Board on the " Puritan " report that it is to the interest of the Government to complete her, but not wholly in accordance with the existing plans, models, and agreements. The modifications are: Side armour to be compound, instead of iron, of a thickness of ten inches to the depth of 4 ft. 6 in. extending along the middle of the vessel, and in wake of turrets, to the distance of 165 ft. 10 in.; from thence the belt will be seven inches in thickness, of the same depth, for 26 ft. 7 in. on either end, terminating with a diminish to four inches, for a distance of 26 ft. 4 in. The lower belt to be four inches thick and 2 ft. 6 in. deep amidships, extending the whole length of the vessel. Armour backing to be of the best Georgia yellow pine instead of white oak.

'Two turrets of Ericsson type, interior diameter 26 ft. 6 in., and height 9 ft. 6 in. mailed with 12-inch compound armour. Pilot-house to be covered with ten inches of same material, and the smoke pipe and ventilator with eight inches. Passages on berth deck to be shifted in against engine and fire-room bulkheads, the space vacated to be used for coal.

'Yellow pine of three inches in thickness to constitute planking of both upper and berth decks, to be increased in the former to the width of three strakes, to four inches in thickness, on either side next to the waterways.

'Deck-house to be abolished, and apartments placed below, leaving platform on bridge between turrets. Armoured ventilator to be increased from eight feet to eleven feet in diameter. Eight boats recommended, one steam cutter, four cutters, one gig, one dinghy (dimensions given).

'The Board concur in a number of suggestions made by the Stevens Board. Displacement in excess of weight, 226 tons. Excess will allow heavier armament and increase of coal. Freeboard of thirty inches. Should a further decrease in weight be desired, the side armour could be reduced half an inch, and the other armour in proportion, leaving the resisting power quite equal to the iron armour designed for the vessel.

'The advantages of moving the passages between the forward and after berth deck are that it gives a more direct communication, fore and aft, increases the coal space, and in case of accident to the boilers, facilitates the closing of the boiler stop-valves.

'Two additional blowers for turrets recommended, and two for fire-room, with engines and connections complete; also that propellers be so lengthened that their surface will be increased 15 per cent.

Cost of additional watertight bulkheads	.	$4,509.70
Cost of moving bulkheads on berth deck	.	1,000.00
Cost of increase in size of boats	.	1,000.00
Cost of additional blowers	.	7,500.00
		$14,009.70 = £2,800
Less cost of compound armour compared with the armour designed for the vessel	.	11,907.33
Less cost of pine backing compared with oak		252.00
		$12,159.33 = £2,431

The Board suggest that, owing to the indefinite tenor of contract of March 3, 1877, for building of hull of "Puritan," before any more work is done a new contract be made, with full specifications and detailed drawings.

'Mr. Pook, Naval Constructor, concurs in the report, with the exception that a more formidable ship could be obtained by the erection of a central citadel, say 120 feet in length, having the turrets on the top at either end. The whole to have 12-inch armoured plate, steel-faced. The upper deck to be carried to ends of ship, to accommodate officers and crew. The additional weight of the superstructure would bring the armoured deck just at, or near, the load water-line, which would be the best position for fighting the ship.

'The Board of officers who examined the double-turreted monitors "Terror" and "Amphitrite" were unanimous in the opinion that, in view of the large sums already expended on those vessels, it is for the interest of the Government to complete them, while differing in their ideas as to how they should be completed.

They were also unanimous in opinion that compound armour should be substituted, for the sides and other armoured parts, for the iron plating originally designed.

'They found that it is not to the interest of the Government to complete the vessels according to the existing plans, but reported that the changes specified should be made to increase their safety and qualities of attack and defence. These changes, in addition to substituting compound armour, are, to substitute for present dimensions of the armour-plating one upper course four feet wide and seven inches thick, extending from the stem to a point five feet abaft the after watertight bulkhead, continuing the course around the stern with plates six inches thick, and below this course another of four inches thickness, two feet wide, extending from the stem to the point aft, where it becomes of a width insufficient for proper fastening ; that the use of the original turrets, pilot-house, armoured smoke pipe and air duct be abandoned, and others constructed of compound armour plates of the thickness given ; the extension of watertight bulkheads to the upper deck.

'The changes will increase the weights, and reduce the freeboard to about 30 inches. The armament will be 10-inch breech-loading steel rifles, instead of muzzle-loading 15-inch smooth-bore cast-iron guns. The increase in weight and displacement will somewhat reduce the speed, but the horse-power cannot be increased without a considerable addition to the weights. The Board advise no change in the motive machinery proposed.

'The cost of completing the vessels as proposed is: For the "Terror," £190,760 ; for the "Amphitrite," £186,360. The new guns and carriages will cost £15,320 for each ship. The total cost to complete the "Terror" will, therefore, be £206,080, and the "Amphitrite," £201,680. Naval Constructor Lenthall made a minority report.'[1]

In order to complete this account of the special types of ships of war constructed in the United States at the period of the rebellion, allusion may appropriately be made to the 'Dunderberg' or 'Rochambeau,' and the 'Onondaga,' which were purchased by the French Government from the United States in 1867. The special features of these ships can be most readily appreciated from the engravings here reproduced from the work of Admiral Paris. His description of them gave an interesting and impartial view of their merits and defects. He regarded them as a useful compromise between the

'Rochambeau' and 'Onondaga.'

---

[1] *New York Army and Navy Journal*, May 15, 1880.

sea-going ironclads and
floating batteries, possessing in consequence the
good qualities and the
defects both of the one
and the other, but capable
nevertheless of rendering
important services, espe-
cially in shallow waters,
where their light draught
is a great advantage.
These vessels are much
more than mere harbour-
defence ships, and at the
same time they possess
the special quality of that
type, the power of with-
drawing into waters too
shallow for the European
sea-going ironclads. The
'Dunderberg' was built
by Mr. Webb, and was
purchased by the French
Government for 500,000l.
The plans give all the
necessary details, show-
ing the form of the ship
above and below the
water, the rig, and the
very remarkable midship
section.

The principal dimen-
sions are—length, 377
ft. 4 in.; length between
perpendiculars, 332 ft. 4
in.; beam at the water-
line, 66 ft. 3 in.; mean
draught of water, 20 feet;
displacement, 7,060 tons;
weight of armour, 1,000
tons. The casemate is
pierced for 22 guns.

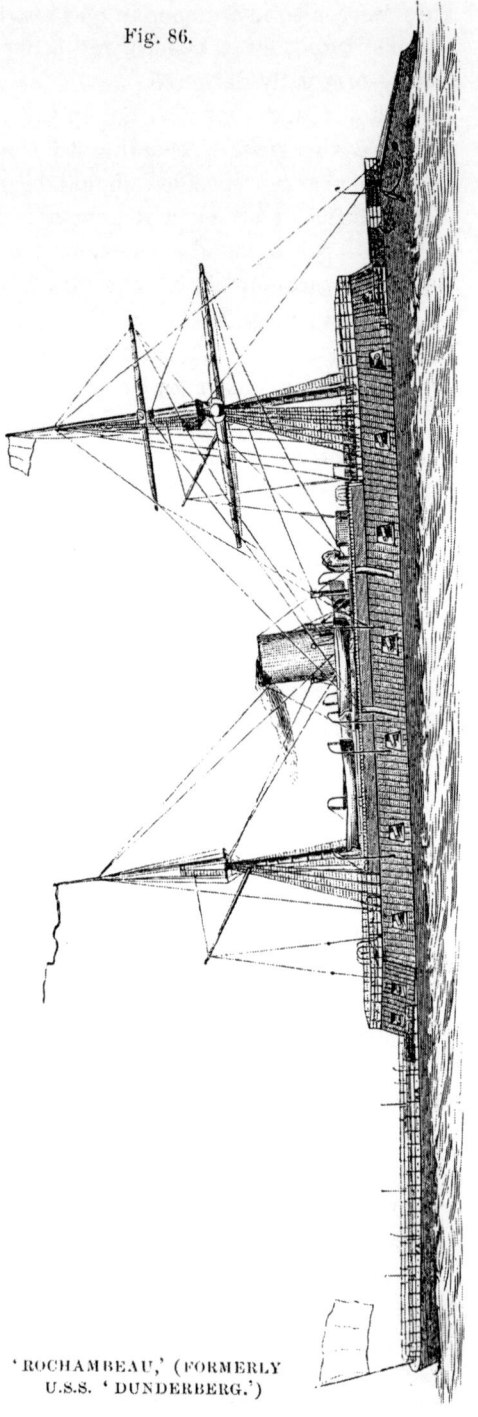

Fig. 86.

'ROCHAMBEAU,' (FORMERLY
U.S.S. 'DUNDERBERG.')

The sides of the ship are built at an angle of 35° from the perpendiculars below the sponson, and at an angle of 55° above it, presenting in fact a total angle of 90°. The object is to deflect the shot, although

Fig. 87.

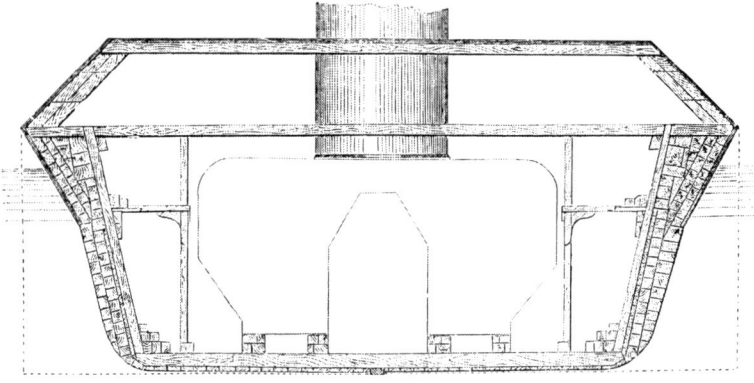

MIDSHIP SECTION OF 'ROCHAMBEAU.'

Fig. 88.

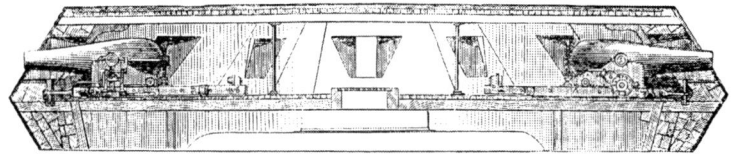

SECTION THROUGH BATTERY OF 'ROCHAMBEAU.'

Fig. 89.

ARRANGEMENT OF GUNS, 'ROCHAMBEAU.'

it is believed, at least in Europe, that with equal height and weight vertical sides are preferable. The armour is constructed of forged iron. The plates are $4\frac{1}{2}$ inches in thickness. These plates were much too thin, even at the time when the 'Dunderberg' was constructed.

When first launched the 'Dunderberg' attained a speed of
11·7 knots at the measured mile. Very important improvements
were, however, effected after the ship had been handed over to
the French Government; and it was stated in an official report
that in the trials at Cherbourg a mean speed of 14·63 knots was
obtained. The 'Rochambeau'—as the 'Dunderberg' was renamed
—did little service under her new flag, and has for some time disappeared from the effective list of the French Navy.

'H.M.S.
Scorpion'
and 'Wy-
vern.'

Before we dismiss altogether the ship-building operations which
had their origin in the conflict between the Northern and the
Southern States, it may be appropriate to refer to the 'Scorpion'
and the 'Wyvern.' The Southern States, having no dockyard of
their own, endeavoured to obtain ironclads from England and France.
Some of those vessels were seized; others were sold. The 'Scorpion'
and the 'Wyvern' were seized and purchased by the British Government. The distinctive features of these ships are shown in the
accompanying figure.

Fig. 90.

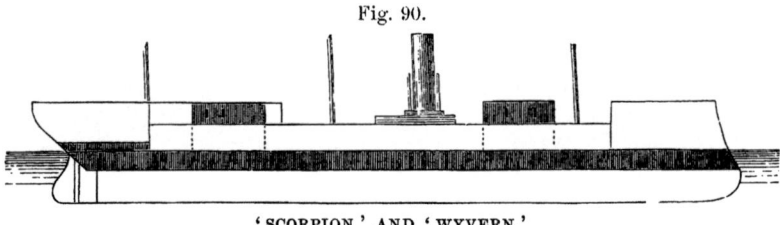

'SCORPION' AND 'WYVERN.'

Their principal dimensions are—length, 220 feet; beam, 42 feet;
displacement, 2,751 tons; draught of water, 15 feet. The engines
are of 350 nominal horse-power, and the speed attained at the
measured mile was 11·5 knots. The turrets are polygonal in form,
and armed with four 12-ton guns.

The 'Rol
Krake.'

We now turn to some of the earlier monitors constructed for
European navies. The 'Rolf Krake' was ordered for Denmark in
1861. Following the narrative of Admiral Paris, it may be mentioned
that this turret-vessel was the first which, under the modest name
of a gunboat, played an important part in the war in 1864. In the
hands of the Danes the 'Rolf Krake' offered a stout resistance to
naval forces very superior in point of numbers, but composed of ships
less efficient for the purposes of maritime war.

The principal dimensions are—length, 185 ft. 2 in.; beam, 38 ft.
3 in.; displacement, 1,325 tons; draught of water, 9 ft. 2 in. The
armour, 4½ inches in thickness, extends from three feet below the

water line to the upper deck. Each of the two towers was originally armed with two 68-pounder guns.

The Prussian naval authorities commenced the construction of ironclads by ordering their first vessel, the 'Arminius,' in England. This ship is a wooden turret-ship, armed with four guns, having a

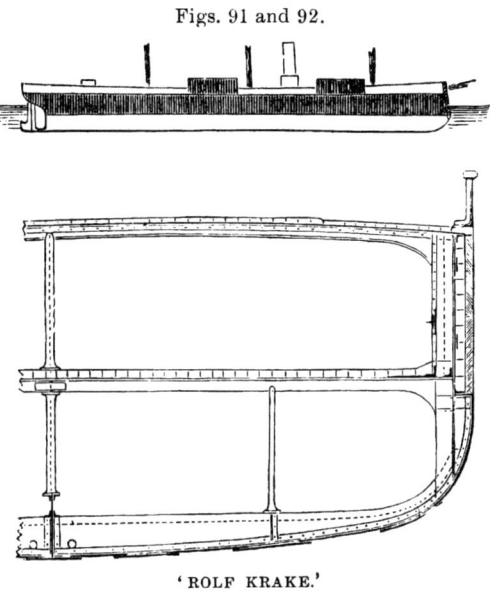

Figs. 91 and 92.

'ROLF KRAKE.'

displacement of 1,500 tons, and specially designed for coast defence. She was launched in 1864. Mr. Samuda was the builder. The design of the 'Arminius' is described by Admiral Paris as almost a copy of the 'Rolf Krake,' with some modification in the distance between the turrets, and some consequential changes in the internal dispositions.

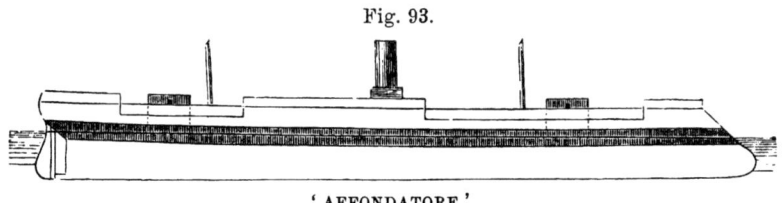

Fig. 93.

'AFFONDATORE.'

In 1866 the Millwall Shipbuilding Company launched the turret-ship 'Affondatore' for the Italian Government. This vessel may be described as a double-turret ram, drawing 19 ft. 7 in. of water, having a displacement of 4,100 tons, protected by armour of 5 inches in thickness, and propelled by machinery of 700 nominal horse-power. The hull is of iron; and the armament consists of 2 guns.

The 'Prince Henry.'   The 'Prince Henry of the Netherlands,' a turret-ship constructed by Messrs. Laird for the Dutch Government, was launched in 1867.

The principal dimensions are—length, 230 feet; beam, 44 feet; depth of hold, 26 ft. 6 in.; draught of water, 18 feet; and indicated power, 2,400 horses. The armament consists of four 300-pounder guns, mounted in two turrets. The 'Prince Henry' is rigged with two tripod masts, and a mizen mast of the ordinary kind. The armour, 4½ inches in thickness, forms a belt in the centre of the ship, and, for a length of 118 feet, in that part of the vessel which is occupied by the turrets and machinery, it rises to a height of nine feet above the water-line. At the extremities the ship is armoured to

Fig. 94.

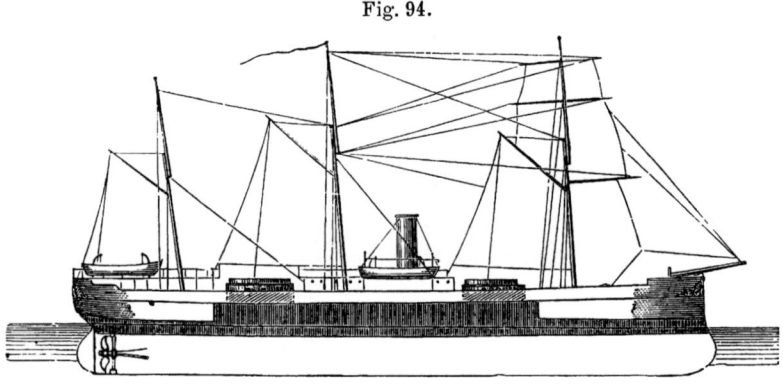

'PRINCE HENRY.'

a height of only two feet above the water-line. The transverse bulk-heads of the central battery are armoured. The turrets, constructed from the plans of Captain Coles, are protected by 5½ inches of plating; they stand, the one before and the other abaft the engine. A pair of 12½-ton guns is mounted in each turret, commanding a complete all-round fire, excepting immediately ahead and astern. The machinery is composed of two engines, each of 200 horse-power, constructed by Messrs. Laird.

Other Dutch armoured ships. The 'King of the Netherlands.'   Other ships of the Dutch navy, most of which were begun at this period, though some were launched later, may be here described.

The 'King of the Netherlands,' the largest armourclad in the Dutch navy, was built at the Royal dockyard at Amsterdam, and was launched in 1874. The principal dimensions are as follows :—

Length between perpendiculars . . 268 feet
Beam, extreme . . . . 49 ft. 10 in.
Depth from keel to upper deck . . 32 ft. 6 in.
Draught of water . . . . 19 ft. 2 in.
Displacement . . . . 5,285 tons
Indicated horse-power . . . 4,630
Speed . . . . . 11 95 knots.

The hull is of iron. The two turrets are each armed with 11-inch
25-ton Armstrong guns. On the upper deck there are four Krupp

Figs. 95 and 96.

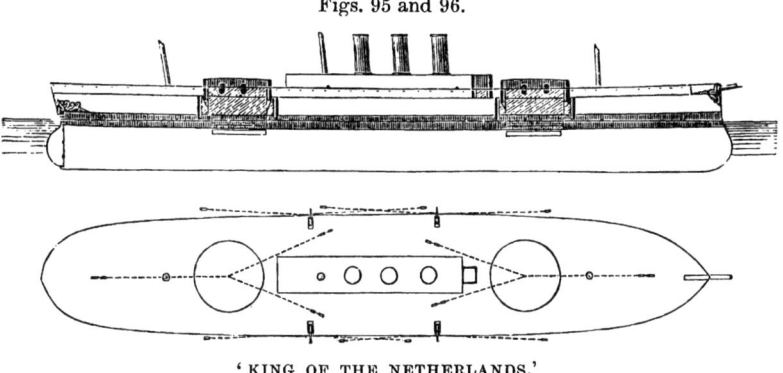

'KING OF THE NETHERLANDS.'

12 c/m. light guns. The turret guns are 10 ft. 10 in. above the
water. The vessel is fitted with spar-torpedoes. The greatest thickness of the armour-belt is 8 inches on a 12-inch backing. The armour
diminishes to six inches at the ends of the ship. The turret armour
is nine inches in thickness, increasing to 12 inches near the gunports. The ram protrudes four feet beyond the bows. There are
two screws with separate engines. The vessel has three funnels,
and carries 620 tons of coal. Each turret has a special turning-
engine and hydraulic apparatus.

Fig. 97.

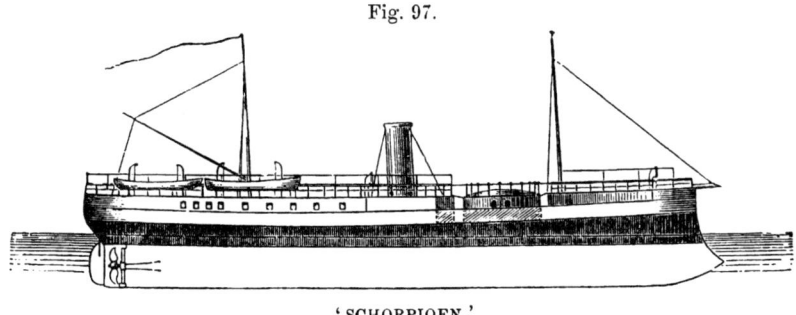

'SCHORPIOEN.'

The Dutch armoured turret-ram 'Schorpioen' was built at La

Seyne by the Forges et Chantiers Company, and was launched on
January 18, 1868. The principal dimensions are—

Length between perpendiculars	193 feet
Beam at the water-line	36 ft. 2 in.
Length to beam	5·35
Draught of water	15 ft. 10 in.
Displacement	2,175 tons.

This vessel is built of iron, and has one turret forward armed with a
9-inch Armstrong gun seven feet above the water. The armour on
the belt has a maximum thickness of six inches on a 12-inch backing,
gradually diminishing to four inches at the extremities. The turret
armour has a thickness of eight inches. Extensive superstructures
have been erected on the upper deck. The engines, also made at La
Seyne, indicate 2,200 horse-power, and work two screws. The maximum speed is 12·82 knots.

Fig. 98.

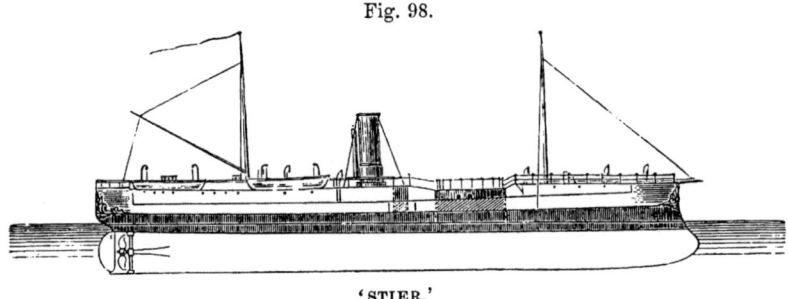

'STIER.'

The 'Stier' which closely resembles the 'Schorpioen,' was built
by Messrs. Laird, and launched on April 10, 1868. The principal
dimensions are—

Length	200 feet
Beam	38 feet
Draught of water	15 ft. 6 in.
Displacement	2,069 tons

The belt is of 6-inch armour, tapering to four inches at the ends of
the ship. It rests on a 10-inch wood backing, supported by a thin
plating of 1-inch iron. The turrets are protected with 8-inch plates,
increasing to a thickness of 11 inches in the vicinity of the ports.
The turrets are armed with two 9-inch Armstrong guns, and can be
turned by either hand or steam power. An armoured pilot-house,
and unarmoured superstructures before and abaft the turret, have been
constructed on the upper deck. The engines, by Laird, indicate 2,200
horse-power, and work two screws, giving a speed of 12·3 knots on
the trial trip.

The 'Buffel' was built by Napier and Sons on the Clyde, and was The 'Buffel.' launched on March 10, 1868. The principal dimensions are:—

Length between the perpendiculars	. 205 feet
Beam, extreme	. 40 feet
Draught of water	. 15 ft. 6 in.
Displacement	. 2,198 tons

The ship is built of iron, and has an armour-belt six inches thick on

Fig. 99.

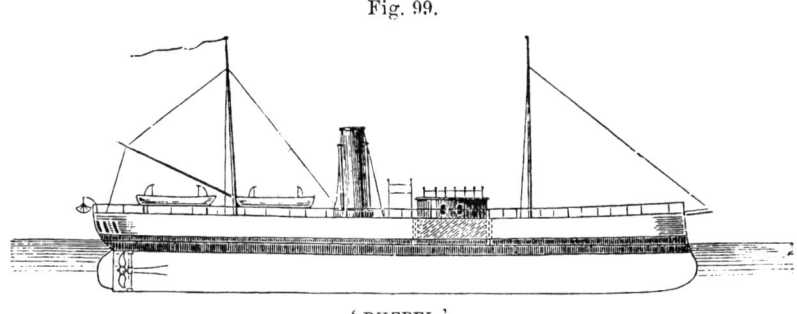

' BUFFEL.'

ten inches of backing. The upper deck is protected with 1-inch plates. The breastwork, in which the turret rotates, has 8-inch armour on 12-inch backing. The armour of the turret, in which are two 9-inch Armstrong guns, is of the same thickness. The engines, made by Napier, and driving two screws, indicate 2,200 horse-power; the speed is 12·7 knots.

The 'Cerberus,' 'Heiligerlee,' 'Tijger,' 'Krokodil,' and 'Bloed- The 'Cerberus,' 'Heiligerlee,' 'Tijger,' 'Krokodil,' and 'Bloedhound.'

Fig. 100.

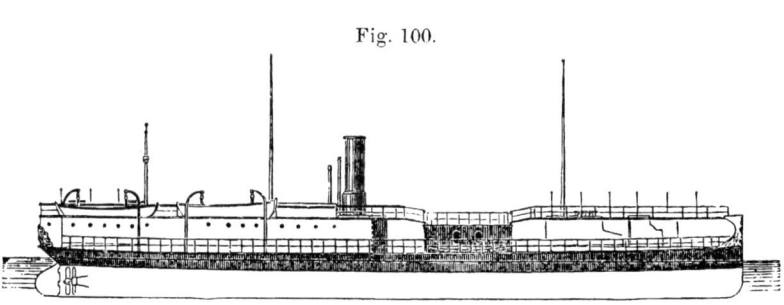

' CERBERUS ' (DUTCH).

hound' are iron turret-vessels, built at English private works, and launched in 1868 and 1869. They have the following principal dimensions :—

Length between the perpendiculars	. 180 feet
Greatest beam	. 44 feet
Draught of water	. 9 ft. 7 in.
Displacement	. 1,530 tons

The armour on the sides is $5\frac{1}{2}$ inches thick, tapering to $4\frac{1}{2}$ at the ends. The teak backing is ten inches in thickness. The turret is protected with 8-inch armour, increasing at the ports to 11 inches. In the turret are two 9-inch 12-ton Armstrong guns. The indicated horse-power is 630; there are two screws, and the speed is nine knots.

The 'Draak' and 'Adder' classes.

The Dutch have two classes of ram-turret monitors. Some are of recent construction. The 'Draak' alone belongs to the first class; seven belong to the second, or 'Adder' class.

Fig. 101.

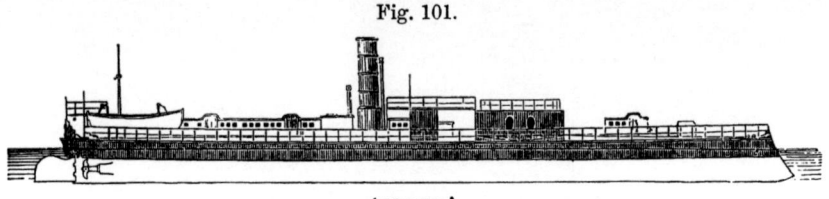

'ADDER.'

seven belong to the second, or 'Adder' class. Their dimensions are given in the table.

Name	Year of Launch	Material of Hull	Displacement	Draught of Water	Ordnance carried	Thickness of Armour		Indicated horse power	No. of Screws	Speed
						Water line	Turret			
			tons	ft. in.		in.	in.			knts
Hyæna .	1870	Iron	1,566	8 10	{ Two 9-in. Armstrong }	$4\frac{1}{2}$	8	680	2	9
Panter .	1870	,,	1,566	8 10	,,	$4\frac{1}{2}$	8	680	2	9
Wesp .	1871	,,	1,566	8 10	,,	$4\frac{1}{2}$	8	680	2	9
Haai .	1871	,,	1,566	8 10	,,	$4\frac{1}{2}$	8	680	2	9
Adder .	1871	,,	1,566	8 10	,,	$4\frac{1}{2}$	8	680	2	9
Linpard	1876	,,	1,525	8 10	{ One 28 c/m Krupp }	$4\frac{1}{2}$	8	680	2	9
Matador	1877	,,	1,650	9 10	{ Two 28 c/m Krupp }	$4\frac{1}{2}$	9	680	2	8
Draak .	1877	,,	2,156	10 10	,,	8	9	800	2	8

In the 'Draak' and 'Matador,' the turret is protected near the ports with 12-inch armour. The other vessels have 11-inch armour.

The 'Huascar and 'Atahualpa.'

Brazilian turret-ships.

At this period several vessels were built for the South American States on the turret system of Captain Coles. The 'Huascar' and 'Atahualpa' were added to the Peruvian fleet, and the 'Bahia' and 'Lima Barros' were built for Brazil. Numerous central battery ships were also constructed, including the 'Independencia' for Peru, the 'Brazil,' 'Cabral,' 'Colombo,' 'Mariz-e-Barros,' 'Herval,' and 'Silvado' for Brazil.

We proceed to give details respecting the more important of the vessels included in the above enumeration.

The 'Huascar' was built for the Peruvian Government by Messrs. Laird Brothers, of Birkenhead, under the directions of Captain Coles. Admiral Paris points to this vessel as one among several successful attempts to produce small armoured vessels, without making too great a sacrifice either of speed or of defensive power. The vessels of this type, like the ' Rolf Krake,' and others which might be cited, seem destined to supersede everywhere the old class of gun-vessel, being infinitely more powerful both in an offensive and defensive sense.

The ' Huascar,' which was launched in 1866, is an iron vessel very strongly built, and divided into watertight compartments, which enclose the turrets, the machinery, and the boilers, and in these vital

Figs. 102 and 103.

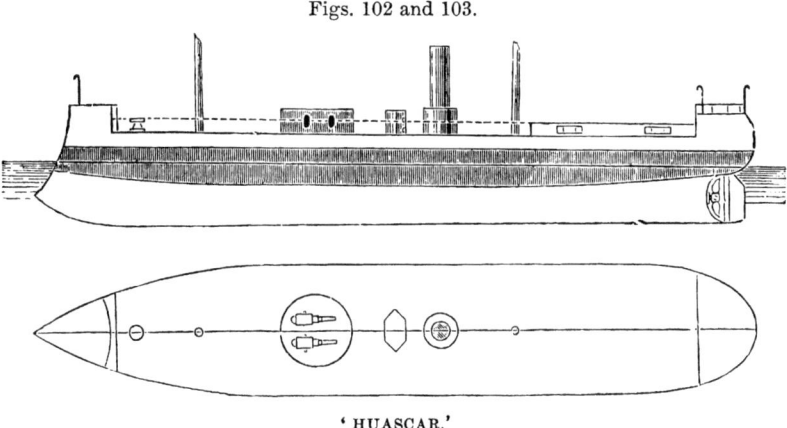

' HUASCAR.'

parts the ship is built with a double bottom. The ' Huascar ' was originally rigged with two masts, the fore mast being upon Captain Coles' tripod principle. The principal dimensions are : displacement, 1,100 tons; length, 200 feet; beam, 35 feet; draught of water, 14 feet; with a freeboard of five feet. The armament consists of two 300-pounder guns in one revolving turret, and three light shell guns on deck. The armour-plating of the turret is $5\frac{1}{2}$ inches thick, worked upon a teak backing of 14 inches. The armour amidships is $4\frac{1}{2}$ inches in thickness, tapering to $2\frac{1}{2}$ inches at the end of the ship. The teak backing on the sides is fourteen inches thick. The deck is protected against a plunging fire, when in action, by 2-inch iron plates fitted to the skylights or hatchways. The bulwark plating being fitted to turn down in the vicinity of the turrets there is no obstruction to the range of fire from the guns. The 'Huascar' is a single-screw vessel, propelled by machinery of 300 horse-power, and capable of steaming at the rate of 11 knots an hour. She sailed from Liverpool on January 17, 1866. At sea the captain reported that much broken water came on board, but no green seas. The passage outwards to Peru was made, in company with the 'America' and the 'Independencia,' by the Straits of Magellan. On clearing the Straits, the vessel was constantly buried in the seas, but arrived safely at her destination. The voyage of this small armoured ship excited considerable interest, and showed that, with proper arrangements for battening down, and furnishing a supply of air to the interior, sea-going ironclads can be built of much smaller dimensions than had previously been thought necessary.

The 'Atahualpa.'

The 'Atahualpa' was another small ironclad built at about the same date for the Peruvian fleet, having a displacement of 1,000 tons, with complete armour protection from end to end 4½ inches in thickness, and armed with four guns, two of which are of heavy calibre.

The (Peruvian) 'Independencia.'

The 'Independencia,' also launched in 1865 to the order of the Peruvian Government, was a ship having a displacement of 2,000 tons, and protected with armour 4½ inches in thickness. The armament consisted of twelve 70-pounder guns and two 150-pounders mounted on pivots on the upper deck. This vessel was lost by running on a rock during an action with some Chilian vessels.

Having been involved in a war with the Republic of Paraguay, the Government of Brazil was led to construct some special vessels for naval operations on the great rivers of South America. With this object in view, the 'Bahia' and some other vessels of similar type, and a number of small monitors, were purchased for the Brazilian fleet. We proceed to give a more detailed account of some of these vessels.

The 'Bahia.'

The 'Bahia' was built by Messrs. Laird Brothers in 1865 for the Brazilian Government. She is described by Admiral Paris as having a single turret erected a little in front of the centre of the vessel, and presenting so great a resemblance to the 'Huascar' that the Admiral did not think it necessary to publish a plan in the collection appended to the *Art Naval*. The turret is armed with two 150-pounder guns. The principal dimensions are : length, 175 feet ; beam, 35 feet ; depth of hold, 11 feet ; draught of water, 8 feet ; tonnage, 1,008. The 'Bahia' has a ram, a poop, and a small forecastle. The bulwarks can be lowered in action. She has a moderate spread of canvas. The 'Bahia' is a twin screw, with machinery of 140 horse-power, and steams 10·5 knots. The armour consists of plates 4¼ inches in thickness, on a wood backing of one foot. The plating diminishes in thickness towards the extremities of the vessel. In the Paraguayan war the 'Bahia' took part in the bombardment of forts armed with 68-pounder guns. Though struck 39 times, neither the armour nor the turret sustained the slightest injury.

The 'Bellona,' now the 'Lima Barros,' was constructed by Messrs. Laird in 1866, also for the Brazilian Government. The principal dimensions are: length, 196 feet; beam, 38 feet; depth of hold, 16 ft. 6 in.; tonnage, 1,330; draught of water, 12 feet. *The 'Lima Barros.'*

The 'Lima Barros' is fitted with twin screws, driven by machinery of 300 horse-power, constructed by Messrs. Ravenhill. Her speed at the measured mile under unfavourable conditions of weather was 11 knots. The armour is 4½ inches in thickness, diminishing towards the extremities; and armour of the same thickness protects the turrets, in which two Whitworth 150-pounder guns are mounted. The voyage to Brazil was accomplished without misadventure at an average speed of nine knots.

Fig. 104.

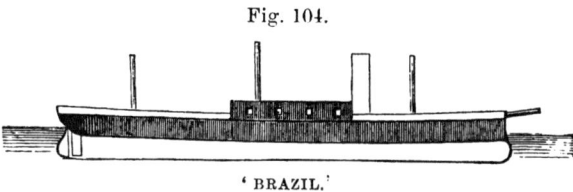

'BRAZIL.'

The 'Brazil,' another vessel in the fleet of the empire whose name she bears, was constructed at La Seyne.

The principal dimensions are: length between perpendiculars, 196 ft. 9 in.; beam, 35 ft. 3 in.; draught of water, 12 feet; displacement, 1,517 tons. The machinery is of 250 horse-power, and the bunkers are capable of containing 170 tons of coal. The 'Brazil' is a central battery ship, with only a narrow belt of armour before and abaft the battery. The depth of the held, however, is so limited that the armour extends to the upper deck. The armour is 4¾ inches in thickness, with a teak backing of 8½ inches. The plans taken from the *Art Naval* give a correct idea of the lines of the vessel, of the arrangement of the armour, and of the mode in which the guns are mounted in the casemate. The armament consisted originally of four 70-pounder Whitworth guns, and four of the ordinary 68-pounders of the British service. This corvette is said to have behaved well at sea, when on the passage to Brazil; she lifted satis-factorily to the sea in spite of her low freeboard—a good quality, *The 'Brazil.'*

which is no doubt due to the concentration of weights in the middle
of the ship. In the trials on the measured mile at Rio Janeiro, a
speed of 11·3 knots was attained. The 'Brazil' was several times in
action on the Parana, and was often struck, but never penetrated by
shot. The Brazilian Government was so satisfied with the vessel
that they ordered a similar ship to be constructed in their own dockyard.

The 'Cabral' and 'Colombo.'   Among the other gunboats with a central battery constructed for
service on the large rivers of South America, the 'Cabral' and
'Colombo,' built by Mr. Rennie of London, plans of which are
appended herewith, deserve mention.

Figs. 105 and 106.

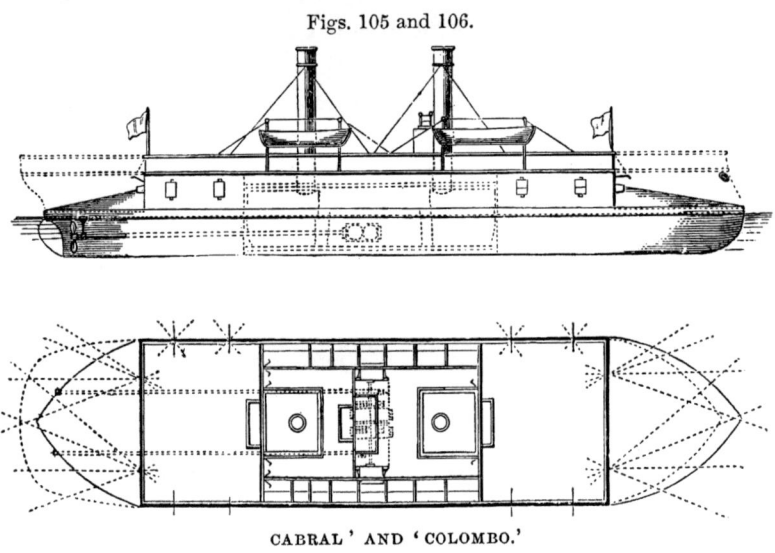

CABRAL ' AND ' COLOMBO.'

Admiral Paris remarks that their length, 160 feet, somewhat exceeds that of the old frigate of 44 guns, the beam being 35 ft. 6 in.;
draught of water, 9 ft. 6 in.; and tonnage 1,032. The machinery is
of 240 nominal, or 750 indicated horse-power, and the speed 10·5
knots. In order to obtain a wide range of fire with the guns placed
in the extremities of the vessel, the ends of the ship both forward
and aft have been cut down to the water's edge; and as it would have
been dangerous to make the passage from Europe to Brazil in this
condition, a superstructure was erected, the outlines of which are
shown in dotted lines in the figure. The armour is of 4¼ inches in
thickness, and extends from end to end at the water-line, and a little
below it. The sloping decks, fore and aft, are covered with 2½-inch
plates. These gunboats were propelled by twin screws, and took an

active part in the Paraguayan war. Their armour proved an effective protection against 68-pounder shot fired at a range of 262 feet. The armament consisted of four Whitworth 68-pounders and four 70-pounders.

Mr. Rennie also constructed two other gunboats, the ' Marriz e Barroz ' and ' Herval.' These vessels are armed with four guns in a central battery, and are propelled by machinery of 240 horse-power.

The ' Marriz e Barroz ' and ' Herval.'

The ' Silvado,' another vessel built to the order of the Brazilian Government, was constructed by M. Arman of Bordeaux, and launched in 1866. The ' Silvado ' is a twin screw, and has two turrets, each armed with two Whitworth 70-pounder guns.

The ' Silvado.'

When ironclads were first introduced into their navy, the attention of the naval authorities in Russia was mainly concentrated on

Russian monitors.

Figs. 107 and 108.

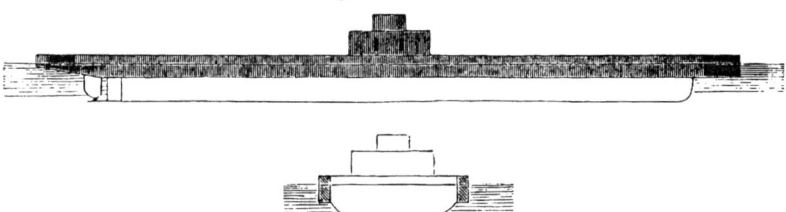

RUSSIAN MONITOR ' BRONENOSEC.'

the coast-defence class. In addition to the vessels before described, ten single-turreted monitors on Mr. Ericsson's plans were commenced simultaneously, and launched in 1864. They were described by Lieutenant Juels, of the Swedish navy, in an article, a translation of which appeared in the *Revue Maritime*. Their armament consists of two 9-inch rifled or 15-inch smooth-bore guns. The vessels are armoured on the laminated system, with five 1-inch plates on a backing nearly three feet in thickness. The turrets are protected with eleven 1-inch plates without backing. The Russian monitors draw only twelve feet of water, and from this circumstance they afford a valuable addition to the defences of the shallow Baltic ports, but they are not seaworthy for ocean service. The engines are of 160 nominal horse-power, and are capable of giving a speed of from six to seven knots. Special engines are provided for moving the turrets, and for ventilation. The displacement of these vessels is 1,566 tons.

Besides the single-turreted vessels already described, the

The
'Smerc.'

'Smerc,' a double-turreted monitor of 1,461 tons, was also built about the same date. The following description is translated from the paper by Lieutenant Juels, from which we have already quoted:—
'The "Smerc" was built in England in 1864 on Captain Coles' system. The "Smerc" has movable bulwarks, tripod masts, a ram-bow, double bottom, and twin screws. The draught of water is 11 ft. 6 in.; the nominal horse-power, 200; and the speed about eight knots. The armour on the hull and turrets is 4½ inches in thickness, increasing to six inches near the ports. The decks are protected by 1-inch armour of two thicknesses.'

Lieutenant Juels states that the 'Smerc' exhibited fair sea-going qualities, in the sense in which the 'Miantonomoh' might be regarded as a sea-going vessel. Viewed in reference to the recent development of naval architecture, she can only be considered as a comparatively weak coast-service ship.

In addition to the vessels already mentioned, the Russians built

Figs. 109 and 110.

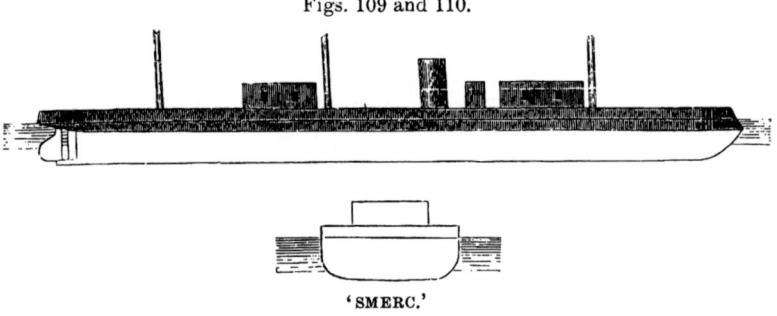

'SMERC.'

The
'Tcharod-jejka' and
'Rous-salka.'

about 1868 two larger monitors of 1,850 tons, the 'Tcharodjejka' and 'Roussalka.' We learn from Lieutenant Juels that these vessels draw twelve feet and steam 8½ knots. Their freeboard amidships is only two feet. At sea they roll very heavily— an angle of 35° having been recorded—a suggestive fact when it is remembered that their metacentric height must be much less than that of the 'Miantono-moh,' whose rolling nevertheless rarely exceeded from 5° to 7°. From their lower freeboard they ought to have derived much more advantage than the 'Miantonomoh' did from the supposed steadying or bilge-keel action of the weather-edge of the deck. The side armour of the 'Tcharodjejka' and 'Roussalka' is five inches in thick-ness, increasing to a thickness of six inches on the turrets, in which are mounted four 9-inch Armstrong guns. The Russian fleet includes thirteen of these smaller turreted monitors.

Among the other sea-going turret-ships in the Russian navy are the 'Admiral Lazareff,' 'Admiral Greig,' 'Admiral Spiridoff,' and The 'Admiral Tchitchachoff.' Particulars of these ships were published in some interesting papers which appeared in the columns of the *Pall Mall Gazette* when the prospect of a war with Russia seemed imminent.

The 'Admiral Lazareff' (the 'Four Admirals').

'The tonnage of these vessels ranges from 3,693 tons in the case

Figs. 111 and 112.

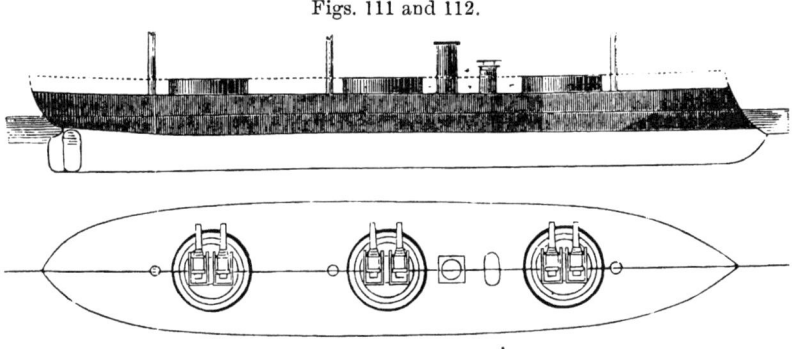

'ADMIRAL LAZAREFF.'

of the last-named, to 3,754 tons in the "Admiral Lazareff." The speed of all these ships under steam may be taken at about ten knots an hour. The "Admiral Lazareff" carries six 15½-ton guns in three turrets; the "Admiral Greig" three 27-ton guns, also in three turrets; and the "Admiral Spiridoff" and "Admiral Tchitchachoff" each

Figs 113 and 114.

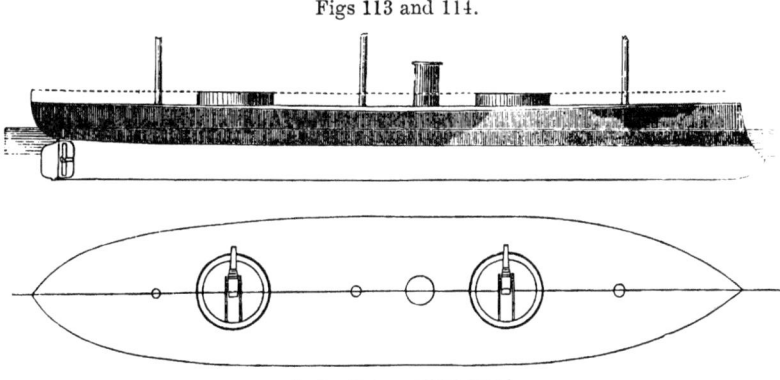

'ADMIRAL SPIRIDOFF.'

two 27-ton guns in two turrets. The two latter vessels are armoured with 6-inch plates, while the other two of the same class are only protected with four inches of iron. All the four ships belong to the class of low freeboard turret-vessels, the height of the deck above the water-line being only between four and six feet. Originally it was

intended that they should be fully rigged ships; but the loss of
the "Captain," a vessel of much the same type, caused the idea
of equipping them as cruisers to be abandoned. As coast-defence
vessels they must be regarded as formidable from their armament.
The projectiles fired by their guns would penetrate twelve inches of
armour at short ranges: but even for the protection of littoral waters
these turret-ships must be classed as inferior to the four vessels of
the "Hecate" class in the English navy.'

Admiral Paris gives the complements of several of the vessels of
which we have given descriptions as follows:—The 'Smerc,' 100;
the 'Roussalka' and her consort, 136; and 'Admiral Greig,' 180
men.

From the foregoing details it will be seen that seventeen of the
twenty-seven ironclads in the Russian navy are of the monitor type,
and fit for harbour defence only. The armour of the thirteen smaller
vessels affords but imperfect protection against the rapidly increasing
power of modern naval ordnance.

Fig. 115.

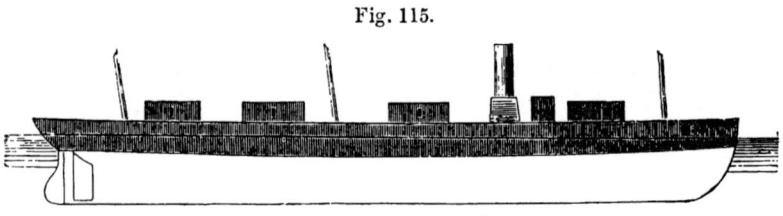

' ROYAL SOVEREIGN.'

English
turret-
ships.

Turning to our own navy, turret-ships were first introduced by the
Admiralty in deference to the persistent advocacy of Captain Coles.
The 'Prince Albert,' which was specially designed for an armament
on the turret system, and a converted line of battle-ship, the 'Royal
Sovereign,' were the first turret-ships actually completed.

The following details are taken from the contemporary notices
published from time to time in the columns of the *Times* by its
able correspondent at Portsmouth; and the author desires to acknowledge his deep obligation to this gentleman for much of the most
recent information which has been brought together in the subsequent pages of these volumes.

The 'Royal
Sovereign.'

The 'Royal Sovereign' was a three-decker of 3,144 tons, pierced
for 120 guns. When Captain Coles so far gained the confidence of
the Admiralty as to induce them to give him an opportunity of
carrying out his turret principle on a large scale, this ship was
selected as being the best for the experimental conversion of a three-

decker into a turret-vessel. She had recently been fitted with engines of 800 horse-power by Messrs. Maudslay and Field. The sides of the 'Royal Sovereign,' after conversion, were composed of three feet of solid timber, strengthened internally with diagonal iron bands, and clothed externally to the usual distance below the water-line with 5½-inch rolled armour-plates. The upper deck beams of wood and iron were double the usual number, and were attached to massive iron knees. One-inch iron plating was laid upon the deck beams, and over the iron plating was laid the deck proper, consisting of 6-inch and 8-inch oak planking. From the side of the ship the deck sloped upwards to the outer circumference of the turrets, which stood like so many circular revolving forts on the crest of a glacis. When the 'Royal Sovereign' was first floated into the outer basin of Portsmouth dockyard after her conversion, she lay alongside the 'Victoria,' screw three-decker of 4,127 tons, 131 guns, and 1,000 horse-power, then fitting out as a flag-ship for the Mediterranean. The *Times* correspondent appropriately called attention to the wonderful contrast between the two ships.

'In the "Victoria" was all the stately pride and grandeur of the wooden period, in, alas! all the combustibleness of its nature. In the 'Royal Sovereign" was visible the iron period in its then latest phase. *Description from the Times.*

'The "Royal Sovereign" made her official trial of speed and power of circling, with full and reduced steam pressure, in Stokes Bay in June 1864. The time occupied in the conversion had been long and the cost great. But the result, in the evident efficiency of the "Royal Sovereign" for the purposes of war, was undoubtedly satisfactory. On reaching the open water of Spithead, with her bulwarks up and her short masts just capping the funnel, she looked like some gigantic gunboat under jury-rig. With her bulwarks down she has the appearance of those American "monitors," which have become so familiar to us from pictures and descriptions, her turrets showing out distinctly along the ridge of the deck.

'Stepping on the "Royal Sovereign's" upper deck, we find that her light iron bulwarks, 3 ft. 6 in. in depth, are thrown down outwards on hinged stanchions. On the crest of the deck stand the four turrets and pilot-house, funnel-casing, hatchways, and ventilating shaft. The foremost turret, standing five feet above the deck, has its top covered by a grating, and is surrounded by a handrail, and thus affords a deck promenade for the officer of the watch or lookout man. The three single-gun turrets are 4 ft. 3 in. above the deck, and have a double line of rails 20 inches in depth around their *Turrets.*

tops, in which the men's hammocks are stowed, and which will thus form capital rifle-pits. The tops of the turrets are closed by heavy angle iron and 1-inch plating, with the necessary man and ventilating holes. The combined iron and wood in the deck is laid upon rolled iron beams and the original wooden beams of the ship, which are fixed so closely together that even if a shot or shell penetrated through the iron and wooden deck, it would be difficult for it to force a further passage through to the deck below.' The pilot-house is plated with 5½-inch armour, and stands between the foremost turret and the funnel-casing.

Compari-
son with
monitors.
The improvements on the American method of working guns mounted in turrets, which were introduced in the 'Royal Sovereign,' were of a very important character, and naturally excited consider- able interest at that date.

In making an historical survey of the progress of naval construc- tion for war purposes, it may not be superfluous to give some detailed account of the changes which were introduced. For this purpose we again refer to the lucid description published in the columns of the *Times.*

'The " Royal Sovereign " differs from most other cupola ships in the provision made for turning the turrets by different appliances of manual power, by rack and pinion inside the turret, by the same appliance outside the turret, and by handspikes worked like capstan- bars on the lower deck, in lieu of one method only by steam. It is in the disposition of the turrets, however, that the "Royal Sovereign" differs most from the American monitors. The American monitors' turrets are nine feet in height above the upper deck, on which their base rests on a brass ring. While thus resting on the upper deck the turret has no means of revolving, so that, when prepared for action, it must be lifted off the deck by a screw wedge driven into the base of a spindle upon the deck below, which spindle bears the same relation to the turret as does the spindle to an ordinary ship's capstan. The turret is revolved, resting upon this central spindle, by geared wheels driven by steam ; the whole weight of the turret being above the plane of the deck, exposed to the enemy's fire, and the turret itself further capped by the pilot-house ; the structure being dependent therefore for its efficiency upon the continued per- fect perpendicularity of an iron spindle which is 13 ft. 6 in. in height. In the case of the " Royal Sovereign," the four turrets have their base and working portion resting upon the lower, and not the upper deck, as with the Americans. Instead of exposing a height of 13 ft. 6 in. to an enemy's fire the foremost or double gun-turret stands only

5 feet, and the three after, or single gun-turrets, 4 ft. 3 in. above the deck. Again, the " Royal Sovereign's " turrets are pivoted in their centres upon wrought-iron cylinders sufficiently large for men to pass through, while the weight is distributed on bevelled wheels over a metal ring in a manner very similar to a railway turntable.

'The ship's armament consisted of five 12½-ton or 300-pounder guns. Two guns were mounted in the foremost turret, and one gun in each of the other three turrets. From the plane of the table on which the guns and their carriages rest, the turrets have an interior height of nine feet. They afford ample space for the crew to work the guns.

'The jamming of the turrets by shot, or broken armour-plating, or bolt-heads falling under their base, was the sole cause of the failure which occurred in the American turret-vessels in the attack upon Charleston. The base of the " Royal Sovereign's " turrets being below the upper deck, there is no risk of accidents of the same nature as those which are so frequently experienced in the American monitors.'

After conversion the speed of the 'Royal Sovereign' at the measured mile was eleven knots. At full power, as a three-decker, she realised a speed of 12·25 knots. The difference is due to her increased immersion, as a cupola ship, of fully three feet.

In July 1864, the ' Royal Sovereign ' commenced a series of trials of experimental firing, under the command of Captain Sherard Osborn, off the Isle of Wight. The experiments were continued, throughout the autumn, in all states of the weather, under the direction of the same officer, off the harbour of Portland, with highly satisfactory results. Viewed in the capacity of a guard-ship only, the ' Royal Sovereign ' fully justified the favourable opinion expressed in the columns of the *Times*. The motion was as easy in a sea-way as that of an ordinary broadside ship. The turret and the guns worked well, and, if the aggressive powers were taken into consideration, in combination with the special powers of resistance, the ' Royal Sovereign' was one of the most powerful vessels afloat at that date. Moreover, the ' Royal Sovereign ' could be manned with a very limited number of experienced seamen, and any trained artillery-men could fight the guns.

It has already been stated that the 'Prince Albert' was the first vessel built by the Admiralty on the cupola principle from original designs. The contract for the construction of this ship was given to Messrs. Samuda, and the arrangement of the cupola was carried out entirely under the supervision and by the advice of Captain Coles.

'Royal Sovereign's' trials.

The 'Prince Albert.'

The 'Prince Albert' was launched in May, 1864. The principal dimensions are : Length between perpendiculars, 240 feet; extreme breadth, 48 feet; depth in hold, 25 ft. 3 in.; displacement, 3,905 tons. The armour is $4\frac{1}{4}$ inches in thickness, on a teak backing of 18 inches. It extends from end to end of the ship, diminishing in thickness towards the extremities to $3\frac{1}{8}$ inches. The upper deck is protected by plating $1\frac{1}{2}$ inch in thickness, similar to the armoured deck of the 'Rolf Krake.' The weight of the iron used in the construction of the hull is 1,399 tons; the weight of the wood backing is 509 tons; the weight of the armour-plating is 255 tons; and that of the cables and hawsers 21 tons. The engines, by Messrs. Humphreys and Tennant, are of 2,128 indicated horse-power; and the draught of water, with engines and armament on board, is about 19 feet. On the upper deck stand the four turrets and the pilot tower. The turrets are placed in the middle line of the deck, which slopes downwards towards the water, and is fitted with shifting bulwarks. Two guns were originally mounted in two of the turrets, and a single gun in the two other turrets; the ship has now four guns in all.

CHAPTER X.

ABANDONING the chronological arrangement which has hitherto been chiefly followed, we shall proceed to treat of the progress of ironclad construction, by taking the ships of the various navies in classes and in groups.

The 'Taureau,' the first coast-defence ram in the French service, was ordered to be built at Toulon in 1863, from designs by M. Dupuy de Lôme. The 'Taureau' is a wooden ship, having a long protruding ram, specially strengthened to resist any strains to which it might be exposed in dealing a blow at an enemy. The hull properly so-called

The 'Taureau.

Fig. 116.

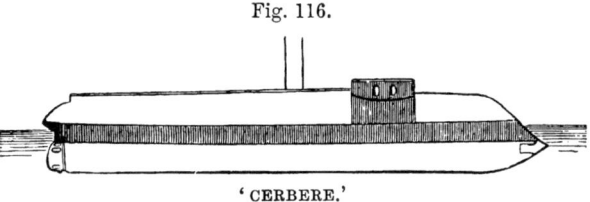

'CERBERE.'

has a freeboard of only 27½ inches. The deck is protected with 2-inch plates. A fixed turret is fitted in the forepart of the ship, pierced with a narrow port in the line of the keel, and armed with a 24 c/m. or 9½-inch gun. It was subsequently decided, whilst the building was proceeding, that the gun should be moveable, and should fire *en barbette*. The hull proper is covered with a 'turtle back' in sheet iron containing the quarters of the crew, and supporting a hurricane deck. The 'Taureau' is propelled by two independent engines, each working a screw.

The 'Taureau' having proved a very successful coast-defence vessel, it was determined to construct four additional vessels of similar type, named respectively the 'Bélier,' 'Tigre,' 'Bouledogue,' and 'Cerbère.'

The 'Bélier' class.

The main features of these designs are described by Baron Grivel, in his work entitled *Nos Nouveaux Navires*. The 'Taureau' must be regarded as the pioneer of the coast-service class. The improvements realised in later examples of the same class will be most readily

Fig. 117.

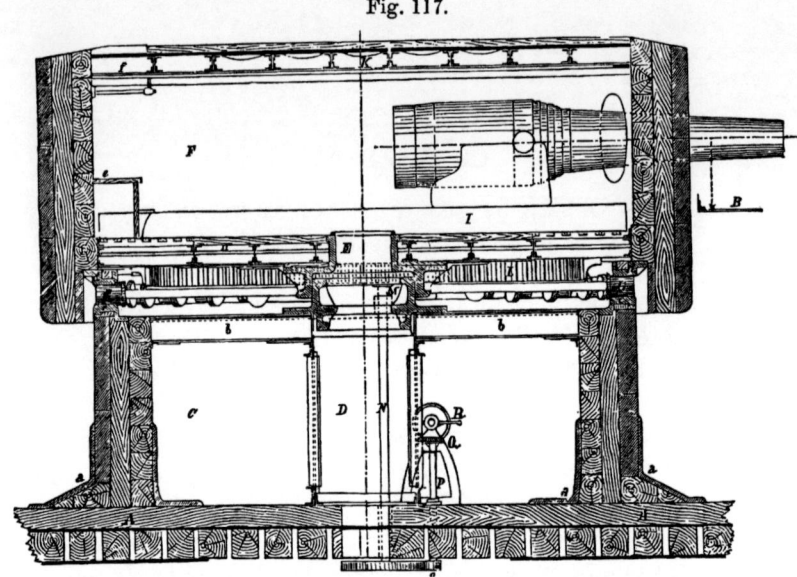

'CERBERE'S' TURRET.

A, Lower deck; B, Upper deck; C, Fixed turret, containing turning gear;
D, Shaft, serving as pivot and ammunition passage; F, Turret.

appreciated by comparing the principal dimensions of the 'Taureau' with the corresponding figures of the 'Bélier.'

	'Taureau.'	'Bélier.'
Length of water-line . .	196 ft. 10 in.	216 ft. 6 in.
Beam, extreme . . .	47 ft. 6 in.	52 ft. 6 in.
Extreme draught of water .	16 ft. 5 in.	17 ft. 9 in.
Displacement . . .	2,456 tons	3,456 tons
Nominal horse-power . .	480	530
Speed	— . .	12·59 knots
Armour at the water-line .	6 inches	8½ inches
Turret	Fixed	Rotatory
Armament	One 24 c/m. (9½-in.), or 15½-ton gun	Two 24 c/m. (9 in.), or 15½-ton guns.

The hulls of both vessels are of wood, the turtle-back or shelter alone being of iron. The 'Bélier' displaces a thousand tons more than the 'Taureau;' and while the displacement equals that of a small ship of the line of former days, the deck of the monitor is only sixteen inches above the water. The smallest opening in the turtle-back would expose vessels of this type to the most disastrous consequences. The 'Bélier' represents a considerable advance compared with the 'Taureau,' in speed, in thickness of armour, and in the height above the water, 2 ft. 3½ in., at which the guns are carried. In order to secure these indisputable advantages, it has been necessary to increase the draught of water, and to make a notable addition to the displacement. The turret of the 'Bélier' is revolving. The mechanical gear for turning the turret is the same as in the American monitors. Baron Grivel objects to the twin-screw system, and considers that the single screw, being better protected, presents decided advantages, for harbour-defence vessels of the 'Bélier' type, which will fight chiefly with the ram. The single screw has been adopted for the new coast-service ships of the 'Tonnerre' and 'Tempête' types.

Fig 118.

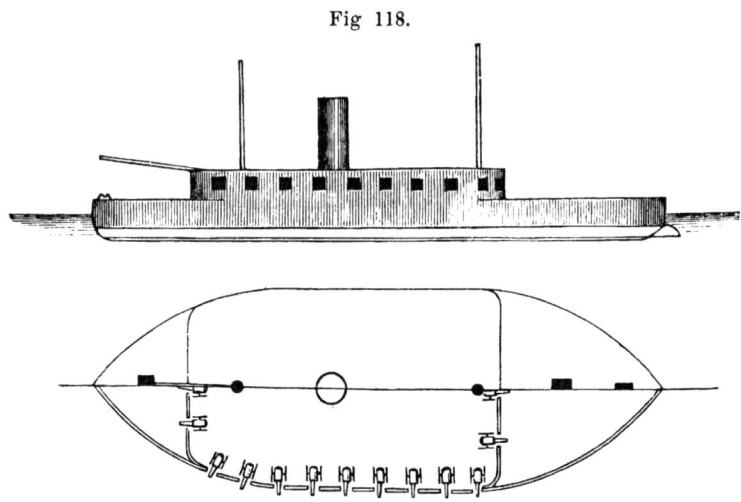

'ARROGANTE,' SHOWING NUMBER OF PORTS.

The armoured gunboat is represented in the French navy by a variety of types including the 'Arrogante,' 'Implacable,' 'Opiniâtre.' The 'Arrogante. The following description appeared in the *Broad Arrow* of March 29, 1879:—'The "Arrogante" was built at Nantes in 1864. Her length was 144 feet, breadth 48½ feet, and displacement 1,338 tons. She was built of iron, and plated with 4¾-inch armour at the water-line and 4½-inch armour on the top-sides. The plates rested upon 16-inch teak backing. Being for coast defence, the draught of water was only 8 ft. 8 in., and the freeboard 3 ft. 9 in. The armament consisted of nine 6-inch guns, which were fired from the upper deck, four being carried on each broadside and one in the bow. The "Arrogante" was propelled with twin screws driven by engines of 120 nominal or 480 indicated horse-power, and steamed 6¾ knots an hour. The total cost was 64,000*l.* From these particulars it will be seen that she was a small, inexpensive, and by no means formidable vessel. With light armament, thin armour, and little speed, she was far from representing the highest development of naval architecture fifteen years ago.

The *Pall Mall Gazette* of March 28, 1879, remarks:—'The "Arrogante" class are only lightly armoured, and would be altogether unable to contend with the far more heavily armed and armoured men of war now common in every European navy.'

In the last edition of the *Carnet de l'Officier de Marine* the armament of the 'Arrogante' is given as follows:—

In the battery: one 19 c/m. or 7½-inch 8-ton gun, and two 24 c/m. or 9½-inch 14½-ton guns.

On the upper deck: one 27 c/m. or 10·6-inch 23-ton gun, one 19 c/m., two 16 c/m. or 6¼-inch 5-ton guns, three 14 c/m. or 62-pounders, and two 10 c/m. or 22-pounders.

Fig. 119.

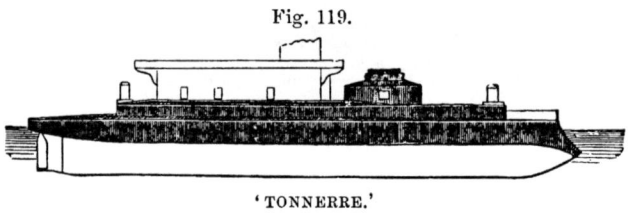

'TONNERRE.'

On March 19, 1879, the 'Arrogante' foundered off the Hyeres Islands, and fifty of her crew perished, at a distance of 1,100 yards from the shore.

In the general revision of the programme of construction for the French navy in 1872, a new type of ship for coast warfare was
'Tempête' and 'Tonnerre' classes. adopted. The second group of French coast-service[1] vessels consisted at first of the three rams of identical type named respectively 'Tempête,' 'Tonnant,' and 'Vengeur,' while the third group included three other rams of identical type named respectively, 'Tonnerre,' 'Fulminant,' and 'Furieux'; to these others of similar type, though of different dimensions and provided with a different armament, are being added. For a detailed description of these vessels we shall

[1] It should perhaps be pointed out that it is intended by the use of the term 'coast-service vessel' in the text to connote a class capable of rather more extended employment than would be expressed by the words 'coast-defence vessels.' Like our own 'Hotspur' and 'Rupert,' the former could proceed to, and be employed on, an enemy's coasts.

avail ourselves of M. Dislere's recent publication on the Maritime Section of the French Exhibition.

The 'Tonnerre,' a first-rate coast-service vessel, was laid down in 1872 from designs by M. de Bussy, Director of Naval Construction, and sent to sea in 1877. The trial trips were completed in 1878. The principal dimensions of this new class are :—

Length of hull at the water-line	241 ft. 9 in.
Beam .	57 ft. 9 in.
Depth in hold	20 ft. 7 in.
Mean draught of water	20 ft. 7 in.
Displacement	5,580 tons
Immersed surface of midship section .	1,099 sq. ft.

The 'Tonnerre.'

Fig. 120

The weight of the hull and backing is 2,000 tons, that of the armour 2,070 tons. The general features of the design are a low hull armoured all round the sides and ends, and covered in by an armoured deck, above which rises a long central breastwork, with one revolving turret above its fore end. The freeboard of the principal deck is 3 feet above the water-line amidships. The breastwork, which is 131 feet long, occupies about half the length of the ship in its central part, and is retired

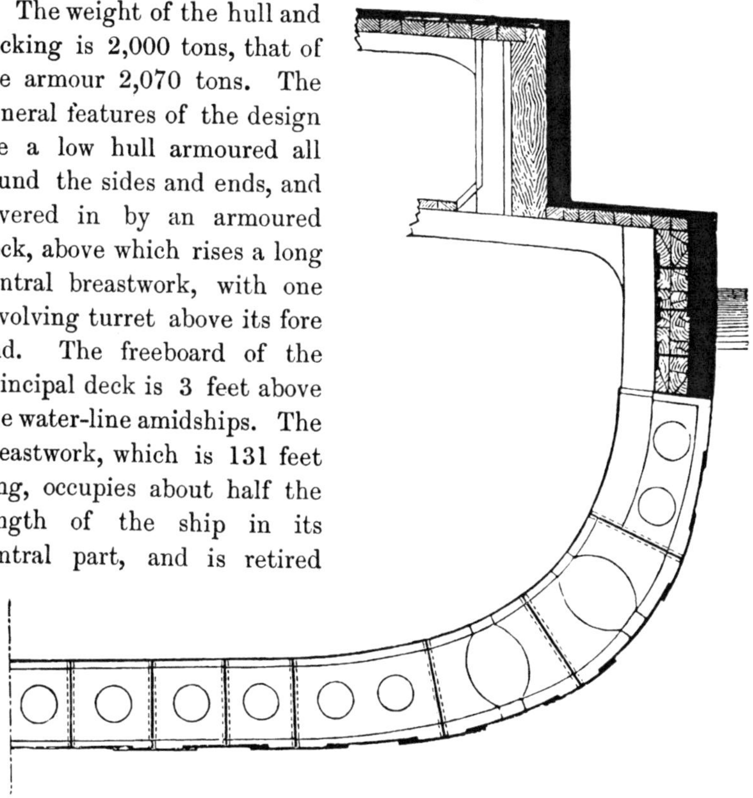

'TONNERRE,' SECTION THROUGH ARMOURED BREASTWORK.

six feet from the ship's side. This breastwork, which has a height of 6 ft. 6 in., contains the revolving turret. A narrow superstructure, eight feet broad abaft the turret, supports the hurricane deck. In the turret, on which stands the captain's conning-tower, are two 27 c/m.

(10½-in.) guns on Armstrong hydraulic-slide carriages, but there is space enough to admit of two larger guns of 32 c/m. (12 inches) if desired. A very high hurricane deck is erected above the breastwork, with hammock nettings along the sides, and a small gun at each corner. On this the boats can be stowed. Four bronze 12 c/m. or 26-pdr. guns are mounted at the four rounded corners of the hurricane deck or *pont d'ouragan*, as it is termed by the French, although *pont de manœuvre* would appear to be a more appropriate designation. Mr. King says (*War Ships and Navies of the World*, 1880, p. 22):—

'The English method of revolving the entire weight of the turret and guns on truncated cones, instead of the objectionable central spindle, has been adopted, but the turret also revolves round a fixed central shaft, 4 ft. 8 in. in diameter, on which is the pilot-house built on top of the turret and protected by armour. From this a clear all-round view can be obtained by the commanding officer, who is at the same time in intimate and close connection with the gunners, instead of being in a distant conning-tower as in the English ships. The armament at present mounted in the turret consists of two rifled guns of the French breech-loading pattern, each about 38 tons in weight and having a calibre of 12½ inches, and four small guns on deck. Another advantage is to be found here in the breech-loading system, which admits the use of a longer gun, thus adding to the power of penetration. Besides, as the gun is sponged and loaded by men inside the turret, the complication of mechanism is reduced, facility and rapidity of firing and loading are increased, and the danger of double-loading, which, it is supposed, caused the explosion on board the "Thunderer," is avoided.'

The funnel stands in the fore part of the hurricane deck. The hammock nettings are placed on the sides, where also the boats are hung on davits. The remainder of the deck is kept free for working the ship. Before and abaft the breastwork a small superstructure, of the same height as the latter, is devoted to the accommodation of the warrant officers.

The hull is built of steel on the bracket system, except the outside sheathing, which is of iron plate. A double bottom occupies two-thirds of the length. There is no keel of the ordinary construction, the necessary longitudinal strength being secured by a double garboard. Eight watertight bulkheads athwartships, and others fore and aft, divide the ship into numerous separate compartments, four of which are occupied by the boilers. The compartments of the hold and the double bottom are kept clear of water by

TONNERRE.

a complete system of pipes and sluice-valves. The stern of the 'Tonnerre' forms an open vault, which closely resembles that of the 'Rochambeau,' and constitutes a very characteristic feature of the French coast-service vessels. The coefficient of weight of hull, not including the backing, is only ·306.

The armour-plates at the water-line belt are 13 inches in thickness, on the breastwork 11¾ inches, and on the turret 13¾ inches. The principal deck, outside the breastwork, and the breastwork deck are protected with 2-inch plates. The engines of the 'Tonnerre' were formerly in the 'Normandie,' but some modern improvements have been introduced. The vessel is propelled by a single screw. There are eight boilers worked at a mean pressure of 32 lbs, with a grate surface of 635·3 sq. ft. At the load draught of 20 ft. 10 in., and with 4,166 indicated horse-power, the 'Tonnerre' attained a speed of 14·7 knots. Starting at a speed of 12 knots, a circle 284 yards in diameter was completed in 3 minutes 48 seconds. The 'Tonnerre' has stowage for 270 tons of coal. The steering apparatus consists of two rudders 4 ft. 7 in. apart from axis to axis, steered with independent tillers. The motion of the steering wheel is transmitted to an intermediate tiller, and thence to the two tillers attached directly to the rudders, and working the latter simultaneously. The supply of ammunition is fixed at a hundred rounds. These vessels are mastless.

The 'Tonnerre' and the 'Tempête' are, in the opinion of Baron Grivel, perfect and well-considered types. The 'Tonnerre,' from her speed and deep draught of water, represents a class of vessel which may be employed to sally forth from the great commercial harbours, and to carry on an offensive defence. The great defect is that she draws eighteen feet of water. It has been thought proper, in view of the necessity of great armour-protection, to resort to considerable displacement and a consequent large expenditure of money.

The 'Tonnerre' having been sharply criticised in the debates in the French Chambers on the Naval Estimates in 1879, M. Lebelin de Dionne was deputed, on the part of the French Admiralty, to reply to the attacks which had been made. He asserted that the vessel steamed one knot an hour faster than the estimated speed. The heeling of the ship, when making the circle, which had been strongly animadverted upon, was due, as he explained, to the diameter of that circle, which was smaller than that of any ship in any navy, and some modifications had been introduced, which would correct the tendency to heel when describing a circle of small diameter.

Captain Tromp, of the Dutch Artillery, tells us that : ' Other vessels of this class were successively put on the stocks ; the " Fulminant " and " Furieux " at Cherbourg, the " Indomptable " at Lorient, the " Terrible " at Brest, the " Caïman " at Toulon, and the " Requin " at Rochefort. The " Fulminant " has the same armour and ordnance as the " Tonnerre." The " Furieux " has thicker armour, but the other details are the same as in the earlier examples of the same type. The other vessels had greater dimensions, the displacement being increased by about 1,600 tons, and the draught of water by nearly 1½ feet. The armour is much stouter, and an armament of 42 c/m. (72-ton) guns is contemplated.'

The
'Tempête.'

The second rate coast-defence vessel 'Tempête,' laid down in 1872 from designs by M. de Bussy, Director of Naval Construction, was launched in 1877.

The
'Tonnant,'
and
'Vengeur.'

The 'Tempête,' 'Tonnant,' and 'Vengeur' belong to the second class of non-rigged coast-defence vessels, and are intended exclusively for the defence of the coasts and harbours of France. Their general plan almost exactly resembles that just described. The differences in point of dimensions are shown in the subjoined table :—

Length at the water-line . . .	241 ft. 6 in.
Breadth at the water-line . . .	57 ft. 9 in.
Depth in hold	16 ft. 9 in.
Draught of water . . .	16 ft. 9 in.
Displacement . . .	4,524 tons
Immersed surface of midship section .	889·6 sq. ft.

The water-line and turret are protected with 11¾-inch plating, and the armoured deck with 2-inch plates. The turret is armed with two 27 c/m. or 10½ inch guns.

In the plan of the hull the 'Tempête' differs from the 'Tonnerre' in the depth in hold, which is reduced by 3 ft. 7 in., and in the displacement, which is less by 1,050 tons. The armour on the belt and the turret has a uniform thickness of 11¾ inches as compared with the 13-inch and 13¾-inch plating of the 'Tonnerre.' The other details of construction and armament are the same. The engines, made at Indret, on the Woolf system, are to indicate 1,500 horse-power. They drive a single screw, and are expected to realise a speed of ten knots.

Of the French coast-defence ships the 'Taureau' was launched in 1863, 'Cerbère' in 1868, 'Bélier' in 1870, 'Tigre' in 1871, 'Boule-dogue' in 1872, 'Tonnerre' in 1875, 'Tempête' and 'Fulminant' in 1876, and 'Furieux' in 1877. The 'Tonnant' and 'Vengeur,' and the other ships of the 'Tonnerre' type mentioned above, are still in construction.[1]

The following description of the French armourclad 'Terrible,' is taken from the *Revue Maritime* for May, 1881 :— The 'Terrible.'

'This cruising armourclad (*cuirassé d'escadre*) building at Brest has recently been successfully launched. The "Terrible" has been built from the designs of M. Sabattier, Director of *Matériel* at the Ministry of Marine. She is intended for coast service [a phrase which it is not quite easy to reconcile with the designation *cuirassé d'escadre* given above; possibly capacity for proceeding to the coast of an enemy not very distant may be implied]. Her dimensions are the following :—

Length between the perpendiculars . .	271 ft. 9 in.
Beam extreme	59 feet
Depth in hold . . .	23 ft. 6 in.
Draught of water . . .	22 ft. 9 in.
Displacement	7,168 tons.

'The armour of this ship, composed of iron and steel, will have a maximum thickness of about 19·6 inches, and will weigh 2,670 tons. The armament will consist of two 42 c/m. (16½-inch) 75-ton guns in turrets, and of four 10 c/m. (26-pounders) on the upper deck.

'The engines, from the Creusot Factory, will have an indicated horse-power of 4,800. They are composed of :—

'1. Two independent engines, on the vertical system with three cylinders, each working a separate screw.

'2. Of four auxiliary vertical engines to work the circulating pumps.

'3. Of four auxiliary horizontal engines, on the Varall, Elwell, and Middleton system, for working the ventilating apparatus.

'The steam-generating apparatus will be composed of four independent groups, each comprising three cylindrical boilers with two furnaces apiece.'

The English colonies requiring ironclads for coast defence, Sir Edward Reed produced a well-conceived design, in which the special features of the Coles and Ericsson systems were combined. In this

[1] Ships building, 'Caïman,' &c. Vice-Admiral Pothuau in his speech on the Navy Estimates, delivered in the French Chamber on November 29, 1878, described the 'Caïman' as intended for a coast-service vessel of the first class, having a displacement of 7,200 tons, to be armed with 72-ton guns, and to be armoured with 22-inch plates. The 'measured mile' speed would be 14½ knots. Though the French have been slow to adopt the revolving turret, they are now adding a considerable number of vessels fitted with it to their navy.

type of monitor a well-armoured breastwork surrounds the base of the turrets, and the lower part of the funnel and the hatchways are also protected. The 'Cerberus' was the first ship of this type, and her construction forms an important incident in the history of armoured shipbuilding.

The 'Cerberus,' 'Magdala,' and 'Abyssinia.'

Two other ships of very similar type, the 'Magdala' and 'Abyssinia,' were laid down together with the 'Cerberus' in 1866. These ships, with a draught of only sixteen feet, carry four 18-ton guns in two turrets, and steam about eleven knots an hour. The armour-plating is 8 to 9 inches thick; the exposed sides are only three feet in height, and the decks are made shellproof, being plated with $1\frac{1}{2}$ inches of iron over ten inches of teak. The displacement is 3,000 tons; the metacentric height is 20 inches.[1] The 'Magdala' and her consort are commended in the *Broad Arrow* as the handiest vessels for harbour defence that have ever been built. The ratio of their offensive and defensive powers to their total displacement has in no

Fig. 121.

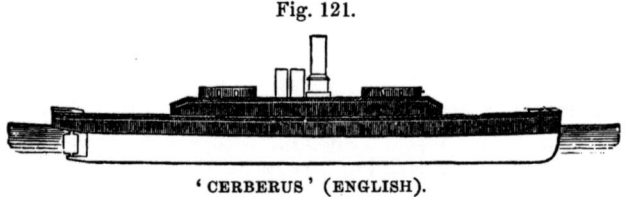

'CERBERUS' (ENGLISH).

case been exceeded without running great risks in regard to buoyancy and stability. They accomplished the voyage out to Bombay, a large portion of the distance being traversed under sail, in the winter season.

The 'Hotspur.'

The 'Hotspur,' the first ship which really fulfilled the idea of a coast-service vessel, was commenced in the same year as the ships 1866 already mentioned. The Admiralty had long hesitated before adopting the 'Monitor' type. The design finally approved presented several important improvements upon the type which had been adopted in America.

The 'Hotspur' may be described as originally a monitor armed with a spur and with a single gun mounted in an oval fixed turret. The base of the turret and the principal hatchways are protected by an armour-plated breastwork, which reaches to within a few inches of the lower sill of the port. The low upper-deck outside the breast-

---

[1] The exact dimensions of these ships are:—

						Length	Beam	Displacement	I.H.P.
Magdala	.	.	.	.	.	. 225 ft.	45 ft.	3,344 tons	1,440
Cerberus	.	.	.	.	.	. do.	do.	do.	1,369
Abyssinia	.	.	.	.	.	. do.	42	2,901	960

work is only 3 or 4 feet above the water. It is protected against the effects of plunging fire by a thick iron-plating. The upper deck being free from any obstruction a perfect all-round fire can be obtained.

M. Marchal gives the following description of the ' Hotspur ':—

' This vessel,' he says, ' is the first armoured ram constructed in England. She is intended specially for ramming, and the gun is only to be used as a preparation for the use of the more formidable weapon. She represents a type of ship which originated with the French Admiralty, who had several rams afloat before the construction of a vessel of the same type was attempted in England.

' A revolving tower was not originally fitted for the protection of the " Hotspur's " gun, probably from the apprehension that it would suffer injury in the sudden shock which might be experienced in ramming. The single 25-ton gun was placed in a sort of battery pierced with four large ports, which rendered the interior extremely vulnerable. It was a nest for projectiles.' The armour is somewhat

Figs. 122 and 123.

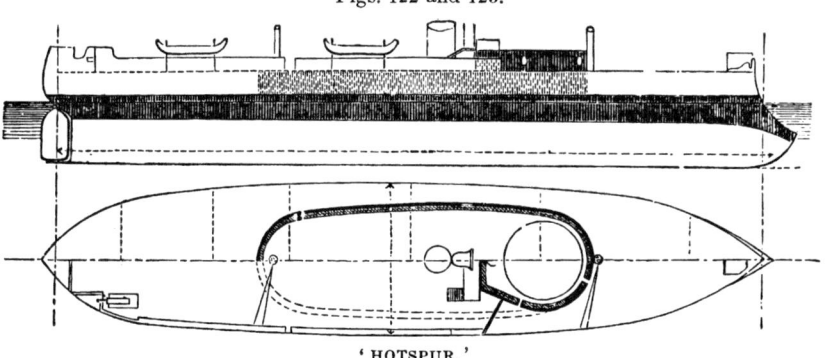

' HOTSPUR.'

thin, being 7¾ inches on the curved parts, and 6 inches on the after bulkhead.

The water-line is protected with armour of eleven inches in the centre, diminishing to seven inches towards the bow and stern. The armour is carried down to the spur in such a manner as to add considerably to its strength. Above the armour is an armoured deck plated with 2½-inch plates in the bow, 2¾-inch in the centre, and 2-inch towards the stern. The 'Hotspur' has been altered in many important respects by Messrs. Laird at Birkenhead. The principal modification has been the substitution of a revolving turret with two guns in the place of the fixed turret with a turntable inside, with which she was originally fitted. The new turret is protected with compound armour, having 2¾ inches of steel on the face, and 5¾ inches of iron in the rear part of the plates.

The following description of the 'Glatton' appeared in the *Times* on the occasion of the 'Hotspur'-'Glatton' experiment :—

'Her sides are encased with iron plates twelve inches at the top, and decreasing in thickness below the water-line. A chain runs round her instead of bulwarks. Above the deck on which one first alights is an iron structure called a flying deck, used more as a look-out than anything else, and which, if destroyed in case of action, would not be of the slightest disadvantage. The "Glatton's" turret rises above the deck to a considerable height, and is protected by immense plates of iron 12 inches thick, increasing to an additional 2 inches near the portholes. The turret is nearly 40 feet in diameter. With their muzzles almost close to the pent-up portholes were the "Glatton's" cannon, consisting of two 25-ton guns—beautiful-looking engines of destruction. By the aid of the

Figs. 124 and 125.

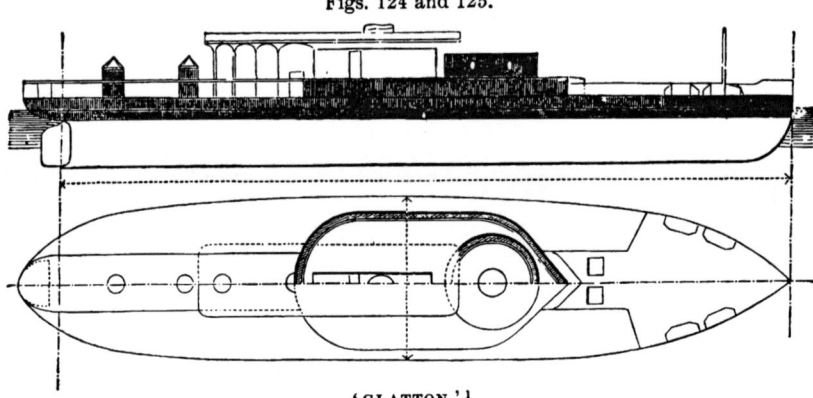

'GLATTON.' [1]

machinery only eleven men are needed to work one of these immense guns, and the turret's crew consists but of 34 men. The turret is made to revolve by either hand or steam-power. The process of lifting the 600-lb. shot into the turret is very easily accomplished by means of pulleys and ropes. The machinery department is exceedingly well worth a visit. The sides of the vessel have armour-plates of twelve or fourteen inches in thickness, decreasing in size as they get below the water-line.'

The remarks of the correspondent of the *Times* may be supplemented by those of the author of *Die Marine*, who says : 'This ship, designed to serve a double purpose, was not a success. It was intended that this ship should, in case of necessity, co-operate with the Fleet, but her seagoing qualities were not such as are required

---

[1] The under-water spur or ram is not shown in the drawing.

GLATTON.

in a cruiser. All that the "Glatton" could do would be to gain the enemy's coast, and take part in an attack on the coast defences ; although the deep draught, which was given her with a view to her keeping the sea, is a serious disadvantage when navigating in the immediate vicinity of the land.'

M. Marchal remarks : ' The " Glatton " was conceived as an engine of war adapted to attack fortresses and naval ports. As at that time the French coasts were chiefly in contemplation, the limitation of the draught of water was not considered of primary importance. The chief aim was to produce the smallest vessel which could carry armour of twelve inches. Hence Mr. Reed, contrary to the wishes of the Admiralty, was able to give the new monitor one turret only. With two turrets it would have been necessary to reduce the plating by nearly $3\frac{1}{8}$ inches.'

It was thought desirable to test the resistance of armour by actual experiment, and the 'Glatton' and the 'Hotspur' were despatched to Portland for that purpose. On July 5, 1872, a series of shots were fired at the 'Glatton' from the 25-ton gun of the 'Hotspur' with results detailed in the following report originally published in the *Times* : ' The first shot went for nothing. The second struck the turret in its weakest part—in the centre of the turret wall, upon a bolt-head, and upon the lower edge of the upper 14-inch armour plate at its longitudinal junction with the lower plate, in perfect line with the mark, although lower than intended. The shot striking thus in the weakest place, lifted the upper plate, or rather forced it upward and over the face of the backing, until its lower edge was separated from the upper edge of the lower plate to a distance of $2\frac{1}{2}$ inches, the upper edge of the lower plate where the shot penetrated being depressed nearly one inch by the sheer downward force of the shot. The shot penetrated beyond the plating to some distance into the timber backing, and then broke up at the base, leaving its head embedded in the teak behind the 14-inch plate. Inside the turret the inner end of the bolt struck by the shot was found to have driven in and fractured the inner skin or iron lining. A score or two of rivet-heads were also shaken from off the skin plating, and there can be no doubt that, had the men belonging to the guns been in the turret at the time, several lives might have been lost and many of the men wounded. One of the inner and one of the outer frames of the turret walls were broken, the timber backing immediately behind the shot's blow was bulged inwards at least seven inches, and the inner skin was burst open by the end of the bolt driven in by the shot to a depth of 4 ft. 6 in., and helped to make matters at first sight look very ugly indeed inside

The 'Hotspur'—'Glatton' experiment, from the Times.

the turret. Still, with all the immense striking force of the shot, estimated at a little over 6,100 ft. tons, there was no thorough penetration. The piece of fractured lining was cut off by the engineers of the ship in a very short space of time, and then steam and hand power being successively applied, all the machinery at its base for turning it, as well as its central bearings, was found to be not in the least damaged, and the turret revolved with the same facility as it did before the shot was fired. The Palliser shot had left a tremendous mark, but, in the opinion of all the officials present, the turret, with its guns, was perfectly fit to go into action. None of the gun-fittings or gear were injured in any way. The shot from the 25-ton gun had, in fact, done its best, and under such favourable conditions as could not well occur in actual engagement with an enemy's ship under steam, and had in the most decided manner succumbed to the turret. The damage done to the inner skin of the " Glatton's" turret in no way affects injuriously the principle of the turret. It merely suggests the necessity for lining the turrets of our monitors with a much thicker inner skin than is the rule at present. Plating of two, three, or four inches in thickness may possibly be adopted for the inner skin lining of our monitors in future. The second shot fired at the turret not only most effectually did the work it was intended to do, but also as effectually did the work which had been laid down for a third shot, intended for the glacis plate, and saved the trouble and time which would otherwise have been taken up in inclining the 'Glatton' and firing the third shot. The mark upon the turret upon which the gun was trained was on the lower ring of armour-plating, between the gunports, and eighteen inches above the bottom of the plating and the glacis plate. The shot was lower than intended, taking the glacis plate in its entire breadth, making a deep indentation, and cracking the plate through, but doing no material damage to the underneath deck plating or beams. From the plate the shot struck the bottom of the turret plating, penetrated to a depth of fifteen inches, and then rebounded broken up on to the deck in front of the turret. No damage whatever was done to the interior of the turret or to any of the gun-fittings or their slides. There was simply the hole the shot had made in the armour-plate to a depth of fifteen inches, and that was all. The inner skin of the turret was not even bulged. This was thought quite sufficient, as establishing in the most indisputable manner the free working of the turret under the heaviest fire, without much danger of being jammed or of damage to the gun slides. Three animals, unwilling occupants of the turret, had also suffered no injury. The ports were next unplugged, and with Mr. Goschen

CYCLOPS.

and other members of the Board present, the guns were loaded with full powder charges and shot, and fired out to seaward over the breakwater. The carriages and gear were found to work in the most perfect manner, and this test brought the trial to a close.'

The powers of the 'Glatton' have recently been increased by fitting her with arrangements for launching the Fish torpedo. Experiments have been carried out from this ship at Spithead, with the view of perfecting the firing of the Whitehead torpedo right ahead when under way. *Torpedoexperiments from the Times.*

In 1870, under the pressure of the anxiety awakened by the Franco-German war, the English Admiralty determined to build four ships, the 'Cyclops,' 'Gorgon,' 'Hecate,' and 'Hydra.' They were of moderate draught, and specially designed for coast service. *The 'Cyclops' class.*

Fig. 126.

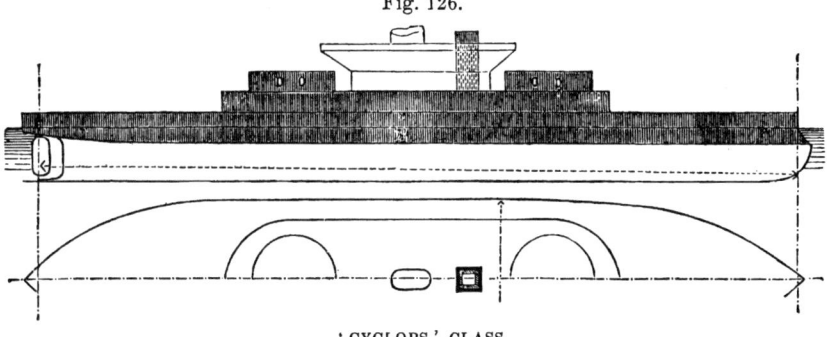

'CYCLOPS' CLASS.

The principal dimensions of the 'Cyclops,' as compared with the 'Glatton,' are given in the following table :—

	'Cyclops.'	'Glatton.'
Tonnage	3,430 (2,107)	4,912 (2,709)
Horse-power	1,660 (250)	2,868 (500)
Armour	8-inch	12-inch
Guns	Four 18-ton	Two 25-ton
Speed	10 knots	12 knots
Coal storage	120 tons	240 tons
Draught	Aft 15½ ft., forward 15½ ft.	Aft 22 ft., forward 20 ft.
Crew	150 men	200 men.

Mr. Barnaby, in his paper *On Modern Ships of War* read at the United Service Institution on January 29, 1872, describes the points of difference between the 'Glatton' and the 'Cyclops' as follows :— 'I come now to the types of "coast-defence ships," viz., the "Glatton" and "Cyclops" classes. The former has 12-inch armour on the sides, and carries two 25-ton guns, with a speed of twelve knots. The latter has 8-inch armour only, and carries four 18-ton guns, with a *Mr. Barnaby on the 'Cyclops' and 'Glatton.'*

speed of ten knots. The cost of the " Glatton " is within 50,000*l.* of the cost of the " Vanguard," and exceeds the cost of the " Cyclops " by 70,000*l.* The ships of the " Cyclops " class cost about 140,000*l.* each for hull and engines complete.'

To make the ' Cyclops ' class thoroughly seaworthy, superstructures are necessary. The necessity for additional freeboard was strongly urged in the course of the discussion on the naval prize essays of 1878. Captain W. Dawson, R.N., said :—

Captain
Dawson,
R.N.

'It is a matter of common sense that ships that won't swim in all weathers are not specially good for coast defence, and that ships drawing 20 feet of water are not essentially the best for the defence of our small and shallow harbours. I may be told that these vessels, referring to the ' Gorgon ' and sister ships, are not unseaworthy because, in the month of June, they are sent a few miles outside deep-water harbours with a squadron of " nurses," provided with boats to pick up their crews, and under one of the most careful Admirals of the Fleet, who would take care that if the barometer falls, they would be sent away from the coast they are to defend into one of the ports near at hand.'

Admiral
Ryder.

The debate was continued by Admiral Ryder:—

'There have been so many Committees, and so much inquiry into the qualification of the various classes of ships, that I dare say that the reports of some of these Committees may have escaped the recollection of gentlemen who perhaps at the time were interested in them. I should like to place on record the opinion of the Committee of Designs, of which Lord Dufferin was the chairman, and six naval officers and numerous civilians were members, of that class. As regards

The
'Gorgon.'

the " Gorgon " class, which Captain Dawson so severely criticised, I think the Committee of which I was a member went almost further than he did in their virtual condemnation of this class as seagoers. Their unanimous report was this, that " if a certain superstructure, extending along a good portion of each side, was not put on they would be safe to go from port to port only in fine weather." That is a very startling statement to make about ships of war. Now that superstructure has not been put on ! I do not know why it has not been put on. It is five years since it was suggested by us that it should be put on, and we carefully considered the phrase given above. I remember there was a considerable discussion about the word " only," but at last it was put in; and those ships are stamped with this character—that they are in their present condition safe to go from port to port only in fine weather.'

It is understood that proposals have been submitted to the

Board of Admiralty from the Controller's Department for this alteration ; and it is much to be regretted that the suggestions of the professional officers have not hitherto been acted upon. On the last occasion when the ' Cyclops' was in commission she formed part of Admiral Sir Cooper Key's Particular Service Squadron. When the broadside vessels were despatched in command of the Admiral to Berehaven, the ' Cyclops' and her consorts remained behind at Portland. If such hesitation was felt as to the despatch of these vessels on a coasting voyage in the summer season, they can scarcely be accepted even as coast-defence vessels for service in the English Channel.

Commander J. B. Haye, in his essay on *Great Britain's Maritime* Commander *Power*, reprinted by the United Service Institution, considered it Haye, R.N. sufficient if the ' Cyclops' class can pass in-shore, and along the coast from Dover to Yarmouth, and enter the Medway or Harwich at any time of tide, and in any but exceptionally rough weather. For the

Fig. 127.

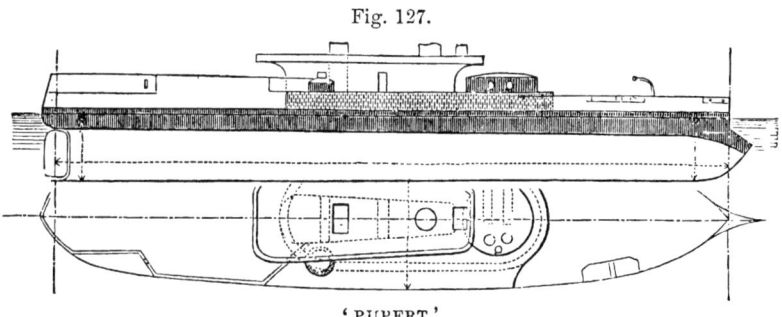

' RUPERT.'

' Glatton' and her subdivision he demands a higher standard of seaworthiness, that of ability to keep the sea during a winter gale in the North Sea. Commander Haye properly remarks that it is a defect common to the ' Cyclops' and all the earlier turret ships that they are unable to carry small guns on the upper deck for defence against torpedo boats without confining the arc of training of their turret guns. Such guns, however, should be mounted on the superstructure, which should be sufficiently strong to receive them. Gun and torpedo boats can be destroyed by very light guns, and these should not be wanting in armoured ships. For most naval operations mixed armaments of light and heavy guns, and flotillas combining armoured with unarmoured ships, are necessary.

The ' Rupert' completes the series of ships of the class now under The consideration. ' Rupert.'

The following description is taken from the *Times* :—

'The "Rupert" is an iron armour-plated turret ship. Her dimensions are : length over all, 250 feet; extreme breadth, 53 feet; depth in hold, 19 ft. 10½ in.; burden, 3,159 tons. The first plate of the "Rupert" was laid in the dock on June 9, 1870. She is built from designs prepared by Sir E. J. Reed, when Chief Constructor of the Navy. The broadside of the ship is protected with heavy armour-plates; above the water-line and on the turret they are twelve inches thick, fastened to a backing of twelve inches of teak, with an inner iron skin 1¼ inch thick. The turret is protected by a breastwork. Though so well armoured and heavily armed, the great feature of the vessel is her ram. The fighting power of the vessel is subservient to the ramming power. The ram, a great mass of iron, projects some nine or ten feet from the bow of the ship. The point, when the vessel is fully loaded, will be about eight feet below the water. The armament of the ship consists of four guns; two 18-ton guns in the turret, and two lighter guns on her weather deck. The armament is protected by a breastwork which completely surrounds the base of the turret, and encloses an elliptical-shaped space, extending over more than two-thirds of the vessel's length. On this breastwork, which is plated with 12-inch iron, a flying deck is laid. The guns are carried eleven feet above the water. The "Rupert" is only intended for coast service. But she will have two light masts and a few small fore and aft sails, which are merely intended to be used under special circumstances as auxiliary to her steam-power.'

This vessel exhibits a great improvement as compared with the 'Hotspur' previous to the recent alterations. The displacement is increased. The turret is moveable, and the base, as in the case of the vessels of the 'Cyclops' type, is protected with a breastwork. The 'Rupert' is a coast vessel capable of doing excellent service.

Fig. 128.

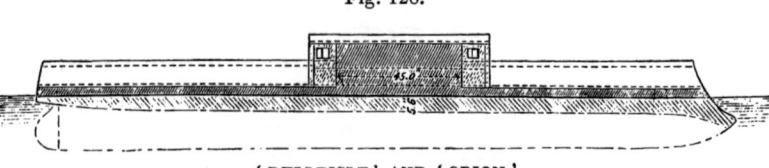

' BELLEISLE ' AND ' ORION.'

The 'Belleisle' and 'Orion.' An addition was made to the coast-service armourclads of the British navy in 1878 by the purchase of the ' Belleisle ' and ' Orion.' These are sister ships, built by Messrs. Samuda and engined by Messrs. Maudslay. In the *Times* of August 12, 1878, the ' Belleisle ' is described as an armour-plated corvette with a raised octagon

BELLE ISLE.

fighting battery amidships, mounting four 25-ton muzzle-loading rifle guns. Two of the guns fight on the starboard, and two on the port side. They are so arranged that they can fire a direct fore and aft or cross fire within a range of ninety yards. There is ample room to work the guns in the battery, which is an octagon of about sixty feet, while the guns, which are somewhat short in the chase, are sixteen feet in length. They are rifled with eight grooves, and on an increasing twist. The shot rises through a lift under the muzzle, and is carried along a bar overhead to the position most convenient for loading, the cartridges also coming up from below through openings on the centre line.

The engines have four cylinders, each 65 inches in diameter, and a 2 ft. 6 in. stroke, making one hundred revolutions a minute. The surface condensers have a total area of 9,000 square feet. The boilers, four in number, have in all twenty furnaces, with a total grate surface of 466 square feet, and a total heating surface of 11,610 square feet. The horse-power indicated on the trial was 4,020.

The general dimensions of these vessels, which were designed by Ahmed Pacha for the Turkish Admiralty, are as follows: length, 245 feet; beam, 52 feet; depth, 22 feet; displacement, 4,700 tons; mean draught of water, 19 ft. 3 in. The thickness of the armour is twelve inches amidships, diminishing as usual towards the extremities, and extending from five feet below the water-line to the main deck. The thickness of the plating protecting the battery varies from $9\frac{1}{2}$ inches to $10\frac{1}{2}$ inches. The side armour reaches to the top of the central battery, which it entirely encircles. The main deck is nearly level with the water, and is composed of 3-inch plates of armour encased in oak. Upon the main deck is erected a spar or hurricane deck, containing the officers' cabins. This superstructure could be shot away in action without injury to the armour-defended battery and submerged hull.

One important feature in the ship is the handiness in answering the helm. An entire circle was made with engines going at full speed in 3 min. 30 sec., and in a diameter of 420 yards. The trial was made with the guns and all the ammunition, excepting powder, on board, and a full complement of coal and stores. The draught on trial was 17 ft. 7 in. forward and 18 feet aft. The mean of six runs, with and against the tide, gave an average speed of 12·99 knots.

On the occasion of the purchase of the 'Belleisle' and 'Orion' a comparison was instituted in the *Broad Arrow* between these vessels and the coast-defence vessels built originally for the British navy. 'The "Paykisherreef," such is the original Turkish name, and the sister

From the Broad Arrow.

ship compare favourably with our own vessels of the same dimensions. They carry 300 tons of coal, which will drive them at full speed for about 3½ days, or a distance of nearly 1,100 miles. The only vessels in the Royal Navy which at all approach the dimensions of the " Paykisherreef" and her consort are the " Hotspur " and " Rupert," the former being somewhat smaller, and the latter rather larger than the Turkish vessels. The " Rupert " is the fairest comparison we can institute ; and her dimensions are 250 feet long, 53 feet broad, displacing 5,322 tons on a mean draught of 22 ft. 6 in. The " Rupert's " armour ranges from twelve inches to six inches, the thickness at the water-line being eleven inches. She carries 350 tons of coal, and her indicated horse-power is 4,200, which gives her about the same distance-steaming power as the Turkish vessels. But the " Rupert " has only two 25-ton guns, and one other of smaller size. It will thus be seen that although the " Rupert " displaces 600 tons more than the " Paykisherreef," she is yet inferior to the latter both in respect to armour and armament. The Turkish vessels draw 39 inches less water, and will each cost probably 20,000l. less than the " Rupert." The price given for the " Paykisherreef," now named the " Belleisle," we believe is about 230,000l., including guns and outfit.'

The ram of these ships projects ten feet beyond the bows under the water-line, eight feet of the ram being a solid forging of iron. The watertight compartments are constructed without any doors. The ' Belleisle ' and the ' Orion ' would be most useful additions to our fleet in the Mediterranean or the Red Sea. They are not adapted for ocean navigation, but their sea-going qualities would be in all probability sufficient for service in narrower waters.

We now proceed to describe several types of coast defenders which have been constructed by the other maritime powers, namely, the Russian circular batteries or Popoffkas, the German armoured gunboats of the ' Wespe ' type, the Brazilian monitor the ' Solimões,' and some smaller and older Danish craft.

Popoffkas. Captain Goulaeff. The circular vessels have excited the deepest interest in naval circles from the distinguished position of their designer and the high praise which Sir E. Reed has bestowed on them. These coast vessels were designed to protect the mouth of the Dnieper and the harbour of Nikolaeff. Captain Goulaeff, in a paper read at the Institute of Naval Architects, introduced his description of the Popoffkas with the following observations: ' It was one of the most important conditions for the defence of the Black Sea coasts that the vessels should float at the very limited draught of water of about thirteen feet. The only then existing types of vessels which fulfilled this condition were the unarmoured gunboats. Every armoured ship, if built of ordinary form, and designed to carry heavy guns and thick armour, required much greater immersion. Unarmoured gunboats, however, were not considered efficient, because a single shot from an insignificant gun is sufficient to penetrate their sides, and sink them with all hands on board. An entirely new class of vessels was requisite to carry heavy guns and armour on a small draught of water, and no type of vessels could have been better adapted to the purpose than the circular; because no hull of any other form and of the same weight could have enclosed so great a displacement upon the same draught of water.'

Among the many innovations introduced by Sir E. Reed, after he went to the Admiralty in 1863, the increased proportions of beam to length as compared with the ships of the monitor type are not the least remarkable   The tendency towards reduction of length reached its culminating point in Messrs. Elder's design for a circular ship for coast defence.   It appeared to Vice-Admiral Popoff that the proposal which Mr. Elder had introduced in 1868 was particularly adapted to the requirements of the Black Sea squadron, inasmuch as it gives the smallest area of side in proportion to any given displacement, and thus combines the twofold advantages of increased thickness of armour with a reduced displacement.

Two batteries, the 'Novgorod' and 'Vice-Admiral Popoff,' were Dimensions. constructed on this system. Their principal dimensions are compared in a table given in Captain Goulaeff's paper :—

	'Novgorod.'		'Admiral Popoff.'	
	ft.	in.	ft.	in.
Extreme diameter	101	0	121	0
Diameter of flat bottom	76	0	96	0
Depth in hold at centre, from under-side of beams to top of the frames of the double bottom .	13	9	14	0
Draught of water ⎰Forward . . .	13	2	12	0
⎱Aft . . .	13	2	14	0
⎰Mean . . .	13	2	13	0
Height of barbette tower from load water-line .	12	0	13	3
Diameter of barbette tower outside . .	30	0	34	0
Height of upper deck at side, from load water-line amidships	1	6	1	6
Displacement in tons	2,490		3,550	
Area of midship section in square feet . .	1,170		1,416	
Engines, nominal horse-power . . .	480		640	
Coal supply in tons	200		250	
Propellers, screw, in number . . .	6		6	

	'Novgorod'	'Admiral Popoff.'
Complement of officers and men, number .	110	120
Armament, breechloading guns two in number, each weighing, in tons	28	41
Smaller guns in unarmoured breastwork . .		4
	ft. in.	ft. in.
Height of armour on side above water . .	1 6	1 6
Depth of armour below load water-line amidships	4 6	4 6
Thickness of armour on sides (including equivalent thickness for the hollow iron girders behind armour) upper strake	0 11	1 6
Ditto lower strake	0 9	1 4
Ditto on barbette tower	0 11	1 6
Thickness of deck plating . . .	0 2¾	0 2¾

The 'Novgorod' was commenced in St. Petersburg on December 17, 1871. The hull was put together, taken to pieces, and forwarded by railway to Nikolaeff, while the boilers were to be sent round by

Fig. 129.

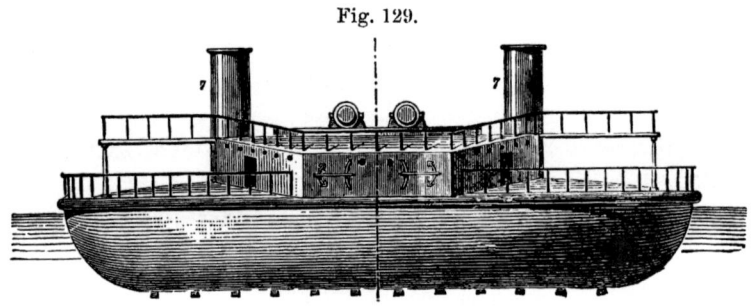

'NOVGOROD' (FROM FORWARD).

sea. The work of putting the separate parts together was begun at Nikolaeff on March 29, 1873.

The 'Novgorod,' from *Die Marine.*

The 'Novgorod,' as it has already been stated, is circular in form and flat-bottomed. The following details of the structure of the hull are taken from *Die Marine*: 'The framework is composed of horizontal circular frames and transverse frames vertical at the sides, extending athwart the flat bottom, and crossing the circular frames of the broadside at right angles. The "Novgorod" has twelve keelsons eight inches in depth, laid parallel to and equidistant from one another. The dimensions of the "Novgorod" are: diameter, 101 feet; draught, fully laden, 13 ft. 2 in.; height of freeboard, 1 ft. 9 in.; displacement, 2,491 tons. The deck rises from the circumference towards the centre, so that in the middle it is 5 ft. 1 in. above the water-line. In the centre stands the turret, forming a concentric circle with the ship. In the turret are placed two 11-inch or 28-ton cast-

iron breechloading guns, mounted on slides invented by General
Pestic. These guns command the whole horizon. The tower stands
twelve feet above the water-line and 6 ft. 11 in. above the deck.

'The "Novgorod" was built of Russian iron. The armour-plating
was manufactured at the Izora works, and consists of two thicknesses
of plating, the inner thickness being riveted to the ship's side. The
outer armour consists of two strakes of armour-plates, of which the
upper strake as well as the armour of the turret is nine inches in thickness, while the lower tiers are seven inches thick. The backing is
formed by 7-inch teak planking. The bottom of the " Novgorod " is
covered with a sheathing of teak and coppered. The deck is of iron,
and is covered with three thicknesses of iron plating of the total
thickness of $2\frac{3}{4}$ inches. The ship has a double bottom, and is divided
into thirty watertight compartments.

' The motive apparatus of the " Novgorod " consists of six screws,
placed parallel to one another in the stern, and driven by six engines
on Woolf's principle, each of 300 indicated horse-power, placed in the
forward part of the ship. The machinery is supplied with steam from
eight boilers. Besides the principal engines, the "Novgorod " is supplied with engines for ventilating, for hoisting the ashes, and weighing the anchor. Two of Friedman's ejectors are fitted for pumping
purposes.

' The " Novgorod " is fitted with an apparatus for the detection of
submarine mines, with which she can operate in all directions. A
light deck-house is constructed forward on the upper deck, in which
accommodation is provided for the captain, the officers' mess, and a
portion of the crew. Below deck are the officers' cabins and the
mess deck for the remainder of the crew. The " Novgorod " was
launched at Nikolaeff on May 21, 1873.'

The diameter of the ' Vice-Admiral Popoff' is twenty feet longer
than that of the 'Novgorod.' The displacement is a thousand tons
larger, and the armour considerably heavier. The principal dimensions are : diameter, 121 feet ; draught forward, 12 ft. 2 in. aft, 14 ft.
2 in. ; displacement, 3,550 tons. The 'Vice-Admiral Popoff.'

The plates on the hull and turret are eighteen inches in thickness.
The deck is protected with 3-inch plates. The number of plates required to enclose the circumference of the hull is 124. The ship is
divided into thirty-six watertight compartments.

Comparative trials of speed have lately taken place between the
' Vice-Admiral Popoff' and the 'Novgorod.' The ' Popoff' attained a
mean speed of eight knots, the ' Novgorod ' did not exceed six knots.
It having been observed that the outer screws produced scarcely any

effect in increasing the speed, they were removed, an alteration which not only lightened the ship, but also added one-third to the cubical contents of the bunkers.

Mr.
Barnaby.

The Popoffkas were highly commended by Sir E. Reed, who made a short excursion in the Black Sea in a ship of this type. Other authorities have consistently refused to recognise the advantages of the circular form. Mr. Barnaby, in his paper *On the Best Types of Ships of War*, said that twenty gunboats going nine knots an hour and carrying a 25-ton gun could be built for the 330,000*l.*, which the 'Novgorod' had already cost. The *Broad Arrow* predicted from the first that the Popoffkas would be a failure at sea. As movable batteries that journal admitted that they might prove useful, although unnecessarily expensive defences; but they strongly advised the Russian Admiralty not to trust them from their moorings in time of war. These anticipations were confirmed on actual trial.

Trials on
the
Danube.

The St. Petersburg *Vedomosti* gives the following account of an experimental cruise of the Popoffkas:—' On June 30 returned to Odessa the two round boats which had been for a trip to the mouth of the Sulina. Four days previously both Popoffkas under the command of Admiral Tchikatchoff, who had hoisted his flag on the " Vice-Admiral Popoff," had gone to the Sulina mouth to see how the steering properties of the vessels would be affected by the current of the Danube. On the following day they arrived at the Sulina, and taking aboard pilots, proceeded without stoppage to the roadstead. Everybody at Sulina hastened to the banks to see the round boats steaming up the river. Against the stream everything went successfully, but when, on the 17th, they raised the anchor to return to Odessa, a curious spectacle occurred. The first to weigh anchor was the " Vice-Admiral Popoff," but no sooner was this operation effected than the vessel began circling round and round across the river, and all the efforts of the engines were insufficient to keep the ship under control. The Popoffka drifted down the river like a log. Only when the vessel got out of the channel into smoother water did the engines regain their mastery over the current. A similar incident occurred to the other Popoffka, the " Novgorod." '

Mr. White, in his lecture on *The Turning Powers of Ships*, states that the principal reason of the uncertain behaviour of the Russian circular ships must be found in the association of a large amount of inertia with a very small resistance to rotation, due chiefly to skin friction. If the inertia and resistance are both small, as happens in shallow-draught gun boats, the vessels quickly acquire angular motion after the helm is put over, but they at the same time sheer off sideways from the course on which their keel-line points, because of the small amount of their lateral resistance.

In 1879, an attempt was made to revive the reputation of the Popoffkas, and the Grand Duke Constantine made a voyage with these vessels from Sevastopol to Batoum. The average speed, however, was only six knots. The 'Popoff,' after landing the Grand Duke, proceeded to Nikolaeff with Admiral Lessovsky, the Minister of Marine, on board. At the mouth of the Dnieper she went ashore, and was not got off until four steamers arrived from Odessa.

In his last publication Mr. King quotes passages from Sir E. Reed's lectures, and supplies some important original criticisms :—

Mr. King, U.S.N.

' It is but fair to the distinguished designer of these vessels carefully to bear in mind that in so far as the " Novgorod " and " Admiral Popoff " are concerned, they have been designed and built purely for service in shallow waters and near the land. . . .

' The " Novgorod " and " Admiral Popoff " have extensive unarmoured houses erected above the armoured decks. The chief of these is a spacious forecastle, which, of course, adds greatly to the buoyancy forward when the sea rises there upon the vessel. I do not think even circular vessels, of very low freeboard, could be steamed against a heavy head sea without such a forecastle, more especially when driven at high speed. . . .

' The chief characteristic of these circular ironclads is that they are purely and simply sea-citadels propelled by steam, and without any attempt to make them conform to the shape of an ordinary ship. The question to be determined hereafter is, is this form of vessel thus originated for coast-defence purposes, and proved eminently successful for that purpose, available under proper modifications for sea-going citadels ?

' I think we may fairly say that, for a seagoing citadel, viewed as a citadel only, apart from other features, the circular form is best, because it requires a minimum amount of armour to protect a given area or volume, or, in other words, a given amount of armour secures the greatest amount of buoyancy. For special purposes some modified form might be preferable ; but speaking generally, the circular form is the best for floating armour to protect an included space, and also for giving that equal all-round cannonade with guns which is so desirable at sea. Starting, then, with this circular armoured citadel, and wishing to propel it at a given speed at sea, there are several ways in which we can deal with it :—

' First. We can put engine-power in it just as it stands without modification ; or,

'Second. We can build ends to it like those of an ordinary ship, protecting those ends by a belt of armour, as in many other ships; or,

'Third. We can build such ends to it and protect the lower parts of them by an under-water deck of armour, as in the "Inflexible"; or,

'Fourth. We can build around it an outer circle of thin iron, with a mere narrow belt of armour analogous to the belt of ordinary ironclads; or,

'Fifth. We can build around it such an outer circle of thin iron, with an under-water deck of armour analogous to that of the "Inflexible"; or,

'Sixth. We can build short ends to it with either above or under-water armoured decks, but of greatly reduced length as compared with the ends of ordinary ships of large beam.

Fig. 130.

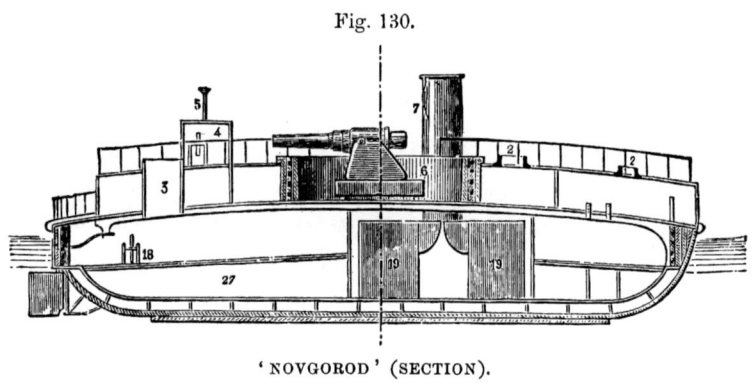

'NOVGOROD' (SECTION).

'The "Novgorod" is the only actual example of the first of these cases that has yet been tried, and we may state roughly that in her 750 tons of armour and 56 tons of guns are carried on a displacement of 2,500 tons, and driven at $8\frac{1}{2}$ knots, with 2,270 indicated horse-power. This confirms what we already know, viz., that such ships will require great power in proportion to displacement. But taking, not the false standard of displacement, but the better (although not perfect) standard of weight of armour and guns as our guide, we shall find nothing very extraordinary in the power required.'

Such are the chief points in Sir E. Reed's lecture. Mr. King did not see these Russian circular vessels, but from an examination of a completely equipped model of one of them and the drawings, he reached the conclusion that, as floating forts designed for shallow water, they do possess some of the merits stated; but even for this purpose, as at present constructed, there are serious objectionable features, some of the most prominent of which are given below : —

Fig. 131.

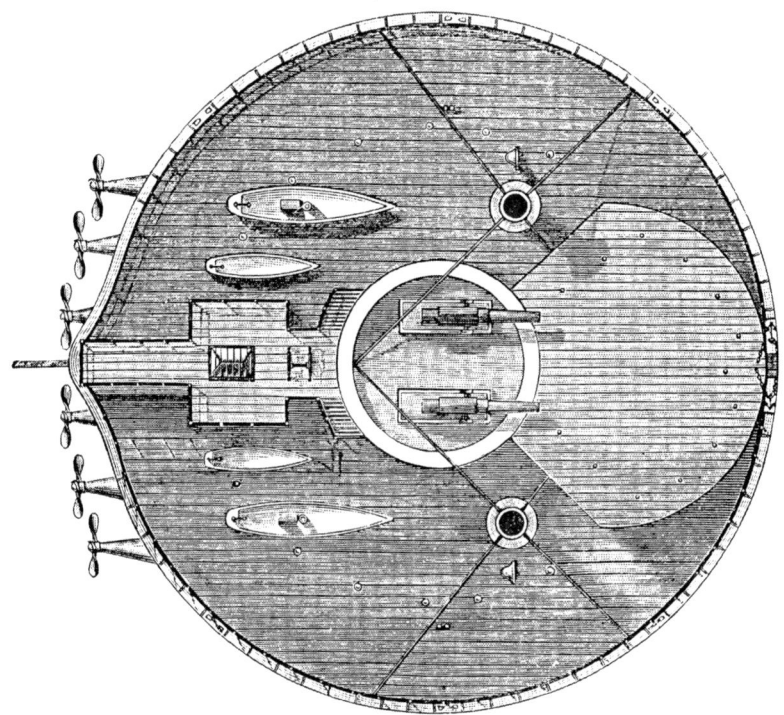

DECK OF 'NOVGOROD.'

Fig. 132.

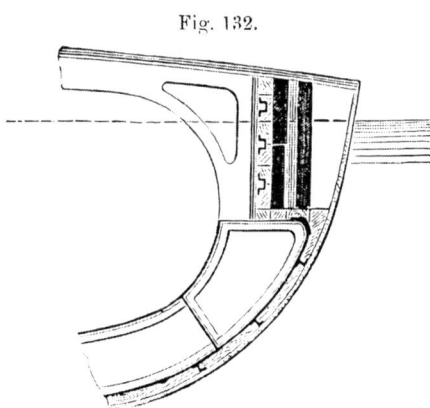

SIDE ARMOUR OF THE 'ADM. POPOFF.'

'1st. As the "Novgorod" is built, there is in the centre an open-top fixed turret, or an iron martello tower, having inside it a revolving platform, on which the guns are *en barbette*. This is the system employed in the upper-deck batteries of the French armoured ships; but in the French ships the towers are located near the sides of the vessels, and high above water, while in the Russian vessels they are located in the centre and on hulls having a freeboard of only eighteen inches. The barbette principle affords very considerable lateral range, but the disadvantages are, as here applied, that it leaves the guns and men working them fully exposed to the fire of the enemy. On shore, artillery officers rarely, if ever, contemplate mounting guns *en barbette* near the level of the water where serious and close action is expected. They seek for a high and somewhat distant position, where the advantages of an all-round lateral and plunging fire are available, and where the exposure of the men and the guns is reduced to a minimum. With a view to remedy this serious disadvantage in some degree, the second vessel constructed, the "Vice-Admiral Popoff,"

Fig. 133.

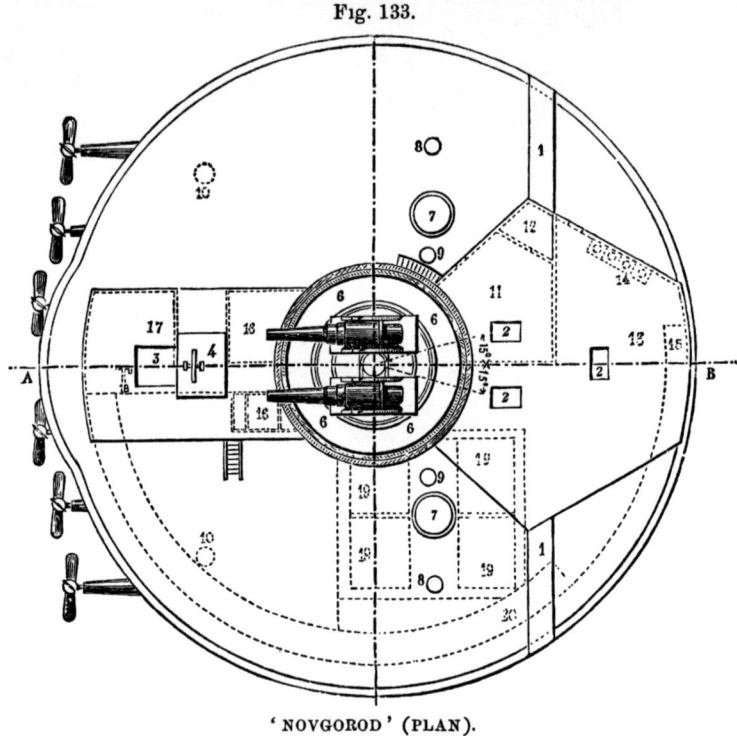

'NOVGOROD' (PLAN).

has been arranged to work the guns on the disappearing principle of Rendel. This change is only a partial remedy; the disadvantage of the open-top tower slightly above the level of the water still remains.

'2nd. The second objection is that the side armour-plates do not extend deeper below the water-line than in ordinary vessels, and as the "Vice-Admiral Popoff" is 121 feet in diameter, there is this large target at all times presented for under-water attack by locomobile torpedoes, instead of the bow or stern alone, as would often happen in the attacks on other vessels. The extra defence against torpedoes gained from the cellular construction by means of the circular system would avail nothing.

' 3rd. The third objection consists in the complication of the motive machinery. There are six screw-propellers, operated by three sets of engines. Two of the propellers have diameters greater than the draught of the vessel, the periphery of the blades extending below the keel. These two screws are three-bladed, and are not worked in shallow water. The writer had considerable experience, during our civil war, on the Mississippi River, in building and operating the machinery of the four wide flat-bottomed gun vessels of the " Milwaukee " class, provided with four screw-propellers, and there obtained a practical knowledge of the complication of the machinery proposed in this case. It is also to be observed that the six screw-propellers are unprotected from attacks of any kind.

' 4th. The fourth and most serious objection to the circular form of vessels consists in the extraordinary steam-power necessary to drive a vessel, say of 121 feet diameter, through the water at a speed equal to that of the ordinary vessel of the same carrying capacity. The weight and space occupied by the machinery would be so great as to leave but little room for all the other requirements.

' Sir Edward Reed says that the " Novgorod " made a speed on the measured mile of $8\frac{1}{2}$ knots; that she has steamed a considerable distance at $7\frac{1}{2}$ knots; and when he made a trip in her the speed averaged $6\frac{1}{2}$ knots. This last is probably the real speed when steaming in ordinary weather for a period of twenty-four hours or more. If the weights of the steam-machinery had been given, and other necessary data, the weights, etc., for higher speeds could be readily estimated.

' The first objection raised to the circular vessel, viz., the open-top tower, could be remedied in future constructions by substituting the revolving turret, and the second objection could be removed by extending the vertical side armour down to the keel. This would entirely protect the vessel from attacks of the moving torpedoes. The third objection may be obviated, but the fourth is insurmountable. Therefore for sea-going vessels, although the form may be changed by adding ends, the principle of construction will not be likely to meet with favour from naval architects, much less from naval officers.'

Admiral Tchikatchoff, in a recent report to the Grand Duke Constantine advocating the creation of a naval reserve, discloses some additional facts, all tending to show that the Popoffka type has been a complete failure.   The cost of the 'Vice-Admiral Popoff' is put down at 420,000*l.*

The Czar's
yacht,
'Livadia.'   Undaunted by their disastrous experiences in their earlier vessels, the Russian authorities have adopted a modification of the round form in the yacht recently built for the Czar to replace the former 'Livadia' which was wrecked in the Black Sea.   A detailed description will be read with the deeper interest, because the yacht is an experimental vessel, and the main features of the design will perhaps be copied in a new armourclad.   The *Times* of December 11, 1880, contains a statement taken from the *Cronstadt Messenger* that an armour-clad resembling the 'Livadia' yacht in design, and to displace 12,000 tons, has been ordered to be laid down by the Russian Government.   It is believed that this has been postponed.

The contract for the new 'Livadia' was entrusted to Messrs. John Elder and Co.   The following account is taken from an article in *Engineering* and from a paper read before an Association of Engineers and Shipbuilders by Captain Goulaeff of the Corps of Russian Naval Architects.   That officer says :—

'This vessel is 235 feet long, 153 feet broad, and has a draught of 6 ft. 6 in.   She might have been a little longer, but on closer investigation it was found that the addition of some 25 feet or 50 feet to her length would not have reduced the resistance in water.   Augmentation of skin friction, not being sufficiently compensated by the improved lines, would have required increased power to drive the larger vessel with the given speed.   She might have been a little narrower to suit the taste of most people, yet the beam of 153 feet cannot be regarded as being too great if we bear in mind the main object of her design, namely, the desire to secure the greatest steadiness.'

As originally designed her displacement was given as 3,920 tons, with coal on board for five days' steaming, and the indicated horse-power was estimated at 10,500.   She is propelled with three screws situated at the stern, one in the middle line of the vessel, and the other two, one on each side, eighteen feet from the line of the centre shaft, and 2 ft. 6 in. before the centre screw-propeller.   The three screws were to be each sixteen feet in diameter, twenty feet pitch, and four-bladed. There are three separate engines with three boilers to each, making nine in all.   The vessel has one rudder placed abaft the centre screw-propeller, and there can be little doubt that, considering the comparative shortness of the vessel, the turning power will be quite effective. The shape of the vessel is described in the *Times* as a sea palace erected on the back of a huge steel turbot, and this is pretty much what it is.

The total depth of the vessel is said to be 46 feet, and of this six feet are below water; but it must not be supposed that the remaining depth of forty feet of side rises vertically out of the water. The greatest breadth is at the water-line, and above this the side falls in rapidly, so that at the middle of the length of the vessel at a height of twelve feet above the water it is twenty-one feet on each side within the breadth at the water-surface. From this point the sides rise vertically, and enclose the saloon and other accommodation, forming a superstructure on the turbot-like vessel or raft. Of course if the sides rose vertically from the water-level, there would be still greater deck room and space for state apartments, but the vessel would then be exposed to blows from the sea tending to render her uneasy, and to thwart one of the main objects of the designer, viz., ease and comfort at sea for the Imperial owner. By rounding the sides in so much immediately

Fig. 134.

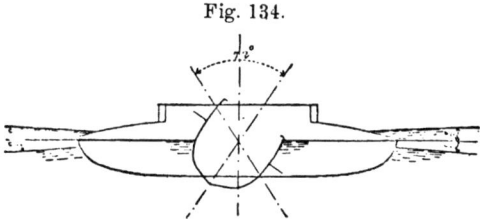

SECTION OF 'LIVADIA' COMPARED WITH SECTION OF ORDINARY OCEAN STEAMER AMID WAVES.

above water, the sea is allowed to wash over this portion, and becomes to a considerable extent a steadying instead of a disturbing element, as has repeatedly been proved in the case of low freeboard monitors. There is still a breadth of 110 feet left in which to arrange the state-rooms, and owing to the immense breadth and stability of the vessel there is no difficulty in arranging two storeys of cabin accommodation, each having much greater height and roominess than is possible in a vessel designed on ordinary proportions of length to breadth.

The lines of the vessel are said to have been decided upon after a series of experiments on paraffin models, carried out by Dr. Tideman of the Royal Dockyard, Amsterdam, in conjunction with Admiral Popoff, and a model in steel twenty-three feet long was made by Messrs. Elder and Co. for further experiments on the Clyde.

A feature worthy of notice is mentioned in connection with the draught of water. A depth of sixteen feet at the stern has been deemed necessary to obtain efficient propulsion. This, however, would seriously interfere with the usefulness of the vessel in waters where shallows abound, and arrangements are to be made for letting water into the forward end of the ship, where the draught of water is only six feet, so as to tilt her up, and thus lift the stern. In this way she will be able to cross the shallows at the mouth of the Dnieper on the way to Nicolaieff.

Captain Goulaeff says :—

'A large superstructure has been built upon the main body of the turbot of the dimensions and of the form just mentioned. This superstructure is of the shape of an ordinary vessel, and because being of usual form, will no doubt gratify the eye of those who are not sufficiently educated to admire the uncovered sides of the lower turbot portion of the ship, which, however, are the very parts that have the greatest share in limiting the rolling at sea.

' The turbot-like lower part of the vessel contains machinery, coals, and stores of all kinds. The steel superstructure rising over it contains accommodation for the crew forward, and for the officers aft, whilst the palace beyond it includes only the imperial apartments and the cabins for the suite.

' This turbot-like portion of the vessel is built of steel, with a double bottom, whose height is no less than 3 ft. 6 in. in the centre. This double bottom is divided into forty watertight compartments, and extends throughout the flat portion of the bottom. At the sides it is superseded by the cells formed by running two vertical bulkheads right round the ship, and subdividing the distance between them and the outside skin into forty other compartments. These side cells, formed of continuous bulkheads, and covered by the plating of the rounded deck, present a very rigid, continuous, annular structure, which has its lower points tied together by the radial girders, forming the bracket framing of the bottom, and by the heavy beams of the rounded deck, also radial, at the top. Thus the turbot-like portion of the vessel is made amply strong enough to withstand those forces which might be experienced in the roughest seas, and the local strains, such as those produced by the powerful machinery with which the ship is provided—particular attention being paid to the structure of the stern, in order to distribute the strains on the brackets supporting the propelling shafts of the side screws.

' The superstructure that rises above the turbot portion of the vessel has been mainly designed to form a support for the palace and deck-houses beyond, in order to raise them so much above the level of the sea as to prevent anything but spray reaching those portions which are intended for the use of the imperial party.

' The palace is not so wide as the steel superstructure, so that all around it on the deck a continuous gallery is formed, which is used for stowing anchors, mooring the vessel, hoisting up boats, steam launches, and a small steam yacht, carried on the davits, which are supported by bridges projecting radially outwards from that gallery.

'It is scarcely possible to enumerate the improvements introduced in all their details. The system of distinguishing red, white, and green electric lights has been worked out under the guidance of His Imperial Highness the Grand Duke Constantine. The system of pumping out the watertight compartments is deserving of special notice, as does also the town-like system of water service, to which, for the first time on board ship, there are added loaded accumulators to produce pressure when the steam pumps are not at work. Machinery has been employed largely to supersede manual labour, and there are no fewer than 23 separate steam-engines on board for different purposes.

'The propelling engines of the yacht, which have been designed by Mr. A. D. Bryce are of a construction decidedly novel, and have been erected in a somewhat novel manner. Their foundation, which is of steel, forms part of the framing of the double bottom, as is also the case, on a smaller scale, in the circular vessels. We hope that, with many other important improvements introduced in these engines, we shall obtain a greater amount of indicated horse-power, as compared with their weight, than with any other marine engine yet constructed (torpedo boats excepted), and that they will satisfactorily answer the problem entrusted by Admiral Popoff to Mr. Bryce.

'The arrangement of propellers forms another very important peculiarity in the design of this vessel.

'The efficiency of submerged screws beneath the ship's bottom had been sufficiently tested previously by Admiral Popoff, but so much as having two-thirds of their diameter entirely below the outline of the vessel is a decided novelty, which, as was expected, will greatly add to their efficiency, as has been corroborated by the recent experiments conducted to that effect, on Loch Lomond, with a steel model of the yacht one-tenth the ship's size. There are three screw propellers of sixteen feet in diameter, spaced 18 ft. 3 in. apart—the centre one being in the line of keel, and each of them worked by an independent engine capable of exerting an indicated horse-power of 3,500.

'Docks capable of lifting vessels of the "Livadia" type for the purpose of painting or repairs, have been already constructed and tested in the Black Sea. The system of single-sided floating docks (known

Figs. 135, 136, and 137.

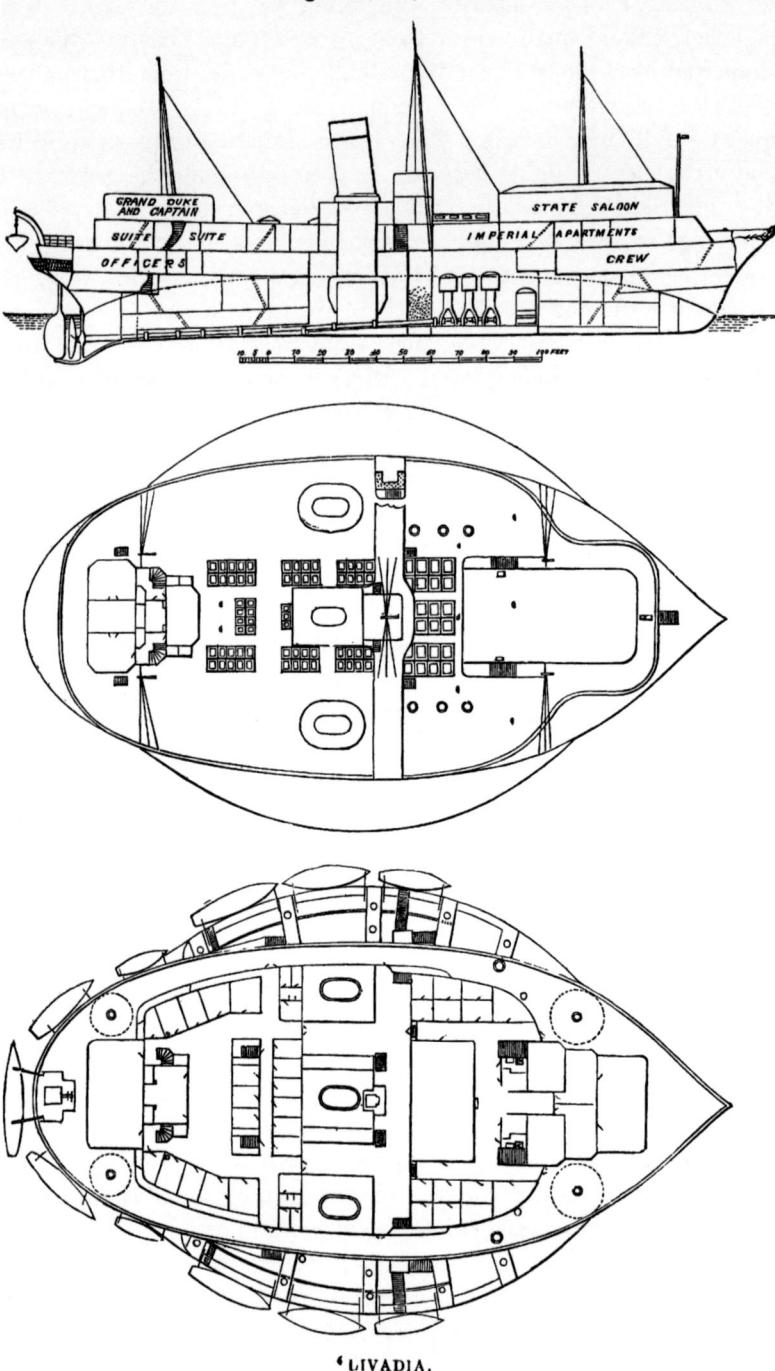

'LIVADIA.

Figs. 138, 139, and 140.

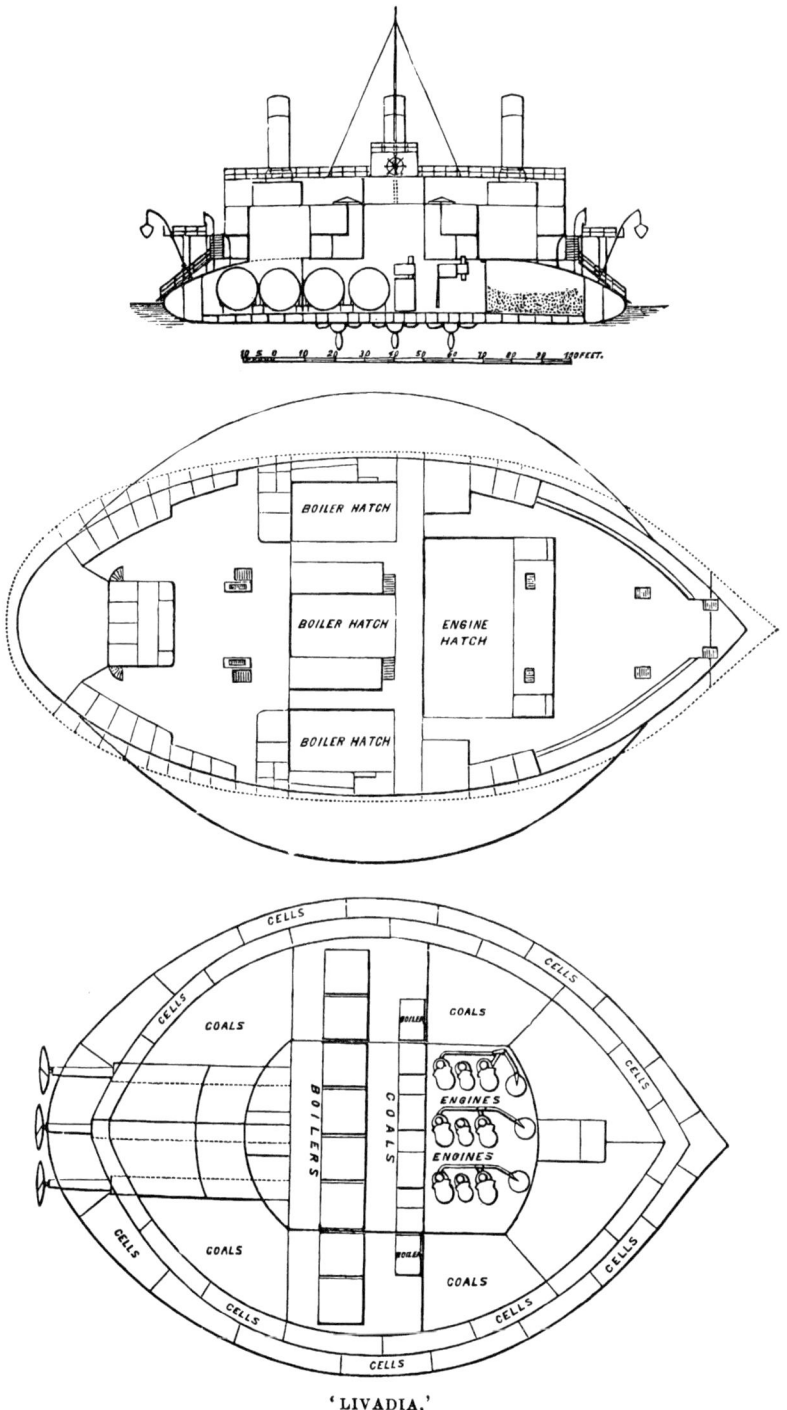

'LIVADIA,'

as Messrs. Clark and Stanfield's system) adopted for extremely broad vessels by Admiral Popoff, does not any longer prevent the construction of vessels of any proportions.'

The ship has proceeded as far as Ferrol in Spain, and has there been detained owing to damage done to the hull by the blows of the sea during her voyage and, apparently, by the doubts which have been felt as to her power of encountering bad weather outside the Mediterranean. Sir E. Reed has given an interesting account of her performances in the following letter to the *Times* of October 30, dated, Ferrol, October 25, 1880.

'The performances of this extraordinary vessel have so immediate a bearing upon the future construction of steamships, both for war and for passenger purposes, that some observations upon her steam trials at the Clyde and her subsequent sea-passages will doubtless be of interest to many of your readers.

'In the articles which you published concerning the "Livadia" before her completion, a higher speed than many expected was confidently predicted for her, and has since been realised. I myself feel some pride in this result, for, although I have had nothing whatever to do with the "Livadia" beyond once visiting her after her launch, and subsequently crossing the Bay of Biscay in her, I have for several years past publicly maintained that ships like the "Livadia," of small length and immense breadth, could be driven at a high speed, and in maintaining this principle I have stood almost absolutely alone in England. Owing to the enterprise of the Russian Government, the matter has now been put to the test, and a ship of only 235 feet long, and with a breadth (153 feet) twice that of the "Inflexible," has at her very first trials, and under some temporary disadvantages, attained a speed of very nearly 16 knots an hour. The power exerted in producing this speed has doubtless been great in proportion to the displacement and section of the vessel, but there is not a greater, nor is there, I am bound to say, a more universal delusion among nautical people than the determination of what is called "economy" by such considerations alone. In the present instance, for example, what was required was to produce a vessel of high speed and of superior steadiness, with large accommodation suitable for an Emperor and his Ministers and suite ; and if that has been accomplished with a given expenditure of steam power, it is idle to say that the same steam power would have driven a larger and more expensive ship as fast. Economy consists in accomplishing your object by the easiest and cheapest method ; the neglect of your object and the attainment of something you do not require is extravagance, however disguised. The disregard of this principle has, in war-ship construction, cost the nations of Europe many a million.

'The "Livadia" as completed has more immersion than was contemplated at the time of her design, and I have ascertained the following figures:—

	Displacement.	Mid section.
As designed	4,000 tons	900 sq. ft.
As tried at measured mile	4,420 tons	1,000 sq. ft.
At departure from Greenock	4,720 tons	1,075 sq. ft.
At departure from Brest	5,070 tons	1,150 sq. ft.

'The reason assigned for these increased immersions is that the experiments of Dr. Tideman at Amsterdam showed that in a ship of the "Livadia's" form, the loss of speed from increased immersion was exceedingly small, and that consequently as the ship approached completion no objection was offered to increase of weight where increased conveniences were suggested, and that many additions were in this way made. For the same reason the quantity of coal taken on board first at Greenock, and afterwards at Brest, was only limited by other considerations. She left Brest with 850 tons of coals on board.

'In view of the exhaustive discussion of the ship's probable speed which you published on July 9 last, it seems unnecessary to again compare the "Livadia" with other vessels, but it may be for the convenience of many readers, whose interest in the question is great, to say that while the immersion was greater than was then anticipated, so also was the power developed. The figures employed by you in July, on Captain Goulaeff's authority, compare with the actual figures of the subsequent trial as follows:—

	Displacement.	Section.	Average indicated horse-power.
Data of July 9	4,000 tons	900 sq. ft.	10,500
Data of measured-mile trials	4,420 tons	1,000 sq. ft.	12,354

The mean speed of six runs was 15·864 knots.

It will be observed that the increases of power and immersion were nearly proportional, so that the comparisons given by you on July 9 remain practically undisturbed. The performance of the "Livadia" at high speed was, therefore, between two and three knots per hour inferior to that of a long fine-lined frigate like the "Shah" of proportional size and power. This difference is so very small, compared with what the nautical world has been predicting, that the full-speed trials of the "Livadia" must be pronounced a splendid success, and a demonstration of the fact which few but myself recognised, namely, that very great breadth of ship is compatible with very high speed.

It is but fair to quote in this connection the following sentence from your article of July 9 : "The new yacht has a far better chance of attaining a high speed than the philosophers of the last century could possibly have conceded to her under their theories of resistance, and it is not by any means extravagant to hope that those may be disappointed who consider it impossible to drive so broad a vessel fast."

'Before we left the Clyde Admiral Popoff showed me a letter which he had addressed to yourself, and in which he had pointed out some of the disadvantages under which the steam trials were made. The success of the ship as regards speed is so great as to render it needless to insist upon these disadvantages, in so far as she is herself concerned ; but it is of great importance to science to have it remembered that it was at her very first trials that a vessel of her proportions steamed nearly sixteen knots. The " Livadia " has three screw-propellers, and while there was but little experience to guide the Admiral in selecting for them the best dimensions, etc., there was none to guide him in fixing their relative positions, pitches, and other conditions. It is also highly probable that even under the best conditions three screws may propel such a form of ship less efficiently than either two screws or one. In view of all the facts, therefore, it appears probable that the deficiency of speed which is solely due to the form and proportions of the hull, as compared with the best ships of ordinary form, is still less, much less than even the trials of the " Livadia " might at first sight suggest.

'Like considerations to these will, of course, apply more or less to all the steam performances of the " Livadia " for the present, but it will nevertheless be instructive to observe briefly her ordinary steaming qualities. On October 14, at her earliest essays at steaming, she steamed at eleven knots per hour with 2,969 indicated horse-power, thirteen knots with 4,770 indicated horse-power, and fifteen knots with 10,037 indicated horse-power. This was in smooth water. At sea, when the wind and waves were moderate, she has run over long distances since we left Greenock with about 4,500 horse-power, at a speed varying from twelve to thirteen knots. It is not easy to select other ships of approximately equal steam power and displacement combined ; but two of our ironclads come near to the " Livadia," and I will give the comparison between them :—

Name of ship.			Displacement.	Horse-power.	Speed.
Penelope	.	.	. 4,394 tons	4,703	12·7 knots
Orion	.	.	. 4,700 tons	4,000	12 knots
Livadia	.	.	. 4,420 tons	4,770	13 knots
Ditto	.	.	. 4,720 tons	4,500	12½ knots

'The speed of the "Orion" given is only estimated, but that is of no consequence, because the object of this comparison is merely to show that the Russian Popoffkas, modified as in the "Livadia," are capable of steaming at ordinary speeds with moderate power, and by no means contrast absurdly, as some suppose, with all other ships.

'I must now say a few words upon the behaviour at sea of this remarkable vessel. In several articles that have appeared in your columns of late the public have been advised not to expect too much from the seagoing performances of the "Livadia." Her extreme lightness of structure has been pointed out, and the probability of her sustaining heavy shocks and great vibration has been mentioned. On July 9 you said: "When waves are encountered at high speed, and the speed of the oncoming waves is virtually added to that of the ship, the qualities of the 'Livadia' will probably be put to by far the most serious tests that await them." This prediction has been literally fulfilled on our passage across the Bay of Biscay. It was fine when we left Brest on Tuesday evening last, but we had only been a few hours at sea when the barometer began to fall and bad weather set in. It would have been prudent, perhaps, to have put back into Brest, considering the very light draught of our ship and the towering heights of deck palaces which are piled upon her lightly-built upper deck. But the Grand Duke Constantine, the Lord High Admiral of Russia, was on board, and considered the opportunity of thoroughly testing the vessel too fine a one to be lost, and we consequently steamed away into the very teeth of a Bay of Biscay gale, which steadily grew angrier and wilder as we advanced all Wednesday, and during that night and the following morning blew at its hardest, accompanied with very heavy seas indeed. The actual rolling and pitching of the "Livadia" at the height of the gale was exceedingly small, never exceeding 4° for the single roll, or 7° for the double roll, or 5° for the forward pitch, and 9° for the double pitch, so to speak. This horizontal steadiness was most remarkable, and, while in very agreeable contrast with my experiences of the last three years at sea in ordinary ships, was full of significance as regards the possible steadiness of gun platforms in ships of war. When we at length had crossed the Bay and got out of the gale, and steamed into Ferrol, not the slightest damage of any description had been sustained, with an exception to be mentioned hereafter, either to the vessel or to her boats, palaces, furniture, crockery, or anything whatever. The dinner-table was laid, the candelabra stood upon it, and the meals were served throughout the voyage, even during the storm of Wednesday evening, exactly as if the vessel had been at anchor in port. The broad covered gallery which extends all round the open deck was never reached by the sea, and it was only during the worst of the weather that even spray invaded it. With a vessel of the very light draught of seven feet in such a gale, and with such high and lumpy waves, the blows of the sea under the flat bottom were at times tremendous; but the confidence of the Grand Duke in refusing to turn back was justified, and both Admiral Sir Houston Stewart, the Controller of the Navy, who was on board, and myself are indebted to his Imperial Highness for a most instructive piece of sea experience. Sailor as Sir Houston is, and intimate with the latest forms and details of naval construction, it was impossible, nevertheless, for him not to profit by this very exceptional voyage on this very exceptional ship.

'Before entering Ferrol one of the small compartments forward was found to be filled with water, and it was soon discovered that one of the bow plates had been stove in, and the plates in the neighbourhood strained and made leaky. My own first impression was that the cellular bow had yielded to the direct impact of the sea during one of the most violent of the shocks which were felt; but a close inspection of the injuries led us to the conclusion that the bow had been struck by some floating wreckage. We are now temporarily repairing the damage, for which, owing to her extreme subdivision into watertight compartments, the vessel is but little the worse.' [1]

The 'Solimões.'   We now come to the armoured vessels for river service. The Brazilian monitor 'Solimões' was designed by the engineers of the Compagnie des Forges et Chantiers de la Mediterranée, under the direction of a Commission especially appointed by the Brazilian Government. The 'Solimões' was commenced on January 2, 1874, and launched on January 2, 1875. Notwithstanding the unusual despatch with which this vessel was built, she is in every way successful, and we venture to think that a short description will not be devoid of interest.

The principal dimensions are as follows—length between perpendiculars, 240 feet; breadth, 58 feet; depth of hold, 13 ft. 9 in.; draught of water, 11 ft. 5 in.; area of the immersed portion of the midship section, 647·75 square feet; displacement, 3,700 tons; thickness of the armour at the water-line, twelve inches; thickness of the deck plating on three laminated plates, three inches.

[1] In May 1881 the 'Livadia' again made a short cruise on the north coast of Spain.

This ship has a double bottom. The mode of construction is a compromise between the bracket frame and transverse systems. The transverse frames extend in one unbroken length from the keelson

Figs. 141 and 141A.

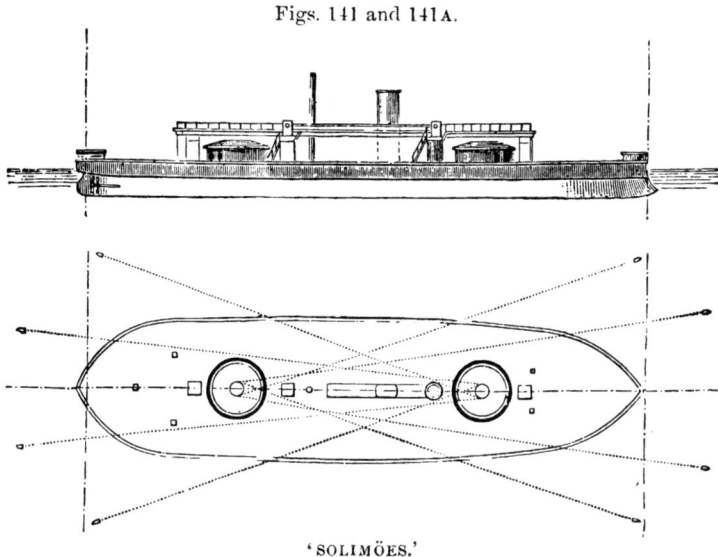

'SOLIMÖES.'

to the shelf-pieces, which carry the armour-plates. The latter, as well as the keelsons, extend in one length from the stem to the stern, while all the other longitudinals are built in short lengths, divided by the transverse frames. The frames, with the exception of every fourth, which is continuous, are built in sections. The hold above the double bottom is divided into seven watertight compartments.

On the deck are two armoured turrets, each carrying two 25 c/m., or 10-inch, 25-ton Whitworth guns. These guns fire solid shot weighing 400 lbs., and shells of from 450 lbs. to 750 lbs. in weight, and from 28 inches to 52 inches in length. These turrets are plated with 12-inch armour on the side in which the ports are cut, and with 11-inch plates on the other sides. Their internal diameter is

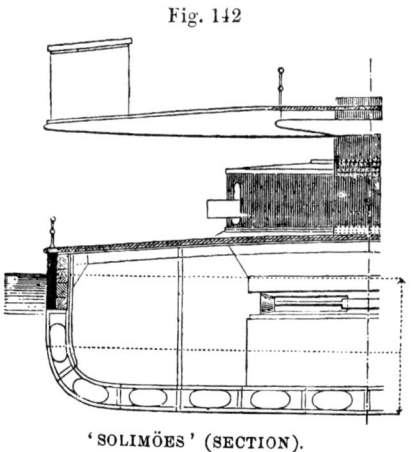

Fig. 142

'SOLIMÖES' (SECTION).

nineteen feet, and the external diameter 26 feet. The guns, when brought into the loading position, are depressed, the muzzle pointing towards the hold, when the gun can be loaded by one man by means of Armstrong's apparatus. There is a third turret, or pilot-tower for the commander, having an external diameter of 8 ft. 6 in., and plated with $3\frac{3}{4}$-inch armour. This tower affords a means of communicating in action with the interior of the monitor.

Three great hatchways are connected by a trunk or shaft 19 feet in height, and built of iron plates, with the flying deck. The latter deck is 154 feet in length, and, with the exception of one section, which is carried out to the full width of the ship, it is seventen feet in width. The central trunk or shaft supplies both light and ventilation to the engine-room and stoke-holes; the other shafts serve as ventilators to the lower deck and the after part of the ship. They are easily removable, and must be cleared away before going into action, in order to secure an uninterrupted range of fire both ahead and astern. The pilot-tower is erected between the central hatchway and the foremost turret. It rises three feet above the hurricane deck, which again stands 4 ft. 4 in. above the upper edge of the turrets.

The three hatchways already mentioned are protected, when going into action, by armoured shutters working on hinges. The central shutter is fitted with numerous perforations for ventilation. When the monitor is at sea in a hot climate, or in action, air is forced into the interior by means of two ventilating engines, one of which expels vitiated, while the other introduces fresh air. The monitor has four of Martin's anchors, which can be worked together at a single capstan. The chain pipes can be closed by india-rubber flaps to prevent the water from penetrating below.

Water can be pumped from the watertight compartments both by steam pumps and hand pumps. The steam pumps also lead directly into a well, which communicates with every compartment of the ship by double pipes extending along the whole length of the monitor, and opening into each compartment by means of a valve. One of the pipes runs through the cells of the double bottom, the other into the space under the stoke-hole.

The machinery for the 'Solimões' was constructed at Havre, from the plans of the engineer of the Forges et Chantiers Company. It consists of two independent engines, each of which drives a screw of ten feet diameter. The eight boilers are cylindrical with two furnaces. The engines on the Woolf system have each two cylinders, and are capable of making 126 revolutions a minute, and developing

2,200 indicated horse-power. The guaranteed speed was ten knots, but the monitor steamed 11¼ knots in the trial trip, and hopes were entertained that even this speed might be exceeded. Two hundred tons of fuel can be stowed in the bunkers. The rudder has an area of 64 square feet, and can be worked either by hand or by a small engine fixed under the foremost turret.

The steering trials of the 'Solimöes' gave the following results:

1. Both engines going ahead at full speed, the helm hard over, the first circle was completed with a diameter of about 321 yards in 5 min. 35 sec.; the second in 6 min. 30 sec

2. With one engine going ahead, and the other astern at full speed, and the rudder amidships, the monitor completed a circle of about 83 yards in 8 min. 40 sec.

3. The engines working the one ahead and the other astern, and the rudder over, the circle, which was completed in 5 min. 45 sec., was still smaller than in the former case.

4. With one engine stopped and the other steaming ahead, the monitor obeyed the rudder, and was easily turned to one side or the other.

Another monitor, the 'Javari,' very similar to the 'Solimöes,' was built at Havre. These monitors are intended both for harbour defence and river service. They are the most powerful vessels in the Brazilian fleet.

The 'Javari.'

The French Admiralty official report on the Exhibition of 1878 gives the following account of two small armoured vessels ' La Plata ' and 'Los Andes,' which had been recently built in England by Messrs. Laird for the Argentine navy. The principal details of these monitors, which are intended for river service, are the following :—

'La Plata,' and 'Los Andes.'

Length at the water-line . . .	180 feet
Beam	43 feet
Mean load draught of water . .	9 ft. 6 in.
Displacement . · . .	1,535 tons
Immersed surface of midship section .	278·6 sq. ft.

The hull has a double bottom, two feet in depth, which is to be filled with water in action, so as to increase the immersion by one foot. At the sides, the double bottom is replaced by a fore and aft bulkhead, distant four feet from the outer plating. The hold is divided into numerous watertight compartments.

The revolving turret is forward of the centre of the vessel. Light central superstructures carry a bridge running fore and aft. They are sufficiently narrow to allow direct fire ahead from the two guns of the turret. They are somewhat wider abaft to give accommodation for the captain, and diminish by 6° the arc of stern fire. The guns are 9-inch Armstrong, and weigh 12½ tons. The armour-plates are eight inches thick on the turret, and twelve inches near the ports. The water-line plates are six inches in thickness amidships, diminishing considerably at the ends. The engines on the compound system develop 750 horse-power. The speed is 9·5 knots.

The following account of the outward voyage of the 'Plata' appeared in the *Army and Navy Gazette* of March 27, 1875 :—

'Argentine monitor " El Plata," St. Vincent, Feb. 28.

'Having arrived at St. Vincent, the second stage of our journey, it may interest naval readers to know our experience of this class of vessel as we find it. On leaving Milford Haven we encountered the

Figs. 143 and 144.

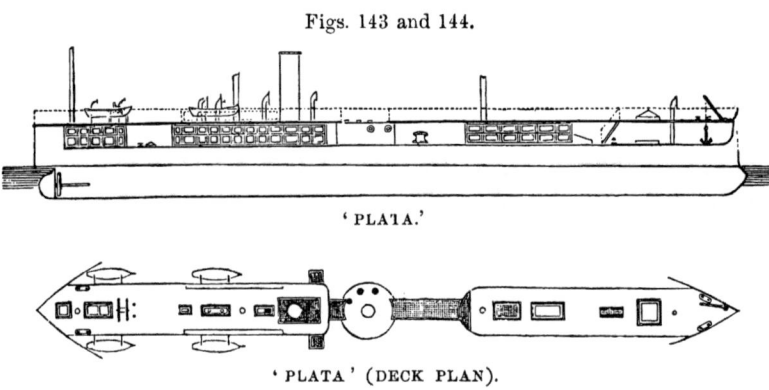

' PLATA.'

' PLATA ' (DECK PLAN).

heavy S.W. breezes and sea which, we read in the papers, you have had nearly ever since. On one day this strengthened into a heavy gale, accompanied by a violent sea which retarded our progress considerably ; as, considering the shape of the bottom, it might be expected to have done. She shipped water plentifully, burying her bows completely at times in the advancing waves, but keeping up her old habit of shaking herself free immediately. Off Cape Finisterre, passed 120 miles to the westward, the wind backed round to the N.E., and making all sail (one square foresail) we ran before it until our arrival at Funchal, in one day accomplishing 216 miles, the time from England being 8 days 3 hours.

' Having completed with coal (71 tons) we proceeded on the 21st for St. Vincent, arriving here this morning, after a very pleasant run of 6 days 19 hours. The remains of the temporary bulwarks, damaged in the bay, were removed at Madeira, not much inconvenience being felt for want of them. Indeed the water playing about the upper wooden deck tended to keep the ship cool below. Instead of the N.E. trades we had a strong S.W. gale on the 22nd, lasting only about twelve hours, followed by S.W. breezes and calms. Leaving Madeira, steaming eight knots, a man fell overboard from the cat-head, and was picked up by the ship herself in five minutes, the low freeboard proving very convenient in this case.

'The engines have worked splendidly hitherto; but the engine-room begins to be unpleasantly hot, the surface condensers causing the thermometer to show 132°; which, however, should not be exceeded. The engines have been worked throughout at 90 revolutions, 120 being full speed; the average speed obtained being six knots, on a consumption of eight tons of coal per diem, or a total of 120 tons since leaving England.

'Now, wishing to contrast this ship with any of about the same offensive and defensive powers in our service, what have we? Here is a seagoing armour-plated turret ship, which has proved herself to be a good sea boat, her only defect being that she is still a little wild to steer; but this could be easily remedied in others. A proof of her good qualities is the absence of desertion among the crew, although it has been rough winter work. Lengthened a little and given more coal bunker space, with one 35-ton gun, or larger, instead of her two 12½-ton guns, she would be very valuable on foreign stations; and a small squadron for home service would be proportionately as effective against any enemy as our large class turret-ships; being more seaworthy, more easily handled, and far less expensive in fuel, crew, and wear and tear. Their use in our colonies, and for river work or shoal water coast on foreign stations, needs no comment.

'This ship is 1,800 tons, on a draught of water of 9 ft. 6 in. aft, and 750 horse-power actual. She carries fuel for (under favourable circumstances) a distance of 2,880 miles, at full speed, consuming ten tons daily. The "Devastation" is more than five times the tonnage, and nearly seven and a half times the horse-power. She has four times the offensive power, but more defensive power also; but the question is, which would be better against an enemy—one "Devastation" with over 500 crew, or four "Platas" with each a crew of 85 men? If the new principle of an extra wooden upper deck 2 ft. 6 in. above the real iron deck, built in watertight compartments, gives such extraordinary buoyancy and easy motion, making a low freeboard vessel seaworthy —would not the same principle, applied to the "Wyvern" and "Scorpion," do as much for them?'

Some light draught armourclads are to be found in the Danish Navy which deserve a particular description. The armoured battery 'Gorm' was begun at Copenhagen in 1867, and was launched on May 12, 1870. The principal dimensions are :—

Length	231 feet
Beam	49 feet
Draught of water	14 ft. 3 in.
Displacement	2,344 tons.

Fig. 145.

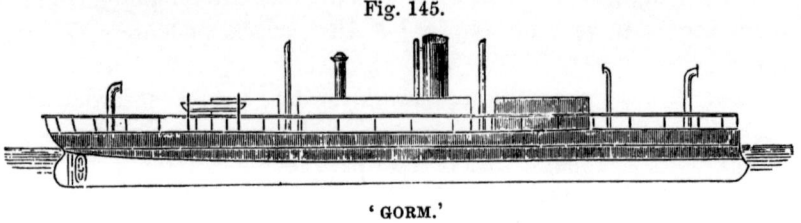

'GORM.'

The hull is of iron, and lies very low in the water. Like another Danish vessel, the 'Lindormen,' the 'Gorm' has only one turret, turned by special steam-engine, though it can also be worked by hand. The armament includes two 10-inch Armstrong guns in the turret,

Figs. 146 and 147.

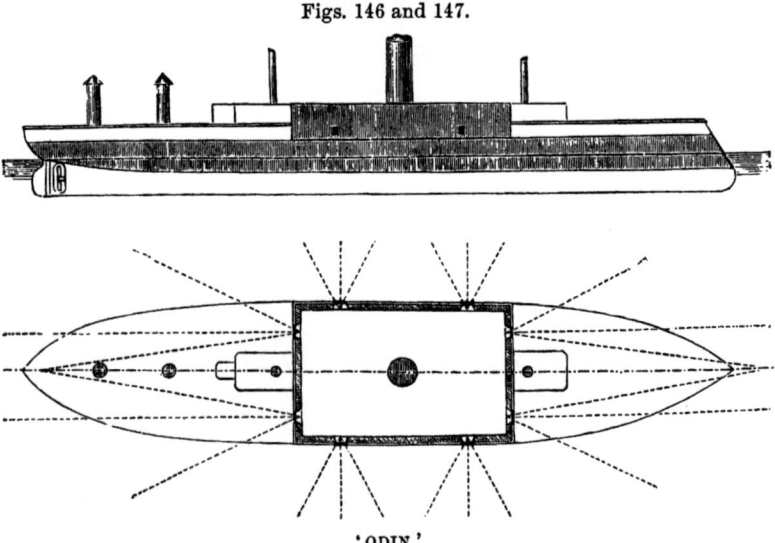

'ODIN.'

and two light cast-iron smooth-bores on the upper deck. The lower port-sill   5 ft. 5 in. above the water. The armour rests on 10·3 inches of teak, and its greatest thickness at the water-line is seven inches. On the turret the armour is eight inches thick, and the backing

$17\frac{1}{2}$ inches. The engines indicate 1,670 horse-power, which gives a speed of 12·2 knots. The 'Gorm' with her ordnance cost 104,000*l*.

The armoured battery 'Odin' was laid down in Denmark in 1871, and was launched in 1872. The principal dimensions are :— The 'Odin.'

Length	.	.	.	.	237 feet
Beam	.	.	.	.	48 ft. 6 in.
Draught of water	.	.	.	.	16 inches
Displacement	.	.	.	.	3,083 tons.

The 'Odin' is built of iron, and has a central battery on deck. Before and abaft the battery are small deck-houses. There are only two light masts for signalling. The ordnance carried is four 10-inch Armstrongs and six light smooth-bore cast-iron guns. The height of the lower port-sill above the water is six feet. The thickest armour on both water-line and battery is eight inches on a 10·3-inch backing. Forward and abaft the armour decreases to five inches. The indicated horse-power is 2,260, and the maximum speed 12·4 knots. The cost of the 'Odin' was 147,000*l*.

We now proceed to describe, from the pages of *Die Marine*, the special type of gunboat which has been produced for service on the coasts of North Germany. A few remarks may here be offered to explain the origin of the plans for the German gunboat 'Wespe.' The 'Wespe.'

'According to the original programme for the fleet, monitors were to be provided for the local defence of the German coast. The continual development of the power of the torpedo showed, however, that such large armoured ships were not necessary, and that smaller vessels were quite sufficient to meet the attack of spar torpedo-boats, and for the local defence of the coasts.

'It became, therefore, a question whether it was not inexpedient to rely solely on armoured vessels for this service, and whether it was not desirable to build instead small unarmoured vessels, carrying one heavy gun. A large number of vessels of this class could be built for the expenditure incurred on a single monitor.

'This course had already been adopted in England, and in lieu of the very limited number of armoured ships, which had been built for coast defence previous to the year 1872, a large number of light-draught vessels had been constructed, armed in the bow with one heavy gun of from twelve to eighteen tons. In France, about the same date, some excellent gunboats had been built, and similar vessels had been introduced in the Danish and Dutch navies. In Russia, too, an unarmoured wooden gunboat had been built, armed with one 26 c/m. ($10\frac{1}{2}$-in.) or 22-ton gun.'

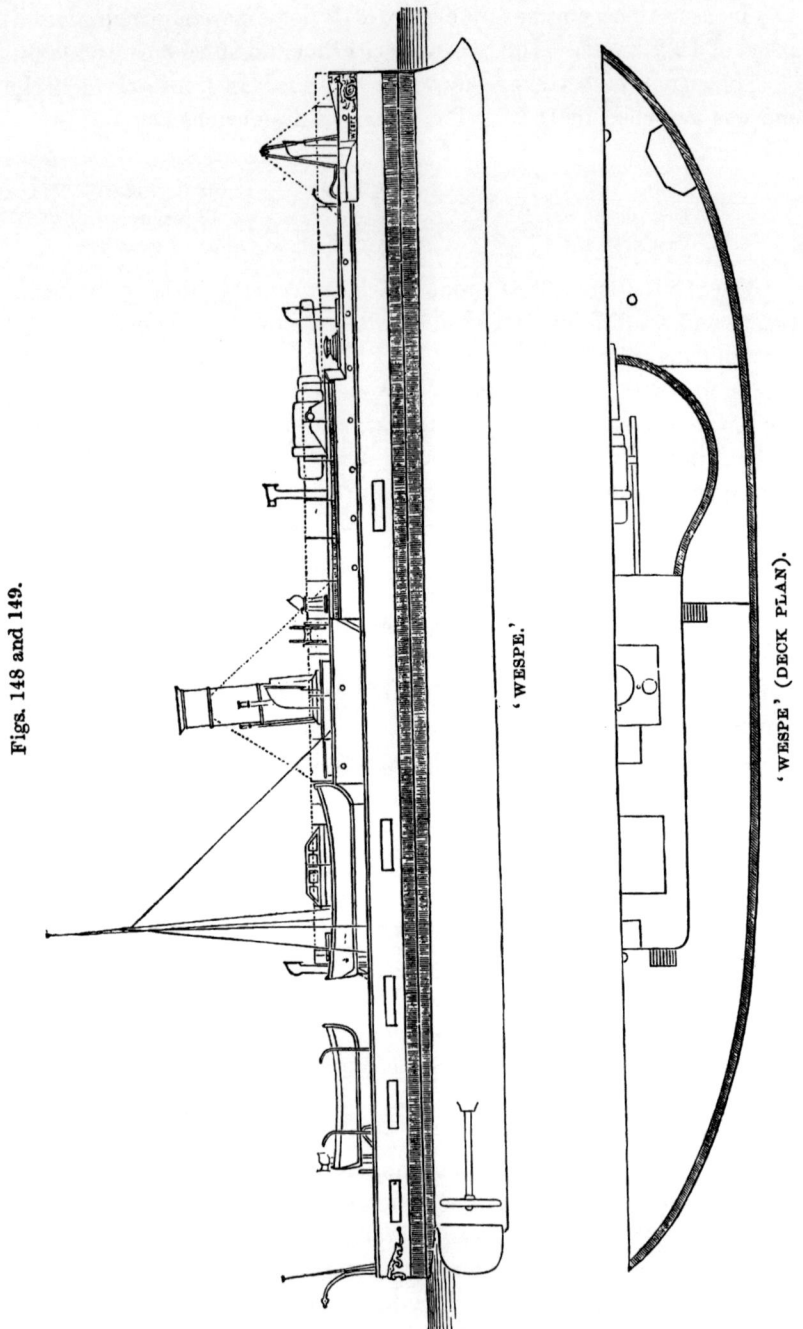

Figs. 148 and 149.

'WESPE.'

'WESPE' (DECK PLAN).

These considerations led to a modification of the original programme, and it was decided to build some small unarmoured vessels for coast defence.

The coast of Germany may be divided for purposes of defence German armoured gunboats. into two separate sections, namely, the Baltic coast, and the coast of the German Ocean, including Schleswig-Holstein. On the former coast the entrances to the harbours, with only two exceptions, are between two parallel piers built out into the sea. By laying down torpedoes and supplementing the torpedo defences with powerful batteries, it can be made impossible for an enemy to force an entrance, and armed vessels become of secondary importance as a means of defence.

The case is very different on the shores of the German Ocean, and specially at the mouths of the Eider, Elbe, Weser, Jahde, and Ems. Here it is of the greatest importance to engage the enemy outside the mouths of the rivers, and to prevent him from gaining a tolerably secure anchorage between the outlying banks, and there make preparations for an attack on the towns situated near the mouths

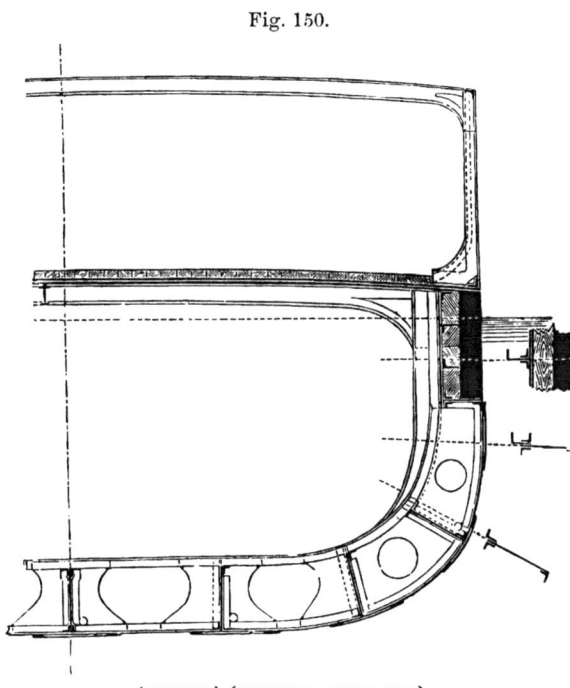

Fig. 150.

'WESPE' (SECTION FORWARD).

of the rivers, or attempting a landing. The vessels designed for the protection of these coasts must under all circumstances be prepared to act on the offensive against the enemy. They must draw as little water as possible, in order to be able to operate in the shoals between the banks. They must also be fitted with the means of laying down torpedoes, which are the more essential for the protection of entrances which cannot be protected by forts or land batteries. Such being the conditions with which the Germans have to deal in organising the means of defending their coasts, unarmoured, heavily armed vessels are indispensable.

An experimental coast-defence vessel was ordered in England, of small dimensions in order to offer a difficult target to the enemy;

and which, while able with its heavy gun to penetrate 8-inch
armour at long range, could avoid an encounter with the ram
by its lighter draught of water. The cost of each vessel would
be proportionately small. It would be nothing more than a
floating gun-carriage. While vessels of this type seemed at first
sight to possess considerable merits, on a fuller consideration they
were not found to be altogether satisfactory. An unarmoured vessel
can only be useful for coast defence when its hull, built of thin
plates, is sheltered behind low earthworks, or a jetty, whence it
can discharge its ponderous projectiles without being exposed to

Fig. 151.

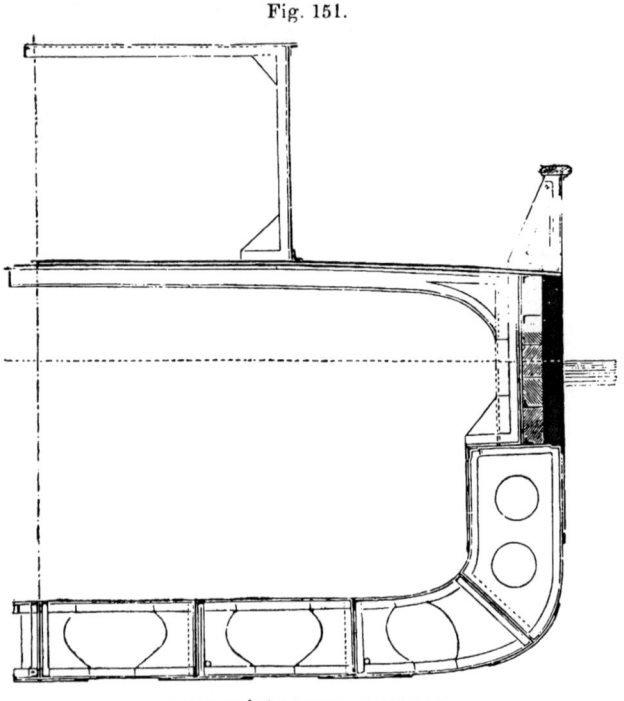

'WESPE' (MIDSHIP SECTION).

destruction by the enemy. For the reasons which have thus been
stated, a considerable reduction was made in the number of small
unarmoured vessels originally proposed for the defence of the North
Sea coast, and some larger armoured vessels were ordered. The
conditions, which the constructors were required to satisfy in their
designs for these vessels, included the following points. They were
to be armed with guns capable of penetrating armour at a considerable range. They were to be protected with armour of a
minimum thickness of eight inches. They were to be seagoing and

handy, of light draught and of moderate speed. The armoured
gunboats of the 'Wespe' type were built in conformity with these
conditions.

They have a length of 142 ft. 9 in., a breadth of 35 feet, a
draught of 10 ft. 2 in., and their displacement, when fully equipped
for sea, is over 1,000 tons. They are armed with a 12-inch 36-ton
gun, mounted in an open circular breastwork, protected with 8-inch
plating, the central axis being twelve feet above the water-line. The
power of this gun is such that it can penetrate stout armour at a
considerable range. These vessels can, therefore, engage ironclads
at a distance beyond that at which the greater number of the guns
in the large ships can inflict any serious damage. They can, therefore, prevent the approach of the large ironclads by the fire from
their guns, and they can shun an engagement at close quarters by
withdrawing among banks and shoals where the larger ironclads are
unable to follow. They run little risk from their inferiority in point
of speed. In the vicinity of the coast the intricacy of the navigation
compels ships, which have an advantage in point of speed, to move
cautiously They possess great offensive power. It would be
difficult for regular seagoing ships, with a high freeboard, to carry
on the broadside the heavy guns which are mounted on board the
'Wespe.' The guns in these gunboats are brought to bear on the
object by the use of twin-screws, and a steam steering apparatus
worked from an elevated platform in the rear of the guns.

As these vessels are designed to engage the enemy end on, the
usual reduction in the thickness of the armour at the bow is avoided,
and the full thickness of eight inches is retained. Protected by this
thickness of armour, and also by its rounded form, the bow is extremely strong. The vessels are protected against a plunging fire
by an armoured deck covered with 2-inch plating. Should their
decks be penetrated, their numerous watertight compartments and
double bottom would probably prevent them from foundering.

The armoured gunboats would have a great advantage in respect
of armament over the light-draught ironclads of an enemy, inasmuch
as the former can be easily penetrated at a considerable range by
the 30·5 c/m. (12-inch) or 36-ton guns of the latter, while the
armoured vessels have little chance of doing injury to the gunboats
with the guns they usually carry. Should they unavoidably come to
close quarters with the enemy, the latter must manœuvre with great
caution in waters with which he is not acquainted, while the gunboat would have a chance of striking a blow with the ram, and is
accordingly fitted for such an encounter.

The armoured gunboats are intended to attain a speed of nine knots with full boiler-power. They have two independent engines, guaranteed to develop a combined power of 700 horses, during a continuous six hours' trial. Each engine drives independently a single screw. The supply of coal in the bunkers has been limited to an amount sufficient for forty hours' steaming at full speed. This limitation has been imposed in order that the gunboats may draw as little water as possible, while employed in the immediate vicinity of the coast. The supply of coal can be considerably increased for 'longshore expeditions, in case the gunboats are not retained at the entrances to harbours.

To improve their seagoing qualities, and make them better

Figs. 152 and 153.

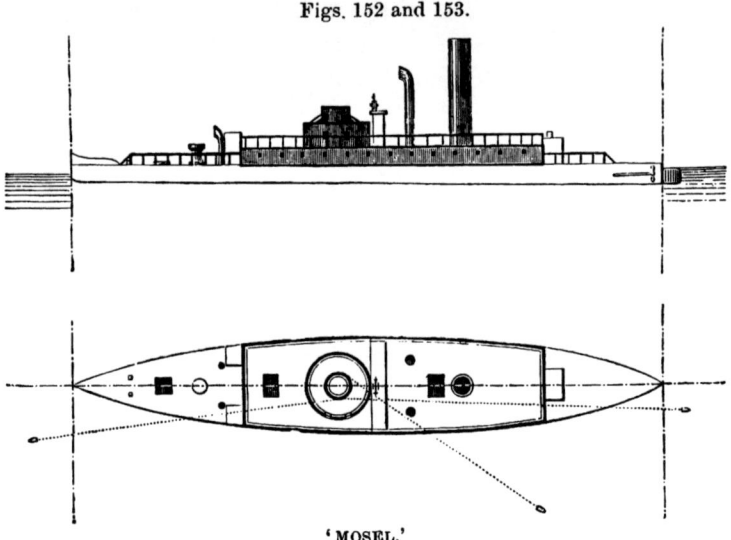

'MOSEL.'

adapted for steaming against a head sea, as well as to provide airy and habitable quarters for the crew, a light iron superstructure has been built, extending along a length of thirty-six feet from the bow to the turret; while in rear of the turret a deck-house is erected, which contains the engine and boiler-room hatchways, the galleys, and communications leading to the cabins of the officers. This arrangement also secures for the engine-room staff a better protected communication with the engine-room in all weathers, while the officers and men on watch can be stationed on the decked roof of the superstructure, where they are less exposed to the wash of the sea.

These vessels are fitted with both steam and hand pumps, of which one is fixed on the lower deck, the other in the after deck-house. They are not masted. The complement consists of two officers and

Figs. 154 and 155.

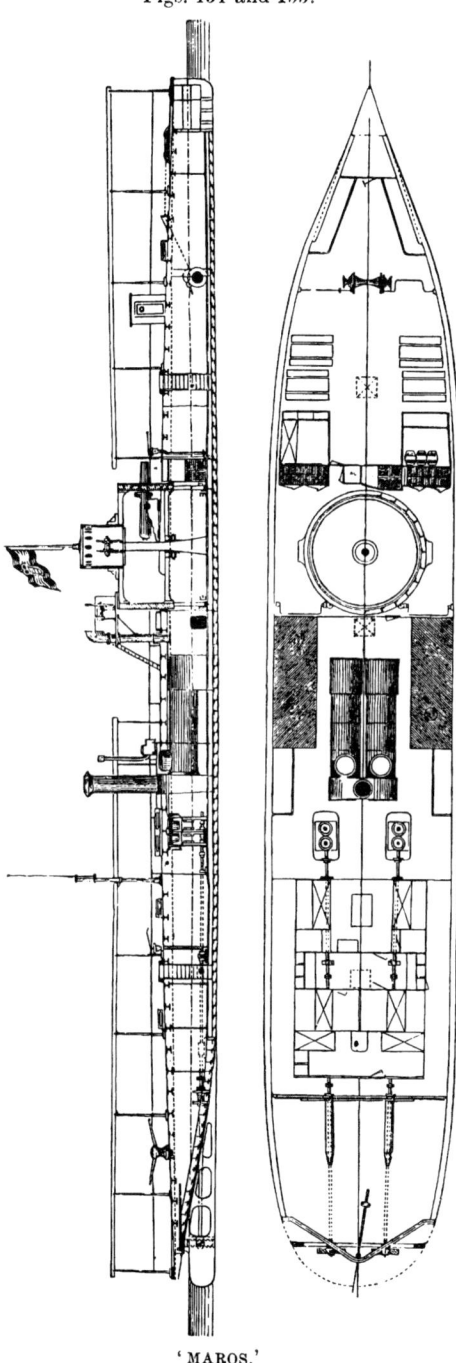

'MAROS.'

62 petty officers, firemen and seamen.

Of the gunboats built under the inspiration of the ideas developed by the authors of *Die Marine*, the 'Wespe,' 'Viper,' and 'Biene' were launched in 1876, and the 'Mücke' and 'Scorpion' in the following year, and several more have since been completed. Eighteen in all were to be built.

The German Government have also built for service on the Rhine the 'Mosel' and 'Rhein.' They are described by Señor Heriz, at pages 45–6 of the *Memoria sobre los Barcos*, as carrying twelve c/m. 36-pounder guns, drawing five feet of water, and having $2\frac{3}{4}$-in. armour. *The 'Mosel' and 'Rhein.'*

For service on the Danube the Austrian Government constructed two iron vessels with one turret and two 15 c/m. (6-inch) guns. They were launched in 1871, and are named the 'Leitha' and 'Maros.' They draw 3 ft. 7 in. of water, their displacement is 300 tons, the thickness of armour at the water-line is $1\frac{3}{4}$ inches, on the turret two inches; in- *The 'Leitha' and 'Maros.*

dicated horse-power, 320 ; speed 8·3 knots. They have twin screws.

CHAPTER XI.

ARMOURED CRUISERS.

WE now propose to deal with the class of cruising ironclads designed for service on foreign stations. They are valuable for the purpose of exhibiting the national flag, and, in time of war, as auxiliaries to the battle-ships. It may, however, be questioned whether the cost in the case of numerous examples of this class is not excessive.

English and foreign armour-clads, for service on foreign stations.

Among ships of the type are the German 'Hansa,' the French 'Victorieuse,' 'Triomphante,' 'Duguesclin,' 'Bayard,' and 'Turenne'; the English 'Shannon,' 'Nelson,' and 'Northampton'; the

Figs. 156 and 157.

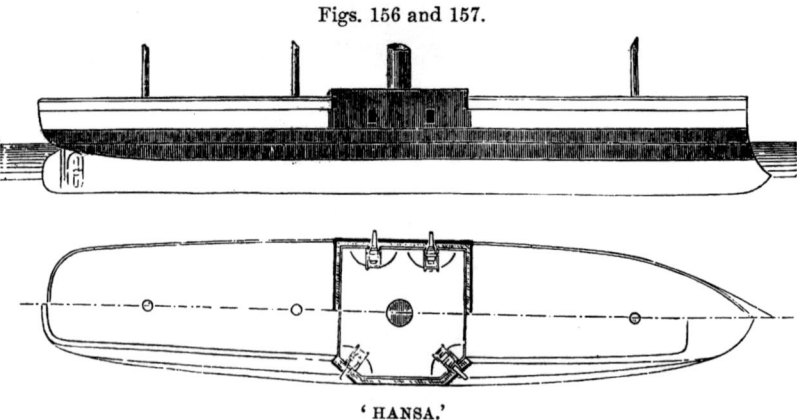

' HANSA.'

Chilian 'Almirante-Cochrane' and 'Blanco-Encalada'; the Portuguese 'Vasco de Gama'; the Russian 'Minin,' 'General-Admiral,' and 'Duke of Edinburgh'; the Austrian 'Don Juan,' 'Kaiser Max,' and 'Prince Eugene'; the Japanese 'Foo-So,' 'Kon-Go,' and 'Hi-Yei'; and the Greek 'King George.'

The 'Hansa.'

The 'Hansa,' a wooden vessel launched in 1873, is designed on the same principle as the 'Belliqueuse.'

The ship is protected by a belt of armour at the water-line, and has an armoured central battery, containing four 21 c/m. (8-inch) guns. On the upper deck, in a projecting casemate, are four more guns of the same calibre. M. Dislère, in his work *La Guerre d'Escadre*, in comparing this ship with the French 'Victorieuse,' displays perhaps a pardonable partiality for the French design. He considers both the offensive and the defensive power somewhat limited, the extreme thickness of the plating being only 6¼ inches. While admitting that the ship, with a displacement not exceeding 3,600 tons, has been kept within reasonable limitations both of cost and dimensions, he contends that, if the comparison be extended to the 'Victorieuse,' commenced about the same date, it will be seen that with an addition of 800 tons to the displacement the armour is considerably heavier in calibre, and the guns on the upper deck have been protected. The speed is about the same in the two ships; but the coal supply of the smaller vessel does not exceed 240 tons. Hence he is of opinion that with an augmentation of only twenty-two per cent. indisputable advantages have been secured, and he draws the conclusion that, desirable as it is to keep down the displacement, there are certain qualities required in each type, and that it is inexpedient to reduce the dimensions to a point which involves a loss of efficiency in essentials.

The 'Victorieuse' may be taken as a typical vessel of the less recent class of armoured ships of the second rate in the French navy. The 'Victorieuse' was laid down in 1869, and launched in 1875. The 'Triomphante,' a sister ship, was laid down at Rochefort in 1870, and launched in 1877. These vessels were built from plans by M. Sabattier, Director of Matériel, and form the sequel to the two earlier classes the 'Belliqueuse' and 'Alma,' which were contemporary with the first ironclad fleet. The 'Victorieuse' is to some extent a reduced copy of the 'Suffren,' 'Ocean,' and 'Marengo.' *The 'Victorieuse.'*

The hull is of wood, except the extremities of the upper works, before and abaft the central battery, which are of iron. The coefficient of weight of the hull, without backing is ·464, and therefore equal to the mean of the coefficients of the 'Suffren' and the 'Trident.'

The ship is armoured from end to end at the water-line, and the immersed part of this belt is covered with a casing of wood, sheathed like the bottom with copper. The battery deck is not armoured, but only plated with sheet iron throughout its length. 'Thwartships and fore and aft watertight bulkheads, rising to the battery deck, divide the hold into distinct compartments. The powder magazines are placed under the stoke-hole and engine-room. The rudder is of wood, with metal braces. There is no after stern-post, or more properly rudder-post.

Details from the Plan.

Length of hull at load water-line . .	253 ft. 7 in.
Beam	48 ft. 3 in.
Depth	19 ft. 6 in.
Mean draught of water . . .	20 ft. 6 in.
Displacement	4,140 tons
Immersed surface of midship section .	808 sq. ft.

The arrangement of the armour is similar to that of the 'Richelieu' class. The thickness at the water-line is ·15 metre, or six inches, and on the battery ·12 metre, or 4·7 inches. The weight of the hull

Figs. 158 and 159.

'VICTORIEUSE.'

and armour is 2,823 tons. The armament is composed of six 24-c/m. or 9·4-inch guns of 14·2 tons. Four of these are in the central battery and two in barbette turrets on the sides and before the funnel. One 19-c/m. or 7·6-inch gun of 7·8 tons, is mounted under the topgallant forecastle, and six smaller guns on the forecastle and quarterdeck. The ship is full-rigged, and has a spread of canvas of 1,780 square mètres (2,000 square yards). The rigging is fitted to set up inboard, so that the turret guns can fire over a portion of the upper deck near the sides.

The 'Victorieuse' is manned by a complement of 310 men. The

engines, manufactured at Indret, are on the compound principle, with three horizontal cylinders, the high-pressure cylinder being in the centre. On the trial trip a speed of 12·75 knots was realised with 2,214 indicated horse-power, and a mean draught of water of 6·36 mètres (22 feet). The quantity of coal carried is 300 tons, a supply sufficient for 1,700 knots at ten knots an hour. The ship is fitted with a single screw. The 'Victorieuse' has a balanced rudder, and on her trial trip at full speed described a complete circle in 5 min. 10 sec., the diameter being about 400 yards.

M. Marchal, comparing this ship with the earlier types, observes that the 'Victorieuse,' which resembles the 'La Galissonière' in the construction and internal arrangements, differs nevertheless from the latter ship in the lines of the after body, which were designed for a single screw, the 'La Galissonière' being a twin-screw. The 'Victorieuse' carries her guns at a height of seven feet above the water-line. The displacement is 4,150 tons. The 'Victorieuse,' like the 'La Galissonière,' is intended for cruising on distant foreign stations, and has a less thickness of armour than the battle ships constructed for naval operations in European waters. The 'Victorieuse' and 'Triomphante' are fitted as rams, which adds considerably to their offensive power.

M. Dislère, in La Guerre d'Escadre, makes the following general observations on the 'Victorieuse' type : 'The "Victorieuse" is a vessel of the same type as the "Alma," though the dimensions and displacement have been considerably augmented, with the view of meeting the ever-increasing exigencies of naval warfare. The "Victorieuse" is constructed of wood, with a central battery. The guns mounted in the battery can be trained to fire on the broadside only, the bow and stern fire being secured in the most complete manner from the guns mounted en barbette in the half-turrets, the mechanism for training the gun and the gun-screws being effectively protected against the projectiles of an enemy. While, however, the type is the same, the offensive power has been considerably augmented. The old corvettes were armed with the 19 c/m. (7½-inch) or 7·8-ton gun only; in the "Victorieuse" guns of 24 c/m. (9·4 inches) or 14·2 tons, are mounted in the central battery. It has further been thought necessary to increase the speed, these ships being intended, in the event of war, to be capable of pursuing the enemy's cruisers. This object can be secured in the great majority of cases with a speed of thirteen knots, a speed which is only exceeded by a few vessels of the most recent construction. This speed has, therefore, been adopted, involving in consequence an addition of one

knot to the speed considered necessary
in the earlier corvettes.   Three hundred
tons of coal can be stowed in the bunkers.
The " Victorieuse " is, therefore, capable
of carrying coal sufficient for steaming a
distance of 2,740 miles at 10 knots.   The
corvettes could not steam more than from
1,600 to 1,700 knots at the same speed.'

There are now being completed in
the French dockyards several second-class
ironclads, among them the ' Vauban,' the
' Duguesclin,' the ' Bayard,' and the
' Turenne.'   The ' Duguesclin,' which
may be taken as a typical vessel of the
recent armourclads of the second class,
was designed by M. Lebelin de Dionne,
an eminent constructor in the French
service, and was begun in 1876.

The
' Dugues-
clin.'

The ' Duguesclin' differs materially
from the ' Victorieuse ' both in the design
and construction of the hull, the disposition of the ordnance, and the vertical and
horizontal armour-protection.   She resembles, in everything but size, thickness
of armour, and power of ordnance, the
' Amiral Duperré.'   The side plating is
cased with a double thickness of wood,
the inner carrying the armour, to which
it serves as a backing, the outer, which
covers the armour, being sheathed with
copper up to a certain height above the
water-line.   The armour is confined to
a belt at the water-line, and the four
barbette turrets are also protected.   The
greatest thickness of the belt is ten
inches, and of the turret armour eight
inches.   The battery deck is armoured
throughout, and laid with sheet iron
below the backing.   Below the armoured
deck the ship is divided into watertight
compartments by seven athwartship and
a certain number of fore and aft bulk-

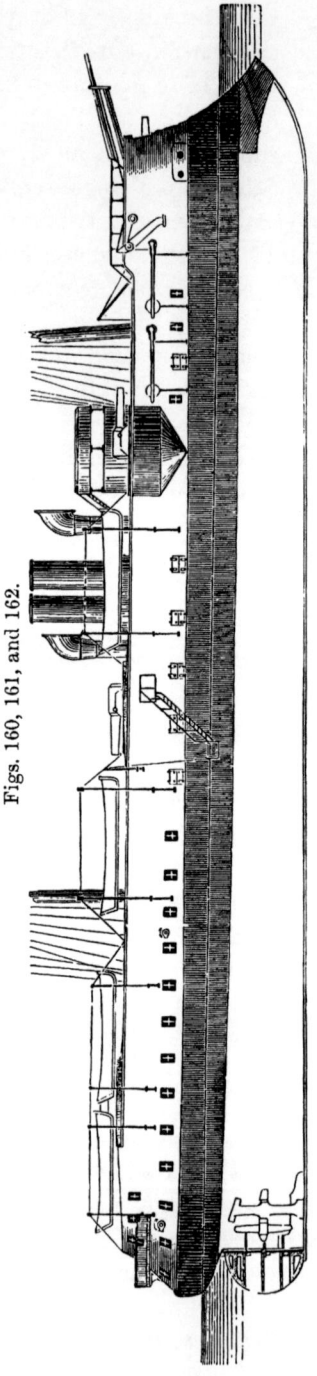

Figs. 160, 161, and 162.

' DUGUESCLIN

heads. The space reserved for the engines and boilers is divided
amidships by fore and aft watertight bulkheads carried up to the

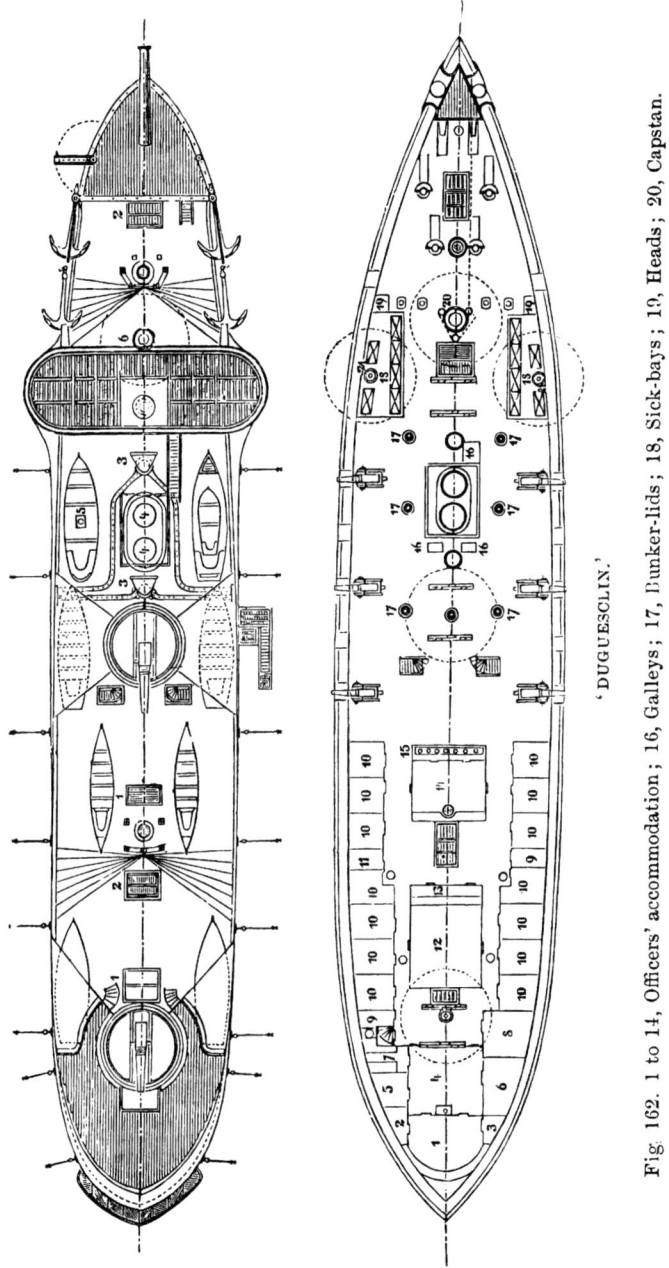

Fig 162. 1 to 14, Officers' accommodation; 16, Galleys; 17, Bunker-lids; 18, Sick-bays; 19, Heads; 20, Capstan.

'DUGUESCLIN.'

orlop deck. The watertight doors are of steel. The keel, stem, and
stern-posts are of wood. The hull is built of steel, and is cased

with wood. The weight of the hull is 2,550 tons, and that of the armour 1,510 tons. The estimated weight of the hull is ·367 of the displacement. This coefficient is ·364 in the case of the ' Dévastation.' The principal dimensions are the following—length at the water-line, 266 feet; breadth, 57 feet; mean draught of water, 23 ft. 4 in.; displacement, 5,882 tons; immersed surface of midship section, 1,075 square feet.

Four heavy guns are carried, one in each of four barbette turrets, of which two are in the forepart of the ship slightly projecting beyond the sides, immediately abaft the fore-rigging. These turrets are well sheltered from a plunging fire of musketry or Gatlings by the bridge, which runs across the ship immediately above them. One gun is mounted in a central turret quite uncovered between the mainmast and the funnel. The fourth piece is in a turret the sides of which rise to a level with the poop deck, in which it seems sunk as in a well. These guns have a calibre of $9\frac{1}{2}$ inches, or 24 c/m. Under the topgallant forecastle a $7\frac{1}{2}$-inch or 19 c/m. gun is mounted, which can be fired right ahead. Six light pieces are distributed on the main deck a considerable distance apart, and are not protected by armour.

The ' Duguesclin' is a full-rigged brig, and spreads 2,701 square yards of canvas. The ram takes the form of a snout tipped with a metal casting of extraordinary length. The ' Duguesclin' is propelled by two four-bladed screws, driven by engines with three vertical cylinders each, fabricated at Indret. They are on the compound system. The shafts protrude for a great length beyond the brackets under the counter, which support the casings in which they work. The boilers are cylindrical, with a grate surface of 414 square feet. The engines are intended to indicate 4,100 horse-power; and it is anticipated that a speed of fourteen knots will be attained. Stowage is provided for 400 tons of coal. The vessel has a moderately fine section, and is fitted with a central keel.

M. Dislère, in the French official publication on the Maritime Section of the recent Exhibition in Paris, makes the following general observations on the armoured second-rates of the French Navy: ' The " Victorieuse " has a displacement of 350 tons in excess of the tonnage of the earlier types, represented by the " Belliqueuse " and " Alma." The additional tonnage has been appropriated almost exclusively to increased offensive power. In the design of the latest example of this class, the " Duguesclin," the increased displacement, which exceeds by nearly 750 tons that of the " Victorieuse," has been appropriated in a very large degree to an increase in the defensive power; and the economy of weight due to the use of steel in the construction of the hull has afforded an opportunity of making further additions to the armour-protection.'

One feature of the equipment of the seagoing armourclads of the French Navy is the arrangement of the towing torpedo. Though the principle is the same, this weapon does not resemble, in outward appearance, that invented by Captain Harvey. It is an elongated cylinder, chamfered away at the ends, to ensure divergence. The attachment to the tow-line is by a span of two legs. The torpedo is usually slung to two light davits or derricks stepped somewhat low down on the ship's side, abaft the main rigging; sometimes the torpedo lies on a kind of bill-board, from which it is moved into a position ready for slipping, by inclining the davits outwards; or it is ejected clear of this by tumblers, somewhat as fitted with sheet-anchors. It is hung by slips to the davits, the foremost one of which is longer than the other, so that the head of the torpedo is directed outwards, and the proper divergence quickly attained. The tow-line is led from forward; it usually comes in on the topgallant forecastle, close to the deck, and is thus kept low enough to clear the fire of the battery guns. From that point it goes through a leading block, as near to the eyes of the fore rigging (inside) as the futtock shrouds permit; and thence through another leading block to a third on the upper deck, abaft the foremast, some feet farther amidships than the bulwarks. It goes from there to the breakwinches, which can usually be placed well under cover, being sheltered laterally by the barbette turrets, and overhead by the bridge or flying deck from which the torpedo is handled. There is apparently no dipping line; but as the present form of towing torpedo has been some years in use, it must be supposed that the simple arrangement just described has been found sufficient to manœuvre it properly.

The positions in which the boats of the new French armoured seagoing ships are hoisted up have evidently been selected with especial care. No davits have been allowed to be fixed so as to seriously impede the fire of the guns. In some ships this difficulty has been completely surmounted; in others less effectually. But in those in which the line of fire is least clear the distribution of the boats has been arranged on a systematic plan. Ingenious arrangements are made for getting both boats and davits out of the way of the guns when necessary, and no rough-and-ready methods of doing so have to be improvised by the crew when clearing for action.

The most original designs and the most marked departures from the ordinary types of ships of war are to be found in the Russian Navy, in which service the belted cruiser first made its appearance, and in which alone are to be found the circular ships of the 'Popoffka' type. The Russian Naval Administration has been the pioneer in the effort to solve the problem of the armoured cruiser, in which great speed is combined with the essential condition of effective armour protection against the projectiles of the greater number of the cruisers with which an engagement may possibly be fought. In point of fact, the armour is sufficient to offer resistance to the projectiles of armed ships, such as the armoured ships of the second class, carrying a still more formidable armament. In pursuance of this policy the Russian Naval Administration has constructed ships in which the water-line is protected like the French armoured vessels of the date

Figs. 163 and 164.

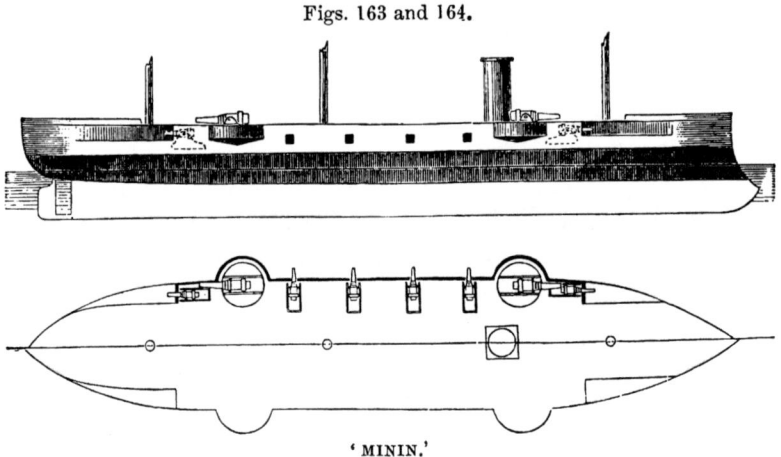

' MININ.'

of the 'Provence' and the 'Bellerophon' by plating six inches in thickness.

The
' Minin.'
The 'Minin,' 'General-Admiral,' and 'Duke of Edinburgh' belong to the class of which we have been speaking. The 'Minin' was constructed, as we learn from Chief Engineer King, as a turret ship on the Coles system, with a length of 298 ft. 3 in., a breadth of 49 ft. 1 in., and a displacement of 5,650 tons. The armament consisted of four guns of 28 tons each, the armour of 12-inch plates on 24-inch backing, and the freeboard was very low. In consequence of the catastrophe to the British vessel 'Captain,' alterations to the 'Minin' were decided upon. The Russian correspondent of the *Newcastle Chronicle* described the modified vessel as being 285 feet long, 48 feet broad, and having a displacement of 4,800 tons. The ship is built with a central battery 98 feet

long, rising ten feet above the water-line. A writer in the *Revue Maritime* says of this vessel : 'The armour, 7 inches thick, exists only on the water-line, which it protects from end to end. Level with the upper edge of the armour is a highly curved deck of iron. The armament, *en barbette* on the upper deck and without protection, is composed of twelve 6-inch, and four 8-inch guns, all on the broadside. Two of the 6-inch and two of the 8-inch guns fire in line with the keel ahead, and two astern. To ensure this result the 8-inch guns are mounted on platforms protruding somewhat beyond the ship's side. All the guns are breech-loaders of Russian construction, mounted on slide carriages with friction compressors. There are also

Figs. 165 and 166.

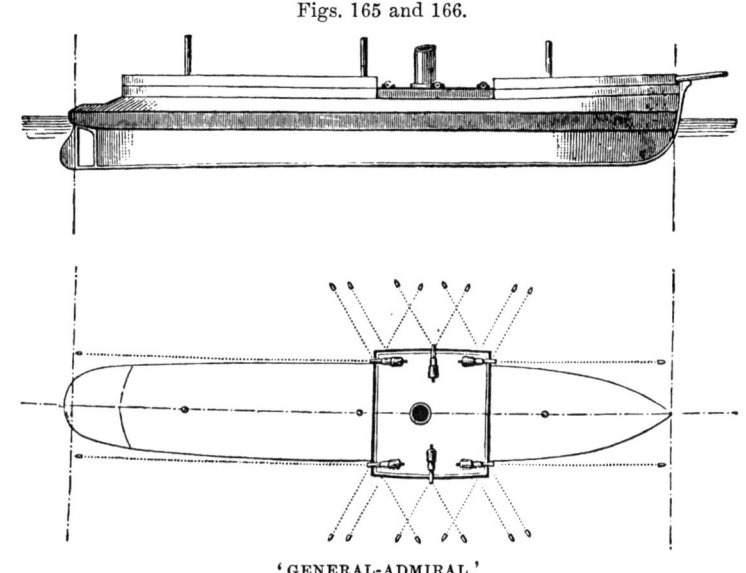

'GENERAL-ADMIRAL.'

twelve light pieces on the hammock-nettings and bridges as a defence against torpedo-boats ; eight are breech-loaders that can be fired eight or nine times in a minute. The " Minin " has a ram and can launch Whitehead torpedoes from above water. She carries an electric light. The hull is divided into watertight compartments by means of athwartship and longitudinal bulkheads. The bunkers are also formed into watertight compartments, and are so placed as to afford protection to the machinery. The vessel is ship rigged and has a large spread of canvas. The machinery, on the compound system, is of 6,300 indicated horse-power ; the speed attained is thirteen knots.'

'In addition to the heavy guns the " Minin " is armed with twelve small pieces, for the purpose of keeping off torpedo-boats ; the vessel is also provided with a spur, and is fitted with tubes for firing the Whitehead torpedo.   A complete electric lighting apparatus has been fitted, and two steam launches have been supplied, for the use either of the spar or the Whitehead torpedo.   Arrangements have been made for protecting the vessel against attack, when at anchor, by means of a complete circle of fifty floating torpedoes.   The " Minin " joined the squadron for exercises at sea, during the whole of one summer, and has lately been despatched to the Pacific.'

Fig. 167.

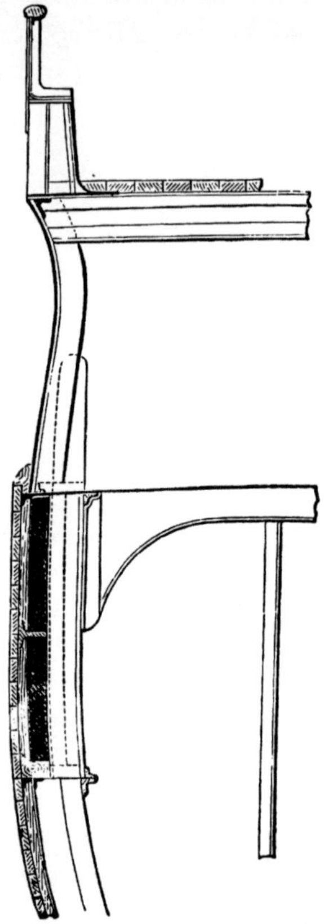

'GENERAL-ADMIRAL' (BELT).

The 'General-Admiral' and 'Duke of Edinburgh.'

The other vessels of the armoured cruiser class, the 'General-Admiral' and the 'Duke of Edinburgh,' were launched the former in 1873, and the latter in 1875.

They were designed to compete with the fast British unarmoured ships 'Raleigh' and 'Boadicea.'   They are built of iron, sheathed with wood and coppered.   The length between perpendiculars is 285 ft. 9 in., the breadth 48 ft. 2 in., the mean draught of water 21 feet, and displacement 4,438 tons.   In weight and dimensions they come therefore between the two British ships just named.   The battery and a belt seven feet wide at the water-line are armoured with 6-inch plates, the remainder of the hull, which is built of iron, being sheathed with wood and coppered.   The battery deck is open-topped, and arranged so as to give both broadside and right ahead and astern fire from corner ports.   It contains four 8-inch rifled guns, and two 6-inch chase guns.   An article in the Revue Maritime et Coloniale, from which extracts have been taken, represents the lines of these vessels to be fine, the engine-power large, and the speed thirteen knots per hour.   They are not provided with spurs to be used as rams, and have neither the speed nor the power of battery possessed by the British ships referred to.

The 'Duke of Edinburgh' has recently been fitted out for a commission in the Pacific, and many alterations have been made in her equipment.   A late account informs us that she is now armed with ten 6-inch breech-loading guns of a new pattern, firing a powder charge of 40 lbs., of which three can be fired right ahead and three astern. There are also fourteen small guns for defence against torpedo-boats. She is fitted for launching Whitehead torpedoes forward and aft. The water-line armour-belt, seven inches at the thickest, tapers to five inches abaft and 4½ inches forward, the rudder-head and steering gear being protected. The ship has twelve boilers set back to back, but there is no longitudinal bulkhead. The coal supply is 950 tons, and the screw can be raised. With 5,200 indicated horse-power a speed of 14½ knots is anticipated.

We have now to consider the English ships, constructed for the same services which have been contemplated in the case of the Russian vessels last described.

The description of the ' Shannon,' as a recent and most powerful The 'Shannon.' type of the second-class ironclad, occupies a considerable space in the work published by Chief Engineer King, of the United States Navy, on *European Ships of War*. The 'Shannon,' he says, was built at Pembroke, and is a new design by the Council of Construction of a special type for a broadside armour-belted cruising ship.

The length between perpendiculars is 260 feet; breadth, extreme, 54 feet; depth of hold, 21 ft. 7½ in.; draught of water, forward 20 feet, aft 22 ft. 6 in.; and displacement, 5,100 tons. She has a full ship-rig, is designed to carry a large spread of canvas, and has a single lifting screw-propeller. Sail-power is intended to be used under all ordinary conditions of cruising.

There are several interesting peculiarities in the construction of Armour. this vessel. The guns, which are to fight upon the broadside, are on an open deck, and without any armour-protection. The armour is limited to a belt extending round the vessel at the water-line, which is not tapered towards the bow, as usual, but ends abruptly sixty feet short of it, at an armoured bulkhead nine inches thick extending across the vessel at this point.

The armour-belt is nine feet deep, five feet of which is under water and four feet above water. It is put on in 12-feet lengths, and extends from the counter to sixty feet from the stem. The thickness at the water-line is nine inches, tapering below as well as above the water. The hull of the vessel is constructed on the usual system, but the double bottom is only 168 feet in length. It is divided into twenty separate watertight spaces, viz., nine principal athwartship watertight bulkheads, and fifteen watertight coal-bunkers. There is no longi-

tudinal bulkhead extending through the vessel, as in all recently constructed armoured ships with twin screws. This element of strength
and safety becomes impracticable in single screw vessels.

The stem has a shifting ram, the point of which is 8 ft. 3 in. above
the keel, and extends eight feet ahead of the stem. This ram is
stowed on board the vessel, the idea being that, as so many accidents
have occurred in time of peace from the ram, and especially in view
of the loss of the 'Vanguard' from the blow by the ram of the 'Iron
Duke, it is best to make it portable and fit it in place only in time
of war. In favour of this plan much can be urged, but it seems to
suggest the questions: first, whether ships on foreign stations will

Figs. 168 and 169.

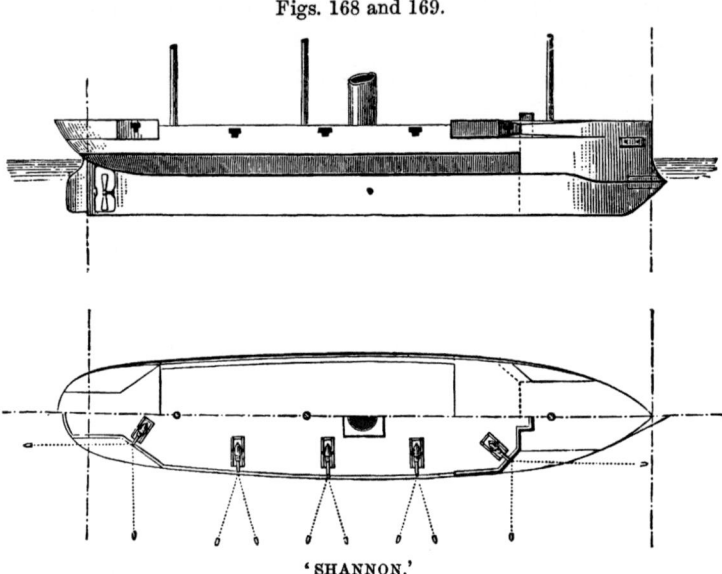

'SHANNON.'

be able in war time to go into docks to have their rams secured in
place ; and secondly, whether, if they should succeed in doing this,
the officers, who up to that time will have been deprived of all
experience, will be able to avoid those accidents which have hitherto
occasionally happened under the most ordinary circumstances, notwithstanding the experience that has been acquired.

The bottom of the 'Shannon,' in common with that of all recently
constructed cruising vessels of the Royal Navy, is sheathed with teak
and zinc. The teak is put on in the usual way, in a single thickness,
with the seams below the water-line uncaulked, for the purpose of
admitting sea water freely between the iron hull and the zinc with
which the planking is covered.

The armament is placed on an open deck, not unlike the un- Armament. covered decks of corvettes. It consists of nine Woolwich guns, two of which are 18-ton guns, protected by armour at the bow from raking fire ahead, six 12-ton guns (three on either broadside unprotected by armour), and one 12-ton stern gun, which is carried on a platform amidships, and is intended to be fought at a port on either side of the deck. This gun is also unprotected by armour. The two 18-ton bow guns can be trained to fire in a line with the keel or to an angle of 90° abaft it.

A writer in *Fraser's Magazine* of February 1878, points out the serious objections to an open battery. He remarks that in the 'Shannon' the stern-chaser, a 12-ton gun, is under the poop deck, but the remaining six guns are completely exposed to rifle fire, and are liable to be disabled by falling spars and rigging. This is, in his opinion, a fatal objection in so large a ship, and it is to be hoped that a future 'Shannon' will have a light spar deck fore and aft.

Mr. King remarks that one of the peculiarities in the design of this ship is the protection by horizontal armour at the top of the belt, and he rightly says that it is an important feature, seeing that the side armour extends only four feet above the water. The lower decks are chiefly composed of iron, rendered watertight, and covered with wood, except the armour deck forward, which is entirely iron. The main deck beams are covered with two thicknesses of iron plates, each about $\frac{3}{8}$-in. thick, under which is wood, thus making the boiler-room, engine-room, and ammunition store impenetrable to anything but very heavy shot or shell. The other decks have a strong plate worked on the end of the beams, connecting them with the outside plating by rivets, rendering them very strong. A second peculiarity is the system of coal-tanks, introduced for the first time at the bow of the vessel. Another noticeable arrangement is the adoption of two ventilating cowls upon the outside of the ship, one for carrying air directly to the stoke-holes, and the other for ventilating the coal-bunkers.

The ship—we are still following the account published by Chief Engines. Engineer King—is propelled by a single screw. The machinery was constructed by Messrs. Laird Brothers, of Birkenhead. The engines are of the compound horizontal return connecting-rod type with four cylinders, two of high and two of low pressure, bolted together similarly to those of the White Star Line of steamers, but placed horizontally. The diameter of the high-pressure cylinders is 44 inches, the diameter of the low-pressure cylinders is 85 inches, and the stroke 4 feet. The condensers are of the ordinary surface type used in the British navy. The diameter of the air-pumps is $22\frac{5}{8}$ inches, and the stroke 4 feet. The diameter of the crank-shaft is $17\frac{1}{2}$ inches. The screw-propeller is of the common Griffith type, two-bladed, and lifting; its diameter is 19 ft. 6 in., and its pitch may be varied from 18 to 22 feet. The boilers, cylindrical in form, are eight in number, each 12 feet in diameter by 12 feet long, and containing two furnaces 3 ft. 8 in. in diameter by six feet in length. They are placed in the vessel back to back, against a longitudinal bulkhead; and, as a consequence, are divided into two sets, with the fire-rooms facing the side coal-bunkers. In this position they are conveniently fired. A transverse bulkhead separates the boilers from the engines, and another transverse bulkhead forward separates them from the hold; hence the central position of the boilers in the vessel, the division into two stoke-holes and protection by watertight bulkheads, gives all the security possible in the event of damage done to the hull by rams or torpedoes.

Designs, compared with earlier types.

Mr. King speaks in terms of high commendation of the progress exhibited in the design of the ' Shannon' over the earlier types of armoured cruisers produced in the Russian navy. In his last edition, however, he adds, ' The trials of this ship have not been as satisfactory as desired. An error appears to have been made in calculating the weights entering into the vessel, and this has been aggravated by additional weights put on board which were unprovided for. As a consequence, the ship is immersed more than was anticipated, besides which alterations became necessary in the topmasts, and the machinery when on trial did not prove satisfactory.'

Alterations.

The alterations in the ' Shannon,' after the ship was apparently almost completed at Pembroke, were very considerable. The correspondent of the *Broad Arrow* reported that the ' Shannon,' when she entered Plymouth Sound in July 1876, was to all intents and purposes ready for sea. Her engines had been tried, and she was masted and rigged. But so far was this from being the case, that she has been under the hands of the Dockyard nearly ever since. Every day something more has been thought of which would benefit the ship, and render her more efficient. Her crew has been increased from 350 to 450 men; Whitehead torpedoes, six 20-pounder torpedo guns, and a number of torpedo fittings have been supplied. The armour to the conning tower has been increased, as also have the armour glacis plates around the hatchways of the lower deck. Armour shutters have been fitted to the engine-hatch, also a heavy windlass and an ejector pump have been supplied. These additional fittings and the increase in the supply of coal from the quantity contemplated in the original estimated displacement, viz., 280 tons to 470 tons, added considerably to the immersion of the 'Shannon.'

Among the additional fittings, though not important in connection with the calculated displacement of the ship, it may not be super-fluous to mention that there was on board a very ingenious and useful apparatus known as Friedman's projector, the invention of a German. The ship has two of these projectors, which are fitted in the double bottom at the forward end. They would be useful in expelling water from the hold, or the armour deck of the ship, if the vessel was damaged in action, and the two together will expel about 700 tons of water per hour through a 9-inch pipe above the water-line. The active agent is steam from the ship's boilers, which, passing through the projector, causes a partial vacuum. The 'Shannon' and the 'Inflexible' are the only two vessels in the Royal Navy yet fitted with this apparatus.

The principle upon which the design for the 'Shannon' was pre-pared has been much discussed by naval critics. In Mr. Barnaby's paper, read before the Institute of Naval Architects, *On some Recent Designs for Ships of War,* he gave the views of the responsible author of the design at considerable length. The paragraphs relating to the 'Shannon,' which was then still on the stocks, may here be appro-priately quoted :— *Mr. Barnaby on the design for the 'Shannon.'*

'*The "Shannon."*—This question of cost leads at once to the "Shannon," an armour-plated ship, designed last year, and now build-ing at Pembroke.

'I have already said that the relative cost of the two unarmoured fast frigates "Raleigh" and "Shah," will be about 50 and 60 respec-tively ; the cost of the ironclad I am about to describe to you will lie between the two, and will be about 54. I will not compare her with the cheaper of the two, but with the more costly, viz., with the "Shah."

'Their relative displacements are, armourclad 5,000, unarmoured ship 5,400, and their engine-powers are 3,500 in the armourclad, and 7,500 in the unarmoured ship; this enormous disproportion of power being necessary to give the three knots of speed which the one will have in excess of the other. When I say that the faster ship carries $12\frac{1}{2}$-ton guns at the bow and stern, and could have them also on her broadside if desired, in place of the $6\frac{1}{2}$-ton guns with which it has been preferred to arm her, I have probably said enough to establish in some minds the incontestable superiority of the "Shah" over the "Shannon."

'Other persons may perhaps care to balance, against the "Shah," the advantage of protection to the hull and engines of the "Shannon"

which is afforded by her nine inches of armour. This ship has a belt
of armour nine feet wide with a deck covering it protected by 1½-inch
plating under the wood, and by shellproof gratings over the hatches.
This 9-inch armour is not tapered towards the bow as is usual, but
ends abruptly sixty feet short of it, at an armoured bulkhead
which descends five feet under water. Before this bulkhead the armour
takes the form of a submerged horizontal deck running forward to the
stem, at a depth of from five to ten feet below the surface. By this
means protection is afforded, so far as the thickness of armour is
capable of giving it, to the buoyancy and stability of the ship, to her
propelling and manœuvring power, and to her magazines. The
armour-bulkhead of which I have already spoken is carried across the
bow of the ship at sixty feet from the stem, rises to a height of twenty
feet out of the water with armour of nine inches and eight inches upon
it to the top of the forecastle, and it turns round at the sides, embracing
the forecastle with arms 26 feet long. It thus guards both decks
against raking fire from ahead, and creates an armoured forecastle, open
only at the rear, for two 18-ton bow guns. Within this armoured forecastle will be the instruments to communicate with the engine-room,
the helm, and the battery. In other respects the ship is unarmoured,
i.e., when engaged upon the beam, her broadside guns are unprotected by armour excepting the two under the forecastle, and as against
an enemy astern the battery is as unprotected as it would be in the
"Shah" or "Raleigh." In these two cases, there would, however, be
always this advantage in the "Shannon," viz., that the men can be
withdrawn under the cover of armour, and the guns being laid on the
broadside, can be discharged by wire when passing an enemy, after
an attempt on either side to ram.

'Compared with powerful, fast unarmoured ships, and engaged
with them, the "Shannon" will have all the advantages of a first-class
ironclad, and would be as unassailable as the "Hercules" and "Sultan."
She would be much more formidable to them than such an adversary
as the "Minotaur," which has twice her bulk, twice her power of
engines, and would cost twice as much money; while the armour of
the "Minotaur" has but little more than one-third the resisting power
of that of the "Shannon." The additional speed of the "Minotaur"
and other ironclads under steam would avail nothing in a fight with
a ship like the "Shah." If I were to compare the "Shannon" with an
ironclad, I should pit against her the latest completed, viz. the
"Swiftsure" and "Triumph," although the cost would stand at 68
for these ships, against 54 for the "Shannon."

'A battle fought upon paper between two ships so dissimilar, in many respects, as the "Shannon" and "Triumph" would hardly be conclusive as to the respective merits of the ships, and I shall not, therefore, go farther into the matter. I have the less hesitation in referring to the "Triumph" in this comparison, because I have in another place spoken in the highest terms I could command of the vessels of the "Triumph" class. I compared them at the same time with the armoured ships of foreign navies, and I should claim the same relative place for the "Shannon." '

It is satisfactory to find that Chief Engineer King fully confirmed the favourable opinion expressed by Mr. Barnaby.

Captain Noel, in his prize essay on *The Best Types of Ships of War*, says, that while he does not wholly coincide with the principle on which this ship is built, he nevertheless regards it as the only approach to what he deems necessary for ironclads or ships of the line.

Commander Noel.

M. Dislère, in *La Guerre d'Escadre*, makes an elaborate criticism of this ship. He says, that, ' If Russia was the first maritime power which acknowledged the necessity of depriving the guns of the protection of armour, for the purpose of combining in one and the same ship some of the qualities required in a cruiser, which might be called upon to keep the sea for months together far from a port at which supplies could be obtained, together with a certain protection for the vitals of the ship, the water-line, the engine, the machinery and the rudder, this programme was only realised by reducing to the minimum the area of the protected surface, and it was the English Admiralty who, in the plans of Mr. Barnaby, first succeeded in producing a ship which, within comparatively limited dimensions, the length being 260 feet and the displacement about 5,200 tons, satisfied tolerably well these numerous requirements.

M. Dislère.

' It will be seen that in the "Shannon," as in other large English armoured vessels, the stern fire is completely sacrificed. No doubt it may be assumed that ships will generally present the stern to the enemy. For ships to be stationed in foreign waters, especially it may be assumed that they will often be called upon to give chase to an enemy; but they may be also compelled to retire before an enemy of superior strength, and is it not possible that guns of heavy calibre may then be found to be extremely valuable? Moreover, if ships of this class were required to take part as auxiliaries in an engagement between line-of-battle ships, would it not be necessary that their guns should be mounted in such a manner that in the *mêlée*, which must follow as soon as an attempt to give the ram to the enemy had failed, and especially at the critical moment when the ships would begin to turn in order to resume the attack, they should have at their disposal something more powerful than a single 12-ton gun.

'The water-line is protected by a belt nine feet in depth, extending from the stern to within sixty feet of the stem. This belt, formed of two strakes of plating nine inches in thickness, and a lower strake eight inches in thickness, preserves the same thickness from the centre to the extremities of the ship. The bow is completely abandoned to the fire of the enemy, but in order to diminish the injurious effects from the influx of water this compartment is filled with coal. The bow compartment extends down to the level of the lower edge of the armour-plating, that is to say, five feet below the water-line. The bow compartment is separated from the lower compartment of the hold by an armoured deck 1½ inches in thickness, which protects the ship from the danger of an influx of water into the forward compartment.

'The "Shannon" is very sufficiently armoured for the greater number of contingencies which may possibly arise; but it may be asked whether it was really useful to protect the guns against a raking fire. By appropriating to the protection of the decks the weight of the armour-plating on the sides of the battery, and on the bulkhead forward, a considerable increase in their thickness might have been secured, and by mounting the artillery upon the upper deck, partly on pivots in the centre, and partly at ports in the side, or on the projecting half-turrets, there would have been a fair chance of escaping the dangers of a raking fire.'

The 'Nelson' and 'Northampton.'
M. Dislère.

M. Dislère introduces his notice of the 'Nelson' with a general description in the following terms:—

'The "Shannon" was held not to satisfy fully the requirements of war, and it was decided, at a cost of 2,260 tons additional, whilst maintaining the principle of taking the protecting armour away from the broadside guns, to protect the stern fire, to increase the offensive power, and, in short, to extend to the after part the system of protection adopted for the fore part of the "Shannon;" in a word, on an ordinary hull terminated by an armoured deck situated five feet below the water-line there is placed amidships a box clad with armour nine inches thick in all parts; the fore and after parts are continued like ordinary constructions in iron; then upon this armoured box is laid an upper "orlop" deck (*faux pont supérieur*) not protected (except forward and aft against raking fire), and finally above this the guns are mounted in a battery in this case completely covered.'

Mr. King.

Chief Engineer King gives a more detailed description. He says:

NELSON.

'The two sister ships " Nelson " and " Northampton," the former under construction by Messrs. Elder and Co., and the latter by Messrs. Napier and Sons, near Glasgow, on the Clyde, constitute a new type of ocean-cruising broadside armour-plated ships. They are the latest productions of armoured vessels by the chief naval architect of the British navy, and in 1876 were pronounced by him before an audience at the Loan Exhibition, South Kensington, to be his ideal of cruising fighting ships.

'The framing is on the usual longitudinal system adopted in the construction of British ships of war, and in this instance the longitudinal frames are made of steel, so as to combine lightness with strength. The double bottom extends for about 150 feet amidships,

Figs. 170 and 171.

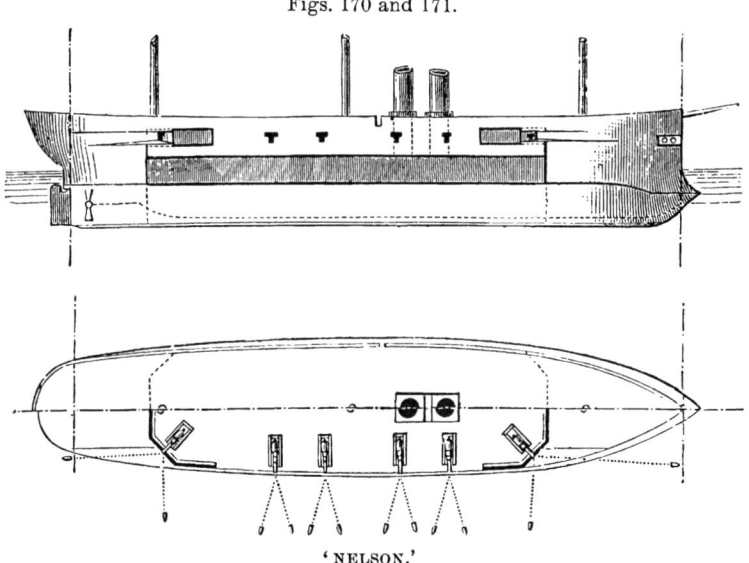

'NELSON.'

and the space between the inner and outer skins is divided into many watertight compartments. According to the system recently adopted for armoured ships, there is a central longitudinal bulkhead, besides numerous transverse bulkheads, underneath the lower deck and wing passage bulkheads. Altogether, including the spaces between the two skins there are ninety watertight compartments; all the doors leading to these compartments are fitted watertight and worked by machinery, and every conceivable precaution has been taken to provide against destruction by rams and torpedoes.

'There are three principal decks, the lower, main, and upper.

'The protecting armour consists of a belt at the water-line of about 181 feet in length amidships, this belt being nine feet deep, four feet above water, and five feet under water. It is put on in two strakes; the upper strake being nine inches thick upon a 10-inch backing of teak, and the lower one six inches thick upon a teak backing of thirteen inches. Extending across the ship at each end of this armour-belt there is an armoured bulkhead, which extends from the bottom of the armour-belt, five feet under water, to the upper deck, and has in all a depth of 22 feet. Its thickness is nine inches above water, tapering to six inches at the bottom. Between the main and upper decks these bulkheads are shaped so as to form corner ports at the fore and after ends of the battery. Between the armour-bulkheads and at the upper level of the armour-belt the lower deck is formed throughout of 2-inch plates, so as to protect the machinery, boilers, magazines, etc. The horizontal armour is a peculiar feature of these ships. For about 57 feet at the fore end there is an armoured deck. This deck is two inches thick and five feet under water at the junction with the armoured bulkhead, but inclines deeper towards the stem, and terminates forward in the ram. There is likewise a horizontal armoured deck of the same thickness and same depth under water, extending from the after armoured bulkhead to the stern. These submerged armoured decks are intended to protect the lower part of the ship before and abaft the armoured bulkheads, and especially the steering gear provided for emergencies.

' As in the case of the " Inflexible," the " Northampton " is partly dependent for buoyancy on the displacement of the bulk of the enclosed spaces forward and aft lying above the armoured deck and below the water-line, and the flooding of these spaces will represent in action so much lost buoyancy. To prevent this loss, however, the ends have been filled up as far as possible by water-excluding stores, such as coal and water tanks; while cofferdams accessible by gratings on the main deck are also provided.

' From the above outline it will be seen that the central part of the vessel for 181 feet in length, in which all the propelling machinery is contained, may be regarded as completely protected from the ordinary shots of the enemy. The ends of the vessel above the submerged decks are entirely unprotected by armour, and may, it is supposed, be riddled with shot without serious injury to the flotation of the vessel. If shot or shell, traversing the unarmoured parts under water should tear away the side plating, it is so constructed that it would rip off from the armoured deck without disturbing the connection between this deck and the plating of the bottom beneath it. With this object in view all the rivets have been countersunk to prevent their heads starting and being converted into projectiles when struck, while the side plating is fixed without the usual transverse framing.

'The armament consists of four 18-ton guns and eight 12-ton guns on the main deck, with six 20-pdrs., three 9-pdrs., one 7-pdr., two Gatlings, and half a dozen Nordenfeldts on the upper or spar deck—the latter being intended for use as torpedo-boat destroyers. Of the 18-ton guns, one on either side forward, and one on either side aft, are situated behind the oblique portion of the armoured bulkhead, and the ports are so cut that these guns can command a cross fire at the bow and stern; the eight 12-ton guns are disposed equally on either side, termed intermediate, and have in front of them the thin sides of the ship only. They are separated by a transverse bulkhead, or splinter skin, one inch thick, intended to cut off each gun's crew from the others. This broadside of guns is designed to be loaded and laid in a close engagement under the shelter of the bow or stern armour, and may be fired by electricity without exposing the crew. The ram is a heavy plate, triangular in shape, set vertically, and terminating in a sharp point about eleven feet in advance of the stem. It is supported by two side plates three inches thick, which may be regarded as a continuation of the armoured deck. The rudder, which is massive, is eighteen feet deep by eleven feet in breadth, and is formed by two thicknesses of deck planking, set in a strong iron frame.

'The vessel has bilge-keels 33 inches deep, formed of two plates riveted together, and extending in length amidships for about 100 feet. The outer bottom of the hull below the water-line is sheathed with a 3-inch thickness of teak, which is covered with zinc. The seams between the strakes of sheathing are left uncaulked. There are to be three masts fitted, as for a full-rigged ship, and the coal-bunker accommodation is sufficient for a long voyage and cruising in distant seas. In time of war it is intended that only the lower masts shall remain standing.

'The novelty of design embodied in the "Nelson" and "Northampton" consists in the system of armouring. As may be readily seen, the object aimed at has been to give thicker plates to vessels of this class over the vital parts, at the expense of the exposed parts, and so to increase the offensive power by carrying a heavier weight of ordnance. .

'While in the "Inflexible" the citadel is thickly armoured to keep out shot and shell, the battery deck of the "Northampton" is wholly unprotected, the safety of the ship being insured, not by keeping out shot, but by interposing as few obstacles as possible to its passage through her.

Armament.

Description of machinery by Mr. Ravenhill.

'The machinery of the " Nelson " was designed and constructed under the direction of Mr. Kirk, the manager of the engineering works of Messrs. Elder and Co. She is fitted with twin screws, each driven by an independent pair of compound engines, with vertical inverted cylinders, of the collective power of 3,000 horses; giving an aggregate power of 6,000 indicated horse-power for both pairs of engines.

Trials, from the *Times'* report.

'The official trial of the "Nelson" took place at Plymouth in March, 1878. At the full-power trial of six hours' duration, the average indicated horse-power was 6,246, with 79·05 revolutions per minute, and a pressure of steam in the boilers of 60 lbs. on the square inch. At the half-power trial of four hours' duration, the indicated horse-power was 3,083, with 63·35 revolutions per minute, and a pressure of steam in the boilers of 60 lbs. The average consumption of coal during the full-power trial was 2·14 lbs. per indicated horse-power per hour; and during the half-power trial 1·47 lbs. of coal per indicated horse-power per hour. This was obtained without the use of the steam blast. The above two results were equal, if not superior, to any equally well authenticated performance up to that time.'

The ' Nelson ' was again put through a comprehensive trial on the measured mile in Stokes Bay in February 1880 :—

For the purposes of the trial, the ' Nelson ' was brought down to her normal load-line of 24 feet forward, and 25 feet aft by 350 tons of water ballast; and she had on board besides about 60 tons of trial coal, in addition to 546 tons of ordinary coal. The sea was what is technically described as ' smooth,' but a lively breeze blew all the time with a force of four from the south-west, and consequently directly abeam throughout the runs. An abundant supply of steam was generated all through the trial without any necessity arising for the use of the blast. The full-power runs were the first completed, the four being made with the tide as near dead water as could be. The following were the results :—

Runs	Time	Revolutions		Knots
	M. S.	Starboard	Port	
1	4 28	81·71	81·94	13·433
2	4 9	81·63	83·85	14·458
3	4 20	81·46	82·38	13·846
4	4 16	80·85	82·96	14·062
	Means	81·42	82·78	14·050

The mean revolutions of both engines were 82·10, the other means being—pressure in boiler, 64·5 lbs.; vacuum, 26 inches starboard, and

26·37 port; pressure in cylinder: starboard engine, 32·75 and 11·90 lbs.; port engine, 32·525, and 11·15 lbs. The indicated horse-power was 6,624·57. Six thousand horses was the contract power, and the excess was readily obtained without any water being necessary to keep the bearings cool. The throttle valves having been adjusted, four runs were next made at two-thirds power, with the following results:—Steam in boilers, 58·75 lbs.; vacuum, 27·12 inches, and 26·50 inches; revolutions, 71; indicated horse-power, 4,125·87; and speed of ship, 12·856 knots per hour. The last progressive trial was made at one-third power, the means being as follow :—Boiler pressure, 59·87 lbs.; vacuum, 27 inches and 26½ inches; revolutions, 58; indicated horse-power, 2,323·47; and speed, 10·537 knots. At the termination of the series of progressive trials, it was determined to make a full-speed trial of the ship with only one of the engines going, the other being for the moment supposed to have been disabled. With the starboard engine at rest a mean speed of 10·600 knots was realised, with 75·64 revolutions, and 2,996·3 horse-power; and with the port engine stopped the result gave 72·25 revolutions, 2,904·06 horses, and a speed of 10·101; from 15° to 17° of helm being required to keep the ship in a straight line.

The machinery of H.M.S. 'Northampton' was manufactured by Messrs. John Penn and Son, of Greenwich; and consists of two sets of inverted three-cylinder engines driving twin screws. Each set of engines consists of three inverted cylinders, having a diameter of 54 inches, and a stroke of 3 ft. 3 in. They are placed between the same perpendiculars on either side of a middle-line bulkhead, and act at equal angles upon the crank-shaft. When working at the full power of 6,000 horses, they are simple expansive engines, with steam at 60 lbs. pressure cut off at about one-fifth of the stroke, and making 85 revolutions per minute. When at full power the steam from the boilers is admitted equally to all the six cylinders and exhausted thence; but when working as compound engines, the steam is admitted to the foremost cylinder of each set only; and from these it is allowed to pass into the other four by a simple valve arrangement, which has been patented by Mr. Penn. The power exerted under these circumstances is 3,000 horses, and the number of revolutions 68. This compound system is also used for any less power than 3,000 horses. The engines may also be worked as simple expansive engines with low-pressure steam. At these reduced powers, which are those ordinarily used by men-of-war when cruising, the ship has all the advantages of compound engines in point of economy, etc.; while there is an actual gain at very small powers in not having a

Machinery of 'Northampton.'

low-pressure cylinder disproportionately large.   While a reduction of
weight per indicated horse-power is thus secured, another advantage
attends the equal-sized cylinders—viz., the interchangeability of parts,
which allows the weight and cost of spare gear to be considerably
diminished.

These engines are the first of the kind which have as yet been
introduced into the service, but the 'Ajax' and 'Agamemnon' are to
be engined after the same model by the same contractors

Trials of
'North-
ampton,'
from *Times*'
reports.On the trial trip of the 'Northampton,' a mean of 6,037 indicated
horse-power and a speed of fourteen knots was obtained.   The mean
indicated horse-power developed in the 'Nelson' was 6,250 horses,
with a maximum speed of fifteen knots.   Further trials of the
'Northampton's' engines were made in November 1879, under
various conditions of engine-power, on the measured mile.   The
details are given in the following extract from the *Times* :—'The one-
third-power trial gave a mean speed of 10·021 knots an hour, the
average pressure in the boiler being 66·8 lbs., the vacuum in the
condensers being over 28 inches, the revolutions per minute 60, and
the total horse-power 2,072·14.   The two-thirds-power runs were
next made, the mean results showing a speed of 12·369 knots and an
indicated power of 4,074·91.   In this series of runs the average
pressure of steam was 63·37 lbs., the vacuum varied from 28·25
inches in the starboard forward condenser to 27·25 in the after
starboard condenser, the revolutions being 74.   During the whole of
the trial it was found that, owing to some defect in the rudder, a
starboard helm of ten points was required to keep the ship in a
straight line ; and it cannot be questioned that this circumstance
both detracted from the speed of the ship and threw much unnecessary
strain upon the machinery.   An attempt was finally made to complete
the full-power runs, but without success.   Some full-power circles
were afterwards made.   With both engines going ahead, the helm
was put hard over to starboard with the steering engine in
8 seconds by 3¼ turns of the wheel, the circle being completed in
4 min. 13 sec.; its diameter was 455 yards.   The time occupied
in putting the helm hard over to port was fifteen seconds, the
circle was 448 yards in diameter, and it was made in 4 min.
5 sec.   With hand gear the helm was put over to starboard in
three minutes, and to port in 3 min. 30 sec.; and it is worth pointing out that while one man sufficed to steer the ship by steam,
it required the services of 24 bluejackets to get the helm over 25
deg.   The starboard circle was made in 5 min. 44 sec., and the port
circle in 4 min. 36 sec., the diameters being respectively 603

yards and 562 yards. The two sets of engines were stopped dead in 17 seconds and 20 seconds, started astern in 9 seconds and 15 seconds, and from going astern they were started ahead in 8 seconds and 10 seconds.'

Shortly afterwards another trial took place. 'Since the last trial, in order to give additional clearance between the propellers and the run of the ship, the diameter of the blades had been reduced by six inches at the leading edge to one inch at the following edge, thus giving a mean reduction of fourteen inches. The draught of water was as nearly as possible the same as before—viz., 24 ft. 9½ in. forward and 25 ft. 3 in. aft. There was no wind, no sea, and as a result very little draught in the furnaces, with a corresponding difficulty in keeping the cylinders, of which there are six, supplied with a full head of steam. A heavy bank of shifting fog lay along the northern shore, which rendered it occasionally difficult at times to discern the buoys and mile-posts. The mean pressure in the boilers was 57·68 lbs.; the average vacuum in all the condensers exceeded 26 inches, that in the forward starboard condenser being 26·68 inches; the mean pressure in the starboard cylinders was 26·549 lbs., and in the port cylinders 26·449 lbs.; and the indicated horse-power of the starboard engine 3,005·19, and of the port engine 3,057·46 horses. The total power developed during the four official runs was thus 6,062·65, which, being in excess of the contract power, was so far satisfactory. But the most extraordinary circumstance is that, while the horse-power developed was about 500 more than before the modification of the screws, a mean speed of only 13·173 knots was realised, or substantially the same as before. There is, consequently, considerable waste of engine-power somewhere, though opinions differ as to the cause. It is quite true that the ship carried about five deg. of starboard helm, by means of which her way was retarded and the useful power of the engines handicapped, but at the former trial the ship carried as many as ten deg. of weather helm, so that the balance, so far as the performance of the ship is concerned, was still more noticeably in favour of the previous trial. The necessity of the starboard helm is attributed to the extra revolutions made by the port engine—the starboard engine making 83·63 revolutions, while the port engine made 85·41 per minute; but this remains to be proved by trials of the ship at various trims. It appears evident from the full-power trial that further modifications will be required in the propellers to secure better speed results, greater blade area being probably necessary to make up for reductions of diameter.'

The cost of vessels of the 'Nelson' and 'Northampton' type may Cost.

be set down at not less than 270,000*l.* for the hull, and 100,000*l.* for the engines and boilers. The sail area of the 'Northampton' is 24,766 square feet, giving a coefficient as regards displacement of 64·26, or considerably higher than that of the 'Bellerophon.' The area of the midship section is 1,242·8 square feet, and the displacement 7,323 tons. Six hundred tons of coal can be carried upon the ordinary draught of 24 ft. 9 in. forward and 25 ft. 9 in. aft. With an increased draught of seventeen inches 1,200 tons of coal can be carried.

Cruise of 'Northampton.' The results of a recent experimental cruise in the Channel are detailed as follows in the *Times*:—' After being commissioned the " Northampton " proceeded on a week's cruise in the Channel for the trial of her guns and machinery, and also for the purpose of ascertaining her behaviour under sail. Mr. Barnaby, the Director of Naval Construction, was present during the whole cruise; Messrs. Penn were represented by Mr. Gosling; and Sir William Thomson also was in attendance. The engines were tried under different conditions of speed, and with and without the blast. They were found to work smoothly, all the parts being easily accessible, and their arrangement very simple. The full power was not realised, but this was attributed to the circumstance that the coal, which was of the ordinary kind, had become deteriorated, and that the stokers, who formed part of the ship's own complement, were somewhat inexperienced. After leaving Sheerness the wind proved light, with a smooth sea all the time. No opportunity was consequently afforded of ascertaining the ship's behaviour in a gale or in a seaway. With a force of wind of from two to three (Beaufort scale), she stayed in ten minutes and wore in 23 minutes ; while close-hauled she was found to carry about 15 degrees of weather helm, thirty degrees being the extreme limit of helm, and her speed about three knots. With the wind abaft the beam and the yards square, she carried ten degrees of weather helm, and realised a speed of 3·8 knots. During the cruise one day was devoted to general quarters firing at a target. The practice was admirable, more especially the electric broadsides, which were delivered at 600 yards with the ship passing the targets at considerable speed. The Gatlings and Nordenfeldts were also tried. Both kinds of guns gave satisfaction, but the former proved somewhat the more rapid of the two. Sir William Thomson's inventions were subjected to very severe practical tests, and were found to answer perfectly. During the gunnery practice the vibration of the compass was inappreciable, even when firing broadsides, and the slightest motion of the ship's head as observed by the land was indicated. On the

other hand, a blank charge fired from a 20-pounder caused the card
of the Admiralty compass to oscillate violently; and it would have
been impossible at any time during the target practice, when the
firing was more or less continuous, to steer except by the untrust-
worthy method of using a liquid compass.   Sir William's sounding
machine was also continuously used during the cruise, and accurate
soundings were obtained in 36 fathoms of water by a couple of men
in four minutes, the ship meanwhile going over the ground at a rate
of fifteen knots.   The rope mantlets on the battery deck in no way
interfered with the guns or with the supply of powder or projectiles,
and it is believed that they will be of great service in action in
reducing danger to life and in producing greater steadiness on the
part of the crew.   The telephone which was connected between the
bridge and the conning tower, and was also led up to the maintop for
the purpose of ascertaining the changes of range at target practice,
turned out a great success.   The only exception was its application
to the engine-room, where the vibration and noise caused by the
machinery prevented its being heard.

'The cruise was perfectly satisfactory so far as the behaviour of
the ship and the endurance of her machinery were concerned.'

The modifications in the design for the 'Nelson' and the 'North-   'Nelson'
ampton' as compared with the 'Shannon' were fully described in the   and
   'Shannon'
columns of the *Broad Arrow*:—'The principle of submerged deck   compared,
   Broad
armour, which was first applied to a slight extent in the "Shannon,"   *Arrow.*
is carried to its fullest limits in these ships.   In the "Shannon" the
guns received but partial protection on the broadside ; in the "Nelson"
and "Northampton" no side armour is to be found except at the
water-line.   The reduction in the area protected by the armour
admits of an increase in the thickness of the plating abreast the engines, boilers, and magazines, while strong transverse bulkheads at the
extremities of the gun-battery protect it from a raking fire.   Further,
it is assumed that a 3-inch armoured deck placed four feet below the
water is a far better provision for keeping a ship afloat, provided
she has sufficient stability, than 12-inch vertical armour at the water's
edge.   The guns are protected against broadside fire with plates of
only one inch in thickness, but instead of employing iron plates, two
thicknesses of half-inch steel plates manufactured by the Siemens'
process had been used.'

The Controller of the Navy expounded the main objects intended   Sir W.
to be realised in the designs of the 'Nelson' and 'Northampton'   Houston
   Stewart.
in a speech delivered on the occasion of the launching of the
'Northampton' on the Clyde.   He said: 'In the designing of the

" Shannon," the " Nelson," and the " Northampton "—the last two
being improvements on the first, and more formidable—he put
specially before them their capacity for the protection of our commerce. They were no part of what was called our battle-ships.
Their object was not to take a place in a close engagement, but to
roam over the seas and drive away those wasps, those unarmoured
fast cruisers, which they were told were to be brought to bear upon
us by stopping our trade and preventing us carrying on that commerce in which we have always taken the foremost place all over
the world. No unarmoured ship would venture to come either near
the " Nelson " or the " Northampton," for they carried guns against
which no unarmoured ship would be safe. The vitals of these vessels,
their engines and boilers, were protected, and he therefore hoped
these ships would be the forerunners of a greater number of such
vessels, which would form what he might call a flying squadron.
They were not for a moment to confuse these with our ironclad
battle-ships.'

It may be hoped that these large and costly ships may be relied
upon to render more effective service in naval battle than seems to
have been anticipated by the Controller in the speech from which
we have quoted. The correspondent of the *Times* remarks that
Captain Fisher regards the ' Northampton ' as practically unsinkable;
and among other merits which she possesses must be mentioned
great coal-stowing capacity, a powerful bow and stern fire under
armour, excellent accommodation and ventilation, torpedo ports above
and near the water-line, and a battery which is not jammed up in a
box, but is spread out along nearly the whole length of the ship.

M. Dislère.   The design has been criticised by M. Dislère as too large and too
costly for ships not intended to take their place in the line of battle.
The defensive power of the ' Nelson ' and ' Northampton ' is quite
sufficient in the majority of cases, but he cannot accept as satisfactory
the reduction in armament. It is composed of four 18-ton guns,
firing two right ahead and two astern, both the former and the
latter being also equally capable of being trained to fire on the
broadside. In addition there are eight 12-ton broadside guns on each
broadside; and lastly six Gatling guns are mounted on the upper deck.
This armament gives—bow fire, two 18-ton guns, weight of broadside
about 800 lbs.; on the broadside, two 18-ton and four 12-ton
guns, weight of broadside about 1,800 lbs; stern fire, two 18-ton
guns, weight of broadside about 800 lbs.[1]

[1] Admiral Scott has made the   of these ships:—'Referring to the dia-
following observations on the armament   gram of the " Nelson " and " Northamp-

For a ship equalling in point of displacement and price the ships intended for the line of battle, while admitting that in the general distribution of weights a sufficiently considerable proportion has been allotted to armament, it must at the same time be remarked that the calibre of the guns is scarcely adequate. The 18-ton gun is not sufficient for an engagement in the line of battle. On the other hand, for service on foreign stations and for the general duties of a cruiser, a displacement of 7,440 tons appears very considerable. In short, if we compare the 'Shannon' and the 'Nelson,' we find, with a slight superiority in speed and some protection at the water-line, almost double the weight of armament sheltered against a raking fire astern, and protected by the deck from falling spars and rigging. This is but a slight gain from the augmentation of forty per cent. in the displacement, and consequently in the cost.

On March 18, 1880, Mr. Barnaby, C.B., read a paper at the Institution of Naval Architects, from which the following extracts are given:— Mr. Barnaby.

'I regret to have to admit the fact that, while the " Nelson " is a 14-knot ship on the mile *without* the use of the steam-blast, the sister ship, notwithstanding that the engines are the perfection of workmanship and material, is at present only a $13\frac{1}{4}$-knot ship *with* the steam-blast. The difference is due mainly to the difference in the performance of the two types of engines, particularly of the propellers, and partly to the fact that, from some cause, the "Northampton"

ton" (now building), so as more clearly to indicate the method which would, I think, largely increase the offensive and defensive power of future cruisers, and render them more than a match for any war vessel afloat, I wish to point out that the aforesaid vessels are to mount four unprotected 12-ton guns, and two partly protected 18-ton guns on *each broadside*. The improvements I propose are, first to exchange these eight 12-ton guns for two 25-ton guns, which, according to the proportions of relative power, would be of equal force to the guns removed ; to exchange the four 18-ton guns for four 25-ton guns, and to bring the armoured bulkheads much nearer, and join them in one solid structure with the cross bulkheads. I would then place one 25-ton gun forward and one aft, *outside* the armour, which would give a total of eight 25-ton guns, six of them fully covered by the same armour as that which forms a first line

of protection to the engines and boilers, the armoured deck being their inner defence. This arrangement would enable the proposed ships to fire five 25-ton guns on either broadside, three 25-ton guns ahead, and three 25-ton guns astern. The broadside of one of these cruisers, which I name the " Collingwood," would consequently be of more than double the power of that fixed for the " Nelson" and " Northampton "; her bow and stern-fire more than treble ; and the whole area covered by the " Collingwood's " fire more than twice that of these ships. This result is obtained by using the same small rear turntables as those by which the 18-ton guns in the " Sultan" and " Hercules," and the 12-ton guns in the " Shah," &c., are turned from port to port.'—From Part II. of a paper, *On the Maritime Defence of England*, R.U.S.I., June 30, 1876.

always needs starboard helm to keep her on a straight course, and this checks her way. When the screws of the " Northampton " are altered, it will probably be possible to greatly reduce the difference between the two ships. I may be permitted to add that the " Northampton " left Spithead for her station with 1,200 tons of coal in her bunkers, and with her gun-deck portsills 11½ feet out of water. The " Nelson " will float under the same conditions about five inches lighter, and will thus have, with 1,200 tons of fuel, nearly a 12-feet height of port.

'The real question concerning the " Nelson " class is, now that they are completed, are they fit for their proposed service? What most people will care about is, what services are the ships designed to perform, and what promise is there of due performance? The ships may be looked at from two points of view. They may be regarded as *armoured ships* having to meet armoured ships, or as *protected cruisers*. The very first duty the class is required to perform is to relieve the " Bellerophon " as the flag-ship on the North American Station. I am therefore almost called upon to compare the two ships, and I believe I am sufficiently alive to the good points in both to be able to compare them impartially, so far at least as they can be compared, without either having undergone the stress of war. The two ships are fairly comparable, for they are about the same size, carry equal crews, and cost about the same money. It is sometimes supposed that the " Nelson " is a type in which armour is greatly reduced in amount. This is not so. It is reduced in extent, but the average thickness is greater, and the total weight is greater in the " Nelson " than it is in the " Bellerophon." Covering-in the entire battery of the " Bellerophon " with armour, and extending the armour to the extremities of the water-line, makes it necessary to be content with an average thickness of the vertical armour throughout the ship of 5·28 inches ; whereas in the " Nelson " the average thickness of the vertical armour is 7·28 inches. So far, therefore, as there is an attempt to protect with armour, the average thickness of the protection will be nearly 38 per cent. more than that in the " Bellerophon." I do not compare the squares of these thicknesses in the usual way, as representing the relative strengths, because for the greater portion of the blows received from shells in action the thinner armour will probably be impenetrable. The armour is suppressed at the ends of the ship, and an under-water deck is substituted for it. Beneath this deck aft is situated the steering gear and the rudder-head, so that it is far more secure than it is in the " Bellerophon," where it is all above water, concealed from view, and protected by thin armour, as is usual in belted ships.

' The " Bellerophon " has greatly the advantage in the weight of the broadside fired from protected guns, and in the fact that, except at the ports, the battery walls are protected against the perforation of most shells, while the central part of the " Nelson's " armament is exposed to the entrance of any projectiles which could get through an inch plate.   But the " Nelson " is much the more heavily-armed ship; the total weight of the armament being, " Bellerophon," 420 tons, " Nelson," 533 tons.   The power of the " Nelson " in the right-ahead and right-astern attack, both offensively and defensively, is also greatly superior to that of earlier ships.   The " Northampton " carries comfortably two 60-feet torpedo boats of sixteen knots speed, in addition to the service of boats required in a flag-ship.   The total weight of the boats carried is nearly forty tons.

' Regarding the class as designed for cruising, it is to be observed that, with 4,000 horses, say two-thirds power, the ship goes in smooth water $12\frac{3}{4}$ knots.   With average coal she may therefore steam at an average ocean speed of $12\frac{1}{2}$ knots, with a consumption for all purposes of 100 tons per day.   For twelve days at this speed the distance covered would be, without the use of sail, say 3,500 knots.   With 2,300 horse-power she obtained in smooth water a speed of $10\cdot537$ knots, so that, with 60 tons per day, she would make a $10\frac{1}{2}$ knots average ocean-speed, and should steam 5,000 knots.   I am fully sensible of the large consumption of fuel for a given speed as compared with the long narrow merchant ship, and of the corresponding loss in coal endurance; but it is always necessary to remember that the ship of war is endowed with a powerful rig, enabling her to cruise under sail for any length of time with no appreciable consumption of fuel, whereas the merchant steamship is helpless under canvas—she can only drift before the wind.   To show the difference in the distribution of the weights in such a ship as the " Nelson " and a first-class passenger steamer of the same displacement and designed for the same average ocean-going speed, 12 to $12\frac{1}{2}$ knots, I have placed them side by side in the following table :—

	"Nelson" Tons.	Passenger Ship. Tons.
Hull	3,017	3,200
Propelling machinery . .	1,030	700
Armour	1,720	—
Armament . . .	533	—
Rigging, stores, and equipment .	633	450
Coal	1,200	3,750
	8,133	8,100
Consumption per hour at 12 to $12\frac{1}{2}$ knots average speed	4	3

' The gain in consumption in favour of the merchant ship is due to the fact that the speed is obtained in her with less engine-power, because her proportions are more favourable to speed, and especially to ocean speeds. The length of the " Nelson " is only 4⅔ times the breadth, while that of the merchant ship is ten times, her length being 420 feet and her breadth only 42 feet.'

Comparative Table: ' Nelson ' class and two other classes.

	Nelson	Northampton	Bellerophon	Iron Duke
Length	280 feet	—	300 feet	280 feet
Breadth	60 feet	—	56 feet	54 feet
Mean draught of water	24 ft. 7 in.	25 feet	24 ft. 8 in.	22 ft. 8 in.
Displacement	7,473 tons	7,652 tons	7,550 tons	6,010 tons
Indicated power of engines	6,624 (twin screw)	6,073	6,520 (single screw)	4,020 (twin screw)
Speed on mile at normal draught	14 knots	13·173 knots	14·17 knots	12·83 knots
Weight of protective plating and backing	1,720 tons	—	1,273 tons	1,082 tons
Average thickness of vertical armour	7·28 inches	—	5·28 inches	5·77 inches
Weight of armament	533 tons	—	420 tons	351 tons
Weight of projectiles in a broadside	1,800 lbs.	—	1,595 lbs.	1,378 lbs.
Weight of projectiles thrown right ahead	800 lbs.	—	230 lbs.	623 lbs.
Weight of projectiles thrown right astern	800 lbs.	—	115 lbs.	628 lbs.
Cubic feet of space per gun in enclosed midship batteries	6,000	—	3,200	4,000
Coal-carrying capacity	1,200 tons	—	645 tons	460 tons
Area of canvas in plain sail	24,770 sq. ft.	—	23,400 sq. ft.	22,750 sq. ft.

Admiral Sir Spencer Robinson. Discussion on the 'Nelson' class. I.N.A.Mar. 18, 1880.

During the discussion on Mr. Barnaby's paper, Admiral Sir R. Spencer Robinson said :—

' There is no ship of war of any nation or country, of anything like the power of the " Nelson " and the " Northampton," which carries the same amount of coal that they carry, and which enables their range of power to be so enormous.

' There will naturally arise a difference of opinion as to whether a ship, with her broadside guns unprotected, and with a very excellent protection elsewhere, is not under somewhat inferior conditions to some other ships. I confess, weighing carefully the good qualities which have been insured by the distribution of the armour against the weakness, if I may so call it, of an opposed battery to a broadside fire, I conclude altogether in favour of the arrangements made in the " Nelson " and " Northampton."

'I have invariably found that sail-power, applied to two screws, after all was of very little use indeed, and that a ship, if you intend to put two screws in her, the less you have to do with masts and sails the better.[1]

[1] The following is from the *Broad Arrow*, November, 1876 :—'The "Nelson" and "Northampton" were designed during the summer of 1874 by the officials of the Constructive Department under the superintendence of Mr. N. Barnaby, Admiral Stewart, and Admiral Boys, the Director of Naval Ordnance. It is only reasonable to suppose that these officers, in carrying out the wishes of their lordships, thoroughly understood them, and were likewise agreed among themselves. During the following winter the turret-ships "Ajax" and "Agamemnon" were designed under the superintendence of the same gentlemen. Of seagoing ironclads it would be difficult to conceive types more diverse in character than are those of the "Nelson" and "Ajax" classes. The former are full-rigged, ship-shaped vessels, with their vital parts protected by 9-inch armour-plates. The fighting portion of each vessel is unprotected except by transverse armour-plated bulkheads before and abaft the gun battery. The guns themselves are fought behind 1-inch plates, which cannot resist any projectile, except, perhaps, the common shell. Palliser shells would find as ready an entrance into the ship as the shot themselves, and the only chance the gunners would have against such projectiles would be that of the shell passing across the ship and out at the other side without exploding. Comparing the "Ajax" type with the vessels we have been considering, we shall find that the former have a comparatively low freeboard, and that their turrets, sides, and the greater part of the water-line are protected by 18-inch armour, and the guns carried weigh 38 tons, as compared with 18 and 12-ton guns in the "Nelson" class.

'Again, the "Ajax" class is but lightly rigged, and almost entirely dependent upon their engine-power, while the rig of the "Nelson" is exactly the same as was allowed for the 131-gun line-of-battle ships of seventeen years ago To us it appeared, at the time the designs were sent out, that these two classes of armour-clad ships represented totally distinct principles in regard to naval construction ; not that they were intended to fulfil different purposes, but that they were two distinct attempts at solving the problem of what is to be the ship-of-war of the future. Our own opinion is that the "Nelson" class represents a very sensible solution of the "armour-plate *versus* gun" difficulty. If you cannot keep a shot out of the ship, then let it in and out as easily as possible ; and by all means prevent splinters. Whatever armour can be carried, let it be as thick as possible, and placed over the vital parts—viz., engines, boilers, and magazine. For the rest, ensure buoyancy and stability by watertight subdivisions, armour-plated decks below water, cofferdams, and steam-pumps. Also, reduce the casualties from shell explosions as much as possible by isolating the guns with shell-proof partial bulkheads. These were the principles kept in view when the "Nelson" was designed, and which are carried out as far as practicable. These, in our opinion, are the leading principles upon which the battle-ship of the future will be constructed. Mr. Barnaby has said that two feet of armour is, in his opinion, the maximum thickness which a ship can be constructed to carry. The 100-ton gun of the Italians has penetrated 22-inch armour, and now a 200-tun gun is being talked of at Woolwich. The gun is certain to be victorious over armour ; hence safety must be sought as much as possible without it.

'The "Ajax" will cost about

'Here, and repeatedly, I have spoken warmly about the necessity of speed for our ships. It is the question of all others that I have most insisted on, and wished in the strongest manner to direct the attention of our naval architects and all people in authority towards.'

The 'Almirante-Cochrane' and 'Blanco-Encalada.'

The ' Almirante-Cochrane ' and ' Blanco-Encalada ' are admirable examples of second class cruising armourclads. They were designed by Sir E. Reed. The following description appeared in the columns of the press on the occasion of the trial trip of the first-named ship : 'The Chilian Government two years ago requested Mr. Reed to prepare a design for an armourclad vessel, whose tonnage should not be more than about 2,000 builders' measurement; to have 9-inch armour at the water-line; to have several $12\frac{1}{2}$-ton guns, with great command of fire on bow, broadside, and stern ; and to have a measured mile speed of from $12\frac{1}{2}$ to 13 knots with twin screws. To fulfil all these conditions, which were quite unprecedented in a rigged sea-going ironclad, Mr. Reed prepared a design, of which the following are the leading features. The length between the perpendiculars is 210 feet ; the extreme breadth is 45 ft. 9 in. ; the depth in hold 21 ft. 8 in. ; the tonnage being $2,032\frac{36}{94}$ tons (builders' measurement). The draught of water forward is 18 ft. 8 in., aft 19 ft. 8 in., and the mean draught 19 ft. 2 in. The height of the port sill from the load water-line is 7 ft. 6 in. The armour is nine inches thick at the water-line, protecting the engines and boilers, eight inches thick in wake of the gun slides, and of varying thicknesses elsewhere on the sides and on the athwartship battery bulkheads. The usual amount of taper is given to the thickness of the armour on the belt forward and aft. Behind the armour the backing is from eight inches to eleven inches in thickness ; with the ordinary arrangement of lon-

450,000l., whereas the "Nelson" is being built by contract for only 350,000l. We can thus obtain four of the latter for about the same price as three of the former type of ship. The "Nelson" can sail as well as steam, whereas the "Ajax" is dependent almost entirely upon her engines. Should the coals run short or the machinery break down while in the middle of the Atlantic, we fear the small amount of fore-and-aft sail carried by the "Ajax" would be of very little service to her in a gale, and the danger would be considerably intensified if she were found near a lee shore in either of these pre-dicaments. Again, the "Nelson" is a habitable ship, ample accommodation being afforded to her officers and crew to the same extent as in the old wooden frigates ; besides which the natural means of ventilation afforded by her style of construction would render her a healthy vessel even in the tropics. On the other hand, the "Ajax" is not a ship in any sense of the word—her crew will have to put up with the many inconveniences which that type is notorious for, and the only ventilation between decks must be by artificial means.'

gitudinal girders worked on the two thicknesses of plates behind armour, the latter being supported by 10-inch frames placed vertically on the inside of the plates behind armour.

'The armament consists of six 12½-ton guns manufactured by Sir William Armstrong and Co. These guns are placed in a central armour-plated battery, arranged as shown on the deck plan. The peculiar recessing of the sides of this battery makes it possible for the two fore guns to command a range of 93°, namely, from right ahead to 3° abaft the beam—the two after guns to command a similar range of 93° from right aft to 3° before the beam—while the two middle guns command a range of 85° extending between 20° from a right-ahead fire to 15° abaft the beam. It can also be easily seen

Figs. 172 and 173.

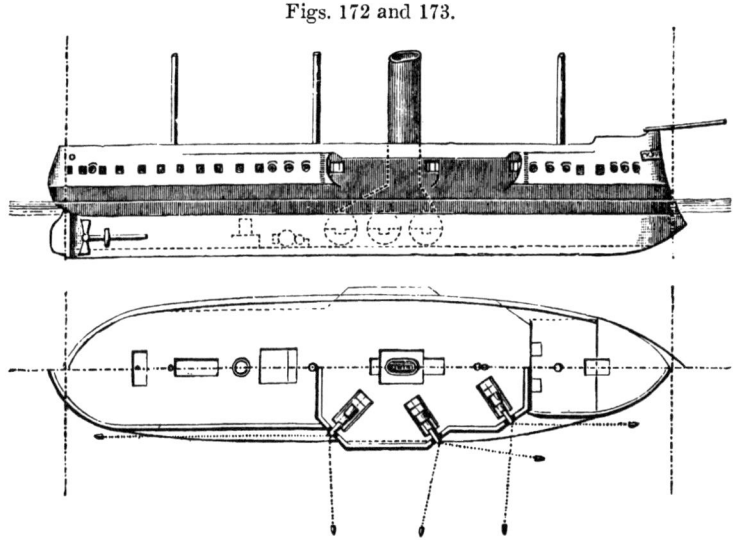

' ALMIRANTE-COCHRANE.'

from the sketch referred to that the three guns on either side can be readily combined in a broadside fire, while the four foremost guns can be worked so as to form a powerful combination for firing ahead. Altogether, then, every point in the horizon is commanded by these six guns in a small and compact battery.

'The speed of the "Almirante-Cochrane" at the steam trial was very nearly thirteen knots, and this was easily sustained continuously when a strong breeze was blowing and the sea rough. The engines, of the most modern compound type, of 500 nominal horse-power, with horizontal cylinders, were manufactured by Messrs. J. Penn and Son for both ironclads. The weight of the coal carried on the trial-trip in the bunkers was 240 tons, and provision is made for additional coal.

'The hull of the vessel is built of iron upon the bracket-frame and longitudinal system, and an inner bottom is fitted throughout the whole length of the engine and boiler-room, as in the most recent ironclads of our own navy. The main deck outside the battery is plated with ¾-inch plating worked on the beams, the deck planking being worked on top of the plating. This gives protection to the magazines, shell-rooms, etc., from a dropping fire.

' A very interesting feature in the designs for these armourclads is, that notwithstanding the double recessed form of the side at the height of the main deck, the top sides along the upper deck are so arranged that they present a fair curved line to the eye, and so improve the appearance of the vessel on deck very much from what it would have been had the recesses of the main deck not been worked out. On the upper deck bridges the eye sees only the usual fair sides of an ordinary ship.

'All the compartments of the double bottom are made watertight; the athwartship bulkheads are provided with watertight doors, the iron platforms are also made watertight, and pumps in connection with a system of pipes are fitted so as to command each and every watertight compartment. Hence, these ironclads are in just as good a position to resist an attack from torpedoes as are the ironclads in our own navy. The bottom of the second vessel, we understand, will be still further protected from the effects of torpedo attack as well as from fouling, by being sheathed with three inches of teak, the outside of the teak to be coated with thin zinc plating, after the manner of the " Audacious," " Rover," and other ships of the Royal Navy.'

M. Dislère. M. Dislère, in *La Guerre d'Escadre*, remarks that the Chilian ironclads are of the same class in point of tonnage as the ' Hansa,' the latter having 3,600 tons, and the former 3,500 tons of displacement. He thus describes the novel features of the Chilian ships :—
' As in the case of the " Hansa," so in the Chilian ironclads the armour belt from end to end is combined with the armoured central battery of the frigates " Kaiser " and " Deutschland," but the battery presents a special arrangement for which there is no precedent in any armoured vessel. The battery in point of fact is composed, so to speak, of two contiguous armoured forts, the aftermost of which projects beyond the other, so that in the angle thus formed a space has been afforded in which a new port has been pierced, giving a direct fire ahead, or at least within 20° of the keel.' Thus in a central battery, which, though of limited dimensions, encloses the funnel, it has been possible to mount six 9-inch 12-ton guns with the range of fire as shown below :

Ahead.

2 guns	9-inch.
Weight of broadside . .	500 lbs.

On the broadside.

3 guns	9-inch.
Weight of broadside . .	750 lbs.

Astern.

2 guns	9-inch.
Weight of broadside . .	500 lbs.

The 'Almirante-Cochrane' was launched in 1874, and the 'Blanco-Encalada' in the following year. At the trial trip of the former vessel Sir E. Reed seized the opportunity of tracing the gradual development of naval architecture for war since the first introduction of ironclads. The 'Defence' and 'Resistance' class were vessels of 3,700 tons, which, as he pointed out, was very nearly double the tonnage of the ship in which they were then sailing, but the 'Defence' had no armour thicker than $4\frac{1}{2}$ inches, while the 'Almirante-Cochrane' had a good deal of armour 9 inches thick, and the strength and resistance of 9-inch armour was at least four times as great as the strength and resistance of $4\frac{1}{2}$-inch armour. Again the 'Almirante-Cochrane' was armoured considerably above and considerably below the water-line from end to end, from ram to rudder, while the 'Defence' was only plated over a little more than half her length. The 'Defence' carried nothing more than the 68-pdr. gun, seven on each side, while the latter ship carried three $12\frac{1}{2}$-ton guns on each side.

Mr. (now Sir E.) Reed, M.P.

Sir E. Reed has still more recently produced three powerful cruisers, of moderate dimensions, for the Japanese Government. They are called respectively, 'Foo-So,' 'Kon-Go,' and 'Hi-Yei.' We take our description from an article which appeared in *Engineering*, November 16, 1877.

Japanese armour-clads.

The principal particulars of the 'Foo-So' are as follows:—

Length between perpendiculars .	220 feet
Breadth, extreme . . .	48 feet
Depth in hold . . .	20 ft. $4\frac{1}{2}$ in.
Draught of water:—	
Forward	17 ft. 9 in.
Aft	18 ft. 3 in.
Height of port from low-water line .	7 ft. 6 in.
Displacement in tons . . .	3,718
Indicated horse-power . .	3,500
Speed in knots . . .	13
Complement of men and officers .	250

Armament :—
    Main deck battery, four 24 c/m. (9·4 in.) guns.
    Upper deck battery, two 17 c/m. (6½ in.) guns to fire
        forward and aft.

The 'Foo-So' carries a supply of coal for 4,500 miles. The armament consists of Krupp guns mounted in a central battery. The guns on the main deck, four in number, weigh 15¼ tons each, and

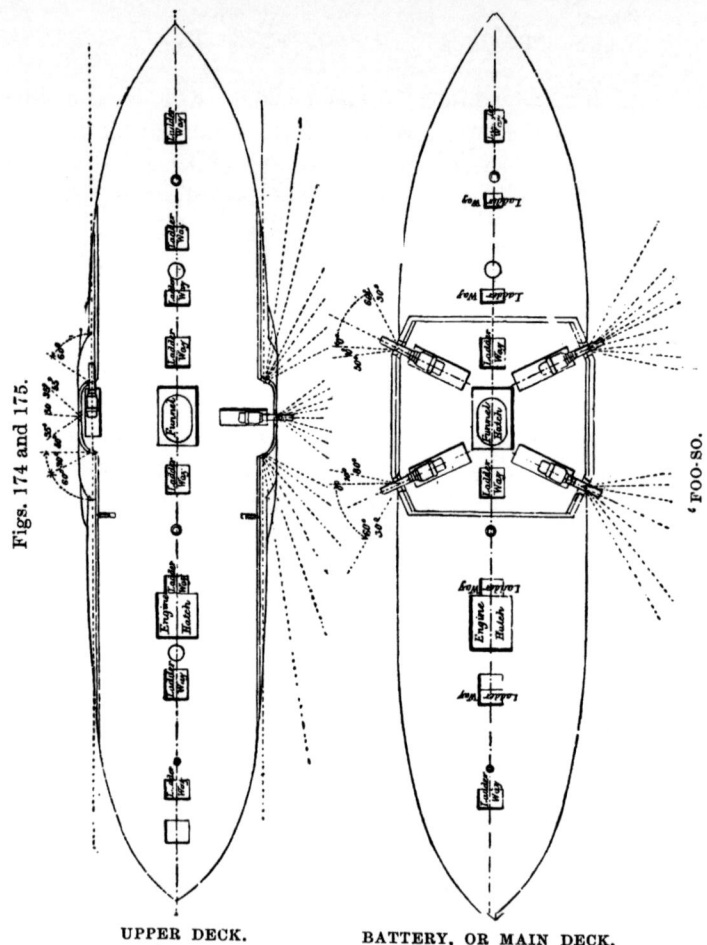

Figs. 174 and 175.

UPPER DECK.　　　BATTERY, OR MAIN DECK.

command a range of fire on the broadside within 30° of the fore and aft line. The guns on the upper deck of 17 c/m. (6½ inch), or about 5½ tons, command the whole horizon. The armour on the sides of the battery is nine inches, and on the athwartship bulkheads eight inches in thickness. The armour is supported by brackets attached outside the frames of the ship, thus allowing a clear line from floor to deck for the frame, and avoiding the usual expensive armour-shelf. The projecting edge of the armour will further act as a bilge keel to reduce the rolling.

The machinery of the 'Foo-So' consists of two pairs of compound horizontal surface condensing trunk engines by Messrs. Penn driving twin screws. The ship is barque-rigged.

Fig. 176.

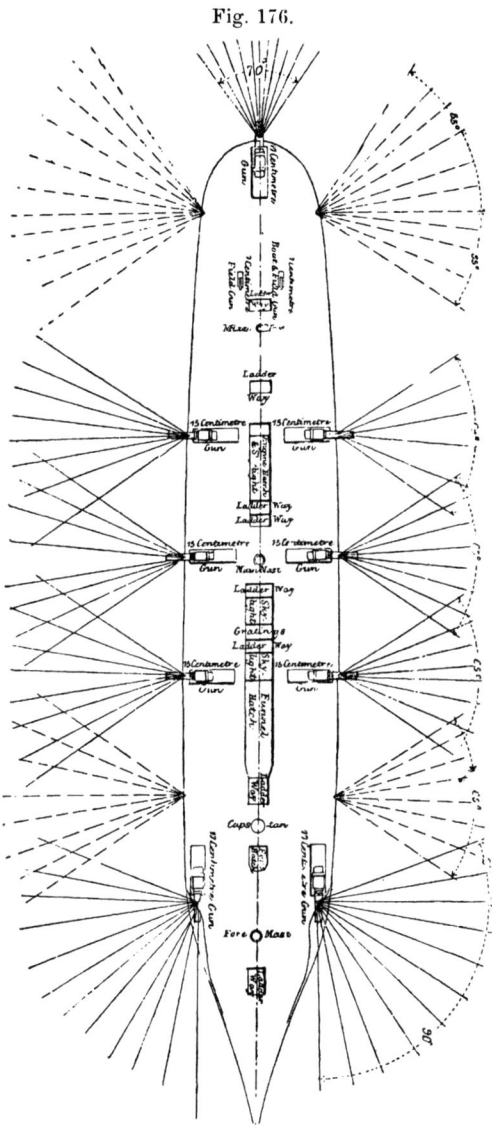

'KON-GO' AND 'HI-YEI.'

The 'Kon-Go' and 'Hi-Yei' are sister vessels; the leading idea being to supply the Japanese navy with ships of the same type as the 'Gem' class lately introduced into the British navy. The later examples of the 'Gem' class are 220 feet long, 40 feet beam, and 17 ft. 6 in. draught, armed with fourteen 64-pdr. 64 cwt. guns on the upper deck, capable of firing two degrees across the bow line forward and within two degrees of the central line aft. They have a speed of from thirteen to $13\frac{1}{4}$ knots, horizontal compound engines of 2,100 indicated horse-power, a large spread of canvas, steer well, and are very handsome. They have, however, no protection above the water-line for their magazines and machinery except such as is afforded by the stowage of coal in the wing bunkers. The Japanese vessels are 231 feet long, 40 ft. 9 in. beam, and 17 ft. 6 in. draught. They are armed with six 15 c/m. (six-inch) or 4-ton guns on the broad-side, and two guns of 17 c/m. (6¾ inches) or about 5½ tons at the bow, and one gun of similar calibre at the stern. They have horizontal compound engines of 2,500 indicated horse-power, and spread 17,000 feet of canvas, the area being exactly the same as that of the larger vessel, the ' Foo-So.' The corvettes each carry about 280 tons of coal. In order to secure the power of fighting the gun right aft, Sir E. Reed has given up the apparatus for lifting the screw, which is fitted in the British ships, and the disconnecting gear will allow of the free revolution of the screw when the vessel is under sail. The Japanese vessels have a great advantage over the British ships as regards boiler space. Their greater length has admitted of much larger boilers, the difficulty experienced in the ' Gem ' class from priming being mainly due to insufficient steam space. The speed anticipated is 13½ knots. The Japanese corvettes are remarkable for one important and most valuable novelty. They are armoured with a 4½-inch belt, extending along the ship at the water-line.

Austrian converted armour-clads.

Three useful second-class ironclads have lately been added to the Austrian navy by the reconstruction of three armoured vessels of an

Fig. 177.

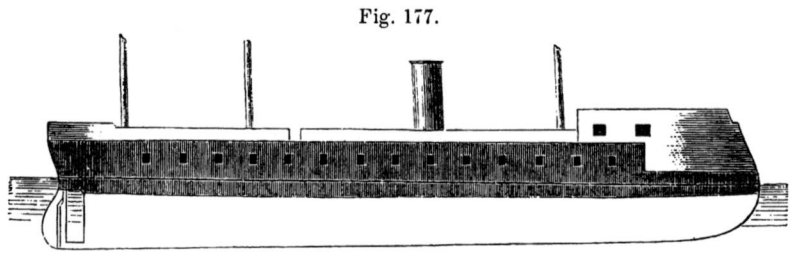

'DON JUAN' (BEFORE REBUILDING).

obsolete type. The Austro-Hungarian ships ' Kaiser-Max ' and ' Don Juan ' launched in 1875, and the ' Prince Eugene ' launched in 1876, are ships originally built of wood, but since rebuilt in iron, bearing the same name as their three predecessors, which were com-pleted in 1862. The hull, deck planking, and backing of the armour have been removed and replaced with iron and Bessemer steel. At the water-line they have been protected with new armour-plates, while the plates protecting the batteries, the engines, and the greater part of the fittings have been removed from the older vessels.

It will not be uninteresting to compare the principal features of the old and the new ships. It will be seen that with the same dis-placement the combination of iron and steel in the hull and the adoption of the central-battery system have been utilised in increasing the offensive and defensive strength.

Figs. 178 and 179.

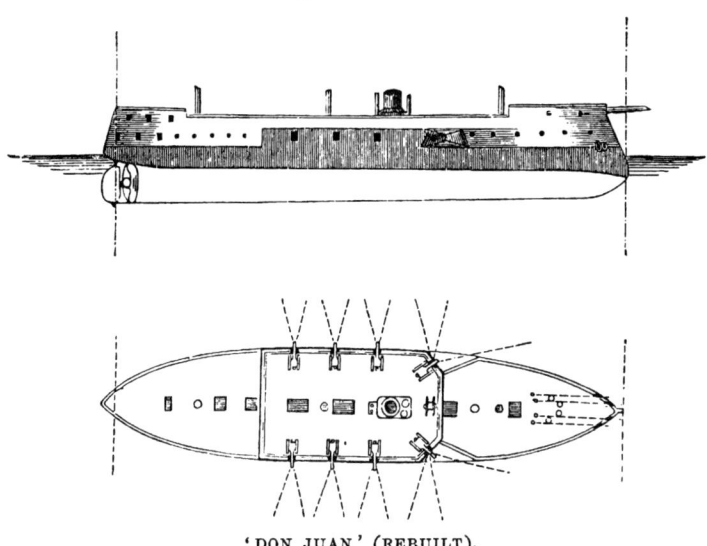

'DON JUAN' (REBUILT).

	New Type	Old Type
Displacement	3,554	3,588 [1]
Length between perpendiculars .	229 feet	221 ft. 10 in.
Breadth	48 ft. 3 in.	42 ft. 9 in.
Depth of hold . . .	21 ft. 3 in.	19 ft. 6 in.
Mean draught of water . .	19 ft. 2 in.	20 ft. 5 in.
Height of portsills above the water	8 ft. 2½ in.	6 feet
Thickness of armour, water-line .	8 inches	4⅔ inches
„ „ battery .	6⅛ inches	4½ inches
Weight of armour . . .	729 tons	606 tons
Armament :—		
Eight breechloading Krupp guns .	21 c/m (8·75 in.)	
Twelve Armstrong muzzle-loaders .		7 inches
Weight of guns . . .	171 tons	144 tons
Coal-supply . . .	380 tons	327 tons

The plans for the two types are by Herr von Romako. By the reconstruction of these three ironclads, the Austro-Hungarian navy recovered its former position. The economy of the operation was such that three powerful vessels were acquired for the cost of one ship of the 'Albrecht' type. The old engines do not realise a speed of more than twelve knots, and the ships are deficient in bow-fire. The

---

[1] So given in Austrian accounts. See *Die Marine*, p. 331.

two foremost guns cannot be trained at a less angle than 35° from

the keel line, but these vessels are efficient for the use of the ram, which in the Austrian navy is regarded as the most formidable naval weapon. The success achieved in the building of these three ships naturally suggested a similar reconstruction of the old wooden ironclads, 'Ferdinand Max,' 'Habsburg,' and 'Salamander.'

The 'Vasco de Gama,' launched in 1876, is another example of an

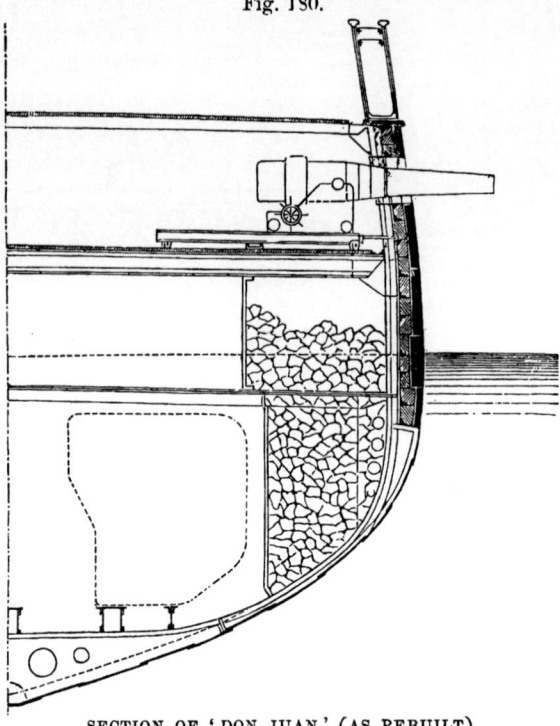

Fig. 180.

SECTION OF 'DON JUAN' (AS REBUILT).

The 'Vasco de Gama.'

economical yet effective armoured coast-defender. This vessel was designed by Mr. Mackrow, and was described as follows in the columns of the *Times*, in a notice of the trial trip, which appeared in that journal:—

'The "Vasco de Gama" is a swift, handy, and powerful seagoing ironclad, mainly intended for the defence of the Tagus and of Lisbon harbour. The displacement tonnage is 2,479 tons. The length over all is 216 feet; the breadth, 40 feet; the depth is 25 feet. The bow is fitted with a ram, and in the fixed octagonal battery, which projects beyond the sides between funnel and forecastle, are two rifled Krupp 400-pdrs., firing ahead, which can be so trailed that the shot will converge at a distance of 300 yards. The guns are of 26 c/m., or 10¼-inches. They are made of cast steel. There is also a stern-chaser throwing shot of 110 lbs. It is of 15 c/m. (6-inch) bore, and, acting in conjunction with the turret guns at after ports, it can converge with either of them upon an object at 90 yards' distance. An all-round fire is thus attained. Four smaller guns are provided for signalling and other purposes. She also carries a Gatling gun by

Armstrong. Great care has been taken in strengthening the bow, the armour-line being carried down to the extreme point of the ram, which is eight feet below the water-line. The ram will thus be firmly supported, and the accident of shots piercing the hull when the bow lifts on the crest of a wave will not be likely to occur. There is a raised forecastle forward, which was designed for protection against the heavy seas sometimes to be encountered at the mouth of the Tagus. A poop aft covers the stern gun. The vessel is built upon the cellular principle, with double bottom, iron watertight decks and bulkheads, having in all 47 iron watertight compartments. She is fitted with three masts, and the foremast is square-rigged, so that

Figs. 181 and 182.

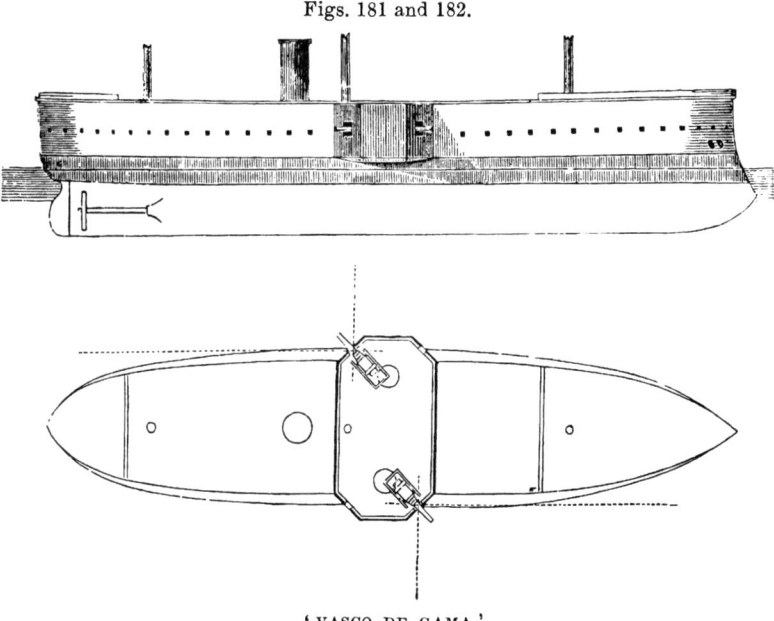

'VASCO DE GAMA.'

the " Vasco de Gama " will be capable of cruising to the Azores or to any part of the Portuguese colonies. Her draught is 19 feet aft, and 16 ft. 10 in. forward, when laden with 700 round of shot and 50 tons of coal, and with water and stores on board.'

The 'Vasco de Gama' is one of the smallest examples of a sea-going ironclad. With a displacement of only 2,500 tons, the water-line is protected by ten inches, and the guns by six inches of armour. The motive machinery, which was furnished by Messrs. Humphreys, Tennant and Co., consists of a pair of vertical compound engines for each of the two screw-propellers. On the measured mile trial, the engines developed 3,625 horse-power, and the ship realised a speed

Compara-
tive size of
'Vasco de
Gama.'

of 13¼ knots per hour. In
four minutes she made a
complete turn in a circle
433 feet in diameter.

The 'fixed octagonal
turret,'—as it is called by
the designer,—is a breastwork converging to a point
towards the bow; and, as the
ship is intended to fight an
enemy bow on, the armour is
disposed so as to give protection in that position, with the
view that the enemy's fire
shall be directed against a
surface placed at such an
angle that penetration will
be difficult.

The total cost has been
reported at 103,880*l.*

The 'King George.' The 'King George' is
another earlier example of a
small ironclad, due to the skilful design of Mr. Mackrow.
This vessel was built by the
Thames Ironworks and Shipbuilding Co. for the Greek
Government. The principal
dimensions are: length 200
feet, beam 33 feet, draught
sixteen feet, depth in hold
twenty feet. The battery and
the water-line are armoured
for the greater part of the
length with plates six inches
in thickness, this thickness
increasing to seven inches
abreast of the battery and
the boilers and engines. The
'King George' is a twin
screw propelled by engines of
300 nominal, or 1,200 indi-

Figs. 183 and 184.

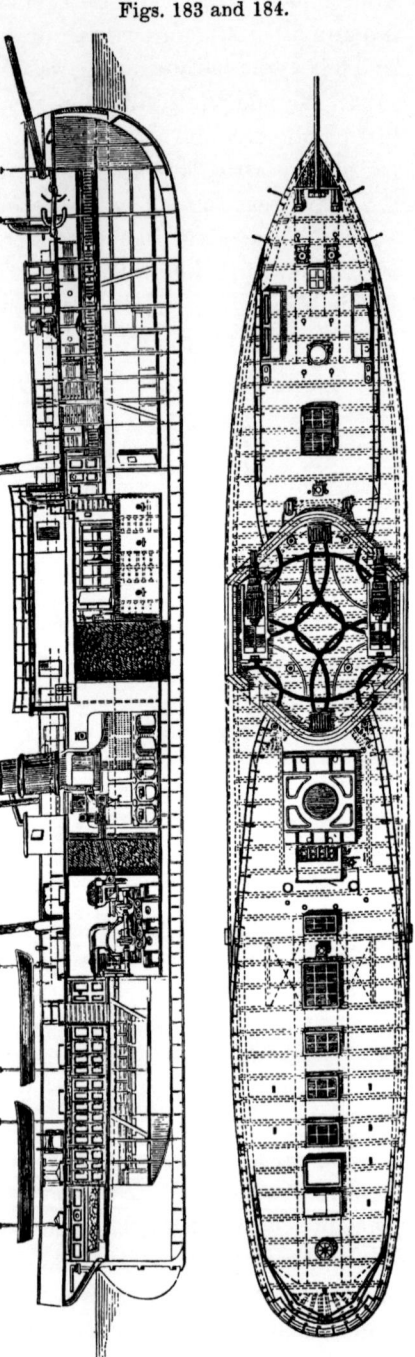

'KING GEORGE.'

cated horse-power. The displacement is 1,774 tons. The weight of the armament is 110 tons; that of the armour 330 tons. Two 300-pdrs. are mounted in the central battery in such a manner as to give a fire almost right ahead or right astern, and a converging fire on each broadside. The plan and the above particulars are taken from the work of Von Kronenfels.

As a conclusion to the present chapter on armoured cruisers, the following observations are quoted from Mr. Trevelyan's speech in introducing the Navy Estimates on March 18, 1881 :— New armoured cruisers.

'There was one department in which, whether we considered our Navy in relation of its great neighbour or in relation to the enormous commerce which in time of war it would be bound to protect—not less than half the mercantile marine of the globe—we had till lately been behindhand. Taking fourteen knots as the standard of high speed, we had only eleven swift cruisers, counting the " Iris " and " Mercury " despatch vessels among them. Fine vessels they were, and no doubt the " Shah " and the " Raleigh," when they had got on board their new armament, would give a good account—a very good account indeed—of any cruiser in the world that was not an ironclad. But the world was a large place ; and eight or ten vessels could not be everywhere, and the safety of our commerce imperatively demanded that the swift cruisers which we had ready at the outbreak of a war should be enough to clear the seas of privateers. Much use, as a war went on, might be made of the armed merchantmen on the Admiralty list ; but we must have royal cruisers to begin with. A commencement was made last year by the late Board in the " Leander " and her two consorts, which, with their partially protected machinery, their great speed, and their excellent guns, would be everything that could be desired for the purpose for which they were devised. The present Board had carried this policy farther. They were pushing on the " Leanders," and they had laid down a fourth " Leander " at Pembroke, to occupy the spare time of the 200 extra men who were working on the ironclads. They had determined, in the new vessels of the "Comus " class, to give an extra knot of speed. But they had done more than this. In their opinion it was necessary to produce a vessel which should not only have the heels of another, but should be able to meet on at least equal terms almost anything she was likely to catch. Great pains had been spent over the form and attributes of a vessel which, in the words of the designer, was intended " especially for independent service on foreign stations, where fast, unarmoured ships may have to be opposed, and where the second-class ironclads of an enemy may have to be met and engaged." On such service it was considered desirable to secure the following conditions: a speed of sixteen knots; a comparatively large number of guns, some of them capable of penetrating the thickest armour of second-class ironclads at long ranges; armour of proof to protect the vitals of the ship; her coal-supply must also be large, and the vessel must have auxiliary sail-power to economise fuel, and a coppered bottom to make her independent of docks. Such a vessel, fit to keep the sea and to sweep the sea, the Admiralty believed that they had got. Her length was to be 315 feet; her extreme breadth, 61 feet; and her tonnage about 7,300. Her horse-power was to be 8,000; her bunkers would hold 900 tons; and her speed on the measured mile would be sixteen knots. She had the great advantage of a twin-screw. She would have a belt eight feet broad and 140 feet long amidships, of steel-faced armour, ten inches thick with ten inches of backing, protecting her engine-room and boilers, three feet above water and five feet below. She would have a conning tower of steel-faced armour; a protecting deck of inclined steel, three inches thick, five feet under water, covering the whole of that part of the ship, both fore and aft, which was not clad in iron. She would carry an armament of four 18-ton 9·2-inch breechloading guns, mounted in barbettes, with protection against bullets, which at a 1,000 yards wound pierce $16\frac{1}{2}$ inches of iron armour, and more than thirteen inches of steel-faced armour. She would carry likewise six 6-inch breechloading guns, equal in range to those which had carried desolation at a distance of five miles into the Peruvian harbours; she would be equipped by boat guns, torpedoes, field-guns, machine guns, and would probably be fitted with a couple of torpedo-boats in addition; and she would have room for over 400 men and officers to work her and fight her. She would combine the speed of the "Leander" with guns of greater power than the "Thunderer" or the "Devastation;" and the Admiralty with some confidence submitted her to the criticism of a nation which thought little of a vessel that could not travel far and fast, and fight sharply and long. She would rank high among cruisers, and high among second-class ironclads; and in the hope that she would meet the ends for which she was designed, it was proposed to lay down one such vessel this year at Portsmouth and another at Chatham. Her hull and engines would cost 400,000l, as against 550,000l. of the "Collingwood," and 150,000l. of the "Leander."'

We add to Mr. Trevelyan's description some additional details, furnished by the Constructor's Department of the Admiralty :—

Ten years ago the armour and the guns of the 'Devastation' and

'Thunderer' were regarded as being sufficiently powerful for battle-
ships of the first class.   Yet by reason of modern improvements they
are inferior to the armour and guns to be carried by the two ships
just designed for cruising—the 'Impérieuse' and 'Warspite.' These
new ships are to carry four guns of superior power to the four guns
of the turret-ships above named, and they are to have besides these
heavy guns a battery of six much lighter guns, but capable of penetrating nearly twelve inches of iron armour.   This armament is to be
carried into action at sixteen knots' speed.   The four heavy guns are
situated at twice the height out of water that they are in the turret-
ships, and they can be fired, three together, in any direction—ahead,
astern, or on the beam.

The ships have very spacious double sides, a double bottom, and
wood and copper sheathing.   They have twin screws and a considerable amount of canvas upon two masts for cruising in favourable
weather without expending fuel.   They will be powerful rams, and
will have the fittings for discharging Whitehead torpedoes from
either side under water.

They will have space in their bunkers for 900 tons of coal.   As
this is about one-third more than the earlier fast cruisers of nearly
equal engine-power can carry, and the consumption of the engines
per mile at high speeds is considerably less, there is marked progress
in the important quality of coal endurance, although the ship of war
still compares in this respect very unfavourably with the passenger
ship of great length, and with large coal spaces in her hold.

The length of the ship is 315 feet, and the displacement 7,300
tons.   This corresponds with a gross register tonnage, in a passenger
ship of the ordinary type with two 'tween decks, of about 4,000 tons.

The length of such a ship would exceed that of these cruisers by
at least seventy feet, and as the engines would be of not more than
half the power, and would be allowed to rise to the upper deck, the
space in the holds occupied by machinery would be far less than
these cruisers require.   In them all the machinery has to be kept
below the level of the water.

It needs to be noted also that ships of war are not required to
steam at full speeds, except in actual combat or in the performance
of manœuvres representing actual warfare, so that the amount of coal
which would be burnt in one day, and would carry the ship in that
time 384 knots at her full speed, would last four days, and carry her
960 knots at the reduced speed of ten knots, and would last longer
and carry her farther still at a lower speed than that.   Twin screws
have also the advantage that a greater distance can be covered with

a ton of coal at moderate speeds with one engine only than with two
engines developing the same power.

One peculiarity in these ships [1] is that their four heavy guns
are revolving guns mounted on turntables, but the armour which
encloses these tables and the loading chamber does not revolve.
The guns will be breechloaders, firing over the parapet of the
armoured enclosure, and are therefore said to be mounted *en barbette*.
The lighter guns are mounted upon the second deck above the water,
and are covered by a spar deck.

[1] For general design of ships of this class see the lithographed plates of various
types of ships appended to this volume.

CUSTOZZA.

CHAPTER XII.

BOW-BATTERY SHIPS.

THE authors of *Die Marine* introduce their description of the bow-battery ships in the Austrian navy with a few general observations on the importance of increasing the offensive power of snips of war in the end-on position.

Offensive power of the 'end-on position.'

It was proved at the battle of Lissa that the ram is a most formidable offensive weapon of naval warfare, destined perhaps to take the first place in future engagements. The manœuvres of each ship were formerly directed to one single object, that of bringing the guns to bear on the enemy in the shortest possible time. The vital object

Fig. 185.

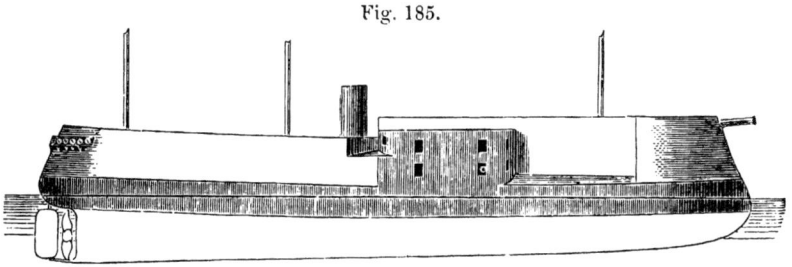

'ARCHDUKE ALBERT.'

must now be to strike the enemy with the ram. It follows that artillery fire must be subordinate to the ram.

With the exception of a few large turret-ships, built in England, all armoured vessels previous to the year 1869 carried their broadside guns in a strongly armoured casemate. 'As a general rule, two heavy guns were carried in the bows, which could be fired nearly in a line with the keel. It is obvious that where such ships are engaged end-on, the broadside guns are reduced to silence, and that, in order to bring them to bear with the greatest effect, the broadside, which is the weakest point, must be exposed to the enemy's stem.

Armoured ships, if struck with the ram at right angles to the broadside, must be destroyed.'

It has also been proved that projectiles, even of heavy calibre, when they strike at oblique angles, inflict little damage. These considerations seem to point to the conclusion that the safety of the ship is best secured by mounting the heaviest gun in the bow. If the bow be turned to the enemy, his projectiles will strike the ship's side at an acute angle, where the armour will offer the most effective resistance. By concentrating in the bow both efficient armour-protection and the combined offensive power of the gun and the ram, it is possible to produce a ship of a more powerful type than one in which the guns are mounted on the broadside, in which therefore it is impossible to make a simultaneous attack with the ram and the guns, and in which too it is necessary to expose the broadside to the enemy's rams in order to bring the guns into action.

Herr v. Romako's designs. The Austrian naval authorities were so fully impressed with the advantages of the bow-battery type, that they decided at the commencement of the year 1868, to suspend the construction of the 'Lissa,' which was already considerably advanced; and the Chief Constructor, the Chevalier J. von Romako, to whom in 1869 the problem was referred for solution, was instructed to prepare designs for two battle-ships, in which it would be practicable to obtain a direct fire ahead and astern for all their guns.

The 'Custozza' and 'Archduke Albert.' The plans for the bow-battery casemate system, were approved by Admiral Tegetthoff, and practically applied in the 'Custozza' and 'Archduke Albert.'

Figs. 186, 187, and 188.

'ARCHDUKE ALBERT' (FORE AND AFT SECTION).

The essential characteristic of the bow-battery type consists in this, that the guns, which were formerly on one deck, are mounted in

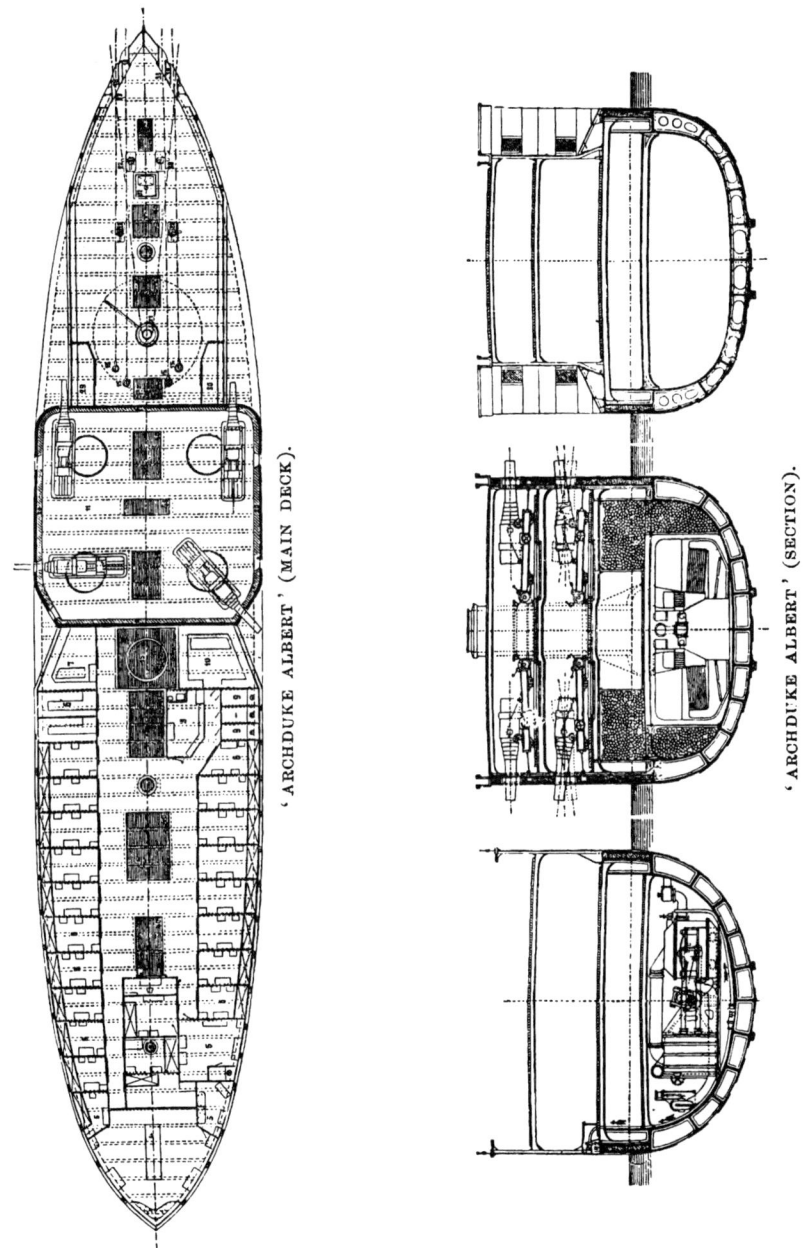

'ARCHDUKE ALBERT' (MAIN DECK).

'ARCHDUKE ALBERT' (SECTION).

equal numbers on two decks. The angles of the foremost armoured bulkhead are cut off, and and pierced with four ports, to which the

guns can readily be shifted from the broadside, by means of turntables sunk to a level with the deck. The unarmoured sides of
the ship recede sufficiently to admit of a direct fire ahead from the
four bow ports. The after end of the corner of the casemate forms
an angle with the keel. Here another port has been opened, from
which a line of fire can be obtained at an angle of 56° from the keel
line.

M. Marchal,[1] who is less partial than the authors of *Die Marine*
to the bow-battery system, points out that the arrangements in
the Austrian ships are almost exactly the same as those of the
'Enterprise' with this disadvantage however, that the weight of the
guns is too great to admit of their being shifted from one port to
another without mechanical appliances. It has been necessary to return to the turntables of the 'Hercules.' Hence results slowness in
the manœuvres; while the interior of the battery is so crowded that
the steering-wheel alone, in addition to the guns, can be protected.
The funnel is outside the battery, though protected, it is true, from
an end-on fire.

Fig. 189.

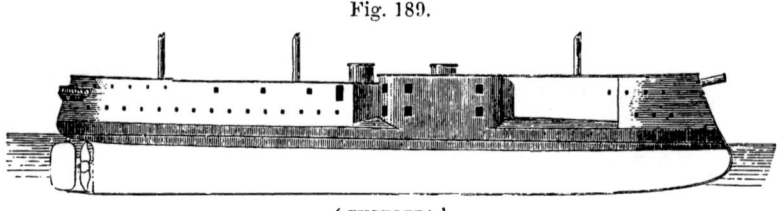

'CUSTOZZA.'

It is contended by the authors of *Die Marine* that the 'Custozza' type combines in a higher degree than any previous vessels
defensive strength with the greatest powers of offence. The fire of the
guns can be concentrated from the strongly armoured bow against
the comparatively ill-defended broadside of the enemy. These advantages were secured without detriment to the qualities of the ships
in other ways. On the contrary, this type possesses exceptional seagoing qualities.

Ironclads are generally decried as bad seagoing ships, a result
which is attributable more particularly to their tendency, when
steaming against a head sea, to roll more deeply than unarmoured
ships. Moreover, while they roll more deeply, they roll quickly.[2]

---

[1] *Les Navires de Guerre.*
[2] This, of course, is intended to apply
to ironclads of the older types. The
rolling of many of recent design is
neither especially deep nor quick.

These peculiarities in their behaviour at sea are mainly attributable to the position of the centre of gravity, which is considerably lower in armoured than it is in unarmoured ships. In consequence of this position of the centre of gravity, there is an excess of stability in the ironclads, and this defect can obviously be remedied by an alteration in the position of the centre of gravity, or, to express it more accurately, by diminishing the stability.

The French ships of the ' Magenta ' class deserve especial mention for their unrivalled merits as seagoing vessels. There is considerable analogy between the ' Magenta ' class and the Austro-Hungarian bow-battery ships, both in the number and weight of their guns, and the plan of mounting the armament on two superimposed decks. The French vessels belong to the earliest era of ironclad construction, and present no features, either of offensive or defensive power, which are worthy of imitation. The distribution of weights, however, was made with judgment, and to this cause are due the moderate and easy rolling movements.

'Magenta' class and Austrian ships.

The bow-battery ships possess considerable advantages in respect of the longitudinal as well as the vertical distribution of weights. It is of the greatest importance to relieve the extremities of the ship, which are not fully waterborne, and to concentrate weight in the centre. The bow-battery ships are highly satisfactory in this point of view. These vessels give superior accommodation both for officers and men. The guns, being placed on two decks, occupy less space longitudinally than in ships where they are mounted on one deck, on which space must also be found for the crew. Another advantage — in M. Marchal's opinion, the sole advantage—of the type consists in the position of the shell and powder rooms in the centre of the ship, under the casemate, and immediately under the guns which are to be supplied with ammunition. The advantages of this arrangement are obvious. The sides of the casemate, with a view to secure simplicity and lightness of construction, are vertical. This gives to the ship an unusually elegant appearance, as compared with ships having an inclined side. This, however, is a very subordinate consideration. It is a point of much more serious importance that the armoured surface of the bow-battery ship is not greater than that of an ordinary ironclad with an equal number of guns, and fitted with a pilot-tower and an armoured shield for the bow guns. Hence it follows that this type, without any increase in their structural strength, can carry armour of the same thickness as ironclads of the ordinary type, with central batteries.

The subjoined table supplies the most important details:

	'Archduke Albert'	'Custozza
Length between perpendiculars	285 ft. 2 in.	302 ft. 3 in.
Breadth at the water-line	56 ft. 3 in.	58 feet
Depth in hold	26 ft. 3 in.	31 ft. 2 in.
Immersed surface of midship section	1,150 sq. ft.	1,223 sq. ft.
Time of completing a circle	5 min. 3 sec.	4 min. 47 sec.
Diameter of a circle	294 yards	306 yards
Maximum speed	13·38 knots	13·95 knots.

Comparison of Austrian ships with each other. The 'Archduke Albert' carries eight 24 c/m. (9·4 inch) Krupp guns; the 'Custozza' carries the same number of 26 c/m. (10·2 inch) Krupps. The thickness of the 'Archduke Albert's' armour at the water-line is eight inches, and on the battery seven inches; that of the 'Custozza' is nine inches at the water-line, and seven inches on the battery. It will be seen that the two ships are very similar in their main features. The 'Custozza,' which is the larger vessel, was built by the Stabilimente-Tecnico-Triestino Company at their works at San Rocco near Mugia, and was launched in August 1872. The engines were made by the same company at San Andrea, near Trieste. The 'Archduke Albert,' built of iron on the cellular system, was constructed at the San Marco works of the Navale-Adriatico Company, near Trieste, and was launched in April, 1872. The engines, like those of the 'Custozza,' were manufactured at San Rocco.

The following comparative table may be interesting:—

	Kaiser	Lissa	Arch. Albert	Custozza
Displacement (tons)	5,810	6,080	5,940	7,060
Proportion of length to breadth	4·56	5·13	5·07	5·20
Draught of water aft	26 ft. 3 in.	28 ft. 6 in.	25 ft. 3 in.	26 ft. 9 in.
Weight of broadside (lbs.)	2,491	3,504	2,337	2,945
Maximum thickness of armour at water-line (inches)	6¼	6¼	8	9
Coal endurance (miles)	1,519	1,420	1,472	1,624

ALEXANDRA.

CHAPTER XIII.

CENTRAL-BATTERY SHIPS.

HAVING examined and described the different classes of coast-service vessels and cruisers, we return to the other descriptions of armour-clad ships.

In all navies the central-battery ships constitute the larger pro-portion of the seagoing armoured fleet actually afloat. The guns are mounted between decks, protected by the thickest plating, and they fire from ports. Heavy guns are also, in some cases, mounted behind armour on the upper decks. Central-battery ships.

The two most recent central-battery ships built by the English Admiralty are the 'Alexandra' (ex-'Superb,') and the 'Téméraire.' Sir E. Reed has built the 'Kaiser' and 'Deutschland' for the German Government. The 'Tegetthoff' belongs to the same type, as well as the ships launched a few years ago for the Turkish Government—the 'Nussratieh,' 'Messudieh,' and 'Hamidieh.' In France the central-battery type has been adopted for the 'Redoubtable,' 'Dévastation,' and 'Foudroyant.'

These battery ships have a moderate amount of armour-protection, and can bring to bear on an enemy's ship considerable offensive power. They have a formidable armament, and great speed, and can keep the sea for a long period without coaling. At present a coal-supply of 550 tons is considered indispensable. It is sufficient for a distance of 2,000 miles at a speed of ten knots. All central-battery ships are masted.

The 'Alexandra' is the most powerful central-battery ship in the English fleet. The following description of that noble vessel ap-peared in *Engineering* :—' The " Alexandra " is a central-battery ship in the best sense—that is, she needs no bow or stern batteries to give her end-on fire. For the first time the English navy really has a masted ship with satisfactory all-round fire, which even the " Monarch " turret-ship has not, for out of twelve guns the new ironclad can fire four, including the two heaviest, straight ahead, and two straight astern. On each broadside from four to six guns can be fought, according to the bearing of the enemy. So far as the fighting portion is concerned, the "Alexandra" is a two-decker, like the six second-class ironclads of the "Audacious" and "Swiftsure" types, launched between 1869 and 1871, and she may be described as a perfected example of the form of war ship shadowed forth in those vessels. They marked a considerable advance made in a long series of usually halting steps, now, by a greater advance still, brought to a satisfactory end in the "Alexandra." We say end, because the central-battery type will bear very little further modification in the

Figs. 190 and 191.

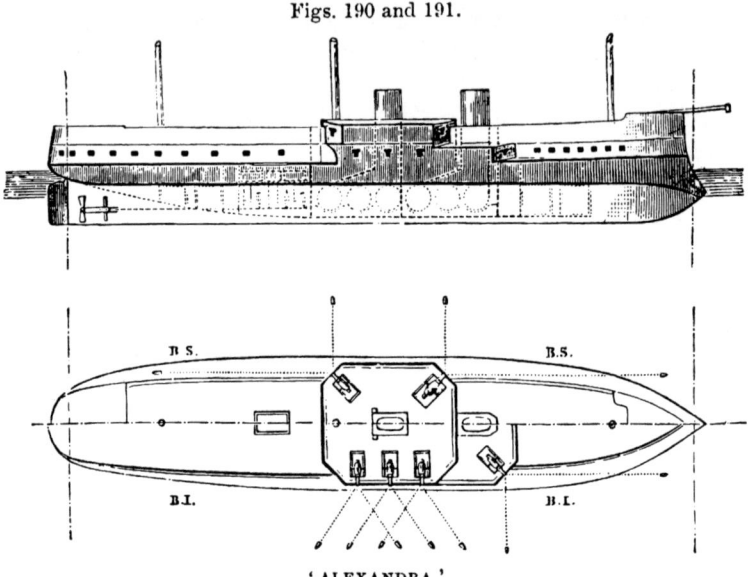

'ALEXANDRA.'

direction hitherto followed; nor do we think that it requires much more. In other words, the "Alexandra" has almost as perfect an all-round fire as is attainable in a broadside ironclad, and as this forms her chief claim to consideration it may be interesting to trace the history of the attempts which have led up to so satisfactory a consummation.

'Taking the "Bellerophon," launched in 1865, as the earliest ironclad in which, as was understood, Mr. Reed was allowed free scope, it will be found that, so far as regards guns of a power worthy of an ironclad, she possessed a broadside fire only. In other words, the central-battery delivered no end-on fire. That was sought to be attained by the unsatisfactory contrivance of a bow-battery on the main deck, the position of which made its use in all but fine weather impossible, while a natural reluctance to overburden the extremity of the ship led to the employment of comparatively thin armour and light guns totally unprotected at the rear. Thus, though the " Bellerophon " was known as a ship carrying ten 12-ton guns, the most important part of her fire, namely, the bow fire, was entrusted to two little 6½-ton guns, indifferently placed and worse protected. For stern fire she had no protected guns at all.

' The next first-class ship, the " Hercules," gained an improved fire from the central battery (18-ton) guns, by the expedient of recesses in the ship's sides, forward and aft of the battery. Advantage was taken of the recesses to make four ports in the ends, or rather corners, of the battery, from which four of the guns were able to fire within a few degrees of the line of keel. If required to fight upon the broadside, these guns, which were mounted on turntables, were revolved to other ports—an arrangement we have always considered very objectionable, since four out of the eight guns, in whatever position fought, had always an open port-hole beside them. Notwithstanding this arrangement, the absence of true end-on fire was so evident that both bow and stern batteries were added, carrying one 12-ton gun in each. These were open to the same objections as the " Bellerophon's," on the ground of indifferent protection and inconvenient position, and the result attained was far from satisfactory. The ship carried eight 18-ton guns, yet one 12-ton gun was all she could bring to bear upon an enemy ahead.

' In the " Sultan " a step was made by adding an upper-deck battery, which, however, mounted only one 12-ton gun on each side, and commanded by no means an all-round fire. At about the same time the idea was carried out in a much more complete form in the " Audacious " class, of which, as already mentioned, six specimens were launched in and about the year 1870. In these the " recessed ports " were abandoned with their complication of turntables and double ports. The main-deck central-battery guns, reduced to three on each side, became again broadside guns and nothing else, but in lieu of the unsatisfactory, not to say mischievous, end batteries of the earlier ships, an upper battery was placed over the other, in which were four guns, firing from corner ports of sufficient width to allow a training of over 90 deg., i.e., from fore-and-aft to broadside fire. The bulwarks were set back, but to a less extent, the necessary space for the guns to point fore-and-aft outside the bulwarks being partly gained by making the upper battery project beyond the sides of the ship, sponson fashion. The guns thus firing end-on were of the same weight, twelve tons, the ships being comparatively small, as those in the main battery, so that end-on fire was at last recognised as equally important with that upon the broadside.

'In the "Alexandra" the upper battery much resembles that of the "Audacious" class, though it does not overhang the sides. But the importance of end-on fire is now conceded to the extent of putting into it the ship's very heaviest guns—the only two 25-ton guns she possesses. The training of these from 2 or 3 deg. *across* the fore-and-aft line forward to several degrees abaft the beam, equal to nearly a hundred degrees, is shown in the plan. There are 18-ton guns with much the same training aft that the others possess forward. These four guns complete the armament of the upper battery.

'To localise the effects of a shell exploding between decks the main-deck battery is divided into two by an armoured bulkhead, which forms a continuation downwards of the forward bulkhead of the upper battery. In the portion which lies under, and corresponds with the upper battery, are six 18-ton guns, three on each side, for broadside fire only. In the forward and detached portion of the main battery are two other 18-ton guns for end-on fire, which they attain by means analogous to those employed to give similar fire to the upper battery guns. Forward of the main-deck battery the whole side of the ship is set back from the level of the main-deck, at the top of the belt, upwards. In other words, the ship, forward of the battery, is narrower above the main-deck than below it, and the two guns, as well as those above, can therefore fire right ahead past the sides. Their arc of training is about the same, or nearly 100 degrees.

'To make the "Alexandra" perfect in regard to all-round fire, the sides should be set back abaft the main-deck battery in the same way as before it, so that the two aftermost guns might fire through corner ports with the same range as the foremost. There would then be four guns firing astern as well as four ahead. But this has not been thought necessary for several reasons. In the first place bow fire is more important than stern fire, and the power of directing two 18-ton guns straight abaft may not unfairly be called reasonably sufficient for a ship of the "Alexandra's" armament, heavy as that is. Then the setting back of the sides from the main deck upwards would involve some sacrifices. It would increase the difficulty of construction, diminish the internal accommodation, and above all, reduce the range and moment of stability. By reducing the amount of side upon which the ship depends to "pick her up," as sailors say, when inclined, it would oblige provision to be made for greater initial stability, and this would be unfavourable to steadiness. We believe, moreover, it is not considered safe to have such large guns as those of the "Alexandra" fired from ports immediately or nearly over each other. This is one reason why the guns above and below are separated so far, and some such separation would have to be made between the aftermost upper guns and any gun which might be required to fire from a similar corner port in the after end of the lower battery. The latter would therefore have to be made much longer, and the present displacement would be not inconsiderably exceeded. For these reasons, we presume, the ship abaft the batteries has been carried up at full width to the upper deck, and only the bulwarks have been set back to allow the aftermost upper battery guns to fire past them.

As already said, the "Alexandra," by virtue of her two-gun decks with end-on fire from *both*, thus approximates very closely, as regards range of fire, to an ideally perfect broadside, or plain central battery ship. The plan is as simple as comparatively perfect plans usually are, and one cannot help asking why a series of most imperfect ships should have been built when reasonable perfection was so easily to be had. When Mr. Reed applied recessed ports, the advantages of wholly recessed sides must of course have occurred to him. Several years ago, in fact, the idea of true fore-and-aft fire from corner ports in a central battery was carried out in a little Greek ironclad, the "King George," built at the Thames Iron Works, and, we believe, in a Turkish ironclad built at the same place. In these vessels the battery was on one deck only, and in the "King George," and we think in the other, it was only bulwarks which were set back, not the topsides. But the idea of thus extending the power of the principal battery was there, and we think it is much to be regretted that the "Hercules" and "Sultan" did not more perfectly embody it.

'Splendid ship as she is, and advantageously as she compares with other broadside ships in the English or any other navy, the "Alexandra" shows, *in places*, that deficiency of protection which is always observable in vessels of her type. Thus the batteries are armoured with only 8-inch and 6-inch armour—the latter a miserable defence against the guns of other ironclads. The reason of course is that the ship must, before all things, be kept above water. There is much to be armoured, and not much to do it with, and when the water-line is fairly secured the batteries are left, to say the least, very unequally protected.

'It should be noted that in the "Alexandra," as in previous ships built on the two-deck battery system, the upper battery serves as a conning-tower, and enables that weight to be dispensed with. It will be seen that the armour forward is carried down over the ram, both to strengthen the latter and to guard the vitals of the ship from injury by raking fire from ahead, at times when waves or pitching action might expose the bows. The magazines, engines, etc., are similarly protected against a raking fire from abaft by a hanging bulkhead across the hold, plated with 5-in. armour.

'The sills of the main-deck ports are nine feet, and those of the upper deck ports more than seventeen feet, above the water. The total weight of armour and backing is 2,350 tons, and of guns and ordnance stores about 660 tons.'

The principal dimensions of the 'Alexandra' are :—

Length between perpendiculars	. .	325 feet
Breadth, extreme	. . .	63 ft. 8 in.
Depth of hold .	. . .	18 ft. 7½ in.
Tonnage	. . .	6,050
Displacement .	. . .	9,492 tons.
Draught of water :—		
Forward	. . . .	26 feet
Aft .	. . . .	26 ft. 6 in.

Mr. King, U.S.N.

The following additional particulars are extracted from Mr. King's *War Ships of Europe*:—

'The system of framing adopted in former armoured vessels has been preserved in its main features. The great weight of armour and machinery, together with the immense power to be developed, necessitates arrangements being made which shall give great strength to the hull. The chief characteristics of the system, as in other vessels, consist in the adoption of an inner bottom and short frame

Internal sub-divisions.

angle-irons connected by bracket plates. Increased strength longitudinally is gained by the use of deeper longitudinal frames than have been employed in many former vessels; an advantage of this feature being that the space between the two bottoms, which is four feet amidships, is roomy and easy of access for cleaning and painting, operations which are essential to the preservation of an iron structure. Facilities are also afforded by these arrangements for letting in water between the bottoms to regulate the trim of the vessel. Provision is made for pumping out any compartment required. In addition to the strength and safety afforded by these numerous watertight cells between the two bottoms, greatly increased strength is obtained by the employment of a heavy longitudinal bulkhead through the centre of the ship, commencing at forty feet abaft the

stem and extending to within forty feet of the stern. The wing passage
bulkheads on either side also form longitudinal divisions of the hold,
and advantage is taken of the transverse bulkheads to form subdivisions for the magazines, shell-rooms, chain-lockers, shaft-passages,
and passages between the engines and boilers. The twelve boilers
are subdivided by bulkheads into four separate sets of three each,
and the engines of the twin screws into two sets. In other words,
the centre longitudinal bulkhead divides the engines of each screw;
it also divides the boilers, six being on either side of it; besides which
there is a transverse bulkhead abaft the boilers, one immediately
before them, and one in the centre of the six. These several watertight bulkheads are so arranged that any one or more sets of boilers
can be worked independently of the others. All communication
can also be shut off from either set of engines, so that if one side of
the ship be damaged the engines on the opposite side can be worked
independently. In the event of damage to the bottom, or accident
by fire or other causes, any one of the compartments can be shut off
or flooded. All the bulkheads are butted at the joints, beautifully
fitted, and strongly secured like a rigid bridge. The watertight
doors on the lowermost deck are fitted with hinges having loose pins,
and are secured when shut by levers placed at short intervals all
round the edges of the doors, which may be worked from either side
of the bulkhead. The doors in the hold are made to slide up and
down, being raised or lowered by screws worked from the main deck.
Flooding arrangements are fitted to the magazines, shell-rooms, and
torpedo-rooms; proper stop-cocks with locks being fitted in each case
to prevent the possibility of water being let in by mistake. Excellent
facilities for pumping have been applied, to be worked by steam or
by hand from the decks. Drain-pipes are placed between the two
bottoms, so as to give control over the water in every compartment,
and to fill or empty them; the former when they are used for
carrying water-ballast; and the latter when they are pumped out in
case of accident.

'The frame spaces and the hollow masts constitute excellent ventilating tubes, the masts especially being good uptakes. On account
of the liability of the inhabited decks to become contaminated,
attention has been given to the necessity of conveying the foul air
away to the upper deck by distinct pipes from the hold and from
the berth decks. This point has not, however, been carried to the
extent it deserves. An important measure lately adopted consists in
providing means for closing all ventilators in event of fire. This is
the more necessary in the case of hollow masts used as ventilating

tubes, for if a fire should occur in the hold, the masts at once become tall chimneys creating enormous draughts to fan the flames. One case of this kind is known to have occurred in the mercantile vessel " River Boyne " only a short time since, and it is probable that there have been other unrecorded cases.'

Machinery.   The ' Alexandra ' was the first cruising armoured broadside ship of the Royal Navy engined on the compound system. The machinery was designed and constructed by Messrs. Humphreys and Tennant, at their works at Deptford.

' As in all recent armoured ships of the royal navy, twin screws are applied to the " Alexandra." Each screw is driven by an independent set of engines with three vertical inverted cylinders of the collective power of 4,000 horses, giving an aggregate indicated horse-power of 8,000 for both sets of engines. The diameter of the high-pressure cylinder is seventy inches, and the diameter of each low-pressure cylinder ninety inches. The high-pressure cylinder is in the centre.

' The engines are raised considerably above the inner bottom of the ship, with the view of preventing damage to them in case of accident to the ship's bottom. The propeller-shafts are in consequence somewhat inclined. The surface-condensers, one to each set of engines, are so fitted as to be worked as common jet-condensers if necessary. They contain an aggregate of 16,500 square feet of cooling surface. The screw-propellers are of the Mangin type, 21 feet in diameter, and work outwards.

' The boilers are twelve in number, divided by bulkheads into four distinct sets. They are placed in the ship back to back against the longitudinal bulkhead. The fronts face the sides of the ship, and they are consequently fired from stoke-holes convenient to the coal-bunkers. An additional advantage in this arrangement consists in keeping the boilers clear of the sides of the ship, and thus making the sides accessible in the event of torpedoes or rams making holes through them. The four sets of boilers are arranged to be used either separately, in sets, or singly. Each boiler contains three furnaces 40 inches in diameter and 6 ft. 6 in. long. The total heating surface is 21,900 square feet, and the pressure of steam to the square inch 60 lbs. The smoke and gases are all carried into one chimney.

' In addition to her main engines she has been fitted with a pair of auxiliary or "turning" engines, one being placed on either side of the central longitudinal bulkhead. These engines are of the direct-acting expansive type, and are similar in every respect to those which were supplied to her Majesty's ship " Swinger " by the same makers.

When the ship is under sail, or when only a low speed is required, these engines will be set to work to rotate the screws, and, as only one boiler will be required to provide the requisite amount of steam, the consumption of coal will be scarcely appreciable, while the relief to the large engines will eventuate in an important saving. They are of 360 nominal horse-power, and although they have not, for obvious reasons, been tested under way, they indicated 600 horses when tried at moorings at Sheerness, and are expected to propel the ship at the rate of $4\frac{1}{2}$ knots.'

At the official trial the horse-power indicated was 8,497·8, and the speed attained 15·089 knots.

'The mind of an officer who has passed his sea life on board wooden ships of war of the old type, and become accustomed to their low dark "between-decks," will be struck with the great additional capacity of our modern men-of-war when he enters the batteries of the "Alexandra," and sees the great rifled guns mounted on Scott's system of wrought-iron carriages, and the unusual height between decks of 10 ft. 4 in. in the upper deck battery, and 9 ft. 6 in. in the main. But lofty and spacious as these battery decks are, his surprise would be still greater upon seeing the mess, or living deck, which has the extraordinary height of 11 ft. 6 in. from deck to under side of beam, equal to the lofty ceiling of a modern dwelling-house. He would also be impressed with the large air-ports, the pleasant, light, and commodious cabins for the officers, the ward-room centrally situated, with a passage between it and the cabins on each side; an arrangement for convenience and comfort unknown to old officers.'

The merits of the 'Alexandra' have been fully recognised both by Mr. King, and by writers in *Engineering*, and other high authorities. Mr. King says: 'The broadside system has proved tenacious of life. For masted vessels it fairly holds its own against the turrets. The hitherto unknown perfection to which it has been brought in the "Alexandra" appears likely to give it a new lease of life, especially in combination with all-round fire from fixed turrets on the upper deck, as in the "Téméraire."' *Merits of design.*

Engineering speaks in terms of equal commendation: 'The "Alexandra" must be taken for what she is—a magnificent specimen of a ship constructed on the belt system, and by no means antiquated on that account. For while her displacement exceeds that of the "Sultan," the largest masted ironclad hitherto built, by only 206 tons, the maximum thickness of armour is increased from nine inches to twelve inches; and instead of eight 18-ton guns and four of

Fig. 102.

'THWARTSHIP SECTION, SHOWING BOTH BATTERIES OF 'ALEXANDRA.'

smaller size, she carries ten of 18 tons and two of 25 tons, a size not hitherto attempted on the broadside.'

The large expenditure on the 'Alexandra,' amounting to 600,000*l.*, will be viewed by the naval administrator as a serious objection to the multiplication of ships of this type.

The 'Téméraire' and 'Alexandra' are, as before remarked, the only two central-battery battle-ships which the Admiralty has constructed in recent years.

The accompanying description of the 'Téméraire' is taken from Mr. King :—

'The "Téméraire," built at Chatham, and completed in 1877, is The 'Téméraire.'

Figs. 193 and 194.

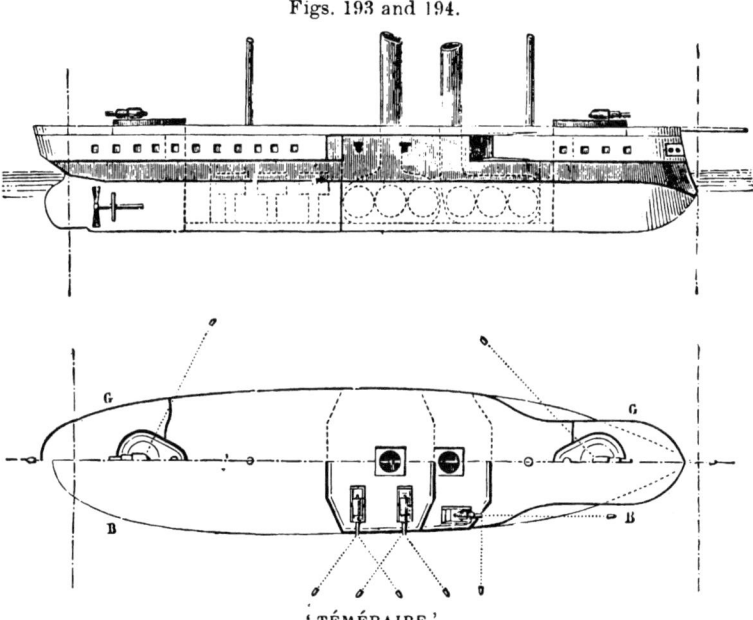

'TÉMÉRAIRE.'

designed for a seagoing ship. Her most important feature—the feature, in fact, which distinguishes her fundamentally from all other armoured ships of the British navy—is that she carries the upper-deck armament in two fixed turrets[1] open at the top, instead of a central-battery. At each end of the upper deck is a pear-shaped tower or battery, standing about six feet above the deck, and measuring about 33 feet in length fore and aft, which is the direction of its longest axis, by 21 ft. 6 in. across. This contains a turntable, on

---

[1] Though, perhaps, the designation is not yet officially settled, it has become customary of late to speak of fixed *bar-* *bette* turrets as 'towers,' the former word being restricted to revolving shields.

which is to be mounted a 25-ton gun,[1] worked by hydraulic machinery, on the disappearing principle; that is, the gun is raised to be fired over the edge of the tower, and immediately after firing sinks under cover to be reloaded.   As the sides of the vessel from the level of the upper deck to that of the main deck are, of course, not armoured at the extremities, a connection is made between the tower and the lower part of the ship by an armoured trunk or tube, so placed that on the gun being revolved, after firing, into the fore-and-aft line, with its muzzle toward the middle of the ship, the muzzle comes just over the opening, ready for the fresh charge to be brought up to it from below.   It must, of course, always be brought to the same

M. Dislère: Observations on Turrets.

position for loading.   The foremost turret is protected with 10-inch armour; the after one with 8-inch.   The guns have a clear sweep round the respective ends of the ship, to some distance abaft or before the beam, as the case may be.   This arrangement is not approved by M. Dislère.   The French engineers have, from the first introduction of armoured ships, entertained a noted antipathy to revolving turrets. They have objected to protecting the guns by a weight equal to that of the guns and their ammunition; to a system which prevented an enemy from being clearly seen; and to the impossibility of getting an all-round fire with two turrets in a line; while the advantages they claimed for the *barbette* system were that an enemy could be clearly seen, and that the freedom and *morale* of the gunners were better assured than in a turret battery.

'The French naturally defend their own system against the opinions of all other European naval authorities.   In the usual sense of the words, the guns in the open battery of the " Téméraire " are not *barbette* guns at all.   They are fired *en barbette*, just as guns in Moncrieff gun-pits are, but they are not *en barbette* at any other time, which is an important distinction.   They and their crews are not exposed to one-half of the risks which attend guns mounted permanently above the parapet of the battery, as is the case in all the French open-top turrets.   The upper deck guns of the " Téméraire " have much more in common with the Moncrieff system of mounting, or even with guns in ordinary turrets, than with the old system of *barbette* firing.   The turrets communicate, as we have seen, by a trunk, not very strongly protected by armour, with the space beneath the armoured deck.   M. Dislère points out that the turrets are thus placed above an unarmoured space, and that a projectile, after having traversed the upper works, might destroy the turrets from below, exactly as if they were unarmoured.'

[1] See lithographed plates attached to this volume.

TEMERAIRE.

We continue the description of the 'Téméraire' from the columns of *Engineering* :—

'Not to obstruct the fire, the bulwarks are kept low, about four feet Description from *En-gineering*. above the deck, an arrangement hardly to be avoided, but likely to be objected to by sailors. The enormously high bulwarks of ordinary men-of-war are liked by the men for the great protection they give against wind and wet; and their absence from the " Monarch "— whose bulwarks, we believe, are a little lower than the " Téméraire's," and perhaps less commodious through being hinged—has often been made a ground of complaint against that ship. On the other hand, the " Téméraire " gains an upper deck with no break in it except the poop and forecastle, and the fixed turrets, which are partly enclosed in them. All recent cruising ironclads have had an upper battery, forming an inconvenient break in the upper deck, and interfering more or less seriously with the working of ropes; this is got rid of in the " Téméraire." The " Alexandra's " upper-deck battery is of this kind, and it may be perhaps useful to describe it, for comparison with the upper-deck armament of the smaller ship. It contains two 25-ton guns forward and two 18-ton guns aft, all firing from corner ports, and with an arc of training extending from a little abaft or before the beam, as the case may be, to a little *across* the fore and aft line. From the upper deck the " Alexandra " can therefore fire— right ahead, two 25-ton guns, converging at a certain distance ; right astern, two 18-ton guns ; right abeam, one of each kind ; and in every other direction, one gun, either of 25 or 18 tons. The " Téméraire," from the upper deck, fires right ahead one 25-ton gun ; right astern the same ; and, through a large arc on the beam, two.

'On the main deck, protecting also the funnel, is the " Téméraire's " double or divided battery, shown in plan, and resembling, except in being shorter, the main-deck battery of the " Alexandra." The foremost part contains two 25-ton guns, the corresponding guns in the " Alexandra " being of 18 tons only. Their arc of training extends from slightly abaft the beam on each side to slightly across the fore-and-aft line, so as to secure a converging fire at some distance ahead of the vessel, as already described in the case of the " Alexandra." These guns, of course, fire from corner ports, and the sides of the ship above the main deck, or top of the belt forward, are set back several feet. The after part of the battery contains four 18-ton guns against six in the " Alexandra," for broadside fire only.

'On the whole, the " Téméraire " fires three 25-ton guns right ahead, against two 25-ton and two 18-ton guns in the " Alexandra ; " on either bow, two 25-ton against one 25-ton and one 18-ton ; right aft, one 25-ton against two 18-ton; on either quarter, one 25-ton against one 18-ton; on either beam, if engaged on one side at a time, two 25-ton and two 18-ton, with a third 25-ton available through only half the usual arc, against three 18-ton guns, with two of the same weight, and one of 25 tons, each available with the limitation just described. Notwithstanding the disparity in the total number of guns, there seems to us not a great deal to choose between these armaments, if the superior accuracy and freedom of range which it is fair to allow to the upper-deck guns on turntables be taken into account. Indeed, we have little doubt that naval officers will generally prefer the armament of the smaller ship. Even if it be allowed that the "Alexandra" might, at the cost of very little extra size, carry 25-ton guns on the main deck in the same way as the "Téméraire," the comparison will not be unfavourable to the latter, especially when it is remembered that her guns, on the whole, are better protected than those of the larger ship. One, though at times exposed altogether, has 10-inch armour, and the *uniform* thickness protecting all the others is eight inches. We believe the armour on parts of the batteries of the "Alexandra" is but six inches thick, and in parts less. The transverse bulkhead dividing the main-deck battery, the chief objects of which are to localise the effects of an explosion in either, and to prevent the broadside guns being raked by shots entering through the corner ports forward, has 5-inch armour. The guns of the "Téméraire" are better defended than those of any other broadside ship we possess, and this fact, coupled with a water-line defence nearly equal to that of the "Alexandra," an armament which many will prefer to hers, and a much less size and cost, should give her the character of being our most successful masted ship. She is at least immeasurably superior to everything, however large, which preceded the "Alexandra."

'The "Téméraire" has not coal-tank ends, having been designed, like the "Alexandra," in the transition time when the present proportion of beam to length in cruising ships was hardly accepted. We presume she will be the last ironclad from which the great advantages of the new system are withheld; the "Nelson" and "Northampton" cruising ships, though smaller, have coal-tanks at both ends, and the "Shannon," an earlier and still smaller vessel of similar type, has a coal-tank forward. Like all belt ships, the "Téméraire" has weak places in her water-line, but amidships, over the most vital parts, she has 11-inch armour, against 12-inch in the "Alexandra," reduced very slightly above and below. At the bow, to guard against exposure to raking fire in pitching, the armour is carried down over the point of the ram, and similar protection is gained for the magazines, etc., against raking fire from aft, by an armoured bulkhead across the hold. This is plated with 5-inch armour. The deck at the level of the top of the belt, outside the main-deck battery, is 1½ inch thick. The hull, which has the usual double bottom, and is divided into very numerous watertight compartments, is built on the well-known bracket-frame system, and it is sheathed externally with wood and copper. As in other recent twin-screw ships, the engine and boiler-rooms are divided into two longitudinally by a bulkhead, to limit the entry of water and its ill consequences to the engines, in case of injury from rams or torpedoes. The weight of the armour and backing is about 2,300 tons, or nearly the same as in the "Alexandra;" the bunkers contain 600 tons of coal; and the guns, ordnance stores, engines, boilers, and all other equipment weigh about 2,200 tons. These weights, amounting in all to 5,100 tons, are carried by a hull weighing 3,300 tons only. The spread of canvas is considerable, but it is carried brig-fashion on two masts only, to avoid obstructing the end-on fire of the upper-deck guns. The loss involved in giving up the mizen mast is not great— indeed we believe that in some large ironclads the weather helm, when sailing by the wind, is so great that it has been found impossible to carry any sail on the mizen.'

The following are the principal dimensions of the 'Téméraire,' with similar information added for the 'Alexandra' for the sake of comparison :—

	'Téméraire'	'Alexandra'
Length between perpendiculars	285 feet	325 feet
Breadth, extreme	62 feet	63 ft. 8 in.
Draught aft	27 feet	26 ft. 6 in.
„ forward	26 ft. 6 in.	26 feet
Displacement	8,412 tons	9,492 tons
Indicated horse-power	7,600	8,600
Speed	14·56 knots	15 knots
Armour:—		
Maximum thickness on belt	11 inches	12 inches
Thickness on batteries	10-in., 8-in.	8-in., 6-in.
Guns of 25 tons	4	2
Guns of 18 tons	4	10
Weight of broadside fire	2,600 lbs.	2,600 lbs.
Weight of bow fire	1,800 lbs.	2,000 lbs.
Weight of stern fire	600 lbs.	800 lbs.
Cost, estimated	£374,000	£521,000

M. Dislère remarks that the reduction of 1,000 tons as compared with the 'Alexandra' has been effected mainly by diminishing the armour-protection of the 'Téméraire.'

Mr. Barnaby, in a paper on *Recent Designs for Ships of War*, read before the Institute of Naval Architects at their annual meeting, drew the following comparison between the 'Alexandra,' at that date called the 'Superb,' and the 'Téméraire':—

Mr. Barnaby on *Recent Designs,* &c. I.N.A.

'The "Superb" and "Téméraire."—I must admit at once that the "Shannon" will not bear comparison with these two ships now building at Chatham; but then it must be remembered that we can have two "Shannons" for the cost of one "Superb" [now the "Alexandra"].

'I will not trouble you with a description of these ships. I will only say of them that they will have but two masted ironclads in the world capable of competing with them, viz., the "Redoutable," now building for the French navy at L'Orient, and the turret-ship building on the Thames for the Brazilian navy.[1] Both the "Superb" and "Téméraire" have very great offensive and defensive power, and present many novel features, some of them, I think, of considerable value.

'The "Téméraire" is, I believe, especially likely to command a large amount of favour in the navy.'

M. Dislère speaks less favourably. He considers that the 'Téméraire' is not an improvement on the 'Alexandra,' and that the smaller types are better adapted to the exigencies of naval warfare.

This description of the 'Téméraire' will be completed by the republication of the accounts of the trials of the engines and torpedoes from the columns of the English press, together with Mr. King's remarks on the working of the barbette guns.

Machinery. 'The steam machinery was designed and constructed by Messrs. Humphreys, Tennant and Co., of Deptford; and the contract provided that the engines should indicate 7,000 horse-power. Though resembling in general appearance and construction the machinery which was supplied by the same eminent manufacturers to the "Dreadnought" and "Alexandra," the engines differ from them in several important details, the principal variations being that, in consequence of want of room, the cylinders are limited to two. They are of the compound vertical inverted type. Each of the twin screws is operated by an independent pair of engines, which with the boilers, are separated by a longitudinal bulkhead. The diameter of the high-pressure cylinders is seventy inches, of the low-pressure 114 inches, the stroke 3 ft. 10 in., and maximum revolutions about seventy. The air-pumps are worked directly from the pistons. The crank-shafts are $17\frac{1}{2}$ inches in diameter, coupled in the centre, and

[1] Now the British 'Neptune.'

the two sections are interchangeable. The screw-propellers are of the Griffith new type, each having a diameter of 20 feet, a pitch of 23 ft. 6 in. (variable from 19 to 24 feet), and an immersion of the upper edge of 4 ft. 10 in. at deep load draught. A novel feature in the design of the engines, introduced here for the first time, has been the employment of wrought iron, steel, and brass to a large extent in lieu of cast iron ; the cylinders, their valves and covers, being the only parts made of that material. Thus the whole of the framing is constructed of wrought iron, the bearings of the crank-shafts being also formed of heavy forgings of the same tough metal, and connected to box-girders of wrought-iron plates ; while for additional security and strength the girders are riveted to the ship's framing, and are thus made to form a part of the general structure of the hull; the cylinders are also supported on wrought-iron box girders placed vertically and strengthened by wrought-iron columns. The whole of the condensing apparatus, including the tube-cases, air-pumps, their connections, etc., are made of brass. The cases are made each in four pieces and bolted together ; they contain 11,236 solid drawn brass tubes 7 ft. $7\frac{1}{2}$ in. in length, with an external diameter of $\frac{5}{8}$ inch ; they are tinned on both sides, and each tube is secured in its place by a stuffing-box tapped into the plate with a canvas washer behind it. The total cooling surface is 14,000 square feet. The water is circulated through the condensers by means of centrifugal pumps, which are driven by independent engines. The valve-faces of the high-pressure cylinders are of phosphor-bronze, secured in place by composition screws. Altogether the whole structure presents an appearance of lightness and beauty, composing a splendid piece of workmanship.

'The steam is furnished by twelve boilers, elliptical in shape, Boilers. containing three furnaces in each. They are placed in the ship back to back, against the longitudinal bulkhead, with the fronts facing the sides of the vessel, and consequently fired with convenient access to the side coal-bunkers. They are divided by bulkheads into four several sets, in the same manner as those in the "Alexandra." Any one set or any one boiler can be worked independently of the others. The whole of the boiler-mountings, including the stop and safety valves and their boxes, are made of composition. The working-pressure of steam is 60 lbs. per square inch, and the boilers have been tested up to 120 lbs. As in other recent twin-screw ships, the engine and boiler rooms are divided into two, longitudinally, to limit the entry of water and its ill consequences to the engine and boilers in case of injury from rams or torpedoes.

Special
engines.

'Besides the main engines described, the "Téméraire" is provided with thirty other steam-engines. These include two pairs of small engines placed near each screw-shaft coupling for the purpose of turning the great engines, when they are not at work, so as to bring the pistons, steam-valves, or other parts to convenient points for examination and adjustment from time to time, as required; two starting-engines for the purpose of starting or reversing the main engines; four feed-engines, for supplying the boilers with water, or drawing it therefrom; two circulating-engines, for forcing water through the condensers; two bilge-pump engines; four pumping-engines, to free the water-bottoms, or to be used in the event of fire or accident to the hull- under water; four engines for hoisting ashes, coal, or provisions; four engines for working the ventilating-fans; one capstan or anchor-hoisting engine; one engine for steering the ship; two engines for working the hydraulic gear of the guns; an engine to charge the torpedo air-reservoir, and an engine to work the electric machine which feeds the lights on the bridge.'

Official
trials.

The measured mile trial in Stokes Bay was made before all the weights were placed on board, the draught of the ship then being 25 ft. 4 in. forward, and 26 ft. 2 in. aft.

Six runs were made over the mile, with and against the tide, with results reported as follows: first, 13·846 knots; second, 15·319 knots; third, 13·636 knots; fourth, 15·859 knots; fifth, 13·636 knots; sixth, 15·721 knots. The mean of the means showed a speed of 14·65 knots, with an indicated horse-power of 7,697. The amount of coal consumed during the trial was 51 tons 2 quarters, being equal to $2\frac{1}{2}$ lbs. per indicated horse-power per hour, a result comparatively low in consideration of the fact that the fires had to be pushed to the utmost, regardless of economy.

Six-hour
trial.

The six-hour trial for endurance was made on September 17, 1878, after all the weights were put on board and the ship ready for sea; the draught of water at this time being, forward, 26 ft. 8 in., and aft, 27 ft. 4 in., or about the same as the estimated draught of the ship. The sea was smooth, and the run was made near Cowes. The following table shows the results of each of the twelve half-hours during which observations were taken, as reported by the *Times* :—

Pressure of steam, in pounds	Vacuum, in inches		Revolutions		Indicated horse-power
	Starboard	Port	Starboard	Port	
49	28·75	28·75	71	70	6,462·98
57	28·75	28·75	74·4	74	7,538·94
57	28·5	28·5	73·6	73·9	7,470·41
57·5	28·25	28·25	74·7	74·4	7,784·19
57	28	28	74·3	74·5	7,562·12
59	28	28	74·2	74·2	7,796·38
56·5	28·25	28	73·6	74	7,447·03
58·5	28·5	28	74·5	74·5	7,517·14
60	28·25	28	73·6	73·7	7,585·61
58·5	28·25	28	74	75	7,586·19
61	28	28	73 3	74·8	7,723·17
59·5	28	28	72·4	72·7	7,644·53

'The means were: pressure of steam in boiler, 59 lbs. Vacuum in condensers— starboard, 28·20 inches ; port, 28 inches. Revolutions per minute—starboard, 73·60 ; port, 74·13. Pressure of steam on square inch of piston—starboard, 26·6 lbs. high, and 11·7 lbs. low ; port, 26·1 lbs. high, and 11·68 lbs. low. Indicated horse-power—starboard, 3,801·09 ; port, 3,782·95. The total collective power developed by the engines during the six hours was thus 7,584·04 horses, or 584·04 beyond the contract.

' Comparing the results with the measured-mile data, and taking four consecutive half-hours, counting from the third, as an equivalent for the mile runs, we have 7,653 horses as compared with the 7,696 horses on the Maplin Sands.[1]

' Subsequently the ship made a trial run at various speeds, under trying conditions of weather, between Spithead and Queenstown, and steaming in a fresh gale she is reported to have made the extraordinary speed of nearly fourteen knots per hour, the wind doubtless being favourable. It is said that during the roughest weather she was remarkably steady, that her barbette-guns might have been easily and effectively worked, and that her after main-deck guns were available the whole time.

' For comparison of the motive machinery of the three recently constructed powerful armoured ships, engined by Messrs. Humphreys and Tennant, the following table is given :— Comparison with 'Dreadnought' and 'Alexandra.'

[1] At this rate of steaming, however, the bunkers of the 'Téméraire,' which should stow 600 tons, would be exhausted in less than three days. The result of a 'full-speed trial' of twelve hours, undertaken by this armourclad on her passage to Tunis in December, 1879, was to demonstrate her mean speed to be between 13 and 14 knots, but exceeding 14 in perfectly smooth water.

—	DREADNOUGHT	ALEXANDRA	TÉMÉRAIRE
Type of engines .	Vertical compound; twin screw; three cylinders driving each screw	Vertical compound; twin screw; three cylinders driving each screw	Vertical compound; twin screw; two cylinders driving each screw
Cylinders:			
Number . .	Six	Six	Four
Diameter . .	Two of 66 inches; four of 90 inches	Two of 70 inches; four of 90 inches	Two of 70 inches; two of 114 inches
Length of stroke .	4 ft. 6 in.	4 feet	3 ft. 10 in.
Diameter of crank-shaft	17½ inches	17½ inches	17½ inches
Screws:			
Diameter . .	20 feet	21 feet	20 feet
Pitch . .	23 ft. 6 in.	22 ft. 3 in.	22 ft. 6 in.
Type . .	Four-bladed Griffith	Mangin	Two-bladed Griffith
Condensers:			
Number . .	Two	Two	Two
Cooling surface .	16,500 sq. ft.	16,500 sq. ft.	16,500 sq. ft.
Type . .	Surface	Surface	Surface
Boilers:			
Number . .	Twelve	Twelve	Twelve
Total grate surface .	820 sq. ft.	780 sq. ft.	780 sq. ft.
Total heating surface .	22,025 sq. ft.	21,912 sq. ft.	19,824 sq. ft.
Six hours' trial:			
Pressure of steam .	60 lbs.	60 lbs.	60 lbs.
Revolutions of engines .	67	64	74
Indicated horsepower .	8,206	8,313	7,518
Speed of ship .	14·52 knots per hour	15 knots per hour	14·65 knots per hour

'The steam steering-gear is operated by a set of Messrs. Brotherhood and Hardingham's three-cylinder engines, which is the first of its type introduced into a ship of war; it required several little alterations and adjustments after the first trial.

Torpedo-fittings.

'The "Téméraire," in like manner with all recently commissioned ships, is provided with the apparatus and appliances for using the Whitehead torpedo. On each side of the vessel forward, above the armour-plating, there has been fitted a tube, the diameter of which is 21 inches, for the purpose of ejecting those instruments of destruction. She is also supplied with the Harvey torpedoes, and with outrigger torpedoes, the latter to be used from steam cutters. Gatling guns are provided for use to guard against the approach of the enemies' torpedo-boats.

'The electric light which proved so successful on board the "Alexandra" has been applied to the "Téméraire," and when tested in the river Medway, in August last, objects were distinguishable for a considerable distance in all directions around the ship.

'The principle of sinking guns entirely under cover from hori- zontal fire behind any sufficient parapet, and raising them only to deliver their fire,' says Mr. King, 'is quite old, and, like very many inventions introduced into European warfare, owes its origin to American genius.

'It was proposed more than twenty years ago by officers of the United States Army for our fortifications, and models were made representing the principle of storing and utilising the force of recoil; *i.e.*, the gun on delivering fire and sinking behind the wall raises a counter-weight, the fall of which again lifts the gun when required; and some years ago Captain King, Engineer Corps, United States Army, successfully applied to one of our forts a carriage of his invention on this principle.

'Captain Eads, of St. Louis, Mo., invented as early as 1861, and soon after successfully applied to the two-turretted gunboats "Winnebago" and "Milwaukie," built at that time on the Mississippi River, a system of mounting heavy guns on a turntable within a rotating turret. The table, with the guns and their attachments, was raised, lowered, and revolved by steam power; the guns were also moved out to the firing positions by the same medium, and the recoil was taken on steam-pressure.

'For the purpose of loading the guns the table was lowered to the berth-deck. The work of construction was done under the Government supervision of the writer. The trial tests of the machinery and firing of the guns to test rapidity and accuracy were personally executed by him, and an official report of the machinery and results of the target-firing was also made by him April 30, 1864, to the Secretary of the Navy, and published in pamphlet form.

'Subsequently Captain Eads invented and patented the principle of raising and lowering guns by the elastic force of compressed air, the mechanical appliances being very similar to those afterwards used by Major Moncrieff in his second invention, where he has substituted for the counter-weight air compressed by the recoil through the medium of water. This part of the Moncrieff invention is thus described :—

'The gun is supported in the firing position on levers, supplemented by a ram working in a cylinder which is in communication with a vessel the upper part of which is filled with compressed air, the lower portion containing water. The air has an initial pressure given it sufficient to raise the gun. When the gun is fired the energy of the recoil drives the ram down into the cylinder, forcing the water up into the air-vessel, thus further compressing the air. A self-acting

valve prevents the water from returning after the recoil has been
completed.   When the gun has been loaded behind the protecting
parapet a valve is opened and the water allowed to flow into the
cylinder.   The air-pressure is thus brought to act on the ram,
which at once raises the gun into the firing position.   No power
beyond that obtained from the discharge of the gun is required for
working the gun, the air-vessel remaining always ready for use.

'The Rendel system as applied to the "Téméraire" is analogous to
that originated by Eads, except that the power used by the former is
applied through the medium of water, that used by the latter being
air.   An important distinction, however, is in the fact that as here
carried out no attempt has been made to store up and utilise the
force of recoil of the gun, that force being taken on a hydraulic
plunger working in a charged cylinder having a safety-valve loaded
to about 750 lbs. per square inch.

'The towers in which the two 25-ton guns are mounted are seven
feet in depth, and are pear- or egg-shaped, the guns being placed
within the broad part of the egg.   The circular platform is rotated by
means of hydraulic presses, which are fitted within the structure of
the platform itself; the platform is arrested by a weighted pawl,
which falls into notches in much the same way as may be observed
in the turntables of railway stations.   The gun itself is raised and
lowered by means of massive forged bell-crank levers, of which the
heads are attached to the trunnions of the gun, and the elbows work
on bearings upon the platform, the extremities being connected with
hydraulic pistons, the outward or inward thrust of which imparts the
upward or downward motion to the piece.   The elevation or depression of the gun is accomplished by means of an elevating arc, which
is actuated by a wheel and pinion after the ordinary manner, and
the radial action of which, in conjunction with that of the lever,
always enables the gun to be brought to the same plane—3° of inclination—for loading.   The sights are fitted to the platform, so that
the gun may be elevated and laid while being revolved into position
for firing, the gunners being at the same time protected by a bullet-
proof shield.   The powder and shell are brought from the magazine
directly to the mouth of the gun without the circumlocution of trolleys, by means of a hydraulic hoist working up and down an armoured shaft or well, 3 ft. 6 in. in diameter, in which also are placed
the pipes communicating with the presses.   The upper storey, so to
speak, of the cradle contains the cartridge, and the lower the projectile.   After the former has been introduced into the gun by a push
of the hydraulic rammer, the hoist is lifted a step higher and the

É. de Marine

KAISER.

projectile and the cartridge are forced home. The rammer, levers, and gearing are placed at the small end of the egg-shaped belt, and are protected by a splinter-proof. Indeed, the gun is the only thing which is exposed in the act of firing. The hydraulic machinery is actuated by a couple of small engines, which may be used either in combination or separately, and which, though placed within the armour-belt below the water-line, are each worked from within the turrets.

'The final trial of the disappearing carriages and hydraulic appa- ratus for loading, training, and working the guns in the towers was made November 13, 1877. Fourteen rounds were fired from the after tower and eleven from the forward, with charges of 85 lbs. of powder, the projectile weighing 530 lbs. Including the firing on former occasions, fifty rounds in all have been discharged from the barbette-guns, sufficient, it is thought, as a test of endurance in respect to the mechanism. Many of the rounds were fired at a floating target, but four were fired against time for the purpose of testing the rapidity with which the gun could be loaded, laid, and discharged, and also of proving the hydraulic gear under such con- ditions. From fire to fire the time was $1\frac{1}{2}$ minutes. The number of men required to work the gun being one man to lay and fire electrically, two men to attend the elevating gear, one man to take charge of the levers for lifting the gun and rotating the platform and five men to manage the rammer and shot-hoist. It is not, however, rapidity of fire which is the most important point, for, considering the weight of the projectile, accuracy is everything, a few fair hits being probably all that will be required to disable an enemy.

'Although the recoil of the gun with the battering charge is very considerable, this enormous force is so absorbed by the water-presses that the recoil upon the cylinders did not exceed an average of twelve inches.'

Trial of gun-fit-tings.

After the close of the Franco-Prussian war, when Germany be- came united, the Imperial German Government deemed it necessary to build up a navy commensurate with the wants and interests of a powerful empire. Accordingly, a number of ships were about that time ordered to be built, including five armoured frigates. The following description of the 'Kaiser' and 'Deutschland' is reprinted from the work of Mr. King.

'The "Kaiser" and "Deutschland," from the designs of Mr. E. J. Reed, late Chief Constructor of the British Navy, were contracted for by Messrs. Samuda Brothers, of London. They were designed as cruisers, have a central battery, and are in general features and arrangement somewhat similar to the British frigate "Hercules," but differ in numerous points of detail. The last one was completed in 1875.

'The "Kaiser" and "Deutschland" are each about 285 feet long, with an extreme breadth of 62 feet, load draught of 24 ft. 6 in., and a displacement of 7,600 tons. They are very strongly framed. The inner frames are of continuous angle-iron, and the longitudinal plates and angle-irons are scored over them. They are built on the bracket-plate system, like the "Invincible" class of ships; with a depth of 40 inches in the vertical keel; while the longitudinals

Figs. 195 and 196.

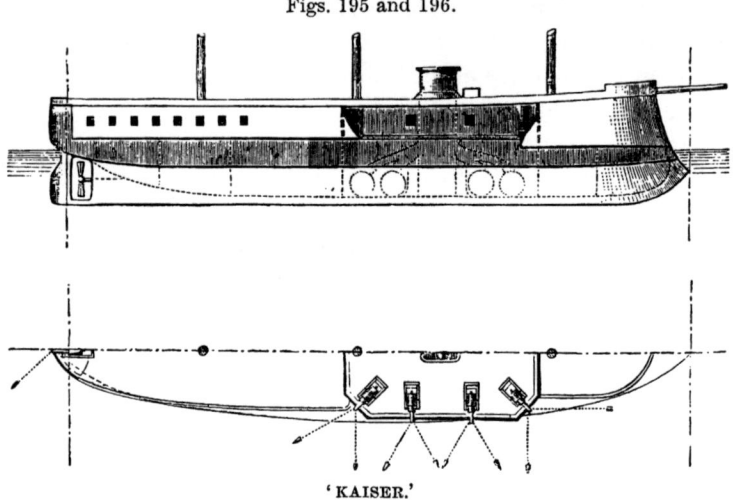

'KAISER.'

diminish to 33 inches in breadth, and then increase to 45 inches at the armour-shelf. There are no wing passages, but they are divided into compartments by transverse watertight bulkheads; and the double-bottom is in 32 watertight compartments. In striking a rock it is expected that not more than four could be filled with water at once; the cubic capacity of each being about 40 tons.

'There is one central battery on the main deck, carrying four guns on each side; of which the forward ones fire 3° within the fore-and-aft line, and thus afford a converging fire ahead, while the embrasures are so arranged that the fire of all the guns on one side may converge at a point 276 feet, or about one ship's length, distant. The battery overhangs the side about 3 ft 6 in. at the forward end and 1 ft. 6 in. at the after end, but is within the extreme breadth of the ship, and the ports are fitted with heavy forgings on a new plan, so as to protect the gunners as much as possible.

'The guns are Krupp 26-c/m. steel breech-loading cannon, having a bore of about $9\frac{3}{4}$ inches, and weighing about 22 tons each. To complete the all-round fire, a Krupp 22-c/m. gun of $8\frac{1}{4}$-inch bore, weighing about 18 tons, is placed on the main deck aft, and is capable of being trained to an angle of 15° on each side of the middle line. This gun is protected by armour. The height of the port-sills above the load water-line is eleven feet. The armour at the water-line, in the wake of the engines, boilers, and magazines, is ten inches thick, and elsewhere on the belt it is eight inches amidships, tapering to five inches forward and aft. In the central battery it is ten inches at the port-sills, eight inches on the sides, and seven inches on the bulkheads. The wood-backing is of teak, ten inches thick,

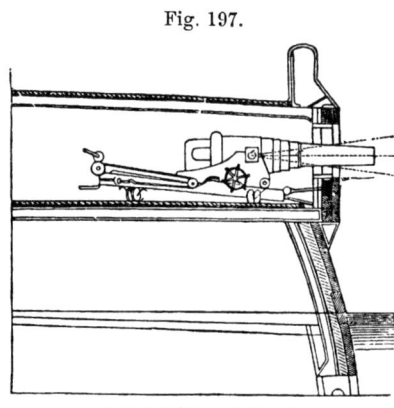

Fig. 197.

'KAISER'S' BATTERY.

placed upon two thicknesses of $\frac{5}{8}$-inch plate, which are supported by 10-inch frames, spaced two feet apart. The armour on the belt abaft the battery extends 5 ft. 6 in. below the water-line and 6 ft. 6 in. above it, while in front of the battery it extends to 2 ft. 6 in. above the water-line up to the lower deck, which is covered with protective plating in two thicknesses, two inches thick for ten feet in front of the battery bulkhead, and $1\frac{1}{2}$ inch thick from this forward. Protection is the more necessary for the deck in consequence of the reduction in the height of the armoured belt above the water-line.

'There is an armoured bulkhead at each end of the battery, the foremost one extending down to the lower deck, in order to protect the engines and boilers against a plunging fire. The upper and main decks and part of the lower deck are also protected with plates. The central battery gives protection only to the boilers and the magazines, which are placed athwartships between the two sets of boilers. The engines are outside the battery; and the deck, which is an extension of the armoured belt, and is covered only with half-inch plating, is the only protection against vertical fire.

'The machinery was designed and constructed by Messrs. Penn and Son. The engines are of the old type, horizontal, direct-acting, with trunks; they are of the collective power of 8,000 indicated horses. The diameter of the cylinders is 122 inches, length of stroke 4 feet, and the greatest number of revolutions per minute 75. A speed of 14½ knots per hour was obtained on the measured-mile trials. The boilers are of the box type, and are eight in number. The vessels are ship-rigged, with an area of 39,000 square feet of canvas when all sail is set, and an area of plain sail of 28,000 square feet. The screws are fixed, and made to revolve when the ships are under sail. The bunkers are capable of containing 710 tons of coal, or sufficient for a distance of 3,400 miles at a speed of ten knots. The circle was completed in 3 min. 32 sec., with a diameter of 452 mètres.' In concluding his description of the 'Kaiser' and 'Deutschland,' Mr. King commends them highly as very powerful armoured frigates.

The following translation from the *Nord Deutsch Zeitung* appeared in the *Broad Arrow* :—

'The "Deutschland" and her consorts will carry the same spars as a second-class ship of the line. They will, therefore, be able to cruise independently of steam. They carry rams, separated from the body of the vessel by watertight compartments, so as to prevent the concussion from a successful stroke against a hostile ship doing serious injury to themselves. They have engines of 8,000 horse-power, a propelling force as yet surpassed only by the English iron-clads "Hercules" and "Sultan" and the German "König Wilhelm." The boilers are heated by 40 fires; there are two chimneys, and the screw is easily detached when the sails are unfurled. Each of these ships will be manned by a crew of 600. Russia as yet has no fully masted ironclad destined to fight on the high seas which can compare with the "Kaiser" and "Deutschland." England has the "Sultan," the "Hercules," and the "Monarch" to match our formidable frigates; and the English "Alexandra" and "Téméraire" are even superior to ours in cuirass and cannon. The French "Friedland," "Marengo," and "Suffren" are also nearly on a par with ours; and the "Redoutable," still in the dockyard, is likely to turn out even somewhat stronger. The fact of England constructing two vessels, and France one, more powerful than the two we are about to finish, aptly illustrates the rivalry existing in this branch of warlike appliances.'

The 'Kaiser' and 'Deutschland' possess a powerful armament. They could use the ram with great effect, and in their defensive power they may be compared with the great majority of armoured vessels of the date of the 'Vanguard,' 'Marengo,' and 'Hercules.'

Four ironclad vessels were ordered by the Turkish Government in the year 1873, two of which were contracted for by the Thames Iron Works Company and two by Messrs. Samuda Bros.

The 'Superb,' one of the vessels ordered on the Thames, was purchased by the Admiralty out of the vote of credit of 6,000,000*l.* The price paid was 453,000*l.* The 'Superb.'

The 'Superb' belongs to the type adopted for the early ironclads of the first rate, in which the bow and stern fire is not secured by the battery guns, but only, as in the 'Hercules' and 'König Wilhelm,' by one or more guns mounted on the upper deck, and in this instance without protection. The dimensions of the 'Superb' are as follows:—

Figs. 198 and 199.

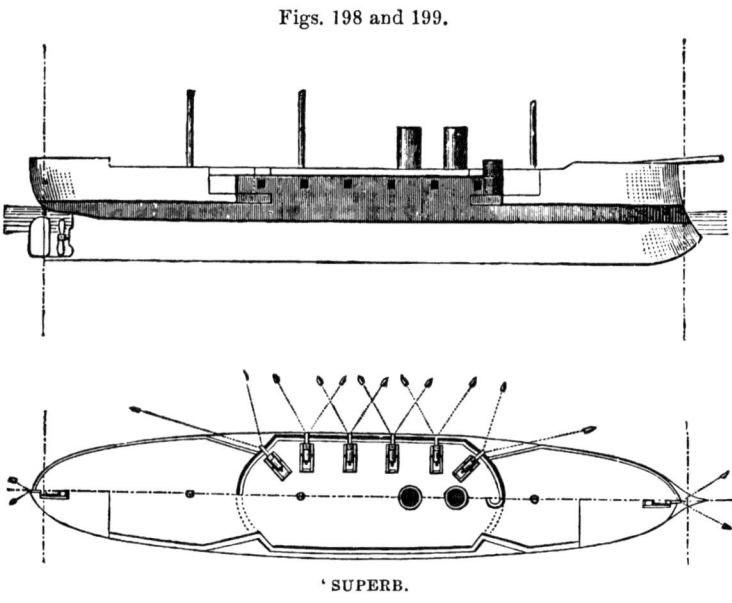

'SUPERB.

Length between perpendiculars	.	.	332 ft. 3 in.
Breadth, extreme . . .	.	.	59 feet
Draught of water, forward .	.	.	24 feet
,, aft	.	.	26 feet
Displacement, tons .	.	.	8950

The battery is 153 feet in length, and the armour-plating twelve inches thick on the sides as compared with nine inches on the 'Sultan.' The 'Superb' has a full rig. The armament consists of sixteen 18-ton guns. When built for the Turkish Government she was only intended to carry twelve guns, by when purchased by the Admiralty it was decided to increase her fighting powers, and the alterations necessary to enable her to carry this increased armament kept her

in the hands of the dockyard workmen about eighteen months. The
original armament was furnished by Sir W. G. Armstrong and Co.,
and consisted of twelve 18-ton guns on the gun-deck, two 6½-ton guns
on the upper deck forward, and one of the same calibre aft. The
armament now consists of sixteen 18-ton guns and a few light pieces.
The engines are by Maudslay and Field, and are on the direct-acting
principle with a single screw. There are two cylinders, 116 inches
in diameter, and the length of stroke is four feet. The indicated
horse-power is 7,431, and the speed 13·78 knots ; the coal-supply is
600 tons.

The battery, which is 153 feet in length, is covered with 12-inch
wrought-iron plates, backed by East-India teak 22 inches thick, with
an inner iron skin 1½ inch thick. The armour is carried down some
depth below the water-line, and raised only a few feet above what
appears to be the main deck, but is really only a spar deck of unarmoured timber. The true main deck is below and is of iron, the
saloons and quarters for officers and men being upon it, but it is
assumed that in time of action all hands will be in the armoured
enclosure, leaving the unarmoured portion to its fate. The hatchways of the main deck close by watertight iron doors, and there are
upwards of sixty watertight compartments in the lower decks and the
double iron skin. The ship is fitted with Paul's steam steering gear,
worked either from the pilot-tower on the upper deck or between the
battery, with hand gear and reserve appliances in case of accident.
The steering apparatus is very powerful, and the ship is said to have
behaved splendidly on her trial trip.

The ' Superb ' left Plymouth in November 1880 *en route* to the
Mediterranean. During the passage from Portsmouth a full-power
trial was made. The machinery worked in a very satisfactory
manner. Over 6,000 indicated horse-power was developed, and no
forcing or blast was required. About nine tons of coal per hour, with
57 revolutions, gave over thirteen knots in smooth water.

The ' Re-
doutable.'

The French ship ' Redoutable,' laid down in 1872 from designs
by M. de Bussy, Director of Naval Construction, marks the first step
on the path of a new and important transformation of the *matériel*, a
transformation suggested by the ideas which were then prevalent in
the English Navy. The new era was characterised by an increase in
displacement, by a very reduced draught of water, and by the abandonment of wood in the construction of the hull. It may be useful
to recapitulate briefly the history of the design adopted for the
' Redoutable.'

Towards the end of 1871 a collection of designs for ships of the new fleet was completed. With respect to armourclads of the first rate it was proposed to abandon the use of timber in constructing the hull, and to protect the decks with armour, at least in the vital parts, which were not defended by the central battery. Armour-protection was also to be provided for engines, boilers, and magazines. In order to increase the bow and stern fire angle-ports imitated from the English Navy were adopted. The question of protecting the guns in these batteries was raised and warmly discussed on several occasions, and definitely settled in the affirmative in 1873.

Deck armour, till then considered as of altogether secondary importance, had become clearly indispensable, now that ordnance was being mounted in such elevated positions on board ship as to increase the dangers to be expected from plunging fire. Amongst the plans proposed that of M. de Bussy, which in many respects departed considerably from the conditions laid down, presented two striking advantages:—a decrease of about 4 ft. 10 in. in the draught of water, and an increase in the thickness of the armour to fifteen inches at the water-line and $9\frac{1}{2}$ inches on the battery. The reduction of the draught of water was secured partly by an increase of beam, as compared with previous designs, and partly by the substitution of steel for iron for the frames, interior fastenings, etc. Iron was still retained for the outside plates of the hull. The diminution of the weight of the hull made it practicable to increase the thickness of the armour as well as to reduce the draught of water. It proved necessary, however, to depart from the limits originally assigned, and to increase the length to 312 feet and the displacement to 8,800 tons.

The principal dimensions of the 'Redoutable,[1] as finally approved by the minister, are as follows: The weight of the hull, including the backing of the armour, is 3,845 tons; that of the armour, 2,360 tons.

Length at the water-line	.	.	.	312 feet
Breadth	.	.	.	$64\frac{1}{2}$ feet
Mean draught of water	.	.	.	23 ft. 9 in.
Displacement, tons	.	.	.	8,796
Immersed area of midship section	.	.	1,351·5 sq. ft.
Proportion of length to breadth	.	.	4·83
Spread of canvas	.	.	.	2,658 sq. yds.

Policy of construc-tion in France.

Dimen-sions.

---

[1] The plan of the 'Redoutable' so closely resembles that of the French 'Dévastation' that the reader may be referred to figs. 200, 201, 202 (pp. 304, 305). The difference mainly consists in the thickness of the armour, and in the continuation of the 'Redoutable's' belt right round the stern.

The hull is almost entirely built of steel, except the external plating, which is of iron. The plan of construction employed is the bracket system amidships. The bottom is double, except under the bow and stern compartments. A longitudinal vertical watertight bulkhead is carried up from the double bottom to the orlop deck.

Armour.   The thickness of the armour-plating is fourteen inches at the water-line; that of the armoured deck is $2\frac{1}{3}$ inches. The armour is arranged in a water-line belt running right round the ship, and brought well down over the point of the snout or ram. The iron ram attached to the bow weighs thirty tons, and the weight of each iron plate is 24 tons. In the central part of the ship is an octagonal battery carried up from the main to the upper deck. The sides, before and abaft this battery, tumble home considerably. This permits of a fore and aft fire from the protected guns inside the battery. The latter bears some resemblance to the upper battery of the 'Audacious' class in the British Navy, but the faculty of firing parallel to the line of keel is secured in the French ship by the tumble-home of the ship's sides, and not by the projection of the battery beyond them, as in the English vessel. On the deck above one heavy gun is mounted on each side, protected apparently by a thin screen of iron, over which it fires *en barbette*. In the model of this vessel, exhibited at Paris last year, a barbette tower was shown on the upper deck, abaft the mizenmast. The bulwarks all round the stern were fitted to let down, so as to give a clear all-round fire to the gun mounted in the tower turret. This gun does not appear in any official list of her armament; and it may have been added, or removed, since the first approval of her design. The guns in the battery are four in number; their calibre is given in one list as $12\frac{3}{4}$-inch (32 c/m.), and in a later one as $10\frac{1}{2}$-inch. Those mounted *en barbette* on the battery are apparently of the latter calibre. There are also eight $5\frac{1}{2}$-inch (14 c/m.) guns distributed about the quarter-deck and forecastle. A certain amount of protection to the upper-deck heavy guns is given by the arrangement of the covering bridge.

Armament.   M. Dislère, in *La Guerre d'Escadre*, supplied the following detailed description of the proposed armament of the 'Redoutable.' The particulars are given here to show the changes which have taken place in the views of the French authorities on the question of armament. Four 32 c/m. ($12\frac{1}{2}$-inch) guns are mounted in a central battery, protected with $9\frac{1}{2}$-inch armour. These guns command a range of fire right ahead or astern, the upper works, both before and abaft the battery, being recessed very considerably inwards. From the two guns firing on the broadside a converging fire can be obtained.

The guns at the stern command a line of fire within 15° of the keel. Two 27 c/m. (10½-inch) guns, mounted in half-turrets on the upper deck, one under the topgallant forecastle, and one on a turntable right aft, have only a musket-proof protection for the mechanical training gear and for the gun's crews. Eight light 14 c/m. (5½-inch) guns are mounted on the broadside on the upper deck. The fire from the heavy guns is therefore distributed as follows :—

				Weight of projectiles
Right ahead	.	.	. 4 guns	3,042 lbs.
On the broadside .	.	. 3 guns	1,997 lbs.
Astern	.	.	. 2 guns	952 lbs.

It will be seen that the armament has been specially arranged for the purpose of bringing the greatest weight of metal to bear on an enemy when engaging in the ' end on ' position.

Captain Von Kronenfels describes the present armament of the ' Redoutable ' as follows : ' Four 27 c/m. (10½-inch) guns are mounted in the central battery ; two guns of the same calibre are mounted *en barbette* in half-turrets ; two more of the same are carried on the upper deck, one in the bows, the other in the stern, on a revolving platform. The armament is completed with six 14 c/m. (5½-inch) guns distributed along the upper deck. The battery guns are carried at a height of 13 ft. 4 in. ; the upper deck guns 20 ft. 6 in. above the water.'

The engines were constructed at the celebrated Creuzot Works. They are on the compound system, and have six horizontal cylinders. The boilers have forty furnaces, with a grate surface of 787½ square feet. The horse-power to be developed is 6,000, which, at the draught of water given above, should give a speed of 14·5 knots. The ship has a single screw and carries 620 tons of coal. *Engines.*

Admiral Pothuau, the Minister of Marine, informed the Chamber that the speed of the ' Redoutable,' with half-boiler power, was thirteen knots, which justified the expectation that she would prove the fastest ironclad afloat. The actual speed was 14·16 knots. Her coal supply is calculated for a distance of 2,800 miles at ten knots.

The ' Redoutable ' has three square-rigged masts.

In 1872 a programme of shipbuilding for the French navy, drawn up by the Minister of Marine, Vice-Admiral Pothuau, was approved by the National Assembly. The Board of Construction prepared designs for the different classes, in accordance with the instructions which they received, increasing the speed and coal endurance, the power of the engines, the dimensions of the ships, and the thickness of the armour. The steady development of the *French programme of 1872.*

power of naval guns, and the consequent increase in the thickness of armour required to resist modern projectiles, have led to frequent modifications in the original plans, all tending to an augmentation of dimensions and of cost. The distinctive characteristic of the new types was to be a considerable addition to the defensive capabilities, whilst retaining the full rig. The necessary consequence was that the displacement was increased from 8,800 tons in the 'Redoutable,' to 9,600 tons in the 'Dévastation' and 'Foudroyant.' The beam and depth in hold only were to be augmented, and not the length. The *maximum* thickness of the armour-belt remained fixed at $13\frac{3}{4}$ inches, but its *mean* thickness was to be much greater than in the 'Redoutable.' The deck was plated from end to end with 2-inch armour. The 27 c/m. ($10\frac{1}{2}$-inch) guns of the battery were replaced by 32 c/m. ($12\frac{1}{2}$-inch), the 27 c/m.

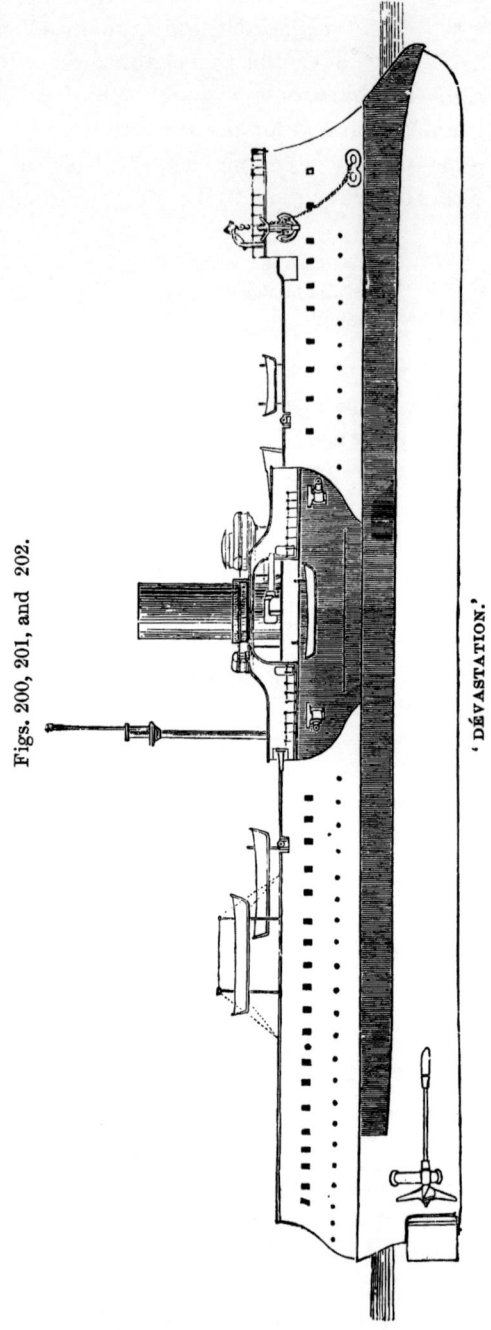

Figs. 200, 201, and 202.

'DÉVASTATION.'

guns on the upper deck being retained. The speed was to be fourteen knots; and the spread of canvas was to be from eighteen to twenty times that of the midship section.

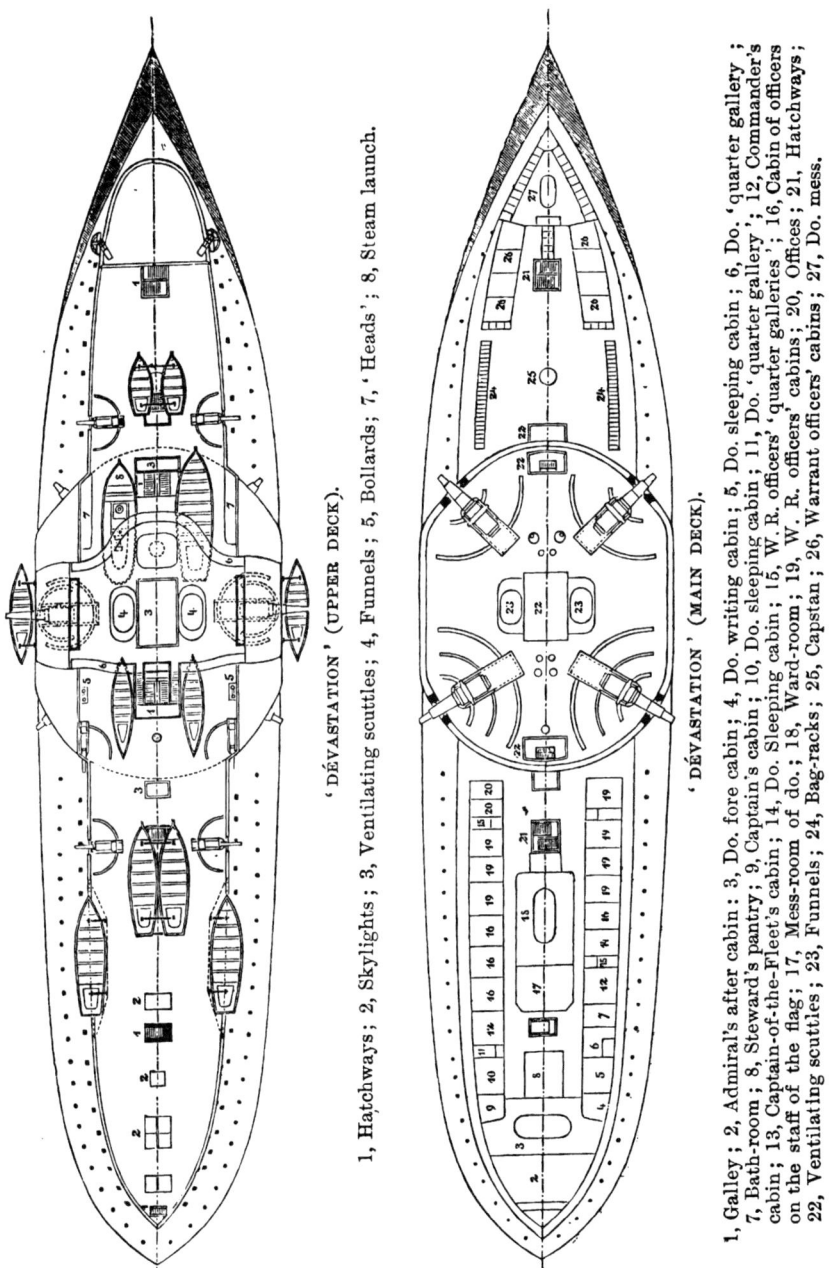

'DÉVASTATION' (UPPER DECK).

1, Hatchways; 2, Skylights; 3, Ventilating scuttles; 4, Funnels; 5, Bollards; 7, 'Heads'; 8, Steam launch.

'DÉVASTATION' (MAIN DECK).

1, Galley; 2, Admiral's after cabin; 3, Do. fore cabin; 4, Do. writing cabin; 5, Do. sleeping cabin; 6, Do. 'quarter gallery; 7, Bath-room; 8, Steward's pantry; 9, Captain's cabin; 10, Do. sleeping cabin; 11, Do. 'quarter gallery'; 12, Commander's cabin; 13, Captain-of-the-Fleet's cabin; 14, Do. Sleeping cabin; 15, W. R. officers' quarter galleries'; 16, Cabin of officers on the staff of the flag; 17, Mess-room of do.; 18, Ward-room; 19, W. R. officers' cabins; 20, Offices; 21, Hatchways; 22, Ventilating scuttles; 23, Funnels; 24, Bag-racks; 25, Capstan; 26, Warrant officers' cabins; 27, Do. mess.

Following up this programme, though departing from it by increasing the thickness of the armour and deck-plating, a proposal was made by M. de Bussy, presented in March 1875, and finally

The 'Dévastation' and 'Foudroyant.'

approved in January 1876, after long consideration and numerous modifications in many particulars, including the substitution of two screws for one. In accordance with these plans, the new ships of the enlarged 'Redoutable' class, the 'Dévastation' and 'Foudroyant,' were laid down at Lorient.

By simplifying and also reducing to the utmost the details of construction, the author of the design has succeeded in obtaining a considerable reduction in the weight of the hull. In comparison with the 'Redoutable,' there is a decrease of 110 tons, notwithstanding the addition of 2 ft. 7 in. to the beam, and of one foot to the depth in hold. The hull is of steel; the side-plating is of iron. The total weight of the hull, including the backing of the armour, is 4,054 tons, or less than 42 per cent. of the displacement. The weight of the armour is estimated at 2,836 tons.

If the experiment succeeds, that is to say, if at the conclusion of a fairly long cruise and of several dockings it is found that the rigidity and general solidity of the two new armourclads leave nothing to be desired, an important question will have been settled, and naval construction will have made a great step in advance.

The principal dimensions of the 'Dévastation' and those of the 'Foudroyant,' on the same plan, are :—

Length at the water-lines	312 feet
Breadth	67 feet
Draught of water	24 feet
Displacement, tons	9,606
Immersed surface of midship section	1,470·6 sq. ft.
Spread of canvas	2,642 sq. yds.

The 'Dévastation' class, though originally intended to surpass other French armour-clads only in defensive power, has been equally strengthened in offensive capabilities by the increase in the displacement over that of the preceding, or 'Redoutable' class. It was in fact impossible to avoid the necessity of arming the class with guns heavier than those of 27 c/m., or $10\frac{1}{2}$ inches. This necessity, which was not quite so apparent in 1872, when the first programme of construction was drawn up, made itself felt soon afterwards; and already, though the ships of the new class have not as yet, in the beginning of the year 1881, been fully tried in long cruises, guns of 32 c/m., or $12\frac{1}{2}$ inches, can no longer be considered sufficient.

The 'Dévastation' is one of the most heavily armoured full-rigged ironclads; the side consists of an inner skin $1\frac{1}{2}$ inch thick, outside which is laid teak backing of $12\frac{1}{2}$ inches, consisting of logs running in a fore-and-aft direction, and upon this rest the 15-inch armour-plates.

DEVASTATION.

The armour-belt has a maximum thickness of fifteen inches amidships, and tapers off to $11\frac{3}{4}$ inches at the ends. The belt is carried to within 28 feet of the after perpendicular, and is there replaced by a thwartship armoured bulkhead of $11\frac{3}{4}$-inch plates, and a deck with 2-inch plates below the water-line. The battery has $9\frac{1}{2}$ inches of armour; the deck is lined with $\frac{3}{4}$-inch and protected with $2\frac{1}{4}$-inch plating from end to end. The hull, as regards system and details of construction, is exactly like that of the 'Redoutable.' Except at the stern the lines are the same. The only difference consists in the addition of a fore-and-aft watertight bulkhead carried up to the orlop deck, fixed on a keelson extending from the fore part of the stoke-hold to the aftermost thwartship watertight bulkhead. The floor is unusually flat, with a shallow central keel, and two side keels, extending from abreast the mizenmast to the foremast.

The armament of the 'Dévastation' consists of four 32 c/m., or $12\frac{3}{4}$-in., guns. Before and abaft the battery, the sides of the ship tumble home, so as to admit of a direct fire ahead and astern within an angle of 15° with the line of keel. In addition, two 27 c/m., or $10\frac{1}{2}$-in., guns are mounted in half-turrets on the upper deck, and command a line of fire parallel to the line of the keel ahead and astern. The training-gear and the guns' crews are protected by light armour from small arms, machine guns, and Shrapnel. The armament is completed with six 14 c/m. ($5\frac{1}{2}$-in.) guns, distributed along the upper deck. It will be seen that the offensive power of the 'Dévastation' is greatest when in the end-on position. The axis of the bore of the battery guns is 15 ft. 6 in., that of the guns of the upper tier is 26 ft. 7 in. above the water. The four 34 c/m. guns being mounted in an enclosed battery, it was necessary to give to the latter a considerable breadth; this was accordingly fixed at 63 ft. 10 in. in order to secure a direct fire in line with the keel. The breadth being so great, it followed that the battery had to be constructed in such a manner that the sides above the water-line projected considerably outwards from the broadside of the ship.

The 'Dévastation' is propelled by twin screws. It had been originally intended to give her only one screw. The alteration was made to secure:— *The machinery.*

(1.) A reduction of the draught of water.

(2.) Adequate protection for the steering gear.

The screws are driven by separate engines on the Woolf system, with three cylinders each. The machinery was made at the Government factory at Indret. The indicated horse-power anticipated was

6,000 horses, and the speed 14 knots. By the use of the steam blast the power can be increased to 8,000 horses. A supply of 560 tons of coal can be carried, which is sufficient for a distance of 2,800 miles, at 10 knots per hour. The boilers are elliptical. The rudder is of the double form, common in the newer French armourclads. The towing-torpedo arrangements resemble those described elsewhere. The spread of canvas, which is 20·1 times the area of the midship section, would be sufficient to enable ships of this class to keep the sea, if deprived of their steam-power.

M. Dislère gives a table of comparison, showing the relative power and distribution of the armament of some of the principal broadside armoured ships.

—	Guns firing right ahead	Weight of projectiles	Guns on the broadside	Weight of projectiles
		lbs.		lbs.
Alexandra . .	4	1,997	6	2,588
Téméraire . .	3	1,799	5	2,396
Dévastation (French)	4	3,042	3	1,997

He claims for the 'Dévastation' greater range of fire, and superior facilities for shifting the guns.

Since 1873, more than forty vessels of various classes have been laid down in France, including a certain number of 'first-rate' armour-clads of the 'Redoutable' type, first-rate coast-service vessels of the 'Tonnerre' type, and second-rate coast-service vessels of the 'Tempête' class. The armoured first-rates, 'Dévastation' and 'Redoutable,' have been already described. Further details are given in a report made by a committee of the Chamber on the estimates for 1878.

The 'Amiral Duperré.' The 'Dévastation' and 'Foudroyant' were begun in January, and the 'Amiral Duperré' in December 1876. The 'Amiral Duperré'[1] is, and appears destined to remain, the most advanced specimen of the class of masted armoured first-rates, having a length of nearly 320 feet, and an estimated displacement of about 10,500 tons. The hull and engines were ordered of the *Compagnie des Forges et Chantiers de la Méditerranée*. The design presents several important features, which distinguish it from those of the ships of the preceding group. The vessel is an enlarged 'Dévastation,' constructed with the object of further increasing the offensive and defensive power. All the requirements of naval warfare had, since the date of the previous plans, become more exacting. Heavier armour, more powerful ordnance, a more complete

---

[1] The design of the smaller 'Duguesclin,' already described, resembles in many points that of the 'Amiral Duperré.' The 'Amiral Duperré' is not strictly a central-battery ship, but is described in this chapter for reasons of convenience.

system of internal subdivision into watertight compartments, were demanded. It was necessary to go to a thickness of 21½ inches for armour; and guns of a calibre of 13¼ inches were the least powerful that could be accepted. The echo of the experimental firing at Spezia seemed as it were to drown the report of the 75-ton guns which were only in contemplation for the French service. It is unnecessary to observe that, if the thickness of the armour-belt be increased, it involves a corresponding diminution of the protection given to the guns. Moreover, the central battery is unsuited to the mounting and working of 13¼-inch guns. Hence it was decided that the four heavy guns of the 'Amiral Duperré' should be placed in armoured fixed barbette turrets, connected with the protected deck by shafts and passages also armoured. The light ordnance was to be increased in number and mounted on an ordinary unarmoured main deck. The central armoured battery has been abandoned, owing to the increase in the size of the guns; but those who look to seagoing and manœuvring qualities will find it more difficult to accept a length approaching 320 feet, and a displacement amounting, according to the dimensions in the plans, to about 10,487 tons. The mean draught of water is kept within proper limits, and the beam is the same, within a fraction, as that of the 'Dévastation.'

The hull is of steel except the stem, stern-post, and skin plating, which are of iron, and is built on the 'bracket-frame' system, with certain modifications. There is a double bottom throughout the portion occupied by the engines and boilers. Before and abaft this space the ship is subdivided into longitudinal watertight compartments. A continuous central keelson extends from stem to stern-post. Below the armoured deck are sixteen thwartship watertight bulkheads. A longitudinal watertight bulkhead also is worked on the keelson in the engine and boiler-rooms, so that each of the two pairs of engines is isolated in a special compartment, while the twelve boilers occupy four distinct divisions. Some of the frames are solid, while others are perforated. The sixth longitudinal girder on each side forms a shelf-piece for the armour. The 'lower' deck is divided by seven thwartship bulkheads resting on the armoured deck.

The subjoined account of and comparison of this ship with the Italian 'Dandolo' are taken from the *New York Army and Navy Journal* of April 3, 1880. The communication had been contributed by Chief Engineer King, U.S.N., from his new work entitled *War Ships and Navies of the World.*

'The "Amiral Duperré," when completed, will be the largest and the most heavily armed and armoured ship ever built by the French.

She is of a type quite different from those which have prevailed in other navies, and possesses some features of more than ordinary importance. She was designed by M. Sabattier, *Directeur du Matériel*, or Chief Constructor of the Ministry of Marine. The keel was laid down at La Seyne by the *Compagnie des Forges et Chantiers de la Méditer-ranée* in December 1876, and the ship was to be completed in 1880.

'The hull is divided into two parts by a longitudinal bulkhead, and subdivided by other watertight transverse bulkheads, containing in all, including the double bottom, nearly 200 cells, thus giving great strength and rigidity to the entire structure, and affording a solid foundation for the motive machinery.

'The vessel is rather peculiar in shape, being almost flat-bottomed and considerably curved above the water-line, the upper deck having less width than the gun deck by about 7 ft. 9 in. The lines forward are very fine.

'The interesting peculiarities in the design are the system of armour and the manner in which the great guns are mounted. The armour is limited to a belt extending around the vessel at the water-line from the extreme point aft to the end of the ram, an armoured deck placed flush with the upper edge of this water-line belt, and the armoured turrets containing the heavy guns. The armour-belt amidships, for protec-tion of the machinery and magazine, has the extreme thickness of

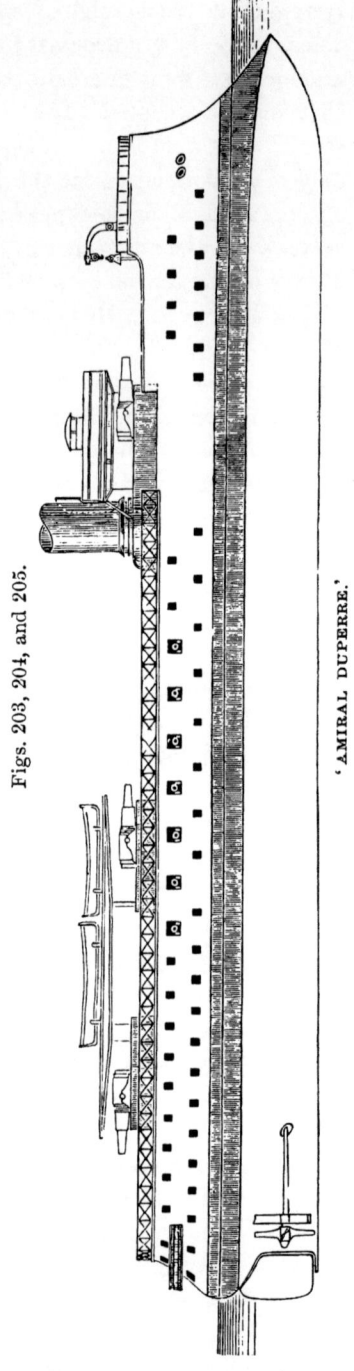

Figs. 203, 204, and 205.

'AMIRAL DUPERRE.'

AMIRAL DUPERRÉ.

21·6 inches, and a depth of 8 ft. 1 in., being 2 ft. 6 in. above the
load water-line, and 5 ft. 7 in. below it.   In other respects the ship

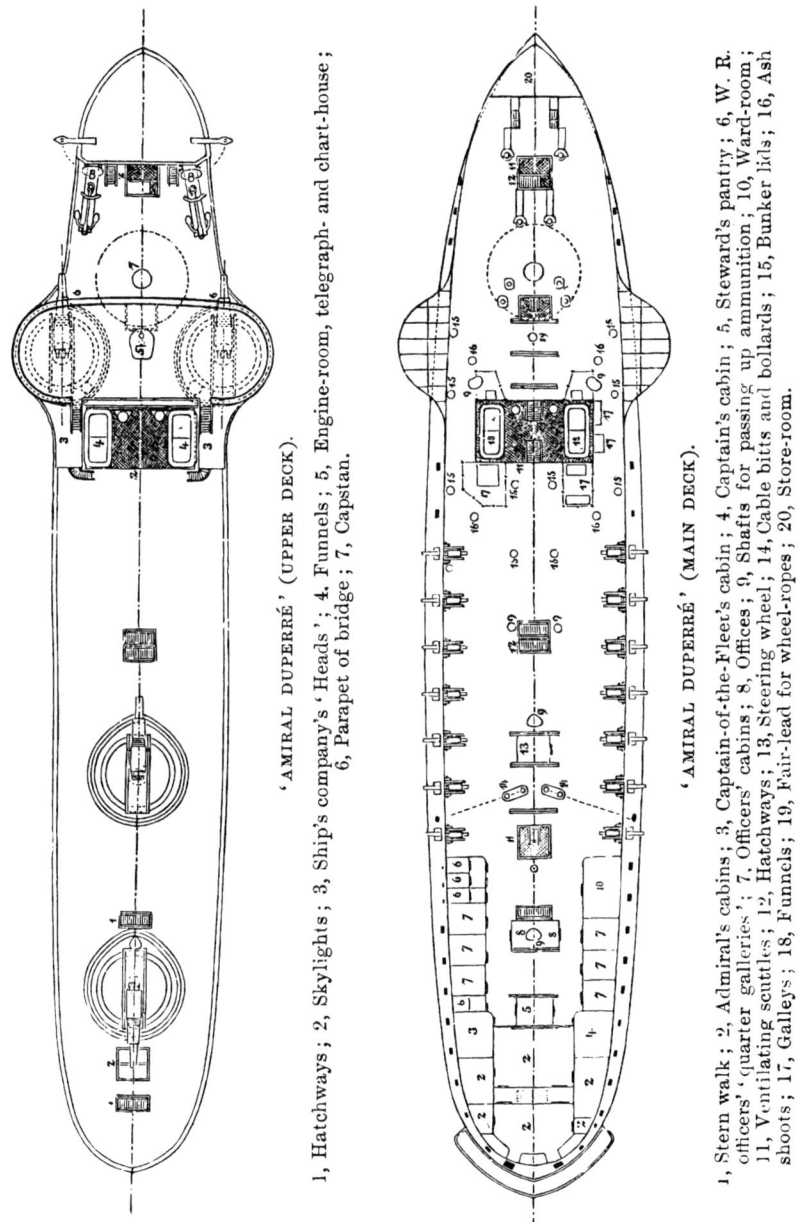

'AMIRAL DUPERRÉ' (UPPER DECK).

1, Hatchways ; 2, Skylights ; 3, Ship's company's 'Heads' ; 4, Funnels ; 5, Engine-room, telegraph- and chart-house ;
6, Parapet of bridge ; 7, Capstan.

'AMIRAL DUPERRÉ' (MAIN DECK).

1, Stern walk ; 2, Admiral's cabins ; 3, Captain-of-the-Fleet's cabin ; 4, Captain's cabin ; 5, Steward's pantry ; 6, W. R.
officers' 'quarter galleries ' ; 7, Officers' cabins ; 8, Offices ; 9, Shafts for passing up ammunition ; 10, Ward-room ;
11, Ventilating scuttles ; 12, Hatchways ; 13, Steering wheel ; 14, Cable bitts and bollards ; 15, Bunker lids ; 16, Ash
shoots ; 17, Galleys ; 18, Funnels ; 19, Fair-lead for wheel-ropes ; 20, Store-room.

is unarmoured, that is, the battery between decks and everything
above the armour-belt, except the towers, is unprotected, and may,

it is supposed, be destroyed by an enemy's projectiles without detriment to stability.

'On the upper deck are four fixed turrets or towers[1] *en barbette,* two of which are placed forward, one on each bow, protruding sponson fashion beyond the ship's side; one stands in the middle of the quarterdeck, and one is abaft the mizenmast. These towers are all armoured with 12-inch plates, and in each is mounted, high above the water-line, a $13\frac{1}{2}$-inch breech-loading rifle, weighing 48 tons. The guns are placed upon turntables, and are worked by steam and hydraulic power. The projection of the bow towers gives the advantage of a line of fire forward parallel with the keel. All four towers have a thin vertical screen of iron running around a portion of their circumference. In the two foremost towers the screen is on the inside, in the tower on the quarterdeck it is on the after side, and in the tower abaft the mizenmast it is on the forward side. The interior of the towers is sheltered from a plunging fire from small arms or machine guns in tops by bridges or hurricane decks, one of which runs forward and aft from the mizenmast so as to cover the two after towers, and the other is forward, extending athwartships over the bow towers.

'The steering gear for ordinary use is on the after bridge, while the conning-tower for the captain's use is forward between the bow turrets. From this tower an all-round view can be gained, and orders transmitted to all parts of the ship. It is protected by an armoured wall enclosing it, and extending athwartships over the bow towers.

'Besides the four heavy guns in the towers, there are fourteen breech-loading 60-pdr. rifles of $5\frac{1}{2}$ inches calibre mounted on the broadside, amidships, between decks. An additional weapon is the ram, which is of wrought iron, and is formed by the stem. It receives the butts of the water-line armour-plates, the lower edges of which are brought down forward nearly ten feet below the water-line to the very point of the ram, which projects about thirteen feet beyond the forward perpendicular, and is formed sharp for ripping.

'The rudder can be worked by steam or by hand as desired.

'The motive machinery was manufactured at the Menpenti Works, and consists of two separate sets of vertical, three-cylinder, compound engines, each set working a screw-propeller. These engines are intended to be worked at 6,075 indicated horse-power, but in emergencies may be driven up to 7,397. There are four independent

---

[1] As hinted in a former foot-note, the designation 'tower' may perhaps be hereafter used for fixed *barbette* turrets.

groups of cylindrical boilers, three in each group. The estimated speed of the ship is 14½ knots per hour.

'The "Amiral Duperré" has no counterpart in the British or any other navy. The advantages claimed for her by the French are these: first, that the great firing angle of depression gained by mounting the guns so high above water—about 27 ft. 5 in.—will enable the gunners to see the enemy more clearly, and, at the same time, give a better opportunity for penetrating their decks, especially in close action; second, that the disposition of the guns is such as to enable them to sweep the horizon with fire in all directions; thus the two forward guns—one on either side—fire from ahead on a line with the keel to 65° abaft the beam, the after guns from dead aft to 36° forward the beam on either side, the midship gun to 52° forward or abaft the beam on either side, while three of the guns can be concentrated on the broadside fire at one point.

'The disadvantages consist, first, in the objectionable open-top towers, which, though high above water where the advantages of an all-round, lateral, and plunging fire are available, expose both the men in them and the guns to the enemy's fire from high and somewhat distant forts, and to the other risks which attend guns mounted permanently above the parapet of a battery. The second objection is the immense weight of the towers, guns, and appendages carried high above the centre of gravity of the ship. This would seriously interfere with the stability in the event of the hull's being pierced below the armour, and hence exposed to the movement of free water within either side passages, while the vessel was pitching and rolling and the guns were being run in and out.

'The "Amiral Duperré" is a masted line-of-battle ship, designed to be sufficiently buoyant to carry coal and stores into any ocean, sufficiently armoured to resist all ordinary projectiles, and armed with guns of sufficient power to meet the enemy under any conditions. There being no ships of her type in other navies with which to draw a comparison, it may be interesting to take for that purpose one of a different type, but having very nearly the same displacement in tons, draught of water, and thickness of armour on the water-line, with power of engines not much greater, and like her designed for ocean work. The vessel which meets these conditions is the Italian mastless, sea-going ship "Dandolo," lately launched at Spezia. The principal dimensions and other data of the two ships are as follows :—

' Amiral
Duperré '
and Dan-
dolo ' com-
pared.

	'Amiral Duperré'	'Dandolo'
Length between perpendiculars . . .	319 ft. 19 in.	340 ft. 11 in.
Breadth, extreme. . . .	66 ft. 11 in.	64 ft. 9 in.
Mean draught of water . . .	25 ft. 9 in.	25 ft. 11 in.
Load displacement . . .	10,322 tons	10,401 tons
Thickness of armour-belt, maximum .	21·6 in.	21·5 in.
System of turrets . . .	{ fixed,open- topped }	revolving
Number ,, . . .	4	2
Total sail areas	24,014 sq. ft.	none
Motive Machinery		
Type of engines	compound	compound
Number of cylinders . . .	6	4
Diameter ,, . . .	61 and 78½ in.	64 and 80 in.
Stroke	39·4 inches	48 inches
Maximum revolutions per minute .	77	80
Indicated horse-power, maximum .	7,396	7,900
Speed of ship per hour, maximum estimate	14·5 knots	15 knots
Total grate surface . . .	729 sq. ft.	811 sq. ft.
,, heating surface . . .	18,756 sq. ft.	22,991 sq. ft.
Armament.		
Number of guns in turrets . .	4	4
,, on broadside . .	14	none
Weight of each gun in turret . .	48 tons	100 tons
,, on broadside .	2·56 tons	none
Total weight of guns . . .	228 tons	400 tons
Weight of broadside metal . .	1·37 tons	3·87 tons
,, bow-fire ,, . .	·82 tons	·29 tons
,, stern ,, . .	·41 tons	1·93 tons
Height of guns above load-water-level, turret .	27 ft. 5 in.	15 ft. 9 in.
,, ,, ,, broadside	14 ft. 3 in.	
Weight of each projectile, turret guns .	915 lbs.	2,000 lbs.
,, ,, broadside guns .	46·3 lbs.	
Weight of each powder-charge, turret guns	165 lbs.	551 lbs.
,, ,, broadside guns	88 lbs.	
Muzzle velocity of projectile, turret guns .	1,475 feet	1,700 feet
,, ,, broadside guns .	1,525 feet	
Total energy of each projectile, turret guns .		40,100 foot-tons
Thickness of iron penetrated at 1,000 yards .	18·9 inches	37 inches

' Both ships are propelled by twin screws. The " Amiral Duperré "
is provided with sail power, which is an advantage in point of
economy, but in some respects is a disadvantage. She is 21 ft. 1 in.
shorter than the " Dandolo " and has more beam, which may give her
some advantage in manœuvring. Her maximum indicated horse-
power, however, measured by grate area being less, with the same
relative displacement and greater beam—the lines being equally good
—the Italian ship must have some advantage in speed. As to
defensive and offensive power, the protection by armour on the

water-line and turrets is equal; but the heavy guns of the French ship are exposed above the parapets to be dismounted by the enemy's fire, and her guns between decks (which are of small calibre, and hence useless, except to riddle the unarmoured ends of the enemy), are unprotected by armour, and, like the ship above the armour-belt, exposed to destruction. Meanwhile, the guns and gunners of the Italian ship, being in revolving enclosed turrets, are not exposed to such risks. The ends of the Italian ship forward and abaft the citadel above the submerged decks, being, like the hull of the French ship above the belt, unprotected by armour, may, it is supposed, be riddled with shot without serious injury to the flotation of the ship. On this point, however, opinions differ, as the discussions upon the stability of the " Inflexible " show.

'The French ship has the advantage of heavy guns mounted high above water, which in close action might be able to penetrate the submerged decks of the Italian ship, while the latter possesses the power of concentrating the extraordinary weight of 3·87 tons of metal at one point, with a total energy of 120,000 foot-tons. Even one 2,000-lb. projectile would be sufficient to destroy the pilot-house or either turret of her antagonist. This is all, however, pure speculation ; for in a contest between two such ships much would depend upon the skill of the artillerymen, and the prompt and rapid execution of evolutions ; while, as extreme precision in firing is impossible without uniformity of range and steadiness of platform, the chances of making fair hits in either case, with the ships in motion and the distance and position changing every minute, would become very uncertain. In the event, however, of a fair hit by a projectile from the 100-ton gun, there can be no question as to the result, it being evident that no armour, whether designed to protect ships or forts, has ever been constructed capable of resisting such a blow.'

The cost of the armoured hull is 450,000l., and of the machinery 120,000l.

The 'Amiral Baudin' and 'Formidable' are at present under construction. The former has been only recently laid down. Both closely resemble in design the 'Amiral Duperré.' Their principal dimensions are :— *'Amiral Baudin' and 'Formidable.'*

Length at the water-line	.	.	.	319 ft. 4 in.
Breadth, extreme	.	.	.	68 ft. 3 in.
Draught of water	.	.	.	26 feet
Displacement, tons	.	.	.	11,141
Area of midship section	.	.	.	1,677 sq. ft.

It is proposed to arm them with three 100-ton [1] guns in turrets and twelve 14 c/m. (5½-in.) guns mounted on the broadside on the upper deck, also eight machine-guns. The armour-belt will be 22 inches in thickness amidships, sixteen inches forward, and fourteen inches abaft. The turrets will be protected with 17-inch, and the deck with 3-inch armour. The twin screws will be driven by two 3-cylinder compound engines. The boilers will be twelve in number, with 36 furnaces. In addition to these two ships, two similar armourclads are to be completed in 1885.

The 'Hoche,' 'Marceau,' 'Magenta,' 'Neptune.'

The *Revue Maritime* of November 1880, states that four new armourclads are about to be put in hand. In the list of ships published in the *Carnet de l'Officier de Marine* for 1881, the names of these vessels are included; they are the 'Hoche,' 'Magenta,' replacing the old wooden hulled ironclad of the name, 'Marceau,' and 'Neptune.' Apparently they are of the 'Amiral Duperré' type, though of less displacement. The designer is M. Huin, Naval Constructor. They are to have the following dimensions:—

Length . . . . . 328 feet
Beam . . . . . 64 ft. 5 in.
Displacement . . . 9,865 tons.

The *Carnet* reports that the hulls are to be of steel; the *Revue*, following the *Moniteur de la Flotte*, states they are to be of iron. The armour of the battery or turrets is to be 15¾ inches thick; that of the water-line is to be 17¾ inches thick amidships, 15¾ inches forward, and 13¾ inches abaft. It is probable, judging from recent experiments, that the turrets of the new vessels will be plated with the steel-faced or compound armour with which those of the 'Inflexible' are protected. The details of the machinery of the 'Hoche' and her sister ships are not yet settled. They are to carry three of the new steel 34 c/m., or 13¼-inch 47-ton breech-loading guns, mounted apparently in barbette turrets, and a broadside armament of eighteen 14 c/m., or 60-pounder, breech-loaders, on the main deck presumably, unprotected by armour.

The 'Custozza' and 'Tegetthoff.'

We now proceed to describe the 'Custozza' and 'Tegetthoff,' two ships which have been highly commended both by M. Dislère and Sir E. J. Reed.

We shall first give a translation from M. Dislère's notice in *La Guerre d'Escadre*, and shall complete our statement by reprinting Sir E. Reed's paper read before the Institute of Naval Architects. 'All the new ironclads of the Austrian fleet belong to the type of ships

[1] *Carnet*, &c., p. 134. 75-ton guns are more likely.

with central batteries, having ports in the angles of the batteries. The plans of Herr Romako, whose earlier efforts in the case of the "Custozza" and "Erzherzog Albrecht" had been so eminently successful, were reproduced in the "Tegetthoff," with such modifications as were rendered necessary by the increased powers both of offence and defence, which had been insisted upon in the new design. The "Custozza" carries an armament of eight 26-c/m., or 22-ton, Krupp guns, mounted on two armoured batteries. Each gun can be fired from two ports, either on the broadside or in line with the keel.

'Armed with guns equally effective from their calibre, and the facility with which they can be trained, the "Custozza" combines

Figs. 206 and 207.

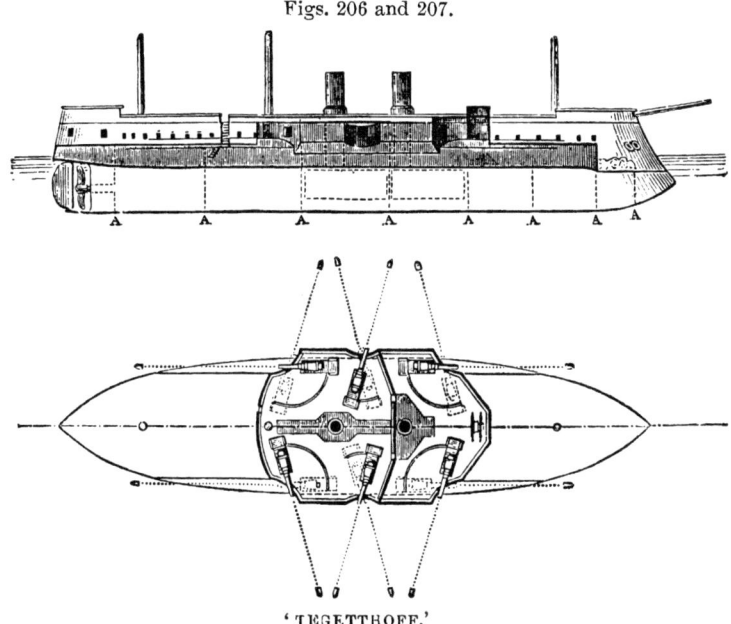

'TEGETTHOFF.'

with this offensive power the advantages of high speed and excellent evolutionary qualities; but in 1874, when the ship was completed, this combination of qualities was no longer accepted as satisfactory. More complete protection was deemed necessary. Armour not less in thickness than that of the "Dreadnought" was asked for. The Austrian Admiralty accordingly decided to adhere to the type which had been found so effective in their earlier ships, but to follow in the line adopted in other navies, and to increase the calibre of their guns and the weight of their armour-plates.

'The problem, therefore, which was submitted to Herr Romako for solution, included the following requirements: to mount on board

ship six guns of very heavy calibre, completely protected; to avoid
the complications of rotation turrets, involving the further risk of
two guns being disabled simultaneously; to protect the water-line
and the battery with the thickest plates which had been applied to
any seagoing ship; to secure a speed of fifteen knots, and a moderate
supply of coal; lastly and above all to keep within a limit of 8,000 tons

Fig. 208.

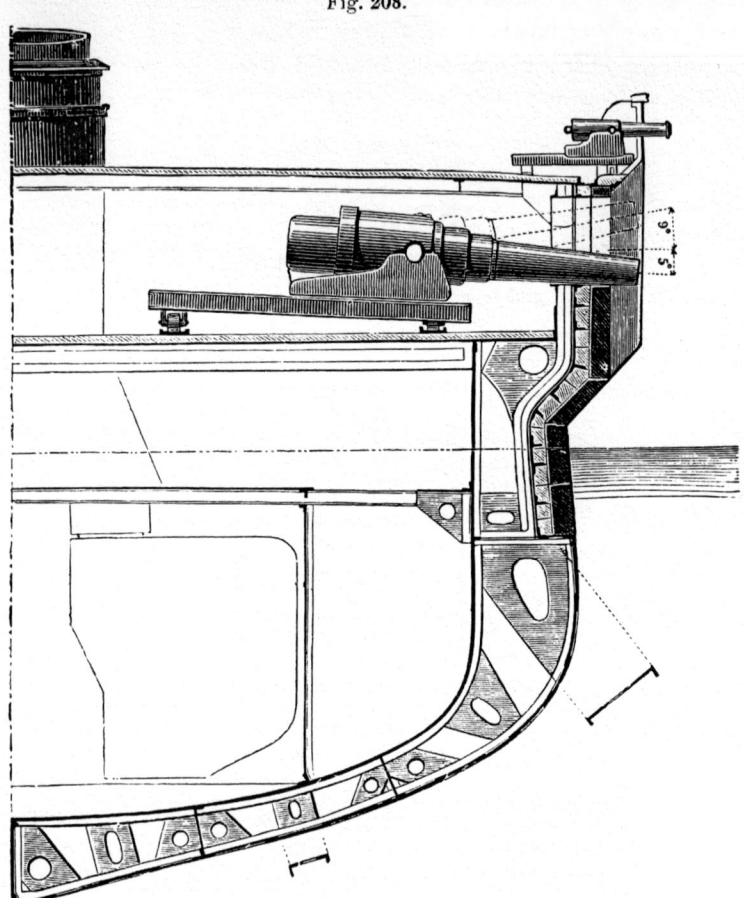

'TEGETTHOFF' (HALF-SECTION THROUGH BATTERY).

displacement, an essential condition having regard to financial considerations.

'The "Tegetthoff" represents Herr Romako's efforts to fulfil the
requirements which had been laid down. The ship is of the same
type as the "Custozza," but it has been necessary to diminish the
area protected by armour. The depth of the belt at the water-line

has been reduced from 11 ft. 9 in. to nine feet. At a distance of 32 ft. 10 in. from the stem, the armoured belt terminates in a transverse bulkhead, the forward compartment being filled with cork. Lastly the battery has only one deck, the height of the guns above the water being somewhat less than that of the guns mounted on the lower deck of the " Custozza." On the other hand, the thickness of the armour has been increased from $8\frac{1}{3}$ inches to 14 inches. Both the battery and the water-line are protected with the same thickness of armour. The horizontal protection has been provided for, by means of $1\frac{1}{2}$-inch plating on the decks outside the battery. Thus the " Tegetthoff " is effectively protected, and must be classed among the most powerful seagoing fighting ships.

'Stowage is provided for 670 tons of coal, a sufficient supply for a distance of 3,000 miles at ten knots, assuming a consumption of 1 kilogramme, or $2\frac{1}{5}$ lbs., per horse-power per hour. The model of this ship exhibits finer lines than had been adopted for any armourclad constructed at the same period.'

Here we leave M. Dislère, and turn to Sir E. Reed's paper, ' On Certain Austrian Ironclads,' read before the Institution of Naval Architects in 1876.

Sir E. Reed on the Austrian armourclads.

He first gives 'the general dimensions and particulars of the ship, and afterwards makes a few observations upon the more marked features of the design. The following figures give her dimensions, calculated elements, etc. :—Length between the perpendiculars, 286 ft. $11\frac{1}{4}$ in. ; length, total, 303 ft. $1\frac{1}{4}$ in. ; breadth on the water-line, 62 ft. 9 in. ; extreme breadth to the outside of armour, 71 ft. $1\frac{1}{2}$ in.; depth of hold, 34 ft. 9 in.; draught of water aft, 26 ft. $7\frac{1}{2}$ in. ; draught of water, forward, 23 ft. 1 in.; displacement with the half of provisions, 7,390 tons ; area of the midship section, 1,301 square feet; area of the load water-line, 14,308 square feet; height of metacentre above centre of gravity of displacement, 14·623 feet; height of metacentre above water, 4·770 feet; distance of the centre of gravity of displacement before the midship section, 3·356 feet; depth of the centre of gravity of displacement below water, 9·853 feet; coefficient of displacement, 0·582 feet; coefficient of water-line, 0·782 feet; coefficient of midship section, 0·82 feet; displacement of an inch immersion at the load water-line, 34·47 tons; weight of armour and backing, 2,160 tons. The armament consists of six 11-inch Krupp guns. Area of sails, 12,165 square feet. Cost of hull, estimated, 172,790*l.* ; cost of engines and boilers, estimated, 81,715*l.* Nominal horse-power, 1,200. Number of cylinders, 2 ; diameter of cylinder effective, 125 inches; length of stroke, 4 ft. 3 in. ;

Griffith's propeller, diameter 23 ft. 6 in.; pitch, 24 feet; number of blades, 2; revolutions per minute, 70. Number of boilers, 4. Area of fire-grate, 850 square feet; heating surface, 25,500 square feet; superheating surface, 1,800 square feet. Pressure of steam, 30 lbs.; number of furnaces, 36; mean indicated horse-power, 8,000; speed, estimated, 14 knots.

'From these figures it will be seen that, although we are not dealing with a ship of the "Inflexible" (English), or of the "Dandolo" (Italian) type, in which armour of excessive thickness is placed over a central citadel of extremely limited extent, we nevertheless have a very powerful ship indeed, with armour of apparently about 13 inches to 14 inches thick, and with a concentrated battery of six 11-inch Krupp guns, each weighing, I presume, about 27 tons. The ship has a belt of armour extending from the stern to within about 30 feet of the foremost perpendicular, where it terminates in a transverse armoured bulkhead, and a stout iron deck going forward to the stem at about 7 feet below water. It would appear from this that the Austrian authorities consider that a strong iron stem, supported by a stout deck near the point of the ram, is sufficient for ramming purposes; whereas in our navy we have thought it better—beginning, if I remember rightly, with the "Rupert" and "Hotspur"—to keep the bow armour, and to carry it down at the stem to considerably below the ram point. We may take it for granted, I think, that the latter, or English, arrangement would at least have the advantage of protecting the ram bow from much local damage in ramming iron vessels, and this is no doubt very desirable where ships are designed primarily as rams—as were the "Rupert" and "Hotspur"—while, on the other hand, where the ram is a subordinate feature—as in the "Tegetthoff"—it may be unnecessary to burden the bow with so much armour-protection. It is worth while to observe in this connection that the Austrians, who have had practical experience of the effects of ramming in actual warfare, have in this, their largest and most powerful ship, preserved a very great length of under-running or spear projection, as shown in the diagram. The projection is 9 feet from the stem at the load water-line, and 19 feet from the stem head.

'I observe next in this ship the Austrian Admiralty have adopted an improvement in armour to which I have for a long time past attached great importance: I refer to the getting rid for the most part of great curvature. Of course armour-plates, if carried round the ends of a ship, must be bent to the curvature of the water-lines, and when imbedded, so to speak, in the sides of a ship of ordinary form and curvature—as has been usual in seagoing ships—they must also be bent crosswise. Now this double curvature of the plates is not only an expensive process, but it is also injurious to the armour-plates in some degree.   To foreign Governments which do not make their own armour-plates, and especially to the Governments of countries very remote from England, the system will further be attended by extreme difficulty in replacing plates injured in battle. This could hardly be accomplished by the slow and expensive process of sending accurate moulds to England for the guidance of the manufacturers.   By so designing the ships that the armour-plates have only to be curved in one direction, all these disadvantages and difficulties are practically got rid of; and therefore, in recent ships which I have had occasion to design for foreign Powers, I have carried out this principle, and Herr Romako, in a letter to me, says:— " With your encouragement I have undertaken to give the stern a form which enables the bending of the plates to be performed in only one way."   I believe I am right in saying that Mr. Barnaby and his colleagues at the Admiralty, as far as practicable, attend to the same thing, although it is, of course, of very much less importance in our Navy than in navies which depend upon foreign supplies of armour, and which are without machines for bending armour-plates.

' The next feature to be remarked in this ship is that the battery is of the projecting type, which so greatly facilitates the attainment of direct fire ahead and astern from a midship battery without excessive recession of the unarmoured parts of the ship before and abaft the battery.   The Admiralty Constructors and myself introduced this arrangement in many cases of upper-deck batteries in ships designed while I was at the Admiralty (most notably in the case of the " Audacious " class), but I do not think the same thing has been done at the Admiralty in the case of the main-deck battery. I have, however, done it myself in several ships for foreign Governments, since I left the Admiralty ; for example, in the German ships the " Kaiser " and " Deutschland," and the Chilian armourclads " Almirante Cochrane " and " Valparaiso." [1]   I cannot recall to mind any previous cases in which this has been done, or even proposed, for main-deck batteries ; but it probably was at least proposed before, and I have a vague recollection or impression that Captain Symonds or Captain Scott once suggested it.   My present object is, however, simply to say that in adopting the system I consider that the Austrian Admiralty have acted wisely, for it has many very great advantages, and no disadvantages of any moment that I have been able to discover, even in

[1] Now called ' Blanco-Encalada.'

a sea-way. If Mr. Barnaby and his colleagues will excuse me for saying so, I think the "Alexandra" might have been improved by these means ; for in her the fore-and-aft fire has only been secured by an enormous depth of recession of the sides beyond the battery, and a corresponding contraction of the upper deck, and other accommodation. In the "Tegetthoff" the overhang is very low and considerable in amount, the battery projecting between four feet and five feet, the spread commencing at 18 inches above the water and terminating at a height of six feet.

'A still more novel feature—one which, although I have seen it suggested before, has never yet to my knowledge been carried out—is to be noticed. It consists in depressing the sides of the ship into curved indentations in wake of the guns, as there shown. The object mentioned to me by Herr Romako, as that which has been sought in the arrangement, is the protection of the gun-muzzles. In mentioning the general form of the battery, and more particularly this feature, he says:—"The ship 'Tegetthoff' is in many regards a novelty, its casemate allowing an all-round fire, avoiding at the same time, by its particular form, the dangerous projection of the muzzle of the midship guns, in consequence of experiences acquired in the battle of Lissa, but which are very little known even in our own Navy." It will easily be seen that in addition to the advantage assigned, this depression of the port likewise possesses the advantage, if designers chose to avail themselves of it, of affording increased horizontal training for the guns, by bringing the pivot in from the line of the ship's side ; and as the armour comes in with the pivot, this end is attained without that enlargement of the port which would otherwise attend it.

'The "Tegetthoff" is also to be furnished with a transverse bulkhead abaft the foremost gun—an arrangement which will prevent the battery from being raked in chasing. This improvement exists in the "Alexandra," where it was, I believe, introduced for the first time by the present Admiralty Constructors. The foremost bulkhead of the battery is inclined forward at a considerable angle to within about 4 feet of the middle line, where it becomes transverse, as shown. Immediately over this foremost portion of the battery at the middle is a very strong pilot-tower, standing well up above both the gunwale and the forecastle. This shows that the Austrian officers who have been in action with ironclads, do not consider such towers unnecessary.

'The above appear to me to be the principal features of the "Tegetthoff." It may be interesting to add that while the outer skin and angle-irons of the hull are of iron, all the remainder is of Bessemer steel, varying in tensile strength from 30 to 33 tons per square inch of section, and possessing this, as I am informed, in combination with 25 per cent. of ductility. This Bessemer steel is produced very successfully in Styria and Carinthia, from which districts of Austria the chief supplies for the "Tegetthoff" are derived. I may further add that in designing this ship much consideration has been given to securing both strength and subdivision, by means of watertight bulkheads between the coal spaces and the boilers and elsewhere.

'I have not hesitated in describing this ship, as above, to mention its various novel features in relation to similar improvements in our own navy where these have taken place; because the whole design, with its many meritorious novelties and combinations, seems to me to reflect the utmost credit upon Admiral Pöckh, Herr Romako, and other Austrian officers who have been consulted, and who have taken part in the preparation of it. It may also be said in this connection that as the primary duty of a naval designer is to produce the best possible design for his employers, so his success and his merit result from the accomplishment of this great object rather than from scheming improvements merely for the sake of displaying originality. I trust this Institution will concur with me in thinking that our thanks are due to the Austrian Admiralty for enabling me to describe, at least in outline, their newest and most important ironclad ship. Perhaps I ought to say, with reference to the very low estimated cost of the "Tegetthoff," that the sums which I have given do not, I believe, provide for anything more than the bare hull and engines.'

The 'Almirante Brown' is an armoured corvette built by Messrs. Samuda for the Argentine Republic, and launched on October 6, 1880. The principal dimensions are:— The 'Almirante Brown.'

Length between perpendiculars	240 feet
Beam	50 feet
Depth from under side of maindeck to garboard strake .	21 ft. 11 in.
Draught of water	20 feet
Displacement, tons	4,200
Speed, knots	$13\frac{3}{4}$
Coal carried, tons	650

The hull is built entirely of Siemens steel. The armour is 'compound' or steel-faced, and consists of a belt nine inches thick at the water-line and six inches thick below the water, 120 feet in length, and protecting the engines, boilers, and magazines. At the ends of the belt there are 'thwartship bulkheads reaching from four feet below the water-line to the main deck. Above the main deck is an

armour-plated battery with double embrasures at the fore end containing in all six guns.　On the sides of the battery the armour is eight
inches and six inches thick, at the ends of the battery seven inches and
six inches. The backing is of teak of an average thickness of ten inches.
The armour-plates are secured to the ship's side with bolts and nuts
screwed from the inside, and so arranged as not to wound the steel
face of the armour.　Horizontal steel-armour $1\frac{1}{2}$-inch in thickness is
worked from the battery to the ends of the vessel, forming a shell-
proof and watertight deck four feet below the water-line protecting

Figs. 209 and 210

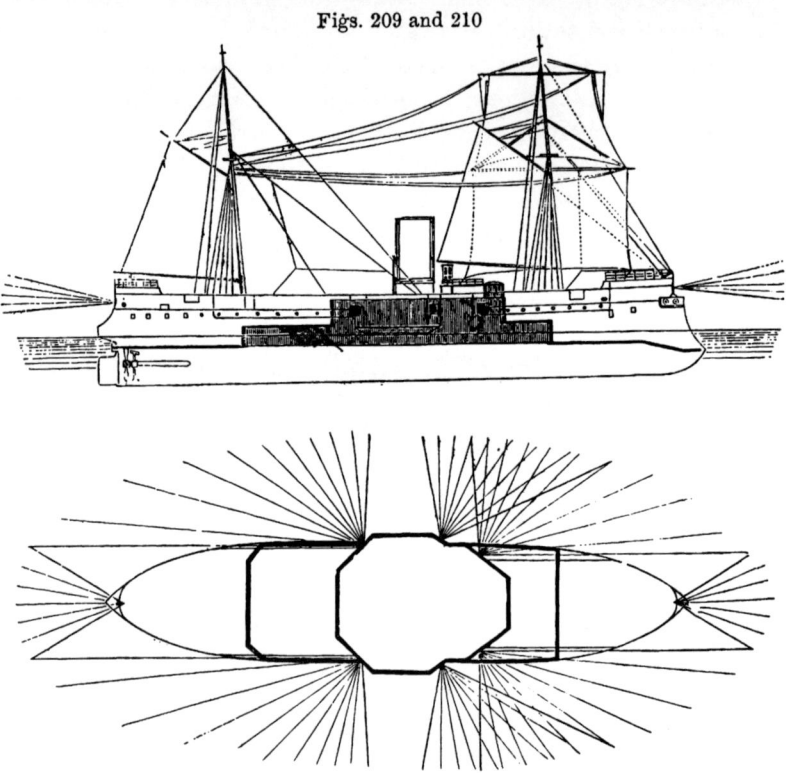

'ALMIRANTE BROWN.'

the steering-gear.　The ship's bottom is cased with 3-inch teak
planking sheathed with zinc.

　　There is a double bottom, and the hull is further subdivided into
numerous watertight compartments by 'thwartship bulkheads and
steel decks.　The ship has two masts, and can spread canvas with an
area of 10,000 square feet.

　　The two screws are driven by two sets of inverted compound
engines of the collective indicated power of 4,500 horses.　Each set

is fitted in a separate engine-room. There are eight cylindrical boilers in four distinct watertight compartments.

The engines, manufactured by Messrs. Maudslay, Sons, and Field, are of the compound type, the high-pressure cylinder being 52 inches, and the low-pressure 90 inches in diameter, with a stroke of 3 ft. 3 in., and making 80 revolutions per minute. Working with one engine only the anticipated speed is put at twelve knots.

The armament consists of six of the new 8-inch breech-loading Armstrong guns of $11\frac{1}{2}$ tons, mounted in the battery and so arranged as to give an all-round fire, and of one similar gun on the upper deck forward and one aft. There are also six $4\frac{1}{2}$-inch guns on the broadside in the upper deck. The coal-supply is sufficient for 18 days' steaming at a speed of ten knots an hour, or about 4,300 miles.

CHAPTER XIV.

MASTED TURRET-SHIPS.

Captain Cowper-Coles' system. THE application of the turret principle to seagoing ships is due to the persistent advocacy of Captain Coles. A design, which he had prepared, was referred by the Admiralty to a committee of naval officers; but they were not sufficiently satisfied to recommend the construction of the ship, as proposed. They thought, however, that the advantages of the system were such as to merit a practical trial, and they advised the Admiralty to prepare plans for a seagoing turret-ship, on their own responsibility. The 'Monarch' was the result of the matured deliberations of the Constructor's Department.

Fig. 211.

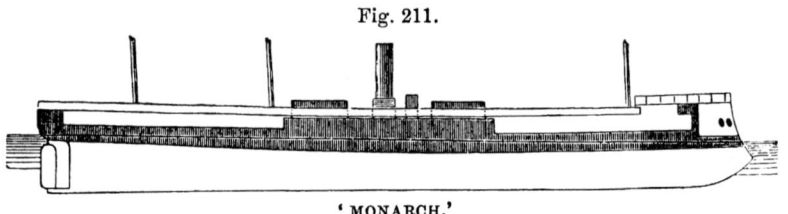

'MONARCH.'

The 'Monarch.' The principal dimensions of the 'Monarch' are:—

Length [1]	330 feet
Breadth	57 ft. 6 in.
Draught of water, forward . .	22 ft. 4 in.
,, aft . . .	26 feet
Displacement, tons . . .	8,322
Horse-power, nominal . . .	1,100
,, indicated . .	7,842
Coal supply, tons . . .	600
The crew's number . . .	575

The 'Monarch' is protected with 8-inch armour, and has a freeboard of 14 feet. The armament consisted of four 25-ton guns, in two turrets, plated with 10-inch and 8-inch armour.

[1] The length is 5·7 times the beam.

The design for the 'Monarch' was sharply criticised by Captain The
Captain. Coles. He insisted on a low freeboard, to decrease weight and present a small surface to the enemy's fire, without sacrificing the rig, and he objected to the limitation of all-round fire by the forecastle. After a protracted negotiation he obtained from the Admiralty permission to design the 'Captain' (1867) in accordance with his own views, in consultation with Messrs. Laird, and without the intervention of the Government naval architects.

In the 'Monarch,' as in the 'Captain,' the direct line of fire from the turrets, both ahead and astern, was obstructed by both the forecastle and the poop.

The height of freeboard of the 'Monarch' is fourteen feet; and the two guns at the bow and stern are protected. The height of freeboard of the 'Captain' was 6 ft. 5 in.; there was one gun in the bows and one astern not protected. The height of the armament above the water was eight feet. The thickness of the armour at the

Fig. 212.

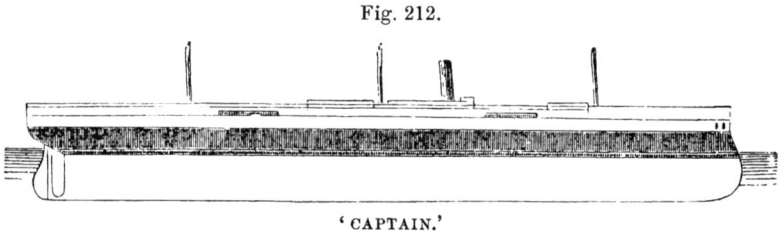

'CAPTAIN.'

water-line was 7 in. by $1\frac{1}{2}$ in.; between the turrets, 8 in. by $1\frac{1}{2}$ in.; and on the turrets, 13 in. by $1\frac{1}{4}$ in. The bridge over the turrets joining the forecastle with the quarterdeck was 24 feet wide. The draught of water was 25 feet forward and 26 feet aft; and the displacement was 7,900 tons. The engines were of 900 nominal, and 6,000 indicated horse-power; and the speed was 14·25 knots an hour. The 'Captain' was fitted with double screws; and described a circle 765 yards in diameter in 5 min. 24 sec.

'The "Captain,"' says Mr. Elgar, 'proved upon trial to be slower under steam, under steam and sail combined, and under sail than the "Monarch;" and owing to some error of calculation having been made in her construction that reduced her intended freeboard of eight feet by two feet, and the failure of her designers to give her a safe amount of stability at angles beyond which the edge of her deck became immersed, she unfortunately capsized at sea under circumstances which are only too well known.'

The performances of the 'Monarch' at sea were in the highest degree satisfactory. The following remarks are from the report, made in 1869, by the Controller of the Navy, Sir Spencer Robinson:

'The "Monarch," a ship of an entirely new class, the only true seagoing turret-ship produced as yet by any navy, is classed by the captain of the fleet, and by other information, as equal in steadiness of platform to the "Hercules," and is spoken of as having behaved in an equally satisfactory manner as the other ships; and also that she could have fought her guns during the gale to which they were exposed. Captain Commerell, in private letters, speaks of the ease, comfort, and dryness of the ship as extraordinary.

'The speed of the "Monarch," both at the measured mile and during the six hours' run at full speed, exceeded that obtained by any ironclad yet built, reaching 14·937 knots at the former, and 14·715 knots per hour at the latter trial. The consumption of coal was less economical than that of the "Hercules" or "Bellerophon," but about the same as that of the "Minotaur" class. Some defects in the pistons, now remedied, appear to have considerably influenced this result. The steering of the "Monarch" under sail, and her general performances under canvas, were not satisfactory, and in consequence the balanced rudder has been somewhat reduced at the fore part. It is believed that this alteration will remedy certain difficulties arising from the first use of this new means of steering, and that the "Monarch" will be found to sail as well as any heavy ironclad ship which is compelled to drag her screw. The handiness of the ship under steam, and in turning the circles at full speed, were on a par with the performances of the "Bellerophon."

'The turret armament of the "Monarch," consisting of four 12-inch rifled guns, when considered with reference to the angle of training and its armour-piercing power at long ranges, places the "Monarch" as one among, if not positively, the most formidable of ironclad seagoing ships in existence; though, until further trial, neither the guns nor their carriages can be deemed satisfactory.'

The launching of the 'Monarch' is an important event in the history of armoured ship-building. She was the first oceangoing turret-ship, and in this experimental vessel it was demonstrated that it was practicable to design a thoroughly seaworthy turret-ship, although for seagoing purposes a central battery presents great advantages over the turret system.

The 'Captain' and 'Monarch' mark the period of 600-pdr., or 25-ton, guns. To resist them, plates of seven inches were manufactured. But plates of at least nine inches were required; and even these could be penetrated by the 600-pdr. at a distance of

PREUSSEN.

2,400 yards. The gun had already gained an indisputable advantage over the armour.

The German vessels, 'Grosser Kurfurst,' 'Friedrich der Grosse,' and 'Preussen,' ex-'Borussia,' and the 'Independencia,' now the 'Neptune,' are the most remarkable vessels which have been built after the plan of the 'Monarch.' German turret-ships.

When the German Admiralty decided, in 1871, to construct turret-ships, they were content to follow the type of the 'Monarch,' with some reduction of dimensions. Of the three sister turret-ships—the 'Preussen,' the 'Friedrich der Grosse,' and the 'Grosser Kurfurst'—the first was built at the private dockyard of the Vulcan Company

Figs. 213 and 214.

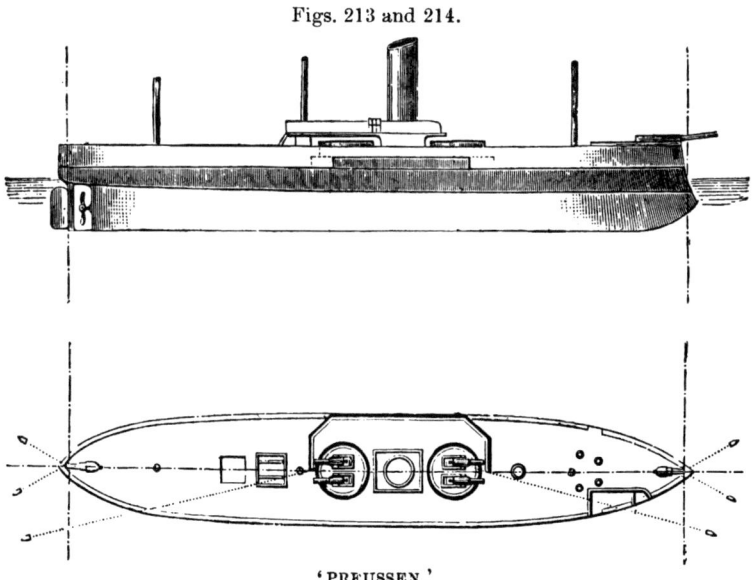

'PREUSSEN.'

at Stettin, and was launched in 1873. The second was built at Ellerbeck, near Kiel, from the designs of Herr Geheimrath Koch, the Chief Constructor of the German Navy. She was launched in 1874, and was completed at the Kiel dockyard. The third was constructed at the Wilhelmshafen dockyard, and was launched in 1875. A writer in the *Broad Arrow* remarks of these ships :—' In general appearance they are similar to the English " Monarch," but they are somewhat smaller, being of only 6,663 tons displacement, while the " Monarch " has 8,332 tons displacement. The armament carried by the German ships is, however, considered by German artillerists to be as powerful as that of the English ironclad, consisting of four

26-c/m. or 22-ton guns, which throw a projectile weighing 410 lbs.

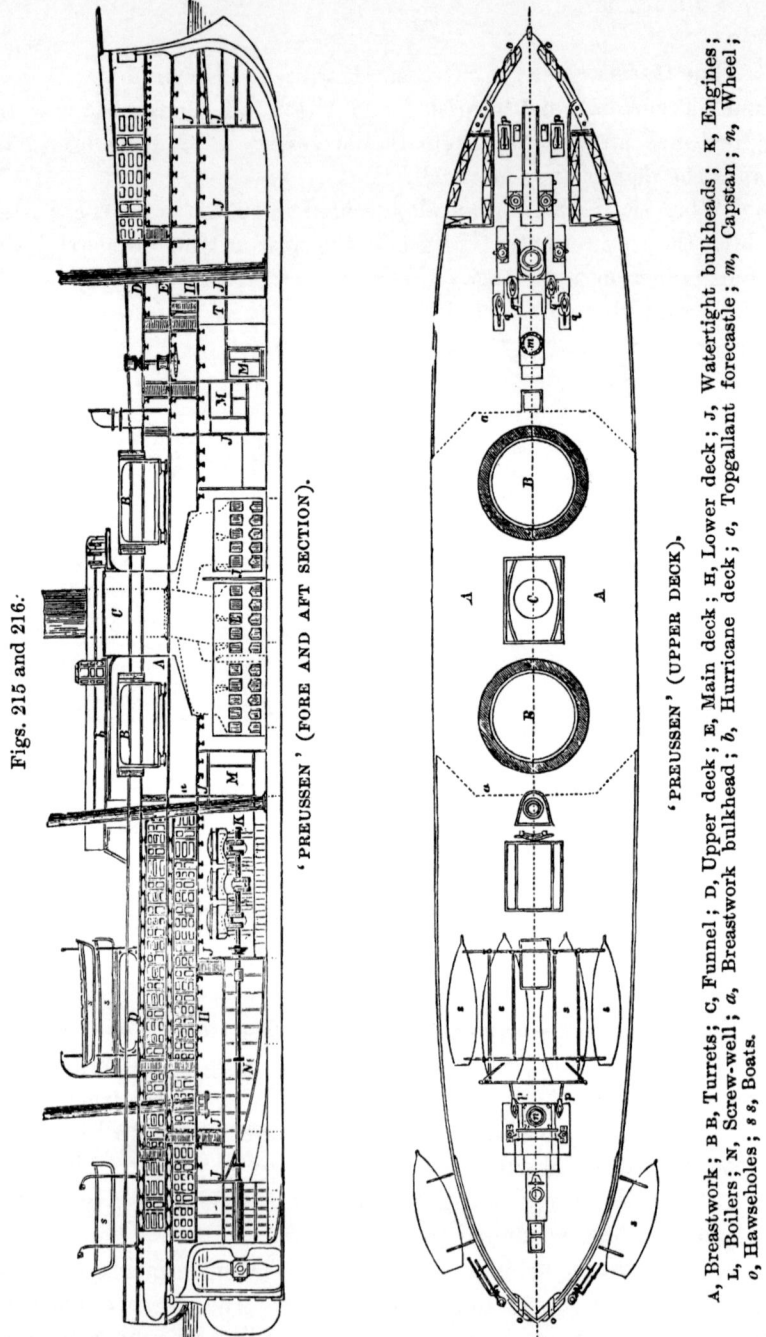

Figs. 215 and 216.

'PREUSSEN' (FORE AND AFT SECTION).

'PREUSSEN' (UPPER DECK).

A, Breastwork; B B, Turrets; C, Funnel; D, Upper deck; E, Main deck; H, Lower deck; J, Watertight bulkheads; K, Engines; L, Boilers; N, Screw-well; a, Breastwork bulkhead; b, Hurricane deck; c, Topgallant forecastle; m, Capstan; n, Wheel; o, Hawseholes; s s, Boats.

with sufficient velocity to enable it to penetrate thirteen inches of iron, while the four 25-ton guns of the "Monarch," though they are somewhat heavier, and throw a somewhat heavier projectile than the Krupp pieces of the German turret-ships, can only penetrate 12½ inches of armour.'

The following description of the 'Preussen' is reprinted in Mr. King's work from the *Zeitschrift des Vereines Deutscher Ingenieure* :—

The 'Preussen.'

'The "Preussen," launched in 1873, is an armoured seagoing turret-ship, similar to the British ship "Monarch." The length

Fig. 217.

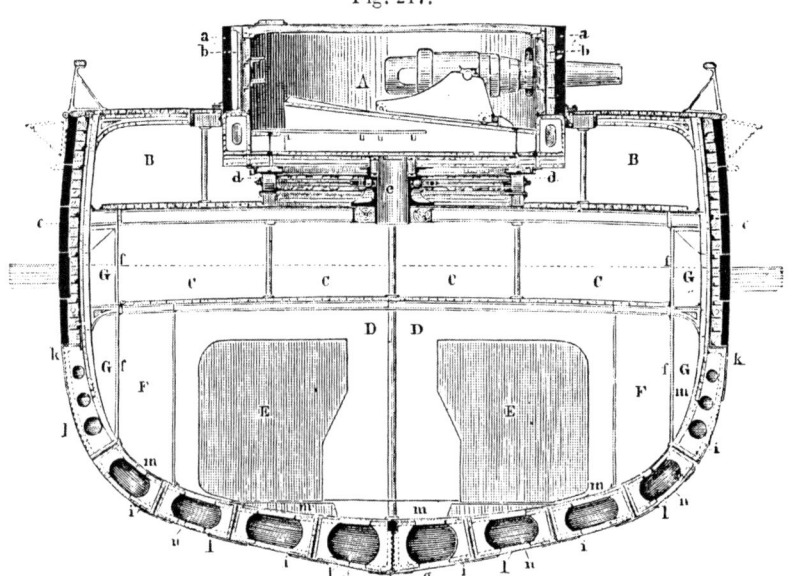

'PREUSSEN' (SECTION THROUGH TURRET).

A, Turret; B, Main deck; C, Lower deck; D, Engine-room and stokehole; E, Boilers; F, Bunkers; G, Wing-passages; a, Turret armour; b, Backing; c, Side armour and backing; d, Turning arrangement of turret; e, Pivot of do.; f, Fore and aft watertight bulkheads; g, Vertical keel-plates; h, Horizontal do.; i, longitudinals; k, Armour-shelf; l, Outside skin; m, Inner skin; n, Double bottom.

between perpendiculars is 308 ft. 6 in. ; extreme length, 318 feet; extreme breadth, 53 ft. 6 in. ; depth from the upper deck to the keel, 34 ft. 10 in. ; displacement, loaded, 6,748 tons; and load-draught of water, mean, 23 ft. 8 in.

'The keel consists of two horizontal plates riveted together, upon which are fastened at the middle, by means of two angle-irons, a vertical plate 3 ft. 10 in. high, extending to the two posts, to which all the plates forming the keel are connected by bolts and rivets.

Four longitudinal frames stand almost vertically upon the outer skin, and their depth, which up to the fourth longitudinal frame is 31 inches, decreases gradually from the keel, running in the same direction as the latter, but approaching it forward and aft as required by the shape of the vessel. These longitudinal frames are made of plates and angle-irons, and are lightened at intervals by large oval holes. The transverse frames from the keel to the fourth longitudinal frame, placed at distances apart of four feet, are made of short angle-irons extending only from one longitudinal to the other, to which they are connected by solid plates, brackets, or angle-irons. The plates have the height of the corresponding longitudinal frames, and those belonging to any transverse frame are connected at the top by means of an angle-iron extending from side to side, through all the longitudinal frames and the keel. The outer skin is riveted to the longitudinal and transverse framing, and to the inner side of the latter the second skin is secured, over a length of 180 feet; the end transverse frames and nine intermediate ones are formed of solid plates, so as to enclose watertight compartments. These compartments are again divided by the vertical keel, and a series of watertight subdivisions are thus formed by a watertight transverse frame at the fore and after ends, the inner bottom plates at the top, the outer skin plating at the bottom, and by the vertical keel-plate and fourth longitudinal frame at the sides.

'Special care is taken to maintain effective communication between the pumps and the whole of the watertight compartments. For this purpose an iron pipe $12\frac{1}{2}$ inches in diameter is placed close to and parallel with the vertical keel-plate over the length of the double bottom; from this pipe, branches extend to the various compartments; the main pipe carries the accumulated water into a reservoir placed under the engine-room, whence it is pumped away by a $12\frac{1}{2}$-inch Downton pump, as well as by all the pumps in connection with the machinery. Four $9\frac{1}{4}$-inch pumps in addition are placed upon the battery deck, each of which can take water from a certain number of compartments; and one can also be used for filling the tanks with drinking-water.

'An armoured battery surrounds the two turrets, which project 6 ft. 2 in. above the upper deck. This battery is separated from the fore and after parts of the vessel by armoured transverse bulkheads; while those parts between wind and water are protected only by an armour-belt reaching from about 6 ft. 2 in. below water to the battery deck. The armoured battery is 90 ft. 6 in. long; it contains the bases of the turrets, and also a second steering-wheel, to be used during action. The armour-plates at the water-line are $9\frac{1}{4}$ inches thick, below the water $7\frac{1}{4}$ inches, and above water $8\frac{1}{4}$ inches; these thicknesses decreasing towards the ends to four inches. Behind these plates there is a backing of teak about $10\frac{1}{2}$ inches thick, which varies with the thickness of the plates.

'The two turrets are each 26 ft. 9 in. in diameter, and are constructed in the usual way. They extend, as already stated, from the battery deck to 6 ft. 2 in. above the upper deck, and are covered with armour at the parts exposed above the upper deck. The armour-plates of these turrets are $8\frac{1}{4}$ inches thick, with the exception of those through which the portholes for the guns are cut, which have a thickness of $10\frac{1}{4}$ inches. The teak backing behind the armour-plates is $8\frac{1}{4}$ inches in thickness. These turrets revolve round strong cast-iron centre-pins secured vertically upon the battery deck; and their weights are taken on conical rollers, placed near the outer circumference of the turrets, which run upon girders laid on the deck. Each turret is worked by a high-pressure engine having two cylinders $10\frac{1}{4}$ by $10\frac{1}{4}$ inches, and also by hand-gear. The ammunition is brought from the battery deck into the turrets through openings; and the tops are covered by plates 1 inch thick. The port-sills of the turrets are 13 ft. $5\frac{1}{2}$ in. above the water-line.

'The armament in the turrets consists of four Krupp rifled guns, about $10\frac{1}{2}$ inches in the bore and 22 tons in weight, two guns of 17 c/m. ($6\frac{1}{2}$ inch) and four of 8 c/m. (3 inch).

'The upper deck is provided in the middle above the turrets with a light platform for the reception of the chart-house, and there is also a raised forecastle. A light screen for the protection of the crew is arranged so that it may be laid down, and be out of the way of the guns of the turrets, which are close to the upper deck.

'The "Preussen" has three masts, made to be used as ventilating-tubes, and she is a full-rigged frigate. The propelling engines are of the three-cylinder type, and the boilers of the box form. The screw is fixed, and fitted to revolve when the ship is under sail.

'The following are the weights of materials used for the hull of the vessel, the masts, and the turrets: Plates, 1,375 tons; angle-irons, 600 tons; bar iron and large forgings, 33 tons; iron for rivets, 115 tons; and cast iron, 100 tons.'

Engines of 'Friedrich der Grosse.'

The engines of the 'Friedrich der Grosse' are of a type well-known in this country, although now almost superseded by compound engines. Three equal and independent cylinders are used, placed side by side, and working cranks set at 120° apart. This arrangement of engine, with trunks instead of return connecting rods, has been advocated in Germany by the Engineer-in-Chief of the German Navy, Herr Geheimrath Coupette, to whose energy is due much of the progress now being made in marine engineering in his country. The type has consequently been much used there in vessels of war. The machinery is very simple, but it cannot compete as regards economy in the use of steam with the compound type.

The following are the principal dimensions, etc., of the engines, given in English measurement:—

Diameters of cylinders . . .	91 inches
„ trunks . . .	37 inches
Effective diameter of cylinders . .	83·125 inches
Stroke . . .	47·625 inches
Diameter of shaft . . .	17 inches
Length of end bearing (two) . .	24 inches
„ middle bearings (four) .	16·7 inches
„ connecting-rod . .	120·5 inches
Diameter of air-pumps . .	26·7 inches
„ circulating pumps (contrifugal)	44 inches
Condensing surface . . .	13,035 sq. ft.
Diameter of propeller (Griffith's) .	21·7 feet
Mean pitch . . . :	22·5 feet
Heating surface in boilers (six) .	17,736 sq. ft.
Grate surface in boilers (thirty furnaces) .	680 sq. ft.
Steam pressure . . .	30 lbs. per sq. in.
Indicated horse-power . . .	5,400

The whole machinery has been constructed by the Markisch Schlesische Maschinenbau und Hutten Actien Gesellschaft (of Berlin and Tegel) from the designs of Herr Jungermann, the 'technical director' of the company.

The speed of these ships is fourteen knots.

M. Dislere.   M. Dislère, in *La Guerre d'Escadre*, criticises the designs of the German turret-ship as deficient in bow-fire, while, on the other hand, the length of the central battery is only sufficient to afford protection to the base of the turrets, the funnels, and the boilers. The hull forward and abaft the battery, notwithstanding the fact that the armoured belt rises but little above the water-line, is protected only by a thinly plated deck. The only protection provided for the lower part of the hull consists in a judicious and elaborate arrangement of coal bunkers.

Armour.   The extreme thickness of the water-line belt is $9\frac{1}{4}$ inches, diminishing rapidly to $7\frac{1}{4}$ inches at the lower strake of plating in the centre, and to four inches at the water-line at the extremities.

With a displacement of 6,700 tons, these ships carry only four 27 c/m. or $10\frac{1}{2}$-inch guns, behind armour nowhere exceeding

9¼ inches in thickness. Both armament and armour are in a marked degree inferior to those of the 'Audacious,' which vessel, with a lesser displacement of 6,200 tons, has an advantage both in speed and in stowage of fuel, and carries ten guns of nine inches calibre. The armour, which nowhere exceeds a thickness of eight inches, is the only point of inferiority in the case of the 'Audacious.'

In the early part of 1878, the Admiralty purchased for the Navy the Brazilian ship 'Independencia,' built by the late firm of Messrs. J. and W. Dudgeon, of Millwall, and renamed her the 'Neptune.' 'Neptune' (late 'Independencia'

The following description of the vessel is compiled from the

Figs. 218 and 219.

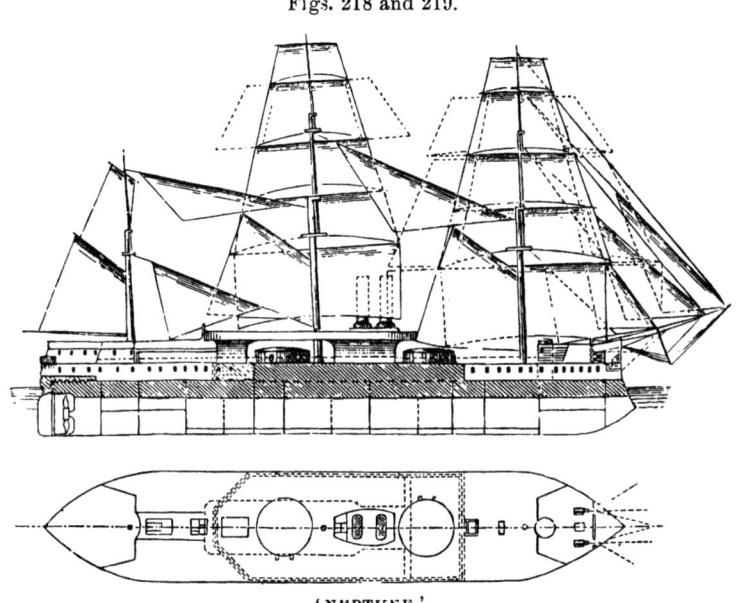

'NEPTUNE.'

Times and other authorities. In this republication the ship will be spoken of by her present name.

'The "Neptune" was designed in 1872, by Sir Edward J. Reed, in accordance with conditions prescribed by a commission of Brazilian officers. The dimensions, draught of water, thickness of armour, size and number of guns, speed, sail-power, and other primary qualities were arranged in concert with this commission. At that time the British ship "Devastation" was being advanced towards completion in the dockyard at Portsmouth, and was exciting great attention in other countries as well as in England, by reason of the enormous powers of offence and defence which were being developed. The twelve and fourteen inch armour on the hull and turrets,

$2\frac{1}{2}$ and 3 inch armour on the decks, and the armament of 35-ton guns constituted a combination of defensive and offensive power, which was not approached by any fighting ships then built, or building, and caused the "Devastation" to be regarded as the type to which all first-class fighting-ships would, in the future, have to approximate. The Brazilian officers desired a ship equally powerful, with the addition of sails. The "Neptune," as completed in 1877, is different in many respects from any other ship, but her typical features may be best described by calling her a rigged "Devastation." She bears, however, a superficial resemblance to the unfortunate "Captain" chiefly due to the upper works, formed by the forecastle, hurricane-deck, and poop, and by her being full-rigged.

'The "Neptune" is a two-turreted breastwork ship of 9,000 tons displacement. The principal dimensions, etc., are:—

Length between perpendiculars	.	.	.	300 feet
Breadth, extreme	.	.	.	63 feet
Depth of hold	.	.	.	16 ft. 6 in.
Mean draught of water	.	.	.	24 ft. 9 in.
Load displacement, tons	.	.	.	8,960

'The central breastwork is 130 feet in length at the top of the belt, and extends to the upper deck, eleven feet above the water-line. This breastwork encloses the boiler and engine-hatches, the scuttles to magazines and shell-rooms, the principal openings for ventilation, and the two circular revolving turrets amidships, one at each end of the breastwork. Before and abaft this breastwork, the armour-plating is continued, in the form of a belt, round the bow and stern. The armour upon the water-line belt amidships is twelve inches thick, with a teak backing of the same thickness, and upon the breastwork it is ten inches, and nine inches, with teak backing ten inches thick. The armour-plating and backing are both bolted in the usual way to the skin-plating of the ship, which consists of two thicknesses of $\frac{5}{8}$-inch plates. The top of the breastwork is protected by plating one inch to $1\frac{1}{2}$ inch thick, and the deck at the top of the armour-belt, before and abaft the breastwork, is also protected by plating two inches to three inches thick. The funnel and engine hatches are completely protected on the breastwork deck by gratings formed of deep armour bars, while the openings in the deck over the armour-belt are fitted with protecting sliding iron shutters of the same thickness as the deck plating. The turrets are plated with armour of 13-inch and 11-inch thickness, the former being placed upon that side of the turret which contains the ports, and the latter upon the other side. This armour is worked upon teak backing of a corresponding thickness; and the whole is secured to the plating of the turrets, which consists of two thicknesses of $\frac{5}{8}$-inch plates.

'Over the breastwork and between the turrets is an erection somewhat similar to the hurricane deck of the "Devastation." It consists of a deck about one-half the breadth of the ship, extending from the fore turret to some distance abaft the after turret, this deck being supported by the casings of the boiler and engine hatches. Upon this deck is a rifle-proof house, containing the steering apparatus and appliances for navigating the ship, the boats, hammocks, steam-winch, ventilating shafts, etc. There is also a poop and a forecastle, the hurricane deck amidships being narrowed abaft the breastwork and continued aft to the poop. Upon this continuation of the hurricane deck are placed the standard compass and steering-wheel. Under the poop are spacious apartments for the admiral and his staff, and cabins for other officers. The forecastle is fitted for working the anchors, and has an armoured bulkhead across the fore part, behind which are placed two 7-inch guns. At the after end of the forecastle is an armoured pilot-tower containing telegraphs and voice-pipes to the engine-room, steering-wheels, battery, etc., and from which the captain will work the ship in action.

'Since the purchase by the British Admiralty extensive alterations have been made for the purpose of obtaining an all-round fire from the turret guns, and the Whitworth 35-ton breech-loaders have been replaced by Woolwich 38-ton muzzle-loaders. This alteration necessitated the enlargement of the turret ports. The bow ports have also been enlarged to facilitate carrying 12-ton Woolwich guns, in place of the 7-ton Whitworths. Top hamper has been reduced by rigging the ship as a barque, alterations have been made in the magazines, shell-rooms, etc., the electric light apparatus, and the electric firing gear improved, and the latest appliances for ejecting the Whitehead torpedoes have been fitted.

'The turret guns are arranged for loading by hydraulic machinery, like those of H.M.S. "Thunderer." Boat guns are mounted at ports cut in the after end of the flying deck amidships for repelling boat attacks; and machine guns are mounted on the poop and forecastle for clearing the deck of boarders.

'The presence of the poop and forecastle prevents a complete all-around fire, as in the "Devastation," but the obstruction thus caused is limited to a few degrees from the fore-and-aft line. These obstructions are necessarily caused by the determination to make the "Neptune" a full-rigged sailing ship. The manner in which this has been done, and the difficulties in the way of it removed or minimised, is one of the most notable features of the design. The foremast is just abaft the forecastle, and is worked from the breast-work-deck ; all fittings in connection with it, and all bitts and the lead of ropes being so arranged that in clearing for action they will all be out of the line of fire. The shrouds to the foremast and also to the mainmast will all be cleared away for action except two shrouds on each side of the mast, which are made larger than the rest and will remain fixed and take their chance of being shot away. The mainmast is between the boiler-hatch and after-turret, and all ropes connected with it will ordinarily be worked on the breastwork deck ; but in clearing for action they will be raised upon the hurri-cane deck, and can be worked there if required. The rigging of the mizenmast is worked entirely from the poop. She will have no royals, but will be fitted with lower square sails, topsails, and top-gallant sails.

'Nep-
tune's'
engines.
'The " Neptune " is not deficient in steam-power, and can steam one knot an hour faster than the " Devastation " or " Thunderer." The engines are by Messrs. John Penn and Sons, and drive a single screw. They consist of one pair of cylinders 127 inches in diameter, with 47-inch trunks, making an effective diameter of cylinder of 118 inches. The stroke is 4 ft. 6 in. The guaranteed number of revo-lutions was 70, and the horse-power 8,500. The boilers are eight in number, working at 30 lbs. pressure. They are contained in two separate watertight compartments, four in each ; so that in the event of one boiler-room being flooded the other could still be worked. The boilers are eighteen feet in length, 10 ft. 6 in. wide, and 12 ft. 9 in. deep. Each contains five furnaces three feet in width. The propeller is 26 feet in diameter, and has 23 feet pitch. The shaft is twenty inches in diameter. The preliminary trial of the machinery was made at the Nore on December 31, 1877, and the official speed trial on February 2, 1878, over the measured mile on the Maplin Sands, . . . where a mean speed of 14·6 knots an hour, with 9,000 indicated horse-power, was obtained.'

In the operation of launching, the 'Neptune' met with an accident. She stopped at the end of the ways, with her after-part overhanging. She was got off and docked at Woolwich ; when the work of restoration proved to be of a very formidable character. It was found necessary to take out and rebuild the whole of the bottom of the ship for a considerable portion of the length amidships. The repairs were carried out by Messrs. Samuda Brothers under the direction of Sir E. Reed.

M. Dislère concludes his description of the 'Neptune' in *La Guerre d'Escadre*, with the following observations :—

'If the "Preussen" and her consorts are slightly reduced copies M. Dislère
on the
'Neptune.' of the "Monarch," the "Neptune" is an enlarged "Monarch," the displacement being increased from 8,450 to 9,370 tons. By this means the armour and armament have been strengthened, though the height of the freeboard of the armoured citadel has been reduced from 14 feet to 11 feet. Hence a notable reduction in the coefficient of safety, although perhaps this question is less important for ships whose armour-belt is considered to be impenetrable. The water-line belt is only 9 ft. 6 in. in depth, of which 5 ft. 6 in. are above the water-line. The extreme thickness seems to be twelve inches, but with very considerable reductions both vertically and horizontally. The thickness of the armour on the battery is ten inches in the lower part, and thirteen inches in the upper part. The turrets are protected with twelve inches of armour. The deck outside the battery is protected with 2-inch plates.

'This ship is covered with zinc, over a sheathing of teak, and is constructed on the bracket system. She has exhibited, as is known, the most striking illustration of the fragility of a system of frames, which, to use the phrase of a French constructor, " cross only the better to cut one another." The "Neptune," having an area of canvas equal to 16·2 times that of the midship section, should be a fair cruiser. With all these advantages, this ironclad does not belong to a type which it is judicious to multiply.'

Mr. King concludes his description of the ' Neptune ' with some Mr. King. remarks of a more favourable tendency. The ' Neptune ' is thirty feet shorter than the ' Monarch ' and has three feet less freeboard, but she has 5½ feet more beam. In comparison with the unfortunate ' Captain ' she is in many respects quite different : the armour is three and four inches thicker, and the guns are 38-ton against the 'Captain's' 25-ton ; besides, she has three feet more freeboard than the ' Captain ' was intended to have, and nearly twice as much as she actually did have ; in addition she is twenty feet longer and ten feet broader. This extra breadth, combined with the freeboard, is doubtless what is relied upon for giving that ample safety against capsizing which the ' Captain ' unfortunately did not have ; at any rate, these differences must give the ' Neptune ' very great stability and power to carry sail, as compared with the ' Captain.'

When we take into view the delay due to an error in launching, and the time that has elapsed since the design was produced, the ' Neptune ' is to be accepted as a powerful ship. The side and turret armour is only one inch thinner than the ' Devastation's, her guns are worked by hydraulic power instead of by hand, they throw heavier projectiles, and have greater penetrating power. Under her new name, the 'Neptune,' this vessel constitutes an acceptable, although a costly, addition to the English navy.

Steam
trials at
Ports-
mouth.

The 'Neptune' was tried [1] in the Solent in May 1880, for the first time since she became an English man-of-war. Though the new armament was on board, the various stores remained to be shipped. As it was essential, however, for the purposes of the trial that she should be as nearly as possible brought down to seagoing trim, sixty tons of water were admitted into the double bottom, which, with the amount of coal in the bunkers, gave her a draught of 24 ft. 10 in. forward and 25 feet aft. She was, therefore, upon an even keel, which is understood to be the normal trim. As she lay deep in the water, the full bows pushed ahead, when driving at full power, a wave which could not have been less than from ten feet to eleven feet in height, and consequently, threw great strain upon the machinery as well as retarding considerably the way of the ship. It was also noticed that a broad channel of dead water followed in her wake.

The ship proceeded to Spithead, when she underwent a pre-liminary trial, but the engines were not pushed beyond forty revolu-tions. Indeed, the temperature in the stokehole, which sometimes was as high as 163°, proved more than the stokers could stand. The steaming was confined to the Solent, with occasional runs beyond the Nab, the opportunity being taken advantage of to make four runs on the measured mile in Stokes Bay. The following shows the result of the four runs on the mile :—First, 14·754 knots ; second, 13·534 knots ; third, 15·126 knots ; fourth, 12·996 knots ; the mean of means giving a speed of 14·216 knots per hour, which was very satisfactory. The result of each half-hour's steaming was as follows :—

Half-hours	Boiler Pressure	Vacuum	Revolutions	Mean Pressure	Indicated Horse-power
1	28½	27	66	20·25	8,001·38
2	28	27	68	21·30	8,627·27
3	28	27	67·5	20·50	8,255·42
4	27	27	66·7	20·45	8,141·38
5	24½	27	66·3	19·50	7,713·17
6	28	27	63	21·00	8,535·66
7	27	27	67·7	20·50	8,276·19
8	27½	27	66·7	19·85	7,895·41
9	23½	27½	63·4	18·75	7,092·25
10	27	27½	64·9	19·65	7,611·97
11	26½	27	65	19·55	7,581·39
12	27½	26	65·5	20·95	8,190·52
Mean	26·9	27	64·2	20·19	7,993·50

[1] From the *Times*, May 17, 1880.

It will be seen that the mean horse-power developed was 7,993·50, which was a very fair success, considering the length of time the engines have been lying idle on board. But the mean result is not a fair test of what the machinery is capable of doing, as is proved by the *maximum* power developed during the trial. With such a temperature in the stokehole, however, it is impossible that the men can work, the more especially seeing that, as the furnaces are stoked amidships, the stokers have fires both in their faces and at their backs. This want of air has also a very serious effect upon the furnaces, which are deprived of a proper amount of draught. The consumption of coal per indicated horse-power per hour amounted to 2·8 lbs. The engines worked very well and afforded unmistakable proof that, though not manufactured for the English Navy, they are equal to any which the same makers have constructed for the English service.

CHAPTER XV.

MASTLESS TURRET-SHIPS.

THE English Admiralty have lately directed their attention mainly to the class of mastless ironclads, as the most formidable fighting ships for the line of battle. The arguments in favour of this type are not far to seek. The masts are an embarrassment when steam is available. There is a great objection to the high freeboard for iron-clad ships. The hulls can be more effectually protected when sunk as far as may be down to the level of the water, like a raft, while only the turrets, armed with colossal guns, are exposed to the enemy's fire.

Mastless ships in England and abroad.

Proceeding on the principle thus indicated, the English Admiralty designed the ' Devastation,' ' Thunderer,' ' Dreadnought,' ' Ajax,' ' Agamemnon,' and ' Inflexible.' Russia followed with the ' Peter the Great '; Italy with the ' Dandolo ' and ' Duilio.'

The leading features of our latest type of battle-ships were summed up in a paper on the unmasted seagoing ships, ' Devastation,' ' Thunderer,' ' Dreadnought,' and ' Peter the Great,' read before the Institute of Naval Architects, by Mr. Barnaby, in 1873.

' Devastation ' and ' Thunderer.'

' Their hulls, engines, boilers, and magazines are protected by twelve inches of armour on the sides, by three inches of armour on the low decks, and by six inches of armour on bow and stern bulkheads in the hold. Each ship carries four guns, each capable of firing shell and shot weighing 700 lbs. each, at a velocity equivalent to about 900 miles an hour. These guns are protected at the breastwork, and above it by at least twelve inches of armour, the faces of the turrets by fourteen inches. The deck forming the glacis to these guns, which is eleven feet out of the water, is protected by two inches of iron beneath the oak. The trial of one of the ships at the measured mile, at her deep sea-line, has shown that she has a speed of $1\frac{1}{3}$ knots over that which was estimated (13·840); and that she will reverse the course at full speed in 1 min. 26 sec. The low hull, and the absence of rigging, are likely to admit of the maintenance of high rates of speed with ease against head winds.'

In another paper by the same authority, on 'Modern Ships of War,' read at the United Service Institution, a comparison is made between the mastless and the masted turret-ships.

'The " Devastation " is the first seagoing ship of war,—properly so called,—designed without sails. The American ships " Monadnock " and " Miantonomoh " carried only a very limited supply of coal, and were never trusted at sea without an escort ; but the " Devastation " class are expected to be able to maintain an independent existence at sea for long periods.

'Comparing the " Monarch " and " Devastation " as to power of endurance under steam, we consider that the average distance which the " Devastation " may be expected to run at five-knots speed, with one ton of coal, is about $5\frac{3}{4}$ knots, so that her 1,600 tons of coal would carry her about 9,200 miles.

'The distance which the " Monarch " would be carried under steam alone at 5-knots speed, by one ton of coal, would be about $6\frac{1}{2}$ knots, and if under sail with sufficient steam-power to keep the screw going, as is always done when the ship is with the fleet under sail, about eleven to twelve knots. Supposing her to have favouring winds, so that she may use her sail in this manner half her time, and to be under steam alone the other half, then it may be assumed that she would be carried about nine knots on an average by one ton of coal, and her coal would then carry her 5,400 miles only, as against the 9,200 of the " Devastation."

' On comparing the resisting power of the armour of the two ships, we see that while the total weight of the " Devastation " including all stores, is only one-ninth greater than that of the " Monarch" the weight of armour carried by the " Devastation " is just twice as great as that carried by the " Monarch." The side armour of the " Monarch " might be pierced by the guns of the " Devastation " at $2\frac{3}{4}$ miles, the charge being 115 lbs. of pebble powder, and the weight of shot 700 lbs. But the armour of the " Devastation " is not penetrable at all by the guns of the " Monarch " if R.L.G. powder is used, and is impenetrable with pebble powder (85 lbs.) at ranges beyond 200 yards. The 14-inch armour on the front of the turrets of the " Devastation " would be impenetrable to the guns of the " Monarch " at any range, but the front turret armour of the " Monarch " would be penetrable at 2,300 yards to the guns of the " Devastation."

' The " Devastation " can be worked by a crew of from 250 to 300 men, while the " Minotaur " requires 700 ; and the cost of the two

ships, exclusive of ordnance and ordnance stores, is about 320,000*l.*
for the " Devastation," and 478,000*l.* for the " Minotaur," which is a
difference of more than 150,000*l.*'

Sir Spencer
Robinson
on ' Devas-
tation.' On another occasion, in the discussion on Captain Noel's paper
on the best types of ships of war, Sir Spencer Robinson thus expressed
his entire confidence in their fighting qualities :—

'The " Devastation " takes to sea four of the heaviest rifled guns
yet constructed in this country. She takes those guns to sea at
a height of fourteen feet above the water. She takes them in two
turrets, protected by 14-inch armour. The hull of the ship that
bears those turrets is protected by 12 and 10-inch armour. There
are bulkheads, which cut off all access of dropping shot from the
vital parts of the ship. She has a speed of 13·8 knots; she can

Figs 220 and 221.

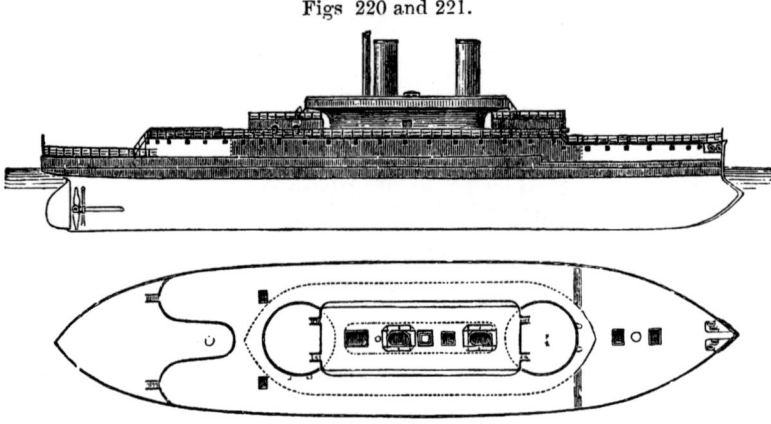

'DEVASTATION.'

reverse her powerful qualities as a ram in 2 min. 2 sec.—that is, she
could be charging in one direction at the rate of sixteen statute
miles an hour, and in two minutes she could be charging in
the opposite direction at the same rate of speed. She has been
in gales of wind on the Atlantic; she has been exposed to such
weather as she could find on the coast of Ireland; she has crossed
the Bay of Biscay; she has done good service in the Mediterranean,
with eminent satisfaction to everybody on board. She carries 1,200
or 1,400 tons of coal, and the radius of her operation is only measured
by the distance that coal will carry her.'

The following detailed descriptions are taken from Mr. King :—

' Devasta-
tion ': Mr.
King's de-
scription. 'The " Devastation " was the first British seagoing mastless ship
built. As originally designed in 1869, she was of the low freeboard,
turret type, 285 feet long, 62 ft. 3 in. beam, and 26 feet mean

draught of water. She was provided with a double bottom; the space between the two skins, which was about three feet deep, being divided, as usual, into a number of separate watertight cells, so that injury to the outer bottom could only result in the filling of one or more of these; and the strength of the hull was arranged so as to give great support to the bow when ramming. The hold of the vessel, also, was divided into a number of compartments by watertight bulkheads across the ship, so that, even in the event of a clean breach being made through both bottoms,—as might be effected by a torpedo, for instance,—being able to confine the water to the compartment or compartments into which the breach had been made, she would still have considerable chance of escape. Her sides, which, except right forward, arose only to a height of 4 ft. 6 in. above the surface of the water, were protected by armour twelve inches thick.

'On the middle of the upper deck there was raised a breastwork or platform about 150 feet in length. The four 25-ton guns were to be mounted in pairs, in two turrets, one at each end of this breastwork. The guns were thus elevated to a height of some fourteen feet above the water-level. The turrets were protected by armour twelve and fourteen inches thick, and the breastwork by armour ten and twelve inches thick. A forecastle extended forward from the fore end of the breastwork at a height of 9 ft. 3 in. above the water-line; but in wake of this forecastle the armour on the sides dropped to a height of only six inches above water, this corresponding to the level of an armoured deck. All the necessary hatchways, openings, etc., into the ship were led up by iron trunks to a light flying-deck which extended between the two turrets, somewhat overlapping each. The vessel was to be propelled by twin screws, one under each counter; each to be worked by a separate pair of engines, so that the ship might be driven by their conjoint action, or by either of them working singly. The total power of the engines was to be 5,600 horses indicated, and the estimated speed was 12·5 knots per hour.

'This was the "Devastation" as first designed. She was the first of the type which it was determined to build from plans prepared at the Admiralty. The great question of that day in England—the comparative merits of turret and broadside armaments for seagoing armoured ships—will still be remembered by all persons informed in the progress of naval construction. So strong were the supporters of certain views with regard to the former system, that, notwithstanding the continued opposition of the then Chief Constructer of the Navy, the order was given for the "Captain," a vessel embodying these views, to be designed and built by a private firm. The " Devastation " represented Mr. Reed's views of what a seagoing monitor should be, and she may be regarded as having been designed to compete with the " Captain." Low sides were adopted, but not in combination with rigging and sails, as was the case in the ill-fated " Captain."

Loss of
' Captain.'

' The " Captain " in the mean time, having been built and sent to sea, was winning a high reputation. She had been launched in March, 1869, and toward the close of 1870 made one or two short but successful cruises. A clever English writer says :—" True, when completed, it was found that a very important element in connection with the design, viz. the weight of the ship, and consequently the draught of water and height of freeboard, had been loosely calculated ; but the error arising therefrom, though by no means small, was not regarded as serious ; and as it did not apparently much influence her seagoing qualities, no special notice was taken of it. Her stability was never doubted by her designers ; nor, indeed, was her critical state ever properly realised by anyone ; any doubt that may have existed was smothered by the confidence of her advocates. The chorus of praise which she elicited on all sides continued to increase, and the question of what the type of British war-ship for the future should be was supposed to be settled in her beyond dispute. Then came the dreadful news that she had gone down during the night between the 6th and 7th of September, 1870, off Cape Finisterre. The wind had not been unusually violent ; the sea had not been exceptionally heavy ; there were no extenuating circumstances ; she had not bravely battled with even ordinary rough weather ; she was proceeding confidently under steam and sail when, in an ordinary squall, she displayed once for all her subtle and treacherous character by slowly turning over and becoming the coffin of nearly the whole of her crew, some 500 men, including a large number of accomplished officers. The people of England were almost panic-stricken at this terrible news. How it could have occurred with the comparatively wide-spread knowledge relating to the subject and the facts and figures of her special case before them, it was difficult to conceive." To remove the doubt which immediately arose as to the safety of the other armoured ships, and particularly as to that of the " Devastation," a special committee was appointed to examine into

Committee
on Designs.

the designs of those vessels. This committee, which consisted of many of the highest professional and scientific authorities in England, met in January, 1871, and made their report concerning the " Devastation " class early in the following March. After numerous calculation's and investigations they came to the conclusion that the stability of the " Devastation " was everything that could be desired, and reported that " ships of this class have stability amply sufficient to make them safe against the rolling and heaving action of the sea." The committee, however, agreed in recommending a plan which the constructors of the Admiralty had proposed with the view of making her still more safe.

' By this plan, which was afterwards adopted, the stability of the ship has been very considerably increased ; and besides this, the accommodation of the officers and men has been very largely augmented. The plan consisted in the addition of side superstructures. They were formed by continuing the ship's sides upwards with light framing, as high as the level of the top of the the breastwork, and continuing the breastwork deck over to the sides. The structures were extended aft on each side a considerable distance beyond the end of the breastwork, providing two spacious wings, which added largely to the cabin accommodation.

' Some other alterations in the design which were suggested by the committee were carried out ; among them may be mentioned the introduction of athwartship armour-plated bulkheads, so as to afford additional protection to the magazines and engines. An alteration of considerable importance had been made some time before, consisting in the substitution of 35-ton guns for the 25-ton guns originally arranged. With these and some other slight alterations the vessel was completed. Her mean draught of water is now 26 ft. 8 in. Her height of side above the water-line is 10 ft. 9 in., except right forward in wake of the foreeastle, where it is 8 ft. 6 in., and right aft abaft the superstructure, where it is only four feet.

' The " Devastation " is propelled by twin screws, each driven by Machinery. an independent pair of engines. These engines, which have been constructed by Messrs. John Penn and Sons, of Greenwich, are of the direct-acting trunk type, and were contracted for prior to the adoption of compound engines. They have cylinders 88 inches in diameter and trunks $36\frac{1}{2}$ inches in diameter; the trunks reducing the effective area of the pistons to that due to a diameter of 80 inches. The cylinders are steam-jacketed both at the sides and ends, and the stroke of the pistons is 3 ft. 3 in. The engines are fitted with expansion gear, which enables the steam to be cut off at any required part of the stroke. The main slide-valves are double-ported, and fitted with an equilibrium-ring. The expansion-valves are of a gridiron form, with a variable stroke and cut-off. The admission of steam to the engines is regulated by equilibrium valves, which are

worked by screws and suitable gearing, led away to the starting platform. To insure ready handling of the engines, small auxiliary
slide-valves are fitted to each cylinder. Each pair of engines is fitted
with a surface-condenser containing 5,432 $\frac{3}{4}$-inch tubes, 6 ft. 3$\frac{1}{4}$ in.
long; the condensing surface for each pair of engines being thus
6,710 square feet. The tubes are packed with screwed glands and
tape packing. The air-pumps and the circulating-pumps are double-
acting, and are worked direct from the pistons. The condensing
water is passed through the tubes and the steam admitted to the
outside. The crank-shafts are in two pieces, with solid couplings
forged on. The turning gear consists of a worm-wheel and worm,
worked by hand by means of a long ratchet lever. The disconnecting coupling is fitted with four steel pins, which can be drawn out of
gear by means of screws and ratchet spanners. The thrust of the
propellers is taken by a bearing fitted with ten movable collars. The
screw-propellers are 17 ft. 6 in. in diameter, and have 19 ft. 6 in.
pitch, and are so fitted that the pitch can be varied from 17
to 22 feet. The number of blades to each is four, and the propellers
are formed on the Griffiths principle. The boilers are eight in
number, of the old kind, containing 32 furnaces, the four boilers
in the forward fire-room having four furnaces each; while of the four
boilers in the after fire-room, two have three and two have five furnaces each. The length of bars is 6 ft. 6 in. and the width of
furnaces 3 ft. 2 in., the total fire-grate area being thus 742 square
feet. The boilers contain in all 2,592 tubes 3$\frac{1}{2}$ inches in diameter
and 6 feet long. The working pressure of steam is 30 lbs. per
square inch. The total heating surface is 17,806 square feet. A
superheater is fixed in each chimney, of which there are two, the
total superheating surface exposed being 1,866 square feet. The
chimneys are telescopic, and are fitted with hoisting gear and shell-
proof gratings at the bottom. The length of the ship occupied by
the engines is 32 feet, and that by the boilers 80 feet: this latter
length being divided into two equal compartments, separated from
the engines and each other by watertight bulkheads. Telegraphs
are fitted between the engine-rooms and the bridge, and, in addition
to the ordinary means of ventilation, fans are fitted, driven by independent engines. A powerful fire-engine is provided, with pipes leading to all parts of the ship. Engines are also fitted for working the
capstans and hoisting the ashes. The weight of engines and boilers
complete, with water in boilers and condensers, and including spare
gear and all the fittings above enumerated is 985 tons, or 2·96 cwt.
per indicated horse-power as developed when working at full power

on the official trial. The following results were obtained on the official trial, on September 2, 1872 :—

Draught of water, forward	.	.	. 26 ft. 4 in.
,, aft .	.	.	. 26 ft. 6 in.
Immersion of upper edge of screw		.	. 7 ft. 2 in.
Pressure of steam in engine-room		.	. 27 lbs.

	Full power	Half power
Revolutions . . .	76·76	63
Mean pressure in cylinders, starboard	22·066	12·88
,, ,, port	21·53	14·41
Indicated horse-power, starboard	3,359·21	1,566·03
,, ,, port .	3,278·5	1,883·89
Speed of vessel (knots) .	13·839	11·900

'Immersed midship section, 1,460 square feet at 26 ft. 5 in. draught.

'Coefficient for midship section, 582.

'During the full-power trial the total power developed by the two pairs of engines was thus 6,637·71 horse-power, and the areas of grate surface, condensing surface, etc., per indicated horse-power, were as follows :—

Fire-grate	.	.	.	. 0·112 sq. ft.
Heating surface	.	.	.	. 2·68 sq. ft.
,, including superheating surface				2·96 sq. ft.
Condensing surface	.	.	.	. 2·02 sq. ft.

'The trial cruises of the "Devastation," made to ascertain the degree of success attained in the design as an engine of war, as well as in respect of seagoing qualities, were made in the summer of 1873; and it may be said with confidence that never before did the proceedings of any single vessel excite so large an amount of public interest. The novelty of her design as an ocean-cruising man-of-war, her odd appearance, and her fighting power, formed constant topics of discussion in the scientific and other papers; but the real source of interest to the English people was doubtless to be found in the fact that the vessel was looked upon by the general public as belonging to the same type as the unfortunate "Captain." Hence, notwith-standing the vital points of difference between the two vessels, to which attention had been repeatedly drawn, her trials were watched with an interest amounting almost to anxiety.

'The preliminary trials had reference principally to the per-formance of the engines, boilers, turrets, and other machinery. The great importance of the first of these will be evident, since the vessel is an ocean-going cruiser without masts and sails, so that she is en-tirely dependent upon her engines for propulsion. As has been seen.

a speed of 13·8 knots per hour was obtained at the measured-mile trial, the engines indicating 6,637 horse-power; and it was shown what distances could be run with the full supply of coal by a series of steam trials at various speeds.

Gunnery trials.

'The gunnery trials were made subsequently at the usual testing-ground off the Isle of Wight. The guns are capable of being raised and lowered by hydraulic pressure through a height of twenty inches, and may thus be placed for firing so as to obtain any desirable degree of elevation or depression in combination with small port-holes. The projectiles used at the trials were 700-lb. Palliser shot, with a battering charge of 110 lbs. of pebble-powder. At the trial the guns were fired first with extreme elevation, and then with extreme depression in all directions round the ship. During two or three trials off Portland and Queenstown, the difficulty of judging of the " Devastation's " behaviour, with reference to the seas that were met with, as compared with the behaviour of ships of ordinary form under similar circumstances, suggested the desirability of prosecuting the ocean trials in company with some other ship or ships of about the same dimensions but of less unusual type. Carrying out this idea, the vessel was placed in company with the "Agincourt" and "Sultan," and thus made to form part of a division of the Channel Squadron. The "Agincourt" is one of the early ironclads, built in 1862–65. She is 400 feet long, and is somewhat heavily rigged with five masts. She is completely protected by armour 5½ inches thick. Her armament consists of twenty-eight guns in a long battery, after the old style of frigates, but although the thickness of her armour and the weight of her guns are now out of date, she is claimed to be one of the best sea-boats in the fleet. The "Sultan," on the other hand, is one of the more modern ironclads. She is short, not much longer than the " Devastation," and is rigged with three masts as a ship. Her armament, consisting of twelve guns, is mounted in a central two-decked battery and protected by thick armour. The water-line is also protected by a belt of thick armour.

'A scientific observer who was on board the " Devastation " during these sea-trials, wrote a highly interesting and valuable account of the proceedings, and, as a matter of interest in relation to the behaviour of this class of vessels at sea, the notable points of his letter are given as follows :—

Seagoing trials.

' " The squadron, consisting of these three vessels, put to sea from Plymouth Sound at the end of August, 1873 ; the programme laid down being to proceed to Bere Haven, on the south-west coast of Ireland, and from this point make occasional cruises into the open

Atlantic, as suitable weather should occur. This programme was pretty strictly adhered to in all respects. The vessels arrived and anchored off Bere Haven on September 2, after a cruise of four days, during which many points of interest came out, although no very heavy weather was met with. For purposes of comparison in pitching and lifting, etc., the ' Sultan ' had the height of the ' Devastation's ' upper deck at side painted on her in a broad white stripe, so that the behaviour of the two ships might be quickly appreciated apart from the records of instruments. The lowness of the extremities of the ' Devastation ' gives a great deal of interest to the pitching and lifting, really the longitudinal rolling, of the vessel. Two trials were made, one on the 9th and the other on the 15th of September. On the first of these occasions she was accompanied by the ' Sultan ' only, and on the second she was accompanied by the ' Agincourt ' only. The seas met with on September 9 were lumpy and irregular, the wind having shifted somewhat suddenly during the previous night. Having got well out to sea, about forty miles off land, the wind was found to be blowing rather north of west with the force of a moderate gale, its speed varying from 40 to 45 miles per hour; and the largest of the waves were found to vary from 300 to 350 feet in length from crest to crest, occasionally reaching 400 feet—the greatest heights from hollow to crest being fifteen and sixteen feet. Going head to sea, at from six to seven knots, both vessels pitched considerably ; the ' Devastation,' however, had the best of it, pitching through smaller angles than the ' Sultan.' The latter vessel was remarkably lively ; at one moment she was to be seen with her forefoot completely out of water, and the next with her bow dipped down to so great an extent that it was difficult to see from the flying deck of the ' Devastation '—although the ships were pretty close together—whether the sea did not really break inboard ; and this, notwithstanding that the bow of the ' Sultan ' rises forward some thirty feet above the surface of the water. On the other hand, the forecastle deck of the ' Devastation ' was repeatedly swept by the seas, to each of which she rose with surprising readiness ; indeed, it invariably happened that the seas broke upon her during the upward journey of the bow, and there is no doubt it is to this fact that her moderate pitching was mainly due, as the weight of the water on the forecastle deck during the short period it remained there acted as a retarding force, preventing the bow from lifting as high as it otherwise would, and this of course limited the succeeding pitch, and so on. The maximum angle pitched through on this occasion, i.e., the angle between the extreme elevation and depression of the bow, was $7\frac{1}{4}°$. Each vessel behaved

extremely well when placed broadside on to the sea, rolling very little.
The trial of the ship on September 15, in company with the 'Agincourt,'
was by far the most severe of any. Early in the morning the vessel
got under way and steamed out to sea, accompanied by the 'Agincourt.' The wind was blowing with considerable force from the
north-west, while the sea was at times very regular, long, and un-
dulating; just the sort to test the rolling propensities of a ship, but
scarcely long enough to be most effective in doing so, either in the
case of the 'Devastation' or 'Agincourt.' The largest waves ranged
from 400 to 650 feet long, and from 20 to 26 feet high. The ships
were tried in almost every position with regard to the direction of
the sea, and at various speeds, the result in point of comparison being
extremely interesting, and, so far as the 'Devastation' was concerned,
very satisfactory. With the sea dead ahead, and proceeding at about
seven knots, the 'Devastation' pitched rather more than the 'Agincourt,' although the great length of the latter compared with that of
the former caused her bow to rise and fall through a much greater
height, giving her the appearance of pitching through a greater angle.
The usual angles pitched through by the 'Devastation,' measuring
the whole arc from out to out, were from 5° to 8°; the maximum
angle pitched through was, however, $11\frac{3}{4}°$. The scene from the fore
end of the flying deck when the vessel was thus going head to sea,
was very imposing. There was repeatedly a rush of water over the
forecastle, the various fittings, riding-bitts, capstan, anchors, etc.,
churning it up into a beautiful cataract of foam; while occasionally
a wall of water would appear to rise up in front of the vessel, and
dashing on board in the most threatening style, as though it would
carry all before it, rushed aft against the fore turret with great
violence, and after throwing a cloud of heavy spray off the turret into
the air, dividing into two, pass overboard on either side. All the
hatchways leading below from the upper deck were closed; it was
not, however, thought necessary to close the doors in the sides of the
trunks leading up from the main hatchways to the flying deck, most of
the men on deck preferring to remain here under the overhang of the
flying deck. It was quite the exception for the water coming over the
bow to get much abaft the fore turret; but this, however, occurred occasionally. The foremost turret makes a most perfect breakwater; it
receives with impunity the force of the water, which, after spending
itself against it, glances off overboard, leaving two-thirds of the deck
seldom wetted. There was one sea which came on board, while thus
proceeding head to sea, which was much heavier than any other: it
rose in front of the vessel some ten or twelve feet above the fore-

castle, and broke on the deck with great force, for the moment completely swamping the fore end of the vessel. A mass of broken water swept up over the top of the fore turret, and heavy volumes of spray extended the whole length of the flying deck, some small portion of it even finding its way down the funnel-hatchway—which had been left uncovered—into the fore stokehole. It should be borne in mind that the angles pitched through, given above, do not measure the inclination of the ship to the surface of the water, but only her inclination to the true vertical. Pitching and lifting are produced by the vessel endeavouring to follow the slope of the waves, or, roughly speaking, to keep her displacement the same as in still water, both as to volume and to longitudinal distribution.

' " As to the depressing effect of the water on the bow, a layer of water one foot deep over the entire forecastle exerts a pressure of 65 tons ; this will produce a change of trim of eleven inches, together with an increase in the mean draught of $1\frac{3}{4}$ inch ; i.e. the draught of water forward will be increased by $7\frac{1}{4}$ inches, while that aft will be diminished by $3\frac{3}{4}$ inches. A layer two feet thick will have double this effect ; one three feet thick will have treble this effect, and so on up to a considerable angle. This follows from the fact that the front slope of the longitudinal curve of stability, up to a considerable angle, is very nearly straight. Hence the effect, even of a large body of water passing over the forecastle, tending to make the vessel dive down head foremost, is small, and of no importance. It modifies, however, the transverse stability. When proceeding head to sea there was no appreciable rolling motion. With the wind and sea on the bow she pitched considerably less than when going head to sea, but rolled through 5° or 6°. With the wind and sea abeam, lying passively in the trough of the waves, the maximum angle rolled through was 14° from port to starboard, $6\frac{1}{2}$° to windward, and $7\frac{1}{2}$° to leeward, and this without perceptible pitching. When, however, proceeding at about $7\frac{1}{2}$ knots, with the wind and sea on her quarter, she rolled through $27\frac{1}{2}$° from port to starboard, 13° off the perpendicular to windward, and $14\frac{1}{2}$° off the perpendicular to leeward, besides also pitching through some 4° or 5°. This is by far the greatest angle she has ever rolled through. It is the apparent period of the waves, i.e., their period relatively to the ship, which operates in making a vessel roll. The motions of the vessel both as to pitching and lifting and to rolling, were extremely easy. She indeed claims to have behaved better than her companion, the 'Agincourt.' Certainly, her rolling motion was somewhat slower, and she rolled less deeply ; when the 'Agincourt' was rolling 17° from port to starboard the 'Devastation' was only rolling 14°. As to pitching, the 'Devastation' may fairly claim to have had the advantage, for, as we have seen, although the 'Agincourt' pitched rather less, her bow moved vertically through a greater distance, so much so that while going head to sea at seven knots she shipped a sea over her high forecastle, showing that she could not be driven under the circumstances at a much higher speed with at least anything like comfort. The behaviour of the vessel generally accorded, with considerable approximation, with what was to be expected under the circumstances from the theoretical knowledge possessed on the subject, and although on no occasion during the trials were the waves quite so long as was wished for, the data obtained have been most valuable in testing and correcting the theory, so that the behaviour of this ship, or of any similar ship, in any weather, may now be foretold with considerable accuracy. The instruments for measuring and recording the behaviour of the vessel were most perfect in their action. They were personally attended throughout the trials by their inventor, Mr. Froude."

'The "Devastation" in 1879 returned from a commission in the Mediterranean. Admiral Inglefield thus spoke of her at a public meeting in London :—" I have just returned from Malta, and I saw the 'Devastation,' having come into port from a long cruise. The captain spoke of the ship as being perfectly seaworthy, wholesome, and comfortable for the men and officers, and everything he could wish."'

The machinery of the 'Devastation' has recently undergone a thorough overhaul by Messrs. John Penn and Sons, the original contractors. On the completion of the repairs, the ship was taken out for a seven hours' trial with the following mean results :—

Steam in boilers, 25·1 lbs.; vacuum, starboard, 22·6 inches; port, 26·02 inches; revolutions, 73 per minute; mean pressure, starboard, 17·56; port, 18·10; indicated horse-power, 2548·17 starboard, 2607·25 port—total, 5155·42. The consumption of coal was 3·15 lbs. per unit of horse-power per hour. The speed of the vessel by cross-bearings was thirteen knots. The working of the machinery was perfect; and although driven for seven hours at the highest speed, no water service was required, nor was there any sign of hot bearings or of any of the casualties and drawbacks so common on protracted trials of machinery. The boilers, which were put on board in 1871, gave a good supply of steam without any signs of priming. The high reputation of Messrs. Penn has been fully sustained by the results of the trials, and it would be impossible for machinery to be better fitted in all respects or to work more satisfactorily.

Simultaneously with the repair of her machinery by the contractors, this turret-ship has undergone an extensive refit. Her armament of four 35-ton guns has been supplemented by six of the new Nordenfeldt guns, which will be fired from the flying-deck, every position being commanded by at least two of these machine guns. A Gatling gun has been also fitted to be fired from the crow's-nest, while another weapon of the same formidable character can be carried to any part of the ship which is best suited to meet the special circumstances of an attack. The ammunition for these guns amounts to 480 cases, or eighty cases per gun, each case containing 600 rounds.

In order to afford a still further means of repulsing night attacks, two electric lamps have been fitted on prominent positions on platforms at the fore and after ends of the hurricane deck. Unlike any apparatus of the kind hitherto introduced into the service, these lights are adapted to burn simultaneously and to illuminate every part of the horizon. But while the 'Devastation' has been enabled to withstand the assaults of torpedo craft by increasing her powers of defence, the advisability of providing her with additional means of meeting the attack by a counter attack has not been lost sight of. The necessary alterations have accordingly been made whereby she will be able to carry a supplementary steam-cutter, suitable alike for purposes of patrol and torpedo warfare.

The 10-inch armour-plates on the breastwork have been pierced for ejecting Whitehead torpedoes, of which twelve will be carried.

Improvements have been made in the sanitary and ventilating arrangements of the ship, the former having been particularly defective during the late commission. At each side one of the coal-bunker shoots has been utilised for the passage of hot air from the engine-room, and during the trial the uprush was to the extent of 1,000 cubic feet per minute.

The merits and defects of the 'Devastation' have been impartially set forth by M. Dislère, in *La Guerre d'Escadre*. The ship is effectively protected, the armour, which is twelve inches in thickness at the water-line, being impenetrable by guns of less than twenty tons, even under the most favourable conditions for attack, 'that is to say at a normal to the surface of the plate, at point-blank range. The deck, covered with 3-inch plates, is more effectively protected than in the great ernumber of ironclads. The upper edge of the armour-belt, however, near the bow, is level with the water-line, and as the superstructure which surmounts it is empty, projectiles of small calibre might penetrate at a certain height, and cause the forward compart-

M. Dislère on the 'Devastation.'

ments to be flooded with water, which rises, when the ship is steaming, to the level of the upper deck. The result must be to cause an alteration of trim, which would gravely impair the steering qualities of the ship.'

The armament, composed of 35-ton guns, mounted in turrets, commanding nearly the whole horizon, and firing, whether ahead or astern, a volley of 1,200 lbs., and on the broadside, a volley of double that weight, is powerful, and can be worked with the utmost facility. It has been found by experiment that it is possible to fire in line with the keel in both directions, and with 14° 10′ of elevation and 3° 10′ of depression. To pass from the extreme elevation to the extreme depression, an interval of thirteen minutes was required. The superstructure easily withstood the effects of the firing, the only injury caused being that the deck was scored by powder which had not been burned.

Finally, the greatest element of offensive power, the facility for ramming, is satisfactorily secured in the 'Devastation.' At full speed both engines going ahead, the full circle, with a diameter of 339 yards, was completed in 4 minutes 34 seconds. With one engine stopped, the time was reduced to 4 minutes 7 seconds, and the diameter of the circle to 261 yards. The extreme inclination did not exceed three degrees.

In the discussion on Mr. Barnaby's paper on unmasted seagoing ships, at the Institution of Naval Architects, according to the *Times* of April 3, 1873, Sir E. J. Reed stated his objections to the alterations as follows :—

Sir E.
Reed on
the altera-
tions in the
'Devasta-
tion.' 'If I had been at the Admiralty and had been compelled to carry the "Devastation's" side up for the purpose of appeasing the apprehensions of certain gentlemen, I should have preferred to have taken the breastwork out, taking down the breastwork as it was. I should have done it for this reason—that the idea and conception of this ship was that she would be without compromise in her fighting powers. But as she is now built, I dislike immensely the idea of a shell coming in, exploding on the outside of this breastwork, and blowing up all the light iron structure in front of the guns.'

M. Dislère's comparison of 'Devastation' with broadside ships.

In *La Guerre d'Escadre*, M. Dislère makes an elaborate comparison between the 'Devastation' and some of the most powerful vessels of that date, including the 'Alexandra,' 'Téméraire,' 'Custozza,' 'Tegetthoff,' and 'Kaiser.' The 'Devastation' alone carries 12-inch guns. She has an immense advantage over every central-battery ship in the bow and stern fire. The facilities for training her guns are far beyond those of any ship armed on the broadside.

The armour-plating is twelve inches, while it is reduced to eleven inches on the 'Téméraire' and less than ten on the 'Kaiser' and 'Deutschland.' The displacement required to secure these advantages is 9,640 tons, or nearly the same as that of the 'Alexandra,' exceeding by 1,000 tons that of the 'Téméraire,' and by 1,500 tons that of the 'Kaiser.' The difference is considerable and proportionately costly, but the price paid for the increased fighting strength is not excessive. The 'Devastation' class may claim to be regarded as most powerful vessels for coast-service, but not as ocean-cruisers. Their grave and insurmountable defect is their deficiency in what the French critic has designated by the term habitability.

In his latest work Mr. King says :—

'When the "Devastation" was first commissioned, she carried the most powerful guns afloat. The recent improvements in the power of guns may be best shown by a comparison between those of the "Devastation" and the Chinese gunboats hereafter described. Both carry 35-ton guns, but the weight of the pieces is the only feature which they have in common. The Woolwich 35-ton gun with which the "Devastation" is armed is twelve inches in calibre, and fires a projectile weighing, with the gas-check, 700 lbs., with a charge of 110 lbs., the muzzle velocity being 1,300 feet per second, and the total energy in foot-tons at the muzzle 8,200, representing an energy of 218 tons per inch of circumference or penetrating power. The Armstrong 35-ton gun,[1] on the other hand, is eleven inches in calibre, fires a charge of 235 lbs., and a projectile of 536 lbs., and possesses an initial velocity of 1,820, and a penetrating power of 358 foot-tons per inch of circumference. The difference is, consequently, important. It may be mentioned that the battering-charge of the "Devastation's" guns has been increased from 110 lbs. to 140 lbs., whereby a higher velocity and greater striking power are secured.'

The following tables give important details of the principal features of the ship :—

Mr. King on the guns of the 'Devastation.'

---

[1] With which the Chinese gunboats alluded to are armed.

Statement of Dimensions and other particulars of Her Majesty's ship 'Devastation,' as estimated at various dates, and as when ready for sea.

Dimensions, &c.	Estimate of April, 1869	Estimate of November, 1869	Estimate of January, 1871	Actual dimensions, &c., as completed in April, 1873.
Length between the perpendiculars .	285 feet	285 feet	285 feet	285 feet
Length of the keel for tonnage .	246 ft. 3⅜ in.	246 ft. 3⅜ in.	246 ft. 3⅜ in.	246 ft. 3⅜ in.
Breadth, extreme . . .	62 ft. 3 in.	62 ft. 3 in	62 ft. 3 in.	62 ft. 3 in.
Breadth, for tonnage . .	58 feet	58 feet	58 feet	58 feet
Depth in hold . . .	18 feet	18 feet	18 feet	18 feet
Burden, in tons . . .	4,406 57-94	4,406 57-94	4,406 57-94	4,406 57-94
Draught of water :—				
Forward	25 ft. 9 in.	25 ft. 9 in.	25 ft. 9 in.	26 ft. 3 in.
Aft	26 ft. 6 in.	26 ft. 6 in.	26 ft. 6 in.	27 ft. 1 in.
Mean	26 ft. 1½ in.	26 ft. 1½ in.	26 ft. 1½ in.	26 ft. 8 in.
Displacement, in tons . .	9,062	9,062	9,090	9,387
Area of midship section, in square feet .	1,449	1,449	1,454	1,487
Height of port sills from load water-line :—				
Fore turret . . .	13 ft. 6 in.	13 ft. 6 in.	13 ft. 6 in.	12 ft. 11 in.
A ter turret . . .	13 ft. 2 in.	13 ft. 2 in.	13 ft. 2 in.	12 ft. 7 in.
Height of upper deck at side from water-line :—				
Forward . . .	9 ft. 3 in.	9 ft. 3 in.	9 ft. 3 in.	8 ft. 6 in.
Amidships . . .	4 ft. 6 in.	4 ft. 6 in.	4 ft. 6 in.	10 ft. 9 in.
Engines :—				
Nominal horse-power . .	800	800	800	800
Indicated horse-power . .	5,600	5,600	5,600	6,650
Speed per hour, in knots . .	12 5	12·5	12·5	13·84
Coals, number of tons . .	1,700	1,600	1,600	1,350
Water :—				
Number of tons . .	16	16	16	30
Number of weeks' consumption .	2	2	2	3
Provisions :—				
Number of tons . .	9·5	9 5	9·5	19
Number of weeks' consumption .	4	4	4	6
Complement of men and officers .	250	250	250	329
Armament	six 25-ton guns	four 30-ton guns	four 35-ton guns	four 35-ton guns
Total weight of armour, in tons (including fastening)	2,307	2,329	2,482	2,581
Total weight of backing, in tons (including fastening) . . .	306	306	306	314
Depth of armour below water-line, amidships	5 feet	5 feet	5 feet	5 ft. 6½ in.
Height of armour above water-line :—				
On sides, amidships . .	4 ft. 2 in.	4 ft. 2 in.	4 ft. 2 in.	3 ft. 7½ in.
" forward . .	6 inches	6 inches	6 inches	nil.
On breastwork, amidships .	11 ft. 5 in.	11 ft. 5 in.	11 ft. 5 in.	10 ft. 10½ in.
" at fore end .	11 ft. 9 in.	11 ft. 9 in.	11 ft. 9 in.	10 ft. 2½ in.

Thickness of armour and backing :—	Armour	Backing	Armour	Backing	Armour	Backing	Armour	Backing
	Inches	Inches	Inches	Inches	Inches	Inches	Inches	Inches
On sides	12 & 10	18	12 & 10	18	12 & 10	18	12 & 10	18
On bulkheads at break of deck forward	12	16	12	16	12	16	12	16
On bulkheads in hold . .	—	—	4, 5, & 6	—	—	—	—	10
On breastwork . . .	12 & 10	18 & 16	12 & 10	18 & 16	12 & 10	18 & 16	12 & 10	18 & 16
On turrets . . .	14 & 12	15 & 17	14 & 12	15 & 17	14 & 12	15 & 17	14 & 12	15 & 17

Thickness of skin-plating behind armour :—				
On sides	1½ & 1¼	1½ & 1¼	1½ & 1¼	1½ & 1¼
On bulkheads at break of deck forward	1½	1½	1½	1½
On breastwork . . .	1¼	1¼	1¼	1¼
On turrets . . .	1¼	1¼	1¼	1¼
Thickness of deck plating :—				
On upper deck, amidship .	2	2	3	3
aft .	1¾	1¾	2	2
On belt-deck . . .	3 & 2½	3 & 2½	3	3
On deck over breastwork . .	1	1	1	2

Statement of Weights and other particulars of Her Majesty's ship 'Devastation.'

Weights, &c.	Estimate of April, 1869	Estimate of November, 1869	Estimate of January, 1871	Actual weights, &c., as completed in April, 1873
	Tons	Tons	Tons	Tons
Water for two weeks . . ⎫ Tare of tanks . . . ⎬	18·8	18·8	18·8	40·0
Provisions, spirits, &c., for four weeks ⎫ Tare of casks . . . ⎬	12·5	12·5	12·5	24·0
Officers' slops and stores . . ⎫ Tare of casks, boxes, cases, &c. . ⎬	12·0	12·0	12·0	12·0
Officers, men, and effects . . .	32·0	32·0	32·0	42·0
Mast and derrick for hoisting boats .	—	—	20·0	20·0
Cables	87·5	87·5	87·5	70·0
Anchors	25·0	25·0	25·0	23·5
Boats	12·0	12·0	12·0	12·0
Warrant officers' stores . . .	34·0	34·0	34·0	50·0
Armament . . . . ⎫ ⎬	355·0 four 25-ton guns	422·2 four 30-ton guns	512·2 four 35-ton guns	514·5 four 35-ton guns
Total weight of rigging, guns, and ship's stores . . .	588·8	656·0	766·0	808·0
Engines, and boilers with water in, including engines for turrets, ventilating and fire service, spare gear, &c. .	970·0	952·0	982·0	1,064·0
Engineers' stores	15·0	15·0	15·0	23·0
Coal	1700·0	1,600·0	1,600·0	1,350·0
Total weight of equipment to be received on board . .	3,273·8	3,223·0	3,363·0	3,245·0
Weight of hull	2,874·0	2,894·0	2,487·0	2,882·0 ¹
Weight of protective deck-plating, including glacis-plates and armoured skylights.	413·0	413·0	522·0	556·0
Weight of armour, exclusive of turret and pilot-tower armour . .	1,604·0	1,626·0	1,542·0	1,629·0
Weight of backing, exclusive of turret and pilot-tower backing . .	266·0	256·0	256·0	254·0
Weight of turrets	590·0	581·0	592·0	622·0
Weight of pilot-tower . . .	—	—	110·0	110·0
Weight of conning-hoods. . .	15·0	15·0	—	—
Total displacement required .	9,035·8	9,008·0	8,872·0	9,298·0
Total displacement per drawing .	9,062·0	9,062·0	9,090·0	9,298·0
Difference	26·2	4·0	218·0	Nil.

¹ This includes the superstructure added in January, 1871, and the additions recommended by the Committee on Designs.

Estimated consumption of coal in the 'Devastation,' at speeds of 10 and 12 knots.

	Speed of ten knots an hour		Speed of twelve knots an hour	
	Total distance steaming	Number of days' consumption	Total distance steaming	Number of days' consumption
	Knots	Days	Knots	Days
Coal carried, 1,600 to 1,700 tons : Statement in Mr. Reed's memorandum on new designs for ironclad ships, dated, March 2, 1869, page 311, report of Committee on Designs of Ships (printed for Parliament) . . .	4,320	18	2,880	10
Coal carried, 1,400 tons : Calculations based on results of measured-mile trial, October 31, 1872	4,580	19	2,890	10
Coal carried, 1,600 tons : Calculations based on results of measured-mile trial, October 31, 1872	5,236	21·8	3,300	11·5
Coal carried, 1,400 tons : Calculations based on six hours' trial, April 15, 1873 . .	4,876	20·31	3,109	10·79
Coal carried, 1,600 tons : Calculations based on six hours' trial, April 15, 1873 . .	5,572	23·21	3,553	12·33

 Except for coast-defence, the Russian fleet is rather numerous than powerful. The 'Peter the Great' and the 'Minin' are the only two vessels on the list of seagoing armoured ships which approach the modern standard of fighting efficiency. The 'Peter the Great was designed after the British ship 'Devastation,' and commenced before the sea trials of that vessel; subsequently modifications were made, and, as completed in 1875, she somewhat resembles the 'Dreadnought.'

Figs. 222 and 223.

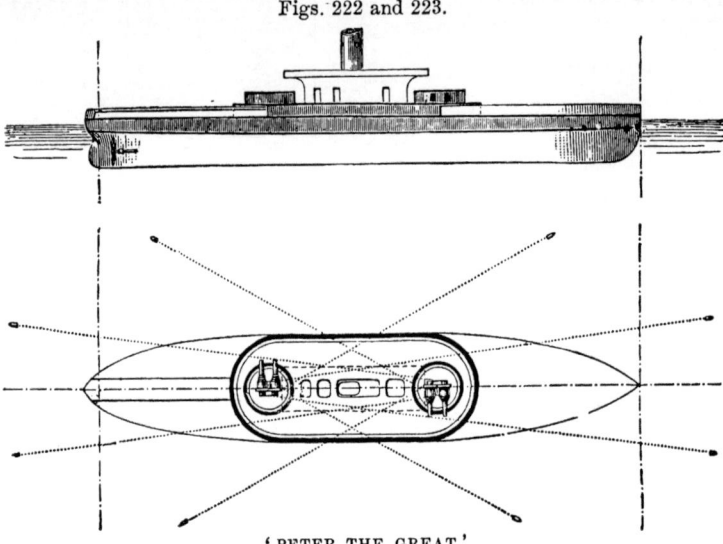

'PETER THE GREAT.'

The 'Peter the Great' has the following principal dimensions, etc. :—

Length between perpendiculars	.	321 ft. 10 in.
„ at load water-line	.	329 ft. 10 in.
Beam, including armour	.	63 ft. 3 in.
Load draught of water, forward	.	22 ft. 9 in.
„ „ aft	.	24 ft. 9 in.
Load displacement, tons	.	9,665
Complement of officers and men	.	315
Armament:—		
In turrets . . .	.	two 12-in. (39¾-ton guns)
		two 12-in. (36½-ton guns)
On deck . . .	.	two 9-inch mortars
		seven small guns
		two Engstrom guns
Maximum indicated horse-power	.	8,000
Actual speed at measured mile	.	10 knots

The hull is of iron, and there is an inner bottom; the system of construction is cellular. The sides are protected with 14-inch solid armour tapering to ten inches forward and eight inches abaft. The height of the side armour above load water-line is ten feet amidships, two feet forward, and three feet aft. Forward and amidships the side armour is carried five feet, and aft it is carried about four feet below the water-line. The thickness of armour on the breastwork is fourteen inches in a single plate. The turret armour is composed of two 7-inch plates 'sandwich' fashion, with hollow stringers in the backing. The deck armour over the breastwork is composed of two layers of $\frac{3}{4}$-inch plates ; over the iron belt it is three inches thick. The glacis plates are of cast brass with one-inch iron on top. The ship carries two hinged spars for torpedoes forward. The cost of the hull was $4\frac{1}{2}$ million roubles ; that of the machinery nearly one million, say 730,000l. in all.

The machinery consists of two engines, each of 700 nominal horse-power, driving two four-bladed screws. Stowage is provided for 1,200 tons of coal, and the consumption is 135 tons in 24 hours. At the reduced speed of nine knots the consumption does not exceed seventy tons, and the supply of coal would suffice for a distance of 3,700 miles. There are 48 furnaces. The ship's complement is sometimes put as high as 374 all told.

The *Pall Mall Gazette* writes as follows :—'The great Russian Speed. ironclad turret-ship " Peter the Great," which Mr. Reed frightened us so much about a year or two ago, has just taken her trial trip at Cronstadt ; and as the vessel is at last afloat and ready for sea it is worth while to examine how she compares in speed and general fighting power with our latest ironclads of similar model, the " Dreadnought," the " Thunderer," and the " Devastation." This last-named is the only one which has as yet been put in commission, and it is satisfactory to observe that in speed at least—one of the most important points in these days —she is far superior to her Russian rival. During her trial at Cronstadt the " Peter the Great " only made $12\frac{2}{3}$ knots an hour, and although it is stated that the trial was most satisfactory, and that she can easily accomplish thirteen knots, those who have watched the doings of our own vessels at the measured mile are well aware that the results obtained there are very rarely surpassed on actual service. If the " Peter the Great " can average twelve knots at sea, her designers may think themselves very lucky. The " Devastation," on the other hand, after having been for some time in commission, steamed about three months ago from Malta to Smyrna in forty-eight hours, or at the rate of $14\frac{1}{4}$ knots an hour all the way —nearly two knots more than the " Peter the Great " could achieve under far more favourable circumstances. In point of armament and thickness of armour-plating the two vessels are almost identical, and the extra 600 tons displacement of the " Peter the Great," due to her 37 feet greater length, is apparently of very little advantage to her. It is evident, therefore, that the " Devastation," being equal in other respects and superior in speed, would be very well able to hold her own with the Russian vessel. Her sister ship, the " Thunderer," being more power-fully armed with two 38-ton and two 35-ton guns, instead of four 35-ton guns, would be a still more formidable antagonist. As to the " Dreadnought," she is considerably larger than the " Peter the Great," carries four 38-ton guns, and, as her steam-power is more than 30 per cent. in excess of either the " Devastation " or the " Thunderer," it is probable that she will be at least as fast as the former vessel, and is certainly, on the whole, the most dangerous ironclad afloat at the present time. In an estimate of first-class ironclads in the *Revue Coloniale et Maritime*, putting the " Inflexible at 100, the " Dread-nought " is rated at 72, the " Peter the Great," at 71, and the " Thunderer " and " Devastation " at 65 and 63 respectively. But the relative power of the " Peter the Great " is much over-estimated by these figures; and if half the stories which are told of the Russian dockyards are true, her construction is defective in many important particulars.'

Comparison with 'Devastation.' It will be interesting to carry still further the comparison of the ' Peter the Great ' with the ' Devastation.' The two ships are con-fessedly rival designs. As may be seen by consulting the list of armoured ships, the dimensions of both vessels are nearly alike. The displacement of the ' Devastation,' when fully equipped, is 9,298 tons, that of the ' Peter the Great ' is 9,665 tons. The indicated horse-power and speed are represented to be equal, while the armour and armament of the ' Peter the Great ' are superior to those of the ' Devastation.' The hull of the latter vessel is protected by 12-inch plates, with eighteen inches of teak backing, and an inner skin of $1\frac{1}{2}$-inch plating. This armour is capable of resisting a projectile striking with a force of 140 foot-tons per inch of circumference. The ' Peter the Great ' is protected by 14-inch plates, resting on ten inches of teak, with hollow stringers in the backing, which are alleged to give an additional resistance, equivalent to two inches of iron, and an inner skin of 3-inch plates. This armour is capable of resisting a projectile striking with a force of 240 foot-tons per inch of circum-ference. The turrets of the ' Devastation' are protected with 14-inch armour, with seventeen inches of teak backing, and an inner skin of $1\frac{1}{2}$-inch plating. The turrets of the ' Peter the Great' are plated with 14-inch armour on fourteen inches of teak, with an inner skin of 3-inch plating. The resisting power of the turrets of the 'Devastation' is equal to 180 foot-tons; that of the 'Peter the Great' turret is equal to 210 foot-tons per inch of circumference.

The armament of the 'Devastation' consists of four 12-inch, 35-ton, Woolwich muzzle-loading guns. The weight of the charge of powder is 121 lbs., that of the projectile 660 lbs. The 'Peter the Great' carries in the turrets four 12-inch breech-loading guns, two of 37 and two of 39 tons, firing a powder-charge of from 130 to 160 lbs., and projectiles weighing 730 lbs.

The central battery of the ' Peter the Great ' is formed, like that of the 'Dreadnought,' by the extension upwards of the armoured belt. The ship is not fitted with a ram.

The deck of the ' Peter the Great ' was awash, fore and aft, in the seas of very moderate height which are encountered in the Gulf of Finland.

In the second edition of his work, Mr. King refers to reports from correspondents, as representing the ' Peter the Great ' to be less successful than had been anticipated. During the winter of 1876–77, when the ship was icebound in the harbour of Cronstadt, and exposed to an atmospheric temperature of from ten to forty degrees below zero (Fahrenheit), the crews were employed in gun-practice. When the ice broke up, and the ship was ordered to cruise, it was found that the hull leaked to a very considerable extent, and that the steam cylinders were cracked, the damage having been caused by vibration from the firing during the time that the iron in the hull and machinery had been under the influence of very low temperature. After being subjected to another trial on the measured mile, the vessel was docked. It is said that the makers of the engines will have to replace the fractured cylinder-covers, an operation which will cost at least 10,000*l.*

A correspondent of the *Times,* writing on the condition of the Russian ironclads, says, with regard to the ' Peter the Great ': ' She is so weak that if driven through the water at a speed greater than eight knots, she shakes to such a degree as to leak in an alarming manner. Although the extent of her longest voyage is the distance between Cronstadt and Revel, her boilers are already under repair, and a commission which was lately assembled to examine her has expressed an opinion that all the large steam-pipes should be renewed. As to her present capabilities, for either offensive or defensive purposes, it is sufficient to say that when her heavy guns are fired rivet-heads fly about unpleasantly. I think I have said enough about this ironclad, the pride of the Russian Navy.'

The *Broad Arrow* observes that 'A ship which can only be steered in the calmest weather, and which even then lets in water " like a sieve," is not of much use as a war-vessel. When to this are added the unfortunate peculiarities that she cannot keep the sea in rough weather, that she is uninhabitable on account of the heat, and that her guns cannot be fired without rupturing her engines, it is evident that the enthusiasm which she has aroused has been entirely wasted.'

In the *Times* of October 18, 1880, we read :—' The *Glasgow News* states that the Russian Ministry of Marine have been so well pleased with the result produced by the engines of the " Livadia," that they have concluded a contract with Messrs. John Elder and Co. for the supply of new engines for their largest armourclad, the " Peter the Great." These engines, which are to be of 7,000 indicated horse-power, are to replace those now on board the " Peter the Great," supplied from Baird's works, St. Petersburg.' It has been reported since that she has arrived in the Clyde for her new machinery.

'Thunderer.' The following description of the 'Thunderer' is reprinted from Mr. King's first work : —

' The " Thunderer " is a sister ship to the " Devastation," and was launched on March 12, 1872, nearly one year after the " Devastation," but was only being prepared for her first commission at the end of 1876. The principal dimensions of the two vessels are alike; they differ only in some details of construction, in the type of propelling machinery, and in armament.

' The " Thunderer," like her sister ship, was designed to be thoroughly seagoing, and to be capable of performing every service which can be required from a first-class modern line-of-battle ship.

' At the date of their construction they were admitted to be the most powerful fighting-ships then laid down. The Committee on the Designs of Ships of the Royal Navy gave their judgment upon them in these words : " They represent in their broad features the first-class fighting ships of the immediate future."

Machinery. ' The " Thunderer," in common with all modern fighting ships, is operated upon in every essential particular by the power of steam. The motive power of the ship is steam, and she contains in all twenty-eight steam-engines and nine boilers. Thirteen of these engines are in pairs, having two cylinders, and the remaining fifteen are single engines, having one cylinder only. Two of the pairs are employed for driving the twin screws, and are termed the propelling engines.

The others are small engines, employed for subsidiary purposes, such
as revolving the turrets, working the hydraulic gun-machinery,
hoisting shot and shell, working the capstans, hoisting anchors and
boats, working the steering apparatus, working pumps for circulating
cold water through the surface condensers, starting the propelling
engines, pumping water from the spaces between the double bottoms,
feeding the boilers, hoisting ashes, and driving fans for ventilating

Figs. 224, 225, and 226.

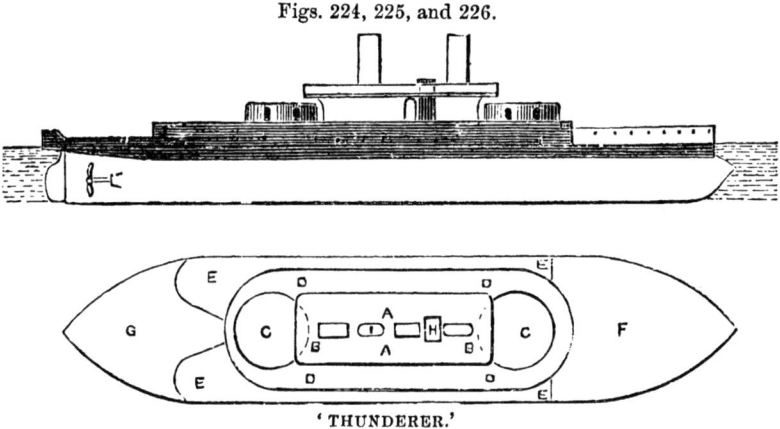

'THUNDERER.'

A, Flying-deck; B, Funnels; C, Turrets; D, Breastwork; E, F, Superstructure
G, Deck.

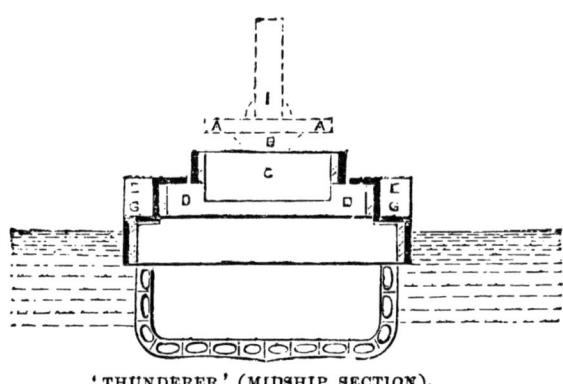

'THUNDERER' (MIDSHIP SECTION).

the ship. In addition to having the great responsibility for all this
machinery and its efficient working, the engineering department of
the ship is charged with the care of all the watertight doors, and all
the valves and pipes in the ship. In short, the interior of the ship
is a vast engineering workshop, requiring great skill and energy to
manage it successfully.

'The propelling machinery of this vessel, as well as that of the

" Devastation," was contracted for previous to the introduction of the compound engine into the Royal Navy. It was constructed by Messrs. Humphreys, Tennant and Co., and is of the horizontal, direct-acting type adopted by that firm, and fitted in several other ships of the navy. There is one pair to each of the two screw-propellers; the cylinders being 77 inches in diameter, and the stroke 3 ft. 6 in. The boilers are of the old box type. In consequence of the explosion of one of the boilers in July 1876, the final official trials at the measured mile were somewhat delayed. The mean indicated horse-power was 6,270, and the speed 13·4 knots per hour.

'Two days after the measured-mile trials on January 4, 1877, a crucial test of the working of the machinery was made by a six hours' continuous full-power run up and down the Solent in boisterous weather, the force of the wind being between 7 and 9, and the sea rough. The following was the mean result of the twelve half-hour performances :—

Pressure in boilers	27·8 lbs.
Vacuum, starboard forward engine . .	27·3 inches
„ starboard after engine . . .	25·79 inches
„ port forward engine . . .	27·99 inches
„ port after engine . . .	25·52 inches
Revolutions per minute, starboard .	75·20
„ port . . .	75·03
Pressure in cylinders per square inch, starboard	19·491 lbs.
„ „ port .	19·25 lbs.
Indicated horse-power, 5,748·97, or 149 horse-power beyond the contract.	

'The best quality of Nixon's steam-navigation coal was used in these trials, and the expenditure was at the rate of 3·14 lbs. per indicated horse-power per hour.

Armament. 'The "Thunderer" was originally fitted, like the "Devastation," with two 35-ton, 12-inch, Woolwich rifled guns in each of the two turrets, mounted on carriages similar to those of the "Glatton," and known as Captain Scott's design; but after Messrs. Armstrong had brought out their system for working heavy guns by hydraulic power, it was decided to introduce it for the first time into the forward turret of this vessel. Accordingly the two 35-ton guns were removed, and guns 38 tons in weight, having a bore of 12 [1] inches, were substituted. The same carriages were retained. When this was written, all the machinery for working these guns had been fitted on board and subjected to the first tests; but as deficiencies usually experienced in new and untried machinery were expected to be developed, no

[1] All other 38-ton Woolwich (M.L.R.) guns have a calibre of 12½ inches.

reports were permitted to be made. Yet it was confidently stated, upon reliable authority, that the result of this first trial on board ship was satisfactory; a proof of which may be found in the fact that the system has been adopted and ordered for the "Dreadnought,"

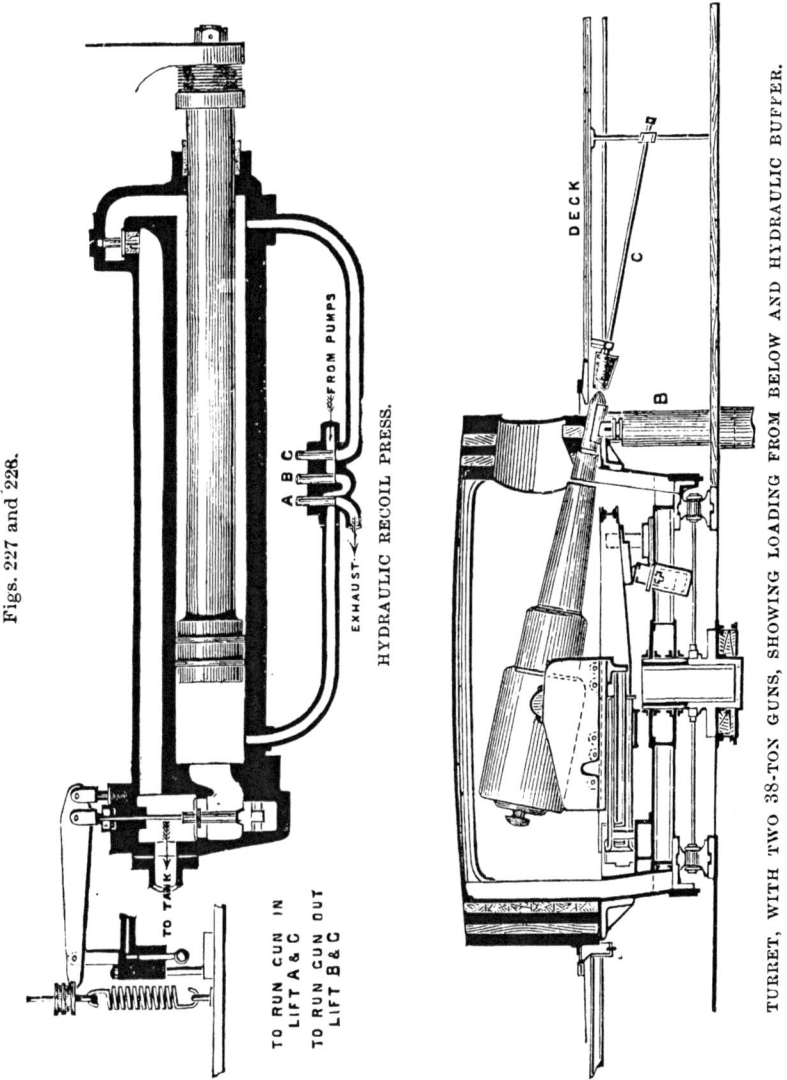

" Inflexible," and other vessels. All British service gun-carriages are at present mounted on their slides in such a manner as to recoil on a dead bearing, but to run out on wheels thrown into action by eccentrics. By placing the carriage permanently on wheels, and trusting more to the compressor to arrest recoil, the operation of "tripping" the carriage, *i.e.* of throwing the wheels into action for running out, is avoided. In 1867 and 1868 a partial muzzle-pivoting carriage was made at the Elswick Works for an 18-ton gun, on the plan of raising and lowering the trunnion-bearings of the gun in vertical grooves formed in the carriage. Captain Scott modified the arrangement by the substitution of hydraulic jacks, in combination with chocks for the screw-lifting gear, and by the application of the jacks to act from fixed positions in the slide or turret-floor on a bow-piece carrying the trunnions. In this form the system has been applied for working heavy turret-guns in the British Navy. It makes the carriage, however, high and topheavy, a disadvantage for naval service which would become more serious with every increase in the weight of guns. The object of muzzle-pivoting is the reduction of the size of the ports. The size of ordnance, however, continues to increase with rapid strides, while the number of men employed to work the guns cannot be much further added to ; and the train of mechanism required to apply the constant and limited power of men to the forces to be exerted in loading and working heavy guns becomes larger and more complicated as the weight of the guns is increased. Hence, the adoption of some inanimate power in the place of mere hand-labour for loading and working heavy ordnance has become an absolute necessity for existing guns, and for those of the immediate future. Adopting the steam-engine as the most ready and convenient source of power, it has been found that that power can be best applied through the medium of water-pressure. The simplicity and compactness of hydraulic machinery, and the perfect control it gives over the motion of heavy weights, especially adapt it for the purpose. Power sufficient for the heaviest guns may be transmitted by water through a very small pipe for long distances and by intricate ways, so that a steam pumping engine may supply power by this means for working many guns.

Hydraulic machinery for working the guns in the fore turret of the 'Thunderer.'
'The fore turret of the "Thunderer" is 31 ft. 3 in. in external diameter, and weighs, including its armament, about 406 tons. It is made to revolve by a steam-engine placed on the hydraulic-room flat, but controlled from within as well as from without the turret. In the arrangement for working the guns they are mounted on their trunnions on wrought-iron carriages, which latter run on wrought-iron slides pivoted at their ends farthest from the muzzle, and at their muzzle ends supported on standards having steps of three different heights, to any one of which the muzzle ends of the slides may be adjusted. Thus there may be given to the gun-carriage,

and therefore to the gun, an inclination which is in addition to, or in subtraction from, as the case may be, the elevation or depression given by the elevating gear on the gun-carriage. This arrangement enables the gun to be elevated or depressed through a large range without involving excessive height in the ports through which the gun is fired. Each gun-carriage is connected by a pendant piece to the rod of a piston which works in a horizontal hydraulic cylinder, placed between the beams forming the slides on which the carriage runs.

' This cylinder performs the double office of checking recoil and moving the gun in or out along the slide. The gun on recoil drives back the piston, and is arrested by the resistance which a valve offers to the escape from the cylinder. This valve is loaded with a spring, which may be adjusted to give any required resistance, and so meet the variations of the force of recoil. It is also partly balanced to lessen the load required upon it. The area of the piston-rod is one-half that of the piston, and the gun is run out by admitting the water-pressure to both sides at once. For running the gun in, the pressure is admitted to the front of the piston only, the exhaust being at the same time opened to the rear. Clack-valves, in connection with a waste-water tank, are used to insure the cylinder being always full, and there is a relief-valve on the front for preventing any excessive strain. On the rear the recoil valve acts as a relief-valve when required. It will happen in some cases that the pressure required on the valve to arrest recoil falls short of that necessary for running the gun in or out, in which case the water admitted to the cylinder for the purpose would lift the valve and escape to waste. This is provided for by making the act of opening the cylinder inlet-valve place an additional load on the recoil valve, retaining it there so long as the inlet-valve remains open. An extra load can be placed on the recoil valve by a small inverted press, having in its normal condition an open communication with the waste-water tank, which communication is closed and the press charged with water under pressure by the first movement of the lever employed to open the inlet-valve of the recoil-cylinder. It was stated that the recoil could be regulated with precision, and that excellent control could be exercised over the movement of the gun on its slide. By the arrangements described the following advantages are claimed : The loading operation is transferred from a confined space in the port of the turret to a roomy and convenient place on the main deck. The dimensions of the turret can be reduced ; four men in the turret, and one outside may direct and control all the movements of a pair of the heaviest guns, and may load and fire them without other help than that involved in bringing up the ammunition; and, finally, far greater rapidity of fire is attainable than would be possible by manual labour.

'When the guns are being fired, ten persons are generally within the fore turret, and in the case of the after turret, where the two 35-ton guns are worked by hand, there are as many as twenty-two persons in the turret. The turret is provided with two ports, above the level of the breastwork or upper deck, through which the muzzles of the guns are run out to be fired. Immediately below these two ports are two other ports, or tubes, made through the wall of the turret and inclined downward, so that, when, by the elevating gear on the carriages, the guns are elevated at the breach and depressed at the muzzle, these tubes will form prolongations of the bore. The outer, or the lower, ends of the inclined tubes are immediately below the breastwork and open into the battery-deck, situated next below the upper deck. It is from the battery-deck that the guns are loaded, the loading being done by pushing the charge, the projectile, and the wad up the inclined tubes and bores of the guns by hydraulic pressure, which gives about 750 lbs. on the square inch to drive the rammer up the bore.

'Besides the two inclined tubes or ports mentioned, there are in the turret two entrance ports by which access is obtained to the turret from the battery-deck, and two other ports which were made for the passage of ammunition to the guns when the armament of the fore turret was to have consisted of two 35-ton guns, loaded by hand from within the turret itself, as in the after turret.

'Two sets of loading apparatus have been provided, placed, respectively, at an angle of about 33° on each side of the midship longitudinal line and aft of the turret. By this arrangement the travel of the turret from the firing position to one of the loading positions need never exceed 147°; besides, in the event of one apparatus being deranged, the other may be used. Each hydraulic loading apparatus of each set consists of a vertically rising platform which receives a trolley, supporting, at the proper inclination, the projectile. This trolley is raised by water pressure so that the projectile is immediately opposite one of the inclined loading-tubes, which, as before stated, are in continuation of the bore of the guns when these are depressed through the 13° required for loading. Immediately in the rear of the trolley platform, and placed in the prolongation of an imaginary line passing through the centre of the gun and tube, is fixed an inclined hydraulic cylinder, containing within it a plunger-rammer which is, by water pressure, forced out of its cylinder and run up the bore of the gun, driving the projectile off the trolley and up the bore. This plunger is in two lengths, which work one within the other telescopically.

'The outer end of the outer joint of the telescopic plunger carries the rammer-head, which is surrounded by a sponge and is provided with a small valve in communication with the water pressure, and is ingeniously arranged to admit water when required to sponge the gun.

'The mode in which the loading apparatus is used is as follows: Method of The gun having been fired, the turret is revolved to the nearer of loading and firing. the two loading positions, and the guns are depressed (which operation goes on simultaneously with that of the revolving of the turret) until the muzzle of each gun is in a line with the loading tube; then, the turret and the gun (as hereafter explained) being locked, the signal is made, by a tell-tale worked from within the turret, "Sponge and load." This signal being received, the lever is moved, the water pressure forces the rammer-head and sponge to the breach end of the bore, and the contact of the pin of the small valve with the breach end opens the valve, allowing the water to escape into the gun. The rammer-lever is now reversed, and the rammer-head is withdrawn clear out of the gun. The cartridge is then lifted by hand into the mouth of the inclined loading-tube, the trolley-lever is moved to raise the projectile, a *papier-mâché* disc-wad is put on the front of the rammer, and the rammer-lever being once more moved, the rammer forces the wad, the projectile, and the cartridge home in the gun. The rammer-lever is once more reversed, and the rammer is thereby brought out of the gun, which is now loaded, and is ready to be raised, and, on the unlocking of the turret, to be revolved into the desired position for firing. With respect to the locking of the turret, it should be stated that there are two bolts to each turret, one is an hydraulic locking-bolt, controlled by a lever within the turret, and so constructed that on being protruded to lock the turret it will, on approaching either one of the two positions in which the turret should be locked for loading, endeavour to arrest the turret at such position; but, if the momentum of the turret should be considerable, this bolt will yield, and will allow the turret to pass some little distance beyond the proper position. The position having been reached, and by the action of the hydraulic locking-bolt, without shock, a second bolt, the dead-lock bolt, worked from the battery-deck, effectually locks the turret.

'The annexed drawing shows a plan of the turret with the guns in the firing position; also the positions in which the guns are fixed when being loaded.

'In firing the fore-turret guns, the operations are as follows:
Assume the gun to have been hydraulically loaded from the battery-
deck, as already described, and the "dead-lock" bolt to have been
removed, the signal, "gun loaded," is given by the tell-tale from that
deck to those within the turret as soon as each gun is loaded. When
both of these signals have been received, the hydraulic bolt is un-
locked and the captain of the turret, by means of a hand-wheel

Fig. 229.

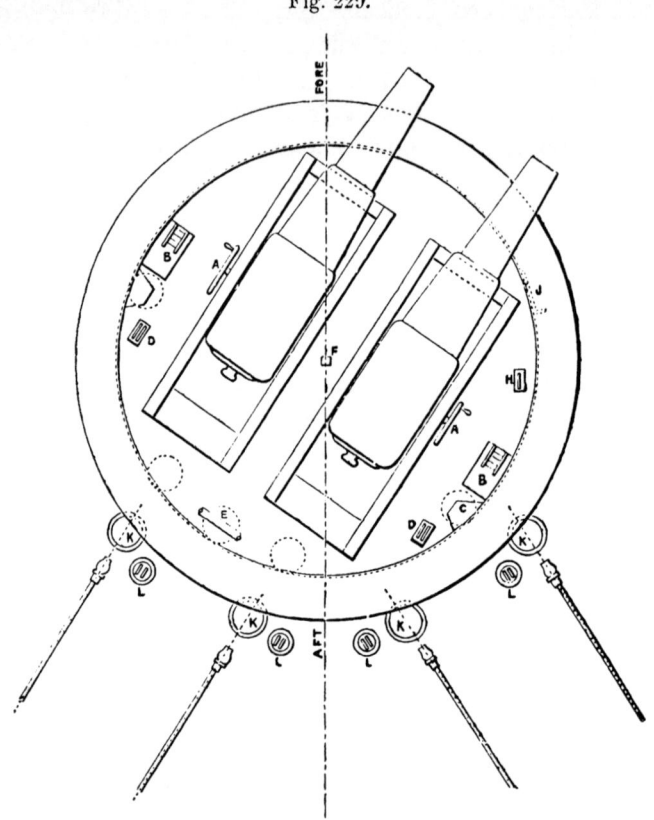

'THUNDERER' (FORE TURRET; FIRING POSITION; BOTH GUNS RUN OUT).

A, Elevating wheels; B, Entrance ports; C, Officer; D, Gun-working valves;
    E, Captain of turret; F, Dial; H, Locking-bolt valve; J, Dead-lock;
    K, Hoists; L, Valves.

within the turret, sets the steam-engine in motion, so as to cause
the turret to revolve in either direction he desires; while this is
being done, No. 1, the captain of the gun, works the elevating gear
so as to raise the gun from the inclined loading position, and on this
being complete, No. 2, who stands at the hydraulic lever, moves it
so as to run the gun out: the gun is then elevated for the required

distance; Nos. 2 and 3 make ready for firing by putting the tube into the vent, and by coupling up the wires or the lanyards (as the case may be) to the firing apparatus. The guns having by the revolution of the turret been brought to bear on the object aimed at, the captain of the turret or of the gun fires it, unless indeed the firing is done electrically from the conning-tower. As soon as the gun is fired, it is run in by the recoil and by the action of the hydraulic cylinder, put into operation by No. 4 reversing his lever.

'When the guns are run in, and even while they are running in, the captain of the turret sets the engine to work to revolve it to the more convenient of the two loading apparatuses, while No. 4 stands by the hydraulic locking-bolt to arrest the motion of the turret at the proper place. The muzzle of the gun is once more depressed into the loading position, and, by the action of the lever of the hydraulic cylinder, is run forward until it is close up to and fair with the loading-tubes in the turret, and in that position is locked to the tube by a stud on the face of the muzzle, ready to be once more sponged out and to be reloaded as soon as the turret is dead-locked.

'There are electrical arrangements by which all the guns in the two turrets can be fired simultaneously from the conning-tower. There are also means by which the guns may be fired either in pairs or independently without the use of electricity: these latter modes of firing are effected in the turrets themselves. Whether the fire be electrical or by hand, it operates on the charge in the gun through the medium of the tube, which may be either an electric or a percussion tube, placed in the vent of the gun.

'An objection raised to this system is the alleged liability to premature explosions in loading, and, as a consequence, the risk of self-destruction to which the ship is thought to be exposed. This objection is, however, it is said, obviated by not depressing the gun for loading to such an extent as to aim a shot below the water-line, and furthermore provided for by a special arrangement for drenching the bore of the gun with water in sponging, and it is entirely removed by the arrangement that has been applied to the "Inflexible," in which the loading-gear is placed so that the gun is little depressed when in the loading position.'

The melancholy details of the catastrophe which occurred on board the 'Thunderer' in the Gulf of Ismid, need not be narrated here. The lessons to be drawn from the disaster will be set forth more appropriately in the special chapter on guns.

The 'Dreadnought' is one of the three mastless vessels which were proposed by Mr. Childers, but though belonging to the same

The 'Dreadnought.'

type as the 'Devastation' and the 'Thunderer,' she differs from them in some very important particulars—the results of growing experience —and exhibits in a concrete shape the steady development which is being made in modern ships of war. The 'Monarch' carries four 25-ton guns in turrets, the armour of which is from seven to ten inches thick; in the 'Glatton' the turret-armour was increased to twelve and fourteen inches. The turrets of the 'Devastation' are of the same thickness as the 'Glatton's,' but are armed with four 35-ton guns; and the 'Thunderer' carries two 35-ton and two 38-ton guns. She was begun in the early days of turret-ships, about the same time as the 'Thunderer' and the 'Devastation,' of which she is an improved type. Owing, however, partly to the loss of the 'Captain,' and partly to the uncertainty existing as to the success of unmasted ·turret-ships, her construction was suspended for some years. Her name was changed from the 'Fury' to the 'Dreadnought,' and about four years ago she was again put in hand. As she floats at present she is a complete museum of all the latest and most approved inventions connected with naval construction.

Mr. Barnaby; Comparison of 'Dreadnought' and other turretships.

In the paper which he read before the Institute of Naval Architects in 1873, Mr. Barnaby described the progressive development of the design for mastless turret-ships, from the 'Devastation' to the 'Thunderer,' and from the 'Thunderer' to the 'Dreadnought,'—then named the 'Fury.' He further compared the 'Dreadnought' with the 'Peter the Great.'

'The "Fury," as re-designed,' he said, 'differs from the "Thunderer" and "Devastation" in many ways. The differences may be briefly stated as follows :—The "Fury," with a speed of over fourteen knots, will be faster, and will be protected with fourteen inches instead of twelve inches; she will have no central superstructure of thin iron, but an armoured tower coming out to the full breadth of the ship, and large enough to berth within it all the officers and crew ; she will have only three feet freeboard for a portion of her length, viz., right forward and aft; she will have economical engines, by which we hope she will steam 6,000 miles with 200 tons less coal than the " Devastation " and " Thunderer ;" her armour will be immersed somewhat more, and especially forward, and her engines and boilers will be cut off from each other by a fore and aft partition. If I add that the cables work under instead of upon the forecastle, I shall have indicated the particulars in which the " Fury " is to differ from the first ships of the class.

'The "Peter the Great " is about ten feet longer than the " Fury," 329 ft. 8 in., and was two inches wider, but the " Fury " has been increased in breadth twelve inches, to 63 ft. 10 in., so that the "Peter the Great" is now ten inches narrower. Her designed displacement is near 10,000 tons, and her indicated horse-power is expected to be 10,000. The "Fury" is to be 10,800 tons, with an indicated power of 8,000 only.'

The following description is mainly from Mr. King: 'The "Dreadnought," built at Pembroke, cannot be called a low free-board ship or a breastwork monitor, for the height from the load water-line to the turret deck is nearly twelve feet, and the super-structure is more properly an oval armoured citadel, of which the sides are those of the vessel carried up to this breastwork deck. In

Descrip-
tion by Mr.
King.

Figs. 230 and 231.

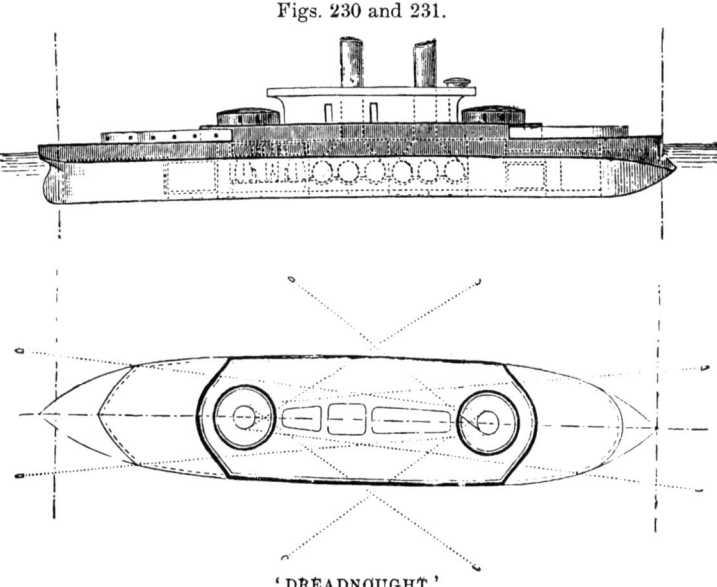

'DREADNOUGHT.'

other words, instead of building a breastwork on the deck of the armoured hull, some 185 feet long amidships, with a passage of, say, ten feet between it and the sides of the vessel, as was done in the "Thunderer" and other low-freeboard ships, the sides of the "Dread-nought" are built up flush to the top of the upper or turret deck. This armoured side rises nearly twelve feet above water, and is 184 feet in length amidships. The design, as will be seen, thus requires con-siderably more armour than would be used if the vessel had been built on the breastwork system, but the advantages derived from having the whole width of the vessel below the upper deck un-obstructed, which affords light and facilities for loading the guns on the hydraulic system and working the turrets, are of importance;

besides which, the increased room admits of comfortable quarters for officers and crew above water.

'The citadel, as before stated, is 184 feet in length, and the height between decks is 7 ft. 6 in. It is armoured with solid plates, eleven inches thick; except at the ends and abreast the bases of the turrets, where the thickness is increased to thirteen and fourteen inches. The increased thickness at the ends is for the purpose of protecting more thoroughly the bases of the turrets, the machinery for working them, and for loading the guns; in short, all the working apparatus enclosed by it. The armour-belt, which is carried entirely round the vessel, is fourteen inches thick at the water-line, tapering to eight inches at the lower edge of belt. It also tapers above water, before and abaft the citadel, as well as towards the ends. This armour-belt, before and abaft the fighting part of the ship, rises only four feet above water, and is intended solely to protect the vital portion of the hull; all parts above it are destructible, and may be riddled with shot without detriment to the fighting or sea-going qualities of the vessel. The turret-deck, or the deck over the citadel, is plated with two thicknesses of $1\frac{1}{2}$ and 1 inch iron respectively, and the main berth-deck below is also plated with the same thickness before and abaft the citadel; of course, no armour on this deck is needed inside of the citadel.

'The turrets rise through the citadel-deck to a height of twelve feet from the base or revolving deck-platform enclosed by the citadel. The diameter of each turret inside of the framing is 27 ft. 4 in., the depth of the framing being ten inches. They are built up with two thicknesses of plates and two thicknesses of teak, in the following manner: first, the shell or skin-plating consists of two $\frac{3}{4}$-inch plates, riveted together and to the framing; on the exterior of this plating is a teak backing six inches thick; outside this, armour-plates seven inches thick; next,

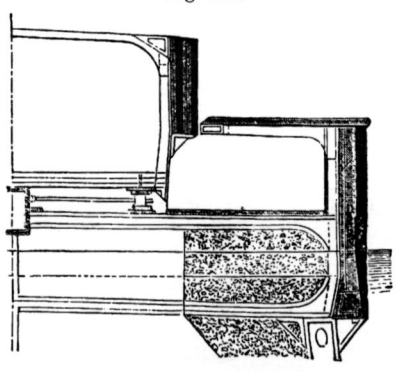

Fig. 232.

'DREADNOUGHT'
(SECTION THROUGH TURRET).

teak backing nine inches thick; and finally, armour-plates outside of all, seven inches thick: the whole being securely bolted together. The plates were rolled at Sheffield, and curved to templates drilled and prepared in place.

'The dimensions of the "Dreadnought" are:—Length over all, 343 feet; length between perpendiculars, 320 feet; extreme breadth, 63 ft. 10 in.; depth of hold, 19 ft. 2 in.; area of midship section in square feet, 1,506 feet; height of upper deck at side from load water-line, 11 ft. 4 in.; and draught of water, 26 ft. 6 in. forward, and 27 feet aft., being a little over that of the "Inflexible" itself, which is 23 ft. 5 in. forward, and 25 ft. 5 in. aft. Her total displacement is 10,886 tons, while that of the "Thunderer" is 9,190 tons.

'The total weight of the "Dreadnought's" hull is 7,350 tons, and the weight of armour, engines, coals, etc., amounts to 3,598 tons. She will carry 1,200 tons of coal, will be provisioned for a month, and will be armed with machine guns, in addition to her turret armament.

'The hull is constructed with the usual double bottom, and contains sixty-one watertight compartments. The ordinary system of divisions and watertight doors is adhered to; including the longitudinal bulkhead, which commences about forty feet from the stem, and extends to nearly the same distance from the stern, thus dividing the vessel in the centre. The flying deck and conning tower are similar to those in the "Thunderer;" and there is also but one mast to be used for signal purposes and hoisting boats. The bottom of the vessel is not sheathed.

'The armament will consist of two 38-ton Woolwich guns in each of the two turrets, all of them to be worked upon Messrs. Armstrong's hydraulic system.

'The "Dreadnought" has been engined by Messrs. Humphreys Machinery. and Tennant. The engines are of the compound type, very similar to those in the "Alexandra," constructed by the same firm.

'There is an independent set of vertical inverted engines to each of the twin screws. Each set consists of three cylinders, the high-pressure exhausting into the two low-pressure cylinders. The diameter of the former is 66 inches; the diameter of each of the latter, 90 inches; and the stroke of pistons, 4 ft. 6 in. All the cylinders are steam-jacketed. The high-pressure jacket is adjusted to the working boiler-pressure of 60 lbs., and the low pressure to 30 lbs.

'The engine crank-shaft is composed of three pieces, interchangeable; each piece has a length of 10 ft. 7⅛ in. and a diameter of 17¾ inches. The diameter of the propelling-shafts is 16 inches, except the lengths in the stern tubes, which are 18 inches. The engines are started and reversed by an auxiliary engine having cylinders 6 inches by 8. The ship is provided with six ventilating engines, two auxiliary fire-engines, four main fire engine pumps, steering-engines, turret-turning engines, capstan and ash-hoist engines, besides the engine and hydraulic apparatus for working the guns ; in all, there are twenty-nine steam-engines on board, and there are 180 valves connected with the ventilating pipes. The screw-propellers are of Griffith's recent pattern, the diameter of each being 20 feet, with pitches adjustable from 21 to 26 feet.

'The steam for the propelling and other engines is supplied by twelve main boilers and one auxiliary boiler. Instead of being arranged in the vessel face to face, as in former ships, so that the firemen have fires behind as well as in front of them, they are placed back to back against the middle-line bulkhead of the ship ; and the firing is done at the sides, convenient to the coal-bunkers. The boiler-rooms are further divided by athwartship bulkheads, whereby four rooms are formed, the forward ones being 42 feet, and the after ones 40 feet, in length. The length of the engine-room, abaft of this, is also 40 feet.

'The engines and boilers are entirely surrounded by the coal-bunkers ; the bunker immediately before the boilers is 22 feet in length fore and aft, and the one immediately abaft the engines is eight feet in length ; there are consequently 152 feet in the length of the ship at the extreme breadth occupied by the propelling machinery and coal. The bunkers contain 1,200 tons of coal.

'The ventilation of the stoke-holes is supplied by fans, supplemented by eight cowls on the hurricane-deck and four others at the side, which are also utilised as ash-hoists. As the ship is mastless, steam-power only is to be used. The total weight of the steam machinery is given as 1,430 tons ; hull and accessories, 7,350 tons ; and all other weights, including coal and stores, 2,170 tons.

Comparison with 'Devastation' and 'Thunderer.'

'The "Dreadnought" is a ship of the same class as the "Devastation" and the "Thunderer," but is as great an improvement upon the latter as that ship was an improvement upon her predecessor. She is in the first place considerably larger than the "Thunderer," and though increased bulk is not itself an improvement, yet in the "Dreadnought" it is combined with so many advantages that it becomes an important gain. While the "Thunderer" is 285 feet between perpendiculars, 62 ft. 3 in. in beam, and 18 feet in depth of hold, the corresponding dimensions of the "Dreadnought" are respectively, 320 feet, 63 ft. 10 in., and 19 ft. 2 in. Or, to put the difference in a more concise form, the load displacement of the "Dreadnought" is 10,950 tons, as compared with the 9,188 tons of the "Thunderer."

'But it is not only in bulk, weight of armour, the size of her guns, and the power of her machinery that the new turret-ship excels the "Devastation" and "Thunderer." She is an improvement upon them in various ways, several of the modifications in the earlier turrets having been introduced during her construction at the suggestion of Admirals Elliot and Ryder. The most important divergence is the erection of a central box in the place of the narrow breastwork in the "Devastation." The unarmoured superstructures in the latter ship were added to the original design in obedience to remonstrances from outside, notwithstanding the opinion of the Committee on Designs that the addition was not necessary for safety. In the "Dreadnought," however, to secure a larger reserve of buoyancy and stability, the breastwork has been carried out flush with the side of the ship, whereby an armoured wall eleven inches thick amidships is obtained. It was proposed to take advantage of this widening of the breastwork to place the turrets out of line with each other, as in the case of the "Inflexible," whereby the whole armament might be fired direct ahead and astern as well as abeam. This idea, however, was not adopted, both the turrets being placed in line as in the "Devastation;" but the increased space has enabled the whole crew, some 380 all told, to be accommodated in the breastwork, which is lit and ventilated from above.

'Another important structural arrangement first introduced here, and since adopted in other ships, is the longitudinal watertight bulkhead between the respective sets of engines and boilers; so that in the event of one set being disabled by rams, torpedoes, or other causes, it can be effectually shut off, and the ship propelled by the other set.

'In the "Dreadnought," again, the armour-belt, which was cut down in the two sister ships, is completed forward, and the recommendations of Admirals Elliot and Ryder for the protection of the fore magazine of the "Devastation" have also been carried out by sloping the bow armour down to the spur. The armour strakes along the length of the breastwork are of a parallel thickness before and aft, while they taper to eight inches in thickness at the stem and stern. The armour on the ends of the breastwork is thirteen inches, and that on the sides eleven inches, except for a length of about twenty feet in the wake of each turret, where the plating is fourteen inches thick.

'The external diameter of the "Dreadnought's" turrets is 32 ft. 3 in., and the thickness of its armour is uniformly fourteen inches, while the other turrets are 31 ft. 3 in. in diameter, and the thickness ranges from twelve to fourteen inches.

'The armament is also more formidable. It consists of four

38-ton guns, all worked on the hydraulic system, while the "Devastation" carries four 35-ton guns worked by hand-power, and the "Thunderer" two 38-ton guns worked by hydraulic power, and two 35-ton guns worked by hand.[1]

'Again, the "Dreadnought" is engined on the compound system, by which means greatly increased power is obtained with reduced consumption of fuel.'

Steam
trials. The contract indicated horse-power was 8,000 horses, as compared with the 'Thunderer's' 5,600. The result of the respective trials of the two vessels, however, showed that while the engines of the older ship developed 6,270 horse-power, those of the 'Dreadnought' were proved to be capable of exerting as much as 8,900 horse-power.

The six hours' trial of the propelling. machinery was made in January 1877. The *Times* reports the results as follows :—

Hour	Vacuum	Revolutions	Horse-power
1	27　and 27·43 in.	67·3 and 67·4	8,201·52
2	27　and 27·18 in.	67·6 and 67·4	8,233·78
3	27　and 27·25 in.	67·4 and 67·3	8,179·94
4	27　and 27·37 in.	66·9 and 67·0	8,177·77
5	27·5 and 27·43 in.	67·1 and 66·9	8,155·93
6	27　and 27·37 in.	66·0 and 66·8	8,207·39

The speed attained was about fifteen knots an hour. The ship was so sensitive that she readily obeyed the slightest touch of the helm.

At the six hours' trial a speed of 14·5 knots was attained.

The mean power developed by the engines was 8,216·28, or 216·28 horses beyond the contract. More could have been readily obtained had the economic purposes of the trial not intervened. The blasts were not used from first to last. Indeed the difficulty was to regulate the amount of steam generated, so as to maintain a steady and uniform power without its blowing off to waste, and, as will be seen from the last column, the variations of power exerted were exceedingly small. The total means of the twelve half-hours were: Pressure of steam in boilers, 60·32 lbs., and in engine-room, 57·32 lbs. ; vacuum in condensers—starboard 27·04 lbs., port 27·33 lbs. ; revolutions—starboard 67, port, 67·18 ; mean pressure of steam on pistons—high, 31·603 lbs., low, 9·137 lbs. One of the most noticeable circumstances connected with the observations was the almost uniform vacuum that was obtained.

---

[1] The 'Thunderer' has now (1881) four 38-ton guns.

The vacuum in the starboard condenser only varied once from 27 inches during the whole time the ship was under way, while that in the port condenser never varied more than half an inch, and that only twice.

The coal burnt on the trial amounted to 50 tons 1 cwt. 10 lbs.; which is equal to 2·27 lbs. per indicated horse-power. The consumption in the 'Thunderer' was 3·14 lbs.; and in order to show the superiority of the 'Dreadnought's' engines from an economic point of view, it may be mentioned that had she been fitted with engines of the same type as those of the 'Thunderer' she would have burnt eighty tons a day more fuel in order to develop the same power. The engines were stopped from full speed in eighteen seconds, and started astern in eight seconds, and from going astern were started full speed ahead in fifteen seconds. The trial passed off without a hitch of any sort, and Mr. Humphreys was warmly congratulated by the officials on board as to the results.

The behaviour of the 'Dreadnought' at sea, on her passage from Pembroke to Portsmouth, is thus described by the *Times* reporter:— *Passage from Pembroke.*

'She left Pembroke Dock together with the "Enchantress," bearing the flag of the Lords of the Admiralty. The wind was fresh and right ahead, bringing up with it a moderately heavy swell from the southward, but she rode the ridges very steadily and sedately. When rounding Land's End, the wind having backed to the eastward of south, there was a cross-sea running, but not sufficient to cause more than a very slight rolling. Plymouth was passed about 5 P.M., steering close in to make her number. The wind had now fallen light, and the sea gone down very much, and a good run was made up Channel; but in the morning watch the wind sprang up fresh and strong, and by the time St. Catherine's was passed, at 8 o'clock, had risen to a gale, blowing right astern. The seas now swept the whole length of her upper deck as they rolled on from behind; yet the motion of the ship was very slight indeed, dipping and rising easily and slowly. As the east end of the island was rounded, the wind was blowing very hard on to the port beam, and the spray at times completely shrouded the ship as the seas broke against her side; but the waves were powerless to produce more than the very slightest roll, indeed, she seemed almost as steady as one of the surrounding forts, over which the spray was breaking in similar fashion.'

The following details of the trials of the loading-gear of the 'Dreadnought' in October, 1878, are taken from the *Times*:—

'The "Dreadnought," double turret-ship, the most powerfully armoured and armed ship afloat at the present time, which has just been completed for the pendant at Portsmouth, went out from Spithead, where she had been previously swung for the adjustment of her compasses, for a trial of her guns and hydraulic gun-gear at the back of the Wight. The trial was an exceptionally important one in many respects, no such heavy charges of powder having been previously fired from any gun afloat. Consequently, not only was the endurance of the gun-carriages and the loading-gear to be determined by a crucial test, but it was necessary to observe the effects of the concussion upon the structure of the ship itself, more particularly within the citadel and upon the upper deck in wake of the turrets.

'The "Dreadnought's" armament consists of four 38-ton

Fig. 233

'DREADNOUGHT' (UPPER DECK FROM FORWARD, LOOKING AFT).

12½-inch unchambered guns, and although they are, therefore, so far as weight is concerned, precisely the same as the guns with which the fore turret of the "Thunderer" is armed, and which are also worked by Mr. Rendel's hydraulic machinery, they measure half an inch more in calibre, and fire a projectile weighing 800 lbs., or 100 lbs. more than the guns of the "Thunderer." Whereas, again, the battering charge of the less formidable ordnance is 110 lbs., the charges which it is deemed useful and practicable to fire from the 38-ton guns of the "Dreadnought" have been increased up to the *maximum* of 160 lbs. Those enormous charges have been adopted since the hydraulic gear was placed on board the ship by the contractors, now three years ago; and although the present carriages and presses were originally designed for the 110-lb. charges, they were found to be not only able to resist the recoils produced by the 130-lb. and 145-lb. cartridges; but, with the aid of some slight assistance from the compressors, equal to the strains resulting from the firing of 160-lb. charges. The pumping engines are so arranged that by means of pipe connections each engine can, in case of the other being disabled in an engagement, be made to work either or both turret gears. These engines, too, are fitted with automatic governors, which enable them to supply the power when it is wanted, while at all other times they merely continue to turn, whereby steam and wear and tear are economised to the utmost extent.

'Before the firing commenced the ship was stripped as if for action. The armour covers were placed over the coaling scuttles, the bow bulwarks were let down, the guard rails and davits lowered, the sashes removed and hatchways battened down, and lamps lighted below. The anchors and other impediments on deck were also doubly secured. The experiments began with the guns in the forward turret, from which, excluding scaling charges, twelve rounds were fired from the two guns from the middle, lower, and upper steps. The powder charges varied from 100 lbs. up to 160 lbs., the projectile in every case being a Palliser shell weighted up to 810 lbs. Two 100-lb. charges were first fired, with an initial velocity of 1,300 feet per second, the recoil being 4 ft. 6 in. Two rounds were next fired with 130-lb. charges, the initial velocity being 1,425 feet. The recoil in the first instance was 6 ft. 1 in., the carriage touching the rear buffer; but on the valve springs being tightened from 1,000 lbs. to 1,100 lbs. to the square inch, the recoil in the other round was found to be 5 ft. 2½ in. In the subsequent rounds with the same charge the compressors were used up to the second adjustment hole, the recoils of each discharge falling, in the case of the left gun to 4 ft. 6 in., and in that of the right gun to 3 ft. 6 in.. A round was next fired from the lower step with 100 lbs. of powder, and an elevation of 3½°, the recoil being 3 ft. 6 in., a subsequent round from the upper step with the same charge giving a recoil of 4 ft. 8 in. Two rounds with 145 lbs. were then fired from the middle step, the compressors being applied to the second hole, the recoils being 4 ft. 8 in. and 3 ft. 11 in., and the initial velocity 1,470 feet. The last two rounds were with charges of 160 lbs., giving a velocity of 1,500 feet per second. They were fired from the middle step without any elevation, the recoil presses being assisted by the compressers up to the 2½ adjustment. The recoils were 4 ft. 10 in. and 4 feet respectively. The firing was then commenced from the after turret, from which, however, only eight rounds were discharged, as it was thought useless to continue firing the smaller charges under conditions which had proved satisfactory when submitted to the severe tests. Two rounds with 130-lb. charges gave a recoil of 5 ft. 6 in. and 5 ft. 10 in. In a similar round from the upper step, and with tightened valve-springs, the carriage on recoil touched the rear buffer at a distance of 6 ft. 1 in. ; while in the following round from the lower step, under like conditions, but with an elevation of $3\frac{1}{2}°$, the recoil was only 4 ft. 6 in. The last test was a salvo, the two guns being fired simultaneously with *maximum* charges of 160 lbs. They were fired from the middle step with the compressors up to the $2\frac{1}{2}$ hole. They were fired immediately over the chains of the shot-hoist on the deck below, with the purpose of testing them, as it was thought possible that they might part when subjected to the jerking strain produced by the concussion. The recoil was 4 ft. 5 in. and 4 ft. 6 in. respectively, and on examination no signs of weakness could be discovered in the hoist-gear. The concussion of the discharge was tremendous, the whole ship heeling over to port 2°. The whistles jumped out of the voice-tubes, the glass from the sashes fell in showers, and the faces of the tell-tales and engine-room telegraphs were also fractured. No indications of distress, however, were observed in the structure of the ship itself, although on the occasion of the trial of the "Thunderer's" gun under less stringent conditions several knees and angle-irons on the breastwork deck were afterwards found to have been fractured and torn from their attachments. The loading gear worked without a hitch, and the pumps gave no trouble whatever. The only defect is in the steam machinery which rotates the turrets, the elasticity of the motive power rendering it occasionally difficult to stop the guns precisely in the loading position, notwithstanding the ingenuity of the locking arrangement. In the "Inflexible," however, the rotating as well as the loading gear will be worked by hydraulic power, a power which is completely under the command of the operator.'

In his latest book Mr. King remarks :—

Mr. King's comparison of 'Dreadnought' with 'Devastation' and 'Thunderer.'

' The improvements of the "Dreadnought" over the other two mastless seagoing ships, the "Devastation" and the "Thunderer," or the difference between them, may be summed up briefly as follows:—The displacement is 1,499 tons more ; the length between perpendiculars is 35 feet greater, with an increase of beam of one foot seven inches, and an increased depth of hold of one foot two inches.

'The structural improvements consist in carrying out the breastwork entirely to the sides of the vessel, and in bringing the forecastle and after-deck up to near the level of the breastwork, or, rather, armoured citadel ; by this arrangement the facilities for working the

guns and ship have been greatly increased and better accommodation provided, besides which the objectionable *cul de sac* that exists
in the other two ships has been obviated, and a high freeboard all
around is obtained, which must make her both a drier ship and a more
comfortable cruiser than either of the others.

'Another important structural arrangement first introduced here,
and since adopted in other ships, is the longitudinal watertight
bulkhead between the respective sets of engines and boilers ; so that
in the event of one set being disabled by rams, torpedoes, or other
causes, it can be effectually shut off, the ship being propelled by the
other set.

Fig. 234.

'DREADNOUGHT.'

On the hurricane deck, looking aft ; practising with the Gatling gun ; method of
lowering a torpedo launch by means of a derrick on the mast.

'The side-armour of the " Dreadnought " varies in thickness from
eight to fourteen inches, while in the other two ships it varies from
ten to twelve inches, besides which it extends $7\frac{1}{2}$ inches deeper
under water than in the other vessels. The external diameter of
her turrets is 32 ft. 3 in., and the thickness of the armour is uniformly fourteen inches, while the turrets of the others are 31 ft. 3 in.
in diameter, and the thickness ranges from twelve to fourteen inches.

'The armament is also more formidable. It consists of four 38-ton
$12\frac{1}{2}$-inch guns, all worked on the hydraulic system, while the " Devastation " carries four 35-ton guns worked by hand power, and the
" Thunderer " two 38-ton 12-inch guns [1] worked by hydraulic power,
and two 35-ton guns worked by hand.

[1] $12\frac{1}{2}$-in. guns have replaced these two.

' Again, the " Dreadnought " is engined on the compound system, by which greatly increased power is obtained, with reduced consumption of fuel.

' The " Dreadnought " may be considered, next to the " Inflexible," the most powerful British ship of war ever floated.'

Observations of M. Dislère

M. Dislère, in *La Guerre d'Escadre*, has made a careful comparison of the ' Dreadnought ' with the earlier ships of the same type. He recognises the marked advance, both in offensive and in defensive power, and in seagoing qualities.

Two 38-ton guns had been substituted in the ' Thunderer ' for two of the 35-ton guns carried in the ' Devastation.' In the ' Dreadnought ' all the four guns were of the heavier calibre, and the dimensions of the turrets had been increased sufficiently to receive the 80-ton guns, should it be found practicable to work guns of that calibre at sea.

The speed had been increased from twelve to $14\frac{1}{2}$ knots, and the supply of coal from 1,370 to 1,630 tons, which amount would be sufficient in each case to carry the two ships about an equal distance.

The increase in the defensive power was less marked. The thickness of the armour at the water-line was thirteen inches in the ' Dreadnought,' and twelve inches in the ' Devastation '; but in the case of the latter vessel, the diminution in the thickness did not exceed $3\frac{1}{2}$ inches, while it was six inches in that of the ' Dreadnought.' The plating of the latter ship at the extremities was thinner therefore than that of the ' Devastation.' The battery was protected with 11-inch plates, as compared with 10-inch plates. The oblique bulkheads at the forward end of the battery were protected with 14-inch plates, in lieu of 305 millimètre or 12-inch plates. For the turrets, 7-inch plates had been substituted for the 6-inch plates of the ' Devastation.' Lastly, if the plating of the deck was only $2\frac{1}{2}$ inches in thickness, in lieu of three inches, it was completely protected with armour, whereas, in the ' Devastation ' the deck was armoured only before and abaft the battery. While the mean thickness was greater, a still more marked alteration had been made in the distribution of the armour, which rises along the whole length of the ship to a height of three feet above the water-line, instead of sinking, towards the bow, to the level of the water-line. Again, the belt was carried down to six feet below the water-line amidships, while it was carried down at the stem in such a manner as to form, as in the case of the ' Devastation,' an integral part of the spur or ram. A bulkhead, covered with 5-inch plates abaft the magazines, protects them from raking fire, when the ship is pitching deeply.

INFLEXIBLE.

The central battery is no longer a fortress in the centre of the ship, with a large deck-space, imperfectly protected, between the battery and the side of the ship, penetrable by projectiles, which might reach the boilers.

The battery in the 'Dreadnought' extends to the full width of the ship, the sides being carried up for a length of about 144 feet to a height of 10½ feet above the water-line. In addition to the protection, other advantages are secured, which are not less considerable in respect to seagoing qualities and facility of construction. If the low freeboard, which is the characteristic feature of the monitor type, is given up, nothing is gained, but rather the contrary, in allowing the deck to be buried in the waves. The forecastle and the poop are formed by an extension of the battery amidships, and afterwards carried forward and aft—though contracted in width—until within a short distance of the extremities:—19 ft. 6 in. forward, and 32 ft. 10 in. aft. Their ends are rounded. The two turrets are connected by a flying-deck, with a considerable overhang. The davits are fitted to the bulwarks, and all the skylights are fitted to this flying-deck.

The various improvements enumerated, in comparing this ship with her predecessors, have not been obtained without corresponding sacrifice. The displacement has been increased from 9,340 to 11,130 tons, involving an augmentation in the cost of not less than 80,000*l*. It is a still more serious disadvantage that the length, already considerable, has been further increased from 285 feet to 320 feet, being an augmentation of more than thirty feet.

The following description of the 'Inflexible' is from Mr. King, with additional matter from later articles in the press. H.M.S. 'Inflexible.'

' The modern man-of-war is much more than an armoured steamer ; she is a great engine of destruction, clad with heavy armour, provided with huge guns which are operated upon by machinery, driven by powerful engines, and fitted with machinery for purposes of all kinds. Year by year the thickness of armour and weight of naval ordnance have gone on increasing together. Mechanical appliances have more and more replaced manual labour, and at the same time the forms of ships have been adapted to the work they have to do and to the conditions under which they must act.'

The 'Inflexible,' which was commenced at Portsmouth dockyard in February 1874, and launched April 1876, is a twin-screw double-turret ship, with a central armed citadel. She was designed by Mr. Barnaby, the Director of Naval Construction at the Admiralty, and 'Inflexible.' Description by Mr. Barnaby.

at a meeting of the Institution of Naval Architects in London, in March 1874, he described her in the following language :—

'This is the ship which the progress of invention in artillery has finally driven us to resort to. Had the manufacture of enormous ordnance been stopped when the 35-ton gun was introduced, we might have been satisfied with the "Fury," now named the "Dreadnought," with her guns of this nature, and her 14-inch armour. But English artillerists were ready to make guns of twice 35 tons, and foreign Powers were known to be building ships to receive such guns.

'There could be no question that we could not allow foreign seamen to have guns afloat more powerful than any of our own, however ready we might have been to allow them to defend themselves with thicker armour. Although, therefore, it was known that the ships in which these guns were to be mounted were to be pro-

Figs. 235 and 236.

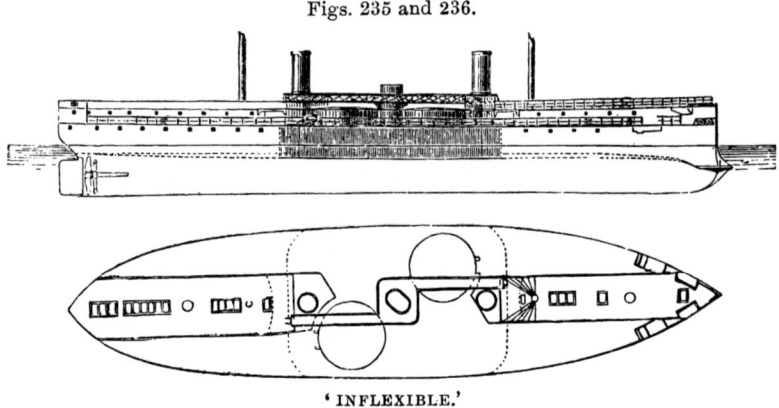

' INFLEXIBLE.'

tected by 22 inches of armour, thickness of armour was not made a ruling feature of the design of the first-class ship which was to mark the next step in advance upon the "Fury"—but the first of the ruling conditions was that she should be able to mount the heaviest guns which could possibly be made now, and by some easy modifications in her construction hereafter, guns of twice that weight when they can be manufactured. The other conditions were that she should have a speed of 14 knots at the measured mile, and that she should not exceed the dimensions and cost of preceding ships. It was found to be possible in conformity with these conditions to protect the hull by two feet of armour.

'I may describe the "Inflexible" to you briefly in the following manner :—

'Imagine a floating castle 110 feet long and 75 feet wide rising ten feet out of the water, and having above that again two round turrets planted diagonally at its opposite corners. Imagine this castle and its turrets to be heavily plated with armour, and that each turret has within it two guns of about 80 tons each, perhaps in the course of a few years guns of twice 80 tons each. Conceive these guns to be capable of firing all four together at an enemy ahead or on either beam, and in pairs towards every point of the compass. Attached to this rectangular armoured castle, but completely submerged, every part being six to seven feet under water, there is a hull of the ordinary form with a powerful ram bow, with twin screws, and a submerged rudder and helm. This compound structure is the fighting part of the ship. Seaworthiness, speed, and shapeliness would be wanting in such a structure if it had no additions to it; there is, therefore, an unarmoured structure lying above the submerged ship, and connected with it, both before and abaft the armoured castle, and as this structure rises twenty feet out of the water, from stem to stern, without depriving the guns of that command of the horizon already described, and as it moreover renders a flying deck unnecessary, it gets over the objections which have been raised against the low freeboard and other features in the " Devastation," " Thunderer," and " Fury." These structures furnish also most luxurious accommodation for officers and seamen. The step in advance has therefore been from 14 inches of armour to 24 inches; from 35-ton guns to 80-ton guns; from two guns ahead to four guns ahead; from a height of ten feet for working the anchors to twenty feet; and this is done without an increase in cost, and with a reduction of nearly three feet in draught of water.

' I cannot attempt to describe the numerous novel and interesting features of such a design, but I may say that no pains have been spared to protect her against underwater attacks by the isolation of the independent engines, the subdivision of boiler compartments, and such further subdivisions as were possible with due regard to proper facilities for moving about. The result is that the ship is perfectly and easily workable, although she is divided into 127 watertight compartments. My belief is, that in the " Inflexible " we have reached the extreme limit in thickness of armour for seagoing ships. The temptation is always great to secure more and more power by the expenditure of ever-increasing sums of money, but it is my conviction that we shall not in any future ship go beyond this expenditure. Some of the ironclads designed ten or twelve years ago cost more than the " Inflexible " will; but succeeding ships were more reasonable in cost until the " Fury " again approached them.

In the " Inflexible " provision has been made both offensively and defensively for an enormous increase in the powers of artillery without any increase in the cost of the ship.'

' The length of the vessel between perpendiculars is 320 feet, and she has the extraordinary breadth of 75 feet at the water-line ; the depth of hold is 23 ft. $3\frac{1}{2}$ in.; freeboard, 10 feet ; mean draught of water, 24 ft. 5 in. (23 ft. 5 in. forward, and 25 ft. 5 in. aft); area of midship section, 1,658 square feet; and displacement when all the weights are on board, 11,407 tons, being the largest of any man-of-war hitherto constructed. She is, as before described, a rectangular armoured castle ; the whole of the other parts of the vessel which are unprotected by armour, have been given their great dimensions for the simple purpose of floating and moving this invulnerable citadel, and the turrets by which it is surmounted. Her immense bulk, unprecedented armament, powerful machinery, and the provision for ramming, and for resisting the impact of rams as well as of shot and shell, have made it necessary that great strength and solidity should enter into every part of the structure.

' While the cellular compartments of the double bottom have a little less depth than in the " Devastation " class, they are built up of heavier angle-irons and plating, and steel has been very largely employed for the purpose of securing great strength with comparative lightness of material. The lower part of the hull is composed of flat and vertical keels, transverse and longitudinal frames, inner and outer bottom plating. The vertical keel is formed of steel plates, $\frac{3}{4}$ inch thick by 40 inches deep, and the flat keel-plates are of iron in two thicknesses of $1\frac{3}{16}$ inch and $\frac{3}{4}$ inch, the two being connected with angle-irons five inches by five inches by $\frac{3}{4}$ inch. On the upper edge of the vertical keel the angle-irons by which it is fastened to the inner bottom-plates are three inches by $3\frac{1}{2}$ inches by $\frac{1}{2}$ inch. The framework of the vessel below the armour is composed of longitudinal and transverse frames. The former, eight in number, are formed of steel plates $\frac{7}{16}$ inch in thickness, the shelf-plate being $\frac{1}{2}$ inch thick. These frames extend as far forward and aft as is deemed practicable. Within the double bottom, which extends through 212 feet of the ship's length, the transverse frames are solid, and are made watertight at intervals of twenty feet. There are also intermediate bracket-frames placed four feet apart. Before and abaft the double bottom, the transverse frames, which are likewise four feet apart, are of the thickness of $\frac{3}{8}$ inch, but are considerably lightened by having holes cut in them, the upper parts at the same time being much narrowed. Additional intermediate frames are introduced in the engine-room in order to secure greater strength. The angle-irons forming the frames vary from $5\frac{1}{2}$ inches by three inches by $\frac{1}{2}$ inch to three inches by $3\frac{1}{2}$ inches by $\frac{1}{2}$ inch. The outer skin plating of the bottom varies from $\frac{15}{16}$ inch in the garboard strakes to $\frac{5}{8}$ inch; with the exception of the ends, where the thickness is increased to $\frac{7}{8}$ inch; and behind the anchors, where the plating is doubled. The plating of the inner bottom, which extends throughout the length of the double bottom, and which, like the outer bottom, is made perfectly watertight, is of the uniform thickness of $\frac{3}{8}$ inch, except under the engines, where it is $\frac{7}{16}$ inch. As is usual in iron vessels, the stem of the "Inflexible" consists of a solid iron forging scarphed at its lower end to the keel-plates. The stern-post and after-pieces of keel, which are formed of the best angle-iron, are also made in a single forging. The rudder is a solid iron frame filled in with wood and covered with iron plates. In consequence of its immense weight—some nine tons— it is made to work on double pintles in combination with the ordinary pintles and braces. It is worked by a tiller 4 ft. 6 in. below the water. Indeed, the whole of the steam steering-gear is placed below the water-line and armoured deck, so that it will be impossible for the rudder-head to be injured by shot or shell during an engagement. To receive the propeller-shafts two iron tubes are constructed, one under each quarter. The forward ends of these tubes, where they leave the run of the ship, are supported by the framework of the hull, which is bossed out in a suitable form for the purpose, the after parts being supported by struts from the ship's bottom. There are four decks—the lower, middle, upper, and superstructure decks—the last being a middle-line erection placed forward and aft above the upper deck for working the ship, carrying and lowering the boats, etc. Outside the citadel the lower-deck beams are covered with iron three inches thick. This deck is depressed at the fore end so as to meet that part of the bow which is intended for ramming, thus conferring upon it greatly increased strength and resistance when engaged in butting an enemy's ship. It may be here stated that the ram of the "Inflexible" is of the spur kind, and though it is fixed at the present time, it may be made to unship. The middle deck consists of $\frac{1}{4}$-inch plating, covered with 3-inch deal planks; while the upper-deck beams in the vicinity of the citadel are covered with 3-inch plating, and in other parts with $\frac{1}{2}$-inch plating. The beams, pillars, and bulkheads for supporting the various decks and platforms, and forming the different compartments and rooms, are arranged and fitted so as to give the greatest possible strength to the sides of the vessel. The largest beams are on the main deck. They are fourteen inches deep, while those on the upper deck are ten inches, and those on the lower deck twelve inches deep. Every beam is either supported by wrought-iron tube-pillars, or is trussed where pillars cannot be erected, the strongest being under the turrets. The two superstructures themselves in no way add to the power of the ship, either for attack or defence. Their purpose in the economy of the ship is to afford accommodation for the officers and crew; and as the structures are erected on the upper deck, this will be of the best kind, with abundance of air and natural light. Their dimensions are: fore superstructure, extreme length, 104 ft. 4 in.; breadth, 21 ft. 4 in.; after superstructure, extreme length, 105 ft. 4 in.; breadth, 30 feet. The frames are formed of angle-iron, seven inches by three inches, placed four feet apart, and between them are intermediate frames made of angle-iron four inches by three inches. The ends are covered with $\frac{3}{8}$-inch plates, and the whole surface with a 3-inch wood deck. The cabin-walls are all coated with Welch's wood-faced cement as a protection against the results of atmospheric condensation. The officers and men together will probably number 350. As a protection against the casualties of war and the sea, the hull is divided by means of the transverse and longitudinal bulkheads into no fewer than 135 watertight compartments, and arrangements can be made for quickly removing any water that may collect within them through collision or other cause. Powerful steam-pumps, among which may be mentioned two of Friedmann's patent ejectors, capable of discharging 300 tons of water each per hour, will be fitted. All the bulkheads are provided with watertight doors of an improved pattern, sluice-valves, man-holes, and watertight scuttles. These doors can be opened from on deck or below. Watertight doors can also be fitted, when necessary, to the bulkheads passing through the coal-bunkers. Each of the watertight compartments has been tested by hydraulic pressure. Great attention has been bestowed upon the question of ventilation, which in ships of the "Devastation" class, and, indeed, in all monitors of low freeboard, has been a source of considerable discomfort and embarrassment. In the "Inflexible" the fresh air will be drawn into the midship part of the vessel through a series of downcast shafts, by means of eight powerful fans, worked by four of Messrs. Brotherhood and Hardingham's patent three-cylinder engines. The air is then conducted into main pipes, which run round the sides of the hull to the extremities, and from these, subsidiary or branch pipes discharge the air in ample quantities to every part of the ship.

'Over the shot-proof deck, at a level a little above the water-
line, comes the middle deck, and the entire space between the two
decks is divided into compartments arranged partly to carry coals
and partly stores packed in watertight tanks, forming further
subdivisions of the space. Next to the sides of the ship the com-

Fig. 237.

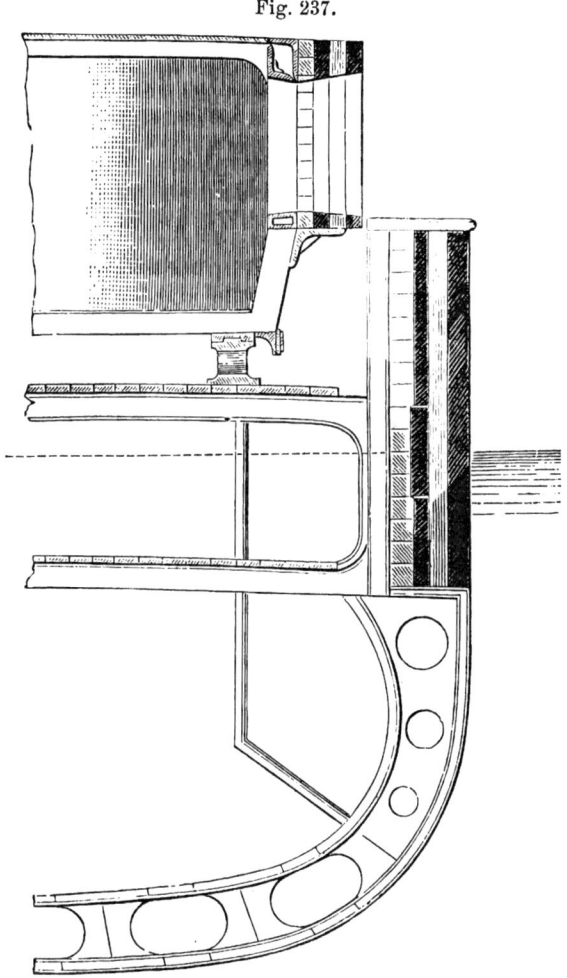

'INFLEXIBLE' (SECTION THROUGH TURRET).

partments are about four feet wide, and are filled with cork, and
inside this again are compartments two feet wide, filled with layers
of canvas and oakum. The cork and canvas compartments are
carried above the main deck four feet and two feet respectively, and
thirty feet forward of the citadel and 37 feet aft of it. Thus, if a shot
hit the unarmoured ends of the vessel at right angles to the water-

line, it would travel through, first, four feet of cork, then two feet of canvas and oakum, then such coal and stores as were unconsumed, and finally pass through oakum and cork to the sea, on the opposite side from which it entered. The cork is, of course, intended as a life-belt to the ship, to give her additional buoyancy when the unprotected ends are riddled and filled with water.

'Since the report of the committee on the stability of the ship was made, a further series of cork chambers have been constructed above the lower deck forward and abaft the citadel; and several tons of cork have also been packed in the larger cork spaces on the lower decks. In the latter case division bulkheads and intermediate cork flats have been introduced and secured to the armour deck.

'The protected portion of the ship is confined to the citadel or battery, within whose walls are enclosed the engines and boilers, the turrets, the hydraulic loading-gear, the magazines, and in fact all the vital parts of the vessel. It measures 110 feet in length, 75 feet in breadth, and is armoured to the depth of 6 ft. 5 in. below the water-line, and 9 ft. 7 in. above it. The sides of the citadel consist of an outer thickness of 12-inch armour-plating, strengthened by vertical angle-iron girders eleven inches wide and three feet apart, the space between them being filled in with teak backing. Behind these girders, in the wake of the water-line, is another thickness of 12-inch armour, backed by horizontal girders six inches wide, and supported by a second thickness of teak backing. Inside this are two thicknesses of skin-plating, to which the horizontal girders are secured; the whole of the armour-backing and plating being supported by, and bolted to, transverse frames two feet apart, which are composed of plates and angle-irons. It will thus be seen that the total thickness of armour at the water-line strake is not less than 24 inches. The armour belt, however, is not of uniform strength throughout, but varies in accordance with the importance of the protection required and the exposure to attack. Consequently, while the armour at the water level is 24 inches in two thicknesses of twelve inches each, above the water-line it is twenty inches in two thicknesses of twelve inches and eight inches, and below the water-line it is reduced to sixteen inches in two thicknesses of twelve inches and four inches. The teak backing with which it is supported also varies inversely as the thickness of armour, being respectively seventeen inches, 21 inches, and 25 inches in thickness, and forming with the armour with which it is associated, a uniform wall 41 inches thick. The depth of armour below the load water-line is 6 ft. 5 in., but as the vessel will be sunk a foot on going into action, the sides will thus have armour protection to the depth of 7 ft. 5 in. below the fighting-line. The armour shelter for the protection of the officers manœuvring the ship is in the shape of a cross, and is plated with iron twelve inches thick.'

It is remarked, in the *Nautical Magazine*, that the ' Inflexible ' is the first instance of the employment of two thicknesses of armour with wood between them on the armoured side of the ship; but the *sandwich* system, as it has been called, has been followed in several cases in the construction of turrets, in the English ships ' Devastation,' ' Thunderer,' and ' Dreadnought,' and also in the Russian ' Peter the Great.' Possibly this has resulted from the practical difficulty of bending the very thick armour to the extreme shapes which are required for turret armour, or perhaps from the difficulty of bending it without injury. The Italian Government, however, have adopted for the turret armour of the ' Dandolo ' single plates nearly eighteen inches thick, and that of our own ' Ajax ' and ' Agamemnon ' is of considerable thickness.

While armour has increased from $4\frac{1}{2}$ inches to 24 inches, the same material has been used throughout. In the early Shoeburyness experiments, the plates were very liable to crack through the armour bolt-holes, and many devices were tried with a view to securing the plates in such a way as not to require holes through the armour. The quality of the armour has been so far improved, however, that for some years past the holes for armour-bolts have ceased to be seriously objectionable.

Colonel Inglis states, as the result of experiment, that the resistance of armour $7\frac{1}{2}$ inches thick made up by one, two, or three plates, varies respectively as 100, 96, and 89 ; and that a single plate $17\frac{1}{2}$ inches thick is about equal to three $6\frac{1}{2}$-inch plates separated by 5-inch layers of teak. If such be the case, the English 'Inflexible' with two 12-inch armour-plates must be superior to the Italian ' Dandolo ' with one plate $21\frac{1}{2}$ inches thick. There is a further consideration. It is exceedingly difficult to make reliable armour-plates of the greater thickness, unless they be narrow. One result of the Spezzia experiments was to prove the great weakness of narrow plates. Every one of the thick plates broke across when fired at by the 100-ton gun.

In the ' Inflexible ' the outside armour is fastened by bolts four inches in diameter, secured with nuts and elastic washers on the inside. The shelf-plate, on which the armour rests, is formed of $\frac{1}{2}$-inch plates, with an angle-iron on the outer edge five inches by $3\frac{1}{2}$ inches by $\frac{9}{16}$ inch. The armour on the fore bulkhead of the citadel is exactly the same in every respect as that on the sides, but the armour of the rear bulk-head is somewhat thinner, being of the respective gradations of 22, eighteen, and fourteen inches, and forming with the teak backing, which is sixteen, twenty, and 24 inches, a uniform thickness of 38 inches.   It may also be useful to mention that before and abaft the citadel the frames are formed of 7-inch and 4-inch angle-irons, covered with $\frac{9}{16}$-inch plates.   The total weight of the armour, ex-clusive of deck plating, is 2,250 tons, and the total weight of armour, inclusive of protective deck-plating, is 3,155 tons.

The most singular feature in the design of the ship is the situation of the turrets.   In the 'Devastation' and 'Thunderer,' and, in fact, all monitors afloat, the turrets are placed at the middle line, an arrangement which, though advantageous in some respects, possesses this signal disadvantage, that in double-turreted monitors only one-half of the guns can be brought to bear on the enemy either right

Fig. 238.

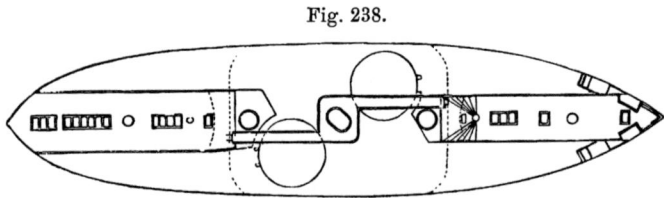

PLAN SHOWING 'INFLEXIBLE'S' TURRETS.

ahead or directly astern.   In the 'Inflexible,' however, the turrets rise up on either side of the ship *en échelon* within the walls of the citadel, the forward turret being on the port side and the after turret on the starboard side, while the superstructures are carried in a fore-and-aft line along the deck.   By these means the whole of the four guns can be discharged simultaneously perhaps, right ahead or right astern, or on either beam, or in pairs towards any point of the compass. Besides these important advantages, the guns of each turret can be projected clear of the ship's side—in the case of the one turret to port, and in the case of the other turret to starboard.

They can then be depressed, so as not only to strike a vessel at close quarters, below the line of the armour, but even to fire down upon the deck, should the enemy be ranged alongside.   The turrets, which have an internal diameter of 28 feet, and an external diameter of about 33 ft. 10 in., are being plated with compound armour. When the vessel was originally designed, it was intended to cover the turret walls with eighteen inches of solid iron armour, backed by eighteen inches of teak.   With the introduction of steel-faced armour, the thickness has been reduced. The inner armour consists of 7-inch iron plates, and the outer of 9-inch compound armour, having a hard steel face $3\frac{1}{2}$ inches thick welded upon iron plating $4\frac{1}{2}$ inches thick.

In 1880 experiments were carried out on a piece of one of the compound 9-inch plates manufactured by Messrs Cammell for the 'Inflexible,' with the best results. Three shots were fired from a 9-inch 12-ton gun, at a distance of thirty feet, with a 250-lb. shot and a 50-lb. charge of powder. The striking velocity was 1,406 feet per second. The shots struck the central portion of the plate two feet apart, in the form of an equilateral triangle. The projectiles used were Palliser chilled shots, all of which splashed, and broke up against the surface of the plate. In no case did they penetrate as far as the iron backing, and caused no other injury, if we except some slight surface cracks confined to the neighbourhood of the points of impact. The saving in weight from the reduced thickness of armour without loss of protection amounts in the 'Inflexible' to nearly 600 tons.

Further experiments of a similar character were recently made at Shoeburyness in the presence of Lord Northbrook and Mr. Childers. The details are taken from the *Standard* of July 22, 1880:—

'A round was to be fired against a compound armour-plate of the description manufactured by Messrs. Charles Cammell and Co., as invented by Mr. George Wilson. The plate was eighteen inches thick, and of large area, weighing many tons. Five inches of its thickness consisted of steel, united at the back to thirteen inches of wrought iron, the entire mass constituting what is termed a steel-faced plate, the steel blending imperceptibly with the iron. Plates of this description have offered great resistance to iron projectiles, including the famous chilled shell bearing the name of Sir William Palliser. The piece of ordnance which was brought to bear against this plate was the $12\frac{1}{2}$-inch 38-ton gun. It was contended that as a Palliser projectile fired from this gun could not possibly penetrate the steel-faced plate, the only useful plan would be to fire at it with a steel shot. On the other hand, it was argued that Palliser projectiles were the service shot, whereas steel projectiles were not used in the British service. It was therefore demanded that the service shot should be fired on this occasion, and this was agreed to. The charge for the gun consisted of 180 lbs. of powder, in cubes of an inch and a half—that is to say, of the P-2 pattern, the projectile weighing 828 lbs. The plate was simply resting against a mass of timber, against which it was held up without being fastened. The range was 227 feet. It was calculated that if the plate were made of wrought iron, eighteen inches thick, without a steel face, it would be penetrated by a chilled iron shot striking it with an energy of 12,300 foot-tons. On the gun being fired under the circumstances described, the velocity was found to be 1,516 feet a second at the muzzle, corresponding to 1,504 feet at the surface of the plate. This would give a striking energy of 12,545 foot-tons, and therefore should have sent the chilled iron shot through had the plate been only of iron. On examination it was found that the projectile, as was expected, had broken up on contact with the plate, driving part of the ogival head into the metal and producing two horizontal cracks extending right and left from the spot where the shot struck. The crack on the left was scarcely continuous, but showed itself as far as the edge. The crack on the right was more pronounced, and probably went to the right edge, but this would not be seen owing to the intervening supports. There was no reason to suppose that either crack extended deeper than the steel, and consequently the plate on the whole may be said to have suffered but little. The contrast between the resistance offered by a steel-faced plate and one of entire iron was therefore very marked. On the other hand, a steel shell fired from the same gun against a 16-inch compound plate with a striking velocity of 12,547 foot-tons broke the plate completely, the projectile itself breaking up. But in this case it was computed that had the plate, sixteen inches thick, consisted solely of iron, it would have suffered similar damage from an iron projectile with an energy of only 9,900 foot-tons.'

The height of the turret ports from the load-line is twelve feet, and a foot less from the fighting-line; and all the plating in the wake of the guns is considerably strengthened.

A very special interest attaches to the armament of the 'Inflexible,' not only because it consists of guns vastly more powerful than any yet mounted in the British Navy, but because these guns are carried and worked on the new and remarkable hydraulic system which has hitherto only been tried in the fore turret of the 'Thunderer.'

Each turret weighs no less than 750 tons, including the guns; and having to deal with a moving mass of such enormous weight, and with the superadded difficulty of a floating, and therefore unstable, platform on which to revolve it, it was determined to commence at this point with the adoption of the hydraulic system of Sir William Armstrong, as developed for gunnery purposes, by his partner, Mr. George Rendel. The revolution of the turrets accordingly will be accomplished by hydraulic machinery, in a manner similar to that employed by the Elswick firm for turning swing-bridges and great cranes. In such cases the weights dealt with have already exceeded

that of the turrets of the ' Inflexible ; ' and so complete is the control
afforded by hydraulic machinery in the movements of heavy masses
in analogous cases, that it is believed the turrets will, by this
machinery, be rotated at any speed, from a complete revolution in
one minute down to a rate as slow and uniform as can be desired.
The advantage of the high speed is plain; that of the slow but
regular rotation will be apparent when it is remembered how much
delicacy of adjustment is necessary for following with accurate aim
an object moving rapidly and at a distance. The power by which
the turrets of the ' Inflexible ' are turned is hydraulic. In the
' Thunderer ' and the ' Dreadnought,' the turrets are rotated by steam,
which is not so certain nor obedient. The hydraulic system offers
the special advantage that it can be stopped dead without locking
gear, and can be made to perform its work so creepingly and uniformly
that the movement of the gun in the turret may be said to resemble
the movement of the minute pointer of a watch. The hydraulic
power is furnished to each turret by a pumping engine working up
to 170 horses, and of the same type as those supplied by the Elswick
firm to the ' Duilio ' and the ' Dandolo,' and to the Chinese gunboat
flotilla. The power thus generated is applied to turn the turret by
two hydraulic engines, one being used as a reserve in case of an
accident happening to the other. The motive power is transferred
to a crank shaft by three oscillating rams, the plungers of which are
$4\frac{1}{2}$ inches in diameter and have a stroke of 1 ft. 6 in. This
crank actuates a pinion which runs in a rack round the base of the
turret and turns the mass. At the trial the turret was rotated
by the port engine in 1 min. 8 sec. with forty-two revolutions of the
engine, and was then reversed in 1 min. 10 sec. with forty revolutions.
The port engine was then disconnected, and with the starboard
hydraulic engine in action the turret was turned in 1 min. 16 sec.
with thirty-seven revolutions, and reversed in 1 min. 18 sec. with
thirty-six revolutions. The pressure on the plungers was 750 lbs. on
the square inch, and the pressure of steam at the pumping engine
68 lbs. The turret was subsequently rotated at a creeping pace, and
was thoroughly under the command of the engineers. Although the
80-ton guns will be worked on a system similar to that adopted in
the case of the 38-ton guns of the ' Thunderer,' yet as the design of
the ' Inflexible ' had not been completed before the decision to work
the guns by hydraulic power was formed, a much more complete
hydraulic gunnery arrangement has become possible. The sponging
and loading apparatus is still, as in the ' Thunderer,' to be placed at
duplicate fixed stations outside the turrets, and under the protection

Method of rotating the turrets.

of the armoured deck of the vessel. The muzzles of the guns are brought to the loading mechanism by revolving the turret and slightly depressing the guns. But there is no special loading-port as in the 'Thunderer.' All that is necessary is to depress the guns to the small angle required for bringing the muzzles below the level of the deck, which is raised and inclined upward at the base of the turrets so as to form a sort of glacis, and to give cover to the muzzles without involving any considerable depression of the gun. By this means the objection brought against the greater depression of the guns of the 'Thunderer' is avoided.

Mounting of the 80-ton guns.

A more important novelty is the manner of mounting the 80-ton guns in the turrets. Hitherto it has been the practice to place all heavy guns upon an iron structure, called the carriage, on which they rest by means of the trunnions. This carriage bears, besides the guns, the mechanism for elevating and depressing the gun, and for 'tripping,' and also in part the mechanism for checking recoil. Besides the carriage, again, there is the slide upon which the carriage runs. In the novel system adopted for the 'Inflexible,' the bold step has been taken of dispensing altogether with a carriage, properly so called. The two guns are mounted side by side in each turret. Each gun is supported on three points. The trunnions rest on blocks sliding on fixed beams bolted down to the floor of the turret, while the breech rests on a third block, sliding like the others between guides upon a beam or table. Behind each of the trunnion-blocks, in the line of recoil, are two hydraulic cylinders, connected

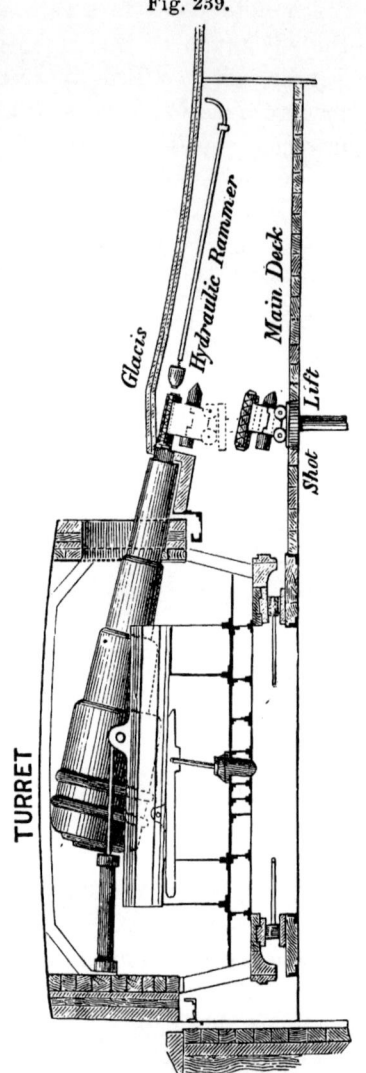

Fig. 239.

LOADING ARRANGEMENTS OF THE 'INFLEXIBLE.'

with them by piston-rods. The cylinders communicate by a pipe, on which there is a valve, which, on the recoil of the gun, opens and allows the pistons to run back slowly, checking the recoil. By reversing the apparatus, the gun can be run out again. The beam on which the breech rests is supported by a third hydraulic cylinder, fixed vertically beneath it.

The following account of an official trial of the 'Inflexible' appeared in the *Times* of November 15, 1878 :—

Trials of the 'Inflexible.'

The trial here described was a six hours' run between Spithead and the Nab. 'A stiffish wind of the force from five to seven blew from the north-west, and the sea was of a decidedly lumpy character. The behaviour of the ship, however, was all that could be desired; and though when driven at full speed against the wind, her prow threw up a massive wave to the estimated height of 8 feet, it subsided almost instantly. It must also be remarked that her draught was about three feet less than when at her load line, her trim being 18 ft. 10 in. forward and 23 feet aft. When she receives her turret armour and other weights on board, the effect of her submerged ram upon the surface water will be less apparent; and as at the same time her twin propellers will be further immersed, the useful power of the machinery will be also increased.

Six hours' run.

'Since the last trial the four-bladed propellers, which were found to be over-much for the engines, have been removed, and two-bladed screws of the Griffith's form substituted, having a diameter of 20 feet, and fitted with a means of varying the pitch from 21 ft. 6 in. to 25 ft. 6 in. They were yesterday set at a pitch of 23 feet. Their surface area, however, is only about a third less than the old four-bladed screws, and, like those of the "Iris," their surfaces are perfectly smooth, the nuts being enclosed within a conical cap. The ventilation, which was simply unbearable on the former occasion, has also been greatly improved in the meantime. Two upcast shafts suck up the heated air from the engine-room on each side of the middle line, and convey it into a trunk below the armour-deck, whence it is discharged into the 6-inch funnel casing. Two shafts have been also fitted behind the cylinder, and communicate with cowls on the pilot tower on the bridge; and besides these, which constitute the additional natural ventilators, there are supplementary artificial ventilators in the shape of fresh-air leads from the fans. The result was that there was an excellent down-rush of fresh air through the engine-room hatches, the hot air escaping at the rate of 2,000 cubic feet per minute, and with a speed of 300 feet per minute. At no time during the most furious part of the trial did the temperature

Screws.

Ventilation.

rise beyond 110° behind the cylinders at the wings. The ventilation of the citadel has likewise been improved by perforated trunks, which discharge into the outer funnel casing.

'Though the heaviest ship afloat, having a displacement of 11,500 tons, the engine-power of the "Inflexible" is relatively much less than that of several ships in the service; while with a positively smaller displacement, the "Dreadnought," "Sultan," "Alexandra," and "Neptune" possess engines which are capable of exerting greater horse-power than those with which this monster turret-vessel has been fitted. Indeed, seeing that her engines have indicated 9,000 horses, being a horse for every ton of displacement, the "Neptune" is the most powerfully engined ship in the navy. While the constant of indicated horse-power to displacement in the "Sultan" is 441·8, the "Neptune" 434·7, and the "Dreadnought" 491·2, the constant of the "Inflexible" is 509·5. The differences are sufficiently startling, and Mr. Barnaby has acknowledged that so far was he from feeling sure that, with the unusual proportions adopted in the "Inflexible" (324 feet long by 75 feet broad), a speed of 14 knots would be realised with 8,000 indicated horse-power, that he had strongly recommended that a new "Inflexible" should not be commenced until there had been a trial of speed with the present one. Should 14 knots be obtained, Mr. Barnaby states he would be the first to thank Mr. Froude for having encouraged the Constructive Department to adopt such proportions in a 14-knot ship, and with such a small proportion of power to displacement. "Nothing like it has been done or attempted before." At the time when the Committee on Designs held their inquiry in 1871, the greatest breadth actually adopted for a seagoing ship of war in any navy was 62½ feet, the proportion of breadth to length in that case being about 5 to 1, and Mr. Barnaby did not hesitate to characterise as "extreme" a proposal to construct a ship of 4½ beams in the length. "Neither Mr. Reed nor the Committee," Mr. Barnaby observes, "expressed any dissent from my view of what was to be regarded as an extreme proportion for 14-knot ships. In 1873, in designing the 'Inflexible' in the light of Mr. Froude's latest investigations, we went beyond this extreme proportion of breadth. This extreme proportion would have made the 'Inflexible' 72 feet wide, and we made her 75 feet." Whether therefore we regard the extreme weight of the "Inflexible" or her proportion of breadth to length, the comparative weakness of her engine-power is not a little surprising. Nevertheless, the gross result of the trial yesterday was so pre-eminently satisfactory, that little doubt need be entertained that with such a large margin of power 14 knots will be realised on the mile.

'As in the case of the hull, the whole of the machinery has been Arrange- constructed with a view of meeting and satisfying the trying re- ment of machinery. quirements of modern naval warfare. The ship, indeed, embodies Mr. Barnaby's essentials, that there should be defence for the pro- pelling power, for the steering power, and for the floating power against the gun, the ram, and the torpedo. In the " Inflexible," therefore, the propelling power and the steering power are duplicated, and the whole is placed under the protection of armour which is proof to all guns below the power of the chambered 38-ton gun. She is propelled by twin screws, an arrangement which has been adopted not only because they have been proved to be more efficient than single screws as regards economy of power exerted, but because they combine the following important advantages in a man-of-war— viz., greater security against total disablement of the propelling apparatus, greater handiness, and the maintenance of manœuvring power in case of serious damage occurring to the rudder or steering gear, and greater facilities for the watertight subdivisions of the engine-room and stokeholes by means of middle-line bulkheads. The screws, which work outwards, are each driven by an independent compound engine. The propelling engines are of 1,200 nominal horse-power in the aggregate, and are guaranteed by Messrs. Elder and Co. to indicate 8,000 horses on the measured mile, though as a matter of fact the contractors felt such confidence in the performances of the machinery that they voluntarily accepted a six hours' trial as a substitute for the now practically obsolete runs on the mile as a test of endurance.

'The engines, which belong to the inverted or " hammer " type, Engines. whereby a longer stroke and a diminution of strains are secured, have each three cylinders—viz., a high-pressure cylinder, 20 feet in dia- meter, and two low-pressure cylinders, with a stroke of four feet. The cylinders are connected by stay-bolts continued to bulkheads, so as to serve as ramming chocks and prevent injury by concussion. Each engine was originally fitted with expansion valves, but this gear has been removed since the previous trial, the expansion being now effected by link motions on the main slides. The faces of the high- pressure cylinders are formed of phosphor bronze, two inches thick, and the liners of the high-pressure cylinders are made of Whitworth fluid-compressed steel, which possesses properties that render it not only extremely light, but, at the same time, much more trustworthy than the ordinary metal used for this and shafting purposes. The piston-rods, which are double and joined by crossheads, are seven inches in diameter, the connecting-rods having a diameter of nine inches, and a length of 7 ft. 6 in. The valves are of the piston kind, the casings being bolted to the cylinders to form receivers. They are worked by link motions and levers, and are reversed by a combination of steam and hydraulic power. The steam from the low-pressure cylinders is exhausted into independent condensers, having a total cooling surface of 16,000 square feet, and in being condensed, it passes through an aggregation of tubes of $\frac{3}{4}$-inch external diameter, of which each condenser has no fewer than 6,650. The surface condensers are also constructed to be worked as common condensers, and each engine is, besides, fitted with a common injection apparatus. The circulating pumps are actuated by separate engines. The air-pumps are formed of gun-metal, with a diameter of 34 inches, and a stroke of 2 ft. 3 in., the water being discharged from below the armour deck, and, together with the feed and bilge pumps, are worked by levers from the low-pressure crossheads. It may also be mentioned that the centrifugal pumps are placed at so high a level in the vessel that in the case of a leakage by which the ship's bottom may be flooded to as great a depth as twelve feet they can be worked with perfect freedom. The engines at starting are assisted by auxiliary steam gear, the valves of which are fitted to the receiver. Then there are double-acting, two-coupled hand pumps, feed donkey-engines with double-acting pumps 4 inches in diameter, bilge donkeys with double-acting pumps 6 inches in diameter, and fire-engines with double-acting pumps $8\frac{1}{2}$ inches in diameter. It may also be stated that the engines which work the circulating pumps are also designed to pump out the bilge in the event of the ship springing a leak from any cause; that the centrifugal pumps can perform the same work in case of emergency; and that a Kingston valve is fitted through the bottom in connection with each fire-pump. The crank-shaft is, for purposes of convenience, formed of three pieces, the diameter of the bearings being $17\frac{1}{2}$ inches. The shaft tubes are of wrought iron, supported by struts, while the shafting, which has an inner diameter of ten inches, and an outer diameter of 16 inches, is formed of the Whitworth steel above mentioned, with solid couplings. Each engine is fitted with a " governor " to prevent racing in stormy weather, and, in addition to the hand gear, small noiseless auxiliary engines are provided for turning the main engines. Altogether the engines weigh 614 tons, or 100 tons less than the contract, while the weight of the propellers and stern fittings is 190 tons each.

Boilers.   'The "Inflexible" is the only ship yet constructed in which the stokeholes—which are divided by a longtitudinal bulkhead—are placed at both ends of the engine-room. This arrangement is not only more convenient, but enables either the fore or the after stoke-hole to be cut off in case of accident without disabling the ship. The boilers, of which there are twelve—eight single-ended and four double-ended—are made of Lowmoor plates, tested to 21 tons lengthwise, and 18 tons crosswise, and are stayed for a working pressure of 60 lbs. The double-ended boilers, of which each stoke-hole contains two, placed along the middle-line bulkhead, are 17 feet long, 9 ft. 3 in. wide, and 14 ft. 3 in. high, and are heated by four furnaces; while of the eight single-ended boilers, four are 9 feet long, 13 ft. 7 in. wide, and 15 ft. 6 in. high, with three furnaces, and the remainder 9 feet long, 11 feet wide, and 13 ft. 4 in. high, with a couple of furnaces, each having a separate fire-box. The whole are clothed with four thicknesses of felt, besides galvanised sheet iron, and are stayed to prevent their moving by concussion in ramming. They are also provided in the interior with zinc plates as a protection against corrosion. In the event of the feed-pumps by which they are supplied with water getting out of order, the boilers are fitted with four auxiliary engines (one in each boiler-room) having separate connections with the boilers. The safety-valves are fitted with springs upon an improved plan. The funnels, of which there are two, stand 65 feet high from the dead plate of the lower furnaces. The bunkers, which are placed at the water-line along the unarmoured sides of the ship, where the entrance of shot or water cannot injure them, are built to store 1,200 tons of coal, and are so arranged that their contents can be approached from the upper and lower compartments independently of each other. The boilers, funnel casings, etc., weigh 522 tons, and the water in the boilers, when full, is estimated at 190 tons.

'Besides the main engines above described, this immense floating machine contains the following auxiliary engines:—A horizontal direct-acting steering engine (Forrester's patent);- two vertical direct-acting fire-engines; a capstan engine (Harfield's patent); a small vertical direct-acting turning engine; two vertical direct-acting donkey engines for pumping out the bilges; four auxiliary feed engines, of the same character as the donkeys, and placed one in each stoke-hole; four of Brotherhood's patent three-cylinder fan engines; a couple of horizontal direct-acting centrifugal engines for circulating the water through the condensers; two reversing engines (steam and hydraulic power combined); two pairs of steam and hydraulic engines for working the shot hoists and the gun-loading apparatus, and turning the turrets; four vertical direct-acting ash hoists; a couple of 40-horse-power engines for pumping out the

Number of auxiliary engines.

main drains ; two steam shot hoists ; two of Brotherhood's 3-cylinder engines for lifting and lowering boats, and four of Friedman's patent ejectors. Altogether, then, the " Inflexible," when commissioned, will have no fewer than 39 engines on board.

' The ship got under way from Spithead shortly after 9, and by 20 minutes past 9 the half-hourly observations were commenced, the engines being in charge of a numerous staff and the stoking being performed by not fewer than 120 stokers in two watches. In order to show the uniformity with which the power was maintained throughout the trial we append the half-hourly returns, merely remarking that with the exception of the last half-hour, when the power developed was over 900 horses beyond the contract, the blast was not once used.

Half-hour	Steam in Boiler	Indicated Horse-power	Half-hour	Steam in Boiler	Indicated Horse-power
1	59½	8,160·38	7	59½	8,250·03
2	60¾	8,602·75	8	61	8,554·67
3	62	8,462·87	9	62	8,373·42
4	62½	8,527·48	10	61¼	8,502·20
5	60½	8,559·53	11	60	8,460·43
6	61	8,476·95	12	60	8,909·00

' Giving a mean power developed of 8,407·30 horses, the number beyond the 8,000 being in excess of the contract. The vacuum in condensers varied from 27 inches, the maximum, to 25¾ inches, the minimum, and the revolutions of the port and starboard engines from 75 to 71·5 per minute. The following were the means :— Steam in boilers, 61 lbs. ; vacuum—starboard, 26·8 forward and 26·8 aft ; port, 26·4 forward and 26·06 aft ; revolutions, 73·98 starboard and 72·45 aft ; pressure of steam in cylinders—starboard high-pressure, 29·61 lbs. ; starboard low-pressure, 10·20 lbs. ; port high-pressure, 29·5 lbs. ; port low-pressure, 9·48 lbs. The total indicated horse-power was 8,407·30, and the consumption of coal per horse was 2·05 lbs. The first throw of the log gave a speed of 14 knots ; but as this means of ascertaining the speed of a ship is only approximate, and as the patent log happened to be carried away while it was being drawn in, four runs were made upon the measured mile in Stokes Bay, whereby all doubt was removed. The results showed that with the tide the " Inflexible " was making 16·143 and 16·216 knots per hour, and against the tide 13·284 and 13·282 knots, thus giving a mean speed of 14·750 knots per hour. The engines worked without a single hitch, and neither the boilers nor the bearings gave the slightest trouble.

'The enormous weight of the vessel, which has a displacement of   Speed.
nearly 12,000 tons, and the bad weather would have excused a
moderate speed; but, in spite of unfavourable circumstances, her
average speed is about 15 knots an hour—a speed which places her,
heavily handicapped as she is, on a par with vessels which have
surrendered certain important advantages to attain speed. The
"Thunderer" the year before attained a mean speed of 13·479 knots;
while the "Téméraire" only attained the mean speed of 14·563 knots;
and in the "Inflexible" the consumption of coal per unit of horse-
power compares favourably with these vessels.

'The "Inflexible" is also to possess sail-power, with respect to the   Proposed
advantages of which considerable diversity of opinion exists. She   rig.
will be brig-rigged, having two iron masts, but no bowsprit or head
gear. In the original design it was proposed to fit her with two pole
masts, with sail set flying for use as steadying sails, and as a stand-by
in the event of total disablement of the machinery; but this was
subsequently modified in accordance with a suggestion of Rear-
Admiral (then Captain) Hood, who strongly recommended that the
idea of having masts in such a vessel should be abandoned. "The
small amount of sail," he remarked in a letter to the Controller,
"which could be carried on the proposed masts would be of very
slight value in the event of the most remote contingency of both sets
of engines being totally disabled, and in action the fall of the masts
might interfere considerably with the delivery of fire from the turrets."
It was, therefore, decided to provide the ship with two masts for
signalling and for crow's nests, but with no yards fitted upon them.
This will still be the fighting trim of the "Inflexible,"[1] but in times
of peace she will carry two lofty masts, with yards and sails. The
lower masts, which are about three feet in diameter, are made of
steel, and are the first of the kind which have been manufactured at
Portsmouth. They are formed in two parts, the lower or permanent
portion being stepped upon the main deck and rising to the top of
the superstructure deck, a distance of 20 feet, where they are joined
to the fore and main masts. The junction is effected by what is
termed a parting joint—an ingenious arrangement, the invention of
Messrs. Finch and Heath, the well-known mastmakers. The upper
and lower parts of the mast are each strengthened at their junction
by a flanged angle-iron collar, the horizontal flanges being accurately
fitted to each other, and the whole is secured by an exterior iron band
or ring. The ring is grooved internally, and when in position this

---

[1] As the 'Inflexible' is masted only   amongst the *mastless* turret-ships.
for peace service, she is here included

groove clutches the horizontal flanges of the collar. When both halves of the ring are in place they are held together by screw-bolts passing through lugs in the ring, and the parting-joint is at least as strong as any other part of the mast. Should it ever be necessary to let go the masts in a storm, or to strip suddenly for action, all that will be required is to unscrew the bolts, whereupon the ring falls off and the mast goes overboard without the deck being injured. When war, however, is anticipated the ship will be docked for the purpose of having her cruising masts lifted out, when she will have wooden pole masts fitted into the tubular sockets. These pole masts will be required for signalling purposes, for derricks, and for enabling her to carry her boats. The length of the steel foremast above the deck is 75 feet, while the topmast is 46 ft. 6 in., and the topgallant mast (including pole) is 39 feet. The total height is thus 160 ft. 6 in., the weight of the steel portion being 12½ tons. The steel mainmast is 78 feet, the topmast 46 feet, and topgallant mast 39 feet long, the total length being thus 163 feet. The weight of the steel is 13½ tons, each of the bands weighing 5¾ cwts. The present purpose is to fit the foremast with a lower yard 79 ft. 6 in. long, a topgallant yard 45 feet, and royal yard 36 ft. 6 in., and the mainmast with spars of like dimensions. The gaff is 45 feet and the boom 64 feet long, while the total contemplated sail area, is 18,500 square feet.'

It has been stated by Mr. Barnaby that the rig of the 'Inflexible' was not introduced in deference to the views of naval officers, but is part of the design of the ship. It will not be a source of peril to the ship in action, because it is distinctly understood that in time of war the ship would carry none of it, except the two lower masts as signal poles. The advantages of the small rig she is to have in time of peace are in every way considerable, and commended themselves to those with whom the final decision rested.

In the 'Inflexible,' the stowage of boats has been a question of considerable difficulty. It has now been determined that the entire complement shall be carried above the after superstructure, where skid beams are being fitted for the purpose. The ship will carry twelve boats, two of which are to be second-class torpedo launches. On the superstructure decks racers and pivots are also being fitted for accommodating the six 20-pdr. guns, which are required for saluting purposes and for defence against boat attacks.

Estimated weights.

The estimated weight of the hull is 7,300 tons. The engines weigh 614 tons. The propellers, shafts, and stern-fittings weigh 151 tons each; the boilers, smoke-pipes, and casings, 522 tons, and the water in the boilers, when ready for steaming, is estimated at 190 tons.

The first estimates of cost were :—

Materials	.	.	.	.	£269,000
Engines and appendages		.	.	.	100,150
Boilers	.	.	.	.	20,600
Labour	.	.	.	.	132,000
Total	.	.	.	.	£521,750

As a new type of a man-of-war the leading features of the 'Inflexible' may be summed up as follows. The armour is confined to the central fighting portion and to the main substructure which floats the ship. An armoured deck seven feet under water divides the vessel into two separate portions. The unarmoured ends are so constructed that the vessel will float even when they are penetrated by shot. The ship has a wide beam and comparatively light draught of water. The deckhouses give a high bow and stern, and the turrets are so arranged as to enable all four guns to be fired, both ahead and astern, or on either beam.

In a letter addressed to the *Times*, Mr. Barnaby made the following observations on the comparative strength of the ' Duilio ' and the ' Inflexible.'

'Inflexible' and 'Duilio.'

'The " Duilio " and " Dandolo " were in course of construction before the design of the " Inflexible " was entered upon, and there will be a greater thickness of armour on all corresponding parts of the sides, bulkheads, and turrets of the " Inflexible " than in the Italian ships.

'When the latter ships were commenced it was intended that they should have guns of about sixty tons each in their turrets, and that their maximum thickness of armour on the sides should be about 22 inches, that on the turrets being about sixteen inches. It was found that a ship could be built, not costing more than the "Dreadnought," and having less draught of water, which could carry such guns as the Italian ships were then to have, with armour about two inches thicker than theirs, and which would not have those special features which had provoked hostile criticism in the "Devastation" type, and which were being repeated in the Italian ships.

'The decision to build such a ship in England appears to have led to increase in weight and power of the proposed guns in the Italian ships, so that guns originally spoken of as 60-ton guns are now understood to be in course of manufacture at Elswick as 100-ton guns. This increase in the weight of the guns has been gained by changes in the arrangement of the armour which have not tended to increase the defensive power of the Italian ships. While the " Inflexible " was commenced many months after these two rivals, she is to be launched before either of them.'

Mr. Reed,
M.P.
Observa-
tions on
stability of
' Duilio.'

The recent discussions on the stability of the 'Inflexible' are fully examined in Mr. King's second edition. He relates that ' During the summer of 1875, or thereabouts, Mr. E. J. Reed, C.B., M.P., made visits of observation to one or both of the great ships building in Italy. After his return to London he pronounced these ships unsafe for battle. He said: " The Italian ships ' Duilio' and ' Dandolo' are exposed, in my opinion, beyond all doubt or question, to speedy destruction. I fear I can only express my apprehension that the Italians are pursuing a totally wrong course, and one which is likely to result in disaster." The charge was promptly met and stoutly denied by the Italian Minister of Marine, from his seat in the Parliament at Rome. He said: " Mr. Reed cannot possibly prove any such statements, because no one but the designer and his con-fidential agents are entitled to have the particulars for making the necessary calculations ; and, in case of a half-built ship, the inten-tions of the designer with regard to the disposition of a great mass of material not yet arranged and specified form part of these par-ticulars."

' The Italians have proceeded to complete these two great ships according to the original design, and trust for both buoyancy and stability to their unarmoured ends. And in their later and far larger ships, the " Italia " and " Lepanto," they have, in full view of Mr. Reed's criticisms, gone still further and abandoned the citadel itself.

Mr. King's
narrative
of the con-
troversy
respecting
the sta-
bility of the
'Inflexible.'

' The " Inflexible," which is of the same type, and of the plans of which Mr. Reed no doubt had knowledge from the time she was laid down in February, 1874, was at this time building, yet nothing was said of the want of stability in this ship. The progress of construc-tion continued rapidly to advance for three and a half years : the completed ship was promised for 1878, and the British public believed that their Government would soon possess the most formida-ble and the most perfect war-ship ever floated, when, suddenly, sur-prise and alarm were created by the announcement that it had become a serious question to one or more naval architects, outside the Admiralty, whether the promised and essential conditions of the safety of the " Inflexible " had been attained. It appeared to a com-petent critic, who had been investigating the subject, that the central citadel of the ship was too small to secure of itself the end designed, and that the added buoyancy in the unprotected ends might, in action, soon be shot away.   The *Times* under date of June 18, 1876, published the result of the calculations, and Mr. Reed brought on the question, on similar lines, in the House of Commons.   The First Lord defended the Admiralty with conspicuous gallantry, treating the criticisms as a departmental attack ; the papers and letters were called for and laid before the House, when it was seen that the naval constructors asserted one thing and Mr. Reed, with no inferior authority, asserted the opposite.   Mr. Reed said that in action the cork and stores might be shot away, and the unprotected ends riddled and water-logged ; and that in such an event the citadel, though intact, would still capsize.   The reply was, that the supposed case was too remote a possibility to be considered, and that without any unprotected ends the ship would still float.   The argument became close and intricate.   The various means of capsizing a ship were considered, as well as the different operations of explosive shells in the destruction of cork and stores.   The varied perils to which the ship would be exposed in battle, with ends riddled—such as the action from the waves, the moving of the " free water " within the ship, the pitching and the rolling, the running out of the guns, and last, but not least, from the action of the rudder as the vessel approached its minimum stability—were all discussed and treated of.

' The essential points in the correspondence may be summarised as follows :—

' First Mr. Reed said : " On visiting the ' Inflexible ' from time to time, I found that the unarmoured ends were so very large in proportion to the citadel as to raise in my mind a doubt as to this important condition being fulfilled.   Observing this, and also the introduction of cork chambers, I designed an ' Inflexible ' in my own office, and had the whole of the calculations made, the result showing that when these cork chambers were destroyed the vessel would have no stability whatever, but would be in a condition to capsize.

' " Second : My objection is not that the ' Inflexible ' and other vessels do not possess that final reserve of stability, after a severe and protracted engagement, which I consider necessary, but that the cork chambers will be liable in action to speedy destruction, and that the ship will then be left without stability." '

Sir E. Reed alleged that, when the ' Inflexible ' was ordered, the Constructor's Department at the Admiralty undertook that the armoured citadel should have ample stability for keeping the ship afloat in an upright position, without any assistance from the unarmoured ends.   He contended that every heavily armoured ship has been designed to comply with this condition. Since the design was first prepared considerable modifications had been introduced, and the 'Inflexible,' instead of having an ample reserve of stability after the unarmoured structure had lost its buoyancy, would not have sufficient stability for withstanding the heave of the sea, or the action of its own rudder.

Sir E. Reed pointed to the engagement between the 'Shah' and the 'Huascar,' and to the fact that the unarmoured superstructure of the Peruvian ship was swept away by the fire of the 'Shah' and the 'Amethyst,' as conclusive evidence of the destructibility of the unprotected parts of the ship. He feared and believed that the cork chambers in action would be speedily and completely destroyed. With the unarmoured ends destroyed, the ship would be overwhelmed by a single torpedo. He pointed out that whereas the original design provided ample stability within the armoured citadel, the Admiralty are now seeking to prove that such stability is unnecessary.

Reply of the Admiralty: Director of Naval Construction.

The reply of the Admiralty officials, laid on the table of the House of Commons, consists of several papers quoted below: First, a letter from the Director of Naval Construction in which, besides giving curves of stability and tables of calculations,[1] he also states: 'But when I say that I regard this stability as being sufficient in view of the possible diminution of the stability by slow degrees by the blowing out of the cork walls and internal solid stores, I desire to add that I regard the possibility of the ship ever being reduced to this state as being infinitely remote, although not absolutely impossible. If the water be kept out of the coal spaces by the cofferdams, as I believe it will be, the ship will retain an amount of stability far in excess of the "Devastation," including her wings added by us. In that case the water will not flow over her decks, as is supposed in the model; these decks will remain as high out of the water as the fore deck of the "Devastation," and we should see no more reason for supposing the sea to wash freely from side to side in those decks than in the "Devastation."

'In order to justify Mr. Reed's objection, it is necessary to assume still further that every atom of solid material, excluding water, in the cellular store-rooms and in the cork walls has been blown out of the ship, and that only the battered iron shell remains, loading down the ship, but giving her no assistance. With regard to that, I say that no heavily armoured ship ever has been designed to comply with such a condition.

[1] See pp. 424, 425.

'I ought, perhaps, to add that the whole of this discussion turns upon the power of the ship to resist the attacks of artillery, and I have endeavoured to show that a fair balance is maintained between thickness of armour and extent of surface covered by armour. But, after all, the power of resisting attacks above water is only one element of the defence. We have also to consider the under-water attack. It would be easy, following Mr. Reed's course, to lay down some principle with regard to these attacks, and to say that no ship is well designed which is not so subdivided as to satisfy certain conditions.'

The second paper is from Rear-Admiral Boys, Director of Naval Ordnance. He said: 'Looking at this as a question of naval artillery, I conceive that the conditions on which Mr. Reed bases his argument as to the safety of the ship cannot be brought about in a naval engagement. These conditions are, practically, that the fore and after ends of the ship are to be utterly demolished. Should the " Inflexible " be made a target for continued practice, or be placed in a position similar to a fort whose walls could be breached by a battery of fixed guns, it is possible that in time the unarmoured parts above water might be destroyed; but I do not think, for the following reasons, it is possible in a naval engagement to commit the havoc below the water that is presupposed by Mr. Reed: Rear Admiral Boys' opinion.

' 1. The difficulty is great of striking a ship at or below the water-line, particularly one of the " Inflexible " type, that will seldom roll.

' 2. The projectiles that would be fired at the " Inflexible " would certainly be armour-piercing, either chilled iron or steel ; and such shell would not burst in passing through the thin iron sides of the ship, as they require the resistance of armour to ignite the bursting charge.

' 3. Considering the few guns that are likely to be carried by any ship engaging the " Inflexible," and the ever-varying distance and bearing that must exist in any future naval action, it is next to impossible that any number of shells could be planted in a ship in such an exact position (even supposing them to burst) as to blow out the cork from the chambers in which it will be fixed.

' Those in charge of the ship must be devoid of all resource if during the intervals of an engagement—for intervals there must be—they could not take some steps, by the employment of stopper-mats or shot-plugs, etc., to prevent the unarmoured ends of the ship from being water-logged ; or supposing the water to come in, to allow it to run into the bilge, to be pumped out by the engines.

' If the ship should get a list from water finding its way into the divisions at either end above the armoured deck, it appears to me there are simple means at hand that can be resorted to for balancing her in an upright position.

'I have no hesitation in saying I do not share, for one moment, Mr. Reed's anxiety for the safety of the "Inflexible" in action, from the effect of artillery fire, as expressed by him.'

Sir Houston Stewart's opinion. The third paper is from Vice-Admiral Sir Houston Stewart, K.C.B., Controller of the Navy, which may be summarised as follows:

'The result which has been assumed in this letter (Mr. Reed's) could, in my opinion, only be arrived at if we can suppose the ship lying perfectly helpless and immovable, and allowing herself to be attacked by an indefinite number of guns. By this means it is possible that a large portion of the unarmoured structure above water might be destroyed; but even then, I fail to see how it is possible to destroy or remove entirely all material, timber, cork, stores, coal or other articles which, while remaining in any portion of the structure, must exclude water or prevent water taking their place. To assume this ship placed in such a position, is, to my mind, representing an exaggerated state of circumstances which could never occur in real warfare.

'Place any other ironclads defended with what is now very weak armour at the extremities in this assumed position, and where would these ships be after a course of such treatment as we are asked to consider likely to occur, during an action, to the 'Inflexible'? because it must be remembered that while we talk of protection from armour we must discard armour of less than a certain thickness. In recent ironclads of large size built in England for foreign Governments from the designs of Mr. Reed, the thickness of armour protecting vital parts is penetrable by guns of 12 tons. In the 'Independenzia,'[1] a ship of 9,000 tons displacement, the engines are protected by not more than 9 inches of armour, which is easily penetrable by the 12-ton gun. In the 'Kaiser' and 'Deutschland' the powder magazines and engines are protected by not more than the 8 inches of armour which is perforable by the 9-ton gun. A few well-delivered rounds from these guns could have but small effect on the unarmoured ends of the 'Inflexible,' whereas they would be fatal to the existence of the above and most other ironclads of their type.'

Admiralty letter. In their official letter to Mr. Reed of June 5 last, the Admiralty view is expressed as follows:—

'The question is to be regarded solely as one to be decided upon the grounds of what is or is not likely to occur in a naval action

[1] Now H.M.S. 'Neptune.'

under shell fire. This subject has been fully investigated by the naval members of the Board of Admiralty and the Director of Naval Ordnance, who are unanimously of opinion that the effects anticipated by you could not occur under the condition of a naval action. Upon these grounds my Lords differ from the views expressed by you, and consider the "Inflexible" to be a safe and most formidable fighting vessel.'

In professional authority and reputation Sir E. Reed, as an ex-Constructor, stands on exactly the same footing with Mr. Barnaby, his successor. His statements necessarily created grave anxiety in the public mind. It was therefore necessary to appoint a committee to adjudicate between the disputants on the technical question on which it was impossible for Parliament to pronounce judgment. The committee was composed of gentlemen in every way qualified to form an opinion. Its president was a distinguished officer, with whom were associated three men of science familiar with naval construction. The suggestion that the committee was not free from bias is inadmissible. The members were Admiral Sir James Hope, Dr. I. Woolley, Mr. G. W. Rendel, C.E., and Mr. Froude, F.R.S. They were appointed in August, and were instructed to consider a series of questions, the investigations of which and the experiments made by them seem to have engaged their time until early in December, when their report was submitted to the Admiralty. The following is a summary of the essential points in their report :—

First: 'The opinion of the Committee is invited as to the probability of the occurrence of the contingencies contemplated by Mr. Reed as being likely to happen early in an engagement, namely, the complete penetration and water logging of the unprotected ends of the ship, and the blowing out of the whole of the stores and the cork by the action of shell-fire.'

'On this point the committee are of opinion that the complete penetration and water-logging of the unprotected ends of the ship, coupled with the blowing out of the whole of the stores and the cork by the action of shell-fire, is not likely to happen very early in an engagement ; further, that it is in a very high degree improbable, even in an engagement protracted to any extent which can be reasonably anticipated. Nor do they think it possible, except in the event of her being attacked by enemies of such preponderating force as to render her entering into any engagement in the highest degree imprudent.

'Question two is divided into two clauses. First it is asked, "Whether there would be any risk of the ship capsizing if she were placed under the conditions mentioned in the previous paragraph,

Committee appointed.

supposing that the water ballast were admitted into the double bottom of the armoured citadel." The committee find that "under the extreme conditions assumed, the ship, even without water-ballast, would yet have stability, and would, therefore, float upright in still water, and we are of opinion that the stability that she would have in that condition, though small, is, in consequence of the remarkable effects of free internal water in extinguishing rolling, sufficient to enable her to encounter with safety waves of considerable magnitude. The ship under these circumstances, however, would require to be handled with great caution. The admission of water as ballast increases the amount of stability, and is thus of advantage as against steady inclining forces ; but on account of the deeper immersion it involves it does not materially increase the range of the stability. When the immersion is such as largely to increase the depth of the water on the middle deck, it appears that the extinguishing effect of such water becomes less vigorous, so that in a seaway the ship would, in the extreme condition, be safer with a moderate than with a very large amount of water admitted as ballast. It must be clearly understood, however, that we should consider the ship in a very critical state if reduced to this condition in the presence of a still powerful enemy. Her speed and power of turning would be so limited as to prevent her being manœuvred with sufficient rapidity to insure her against being effectively rammed, or so as to avoid a well directed torpedo, while the small residuum of stability she would possess would not avail to render such an attack other than fatal. Her guns would also have to be worked with great caution, and under restrictions imposed by the high angle to which their combined movements would in broadside firing heel the ship. We have already expressed our opinion that it is in a very high degree improbable that the ship would be reduced to this condition, even in a protracted engagement."'

The second interrogatory is, 'Would she retain a sufficient amount of stability to enable such temporary repairs to be executed as would enable her to reach a port.' The committee think that the destruction, implied by the extreme condition assumed, would be such that nothing effective could be done in the way of repairs at sea under any circumstances.

Question three is also divided into sections. The first is, 'Whether, all points considered, in so far as can be ascertained from the designs and calculations, the "Inflexible" is a safe seagoing vessel.' The committee are of opinion that in the intact condition the 'Inflexible' is a safe seagoing vessel. The consideration of her safety, when not in an intact condition, properly falls under the investigation connected with the subsequent stages of the inquiry.

'The second interrogatory is, "Whether, when the amount of damage to which the unprotected ends would be exposed in action is borne in mind, sufficient provision has been made to insure, in all human probability, her safety under such conditions." We have first to consider what is "the amount of damage to which the unprotected ends would be exposed in action." We do not hesitate to say that the complete destruction implied by riddling and gutting is so extreme an assumption that it may be regarded as a very highly improbable event even in a protracted engagement; yet recognising the extravagance of one assumption does little toward enabling us to fix a reasonable one, and there is no sufficient basis either of actual experience or of experiment on which to decide what amount of damage to the ends is probable. Nor can we take refuge in adopting and providing for the extreme case as covering all others, because provision cannot be made for the safety of the ship in one way without prejudice to it in another, and to give undue prominence to any one provision for its security becomes a serious error where only a just balance can give the best general result. For example, any extension of the citadel in favour of the unprotected ends would necessitate a corresponding reduction of thickness of the armour on the citadel. To the best of our judgment, the condition represented under the letters e or f in the Parliamentary papers is that which might be fairly assumed to represent the greatest amount of damage the ship would be likely to suffer in any action. This condition represents the unprotected ends completely riddled and water-logged, but the materials and cork remaining and adding buoyancy. Under e the whole of the coal is assumed in place, under f it is assumed to be removed. In adopting it we include any state of partial removal of material and partial riddling which may be regarded as its equivalent. We find that the ship, if reduced to this condition, would possess both buoyancy and stability enough to enable her to face all contingencies of weather, and to exercise all her powers, subject, however to the limitations of speed which may be imposed by the character and position of the wounds in the ends, and which might be very serious. The united movement of all her guns from the loading to the firing position would not heel her more than $2\frac{1}{4}$ degrees, and the heel due to her circling at the highest speed attainable would not be an element of danger. The actual range of her stability would be not less than 35 degrees, which is considerably below the standard provisionally laid down by the Committee on Designs, and referred to

in the Parliamentary papers submitted to us. That standard, however, requires revision by the light of more recent investigations of
the theory of rolling. It would be, at any rate, inapplicable to the
present case, because the very water-logging of the ends, which so
reduces the range of stability, has a most remarkable effect in preventing rolling. Should the damage to the ends go beyond what we
contemplate, the ship would still be in no immediate danger of being
placed *hors de combat*. The transition from the condition *e*, in which
she may be said to begin to have her efficiency impaired, to that extreme in which she must be regarded as in a critical state in the
presence of an enemy, is necessarily a gradual one, because it follows
only the progress of destruction of the ends, and can only be completed with that destruction. It cannot be said that the armoured
citadel is invulnerable, or that the unarmoured ends are indestruc-
tible, although the character of the risks they run is different. But in
our opinion the unprotected ends are as well able as the armoured
citadel to bear the part assigned to them in encountering the various
risks of naval warfare, and therefore we consider that a just balance
has been maintained in the design, so that out of a given set of conditions a good result has been obtained.'

The preceding paragraphs give a summary of the report. In the
report itself the committee go into details. Among other points the
committee refer to the great difficulty which exists in hitting objects
at sea with any degree of precision and accuracy. 'Among the chief
sources of error in an action at sea are, the motion of the attacking
vessel, the motion of the attacked vessel, the smoke of both vessels,
the rolling and pitching of the vessel forming the gun-platform, the
imperfect knowledge of the distance of the object aimed at, the action
of the wind in deflecting the shot. As regards the error from imperfect knowledge of distance, the means of ascertaining which at sea are
at present very rude, it is to be remembered that the high speed at
which modern ships of war engage causes them to change their distance with great rapidity. For instance, two vessels approaching, or
receding from each other at the rate of twelve knots vary their distance
apart at the rate of forty feet per second. Errors of range from this and
other causes are, as might be expected, much in excess even of errors
of direction, and a target which is low and wide, like the ends of the
" Inflexible," is much more difficult to hit than one which is high
and narrow. Rifled projectiles are very devious after ricochet, so
that if they fall short of the mark they have little chance of producing effect, while, if they go over, they are equally thrown away.
As regards the effect of the rolling of the ship upon the accuracy of

fire, the gun is generally fired at the middle of the roll, when the deck is nearly horizontal. At such time the speed of the roll is the highest and the disturbing effect greatest, rendering it a matter requiring great skill and practice to make anything like accurate firing, even at short ranges.

'It is to be regretted that there are no exact records of the results of naval firing. The custom is to record it by ocular estimate made from the ships from which the practice is carried on. We are, therefore, only in a position to say that such records as we have had before us confirm, so far as they go, the conclusion we have arrived at as to the improbability of a very large number of shells being planted in the unprotected ends. The unarmoured structures in question arise nine feet above the water, and extend seven feet below it in the fighting condition of the ship. Their length is about 110 feet in front and in rear of the central citadel respectively. The structures to be destroyed are thus about 220 feet long in broadside view, by 16 feet high, nearly one-half of which is below the water-level, and can only be reached by shells entering obliquely or when the side of the ship is partially laid bare by the action of the waves. Shells striking at or about the water-line may rip up the middle deck and let water into the compartment pierced, although it is expected that the canvas and oakum with which the cofferdam is charged will materially obstruct the inflow. Shells cannot, however, lift and blow out all the materials packed in the compartments except they enter very obliquely, which implies long range and consequent greatly increased inaccuracy of fire. The immersion of the vessel occasioned by the admission of water would in itself add to the difficulty of reaching and removing the materials below the water. Viewed obliquely or directly ahead or astern, one or other of the unarmoured ends would derive a considerable amount of protection from the central battery. Shells very rarely make large breaches where they enter the side of an unarmoured vessel. The process of ignition of the bursting charge, commenced on impact, takes a sensible time to complete, and the velocity of the shell being high, and but little diminished by the slight resistance offered by thin plating, it passes on at least six feet to ten feet—corresponding roughly with a time of $\frac{1}{130}$th part of a second—before actual explosion takes place. It therefore enters as a shot by a hole of its own figure, and not greatly exceeding it in size, and from the point at which explosion takes place the fragments go forward in a cone of dispersion, expending themselves in indenting and cutting intervening bulkheads and the opposite side of the ship. The cork wall and cofferdam being only six feet thick in all, most of the shell may be expected to pass through them and to open in the spaces inside, unless striking very obliquely. The most effective armament to bring against the "Inflexible's" ends alone would undoubtedly be one of numerous shell-guns. In an ironclad such an armament is incompatible with armour of a thickness to be of the least avail against the "Inflexible's" guns. It must be a broadside armament, and this carried at a sufficient height above the water-level to be worked in a seaway would involve an extended area of armour incompatible with great thickness. We cannot, therefore, conceive an enemy deliberately adopting the tactics of using or building such ironclads with a special view to attack the unprotected ends only, nor, considering the difficulty of naval fire, do we think firing could be very successfully directed at particular portions of the ship, such as the ends, instead of against the ship as a whole. If called on to engage land forts mounting numerous shell-guns, the exceptional range of her great guns would enable the "Inflexible" to choose her distance, and to engage beyond the range at which guns of such inferior power could strike frequently or with effect. She could also, in case of need, always retire out of action, and choose her own time for renewing an engagement. Probably the most effective mode of bringing a destructive shell-fire to bear on the "Inflexible" would be by a flotilla of gunboats concentrating their fire upon her.

'The committee compare the "Inflexible" as she is with a new "Inflexible," having her armoured citadel drawn out in length so as to render her much more nearly, if not absolutely, independent of the unprotected ends, the thickness of the armour being of course reduced in proportion to its extended area. It may be assumed that an addition to the citadel of at least 30 feet in length would be necessary to satisfy this condition. The thickness of armour would then be in the new ship 21 inches as compared with 24 inches in the present one. If we now suppose the actual "Inflexible" to meet in conflict the new "Inflexible," both being armed with the most powerful guns existing, which are capable of piercing 22 inches of armour, the new ship with her 21 inches of armour would be in immediate danger of receiving a mortal wound by the penetration of her citadel, where the vital parts are so crowded together that one blow might be fatal, and would almost certainly seriously cripple her. The possibility of ultimately crippling the enemy by a multiplicity of slight wounds in his unarmoured extremities would do little or nothing practically to diminish the disparity arising from the fact that one ship possessed penetrable and the other impenetrable armour

Great accuracy of fire would only render it more certain that the penetrable citadel of the supposed new ship would be struck and pierced before the destruction of the ends of the other ship could be completed. In such a case the conclusion seems inevitable that the actual " Inflexible" would be greatly the superior vessel, and if any increase in the power of existing guns takes place, the same argument would induce a shortening and thickening of the armoured citadel walls rather than the reverse. Nor would there appear to be a corresponding loss of advantage to the actual " Inflexible" as compared with the supposed new one, in the event of her having to engage weak ironclads or unarmoured vessels which might be able

Fig. 240.

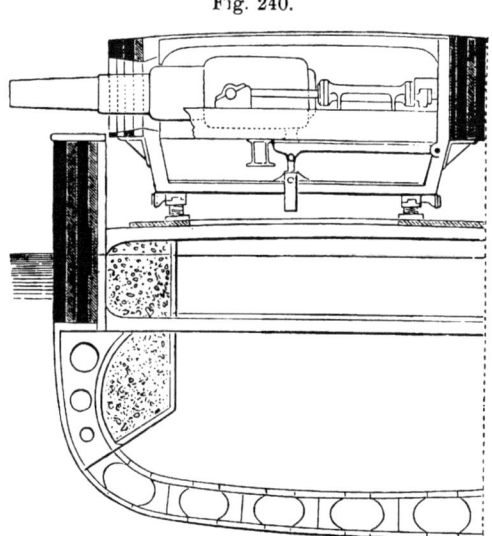

THE 'INFLEXIBLE'S' GUN (SECTION THROUGH TURRET).

to bring against her numerous shell-guns equally useless against 21-inch and 24-inch armour, and therefore only able to attack the unprotected ends ; because, conceding to the " Inflexible" the same accuracy of fire which must be assumed for the enemy before we can contemplate the fire of the shell guns destroying the unprotected ends, either " Inflexible " would have speedily planted among her opponents the few blows necessary to disable them.'

The committee conclude with the following recommendations :—

' 1. Looking to the unexpectedly great demand on the ship's longitudinal stability which may possibly ensue under the circumstances referred to . . . we think it deserving of careful consideration whether it will not be advisable to extend the cork chambers longitudinally to the extreme ends of the ship and upward to the upper deck.

'2. We suggest for consideration that the travel of the guns on their slides should be reduced, and that they should either be so placed in the turrets that they may range equally on each side of the centre, or otherwise that a slight alteration of the distribution of weight in the turret should be made for the purpose of bringing the centre of gravity of the turrets and guns over the centre of evolution when the guns are at the middle of their range on the slides. At present the inclining moment due to the running-out of the guns is over 1,600 foot-tons, and becomes a serious element of danger as the ship approaches the riddled and gutted condition. It might, by the measures proposed, be reduced to little more than one-third of that amount.

'3. We note that the total pumping power which the "Inflexible" will possess, including the use of the circulating pumps, is capable of throwing out 4,500 tons of water per hour; and it is understood that in providing that amount of power a large increase (probably in the ratio of 2 to 1) has been made in the proportion of pumping power to displacement hitherto adopted.

'Notwithstanding this increase, the pumping power is very dis-proportioned to the enormous extent of the leakage to which a modern ship of war is subject in action. The 4,500 tons per hour might be thrown out by 200 horse-power well applied, and it appears to us to be a conclusion, not to be admitted except after the most exhaustive inquiry, that a ship which has at her disposal for motive purposes 8,000 horse-power should not have more than 200 available for pumping purposes when she has been struck in a vital part by ram or torpedo.

'We do not pretend to say how large a proportion of the engine-power could be made available, but we think it right to draw atten-tion to the subject as one demanding grave consideration.

'4. Having expressed the opinion that future progress in the construction of armoured ships lies in the adoption of an efficient system of armour, combined with some cellular or equivalent struc-ture, we cannot but feel desirous that the best mode of dealing with shot and shell in the unarmoured portions of the ends should be made the subject of careful and systematic experimental inquiry. Such inquiry should embrace not only the form and distribution of the cells themselves, but also the best material, if any, with which they might be wholly or partially filled. It is to be re-gretted that a similar recommendation of the Committee on Designs was so imperfectly adopted ; but even the partial experiments made in 1872 added materially to our information, and, so far as they went, they justified the adoption of the cork-filled cells and oakum and canvas packed cofferdams of the " Inflexible." If, however, as we believe, the time has come when cellular structures must form an important feature in a ship's design, the area and scope of such experiments should be greatly enlarged ; and we strongly recommend this subject to the serious consideration of their Lordships.

' 5. Results which have been obtained in the course of the experiments at Torquay on the resistance of ships show that a considerable increase of the extreme breadth of the " Inflexible," if accompanied by a corresponding fining of the ends so as to keep the displacement unaltered, would, if anything, diminish the resistance of the intact vessel to propulsion at full speed. Supposing the ship thus increased in beam by 10 feet and the citadel shortened so as to retain the same perimeter and thickness of armour, her transverse stability would then be about doubled in the e and f conditions, and in the riddled and gutted conditions would be more than it now is in condition e or f.

' Her longitudinal stability in the riddled and gutted condition would be reduced 10 per cent., but would not be diminished in condition e, and scarcely appreciably so in f. The increase of beam would also add to the area of the citadel in a horizontal plane, and thus increase the buoyancy in the riddled condition.

' We note that the beam of the " Inflexible " was limited by the consideration of the width of the docks available for her repair, but we doubt if this consideration ought to outweigh the great advantages which a further increase of beam would give to vessels of the " Inflexible " type. We are the more inclined to doubt it because at present docks capable of accommodating vessels of any breadth can be constructed of iron rapidly, and at no serious cost in comparison with that of such vessels as the " Inflexible."

' We therefore, in conclusion, desire to bring under the very serious consideration of their lordships the necessity, before proceeding with the construction of more vessels of the type of the " Inflexible," of thoroughly investigating whether by more beam their safety may not be largely increased without impairing their speed and efficiency.'

It is impossible to secure immunity from risk in battle. If this much discussed question should ever be practically tested in actual warfare, the 'Inflexible' in like manner with the 'Nelson' and ' Northampton' having unprotected ends, as well as other British

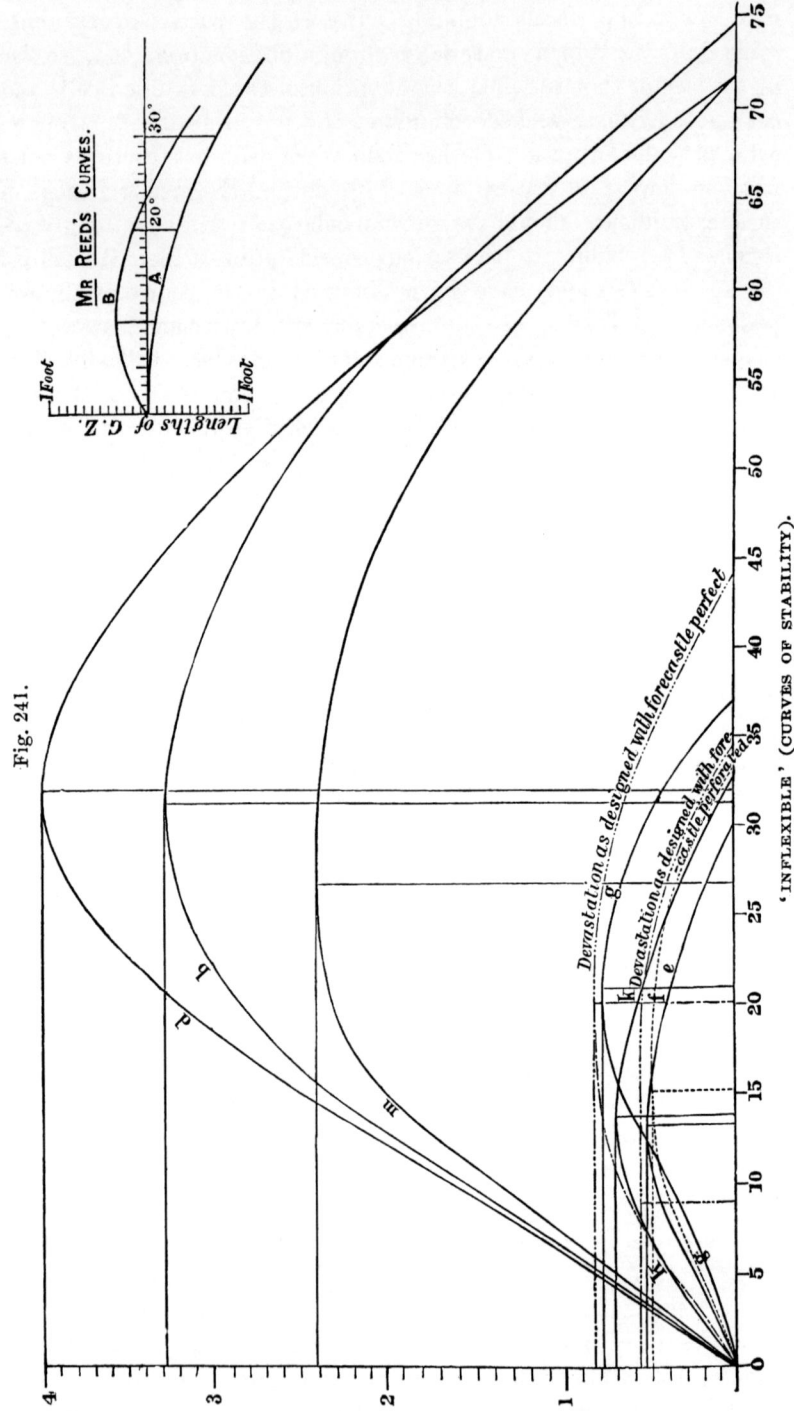

Fig. 241.

'INFLEXIBLE' (CURVES OF STABILITY).

Mr Reed's Curves.

Lengths of G.Z.

armoured ships, if engaged by a powerful enemy, will encounter greater risks of being sunk from the attacks of rams and torpedoes than from the effects of artillery fire.

TABLES OF CALCULATIONS.

Table I.

Condition	Draught	Displacement	Deck enters Wa'er	Angle of Maximum Stability	Maximum G. Z.	Range	Metacentre above C. G.
	ft. in.	tons	deg.	deg.	feet	deg.	feet
b, ship complete, cork in place	24 7	11,500	14	31·2	3·28	74·3	8·25
d, as in *b*, but in light condition . . .	21 10	10,000	18	31·7	3·935	71·5	8·53
e, fully equipped; ends riddled	26 8½	11,500	11	13·5	·568	30·0	2·0
f, as in *e*, but coal between decks (800 tons) removed .	26 1	10,700	11½	15·4	·534	32·2	3·09
g, as in *e*, but in light condition . . .	23 9	10,000	15	20·8	·794	36·8	2·22
k, as in *e*, but supposing the water in the ship when upright locked . .	26 8½	12,668	11	13·9	·705	32·0	
m, as in *k*, but supposing maindeck kept free of water .	26 8½	12,668	11	27·4	2·42	71·5	

Table II.

Condition of Ship (intact Draught 24 ft. 7 in.)		Draught	Top of middle deck above water
		ft. in.	ft. in.
1. Ends riddled, and one-third of buoyancy of ends clear of coals retained, but water excluded from cofferdams and coal-spaces between decks	Coals between decks in	25 4	1 3
ditto. ditto.	Coals between decks out	23 7½	2 11½
2. Same as No. 1, except that the one-third of buoyancy of ends referred to is neglected	Coals between decks in	25 9	0 10
ditto ditto.	Coals between decks out	24 0	2 7

The following table is given on page 10 of the official report:—

—	'Inflexible' as assumed in model, unarmoured ends giving no stability	'Devastation' with forecastle riddled, and giving no stability
Maximum stability . .	6,532 foot-tons	5,237 foot-tons
Angle of maximum stability .	13½ degrees	9 degrees
Range	30 degrees	34½ degrees

General
observa-
tions.

As to the consequences which must ensue in the event of the complete penetration and water-logging of the unprotected ends, and the blowing out of the cork by shells, there was no difference of opinion between Sir E. Reed and the committee. Both agreed that the ship would be in a very critical state. The committee, however, were at total variance with Sir E. Reed as to the probability of such a destruction of the unarmoured ends. The contingency contemplated by Sir E. Reed was, in the view of the committee, so extreme an assumption that it might be regarded as a highly improbable event, even in a protracted engagement. On this vital point, therefore, Sir E. Reed was at issue with the committee, the Board of Admiralty, and the Council of Construction at Whitehall.

By the House of Commons this question was viewed mainly as a question of the relative credibility of evidence. No one doubted Sir E. Reed's competence or sincerity; but his opinion could not be accepted as conclusive. It lay more strictly within the sphere of the naval officer than that of the naval architect to form an estimate of the probable results of a naval action.

We have already seen that the naval advisers of the Admiralty did not share Sir E. Reed's apprehensions as to the destructibility of the unarmoured ends of the 'Inflexible.' On the other hand it is certain that it would materially add to the value of the ship, if the stability of the armoured citadel could be increased. Let us therefore examine the various suggestions which were made for this purpose.

Sir E. Reed, in a memorandum prepared for the consideration of the committee, suggested that a large addition should be made to the stability of the citadel of the 'Inflexible,' and that the ship should be relieved of a large portion of its immense superstructures, which the moment their own unprotected bouyancy was gone, would inevitably overpower and overwhelm the armoured structure.

Mr. Barnaby entirely objected to this proposal. He urged that to lengthen the citadel, and, therefore, diminish the thickness of the armour, was to sacrifice the vital for that which was not vital. A single shot sent through the armour might disable the ship, but no single shell in the unarmoured structure could possibly do so.

The committee concurred with Mr. Barnaby in his objection to the proposed change. An addition of thirty feet to the armoured citadel would render the 'Inflexible' independent of the unprotected ends. The thickness of the armour would then be in the new ship 21 inches as compared with 24 inches in the present one. If the actual 'Inflexible' were to engage the new 'Inflexible,' both being armed with the most powerful guns now existing, the new ship with 21 inches of armour would be in immediate danger of receiving a mortal wound by the penetration of her citadel; and when the vital parts are so crowded together that one blow might be fatal, the conclusion seemed inevitable that the actual ' Inflexible' was much the superior vessel.

Other suggestions, however, of a more practicable kind were made by the committee. They recommended the extension of the cork chambers, that the travel of the guns on the slide should be reduced, and that the pumping power should be increased.

The committee made a most valuable suggestion with reference to future designs. They pointed out that if in the original design for the 'Inflexible' the beam had been increased by ten feet, and the citadel shortened, so as to retain the same perimeter and thickness of armour, the transverse stability would then be doubled in the event of the ends being riddled in action. The beam of the 'Inflexible' was limited with reference to the width of the docks in Her Majesty's yards. It is obviously desirable to increase the width of the entrances, so as to make them available for the types of vessels which modern naval science demands. Owing to the insufficiency of beam the Italians, though they have placed the turrets, like those of the ' Inflexible,' *en echelon* on either side of the keel, have been able to obtain a bow fire from three guns only, and the arrangement of machinery and boilers is much less symmetrical than in the 'Inflexible.'

If on further consideration more stability had been considered necessary in the ' Inflexible,' it should have been obtained by reducing the weight of armour. Any important structural alteration would involve an immense outlay and long delay. The costliest alterations would not make the altered ship as satisfactory as a new design.

It is doubtless very desirable that our armoured ships should possess a more ample margin of stability than is provided in the armoured citadel of the ' Inflexible.' The ideas of the committee and of Sir E. Reed on this point were in entire accord. To secure this important object it may be desirable that the ironclads of the future should have less length and more beam, but whatever alterations may be decided upon hereafter, the Admiralty have undoubtedly been well advised in completing the ' Inflexible' without attempting any material structural alterations. Enormous sums have been wasted in the alteration of ironclads during construction. Ships so large and complicated necessarily take long to build. Naval architecture for war is in a state of perpetual change. A design which was in advance of the times when the keel was laid, is sure to leave something to be desired before the ship approaches completion. Such disappointments will, however, occur less frequently if greater expedition be used in the process of building. Alterations of matured plans should never be attempted. Much waste would have been avoided if these principles had been adopted by the successive Boards of Admiralty.

M. Dislère on the 'Inflexible.'
M. Dislère, in describing the 'Inflexible,' concludes by saying: 'The ship may be described as follows: A hull completely immersed, 6 feet 6 inches beneath the water-line, is covered with an armoured deck, protecting it from projectiles striking it at an oblique angle. It contains the machinery, boilers, and stearing gear. Amidships is a citadel, 16 feet in height, 100 feet in length, and 76 feet in breadth, completely armoured, and carrying in its upper part two turrets, placed diagonally. The upper works of the ship are a continuation of the armoured citadel, but are completely unprotected. . . . Continuing the comparison with the "Devastation" and "Dreadnought," the increase of beam has afforded the means of greatly improving the evolutionary qualities, by giving to the ship a flatter floor. The mean draught has been reduced by 33 inches. By increasing the displacement, and by taking the decided course of abandoning to the waves the extremities of the ship at the water-line, an ironclad has been built, which, at sea, will behave much more satisfactorily than her predecessors, and in which the conditions of habitability will be adapted to the requirements of a long cruise. The other advantages obtained will not be less conspicuous. Four 80-ton guns are substituted for 38-ton guns, and the bow fire is obtained from four guns instead of two. The armoured protection is also much increased.'

'Inflexible's' Whitehead torpedo apparatus.
The gear for launching the Whitehead torpedo is of a most elaborate and complicated character, and exhibits a great advance upon the various systems at present adopted in the service. The 'Inflexible' is pierced with four torpedo ports forwards, two upon each bow, of which one is situated above and the other ten feet below the water-line. The means adopted for discharging the Whitehead above the water do not call for any remark, being substantially the same as those employed upon the 'Dreadnought' and the 'Téméraire.' But the under-water system is as much an improvement upon that of the 'Glatton,' as the 'Glatton's' is an advance upon that of the 'Vesuvius.' The contrivances for enabling the torpedo to be traversed without allowing any water to enter from outside are particularly ingenious; while the workmanship, which has been

wholly executed under the superintendence of the dockyard engineering staff, exhibits the perfection of mechanical skill. The impulse-tube consists of a massive cylindrical iron casting, mounted upon a traversing carriage travelling upon a rack-racer, and resembling in its main features the gun-platforms on board ship. But while the breech of the tube can be moved over an arc by means of a three-cylinder Brotherhood engine driven by compressed air, the head is fixed in a brazen cup-and-socket joint, which is permanently fitted to the side of the ship, and which allows the same freedom of movement to the cylinder as a chandelier receives from a similar joint in the ceiling of a drawing-room. Inside the cup is a valve for admitting and excluding the water. The valve consists of a demi-globe or inner shell, and fits so perfectly against the interior surface of the cup that no packing is required to make it watertight. It is worked by means of bevelled pinion-gearing from the rear, and as it rotates it is made either to cover or expose the aperture through which the projectile is discharged.

When it is intended to fire a torpedo, an open guide is run out through the cylinder to a distance of about ten feet from the ship's side, the purpose being to protect the engine from the currents produced by the way of the ship, and until it gets into still water and feels the full force of its self-contained machinery. This guide, which has a section like the letter **C**, fits into the head of the cylinder and is grooved so that the convex edge of the valve may bite into its concave surface. After being charged, the torpedo, which is of the ordinary 14-inch service type, is inserted in a brass tube, which is made to run upon castors and to fit like a lining into the iron cylinder already described, and into which it is forced by means of a ram which is placed for convenience on the top of the casting. Once in, the rear end of the cylinder is hermetically closed and the sea valve opened. The water thereupon rushes into the tube, so that the torpedo is actually afloat while it is still in the ship. When all is ready the officer in the conning tower upon the hurricane deck touches the electric firing key, the compressed air is admitted to the impulse piston at the rear of the cylinder, and the torpedo is forced out of the ship with great velocity. The cup valve is then closed, and the water which is left in the cylinder is allowed to drain into the double bottom, after which a second Whitehead can be got ready for firing. The compressed air used for charging and discharging the torpedoes is produced by eight pumps, worked in sets of four on each bow, and can be used either together or separately. The reservoirs are, or rather will be, placed between the beams overhead.

They consist of two nests of pipes, each pipe being 6 feet long and 3 inches wide, and numbering altogether about 54. They are tested to withstand a pressure of 1,500 lbs. to the square inch, the *maximum* power of the pumps, although, as a matter of fact, 200 lbs. pressure is ample to supply all the force that is necessary to project the torpedo into the sea. After the utmost pressure has been supplied to the reservoirs, the engines will "creep" until further power be required, the surplus being allowed to blow off at the escape valves. The machinery will prove very costly, and additional expense has been unexpectedly incurred by reason of heavy brass castings being required to connect the head of the firing tube with the side of the ship.

On December 16 and 17, 1880, the 'Inflexible's' guns were fired, the ship being under way off the Nab. The result was very satisfactory. The engine-room and citadel were lighted with the Brush electric light, which stood the firing perfectly.

'Ajax' and 'Agamemnon.' Comparison with 'Inflexible.' The 'Inflexible' having been accepted as the type of the future British line-of-battle ship, the 'Ajax' was laid down at Pembroke in 1876, and the 'Agamemnon' at Chatham in the same year. They differ from the 'Inflexible' in dimensions, but not in type.

Their principal dimensions, as compared with those of the 'Inflexible,' are:—

Length between perpendiculars, 40 feet less; beam, 14 feet less; mean draught of water, 23 ft. 4 in., as against 24 ft. 5 in.; displacement, 8,402 tons, as against 11,406 tons. The length of the citadel is 104 feet, instead of 110 feet; the armoured deck outside of the citadel is 5 ft. 10 in. below the water-level, instead of 7 feet; and the freeboard is 9 ft. 6 in. The cork chambers extend forward of the citadel 30 feet, and abaft it 37 feet. They are twelve feet in depth, rising from six feet below to six feet above the water-line. The cofferdam is of the same depth, and is two feet wide.

Citadel.

Like the 'Inflexible's' the armour is in two thicknesses with wood-backing between, in this respect differing from the 'Devastation' and all former ships, where a great point was made of keeping the armour in one thickness only, it having been found up to certain thicknesses that the resistance to penetration varied nearly as the square of the thickness, and hence one thick plate was considerably stronger than two plates of the same total thickness. The outer thickness of armour on the citadel will probably be of steel, ten inches in thickness, or compound.

Armour.

The armour rests on eleven inches of backing fitted between vertical iron girders eleven inches deep. In rear of this backing is the second thickness of armour, and behind this about seven inches of teak backing fitted between horizontal girders of an equal depth. These are attached to the shell plating of the ship, which is in two thicknesses, each $\frac{1}{2}$ inch, through which also the whole of the armour and backing is bolted. Inside of this plating are the deep frames of the ship. The total thickness of wood backing on the citadel is

Figs. 242, 243, 244, and 245.

SECTION THROUGH UNARMOURED PART.　　SECTION THROUGH CITADEL

' AJAX ' AND 'AGAMEMNON.'

eighteen inches, the same as that of the thickest armour, but like the armour it varies in thickness at different parts. The 3-inch armoured deck is also made up of two thicknesses, one being two inches the other one inch thick. The turret armour is to be steel-faced in one thickness.

The hull is built on the longitudinal and bracket-plate system with a double bottom, as is customary in heavy ships of war, and it is well divided into watertight compartments. Especially is this so in the engine and boiler space, where a marked improvement has been made in this respect of late years in our Navy.

Passing from the citadel to the unprotected portion of the vessel, it should be noticed that the invaluable protection of horizontal armour is largely used. The thickness is no less than three inches on the upper deck; and the lower decks, both before and in the rear of the citadel, six feet under water, are protected with similar armour. In addition to the ordinary decks—the lower, middle, and upper— there is a superstructure, running lengthways with the keel and erected above the upper deck, for the purpose of working the vessel.

Dimensions.

The 'Thunderer' has no cabin accommodation above her low fighting deck, and the daylight has to make its way below through some scanty perforations. The 'Agamemnon,' on the other hand, will be able to accommodate most of her crew on a well-lighted mess-deck above the water-line.

The principal dimensions of the 'Agamemnon' are:—

Length between perpendiculars	280 feet
„ over all	300 ft. 9 in.
Breadth	66 feet
Draught of water, forward	23 feet
„ aft	24 feet
Depth of hold from top of citadel . . .	21 ft. 4 in.
Area of midship section	1,402 feet
Displacement	8,492 tons
Freeboard	9 ft. 6 in.
Depth of armoured deck below water-line . .	5 ft. 10 in
Number of turrets	2
Diameter of turrets, external . . .	30 feet
Height of top of turrets above water-line . .	17 ft. 6 in.
„ port from water-line . . .	10 ft. 7 in.
Projection of ram	9 feet
Depth of point of ram below water-line . .	9 feet
Width of forward superstructure . .	16 feet
Length of forward superstructure . . .	82 feet
Width of after superstructure . . .	29 feet
Length of after superstructure . . .	92 ft. 6 in.
Height of superstructure, extreme . . .	7 ft. 9 in.
Distance between outer and inner hulls, amidships .	3 ft. 2 in.
Distance between outer and inner hulls, near bilge .	2 ft. 8 in.
Distance between outer and inner hulls, near water-line	3 ft. 10 in.
Citadel-armour, at water-line, 10 inches iron, 9 inches wood, 8 inches iron, 10 inches wood, and $1\frac{1}{4}$ inches iron; total thickness.	3 ft. $2\frac{1}{4}$ in. M.L.
Armament in turrets	four 38-ton M.L. guns
„ superstructure . . .	two 6-in. B.L. guns
Complement of officers and men . . .	325

Number of engines (inverted 3-cylinder) . . .	2
„ cylinders	6
Diameter of cylinders, high and low . . .	54 inches
Stroke of pistons	3 ft. 3 in.
Indicated horse-power, maximum . . .	6,000
Diameter of crank-shafts	14½ inches
Number of screw-propellers	2
Diameter of screw-propellers . . .	18 feet
Number of boilers, (return tubular) . . .	10
„ furnaces	28
Total grate-surface	647 sq. ft.
„ heating-surface . , . , .	18,062 sq. ft.
Estimated speed	13 knots
Coal-supply	700 tons

The following notice appeared in the *Times*, on the occasion of the launch of the ' Agamemnon,' in 1879:—

'The ship herself is a child of controversy. From the first, since her keel was laid, she has been the subject of anxious thoughts and of restless argument. To this it is due that, although so far back as the spring of 1876 she was first put on the stocks, the autumn of 1879 has come round before she is even launched, and that more than three years have elapsed before her hull even is complete. Were it not for this, there would be little in her construction to call attention to. For she is a copy—in some respects a servile copy—of the " Inflexible," and it is difficult with ships as with pictures, however good in themselves, to excite enthusiasm about replicas or copies. The launch of the " Agamemnon " is, however, worthy of some notice on other grounds than those we have mentioned. She serves to remind us that she is the first ironclad laid down in the Royal Dockyards since the " Inflexible " was commenced, and that from 1874 to last year the " Agamemnon " and " Ajax " have represented the new ironclad construction which it has been thought fit to intrust to the dockyards. And the " Inflexible " is not even yet ready for sea. These two facts are sufficiently instructive as to the rate of progress which is thought satisfactory in regard to ironclad construction.'

'It has been pointed out by some of our contemporaries,' observes a writer in *Engineering*, 'that the " Agememnon " was designed three years ago, that it has taken this time to complete her sufficiently for launching, and that the " Inflexible," which was designed six years ago, is not yet completed. It is a question worthy of serious consideration whether this time could not be much shortened by greater simplicity of construction without adding to the weight or at all diminishing the strength of the ships.

'In the three new ships, the " Colossus," " Conqueror," and

' Majestic," just commenced, steel will be largely used for the plating, and will be so far an advance upon the "Agamemnon;" but when it is said that these ships will, "in all probability, be out of date before they are well finished," the question arises whether it would not be wiser to order fewer ships from one design and to push what are ordered more rapidly towards completion.'

To return to the notice in the *Times* :—

' Although during the present year four new ironclads have been laid down, for five years it was found sufficient to commence and complete one ironclad and to commence and partially build two ; not, be it remembered, with starved estimates or stinted labour, but with a vigorous application of both. Perhaps Mr. Brassey may find in this fact a possible corrective to his ideas of highly-paid energetic constructors rivalling one another in competitive plans of ocean-going cruisers and monitors. The rivalry might become too intense with the limited chance of designing an ironclad once every three or four years ; or, worse still, the enthusiastic and highly paid ones might be found eating their hearts out for want of proper employment, or, from the same cause, failing when the moment for exertion arrived. It is true that the navy has had other additions made to it in this period. The ocean-going ironclads " Alexandra " and " Téméraire," launched at Chatham three or four years ago, should not be forgotten, nor the " Shannon " and " Dreadnought " at Pembroke, while private enterprise has given the navy the " Nelson " and " Northampton," two more ocean-going ironclads, which were built by the Messrs. Napier, at Glasgow. And, to come to a more recent date, for the vessels we have mentioned are a little antique, the vote of credit enabled the Government last year, by a stroke of the pen, to supply the deficiency in construction of previous years by the out-and-out purchase of four ironclads. But as the Constructive Department at Portsmouth lived on the " Inflexible " for an unspeakable length of time, so the constructors at Chatham contrived to live on the " Agamemnon," while they revelled in dreams of the monsters continually promised them. In the case of Chatham, however, patience has been rewarded, for side by side with the " Agamemnon " lies the " Polyphemus," whose ribbed roof and sides betray but little to the uninitiated what its future appearance will be ; and further on is the " Conqueror," the new steel ironclad, which is being vigorously proceeded with. Before quitting this subject it should be noted that during the past five years, if the building of ironclads has halted, unarmoured construction has been prosecuted with energy, and with a success as to result and as to fertility of resource which could hardly have been anticipated. In torpedo vessels, dispatch vessels, cruisers, and gun vessels, remarkable progress has been made, which is due chiefly to the boldness with which experiments in steel construction have been carried out, and the success with which these efforts have been crowned. But while our constructors have in this direction shown ingenuity or enterprise, and have, in fact, theorised successfully, in ironclad construction they have, it would almost seem, come to a standstill. True, with a vigorous determination, Mr. Barnaby has set to work to apply steel to the purposes of ironclad construction, and to render it useful to this end; and it is possible now to say that his expectations have been realised and his efforts proved successful. Still, for the present, there does not seem much room for the hope that any new departure is likely to be taken in ironclad architecture, or that, for some time, we shall be able to do better than follow cautiously, if progressively, in the beaten track. The " Colossus," " Conqueror," and " Majestic," whose construction has just been commenced, will represent the latest efforts in the direction of substituting steel-plated for ironclad ships; but they will in all probability be out of date before they are well finished, as the " Agamemnon," on the day of her launch, is out of date compared with them. To return to the " Agamemnon." If she is like the " Inflexible," she is much smaller, and represents the attempt to reduce the size of ironclads without impairing seriously their power. This reduction of size implies, what it is by no means unimportant to recollect, diminution in cost; and when it is further recollected that an ironclad like the " Inflexible " costs fully 800,000l., reduction means a great deal. The " Agamemnon " has, then, a length of 280 feet compared with 325 feet for the " Inflexible," a breadth of 66 feet compared with 75 feet, and a displacement in tons of about 8,500 compared with 12,000 for the other vessel. She will carry heavier armour than any other vessel in the navy except the " Inflexible," the two revolving turrets being plated with iron $1\frac{1}{2}$ feet thick. The turrets, which are placed en échelon, will contain each two 38-ton guns, and are each of them revolving. Her power of attack is not confined to ordnance; for she will be armed with Whitehead torpedoes, for which she is provided with the means of ejection from the armoured sides of her citadel. To say that she is rather an unsightly vessel is hardly necessary; but what she wants in appearance is made up in power. It is no exaggeration to describe her and her sister vessel, the " Ajax," as among the most formidable ironclads afloat. Although both of them are modelled on the " Inflexible," they may perhaps be best compared with the " Dreadnought " and "Devastation," especially in regard to size and armament. When complete they will help materially to provide the navy with a fleet of the most powerful monitors in the world, the names of which alone are sufficient to justify such an assertion, including as they do the "Inflexible," "Ajax," "Agamemnon," "Dreadnought," "Thunderer," "Devastation," "Superb," and "Neptune." A provision of a novel kind calls to mind the controversy which arose on the stability of the "Inflexible." The watertight compartments of the "Agamemnon," instead of being empty, are to be filled with cork, the object being to prevent her from sinking if struck below the water-line. We have already referred to the citadel of this vessel, and in describing her she may be stated to be an ironclad of the centre citadel type. By this is meant that she is built with an invulnerable citadel, or central compartment, which is kept afloat by the two unprotected ends of the vessel.'

Steel armour on turrets.

The loading and working of the guns will be performed by means of hydraulic machinery. The 'Agamemnon' and 'Ajax' are to have their turrets armoured with steel-faced composite plates. These are the most costly plates yet used in the construction of Her Majesty's ships, and those required for the turrets of these two ships will cost 50,000*l.* In the experiments with the composite armour manufactured for the 'Inflexible' it was found that three inches of steel face was amply sufficient to pulverise chilled shot of moderate weight and prevent penetration, and that the ductility of the iron-backing was unquestionably a defence against racking. There was every reason to believe that an extra depth of iron would preserve the integrity of the plate, and prevent its falling to pieces under the blows of continuous direct firing. In the 'Ajax' and 'Agamemnon' therefore, it has been determined to get rid of the inner ring of armour, and to manufacture the compound armour for the turrets of a single thickness, instead of two thicknesses as in the 'Inflexible.' The plates will accordingly be sixteen inches thick, the steel on the face being $5\frac{1}{4}$ inches and the iron $10\frac{3}{4}$ inches.

The speed of the 'Agamemnon' is estimated at thirteen knots. She is fitted with twin screws, and is designed to carry 700 tons of coal, which is equivalent to from five to six days' steaming at full speed. She will carry a crew of about 350 men, of whom about one-third may be set down as stokers, artisans, and engine-room men, while fifty more will be marines; only half of the crew of a modern turret-ship consists of bluejackets and boys.

The weight of armour and backing approaches 3,000 tons, and the weight of the guns and ammunition slightly exceeds 400 tons.

The ' Ajax,' the sister ship to the 'Agamemnon,' was launched at Pembroke Dock on March 10, 1880. The ' Ajax ' was laid down on March 21,.1876.

It is impossible to review the historical development of our iron-clad fleet without being impressed with the sudden and portentous change in the fundamental principles of naval architecture for war, which has been introduced within a comparatively limited period of time. Confining our attention to a few salient features, we find that the earlier ironclads, the long ships of the ' Minotaur ' class, com-pletely protected from stem to stern, were speedily superseded by shorter vessels, with a central armoured battery, and a belt at the water-line. This is seen in the 'Bellerophon' and subsequent vessels, as well as in some small wooden converted ships. This change enabled the armour to be thickened, and simultaneously the length of our first-class ironclads was reduced from 400 feet to about 300 feet. The ' Bellerophon ' type remained in favour for an extended period as the most suitable for the masted sea-keeping ironclad cruiser. The next great type introduced, apart from vessels for coast or harbour defence or special purposes, was the heavy mastless monitor such as the 'Devastation,' which made up in some degree for the absence of masts and sails by an unusually large supply of coal. By this great change we were enabled to rise at a bound from 8-inch or 9-inch armour-protection to 14-inch armour, and from 18-ton to 35-ton guns. Here, also, it will be noticed we return to complete protection.

The central battery was superseded by the citadel ships. This type, like the ' Bellerophon ' and the ' Devastation' types, was un-doubtedly projected by Sir E. J. Reed before he left the Admiralty, although not worked out by him in detail. Foreseeing that the time was approaching when side armour must be still further thickened to withstand the growing power of artillery, he proposed to confine it to a central citadel at the middle and broadest part of the ship, which would protect the vital parts and be sufficiently large to insure the buoyancy and stability of the ship in action, while side armour at the ends of the ship was discarded, and a thick armour deck sub-stituted for it six feet below water.

The ships of the new type admitted, and indeed required, a large addition to the beam, as compared with ships of the elongated forms hitherto adopted. In the ' Inflexible' these novel features received a still more marked development. The beam especially was increased in quite unprecedented proportion to the length of the ship. This type of ship, as embodied in the ' Inflexible,' has been reproduced in the

'Agamemnon,' the 'Ajax,' and the more recent heavy armourclad ships designed for our Navy. In one important particular the 'Ajax' and 'Agamemnon' are inferior to the 'Inflexible.' The central armoured citadel is not, as it is in the case of the 'Inflexible,' of sufficient displacement to secure the stability of the ship, should the unarmoured ends be destroyed.

'Colossus' and 'Majestic.'

The plans for the 'Colossus' and 'Majestic,' and the 'Conqueror' were originally sketched out in a speech by the First Lord of the Admiralty in the House of Commons on the vote for Dockyards and Naval yards in the estimates for 1878–79. 'Those who took an interest in shipbuilding would understand the ship better if he described it by a type that was known. . . . It was purposed that two improved "Agamemnons" should be laid down, and that they should be armed with guns of about the same power as those of the "Dreadnought," that was, of about 38 tons mounted in two turrets. Those guns, and the citadel within which they would be worked, would be protected by the same armour as the "Ajax" and the "Agamemnon" —viz., a *maximum* of 18 inches, the *maximum* in the "Dreadnought" being 14 inches. The engine-power would not exceed that of the "Ajax" and "Agamemnon," but would be capable of producing a speed of 14 knots, or one knot higher speed than the "Agamemnon" class would have. This would be done by increasing the length of the ship to that of the "Dreadnought" and "Inflexible" and suitably arranging the form. The machinery and all the vital parts of the ship would be protected either by horizontal or by vertical armour. The ships would be capable of ejecting torpedoes below the water or from behind armour, and of being employed as rams. They would be much smaller and less costly than the "Dreadnought" and "Inflexible." The displacement would be about 9,000 tons, while the "Dreadnought" and "Inflexible" were over 11,000 tons, and the "Ajax" and "Agamemnon" were about 8,500. The alteration in these new ships would be that they would have a larger supply of coal, be able to keep the sea for a longer period, and would have greater speed, but in other respects they would be very similar to the "Ajax" and "Agamemnon."'

The 'Conqueror.'

The speaker went on to describe another ship, which has received the name of the 'Conqueror,' and which, he said, was intended to be an improved 'Rupert.' The 'Rupert' would commend herself to the judgment of naval officers as being a handy and convenient vessel. It was proposed to build another vessel of the same class, with more powerful guns in her single turret, namely, guns of 38 tons instead of eighteen tons, with economical engines of modern type and great coal-endurance. It was proposed to build the hull of steel, and it was hoped that the experiments that had been made with steel armour would justify its use for the armour of that ship and the new 'Agamemnon,' so that the advantage of great resistance to penetration might be secured without cracking. Up to the present time they had not been successful in obtaining a steel plate which altogether answered the expectations they had formed, but he was in great hopes that the ingenuity, the skill, and the determined perseverance of the manufacturers of steel plates would ultimately produce plates capable of resisting a blow without cracking. If they could do that, they would obtain a very valuable result indeed.

The principal dimensions of the three vessels referred to are as follows:—

	'Colossus' and 'Majestic.'	'Conqueror' (Modified 'Rupert ').
Length between perpendiculars .	325 feet	270 feet
Breadth, extreme . . .	68 feet	58 feet
Draught of water, mean .	25 ft. 9 in.	23 feet
Displacement . . .	9,150 tons	6,200 tons
Indicated horse-power of engines .	6,000	4,500
Estimated speed in knots .	14	13
Coal-supply . . .	950 tons	
Maximum thickness of armour .	18 inches	12 inches
Complement of officers and men .	345	
Principal armament . .	four 42-ton b.-l. guns, and four 6-in. b.-l. guns	two 42-ton b.-l. guns, and four 6-in. b.-l. guns

The *Times*, of June 10, 1879, contained a more detailed description of the 'Colossus':—

Times' description of 'Colossus.'

'Without formality or parade of any kind the keel plates of the new turret-ship "Colossus" have been laid down in No. 5 slip at Portsmouth, the blocks on which they rest having a slope towards the water of five-eighths of an inch to a foot. It was hoped that the First Lord of the Admiralty or some other high official at Whitehall would have gone down to Portsmouth to clinch the first rivet; but as the keel plates, vertical keel, and butt straps were all in position, and as no intimation had been received at the dockyard of any desire on the part of their lordships to take part in any ceremony on the occasion, the riveting has been commenced, and the construction of the new vessel is now proceeding in the usual course under the superintendence of Mr. W. B. Robinson, chief constructor; Mr. J. C. Froyne, constructor; and Mr. Coward, foreman of the yard.

'The "Colossus" is the first steel ship which has been laid down in the Portsmouth yard, and consequently differs from the "Inflexible," which is wholly built of iron. While, however, the vertical keel, flat keel, garboard strakes, bracket and solid frames, longitudinals, inside and outside plating, and bulkheads will be all formed of low steel, it has been deemed advisable to construct the heavy forgings, such as the solid stem and the stern-post, as well as the afterpiece of keel, of iron. The vertical keel plates are $\frac{1}{2}$ inch in thickness, and 38 inches deep; while the flat keel is composed of plates in two thicknesses, the upper being $\frac{5}{8}$ inch and the lower $\frac{3}{4}$ inch. The flat and the vertical keels are connected together by angle steels, and similar angle steels run along each side of the upper edge of the vertical keel. As it has been found that these bars are liable to fracture in the flanges and rivet-holes, owing

Figs. 246 and 247

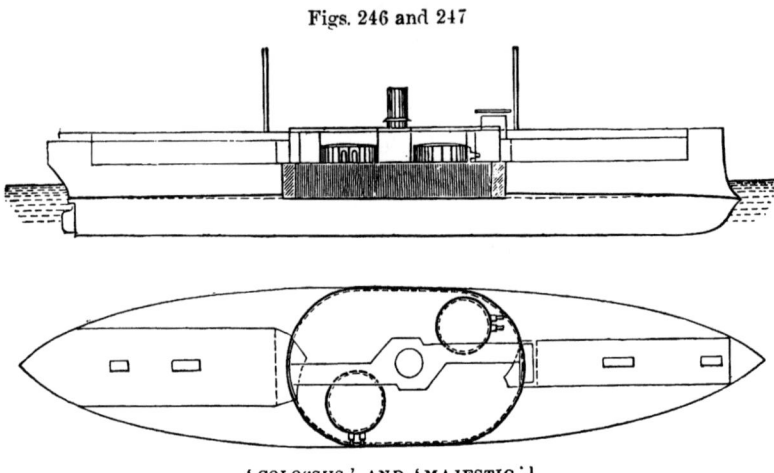

' COLOSSUS ' AND 'MAJESTIC.' [1]

to causes which the usual tests have not been able to discover, Mr. Barnaby has insisted upon very stringent precautions being observed in dealing with a material apparently so erratic in its behaviour as steel. All plates or bars which can be bent cold are to be so treated; and if the whole length cannot be bent cold, heating is to be had recourse to over as little length as possible. All plates or bars which have been heated for bending or flanging are to be annealed afterwards over the parts which have been heated; and if desired, exceptionally long or quickly curved bars, such as frames, may be formed of shorter pieces with the butts suitably shifted and strapped. No bar or plate which exhibits signs of failure in working

---

[1] Mr. W. H. Smith, when First Lord of the Admiralty, kindly permitted the Constructors' Department to furnish the plan in the text.

is to be put into a ship; but pieces should be cut from such plates and bars and subjected to quenching and tensile tests. In the outer bottom plating, again, the holes which are to be countersunk should be punched about $\frac{1}{8}$ inch less in diameter than the rivets which are used, the enlargement of the holes being made in the countersinking, which should in all cases be carried through the whole thickness of the plates. All butt-straps to plating forming an important feature in the general structural strength, should have the holes drilled, or be annealed after the holes are punched. Snap-riveting is only to be employed for internal work of subordinate importance; but on stringers, deck-plating, and other parts subjected to considerable tensile strain countersunk riveting is to be used, and the holes treated similarly to those in the outside plating. Acting on these principles, Mr. Barnaby is satisfied that steel bottom-plating needs neither drilling nor annealing after punching. Iron rivets only are used.

'Though resembling the "Inflexible" as to citadel, turret arrangement, and other important particulars, the "Colossus," which is a sister ship to the "Majestic," now being built at Pembroke, embodies no less important departures from the monster ship, not only as regards the material used in its construction, but in the proportions of the hull itself. The "Inflexible" was designed in accordance with the investigations of Mr. Froude, but it is clear from Mr. Barnaby's own admission that the Constructive Department was by no means satisfied that the actual performances of the ship under steam would tally with the theoretical conclusions which had been confidently put forward, and which, it was contended, had been verified by model experiments. No vessel with the like proportions had ever been attempted before. In 1869 Mr. Reed seems to have sketched the outline of a ship which had $4\frac{1}{2}$ beams in its length; but this quotient was considered so extreme by the present Director of Naval Construction that in reporting in 1871 upon Mr. Reed's investigations Mr. Barnaby stated before the Committee on Designs that he supposed he had been waiting for an assured success with such steps as he had taken before proposing to adopt it. Nevertheless, in designing the "Inflexible" in the light of Mr. Froude's latest investigations, the Constructive Department went beyond the proportion of breadth to length which Mr. Barnaby had pointed to as "extreme." For, while this proportion would have made the "Inflexible" 72 feet wide, she was actually given 75 feet of beam ($4\cdot32$), which was as great as any of the existing docks could accommodate. But so far was Mr. Barnaby from feeling sure that with the unusual proportions adopted in the "Inflexible" fourteen knots would be obtained with 8,000 indicated horse-power, that he had strongly recommended that a new "Inflexible" should not be commenced until there had been a trial of speed with that ship. And with his usual frankness he added that if a speed of fourteen knots were realised he would be the first to thank Mr. Froude for having encouraged his department to adopt such proportions in a 14-knot ship, and with such a small proportion of power to displacement. There were, however, other considerations than those of speed which induced the Department to adhere for the present to $4\frac{1}{2}$ beams in the "Ajax" and "Agamemnon." Mr. Barnaby was indeed, doubtful whether if they were made shorter a satisfactory rate of speed could be obtained ; but he was also of opinion that sufficient bilge keel could not be given them to check rolling and make them comfortable, that sufficient depth of armour could not be provided to prevent the unarmoured bottom being exposed to shot, that with a shorter citadel the four guns could not be fired abeam, and that if the ships had been made wider the ends must have been fined, which would have necessarily cramped the accommodation at the ends for the officers and men.

'It would appear as if the theoretical doubts of the Director of Naval Construction had received confirmation from the actual performances of the "Inflexible." At the six hours' trial of the machinery of this ship, which was made under the superintendence of Mr. Barnaby and Mr. Wright themselves, as much as 8,407·30 horsepower was developed by the engines, and a speed on the mile of nearly fifteen knots was realised. As far as the contractors were concerned, these results were highly satisfactory, but it must be remarked that, so far as regards the ship herself, she was three feet short of her estimated load draught, being only 18 ft. 10 in. forward and 23 feet aft. Whether with greater displacement and wave resistance the "Inflexible" will practically justify Mr. Froude's calculations and Mr. Barnaby's adoption of them is a matter upon which we can form no opinion ; but it is clear that in the design and proportions of the "Colossus" very important changes have been introduced. Not only is the new ship to be five feet longer than the "Inflexible" between perpendiculars, but she is to be no fewer than seven feet narrower, so that her coefficient of fineness exhibits a noteworthy return to old-fashioned principles, and brings her nearer in form to the "Dreadnought." The "Colossus" will be a twin-screw double-turret ship, measuring 325 feet between perpendiculars, and 68 feet in extreme breadth, while her draught forward will be

25 ft. 3 in. and aft 26 ft. 3 in., thus giving her a mean load draught of 25 ft. 9 in. The height of her deck from the water-line—in other words, her freeboard—will be 9 ft. 6 in., and the depth of her hold 23 ft. 7 in. Her total displacement is 9,150 tons, or upwards of 2,000 tons less than the "Inflexible." She will be engined by Messrs. Maudslay, Sons, and Field, with engines constructed to indicate 6,000 horses on the official trial, and she is expected to realise a measured mile speed of fourteen knots. Her greater fineness of form and superior coefficient of power, as compared with the older ship, will probably make this expectation very readily realised. She will be provided with bunkers to enable her to carry 950 tons of coal. It is, of course, to be expected that various modifications will be made in her design during the two years or so which it will take to construct her, and many details have been purposely postponed for future consideration. It was originally intended to protect the sides to six feet below the water-line, by eighteen inches of armour in two thicknesses, and the turrets by sixteen inches of armour, also in a couple of thicknesses, while the exposed decks will be armoured to the extent of three inches. But so satisfied is Mr. Barnaby as to the advantage of facing iron armour with hard steel, that it is proposed to apply it for the protection of the sides as well as the turrets of ships. The first trial will be made upon the three new vessels now in course of building—the "Colossus" at Portsmouth, the "Majestic" at Pembroke, and the "Conqueror" at Chatham. The armour in these instances will be eighteen inches thick at the water-line, tapering below to a less thickness.

'Like the "Inflexible," and other modern turret-ships, she will have a central armoured citadel, about one-third the length of the ship, and rising well out of the water; and two submerged ends on which are raised unarmoured structures, which complete the form of the vessel and provide liberal space for her crew of 400 officers and men, stores and fuel, besides providing these portions of the ship with the necessary stability. The turrets will be placed *en échelon*, so as to command a fore-and-aft fire from all the guns. The guns will not be of such weight and calibre as those of the "Inflexible," which is to be armed with 80-ton guns, but will be of a powerful nature and of a modern type. The precise description is not yet decided upon, but they will probably be superior to the 38-ton guns. The "Colossus" will also carry six light shell-guns on the superstructures, boat and field guns, and four or six Nordenfeldt guns, and will be fitted with gear for ejecting Whitehead torpedoes from a transverse battery under the forward armour-deck. She will

not be rigged, but will be provided with a derrick for getting the
boats in and out, and with a special arrangement for carrying a couple
of torpedo launches of the Thornycroft or Yarrow pattern. More
than usual care has been taken to divide the ship, by means of large
transverse and smaller transverse and longitudinal bulkheads, into
water-tight compartments, upon which her safety will mainly depend
against under-water torpedo attacks. As in the case of the " Inflexible," a fore-and-aft divisional bulkhead will be carried through
the engine and boiler-rooms, thereby materially adding to the security
of the vessel in case of injury to the bottom in wake of these compartments, and the coal bunker and wing passage bulkheads are to
be specially stiffened as a further protection of the structure against
torpedoes. The principle of defending the stability of the ship in
action by cork spaces and cofferdams will receive additional development on board. The weight of the hull is estimated at 6,150 tons,
and its cost at 240,000*l.* for material, and 205,000*l.* for labour, exclusive of its equipments.'

The progress made in the construction of the ' Colossus,' up to
January 1880, is thus recorded in the columns of the *Times*:—

' Rapid progress has been lately made in the construction of
the double-turret armourclad ship " Colossus," at Portsmouth. The
keel was laid on June 5 last year, and at the present time it is
computed that 570 tons have been placed upon the blocks. The
work will now, however, go on with less despatch, as the men engaged in preparing the plates and frames in the workshops have been
taken from task-work, and overtime has been forbidden; and as,
under the new conditions, the hands employed upon the ship itself
cannot be supplied with the necessary amount of prepared material
to work into the hull, the number has been reduced. The "Colossus,"
which is the first steel vessel built at Portsmouth, may be roundly
stated to have been advanced as far as three-quarter frame. As the
middle part of the ship was the first to be laid off, the citadel is
somewhat more forward than the ends, though the work is proceeded
with as uniformly as possible. The whole of the keel plates are not
only in position, but have been riveted and caulked throughout. The
frames and intercostal frames of the citadel are fixed, and nearly
the whole of the plating in wake of the side armour has been completed, as well as the armour shelf. The iron beams for supporting
the turrets are well advanced, the transverse bulkheads within the
citadel have been erected, and the longitudinal bulkhead, with its
stiffeners formed of steel columns, is well-nigh completed. Indeed,
with the exception of the bunkers and the wing passages, the central

portion of the structure up to the turret deck is in a very forward
state. The forepart of the ship is also in an advanced condition.
The lower part of the prow is in position, and the workmen are employed in erecting the continuous longitudinals, which converge at the
stem and thus give support to the ram. The middle and upper part
of the prow are being shaped and finished in the armour-plate shop.
Some progress has also been made in laying down the armoured deck
forward, which protects the magazines, and secures the buoyancy of
the structure. This is composed of 3-inch armour in two thicknesses
of 1-inch and 2-inch plates, with a dip from the horizontal as it nears
the stem so as to give strength to the centre of the ram. The after
portion of the ship is in a less advanced condition than the other
parts. Here, again, however, the work is being pushed forward ;
and, in order to save time, while the upper rudder-post and the
rudder-pawl are being prepared, the lower post has been dropped into
its place and is being drilled, after which it will be lifted out of
position and welded to the upper post, when the united forging will
be worked into the hull. Mr. Coward, a foreman of the yard, is in
charge of the work.'

Mr. King has compiled the following description of the
'Conqueror':—

'This ship, now building at Chatham, is a mastless, seagoing, Mr. King's
twin-screw, single-turret steel ship, but of a type quite different from description
any vessel that has preceded her. She is a citadel vessel, but not to queror.'
the same extent as those just described, since she does not depend
upon the citadel or upon cork chambers for her reserve of stability, in
the event of being pierced by projectiles.

'The protection of the vital parts of this ship consists of a steel-
faced armour-belt, extending from the point of the ram to within
nineteen feet of the after perpendicular. This armour belt is twelve
inches thick at the water-line amidships, tapering to eleven inches
and $8\frac{1}{2}$ inches below water and at the ends, and backed by teak
having a varying thickness of ten, eleven, and $13\frac{1}{2}$ inches. At its
termination astern, an armoured steel-faced bulkhead, $11\frac{1}{4}$ inches
thick, extends across the vessel. From this point to the bow, below
water, is an armoured steel deck $2\frac{1}{2}$ inches thick.

'Rising above this deck to the height of 9 ft. 6 in. above the load
water-line is the citadel. This is of sufficient length only to enclose
the lower part of the turret and its machinery, the entrance to the
conning-tower or pilot-house, and the chimneys of the boilers. It
commences 83 feet from the bow, has a length on the middle line of
102 feet, and is protected both on the sides and on the ends by steel-

faced armour, varying in thickness from 12 to 10½ inches, backed by teak of equal thickness. The deck over the citadel is covered with 1¾-inch steel plates, and this deck is carried forward to the bow, thus affording comfortable quarters above water for the crew. Immediately in the fore part of the citadel, and rising above it, as in the "Inflexible," is the turret, which is 22 feet in internal diameter, built of steel-faced armour, twelve inches thick, backed by an equal thickness of teak. In this turret will be mounted two 43-ton breech-loading guns, being the first British breech-loaders ever mounted in a turret. These guns will be much more powerful than the 38-ton guns of the "Dreadnought."

Figs. 248 and 249.

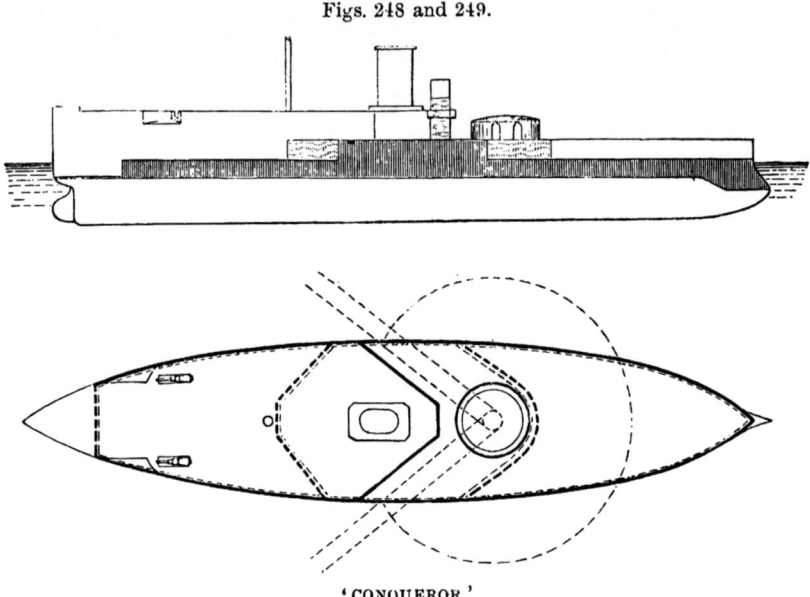

'CONQUEROR.'

'Between the turret and the chimney is the armoured conning-tower, rising high above the turret. From this tower to the stern is an upper deck, elevated above the citadel, and under this are the quarters of the officers, situated so high above water as to afford natural ventilation and ample light. The rudder is deep below water, and is worked under protection. The bow is fitted with a ram.

'The leading features of this ship may, therefore, be said to be: first, that the protection of her vital parts against an enemy's projectiles is so ample, that, if the stern and upper works and even the citadel should be damaged, stability would still be preserved; second, that the unarmoured structure, rising high above the submerged vessel, affords comfortable quarters and removes the objections raised against low freeboard monitors. Altogether, the " Conqueror " is the best specimen of a single-turret vessel yet laid down. Perhaps the principal, if not the only, objection which may be urged against her will be her large size and cost, considering that she carries but two heavy guns, and that they do not have an all-round fire.'

The following are the principal dimensions and particulars :—

Ship.

Length, extreme	288 feet
Length between perpendiculars . . .	270 feet
Breadth, extreme	58 feet
Depth of hold, from inner bottom to under side of lower-deck beams	21 feet
Draught of water, forward	22 feet
„ aft	24 feet
„ mean	23 feet
Displacement	6,200 tons
Area of midship section . . .	1,145 sq. ft.
Height of upper deck at side from load water-line .	9 ft. 6 in.
Internal diameter of turret . . .	22 feet
External diameter of turret	27 ft. 10 in.

Armour and Backing.	Armour	Backing
Thickness on sides (steel-faced) .	12, 11 & 8½ in.	10, 11 & 13½ in.
„ bulkheads (steel-faced) .	11, 11½ & 10½ in.	9 inches
„ turrets (steel-faced) . .	12 inches	11½ inches
„ of steel plating on upper deck over battery	—	1¾ inches
Thickness of steel plating on lower deck .	—	2¼ inches
Thickness of steel plating on deck under water abaft armoured bulkhead aft .	—	2½ inches

Motive Machinery.

Type of engines (vertical compound) . .	3-cylinder
Number of engines	2 sets
Diameter of cylinders, high pressure .	54 inches
„ „ low pressure . .	70 inches
Stroke of pistons	3 feet
Diameter of screws	14 ft. 6 in.
Pitch of screws, about . . .	17 feet
Number of boilers	8
Pressure in boilers	60 lbs.
Grate surface	500 sq. ft.
Heating surface, tubes, about . .	11,000 sq. ft.
Indicated horse-power, maximum . .	4,500
Estimated speed per hour . . .	13 knots

Armament.

Guns in turrets	two 40-ton breech-loaders
,, on broadside	two 6-inch breech-loaders
Stowage	for 150 rounds per gun

New ships for the Italian Navy; programme of 1877.

According to the programme sanctioned by Parliament in 1877, the strength of the Italian fleet is to be raised to the following standard :—

16 battle ships of the first class,
10 battle ships of the second class,
20 cruisers of the third class.

It is quite uncertain when this programme will be completed. It is assumed at present that in 1888 the list of ironclads will comprise eleven ironclads of modern construction, and diminishing in tonnage from 5,800 to 2,000 tons. Of the ships of recent type of 10,491 tons the 'Duilio' is in commission and the 'Dandolo' is already far advanced, and of the four large ships of 13,700 tons originally proposed, two have been commenced, and two smaller ships of 9,000 tons may possibly be completed at the date mentioned. The Italian naval administration has not escaped the embarrassments and the doubts which have been felt elsewhere. By its vote of December 20, 1880, the Chamber has approved a decision of the Minister of Marine not to build the third and fourth ships of 13,700 tons. Future ships are not to exceed 9,000 tons displacement.

The 'Duilio' and 'Dandolo.'

We now proceed to give descriptions of the most recent designs. The 'Duilio' and 'Dandolo' are mastless turret-ships of the largest class. The 'Duilio' was commenced at Castellamare in 1872, launched in 1876, and made her trial trip in January, 1880. The 'Dandolo' is building at Spezia, on the Mediterranean, having been commenced a year later, and will not probably be completed before 1882.

For their general design the naval authorities accepted the view of the British committee on designs, and trusted both for buoyancy and stability to their unarmoured raft. They, moreover, placed the turrets as they are placed in the 'Inflexible.'

The following are the principal dimensions and elements of these two ships :—

	'Duilio'	'Dandolo'
Year in which their construction was commenced	1872	1873
Year in which one was and the other will be entirely completed . . .	1880	1882
Place of construction . . .	Castellamare	Spezia
,, completion . . .	Spezia	
Materials of which the vessels are built . .	iron	

DUILIO.

Dimensions.

Length between perpendiculars . . .	340 ft. 11 in.
Breadth of beam, extreme . . .	64 ft. 9 in.
Depth of hold	21 ft. 11 in.
Draught of water, forward . .	25 ft. 5 in.
,, aft . . .	26 ft. 5 in.
Displacement at deep load-line . .	10,401 tons
Area of immersed midship section . .	1,466·6 sq. ft.
Projection of ram forward of perpendicular	9 feet
Immersion of ram at deep load-line .	14 feet
Number of compartments . . .	102
,, turrets	2
System of turrets	revolving
Interior diameter of turrets . .	25 ft. 9 in.

Armour.

Thickness of armour at water-line . .	21·65 inches
,, ,, on upper redoubt .	17·71 inches
,, ,, on turrets . .	17·71 inches
,, of wood-backing at water-line .	23·62 inches
,, ,, of upper redoubt	19·68 inches
,, ,, of turrets .	11·81 inches
Depth of immersion of armour . .	5 ft. 3 in.

Armament.

Number of guns	4
Weight of each gun . . .	100 tons
Calibre of each gun . . .	17·72 inches
Weight of broadside metal . .	3·87 tons
,, bow-fire metal . .	2·9 tons
,, stern-fire metal . .	1·93 tons
Height of main deck above water . .	11 ft. 6 in.
,, battery-deck above water	15 ft. 9 in.

Motive Machinery.

	'Duilio'	'Dandolo'
Kind of engines . . .	ordinary	compound
Name of constructor . .	Penn	Maudslay
Indicated horse-power . .	7,710	7,900
Number of cylinders . .	4	4
Diameter of cylinders . .	93·5 inches	64 and 120 inches
Stroke of pistons . . .	39 inches	48 inches
Number of revolutions of engine per minute .	84	80
Number of screw-propellers . .	2	2
Diameter of screw-propellers . .	17 ft. 2 in.	16 feet
Pitch of screw-propellers . .	19 ft. 6 in.	19 feet
Speed of ship . . .	15 knots	15 knots
Number of boilers . . .	10	8
,, furnaces . . .	40	32
Grate surface . . .	899·6 sq. ft.	811·6 sq. ft.
Heating surface . . .	23,775 sq. ft.	22,991 sq. ft.
Boiler pressure . . .	30 lbs.	60 lbs.
Number of funnels . . .	2	2

Weights.

Weight of hull	. . . . .	3,395·5 ton
,, armour	. . . . .	2,559 tons
,, wood-backing	. . . .	239 tons
,, guns, their machinery, ammunition, etc. .		990 tons
,, coal carried in bunkers	. . .	1,279 tons

The hull is built of iron and steel on the cellular system. The double bottom extends for upwards of 230 feet in length, and is divided both longitudinally and transversely into a great number of watertight compartments. Each compartment is provided with a branch tube, which is connected with one principal tube in communication with powerful steam-pumps. The tubes are, of course, fitted with the necessary valves, so that in the event of damage to the bottom of the vessel, or for any desirable purpose, any one or more of the compartments may be drained or filled with water.

There is a central armoured citadel or compartment 107 feet in length and 58 feet in breadth, which descends to 5 ft. 11 in. below the water-line. It protects the machinery and boilers, the magazines and shell-rooms, and a portion of the machinery for working the turrets and guns. Forward and aft of this citadel, the decks, which are 4 ft. 9 in. under water, are defended by horizontal armour. Over this citadel is built a second central armoured compartment, which encloses the bases of the turrets and the remaining portion of the mechanism employed in loading and working the guns. Lastly, above this second compartment rise the two turrets. The turrets are placed at each end of the armoured citadel,—not in an even line with each other, but diagonally at opposite corners of it, with the centres at the distance of 7 ft. 8 in. from the longitudinal centre line of the vessel, so that one turret is on the starboard side and the other on the port side. The effect of this arrangement is to render possible the discharge of three guns simultaneously in a direction parallel with the keel.

Only the central portion of the ship and the two turrets are protected by vertical armour. In order to determine the best material and method of construction for their armour-plates, a course of experiments was undertaken at Spezia with the 100-ton gun and guns of ten and eleven inches calibre, discharged against targets constructed on four different systems of steel and iron from three manufacturers. The result of these experiments induced the Italian Government to adopt steel for armour in preference to iron. They were led to this determination for the reason that the projectiles fired from the 100-ton gun failed to pass through a target faced with 22 inches of that metal, while similar projectiles from the same gun perforated tar-

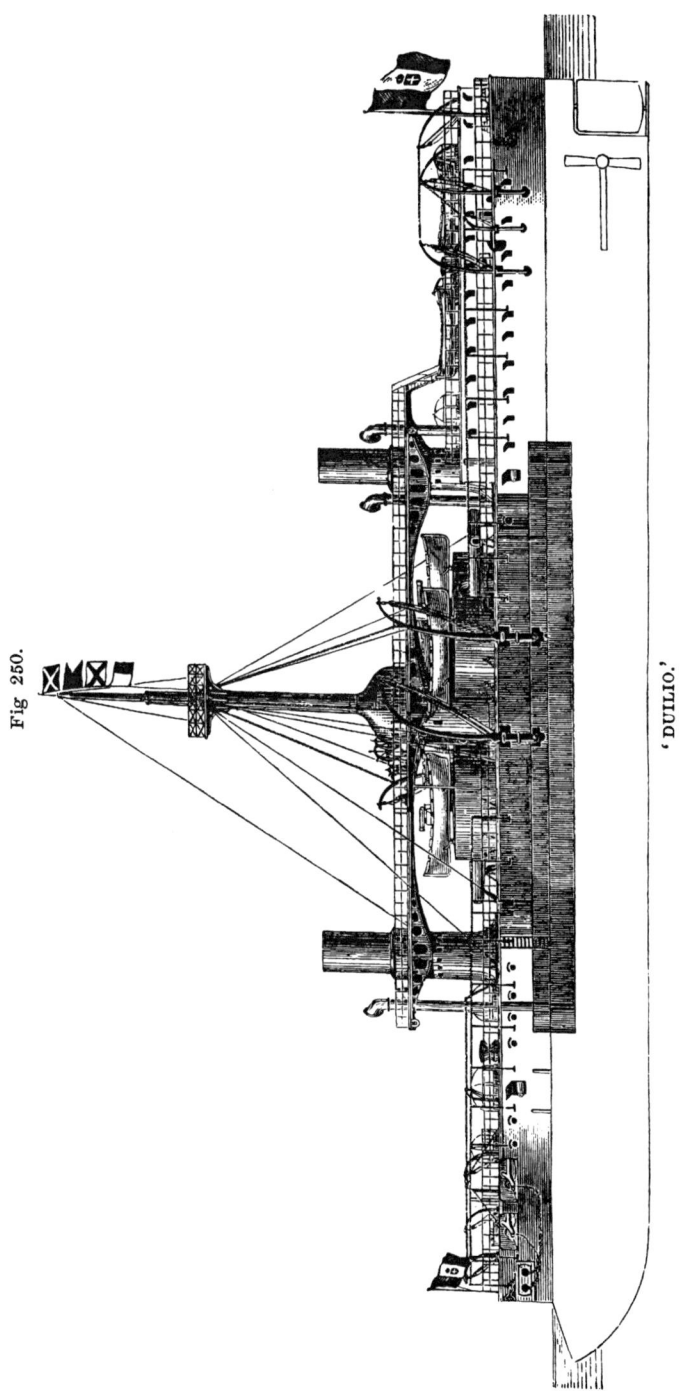

Fig 250.

'DUILIO.'

gets composed of iron plates of the same thickness. The armour of the central portion of the vessel is 21·65 inches in thickness. The armour of the turrets is composed of solid plates 17·71 inches in thickness, resting upon teak backing. The decks are protected by horizontal armour of iron and steel, the former being under the latter.

The original intention was that the armament should be composed of two 60-ton guns in each turret; subsequently it was decided to employ 100-ton guns, and the opinion prevails that this decision was reached after the fact became known that the 'Inflexible' would be armed with the 80-ton guns. These 100-ton guns, four for each ship, have been manufactured by Sir William

Figs. 251 and 252.

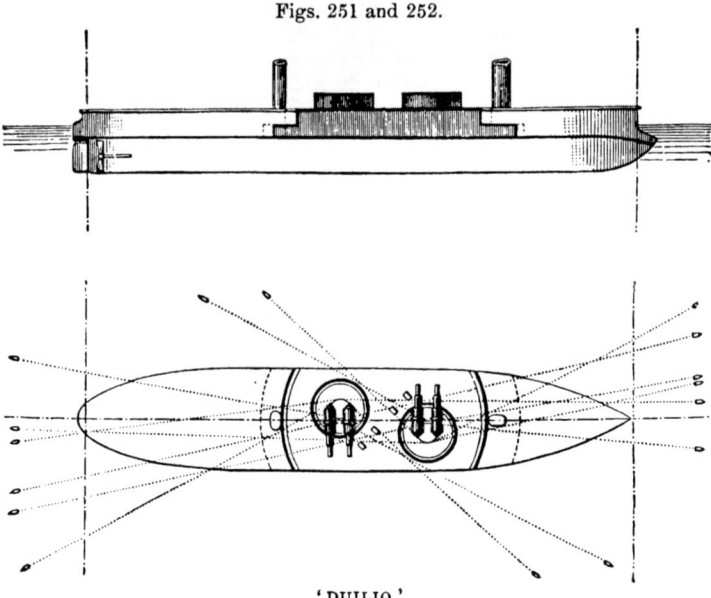

'DUILIO.'

Armstrong at the Elswick Works, Newcastle-on-Tyne, England. They are muzzle-loading, and are built upon the well-known Armstrong system. The 'Duilio' is armed with a heavy projecting ram, and she is also to be provided with apparatus for discharging the Whitehead fish-torpedoes. Besides these powerful means of offence, there is to be an arrangement for carrying a rapid torpedo-boat.

The 'Duilio' is driven by twin screws. The motive machinery has been furnished by Messrs. John Penn & Sons of Greenwich, and consists of that firm's old type,—a pair of trunk engines to each screw. The steam is supplied by the ordinary box-boilers.

The heavy forgings for the ship were made in Italy. The frames, beams, and plates for the hull—in fact, all the iron and steel entering into the construction of the vessel—were made in France. All the armour-plates were ordered from Cammell and Co., Sheffield, England, and the guns and machinery for working them are also of English manufacture, thus leaving only the construction and labour entering therein to be performed by the Italian engineers.

Steam Trials.—When the ship was ready for trial with all weights on board, the mean draught was 26 ft. 9 in., or one foot more than was calculated in the designs. With this draught, on February 16, 1880, a speed trial was made on the measured mile, when, with 84 revolutions of the engines and 7,710 indicated horse-power, a speed at the rate of fifteen knots per hour was realised.

The 'Duilio' is armed with four of the heaviest and most powerful guns now afloat in any ship, and it was believed that if successful in all respects she would be the most formidable fighting-machine, both for offence and defence, in the waters of continental Europe. It remains to be seen whether this estimate is a correct one, or whether the prediction of the eminent ex-Chief Constructor of the British Navy—that she would capsize in the first engagement if seriously injured by shot in the unprotected parts—will be fulfilled.

The recent trials of the guns, after being mounted on board the ship, were attended with a serious disaster in the rupture of the inner steel tube and complete separation of the outer coils of one of the pieces.

The 'Dandolo,' the sister ship of the 'Duilio,' as it has already been stated, will not probably be completed until the end of 1882. The financial resources of the Italian Admiralty will doubtless have been taxed to the utmost during the past year to complete the first of the great ships. The 'Dandolo' is to be in essential features of construction the same as her sister, but with an important difference in the machinery. This has been designed and furnished by Messrs. Maudslay, Sons, and Field, of London, and consists of a pair of their inverted vertical compound engines giving motion to each of the two screw-propellers. The engines are to be supplied with steam from eight boilers fired from both ends, having in all thirty-two furnaces, four of the boilers being placed forward and four abaft the engines. The pressure of steam is to be 60 lbs. per square inch, the maximum indicated horse-power 7,900.

The estimated cost of each of these ships, exclusive of armament, is 700,000*l.*

There is a positive limit to the dimensions of every construction, beyond which it is not wise or safe to go. This point was over-reached in the case of the mercantile ship 'Great Eastern,' the cost of which to the owners was very great.

It is reasonable to believe that the Italian naval authorities have gone beyond the judicious limit in the designs of their last ships laid down. The great cost of the guns and the machinery to work them, the still greater cost of the ship, and the expense of maintaining the stupendous and unwieldy bulk, will probably not be the most serious of the difficulties. Practical questions of the working of the guns and the motive machinery will have to be tested.

The 'Duilio' has now (July 1881) been some time in commission, and has made several short cruises, but it does not appear that she has been exposed to any severe trial either by wind or sea. The official report of her voyage, as one of the squadron of honour attending the King and Queen of Italy on their visit to Sicily in January 1881, has been published. In this her commander, Captain Caimi, pronounces her seagoing qualities to be 'excellent.' But, as during the most trying weather met with, she was able to lower a boat and keep it rowing about for two hours in search of a man who had fallen overboard, it is evident that her capabilities were not tested very severely.

Height of Axis of Guns above the Seagoing Water-line in the Ships under-mentioned.

Port-sills are about two feet lower, except in barbettes.

Ship's name	Main deck	Upper deck
Bellerophon, 7,550 tons .	9 ft. 3 in. amidships	16 ft. 7 in. amidships (unarmoured)
Monarch, 8,320 tons	9 ft. 7 in., stern gun (armoured)	18 ft. in turrets and at bow (armoured)
Alexandra, 9,490 tons .	10 ft. 10 in. amidships (armoured)	19 ft. 8 in. amidships (armoured)
Vauban, 5,800 tons . .	8 ft. 2 in. amidships (unarmoured)	22 ft. amidships (armoured barbettes)
Océan (Fr.), 7,700 tons .	14 ft. 5 in. (armoured)	27 ft. 5 in. (armoured barbettes)
New Cruisers, 7,300 tons .	13 ft. 10 in. amidships	21 ft. 5 in. amidships
Amiral Duperré, 10,320 tons . . .	14 ft. (unarmoured)	27 ft. amidships (armoured barbettes)
Duilio . . .	—	15 ft. 9 in. turrets (armoured)
Nelson (with 1,200 tons of coal) . .	—	13 ft. 6 in.

SACHSEN.

CHAPTER XVI.

MASTLESS BARBETTE SHIPS.

ACCORDING to the programme, the ironclads of the German navy are divided into three groups :—

I. Armoured seagoing, or ocean-service ships.

II. Armoured ships, the employment of which is chiefly limited to home waters, and which are therefore more or less intended for coast defence.

III. Armoured vessels for local coast defence.

To the first group belong the ironclad frigates already finished. Several vessels included in the coast-defence class are completed, and eight armoured gunboats and two monitors are under construction.

On July 1, 1877, the ' Sachsen,' the first of the six armoured ' Sachsen.' corvettes included in the second class, was launched from the slips of the Vulcan Joint-stock Engine Building Company, at Bredow, near Stettin. The ' Sachsen ' has already been tried at the measured mile. Three other vessels of the same class are in progress, of which the ' Bayern ' and ' Wurtemberg ' will shortly be ready for the pendant.

The ' Sachsen ' exhibits so many special features, and differs so widely from any armourclads hitherto constructed, that a short explanation of the principles adopted in the construction of this most important addition to the naval power of Germany may prove of interest.

The following description is taken from Mr. King, with additional matter from the *Revue Maritime* :—

' The dimensions of the " Sachsen " are :

Length between perpendiculars	.	.	213 ft. 3 in.
Breadth, extreme	.	.	.	51 ft. 4 in.
Depth	.	.	.	26 ft. 3 in.
Load draught of water	.	.	19 ft. 8 in.
Displacement	.	.	.	7,135 tons

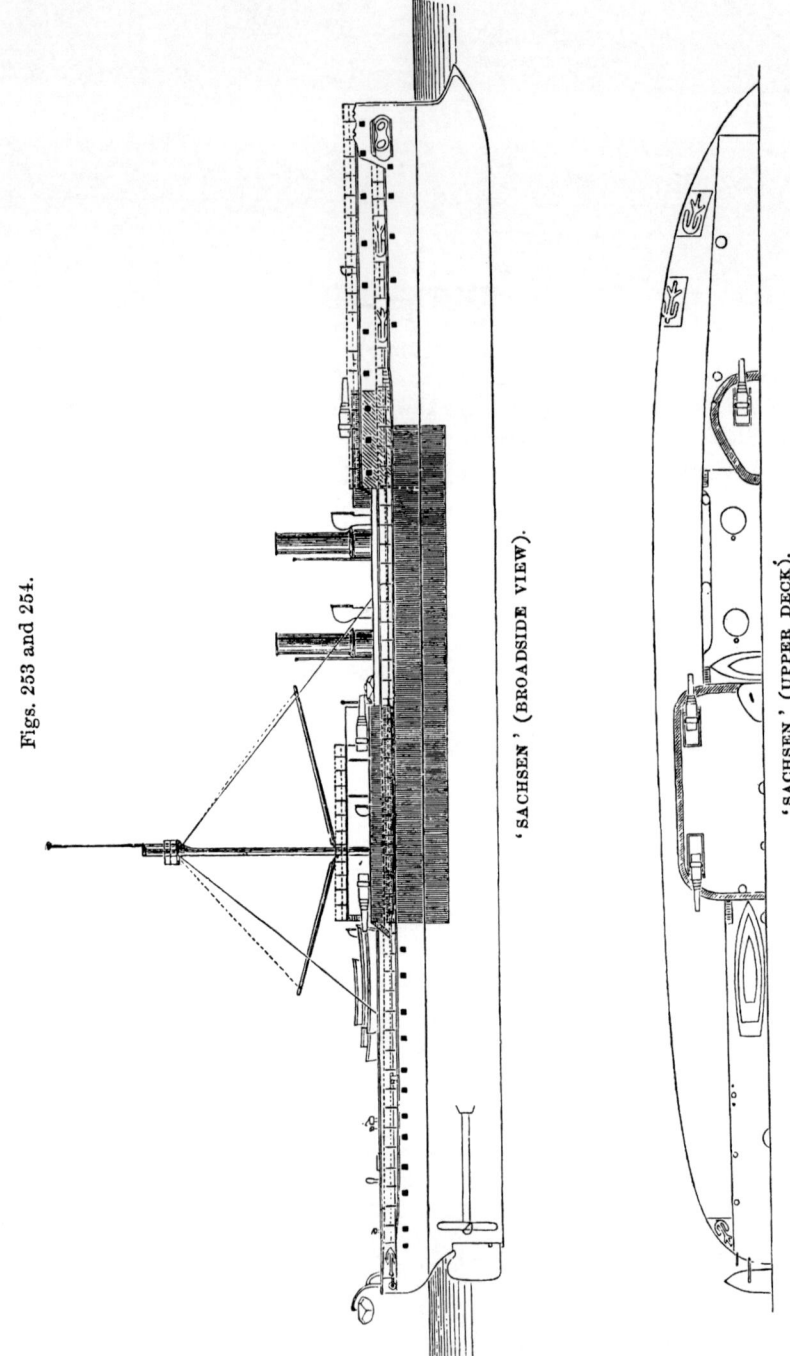

Figs. 253 and 254.

'SACHSEN' (BROADSIDE VIEW).

'SACHSEN' (UPPER DECK).

The " Sachsen " is a double-barbette citadel-vessel, similar in many respects to the late English designs, but having the batteries placed in a line with the keel. A German writer describes the vessel in this manner: " The conditions to be fulfilled by this class, in their *rôle* of chief defenders of the German coast, are light draught, in order to be able to enter the eastern harbours, and equality in offensive and defensive strength with the armoured ships of opposing nations. These demands have been complied with in the calculations for the building and equipment, wherein many new arrangements and departures from earlier contrivances show themselves.

Fig. 255.

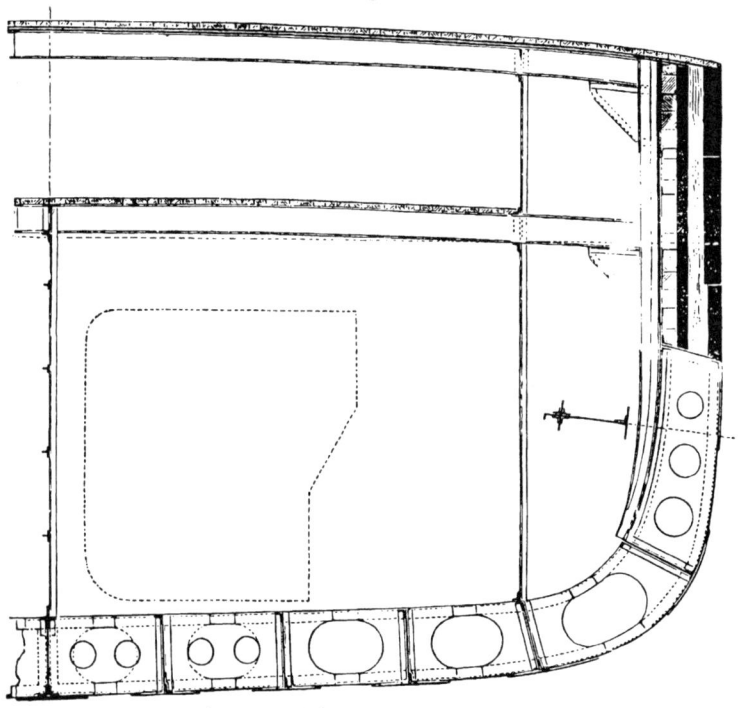

'SACHSEN' (HALF MIDSHIP SECTION).

' " The application of ironclad frigates to the business of fighting on the high seas demands also strong armour to give sufficient resistance to the ever-increasing calibre of the enemy's guns, without making the limits of mobility, manœuvreing, and seaworthiness too narrow. After entering into considerations from this point of view, the armouring of the ship the whole length of the water-line was deemed unnecessary; furthermore, it was considered sufficient if this armour existed as a casemate only, and in the middle of the ship,

for the protection of the machinery, etc.   The application of side
armour was therefore entirely renounced."'

The armour is composed of two plates, the inner six inches, the
outer plate ten inches in thickness.
Each plate rests on a backing of
$7\frac{5}{8}$ inches of teak.   There is an
inner skin of iron $1\frac{1}{4}$ inches in
thickness. The total thickness of
the ship's side is therefore 33 inches,
including about $17\frac{1}{4}$ inches of iron.

The ends of the ship being unarmoured along the water-line, with
a view to insure the whole under
part of the vessel against destruction by shot, an ironclad deck is
built forward and abaft the armoured
casemate about 6 ft. '6 in. under
water, so that the under part of the
ship is completely closed from above,
and the destruction of the side walls
is only possible down to the level of
the armoured deck.   A cork girdle
about 3 ft. 3 in. wide, and of the
same thickness, is fastened on the
inside, forward and abaft the casemate, for the protection of the ship
against sinking, in case of damage
by shot to the unarmoured part.
For further security to the remainder, the under portion of the
ship is divided into a greater
number of cells, and the interior is
divided amidships by a watertight
bulkhead, extending the full length
of the ship. Each of these halves is
again divided by sixteen watertight
cross-walls into an equal number of
watertight compartments, and each
of these compartments is again split
up by vertical and horizontal walls;

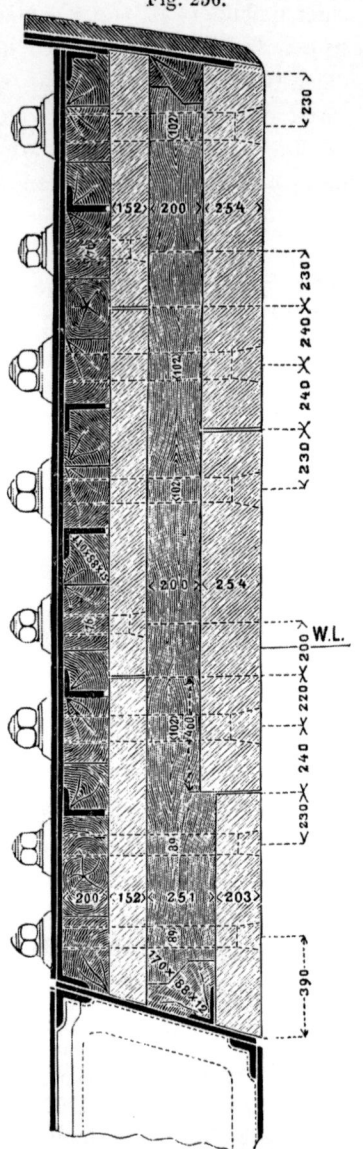

Fig. 256.

'SACHSEN'S' ARMOUR.
(In millimètres.)

so that the ship's body under water presents a web of 120 cells.   As
the joints of each cell are closely made, a leak caused by a ram-

ITALIA.

thrust or a torpedo can only affect a small part of the ship. A system of pump attachments is provided for the speedy expulsion of water from any leaky cell.

The casemate is protected from above by a 2-inch wrought-iron deck. Upon this are situated two armoured fixed barbette turrets or batteries in the line of the keel, protected by ten inches of iron. In the after turret are mounted four 10¼-inch guns, and in the forward turret two guns of the same calibre instead of one 12-inch gun as first arranged. All the guns are mounted *en barbette* behind armoured breastworks, in order that they may command a wide range of fire. They are divided, two guns being now mounted in an oval turret, open at the top, in the fore part of the ship, while four guns are in a large turret, or rather open battery, somewhat abaft the midship part of the vessel. Two 10¼-inch guns, in addition to the guns in the fore turret, can be fired ahead, the other two can be fired astern, and four can be laid at a vessel on the beam. The guns are high above the water, and will command the deck of an enemy with a less lofty freeboard.

In the after battery is placed an elevated pilot-house. A lance-shaped ram, about 9 ft. 10 in. long, is fitted to the bow; and means have been prepared for launching torpedoes.

The vessel is propelled by two separate pairs of engines, each working up to 2,800 horse-power, and driving each a four-bladed screw propeller. The requisite steam is generated by eight boilers in four groups of two in each group. They are situated so that the coal can be conveniently passed into the fire-room. The speed is fourteen knots.

Forward and abaft the casemate, and above the cells, are built quarters for the officers and crew, and upon the bow is a super-structure for protection against heavy seas. This last is built of such a width as to permit a forward fire from the two after guns. Special machinery is provided for ventilation, steering, hoisting anchors, and pumping. The 'Bayern,' a sister ship, has been launched, and the 'Baden,' and others of the same type, are under construction.

Mr. King gives the following description of the Italian ships 'Italia' and 'Lepanto':—

'These two monsters, the "Italia" and the "Lepanto," are now in process of construction, the former at Castellamare and the latter at Leghorn. They were laid down in 1877–78, and the construction of the first will not probably be completed in less than four or five years.' *The 'Italia' and 'Lepanto.'*

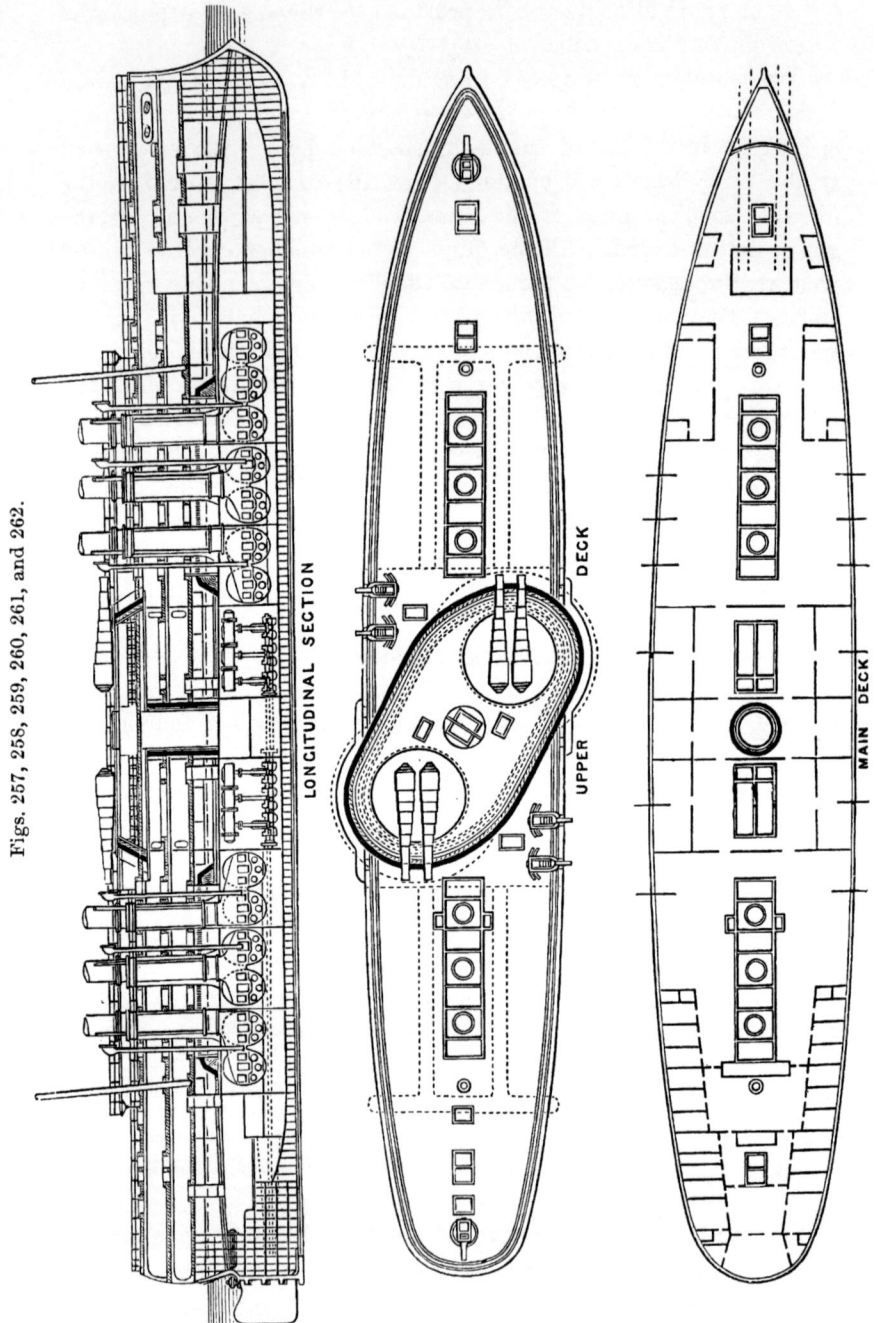

Figs. 257, 258, 259, 260, 261, and 262.

LONGITUDINAL SECTION

UPPER DECK

MAIN DECK

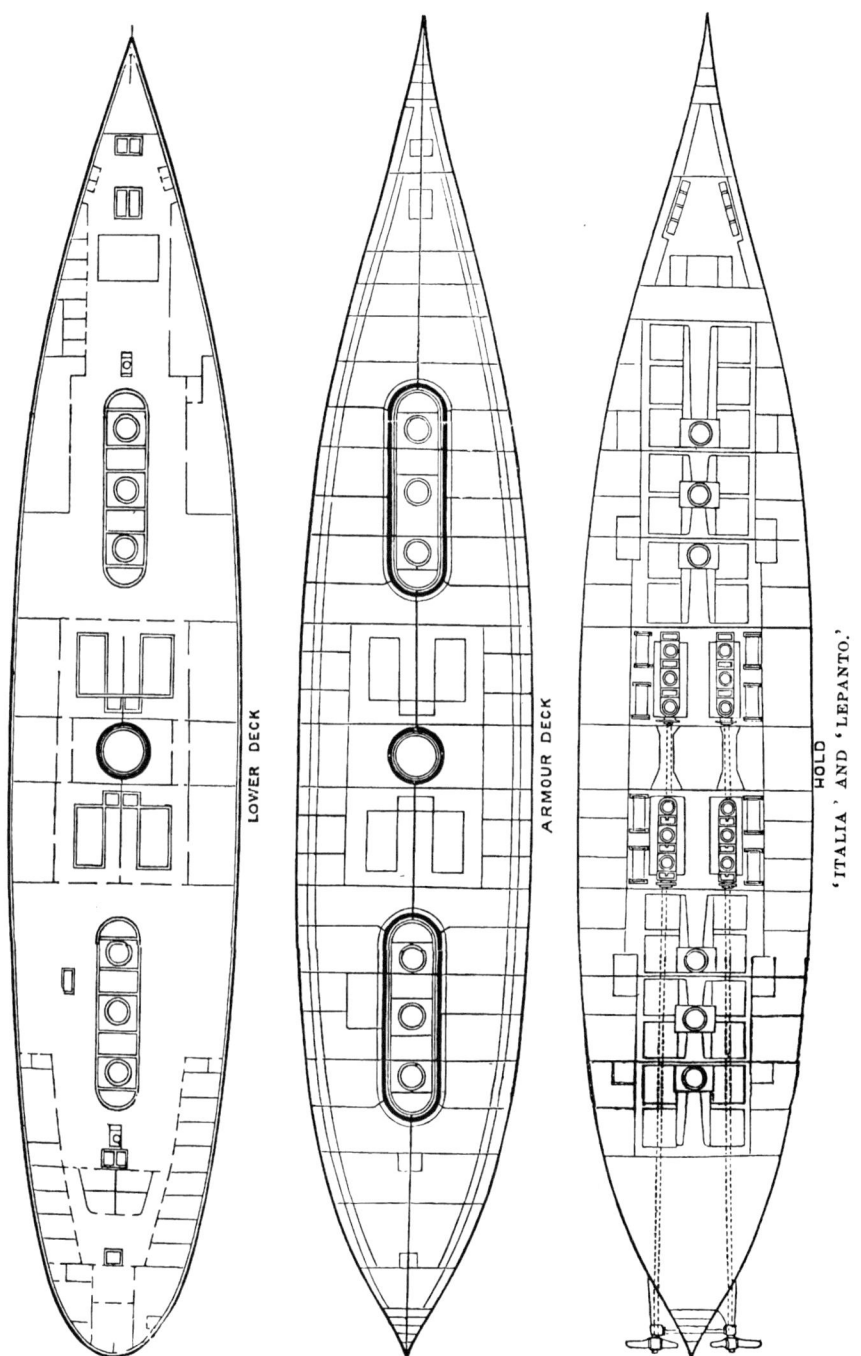

LOWER DECK

ARMOUR DECK

HOLD

'ITALIA' AND 'LEPANTO.'

The drawings exhibit the type of these powerful ships, the disposition of the batteries, the armour and motive machinery, and the arrangement of the watertight bulkheads and decks.

'It will be seen that the bold step has been taken of dispensing entirely with side armour; and that the great guns, of which there are four Armstrong breech-loaders of 100 tons weight, are to be mounted on the upper deck in pairs *en barbette*, in a peculiarly-placed armoured casemate, so arranged as to permit a fire of the guns either on a line with the keel, fore and aft, or in pairs on either beam, or towards any point of the compass.

'The hull is of steel, the lines fore and aft being very fine, and is to be sheathed with wood. It is constructed with the usual double bottom, 3 ft. 3 in. between the skins amidships, and divided into

Fig. 263.

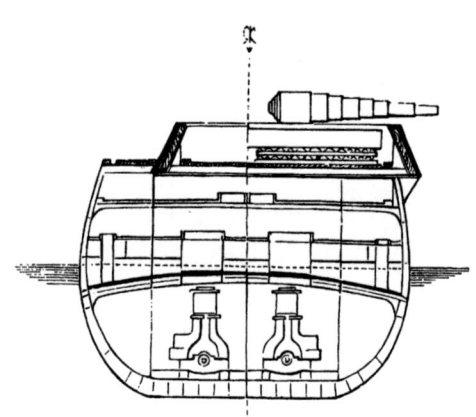

'ITALIA' AND 'LEPANTO' (SECTION THROUGH BARBETTE).

numerous separate cells. Great strength is given to the structure by the bulkheads and decks. Two longitudinal, watertight bulkheads extend for the length of 254 ft. 6 in. in the ship. These, together with the transverse bulkheads, divide the hull into fifty-three large compartments, which are again subdivided horizontally by four watertight decks. The first of these is the armoured deck, 5 ft. 6 in. below the water-line at the sides of the ship, and protected by three inches of iron or steel. This deck extends from stem to stern, and is incurvated at both extremities, meeting at the bow the extreme point of the ram, and thus adding material strength where most needed in the event of ramming an enemy. Immediately above this armoured or lowest deck is another, six feet above the water-line, constructed of thin iron or steel, and covered with wood. The side compartments between this and the lower deck just named, which are divided into watertight cells, are to be filled with cork, as in the " Inflexible." There is, however, this important difference, that, whereas the last-named ship has a long citadel at the middle of her length, protected by heavy armour, and relies upon cork only at her extremities, in the " Italia " the cork and watertight cells afford the only means of preserving stability when the sides are penetrated near the water-line.

' Next comes the third or battery-deck, at a height of fourteen feet above the water-line, upon which are to be carried twelve guns of six inches' calibre, whose power will be moderate compared with the great guns in the armoured citadel, but whose lighter metal will admit of rapid, continuous, and concentrated fire. Situated 7 ft. 9 in. above this battery-deck, and 25 feet above the water-line, is the fourth or upper deck, supporting the casemate battery, 7 ft. 6 in. in height, in which are to be placed the great guns, symmetrically disposed in the quadrantal arcs at each extremity of the oval. From within this battery the guns are to be fired *en barbette*, being supplied with ammunition from below the armoured deck through armour-plated cylinders or shafts of nine feet inside diameter.

' It will thus be seen that armour is only used to keep out shot and shell from the engines and boilers, the magazines, shell-room spaces, and the channels leading therefrom to the upper deck ; and to protect the guns in the casemate when not elevated above the battery, and the gunners employed in firing them. But all other parts of the ship above the armoured deck, all the guns not in the casemate, and all persons out of the casemate and not below the armoured deck, will be exposed to the enemy's projectiles.

' Remembering that the whole of the controversy raised by Mr. Reed, late Chief Constructor of the British Navy, about three years ago, respecting the "Inflexible," related to the limitation of her armour to the central portion of the ship, it will appear a bold defiance of the principles laid down by that gentleman, to abandon side armour altogether as a means of preserving stability when the ship is pierced at the water-line.

' *Motive Machinery.*—This has been designed by Messrs. John Penn and Sons, and is under construction at their well-known works at Greenwich, England. The engines will consist of two sets, of the three-cylinder, vertical, inverted type, to each of the two screw-propeller shafts, making twelve cylinders in all ; and the steam will be supplied by twenty-six boilers, with three furnaces each. Twelve of the boilers will be located in three groups aft of the engines, and fourteen in three groups forward of the engines. The after boilers are placed far aft and the forward boilers far forward, and between the after sets and forward sets of engines there is a space for the passage of the ammunition-shaft. The after boilers are placed sufficiently high above the keel to admit the passage of the screw-shafts under them.

'The engines are of the same type as have been supplied by Messrs. Penn to the British armourclads "Northampton" and "Agamemnon," the cylinders being of equal diameters, applied to cranks set at equal angles. The steam and exhaust valves are so arranged as to allow the engines to be worked either on the compound or the non-compound system, as desired.

'Such stupendous engine-power as has been designed for the "Italia" is, of course, required only exceptionally, a moderate power being sufficient primarily and under normal conditions; consequently, the arrangement of the engines here applied possesses several advantages over that of two very large sets of engines to each screw-shaft. First, the objectionable great weight of the working parts of the engines is avoided. Second, under all ordinary conditions of cruising, the two after sets of engines and the after groups of boilers alone will be employed, and they will be worked on the compound system. It will be only in exceptional cases that the necessity for the full speed of the ship will require all the twenty-six boilers and the twelve steam cylinders.

'The total grate-area of the seventy-eight furnaces is 1,521 square feet. Calculating the power of the engines and the speed of the ship from this element, as compared with that of some other of the latest armoured ships put afloat, the combined engines of the "Italia" ought to develop an indicated horse-power of not less than 15,000, and a speed of sixteen knots per hour at sea—a greater power than ever before placed in a single ship, and a speed greater than ever attained by any war-vessel afloat, the "Iris" and the "Mercury" excepted.

'The following are the correct principal dimensions and other particulars:—

Ship.

Length between perpendiculars	.	.	.	. 400 ft. 6 in.
Breadth of beam at water-line	.	.	.	. 72 ft. 9 in.
„ „ upper deck	.	.	.	. 65 ft. 6 in.
Draught of water, forward	.	.	.	. 25 ft. 6 in.
„ „ aft	.	.	.	. 30 ft. 6 in.
„ „ mean	.	.	.	. 28 feet

Area of immersed midship section	1,770 sq. ft.
Displacement at load draught . . .	13,480 tons
Length of armoured tower on fore and aft line .	88 ft. 6 in.
Breadth of armoured tower across ship (extreme) .	72 ft. 6 in.
Length of armoured tower, *per se*	96 feet
Breadth of armoured tower, *per se* . . .	52 ft. 9 in.
Distance of stem from armoured tower . . .	170 feet
Thickness of sides of tower, including armour .	3 ft. 3 in.
,, iron armour on tower . . .	21 inches
Height of centre of heavy guns above water-line .	32 ft. 8 in.
,, top of tower above water-line . .	30 feet
,, upper deck above water-line, forward .	25 feet
,, ,, ,, aft . .	23 feet
,, ,, ,, amidships .	22 ft. 6 in.
,, between upper deck and battery-deck .	7 ft. 9 in.
,, ,, battery and second deck . .	7 ft. 9 in.
,, ,, second and armoured deck .	7 ft. 6 in.
Depth of lower deck below water-line amidship at sides .	5 ft. 6 in.
,, hold under lower deck . . .	21 feet
Extension of ram beyond forward perpendicular .	6 ft. 4 in.
Distance of point of ram below water-line . .	8 ft. 6 in.

Motive Machinery.

Number of engines	4 sets
,, cylinders	12
,, propellers	2
Diameter of propellers	19 ft. 6 in.
Number of boilers	26
,, furnaces (three to each boiler) . .	78
Length of ship, fore-and-aft, occupied by engines, coal, and boilers	250 feet

'The estimated weights of the hull, armour, etc., are approximately as follows :—

Hull	5,000	tons
Armour of armoured deck . .	1,200	,,
,, citadel . . .	900	,,
,, ammunition-shaft .	246	,,
,, chimneys . . .	552	,,
Total weight of armour .	2,898	,,
Teak backing	114	,,

'*Armament.*—The armament is to consist of four of the most powerful guns ever constructed, the 100-ton Armstrong breech-loaders, mounted in the citadel on the upper deck at the extraordinary height of 32 ft. 8 in. above the water-line; eighteen 6-inch Armstrong breech-loaders of the new pattern, mounted on carriages designed by Captain Albini; six of which are carried on the upper deck, one being a bow-chaser and another a stern-chaser, and twelve on the deck next below. There are also four ports provided for the purpose of ejecting Whitehead torpedoes, while the ram will constitute another powerful weapon.

'The 100-ton guns are now being manufactured by Sir William Armstrong, and will be the first heavy guns on the breech-loading system ever turned out in England; indeed, the heaviest breech-loaders [1] ever manufactured. They will be mounted in pairs on revolving platforms within the tower, and will be worked by the remarkably ingenious hydraulic system developed by the talented engineer and partner in the Elswick firm, Mr. George Rendel. The principle is the same as applied to the barbette guns of the British ship " Téméraire."

'The cost of each of these ships completed, exclusive of armament, is estimated at 766,900*l.*'

'Italia' from M. Dislère. Additional particulars and criticisms are given in the following translation of a notice communicated to the *Revue Maritime et Coloniale*, by M. Dislère.

The armour of the breastwork will be 18 inches of steel, or possibly wrought iron faced with hard steel, which has been found to give the best results. The steel employed in the hull is manufactured by M. Schneider, and is somewhat like the mild steel lately brought into use in ship-building.

M. Dislère gives a higher power to the engines than was anticipated by Mr. King. The vessel is to be propelled by two screws of nineteen feet diameter; each of them being worked by an engine of six cylinders. The boilers will be twenty-six in number. The power expected is to be 18,000 horse-power, and it is hoped that a speed of sixteen knots may be attained.

The usual amount of coal is 1,500 tons, but she can carry 2,500 tons. At low speed she could cruise without once putting out the fires for a period of six months.

M. Dislère, writing when the 'Italia' was first laid down, remarked of the armament, that ' it would seem probable that it will be composed of four guns of 100 tons, mounted in pairs on turntables. The form adopted of a casemate surrounding the two turntables, instead of two separate turrets, as on board the " Dandolo," has for its object the diminution of weight.

'It seems strange that a protected deck placed below the water-

---

[1] Mr. King is here not quite exact. The Italians have themselves made a breech-loader of rather more than 100 tons weight, which has been in position in a coast battery near Spezia for nearly two years. It is made of cast iron and steel on the French system, and has given most satisfactory results. It is not, however, considered a naval gun.

line and running throughout the entire length of the ship should have been adopted. Where there is no side armour, before and abaft, the armoured deck is necessarily placed below the dividing compartments; but where there is the protection of an armoured belt, it is evident that the plated deck ought to be carried to the upper part of that belt, instead of creating a sort of reservoir, in which projectiles striking in a plunging direction must necessarily explode.

'It is very probable that these early *data* will be modified hereafter, but they are not the less interesting as characteristics of the new steps made in the building of gigantic ships. It may be that this will be the last of these structures, and that, instead of seeking to produce marine colossi, a return will be made—in displacements of 8,000—to the dimensions of manageable ships, and to a cost so far reduced that our total resources will no longer be at stake on one or two elements of a problematical success.'

A correspondent of the *Standard* summarises the leading features of the 'Italia' and 'Lepanto' as follows:—

'Their floating powers are preserved by a cellular raft body, which is partly above the water-line and partly below it, standing on an armoured deck below the water-line, which will deflect a shot upwards, and prevent it from going through the bottom. They have double sides, also cellular, some ten or twelve feet apart, and each watertight division of the hold is made as small as possible. The cellular raft body is stowed with coal, so that water entering there will find the space into which it would flow occupied by material which already forms one of the weights carried by the ship.

The *Standard*: leading features of the two ships.

'It will be observed that the main principles are to protect the battery and its communication with the magazine with armour; to keep all the other vital parts of the ship below the water-line; to fill up the space into which water could penetrate through a shot-hole with coal, and to divide the entire hull into as many cells as possible, each of them keeping out the water when others are flooded. Protection against torpedoes is gained by the space left between the inner and outer walls of the ship and by her great speed. Each of the guns in the battery has a light bullet-proof shield above it, which moves with it and protects the gunners from the fire of rifles and machine guns. The rest of the battery is open to the air, and this appears to be, from one point of view, a great advantage. The gas from burning gunpowder is of a suffocating description, and it is said that the men who were in the turret of the "Duilio" when the 100-ton gun burst suffered much from the poisoned air. Hutchinson, an *employé* of the Armstrong firm, reports that his greatest anxiety was to keep his mouth shut, and not breathe the vitiated atmosphere before he could escape into the open air.'

Contro-versy as to the sta-bility of the 'Duilio.' The controversy as to the stability of the 'Inflexible' drew widely divergent opinions from Sir E. Reed and Mr. Barnaby on the characteristic features of the designs for the 'Italia' and 'Lepanto.' The following passage occurs in a memorandum addressed by Mr. Barnaby to Sir E. Reed on April 16, 1877:—

'The Italians, for the "Duilio" and "Dandolo," trust for both buoyancy and stability to their unarmoured raft.

'In their later and far larger ships, "Italia" and "Lepanto," they have gone farther still and surrendered the citadel itself, abandoning side armour entirely. I am not at all confident that the Italians are not in the right, and I have recommended a large experiment to settle that question.'

Sir E. Reed's view is that the completed ship should have stability from her protected structure alone.

Replying to Mr. Barnaby on May 18, 1877, he says:—

'Every heavily armoured ship . . . has been designed to comply with the condition that I am contending for, with the exception of the ships under notice, and of the Italian ships "Duilio" and "Dandolo," which are exposed, in my opinion, beyond all doubt or question to speedy destruction.'

Mr. Barnaby, in a later utterance, gives a general outline of the policy now adopted by the Constructor's Department in relation to armour-protection:—

'As to the sea-going fleets we have already proceeded far in stripping the armour from their sides, and coming back to the old condition, but with this important difference: the vital parts of the fighting machine are protected against the enemy's guns to such an extent that no single shot or shell shall be capable of disabling it. This protection, however afforded, appears to be indispensable in ships designed under such conditions of warfare as now exist. This is the nature of the protection given to the great Italian first-class battle-ships "Italia" and "Lepanto." They are to have enormous power of engines and guns, but they are not ironclads. They are protected ships, and it cannot be denied that they are also armoured ships. They have an underwater deck of 3-inch armour, weighing about 1,200 tons, and they have probably an equal weight of armour of eighteen to twenty-seven inches protecting their internal vital parts.'

According to the most recently published statements, the 'Italia' and 'Lepanto' will have a displacement of not less than 13,700 tons.

HELIGOLAND.

The original estimate of cost was 17,000,000 lire, or 680,000*l*. It is now certain that the cost will exceed 19,720,000 lire, or nearly 789,000*l*. The total cost of the four large ironclads of the Italian navy will exceed the estimate by no less than 8,000,000 lire, or 320,000*l*. The 'Italia' was launched at Castellamare in September, 1880.

The 'Helgoland,' the largest ship built in Denmark, was begun in 1876 and launched on May 9, 1878. The hull is of iron. The dimensions are as follows:

The Danish armour-clad 'Helgoland.'

Length	. 274 ft. 6 in.
Breadth	. 59 ft. 2 in.
Draught of water	. 18 ft. 6 in.
Tonnage	. 5,347 tons
Horse-power, indicated	. 3,700
Speed	. 12 knots

The armour at the water-line is twelve inches, but is tapered off gradually towards the bow and stern to a thickness of eight inches; it has a strong 10-inch backing and a double iron skin. The ship has a fixed battery amidships with 10-inch armour and 10-inch backing. The upper deck outside the battery is covered with 2-inch iron plating and the top of the battery with $2\frac{3}{4}$-inch. A 'traverse' consisting of 2 × 3 inch iron plates divides the battery into two parts. On the top of the battery is an unarmoured turret. The hull is divided into watertight compartments.

The armament consists of one 30 c/m. (12-inch) Krupp gun in turret, four 26 c/m. ($10\frac{1}{2}$-inch) Krupp guns in the battery, and five light Krupp guns on the upper deck. The complement is 300 officers and men. The 'Helgoland' is propelled by twin screws. The firm of Burmeister, of Copenhagen, were the builders, and the cost was 264,000*l*.

The 'Collingwood' will be the first regular barbette ship built for the British navy, the barbette turrets of the 'Téméraire' being combined with a common form of the broadside armament. This ship was begun at Pembroke in July, 1880.

The 'Collingwood.'

The principal dimensions, etc., are :—

Length between perpendiculars	. 325 feet
Breadth, extreme	. 68 feet
Depth in hold	. 25 ft. 5 in.
Draught of water, forward	. 25 ft. 3 in.
„ aft	. 26 ft. 3 in.
Displacement	. 9.150 tons
Height of upper deck at side from water-line	. 10 ft. 6 in.

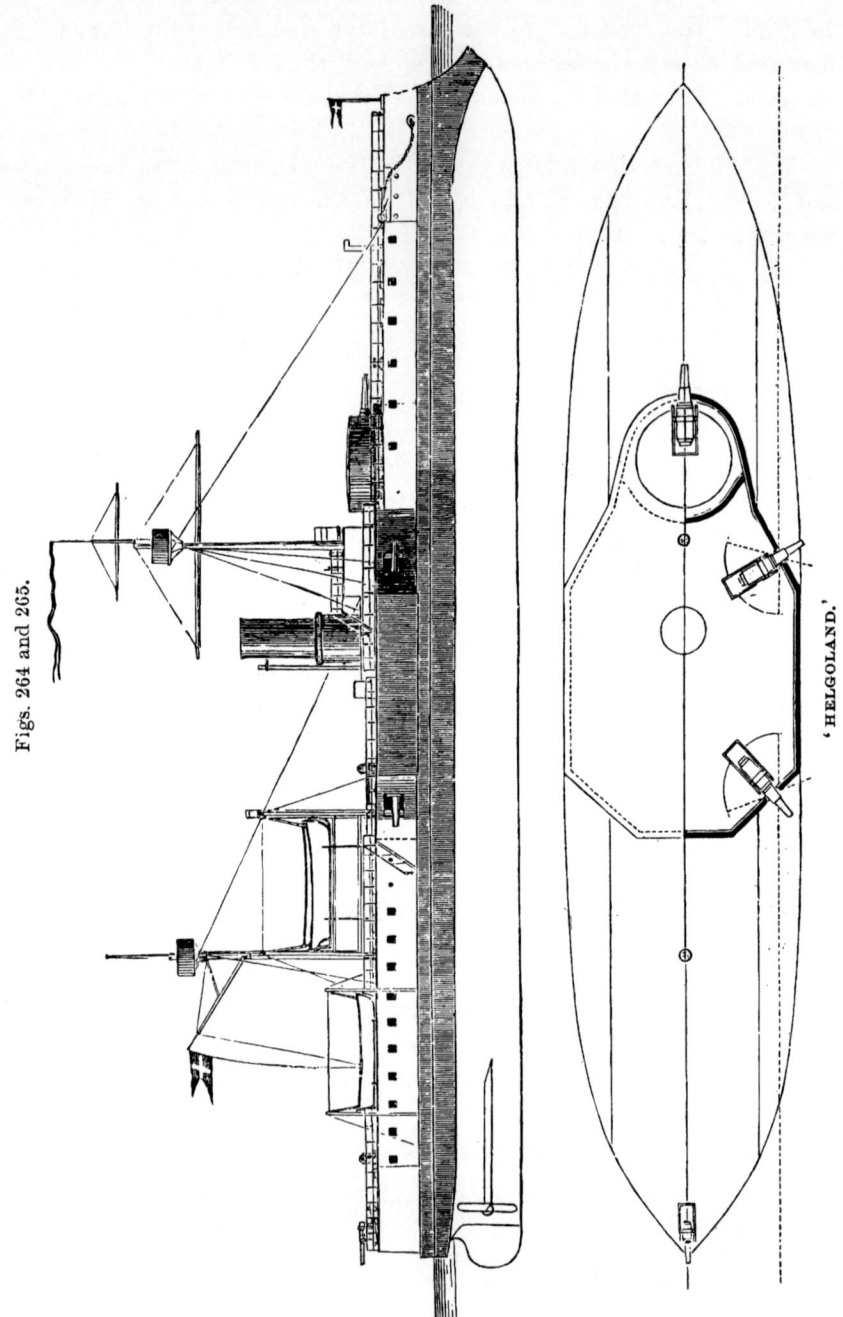

Figs. 264 and 265.

'HELGOLAND.'

COLLINGWOOD.

Height of barbette ports from water-line	$\cdot\begin{cases} \text{19 ft. 3 in.} \\ \text{20 ft. 3 in.} \end{cases}$
Indicated horse-power . . .	. 7,000
Coal-supply	. 950 tons
Complement of officers and men .	. 345

Figs. 266, 267, and 268.

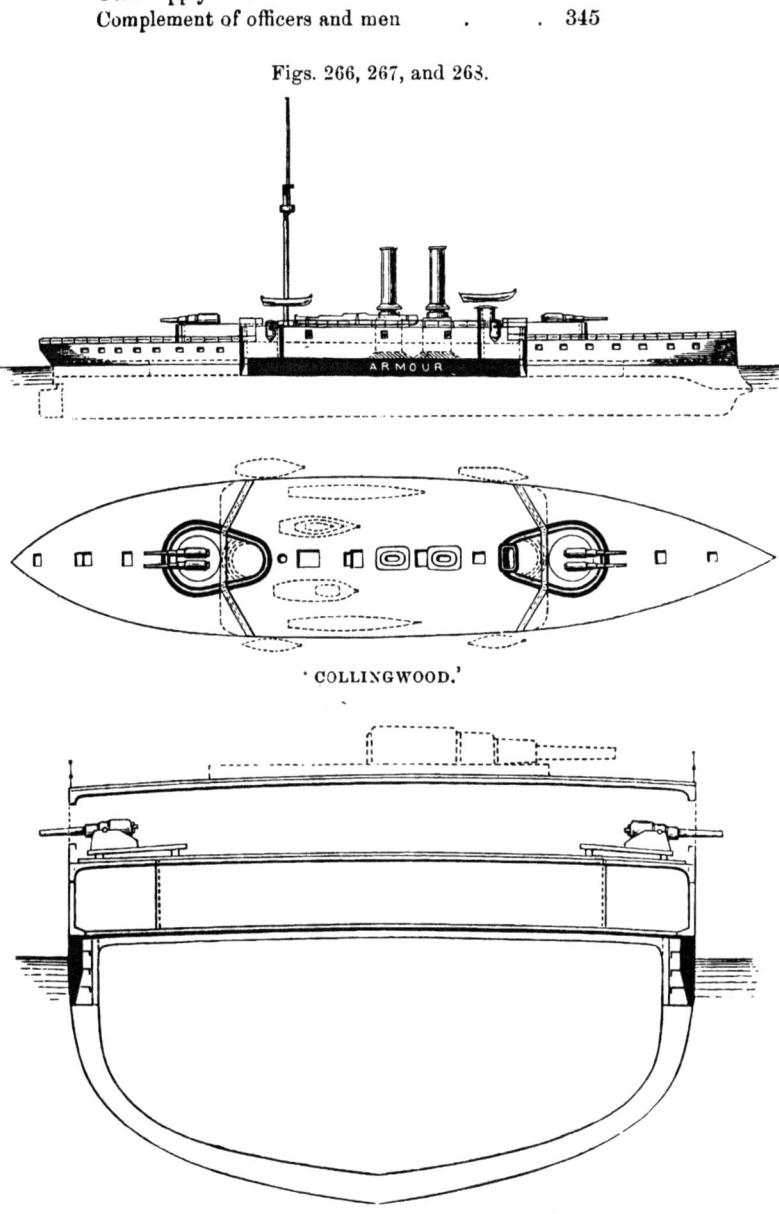

'COLLINGWOOD.'

'COLLINGWOOD' (MIDSHIP SECTION).

The armour on the sides of the barbette is to be fourteen and twelve inches thick, on the 'screen bulkhead' six inches, and on the belt eighteen inches at the sides and sixteen inches at the ends. The armament will consist of four 43-ton breech-loading guns in the barbette, and six 6-inch guns on the upper deck.

Though not belonging to any of the before-mentioned types, the ship described below may fittingly conclude the list of those of which accounts have already been given.

The following description of the 'Polyphemus' is taken from *Iron* of August 2, 1879 :—

The 'Polyphemus.'

'The torpedo ram "Polyphemus," now being constructed in Chatham Dockyard, appears likely to be the most extraordinary ship that has yet been built. She is novel and peculiar alike in form, structure, fittings, and arrangements of armour-protection ; while her weapons of attack are such as will necessitate her being fought dif-

Fig. 269.

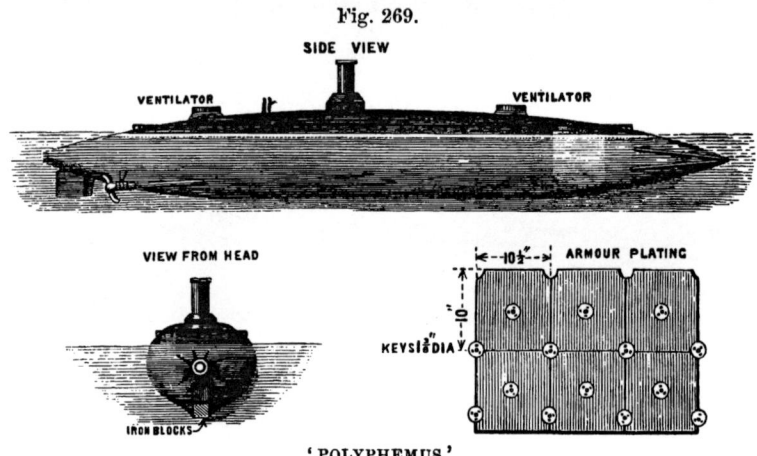

'POLYPHEMUS.'

ferently from any other war ship. Her design was described by the late Mr. Ward Hunt in the House of Commons on March 12, 1877, as being " of a kind as yet unknown in any part of the world, but which had been much talked about, and has been at last forced upon me by that gallant officer who stands at the head of the veteran list of the navy—viz., Sir George Sartorius, who has shown that although his age is great his mind is still youthful, and that he is willing to receive new ideas and able to inculcate them." The leading features of the " Polyphemus " are a strong ram bow, a powerful torpedo battery, great speed and handiness, moderate size, and a small extent of surface above water exposed to the enemy's fire, such portion of the vessel as is above the water-line being convex in form, so as to deflect any projectile that may strike it. The appearance she will present when at sea will be that of a cylinder, floating on its side and deeply immersed, which is tapered at the ends to form a bow and stern.

The top of the cylinder will be 4 ft. 6 in. above the water-line, and will be flattened over a large portion of its area to form a deck. The whole of this flattened cylindrical surface will be plated over with steel armour, and will cover in and protect the ship and all her machinery and fighting appliances. The armour is made up of two ½-inch thicknesses of Landore-Siemens steel, one being the skin of the ship, on which are laid 1-inch plates of Whitworth compressed steel. The ship proper as she will thus appear will be surmounted by a light structure carrying a hurricane deck of about two-thirds her length, and upon this deck will be seen a signal-mast, funnel, pilot-tower, boats, and other fittings. The curvature of the sides is carried down several feet below the water-line, and armoured to that depth. Below this point the section assumes a V form, and ends in a sharp angle at the keel. A complete cross section of the vessel is similar to that of a peg-top. The flattened convex curvature of the upper part of the peg-top would represent the part of the " Polyphemus " that is above water, and the lower portion, which ends in a point, would also represent the part of the ship that is below water. If the peg-top be imagined to float in water at a depth below where its breadth is greatest and where the section thus begins to curve towards the centre line, a rough idea may be obtained both of the form and proportions of the above and under water parts of the " Polyphemus." The " Polyphemus " is 240 feet long between perpendiculars, 40 feet in extreme breadth, and will have a load draught of 20 feet. Her displacement will be 2,640 tons. The convex armoured deck will be 4 ft. 6 in. above the water-line, and will be completely plated over with steel armour 3 inches thick. This armour will be carried to a depth of six feet to seven feet below the water-line. The " Polyphemus " will not be fitted with masts or sails, but will carry a pole for signalling purposes and for making observations from. She will be propelled by twin screws, and will have two pairs of high-pressure compound horizontal engines, which are being constructed by Messrs. Humphreys and Tennant, Deptford. Each high-pressure cylinder will be 38 inches in diameter, and the low-pressure 64 inches. The stroke will be 45 inches. The boilers will be of the locomotive type, twelve in number, and will be made of steel. They will work up to a pressure of 110 lbs. per square inch. It is estimated that the engines will indicate a collective power of 5,500 horses, and that the speed of the ship will be seventeen knots. The coal-supply is 200 tons.

' The only offensive weapons the " Polyphemus " will possess are a powerful ram bow and Whitehead torpedoes. She will have no guns at all, except a few light shell guns and machine-guns on the hurricane deck for the purpose of repelling boat or torpedo attack. The

Offensive weapons.

ram will consist of a very strong spur, which will project twelve feet
in advance of the stem of the ship, and is so placed that it will strike
several feet below an enemy's armour. It will be connected to the
stem and bow by deep web plates and angles on each side; the former
being a continuation of the 3-inch deck armour, which is curved
downwards at the bow and carried under water till it reaches the
level of the spur. The spur is being fitted so that it may be un-
shipped and taken off the stem when not required for active use.
Under the ram is a torpedo port, which will enable Whitehead torpedoes to be ejected right ahead of the ship. There are also two
torpedo ports on each side amidships, from which they will be ejected
on the broadsides. The ports and apparatus for working the torpedoes
will be upon the system fitted in the " Vesuvius " and " Glatton."
All the torpedo ports are below water, but it is understood that this
under-water attack will be supplemented by torpedo firing above
water from the armoured deck upon the system adopted in ordinary
torpedo launches. Above the armour-plated portion of the hull a
hurricane deck is fitted for about two-thirds of its length. This
deck is about one-half the extreme breadth of the ship. Communication is made between the hurricane deck and the interior of the
ship by openings cut through the armoured deck. The openings
thus cut are protected by glacis plates and armour and by casings,
which are carried up to the hurricane deck. The boats are carried
upon the hurricane deck, and the ship is steered and worked from
it. An armoured pilot-tower with protected means of access to the
lower part of the ship, is placed at the fore end of the hurricane
deck, and fitted with steering wheel, telegraphs, voice-pipes, apparatus
for firing off torpedoes, and all other appliances for conning and
working the ship. A few light shell or machine guns will also be
carried on the hurricane deck, as we have stated, for repelling
boarders or torpedo boats.

Material of
hull.

'The "Polyphemus" is built throughout of steel. The frames
are of Bessemer, and the bottom plating of Landore-Siemens steel.
She is constructed upon the usual system of transverse bracket
frames and continuous longitudinals, and has a double bottom the
whole length of the ship right up to the upper deck. The subdivision
of the lower part of the ship into small watertight compartments has
been carried as far as appears possible. The double bottom is split
up into a large number of cellular spaces, and the hold is divided by
a longitudinal middle-line bulkhead, and numerous transverse bulkheads. The boilers are contained in four separate watertight compartments of the hold, three being placed in each; and each pair of
engines is also contained in a separate watertight compartment. The

advantage of such an arrangement is sufficiently obvious in view of the possibility of one of the boilers or engine-rooms being bilged by a blow from a ram or torpedo. The double bottom is arranged so as to include the coal-bunkers, as in the " Devastation " and the " Inflexible." By these means buoyancy is gained if one of the compartments is opened up to the sea, as the water can only find its way among the interstices of the coal, and a large quantity is thus kept out of the ship. The cabins and accommodation for the crew will all be below the armoured deck, and will be ventilated artificially, as in the ironclad monitors. They will be lighted throughout by the electric light, which is already being fitted in several ironclads, and is likely to become extensively used for this purpose. An electric light will also be fixed in the look-out on the pole-mast, for reconnoitring and signalling purposes.

'The most remarkable and novel feature in the ship yet remains to be described. The bottom plating on each side, instead of ending in a keel, or flat keel-plate, at the middle line, is formed into a recess ; so that in place of a keel there is a rectangular groove, 1 ft. 8 in. wide and 3 feet deep, taken out of the bottom of the ship. This groove or recess is intended to be filled with cast-iron ballast up to a weight of 300 tons. The ballast will be cast in several lengths, and will be so attached to the ship that, in the event of a compartment becoming bilged, and its being desirable to lighten the ship, the ballast can be let go and dropped from any part, as may be required. The draught and trim may thus be regulated to a certain limited extent should the vessel be damaged in action. This is a point that will probably be discussed among constructors. The object of carrying the ballast seems to be to keep the ship down in the water, and prevent the deck from becoming too much exposed when the ship is uninjured ; but should she become still further immersed from any cause, the dropping of the ballast will somewhat relieve and lighten her. The utmost effect of the dropping of the ballast will be to enable the vessel to float twelve to fourteen inches lighter after it has been dropped than she would do before. In other words, although her armoured deck is only 4 ft. 6 in. above the water, and this height only is exposed to the enemy's fire, the surplus buoyancy, on account of the ballast, will be the same as though the armoured deck stood 5 ft. 6 in. or 5 ft. 8 in. above the water-line. It will be obvious that this quantity of ballast, amounting to about one-ninth of the whole weight of the ship, cannot be carried about for nothing. It adds to the work the engines have to do, and a greater expenditure of engine-power for a given speed will be required to enable the ship to drag the ballast about with her. The additional engine-power

'Ballast keel.'

that will be required to drive the "Polyphemus" at full speed, after adding the ballast, will necessitate an increased coal-consumption of nine to ten per cent., and a corresponding reduction in coal-endurance. It will hardly be considered necessary to carry about all this dead weight in time of peace ; and it will be a question for practical consideration whether the carrying of it about in time of war at a cost of reduction in speed, or in coal-endurance—and this in a ship whose coal-supply is very small for her power—will be compensated for by the armoured deck being 4 ft. 6 in. out of water, instead of 5 ft. 6 in.

'The "Polyphemus" is more or less of an experimental character, and the building of future ships, possessing some or all of her characteristics, will depend upon the results of her trials. She is not likely to create a great revolution in war shipbuilding, or to show that guns are unnecessary in a fleet. Indeed, it must be evident that there are many operations—such as the bombardment of fortifications—which could only be carried out by ships armed with guns. The question respecting the "Polyphemus" is not whether such vessels as she are to supersede gun-vessels, but whether she may not serve the more humble, though very useful, purpose of starting a type of war ships that will be valuable auxiliaries in action. Mr. Ward Hunt, on the occasion before referred to, spoke of her as follows :—

' " This vessel must of course, to a certain extent, be regarded as an experiment, and, even supposing it to be a success, I could not propose it to the House as being likely to supersede all other kinds of fighting ships, but only as a useful adjunct to a fleet in case of war. Probably it would not be desirable that she should be kept at sea for a long period at a time, but I venture to think she will prove a very formidable weapon, and, if she should be a success, she may perhaps be regarded as a sort of rival to those monstrous ships with tremendous armour that we hear spoken of as likely to be built in some foreign ports." '

The 'Polyphemus' was commenced in September 1878, and was launched in June 1881. When afloat she was thus spoken of in the *Standard* :—

' Having her engines and boilers in, but neither her armament, her stores, nor her ballast, her weights, it will be well understood, were not as they should be. But by putting some 30 tons of pig ballast forward, and about 15 tons of water in one of the forward recesses, the vessel floated, light it is true, but still very prettily, drawing 13 ft. 6 in. forward, and 15 ft. 8 in. aft. Her proper draught, when the 830 tons additional of materials are aboard, will be 19 ft. 6 in. forward, and 20 ft. 6 in. aft.'

CHAPTER XVII.

UNARMOURED CRUISERS AND SPECIAL VESSELS OF THE
CHIEF NAVAL POWERS.

Section I.—*British Unarmoured Vessels.*

THE navy has other duties to perform besides those of fighting
battles on the high seas and defending the coasts. It must protect
the merchant shipping and prevent the enemy from adding to his
resources by the capture of property at sea. This third duty devolves
on vessels of the cruising classes.

The impulse given to the construction of the modern cruising
ships is due to the War of Secession in America. The incidents of
the careers of the 'Sumter' and 'Alabama' are well known. In
1863 it was resolved to build special vessels for service as cruisers.
They were to be capable of overtaking the Confederate vessels, and
of driving the mercantile marine of a hostile country from the seas.
As a principal object of their existence was the annihilation of an
enemy's commerce, they were not to take part in an engagement
unless an opportunity favourable to themselves presented itself. If
they should encounter a more powerful opponent they were to take
to flight. Their especial duty being to injure and annihilate, they
were not to do battle with an enemy of greater strength. The
'Idaho,' which was the first vessel built for the special service which
has been described, was a complete failure. The ship had scarcely
been completed when the engines were removed, and she was converted into a sailing store-ship. The second attempt to produce a
cruiser of extreme speed was only a degree more successful. The
seven cruisers of the 'Wampanoag' type were intended to attain
a speed of 17 knots, but on their trial trips they hardly exceeded
15 knots. Their length over all was 341 feet; their displacement
4,000 tons. They were to carry sixteen 10- and 11-inch smooth-
bore cast-iron guns on the broadside on the upper deck, and one
revolving 60-pounder rifled gun in the bows. Their bunkers were to

[margin notes:] Cruise of the 'Alabama' and 'Sumter.'

The 'Idaho.'

The 'Wam-panoag.'

contain 1,000 tons of coal, sufficient for a distance of 5,600 miles at 10 knots. Owing to their moderate draught of water, about 18 ft. 4 in. to the 'load' water-line, their screws proved ineffective. The weakness of structure incidental to their great length, and the use of wood as the material for the construction of the hull, was compensated by a system of diagonal and longitudinal stringers and plates, by which the hull was bound together from stem to stern and from the upper deck to the keelson. These were the finest ships of the kind which existed at the close of the War of Secession, and they introduced the era of fast cruisers. These pioneers of the type were followed, both in England and in France, by vessels believed by the builders of their respective countries to be better adapted for the work for which they were designed.

H.M.S. 'Inconstant.' The 'Inconstant,' the first ship of the new class, was laid down at Pembroke on November 27, 1866; and was launched on November 1, 1868. This vessel attained a speed on the measured mile of

Fig. 270.

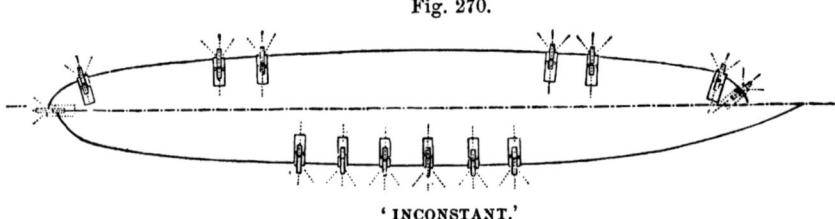

'INCONSTANT.'

sixteen knots with full boiler, and thirteen knots with half-boiler power. The coal-supply was sufficient for two and a quarter days' steaming with full boiler power; for nine days at ten knots an hour; for twenty-three and a half days at seven knots; and for forty-three days at five knots. Under sail the speed and handiness were remarkable, and the 'Inconstant' could without difficulty keep her station in a sailing squadron.

It was obvious that ships exceeding 330 feet in length, however strongly their timbers might be fastened, could not be constructed of sufficient strength of wood. Sir E. Reed accordingly proposed to build the cruisers of iron, to case them with wood, and to sheathe the bottom with copper, the latter device seeming indispensable in the case of ships designed to undertake long voyages and to remain out of dock for a lengthened period. This system of construction was adopted for all the larger cruisers built after the date of the 'Inconstant.' The figure shows the arrangement of the 'Inconstant's' guns.

Admiral Scott has made the following criticism on this arrangement:—

'Her 12-ton gun-carriages are placed upon slides which are too long and two feet too far inboard; this consequently interferes with the passing of powder and shot behind them. On the other hand, from her guns being so far inboard, the sights for pointing them are blocked by a slight roll, and the fire and smoke from the discharge are not carried sufficiently far from the ship's side. This vessel is also deficient in bow and stern fire, which might easily be given.'

Two smaller vessels, the 'Active' and 'Volage,' were laid down almost simultaneously with the 'Inconstant.' They were designed for similar services, but their dimensions were more restricted. These vessels are quite large enough for the special duties required of cruisers. Sir E. Reed, however, was of opinion that it was more politic to expend a given sum in the construction of a smaller number of ships of the 'Inconstant' class than a larger number of the 'Volage' class. He thought that the moral influence of the nation was more powerfully sustained in time of war by making number subordinate to quality, and that the inferiority of $1\frac{1}{2}$ knots in the speed of the 'Volage,' as compared with that of the 'Inconstant,' might—if a ship escaped from pursuit in consequence—exercise a demoralising influence, not only on her ship's company, but throughout England. In consequence of this opinion the smaller vessels were for the time abandoned; and in 1873 the 'Shah' (formerly the 'Blonde') and the 'Raleigh' were commenced. {The 'Active' and 'Volage.'}

The greater number of the American corvettes had now been launched. A trial of one of them showed that the high hopes which had been entertained of their performance were fallacious. It now appeared no longer necessary that the English corvettes should possess such extraordinary power and speed, qualities which necessarily required very large displacements. The Admiralty, however, still believing in the wisdom of the policy which they had previously adopted, decided to follow a totally different course from that which all other navies had been compelled by financial considerations to follow. So far from diminishing the size of their ships, increased displacement was given to the new designs.

The 'Shah,' termed an 'iron screw-frigate,' was launched at Portsmouth in September, 1873. The hull, built of iron, is cased with wood on the plan adopted in the 'Inconstant.' The principal dimensions are:— {H.M.S. 'Shah.'}

Length between perpendiculars . .	334 ft. 8 in.
„ of keel for tonnage . .	298 ft. 5 in.
Breadth, extreme . . .	52 feet
„ for tonnage . . .	51 ft. 6 in.
„ moulded . . .	50 ft. 4 in.
Depth in hold . . .	17 ft. 6½ in.
Burden in tons (O. M.) . .	4,210
Displacement (ready for sea) . .	5,700
Load draught of water, forward .	21 feet
„ „ aft . .	25 feet

The coal-supply is about 950 tons, a quantity which at half-boiler power would enable her to keep under steam for nine days; or at full power for four days. The armament originally was sixteen 6½-ton guns on slides, and two 64-pounders on common truck carriages on the main deck, and on the upper deck two 12-ton guns, and six 64-pounders. The 12-ton guns on the upper deck are carried one at each end of the ship, turntables being fitted so as to shift them from side to side. These guns are covered by the poop and forecastle, which give protection from rifle-fire and falling spars in action. The ports are recessed, and allow a great range of fire. The foremost gun fires from two ports of a side, and commands an arc of from 23 degrees abaft the beam to five degrees across the keel, or a total range of 118 degrees. The poop is a novel feature in the ship; and the armament was considered a great improvement on that of the 'Inconstant,' the heavier guns being carried on the upper deck, where they can be given the greatest possible range, and be available when main deck guns could not be used.

Hull of 'Shah.'

The ship is divided, by means of watertight bulkheads and flats, into twelve compartments; the iron-plating is covered on the outside with two thicknesses of carefully selected teak planking; the inner thickness is secured to the ship with iron fastenings, the outer thickness is secured to the inner by metal fastenings. Great care is taken to prevent any galvanic action between the iron of the hull and the copper with which the outside planking is covered. For the same reason the after part of the keel, together with the stern and rudder-posts, has been made of gun-metal. These and the rudder were all cast in Portsmouth dockyard, and weigh about fifty tons. The ship's side on the main deck is lined with paper half an inch in thickness, a contrivance intended to prevent the spread of splinters, which would be caused were the sides lined in the ordinary way with wood. The dimensions of the 'Shah' and the 'Inconstant,' are approximately the same, the main difference consisting in the addition of a few feet to the length in the former ship, while steadiness of platform and additional stability have been obtained by increased beam. The engines were manufactured by Messrs Ravenhill and Co., the contract power being 7,500 horses indicated. They have horizontal return connecting-rods and surface condensers, and the cylinders are 116½ inches in diameter, the length of stroke being four feet. The ship is propelled by a single screw.

Trials on the measured mile took place in December, 1875. Trial trip
of 'Shah.' The ship had only a few days before been taken out of dock, so that her copper sheathing was free from weeds ; there was little or no wind, and the sea was perfectly smooth. The trim was adjusted by means of seventy tons of iron ballast, disposed on each side on the upper deck to make up for the difference of the weights on board, and so bring the ship to the same draught as on a former trial, viz. 21 ft. 7 in. forward and 25 ft. 7 in. aft. The safety valve was loaded to 32 lbs. The following figures were obtained from six runs upon the measured mile, with and against the tide, at full power :— The pressure of steam in the boilers was 29·5 lbs., and the vacuum in the condensers 27 lbs. forward and 26·41 aft. The highest number of revolutions per minute was 67·79 ; the mean per minute 66·08 ; and the mean per mile 245·66. The mean pressure of steam in the cylinders was 19·941. The results of the runs were—first mile, 16·744 knots, with 67·50 revolutions ; second mile, 16·143 knots, with 67·79 revolutions ; third mile, 16·901 knots, with 66·76 revolutions ; fourth mile, 15·385 knots, with 65·38 revolutions ; fifth mile, 16·981 knots with 65·09 revolutions ; and sixth mile, 14·876 knots, with 63·96 revolutions. The mean was thus 16·258 knots an hour, and the mean number of revolutions 66·08 per minute. The mean horse-power developed was 6,868·87. With five feet greater length, two feet more beam, a foot more immersion, and with fewer revolutions and less horse-power, the ' Shah ' realised only half an knot per hour less than the sister frigate, the ' Inconstant,' and this in spite of the difficulty experienced in preventing the metal from running out of the bearings when driven at a high rate of speed. The brasses at the time of the trial under review were new ; and, although the precaution was taken of gradually working up the steam by preliminary trips up and down the Solent, the bearing became so injuriously heated that it was deemed necessary to keep a couple of 2¾-inch hoses constantly playing upon the heads of the connecting rods. This will serve to explain the fact shown above, that from the second run—when 67·79 revolutions per minute were obtained, there was a gradual reduction in the number, the effect of the heated bearings being aggravated by the loss of steam withdrawn to work the engines which fed the hoses.

At the conclusion of the full-power trial, four runs were made under half-boiler power, with the following results : the pressure in five boilers was 31 lbs.; the vacuum in the condensers was 27·81 forward, 27·12 aft ; and the mean pressure in the cylinders 12·212. The highest number of revolutions per minute was 51·61, the mean per minute 50·47, and the mean per mile 238·25. The horse-power realised was 3,212·83 and the speed attained 12·928 knots. The engines were stopped in 42 seconds under full power, and in 18 seconds under half boiler-power. They were started astern in 28 seconds and seven seconds, and going astern they were started ahead in 14 seconds and 11 seconds. The temperature on deck during the day was 44 degs. (F.), and the highest reading of the thermometer in the middle stoke-hole was 104 degrees.

H.M.S. 'Raleigh' — The 'Raleigh,' though of smaller dimensions, is designated, like the 'Shah,' in the official navy list a 'frigate.' The hull is of iron sheathed with wood, and she has the following principal dimensions :—

Length	298 feet
Breadth, extreme . . .	49 feet
Depth in hold	19 ft. 11 in.
Draught of water, forward . .	21 ft. 11 in.
„ aft . . .	24 ft. 10 in.
Displacement, tons . . .	5,200
Indicated horse-power . . .	6,158

The 'Raleigh,' like the other frigates of the group to which she belongs—the 'Inconstant' and the 'Shah'—is a perfectly-built iron ship, divided internally into watertight compartments, and with an outer casing of double wood-planking, the inner skin of wood-planking being lapped on to the iron hull with iron screws, and the outer skin on to the inner wood skin with joints broken. On this outer wood skin is nailed the copper sheathing of the hull below the load-line. The 'Raleigh' is fitted with three coaling ports on each side—an idea imported from America—opening into shoots on the lower deck which lead direct into the bunkers below, a very excellent arrangement for several reasons. She, however, has no steam capstan or steam steering apparatus.

The present armament of the 'Raleigh' is arranged on the following plan : Upper deck.—Two 12-ton 9-inch revolving guns, mounted one under the forecastle and one under the demi-poop, four converted 71-cwt. 64-pounder guns, two on the broadside, and two as stern-chasers. Main deck.—Two 64-pounders as chase guns, and fourteen of the new pattern, 115-pounder or 7-inch 4½-ton shell-guns on the broadside. The total weight of the guns carried by the 'Raleigh,' with their carriages and slides, is 108 tons 16 cwt. 1 qr. The change in the main-deck armament from fourteen 71-cwt. 64-pounders to fourteen 90-cwt. 7-inch 115-pounders has given an increased weight of nearly 39 tons.

The engines, constructed by Humphreys, Tennant and Co., are of the horizontal direct-acting, return connecting-rod type, and intended to indicate 6,000 horse-power. Their principal dimensions are as follows : —

Number of cylinders	2
Diameter	8 ft. 4 in.
Stroke	4 ft. 6 in.
Piston rods, four to each piston, diameter	7 inches
Back trunk, one to each piston, diameter	1 ft. 6 in.
Slide valves, vertical, double-ported, travel	10¼ inches
Depth of valve	5 ft. 10 in.
Width of valve	5 ft. 1½ in.
Depth of ports	5 ft. 2$\frac{7}{16}$ in.
,, bars in extreme ports, two in each	2 inches
,, ,, other ports, two in each	1 inch

The expansion valves are horizontal and of the gridiron type, placed above the slide casing, and worked from rocking shafts by means of eccentrics on the main shaft. The cut-off ranges from 3½ inches of the stroke onwards, and is varied by moving the end of the eccentric rod along a quadrant arm on the rocking shaft. There is one surface condenser to each cylinder. The air-pumps are 25½ inches in diameter, double-acting, and worked direct off the pistons. The circulating pumps are centrifugal, and driven by separate engines with 12-inch cylinders and 12-inch stroke, exhausting into the condensers ; the water is forced through the condensers outside the tubes.

The condenser tubes are vertical, and there are 6,740 in each condenser. Their dimensions are as follows :—

Diameter, inside . . .	½ inch
,, outside . . .	$\frac{5}{8}$ inch
Length between tube-plates . .	6 ft. 6½ in.
Cooling surface	12,000 sq. ft.

The starting gear can be worked by hand or steam. A Silver's governor is fitted. The propeller is by Hirsch, two-bladed, 26 ft. 8 in. pitch, and fitted for being raised when the ship is under sail alone. The number of boilers is nine ; but two of them are small and intended for auxiliary purposes; these are together equal to one of the large boilers. The chief dimensions of the boilers are as follows:—

Number of funnels	2
„ furnaces	32
Length of fire-grate	6 ft. 10 in.
Breadth of fire-grate	3 ft. 3½ in.
Area of fire-grate	720 sq. ft.
Number of tubes	2,880
Length between tube-plates	6 ft. 4 in.
Diameter outside	3 inches
Tube heating surface	14,300 sq. ft.
Number of superheaters (steam pass ng through the tubes) .	2
Number of tubes	248
Diameter of tubes inside	2 inches
Length ・	9 feet
Superheating tube surface	1,170 sq. ft.

The boilers are of the ordinary 'box' kind, pressed to 30 lbs. on the square inch.

A writer in *Engineering*, from which paper this account of the 'Raleigh's' engines is taken, remarks:—

'We observe that rather than round off the lower back corners of the two forward boilers to meet the change of shape in the hull, they have been raised to a higher level. By this means the furnaces have been kept their full length, and the boilers are not so liable to foul, while they are more easily cleaned at the backs of the furnaces; but an inconvenient, if not a dangerous, break has been made in the level of the stoke-hole plates, and to keep the crowns of these boilers under the water-line like the others, part of their steam space has been sacrificed. We were not surprised to hear of their priming; and we think that altogether the disadvantages of the arrangement outweigh its advantages.'

The steam starting-gear is a great advantage, and one not common in Her Majesty's ships. The arrangement in the 'Raleigh,' consisting of a small pair of engines working at a comparatively high speed, is better than that of a single steam cylinder *assisting* the hand gear—better, because it does the work by itself, and is more easily controlled.

The immersion of the 'Raleigh' having been considerably increased over the original design since her official trial in April, 1874, she was subjected to further trials at full power to determine wh t she can do under conditions not anticipated when she was designed. These extra trials were made at Portsmouth in September, 1874; one being for six hours at full power, the other over the measured mile ; and the results are given in a table, together with those of the original measured mile trial at Sheerness.

Trials of H.M.S. 'Raleigh.'

	April 1, 1874		September 2, 1874	September 18, 1874
Date of trial .	April 1, 1874		September 2, 1874	September 18, 1874
Kind of trial .	Measured-mile		Six hours	Measured-mile
Where tried .	Maplin Sands		off Portsmouth	Stokes Bay
Draught:				
Forward . .	19 ft. 6 in.		21 ft. 10 in.	21 ft. 11 in.
Aft . .	23 ft. 6 in.		25 ft. 2 in.	24 ft. 10 in.
Mean . .	21 ft. 6 in.		23 ft. 6 in.	23 ft. 4½ in.
Ship by the stern .	4 feet		3 ft. 4 in.	2 ft. 11 in.
Screw:				
Diameter . .	21 feet		21 ft. 1 in.	21 ft. 1 in.
Length, greatest .	3 ft. 2½ in.		3 ft. 3¾ in.	3 ft. 3¾ in.
Upper edge, immersed .	10 inches		2 ft. 5½ in.	2 ft. 1½ in.
Force of wind .	4 to 5		3 to 5	3
State of sea . .	Smooth		Moderate	Smooth
Steam pressure and temperature :	Full power	Half power		
Boilers . .	32·7 lbs.	29·1 lbs.	27·4 lbs.	28·3 lbs.
Superheaters .	mean 310°	370°	mean 325°	mean 320°
Engines . .	31·2 lbs., 274°	27·6 lbs., 282°	25·9 lbs., 289°	26·8 lbs., 281°
Vacuum:				
Forward . .	27·6	27·4	27·0	26·8
Aft . .	26·9	26·4	26·5	26·8
Revolutions per minute . .	73·9	58·5	68·8	69·6
Indicated mean pressure . .	19·8	13·8	19·1	19·2
Indicated horsepower .	6,157	3,413	5,541	5,639
Speed of vessel .	15·503	13·455	Calculated 15·139	15·320
Revolutions per knot	286·0	260·8	272·5	272·5
Slip per cent. .	20·28	12·6	16·35	16·35
Temperatures :				
Deck . .	56°		65°	64°
Engine-room .	77°		87°	83°
Stoke-hole, aft .	105°		118°	108°
„ fore .	118°		110°	92°
Kind of coal used on trial . .	Nixon's Navigation			

When at sea and under very favourable conditions of light winds and smooth water, the rate of speed ought to be fourteen knots per hour, being a deduction of 1·25 knots per hour from the measured mile rate, so long as the stokers can keep a pressure of steam in the boilers sufficient to maintain the revolutions of the engines above sixty-seven per minute.

The ' Boadicea,' officially designated an ' iron screw corvette cased with wood,' was the pioneer of a new class of men-of-war, intermediate between the ' Shah ' and the ' Inconstant ' on the one hand, and the ' Active ' and the ' Volage ' on the other. The two latter are wood-sheathed iron corvettes. They displace 3,078 tons, and have engines which work up to 4,015 horse-power. In point of stability it was acknowledged that these ships were somewhat deficient. Their armament was not universally approved. They carry their guns on the upper deck ; and the absence of a covering deck was considered a grave defect by naval men, though it was approved by the Committee on Designs.

In reference to the objections which had been raised, the professional naval architects on the staff of the Controller of the Navy were directed to design the smallest ship possible which would meet the conditions of a covering deck combined with good seagoing properties. From this resulted the ' Boadicea ' class of ships, of which there are three examples, the ' Boadicea,' the ' Bacchante,' built at Portsmouth, and the ' Euryalus,' at Chatham. The following are the principal dimensions of the ' Boadicea ':—Length between perpendiculars, 280 feet ; length over all, 315 feet ; extreme breadth, 45 feet ; depth in hold, 15 ft. 7 in. ; burden in tons, $2,679\frac{15}{94}$; displacement when fully equipped for sea, 3,912 tons ; height of ports from load-water line, 8 ft. 9 in. ; height of freeboard, 14 ft. 3 in ; and draught of water, forward 20 ft. 9 in., aft 23 ft. 3 in., mean 22 feet. The transverse frames, which are of angle irons three inches by $3\frac{1}{2}$ inches by $\frac{7}{16}$ inch, and riveted to reverse frames of nine inches by $3\frac{1}{2}$ inches by $\frac{7}{16}$ inch, are 3 ft. 6 in. apart. These frames are continuous from gunwale to gunwale ; while another source of transverse strength is obtained from the watertight bulkheads, of which there are ten. The ship is thus divided into eleven main watertight compartments ; and in addition to these the engine and boiler-rooms are protected from injury from ramming by means of the longitudinal bulkheads forming the coal bunkers, which are situated on each side of the engine and boiler-rooms, and are capable of storing 400 tons of coal. There are other small compartments constructed on the watertight principle, such as the magazines and chain lockers. In order to give longitudinal strength to the structure, continuous longitudinal frames are fitted, varying in breadth from 27 inches to twelve inches. The outside iron plating varies in thickness from $\frac{7}{8}$ inch at the keel plate to $\frac{7}{16}$ inch in the bottom and side plating. Against the bottom plating there are worked two layers of teak sheathing, each three inches thick, the inner thickness being fastened with iron screw bolts tapped through the bottom plating and nutted on the inside. The outer thickness of sheathing is fastened to the inner thickness by means of metal screws. Under water the 'Boadicea' is of precisely the same form and dimensions as her sister, the 'Bacchante,' but the iron hull of the former is slightly smaller than that of the latter, in consequence of her having, as we have said, two thicknesses of wood on the bottom as compared with the 'Bacchante's' one. The purpose of the two thicknesses is to completely insulate the iron hull from the copper, with which the 'Boadicea' is sheathed over all, while in the case of the 'Bacchante' the one thickness is intended to admit the water to the iron hull in order that an electric battery may be formed by the iron, the zinc sheathing (which is substituted for the ordinary copper), and the sea water, so that, as a result, the iron of the hull may be preserved at the expense of the positive metal—the zinc sheathing. The difference in the wood sheathing leaves the iron stem of the 'Bacchante' exposed and ready for ramming, whereas the stem of the 'Boadicea' is covered with wood and coppered, and is therefore unsuitable for effective attack by ramming. Advantage was taken of this difference in the teak sheathing by Vice-Admiral Sir W. Houston Stewart, the Controller of the Navy, to order a head-knee and a figure-head of the 'Queen of the Iceni' to be fitted to the 'Boadicea.' The latter is an excellent piece of carving, and makes the corvette look as handsome as some of the old frigates. The 'Boadicea' has no double bottom. She is steered by hand power. To the head of the rudder, which is fitted in the ordinary way, is attached a tiller, the fore end of which works across the ship in a slide, and is connected by chains with the steering wheels on the main and upper decks. The ship is provided on each side with a conning house, constructed of $\frac{3}{8}$-inch iron plates.

The complement of men and officers is 350, and in a ship of the 'Boadicea' class great comfort is secured for the crew from the messes being on the main deck, where there is an abundance of light and air. The covered deck also affords protection for the men working the guns. The principal cabins are situated on the main deck, the remainder, together with the ward-room, being on the lower deck and on the after side of the engine-room bulkhead. The 'Boadicea' is ship-rigged. The authorities have introduced some important alterations in the armament. At first she carried sixteen $4\frac{1}{2}$-ton 7-inch guns, throwing a common shell of 116 lbs. 12 ozs., the full charge being 14 lbs., and the reduced charge 10 lbs.; but as the guns of this nature have been ascertained to be sufficiently strong to stand the strain of increased charges, it is proposed to fire them with battering charges of 22 lbs. of pebble powder, and with double shells of the weight of 156 lbs. and Palliser shot weighing 113 lbs. The gun will thus be not inferior in power to the $6\frac{1}{2}$-ton 7-inch guns, the only difference being that in the case of the latter gun the battering charge of the same weight is composed of R. L. G. instead of pebble powder. To enable the $4\frac{1}{2}$-ton guns, however, to fire the additional weight of cartridge and projectile, it was necessary to fit them with the 'Bacchante's' slides and carriages, and to provide them with hydraulic buffers. It was also considered advisable to strengthen the port sills to enable them to take a drop bolt in lieu of the existing fixed pivot, and thus provide against the greater recoil produced by the heavier powder charges.

The estimated cost of the engines is 68,000*l.*; the estimated first cost of the hull was 113,160*l.*, and the estimated last cost 140,000*l.* These figures have been somewhat exceeded.

The engines were constructed by Messrs. Rennie to develope 5,250 horse-power. In common with all the engines now being constructed for ships of the Royal Navy, those of the 'Boadicea' are on the compound principle. There are three cylinders, one high-pressure, which is 73 inches in diameter, and two low-pressure, each of which is 93 inches in diameter. The stroke is four feet. The two low-pressure cylinders have been adopted to avoid the risk involved in making good castings of the size that would be required if the engines had been designed with one low-pressure cylinder. The estimated speed was 15 knots. At the full-speed trial in Stokes Bay on October 20, 1876, the 'Boadicea' steamed 14·8 knots, with a displacement of 3,918 tons and 5,134 indicated horse-power.

H.M.S. 'Bacchante.' The 'Bacchante' is an iron corvette cased with wood of the same type as the 'Boadicea.' The principal dimensions are as follows:— Length over all, 317 feet; length between perpendiculars, 280 feet; extreme breadth, 45 ft. 6 in.; breadth within mouldings, 43 ft. $11\frac{1}{4}$ in.; depth in hold, 15 ft. 7 in.; draught of water, 20 ft. 7 in. forward, and 23 ft. 3 in. aft; and total weight, or, in other words, the displacement of the ship when fully equipped for sea, 4,070 tons. It will thus be seen that the 'Bacchante' comes midway in point of size between the 'Shah' and the 'Volage,' and may therefore be said to approach the ideal of an unarmed cruiser. The keel consists of a vertical iron keel, composed of intercostal plates $\frac{3}{4}$ inch thick, united to a continuous longitudinal plate $\frac{3}{4}$ inch thick and 27 inches deep; a flat keel-plate connected by an angle-iron to the intercostal plates; and below this a wooden keel to receive the lower strake of the wood sheathing. The stem is wholly of iron, and supported with breasthooks fixed at the ends of the longitudinal frames and at other places. The stern-posts and after-piece of keel are also of iron, the latter as well as the body-post being of one forging. The framing of the vessel is formed of a combination of transverse and longitudinal frames. The former consists of an outer angle-iron, 3 inches by $3\frac{1}{2}$ inches by 7-16th inch, and a reverse angle-iron 9 inches by $3\frac{1}{2}$ inches by 7-16th inch, with intermediate frames of intercostal floor-plates throughout the midship part of the ship, the whole being firmly united to the longitudinal frames, and for the most part constructed similarly to the vertical keel. Special means have been adopted for strengthening the framing of the after part of the vessel, so as to support the shaft tube and otherwise enable it to resist the violent action of the screw. The iron plating forming the inner part of the skin is generally $\frac{1}{2}$ inch in thickness, with the exception of the garboard strakes, which are an inch thick. The plating is worked next the frames, to which it is riveted. The wood sheathing is worked upon the skin, and is in two thicknesses from a few feet below the water-line and upwards throughout the midship part of the ship's side. The remaining portion of the planking is in one thickness only. The edges of the wood sheathing are not caulked, but are worked close-jointed. This is to allow the water to gain access to the iron skin, whereby a galvanic battery may be set up, and the plating of the hull be preserved at the expense of the zinc. As soon as the ship is docked the zinc sheathing will be placed over the wood casing from the water-line downwards. It is also useful to remark that the casing is secured to the skin plating by nut and screw bolts, those of the bolts which are above the zinc being galvanised, but those behind the zinc remaining unprotected. The interior of the ship consists of the iron bulkheads, beams, stringer plates, deck flats, and pillars, which support the decks and the various compartments into which the vessel is divided. The beams for supporting the decks and platforms are all of iron, those beneath the heavy guns on the main and upper decks being not less than twelve inches deep. The 'Bacchante' is fitted with three iron masts, and is ship-rigged.

Though built from the same lines, the 'Bacchante' differs in several features from the 'Boadicea.' In the latter ship the after-piece of the keel, the stern-posts, and the rudder-frames are of metal; she has also two thicknesses of wood casing throughout, and is, moreover, sheathed with copper. The 'Boadicea' has also a knee-head and a figure-head, while the 'Bacchante' is provided with a ram bow fitted with a running bowsprit, which will enable her to ram with effect all wooden and unarmed ships.   Having only a single thickness of wood, the difference has been equalised by making the iron hull of the 'Bacchante' slightly wider than that of the sister ship.

The height of her ports above the load water-line is 8 ft. 9 in.; and the height of her freeboard 14 ft. 3 in.   The quantity of coals carried is 400 tons, and the complement of officers and men 350.

The estimated cost of the engines was 72,000*l.*   They were manufactured by Messrs J. and G. Rennie, Blackfriars Road, London, and have developed the greatest power through a single screw shaft of any compound engines yet tried, while the several diagrams taken from the cylinders show that the engines give considerable uniformity of power in the high and low pressure cylinders at all speeds.   They are of the horizontal return-action type, and consist of three cylinders, the high-pressure engine being 73 inches and the two low-pressures 92 inches in diameter, with a stroke of four feet.   The cranks in connection with the low-pressure cylinders are on the same plane, but in contrast as regards throw, the centre crank being at right angles with them.   The boilers supply steam at an initial pressure of 70 lbs., but the engines are adapted to work steadily at very low as well as at very high powers, as well as at various powers between the extreme limits.

The following are the results of the official steam trial in August, 1879 :—

	Full power	Two-thirds power	One-third power
Steam in boilers . .	70 lbs.	69·5 lbs.	67·5 lbs.
Vacuum, forward . .	26·62 in.	26·87 in.	26·85 in.
„ aft . . .	26·62 in.	26·25 in.	27·0 in.
Revolutions per minute .	76·01	66·36	54·13
Mean pressure, high . .	30·425 lbs.	29·10 lbs.	20·30 lbs.
„ low . .	12·512 lbs.	7·825 lbs.	4·65 lbs.
Total indicated power .	5,412·28	3,633·43	1,926·50
Speed of vessel, knots .	·15·061	13·633	11·693

Nothing could be more satisfactory than the manner in which the machinery worked throughout, the horse-power developed being 200 in excess of the contract.   The speed also fully justified the expectations of the designers of the ship.   The ship was tested in turning at full and half power with the following results :—Under full power the starboard circle was made in 5 min. 46 sec. (diameter 687 yards), and the port circle in 7 min. 23 sec. (diameter 732 yards): and with half power the starboard circle was completed in 5 min. 34 sec. (diameter 530 yards), and the port circle in 5 min. 41 sec. (diameter 538 yards). Twelve men were required at the wheel. The engines were stopped in nine seconds; being stopped, they were started astern in eleven seconds, and from going astern they were started ahead in nine seconds, being under perfect control.

The 'Euryalus,' another iron wood-cased corvette, was laid down H.M.S. in November, 1873, and has a displacement of 3,932 tons, or in 'Euryalus.' builders' measurement, a tonnage of 1,906 tons. This gives her superiority in size over the 'Active,' whose displacement is only 3,078 tons, and a considerable inferiority to the 'Shah,' whose displacement is 6,040 tons. Like the sister ships, the 'Boadicea' and 'Bacchante,' she holds, therefore, a middle position between the large unarmoured cruisers like the 'Shah,' 'Inconstant,' and 'Raleigh,' and the small corvettes, the 'Active' and 'Volage.' The length is 280 feet; breadth, 45 ft. 6 in.; draught of water—forward, 20 ft. 4 in., and aft, 22 ft. 10 in.; indicated horse-power, 5,250. The armament consists of two revolving $4\frac{1}{2}$-ton guns; 14 similar guns to be used on the broadside; and two 64-pounder chase guns. From this it will be seen that the 'Euryalus' does not carry any guns of armour-piercing power. In the case of the $4\frac{1}{2}$-ton gun, no Palliser projectiles, whether shot or shell, are used. The shells in use are the 107 lbs. 4 oz. common shell, the 115 lbs. 10 oz. shrapnel, and case-shot of 69 lbs. The $4\frac{1}{2}$-ton gun is, of course, vastly superior to the old-fashioned 64-pounder, which uses only 56 lbs. 14 oz. common shell, 65 lbs. 10 oz. shrapnel, and 50 lbs. $8\frac{1}{2}$ oz. case-shot.

On July 5, 1878, at the full-speed trial in Stokes Bay, the 'Euryalus' attained a mean speed of 14·7 knots with 5,271 indicated horse-power.

We now proceed to describe an unarmoured vessel, to which more H.M.S. than ordinary interest attaches. The 'Iris' is remarkable, not only 'Iris.' from the hitherto unapproached speed attained on the measured mile, but also from the extended use of steel in the structure of the hull.

'The "Iris,"' says Mr. W. H. White, 'was the first ship built in England in which mild steel was employed; and the first vessel of the Royal Navy wholly built of steel.'

The principal dimensions of the 'Iris' are—length between perpendiculars, 300 feet, and over all, 333 feet; extreme breadth, 46 ft. 1 in.; depth in hold, 16 ft. 3 in.; length of poop, 78 feet; mean draught, 19 ft. 9 in.; displacement, 3,750 tons; and midship section, 777 square feet. Unlike the steel vessels of the 'Comus' class, she is not sheathed with wood, but has the hull simply protected by composition. The plating varies from $\frac{3}{8}$ inch to $\frac{1}{2}$ inch in thickness, and is riveted to the longitudinals and perpendiculars by wrought-iron rivets $\frac{3}{4}$ inch in diameter. There are 83 frames, those

Figs. 271, 272, and 273.

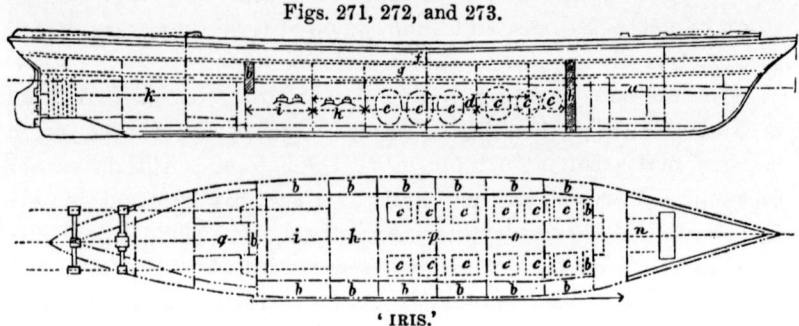

' IRIS.'

a, Foremost platform; b, b, Coal bunkers: c, c, Boilers; f, Upper deck; g, Lower deck; h, i, Engine-rooms; k, After platform; o, p, Stoke-holes; n, q, Holds.

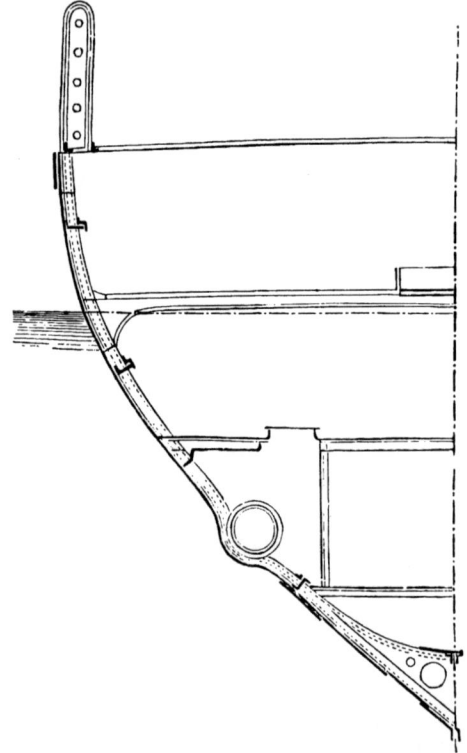

' IRIS ' (SECTION ABAFT DOUBLE BOTTOM).

forward and aft being three feet apart, and those amidship four feet apart, and, as they are crossed by longitudinal Z-shaped girders, no part of the ship's side is unsupported for more than four feet square.

The armament consists of ten 64-pounders, eight side and two revolving, the latter being mounted on the poop and forecastle, so that the recessed ports which have been cut in the corvettes of the 'Boadicea' class for the purpose of securing fore and aft fire, will be dispensed with. The broadside guns, which are worked on the upper deck, have no protection beyond the ⅜-inch plating which forms the top-sides and runs up so as to give an exceptional height of bulwark and freeboard. A 9-pounder and a 7-pounder field-piece complete

Fig. 274.

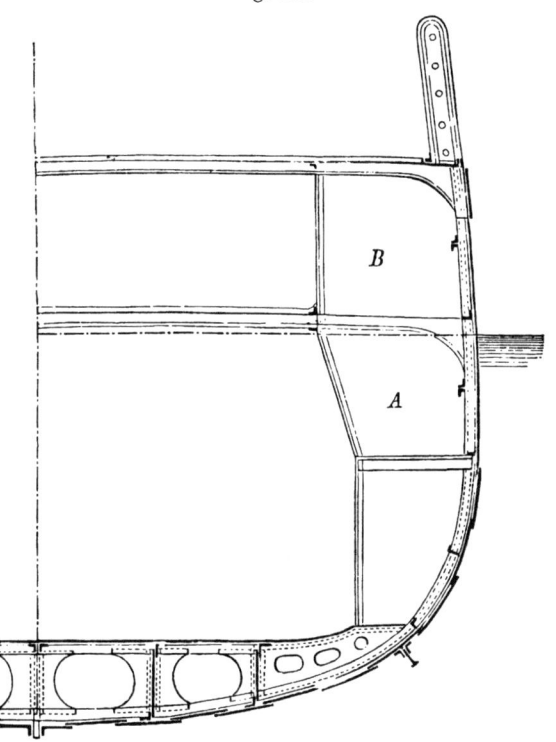

'IRIS' (MIDSHIP SECTION).

the armament, which is undeniably light. The 'Iris' is fitted with the Whitehead torpedo. She is square-rigged forward, has wooden masts, and is steered by hand-gear. The complement is 250. The steering is performed by the ordinary wheel fitted with Rapson's patent connecting-gear, and Frayne's patent break for use in turning at a high rate of speed or in heavy weather.

The wardroom and the cabins of the captain and wardroom officers are all under the poop, in the front of which is a watertight bulkhead extending down to the ship's bottom. The gunroom, engineers'

berth, and the warrant officers' cabins and messplace are all on the
lower deck aft; and the sick bay, dispensary, and engine-room arti-

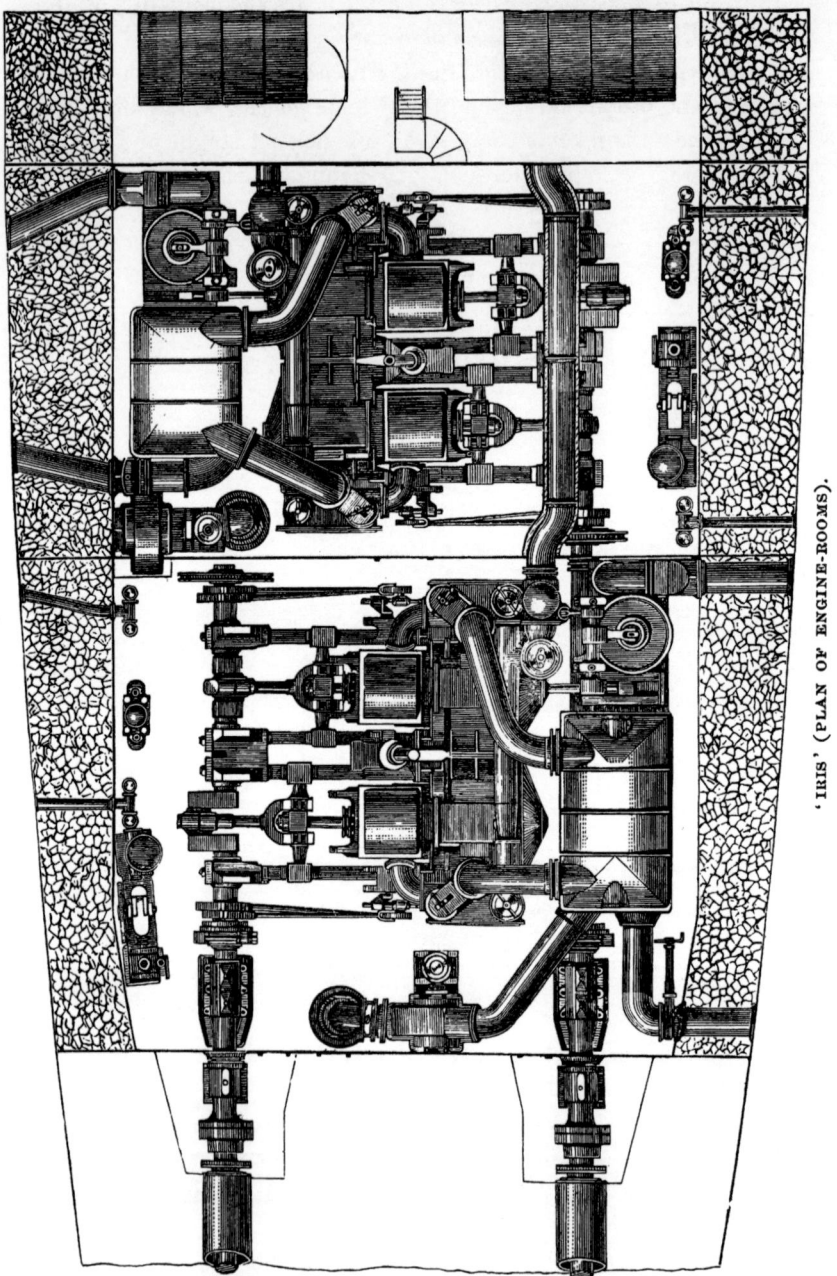

Fig. 275.

'IRIS' (PLAN OF ENGINE-ROOMS).

ficers' berth are also on the same deck—one compartment further
forward. The magazines, shell-rooms, and storerooms are on the iron

flat below the lower deck. The whole of the lower deck forward is devoted to quarters for the men, and is very spacious and commodious. The forecastle is to be fitted up for supernumeraries, the afterpart being closed in by a watertight bulkhead which is carried down to the bottom of the ship.

Fig. 276.

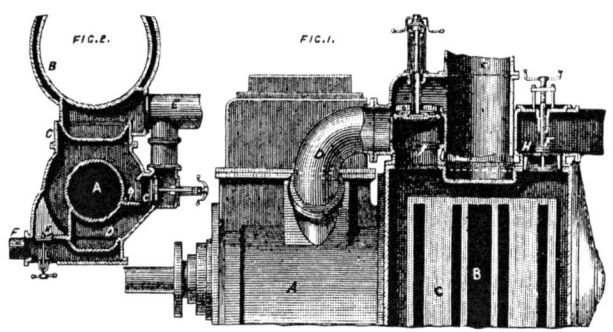

'IRIS' (ARRANGEMENT OF CHARGE VALVES).

Like the hull of the ship itself, the engines, which are manufactured by Messrs. Maudslay, Sons, and Field, are of novel construction, there being nothing resembling their cylinder and valve arrangements in the service, with the exception of those which were fitted by Messrs. Maudslay to the machinery of the 'Sirius,' corvette, in

Fig. 277.

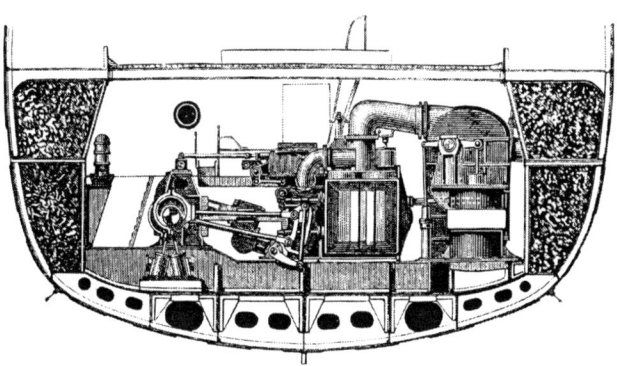

'IRIS' (SECTION THROUGH ENGINE-ROOM).

1867. The ship is propelled by direct-acting, horizontal, compound four-cylinder engines designed to turn twin screws. They are driven with 60-lb. pressure of steam, are intended to work up to 7,000 indicated horse-power, and are calculated to make about 95 revolutions per minute when developing their contract power. There are in all four high-pressure cylinders, having a diameter of 41 inches, and four low-pressure cylinders, with a diameter of 75 inches, the stroke being three feet. Each high-pressure cylinder is bolted to the front of the low-pressure cylinder with which it works. It is also, for the purpose of economising length, partly recessed into it, and one piston-rod carries the two pistons. The engines are placed in separate engine-rooms divided by a watertight doorway, the starting platforms of each pair of engines being situated close to and conveniently adjoining the doorway. The narrow beam of the ship, in proportion to the size and power of the engines, has rendered it necessary to place the starboard engine in front of the port engine, so that the body of the ship is filled with machinery.

The requirements of the vessel having greatly limited the weights of the engines, the piston-rods have been connected to wrought-iron crossheads working on guide-rods which form the connection between the main crankshaft bearings and the cylinders, and to each of which they are bolted with strong T ends. The surface condensers, which are constructed entirely of brass, are placed in the wings behind the cylinders. The condenser in the forward engine-room is fitted with 5,290 tubes, seven feet long, and $\frac{5}{8}$ inch in diameter in the inside; while the after condenser contains 7,024 tubes of the same internal diameter, but with a length of only 5 ft. 3 in. The total cooling surface is 14,000 square feet. The air-pumps are of the upright single-acting description. They are placed at the rear of the cylinders, and are worked by bell-crank levers direct from the piston of the foremost low-pressure cylinder in each compartment, an arrangement which was deemed expedient on account of the limited space in the engine-rooms. The slide valves of each pair of cylinders are worked by one link, and the engines are fitted with steam starting and reversing gear. The crankshafts are double throw, and were forged by the Thames Iron Works Company. The line of screw shafting, which is hollow, is constructed of Whitworth compressed steel, with a 9-inch hole through its centre; and it may be mentioned that the low-pressure cylinders are each lined with working barrels of the same metal. The engines give motion to a couple of four-bladed screw-propellers, 18 ft. 6 in. in diameter, and so adjusted that the pitch can be varied from 17 ft. 6 in. to 22 ft. 6 in. At the preliminary trial the pitch was set at 18 ft. 8 in, but, as the engines could not take all the steam that was generated, the pitch was subsequently reduced to 17 ft. 6 in. The outer edges of the blades are unusually fine, and to show their great power relatively to the size of the ship, it may be stated that their outer edge comes to within 3 ft. 5½ in. of the extreme beam. In order that the screws may obtain a good supply of water and exercise their full power of thrust, the tubes are carried out fifty-one feet from the body of the ship.

Steam is furnished by twelve boilers of slightly different dimensions in order to meet the varying line of the ship's bottom. They are placed at the wings, and are fired amidship. They are also disposed into two watertight compartments, six in each, the object being that if one set of boilers were rendered useless by reason of the compartment becoming flooded, the engines could be driven from the other set; and with this contingency in view, the steampipes connecting the boilers with the engines have an outer metal covering, to prevent the radiation of heat in the event of their being surrounded by water. It also deserves to be mentioned that the doors in the watertight bulkheads which separate the fore engine-room from the stokeholes, and the stokeholes from each other, are placed near the top instead of upon the flat. Should the ship, therefore, be rammed, the inflowing water would be confined to one compartment sufficiently long to enable the doors to be leisurely closed. The stokeholes are admirably ventilated by wide annular spaces in the two funnels, up which the hot air rushes and causes a correspondingly vigorous inflow of fresh air through the cowls and funnel casings. The boilers are fitted with 2,898 brass tubes, 6 ft. 6 in. long, and 3¼ in. external diameter, the total heating surface being 18,700 square feet. There are in all 32 furnaces, each seven feet long by 3 ft. 1½ in. wide, and possessing a total area of grate surface of 700 square feet. In order to save weight as far as possible, the outer shells of the boilers are made of the Landore Company's mild steel, of similar quality to that of which the hull itself is built. The stop-valves can be worked from the main deck, and are also to be worked from the upper deck. The 'Iris' carries 500 tons of coal in the ordinary bunkers, and 250 tons additional in the reserve bunkers. The total weight of the machinery, with water in the boilers and condensers, is about 1,000 tons, and the contract price is 93,000*l*.

The 'Iris' is the first ship in the service which has been specially fitted for working with steam at atmospheric pressure. Mr. Sells, a gentleman connected with the contractors' firm, has patented an ingenious duplex valve arrangement, whereby the communication between the exhaust of the high-pressure cylinders and the low-pressure slide chest is cut off, and the steam passes instead into the main exhaust pipe, while at the same time other valves are opened, which admit steam directly from the boilers into the low-pressure cylinders.

We quote from the *Times* the following particulars of the trials of H.M.S. ' Iris ':—

'Whatever doubts may have been entertained with respect to the speed performances of the "Iris," steel despatch vessel, were conclusively set at rest by the long and varied trial to which she was subjected on the measured mile in Stokes Bay. She was proved to be not only the quickest ship in the navy, but the quickest ship afloat, having surpassed the highest speed realised by the "Lightning," torpedo vessel, and even outstripped the most sanguine expectations of Mr. Barnaby, her designer. The "Iris" was in every respect an essentially experimental craft. There was nothing resembling her in the service with reference to the proportion of midship section to length, the extreme fineness of her entrance and run, and the ratio of her enormous horse-power to displacement ; and as a result there were only very imperfect data to guide the Constructive Department as to her probable performances from the actual performances of previously existing ships. It was, therefore, necessary to obtain a constant for guidance hereafter, and to establish her coefficients, and this was rendered all the more indispensable, seeing that the "Mercury," a sister vessel, in which everything has been sacrificed to speed, was being rapidly brought forward at Pembroke. The results of her first trial at Portsmouth were undoubtedly disappointing. Mr. Barnaby had calculated that, with the engines developing 7,000 horse-power, a speed of $17\frac{1}{2}$ knots an hour might be realised; but the fact remained that, while the engines indicated 500 over the contract power, the full power runs only gave a mean speed of 16·6 knots, the revolutions per minute being 91. There were, however, grounds for thinking that the comparative failure was due, not to the form of hull, but to some defect in the machinery. The "Iris" was propelled by two four-bladed screws, each $18\frac{1}{2}$ feet in diameter, with a pitch of eighteen feet, the joint disc area being considerably greater in proportion to the engine-power than is common in single-screw ships, while the surface of the blades was also exceptionally large. On the trial it became evident that the engines were over-weighted by the screws, and that the friction and drag which were set up materially detracted from the effective power of the machinery. It was accordingly arranged, for experimental purposes only, to remove two of the four blades on each fan and to make a series of progressive trials in order to see what improvement would result from a reduction of the blade area and a consequent relief to the engines. According to an analysis which has been made by Mr. W. H. White, of the Admiralty, the highest power developed under the novel conditions was 4,369 horses, the corresponding speed 15¾ knots, and the revolutions 89. With the four-bladed screws 15⅛ knots had required 5,250 horse-power, and 4,369 horse-power would have sufficed for 14⅜ knots only. It was not considered desirable to press the extemporised two-bladed screws by running at any higher speeds, nor by their form or pitch were they adapted for use as two-bladed propellers; but enough had been done to show that the performance of the ship could be greatly improved by a modification in the size of the fans. The purpose of the trial was to practically test the accuracy of the deduction. The ship was trimmed by ballast and coal to 15 ft. 8 in. forward, and 20 ft. 6 in. aft, and was thus brought down to her intended load-line; and the new experimental four-bladed screws were 16 ft. 3 in. in diameter, and had a pitch of 20 feet. While the diameter had been reduced the pitch had been increased, the ratio of screw disc to area of midship section being thus much less than on the original trial. The blades were smoothed to prevent friction, and conical caps had been tapped into the bosses over the nuts which secure the screws to the shafts, for the purpose of preventing the wave which has been found to follow a bluff ending, whereby the resistance against which the ship has to contend in passing through the water is augmented. The result of the trial was in every respect more than satisfactory. Four full-power runs were made on the mile with the following surprising results: Steam at engines, 62 lbs.; vacuum, 27 inches; revolutions, 96 starboard and 98 port; horse-power, 7,734·85; speed of vessel, 18·572 knots. The engines thus developed fully 700 horses more than the contract; while the ship realised two knots in excess of the speed obtained from the larger screws, and fully a knot more than the Constructive Department anticipated to get out of her. Four runs at 16½ knots gave 5,132·16 horse-power, with 86 revolutions. This, as will have been seen, was the utmost speed realised at the original trial with 7,500 horse-power, and 91 revolutions. Two runs at twelve knots gave 1,837·14 horse-power, with 62 and 60 revolutions, and two runs at 8 knots gave 607·25 horse-power, with 41 revolutions. The engines were also turned as slowly as possible with the steam at only a little above the atmospheric pressure, when the following data were obtained: revolutions, 24 starboard, and 19 port; vacuum, 28 inches; power indicated—starboard engines 127, port 59; making a total of 186 horses. There were scarcely any vibrations noticed, although at the previous trials the shaking of the ship was excessive.

'In material, construction, and dimensions, and in the power and description of the machinery, the "Mercury" is a sister ship to the steel despatch vessel, "Iris," which has completed her trials at Portsmouth and is ready for commissioning. The only difference has reference to appearance, and is a mere matter of detail of no practical importance. The "Iris" has an overhanging bow, a figure-head being placed on what is termed the "knee of head," while the "Mercury" has a perfectly straight stem. She was built at Pembroke from Mr. Barnaby's designs, and is engined by Messrs. Maudslay, Sons, and Field. As was the case with the sister ship, everything has been surrendered in the "Mercury" in order to secure a high rate of speed. She is entirely unprotected, her entrance and run are as fine as a racing yacht, and her machinery, which fills the major portion of the hull, is guaranteed to develop 7,000 on the trial trip. She is built of Landore mild steel, and measures 300 feet between perpendiculars, 46 ft. 1 in. in extreme breadth, 16 ft. 3 in. in hold, and has a displacement of 3,750 tons. The armament consists of ten 64-pounders, including a couple of revolving chase guns which will be mounted on the forecastle and the poop. The area of midship section in the "Mercury" is 771 square feet, and the height of the ports from the lower water-line is 10 ft. 7$\frac{1}{2}$ in. ; the water tanks will carry 32 tons, and she has accommodation for 34 tons of provisions, besides having bunkers to convey 500 tons of coal.

'The trials can scarcely be said to possess the same interest for engineers as the experimental cruises of the "Iris" in 1877–78. Built on the same lines and engined in precisely the same manner as her predecessor, her performances under defined conditions of power and screw could have been well-nigh foretold. The "Iris" was tested under way with four varieties of twin propellers, and the screws which have been fitted to the "Mercury" are the four-bladed screws of the third series of experiments which gave a speed of 18·57 knots, with 7,714 of indicated horse-power. These results, it is true, so far as speed on the measured mile was concerned, were subsequently surpassed by the work of a special two-bladed screw, which gave 18·587 knots, with 7,556 indicated horse-power, but the small improvement in speed under full power did not compensate for the increased vibration produced throughout the ship at all speeds except the maximum. No. 3 screws were, therefore, adopted, though had time permitted it was intended to continue the experiments. The diameter was 16 ft. 3$\frac{1}{2}$ in., while the pitch at the forward edge of the blades was 18 ft. 11$\frac{1}{2}$ in., at the after edge 20 ft. 11$\frac{1}{2}$ in., and the mean pitch as measured 19 ft. 11$\frac{1}{2}$ in. The disc area of the blades was 288 of the whole disc. The blades were curved aft a little towards the tips, with a view of keeping the points rather further away from the A brackets, and of checking in some degree any centrifugal tendency of the water acted upon. The blades, which were constructed of gun-metal, were polished on both sides to reduce friction, and the edges were made sharp. The original bosses to which the blades were attached had each a conical tail-piece added. The vessel left the Tidal Basin for a six hours' continuous full power trial, and after clearing the harbour the engines were gradually worked up to full speed. The trial commenced at a quarter-past 8, a run being made down the Channel as far as St. Alban s Head. The force of the wind was from 3 to 4, and the direction abeam, the sea being quite smooth at the time. The draught was 15 ft. 8 in. forward, and 20 ft. 6 in. aft, which was precisely the trim of the "Iris" during her experimental trips. At the preliminary run the mean pitch of the screw was fixed at 20 ft. 8 in., from which 7,025 horse-power was realised. This was so far satisfactory, as the result showed 25 horses over the contract; but as the engines could not take all the steam that was generated and still better results were expected, the "Mercury" was subsequently docked and the pitch confined to 20 feet, which, again, was the pitch of the "Iris's" fans in the trial to which allusion has already been made. Singularly enough the engines could have taken more steam than could be obtained, the mean number of revolutions per minute having increased from 91 to 95. The following table gives the average results for every half-hour during the six hours' official steaming :—

Steam in Boilers	Vacuum		Revolutions		Indicated power		Total Indicated Horse-power
	S.	P.	S.	P.	S.	P.	
63	27½	26¾	91·4	91·1	3,500·68	3,285·64	6,786·32
65	27½	27¼	96·3	95·9	3,744·70	3,654·63	7,396·33
64	27½	27¼	96·2	95·7	3,619·10	3,561·87	7,180·97
64	27½	27¼	96·3	96·2	3,604·46	3,513·60	7,118·06
62	27½	27½	96·4	95·9	3,516·52	3,557·42	7,073·94
64	27½	27¼	97·7	96·2	3,681·90	3,586·70	7,268·60
65	27½	27¼	97·6	96·7	3,537·57	3,616·08	7,152·65
62	27¾	27¼	96·5	95·5	3,481·49	3,437·74	6,919·23
60	27¾	26¾	95·5	97·4	3,473·43	3,489·43	6,962·86
62	27¾	27	94·7	93·7	3,429·12	3,356·44	6,785·56
58	27	27	93·7	92·2	3,202·85	3,137·45	6,340·30
61	27	27¼	93·3	91·3	3,380·97	3,189·41	6,570·38

'These results were scarcely as satisfactory as at the preliminary trial, for while some of the observations showed that the engines were indicating 7,396 and 7,268·6 horses, the mean of the whole run gave a total indicated power of 6,953·07, being 3,514·14 by the starboard, and 3,438·93 by the port engines, or a little below the guaranteed power. It will be seen that only on two occasions did the pressure in the boilers reach 65 lbs., to which the safety-valves were loaded, while near the end of the trial the pressure fell as low as 58 lbs. The cause of this was undoubtedly a failure in the supply of the smokeless coal, which is generally used on steam trials, and the necessity for resorting to north-country coal. By these means not only was the heat in the furnaces reduced, but the tubes partly choked by the thick smoke. The vacuum was exceedingly regular and satisfactory, the mean being 27·43 inches in the starboard, and 27·14 inches in the port condensers. The other means were: steam in starboard cylinders, 39·737 and 11·087 lbs.; and in port cylinders, 39·341 and 10·85 lbs.; revolutions, 95·5 starboard, and 94·5 port. A mean of a couple of runs on the mile in Stokes Bay gave a speed of 18·055 knots. These runs were made during the 10th and 11th half-hours, when the steam-pressure was low, and when the feed to the boilers had become somewhat irregular. The coal-consumption averaged 2·35 lbs. per indicated horse-power per hour. The steam-steering gear was found to act admirably, one man being able to steer the ship, where otherwise sixteen would be required to get the rudder over fifteen degrees. By steam power the helm is put hard over 24 deg. Although the Government officials were well satisfied with the working of the engines during the six hours' run, it was thought desirable to try the ship for speed on the measured mile, and thereby institute a comparison between her performances and those of the "Iris." This trial led to some astonishing results. The day was exceedingly boisterous, the wind having the force of between five and six, and the sea rather rough. The direction of the wind was W.S.W., and thus almost directly ahead and astern during the runs in Stokes Bay. After an hour's preliminary cantering, the ship was placed upon the mile with the following result, the boiler pressure being 64·75 lbs. :—

—	Revolutions	Indicated horse-power	Knots
First mile . .	97	7,471·09	18·274
Second mile . .	98	7,451·78	19·149
Third mile . .	97	7,537·97	18·848
Fourth mile . .	98	7,594·98	18·750

The mean of all the means gave the remarkable speed of 18·876 knots per hour, thereby beating the "Iris," which realised a mean speed of 18·54 knots, and proving the "Mercury" to be the swiftest full-sized ship afloat in any navy of the world. Indeed, it is difficult to conceive of a ship of her size being driven through the water at the rate of close upon 22 miles an hour. The horse-power developed was also more than satisfactory, since the mean reached a total of 7,513·95, which is greatly in excess of the contract, the mean revolutions per minute being 93·44 starboard, and 97·26 port, and the average vacuum, 27·5 starboard, and 27·12 inches port. The engines were subsequently worked with the jet injection, the results obtained being 4,214·92 horse-power, 80 revolutions, and a vacuum of 25 and 23·5 inches. The exhaust into the low-pressure cylinders was next cut off, and all the eight cylinders worked direct from the boilers, as common engines, for the purpose of ascertaining with how low a pressure the machinery could be worked in action. The pressure in the boilers was reduced to 60 lbs. above the atmosphere, and was then gradually further diminished to the atmospheric pressure. Under the latter condition 60 revolutions were obtained. The engines were next stopped, and started again at 5½ lbs. above the atmospheric pressure ; and were afterwards worked at full power to bring the ship into harbour. Before the close of the trial, however, the engines were stopped, the starboard engine .in 34 secs. and the port in 37 secs. ; being stopped they were started ahead in 12 secs. and 10 secs. respectively ; and going astern they were started ahead in 17 secs. and 10 secs.'

A further trial of the 'Mercury' took place in September 1879. Six hours' The weather was all that could be desired. There was no wind save trial. what the ship made in passing, and the sea was as smooth as a duck-pond. In the after part of the trial the wind somewhat freshened, but at no time did it exceed the figure 2, and might, consequently, be thrown out of the calculations. The 'Mercury' left Portsmouth harbour at 8 o'clock, and having rounded the Warner and the eastern end of the Isle of Wight she made a straight course for Portland. At a quarter to nine the fires in the furnaces were burning with intense heat, care being taken on the present occasion to use nothing but Nixon's steam navigation smokeless coal ; and, as a full head of steam had been obtained, the half-hourly observations were begun as early as a quarter to nine. Portland was reached at 45 minutes past 11, being the quickest passage on record. The ship was then turned round for the three hours' homeward run, the tide being against her in both directions. A large circle was made in turning in order to reduce the grind upon the engines as much as possible, but, as will be seen from the following series of observations the helm nevertheless exercised a very appreciable deterrent effect upon the engines, a couple of revolutions per minute being lost in going round :—

Steam in Boilers	Vacuum		Revolutions		Indicated Horse-Power		Total indicated Horse-Power
	S.	P.	S.	P.	S.	P.	
66	27¾	27	95·87	94·53	3,852·23	3,679·21	7,531·44
65½	27½	27	98·20	96·66	3,875·45	3,756·31	7,631·76
65	28	27	97·13	96·00	3,821·59	3,643·98	7,465·57
66	27½	27	98·20	96·73	3,901·38	3,738·32	7,639·70
65	27½	27	97·53	96·00	3,816·14	3,616·24	7,432·38
64	27	27	97·13	95·70	3,786·50	3,606·45	7,392·95
61½	27	27¼	95·90	94·90	3,588·66	3,443·90	7,632·56
64	27	27	96·36	94·83	3,670·01	3,532·59	7,202·60
65½	27¼	27	97·00	95·56	3,762·63	3,645·54	7,408·17
62½	27	27	95·70	94·46	3,639·49	3,381·72	7,021·21
62½	27	27	96·03	94·77	3,654·34	3,439·19	7,093·53
59	27¼	27¼	94·43	93·11	3,459·45	3,272·86	6,732·31

It will thus be seen that the *maximum* power developed at any time during the trial was 7,639·70 horses, and that, near the conclusion of the run, dirty grates and exhausted energy on the part of the stokers (who had to work in an atmosphere rising occasionally to a temperature of 140 deg.) produced the inevitable result in loss of steam, revolutions, and power. The vacuum was remarkably high and regular from first to last. The following are the means of the six hours:—Steam in boilers, 63·87 lbs.; vacuum, starboard 27·29 inches, and port 27·04 inches; revolutions per minute, 96·66 starboard, and 95·26 port; mean pressure of steam in cylinders, starboard, high 41·77 lbs., low, 11·56 lbs.; port, high 40·46 lbs., low 11·18 lbs.; indicated horse-power, starboard engines, 3,735·65, port engines 3,563·02; total indicated horse-power 7,298·68, or nearly 300 horses beyond the contract. The 'Iris' at the six hours' trial attained only 7,072 horses. The mean speed realised by the 'Mercury' during the entire run reached 18·6 knots per hour. This marvellous speed has been excelled both by herself and her sister ship on the measured mile, but on no occasion has so high a rate of speed been maintained for so long a period. The working of the machinery and boilers was in every respect satisfactory. The quantity of coal consumed during the trial amounted to 1,044 cwts., giving 2·72 lbs. to every unit of horse-power developed. In the 'Mercury' cast iron of additional strength has been substituted for the wrought iron guides of the piston-rod heads in the 'Iris'; and in both ships considerable mechanical ingenuity has been requisite to keep the vital parts of the engines below the water-line. The boilers are fitted with automatic stop-valves. Should a boiler, therefore, be pierced by shot in action, the valve would close of itself and the steam from the other boilers would be prevented from escaping through the shot-holes. The valve would also be of service in case of boiler explosion.

The policy, represented in its extreme development by the 'Iris' and 'Mercury,' has been followed up by the Admiralty in the construction of several vessels, capable of steaming sixteen knots. We give a short description of the new class, taken from *Iron* of November 12, 1880. The writer begins with a reference to the absence of protection in the 'Iris' and 'Mercury':—

'In these ships,' he says, 'more or less provision has been made to compensate for the absence of armour, by watertight subdivision and by coal-protection: still they have to run the risk of being penetrated in a vital part, and sent to the bottom by a single shell.

'In view of this the late Government caused designs to be prepared for three fast cruisers of similar dimensions and form to the "Iris" and "Mercury," but with engines of 5,000 indicated horse-power, against 7,500 in the other ships. The weight thus saved in the engines is to be utilised in fitting a steel protective deck $1\frac{1}{2}$ inch thick, extending over the engines, boilers, and magazines, and in increasing the space for coal. The armoured deck is to be slightly below the water at the middle line, and curved down so as to be considerably below it at the sides. The present Government approved this design, and have contracted with Messrs. R. Napier and Sons, of Glasgow, to build three ships in accordance with it, to be named the "Leander," "Phaeton," and "Arethusa." The engines—also by Messrs. Napier—are to be twin-screw, horizontal, surface-condensing, with high pressure and all the latest improvements, to develop collectively 5,000 indicated horse-power. With this power a speed of sixteen knots is anticipated, but it is possible that hereafter arrangements may be made for working with a closed stokehole and forced blast, in which case a speed equal to that of the "Iris" and "Mercury" may be obtained.

The principal dimensions of the "Leander" class are:—

The 'Leander,' 'Phaeton,' and 'Arethusa.'

Length between perpendiculars	. .	300 feet
Breadth, extreme	. .	46 feet
Draught of water, forward	. .	17 ft. 6 in.
„ aft	. .	20 ft. 6 in.
Displacement in tons	. .	3,748
Coals, tons	. .	725 (room in bunkers for 1,000 tons)
Armament:—		
Breech-loading rifle-guns (side)	. .	8 6-inch R.B.L.
„ „ guns (revolving)	. .	2 6-inch „

10

'The new cruisers will each carry two second-class torpedo-boats, and will, of course, be fitted with torpedo-gear, machine guns, and other appliances of modern naval warfare. The rig is to be very light, with square yards on the foremast, and fore and aft sails only on the main and mizen.'

We now turn to vessels of older date than those last described.

H.M.S. 'Rover.'

The 'Rover' belongs to the same class as the 'Active' and 'Volage.' The dimensions of the ship are, length 280 feet, breadth 43 ft. 6 in., displacement 3,494 tons. The armament consists of sixteen 64-pounders, and two 90-cwt. revolving guns. The engines are of 4,750 indicated horse-power, and were manufactured by Messrs. Ravenhill, Easten and Co. The vessel has a straight stem, and embrasures have been built into the poop and forecastle, to allow the revolving guns to carry on a fore and aft fire with power to sweep the sea over an extent of ninety-five degrees. The principal novelty in the construction of the 'Rover' is that the sheathing consists of zinc instead of copper, which scientific authorities believe will not be subject to such rapid deterioration as the copper.

The final trial took place in the Solent. Considerable difficulty had been experienced in Chatham in getting the contract horse-power (4,750) out of the engines, in consequence of heated bearings and the priming of the boilers; and, although at the previous trial as many as 4,963 horses were realised, or 217 more than the pre-scribed standard, the pace proved somewhat disappointing, since the mean speed obtained was only $14\frac{1}{2}$ knots, or about a knot short of what was expected. It was, therefore, determined to give the ship another trial at Portsmouth, where the course is not only more sheltered than the Maplin Sands, but the water is deeper, and where she would have the benefit of the experienced stokers of the Steam Reserve. The trial was inconclusive, but so far as it went highly promising, and the results in the end proved satisfactory.

The force of the wind was two, and as the sea was perfectly smooth, a better day could not have been desired for testing the power of her machinery to the utmost. The vessel got under weigh at half-past nine, but it was not until half-past twelve that she made the first run on the mile. The boiler unfortunately showed symptoms of priming from the beginning, and at times, when the fires were pressed, a shower of dirty water fell in the engine-room and upon the deck. Subsequently a gland was blown out, and the double mishap produced the delay. After a preliminary canter up the course, two runs against and with the tide were made, realising a mean speed of 14·689 knots an hour. As there was afterwards a falling off of steam power, and as, moreover, the spring of the safety-valve happened to break, the trial had to be postponed until another day. The load on the safety-valve was 70 lbs., the pressure in the boilers 58 lbs., the mean number of revolutions per minute 63·07, and the indicated horse-power 3,725. The screw worked beautifully, the vibration when under steam being almost imperceptible.

Smaller in size and of less speed than the 'Active,' is the class of steel and iron corvettes known as the ' C class,' from the initial letter of the names of the individuals composing it. In these vessels facilities for keeping the sea for long periods have not been sacrificed for the sake of high speed ; but at the same time they are provided with sufficiently powerful engines to drive them at a very fair speed through the water. The engines work up to 2,300 indicated horse - power ; while the engines of such old corvettes as the 'Challenger,' which has almost exactly the same displacement as the ' Comus,

The 'C class.'

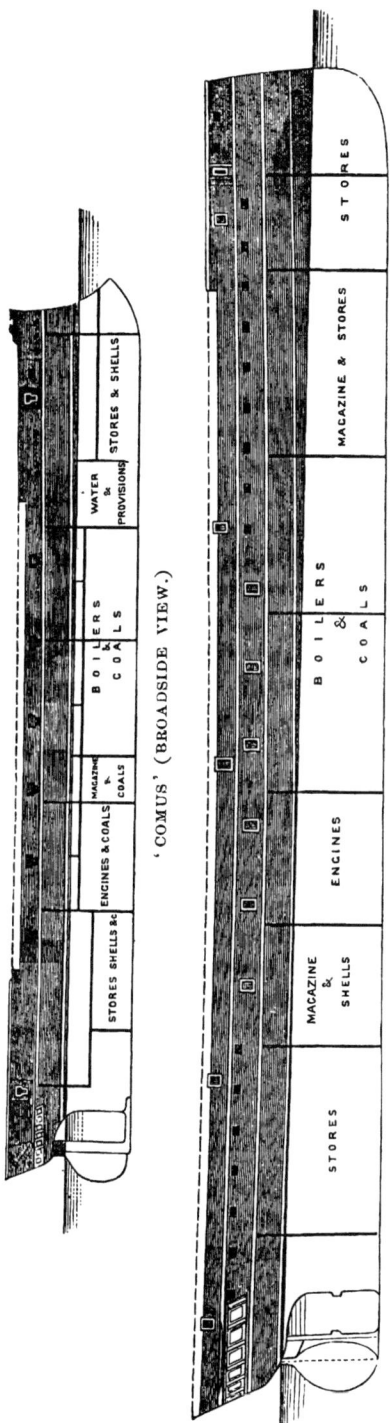

Figs. 278 and 279.

'COMUS' (BROADSIDE VIEW.)

STORES & SHELLS

WATER & PROVISIONS

BOILERS & COALS

MAGAZINE & COALS

ENGINES & COALS &c

STORES SHELLS &c

'INCONSTANT' (BROADSIDE VIEW).

STORES

MAGAZINE & STORES

BOILERS & COALS

ENGINES

MAGAZINE & SHELLS

STORES

can only develop 1,261 horse-power. Of moderate size—their displacement being 2,385 tons—armed with two 7-inch and 12 lighter guns, all of which throw a projectile with a velocity sufficient to penetrate eight inches of armour; of great structural strength; with an armoured deck three feet below the water-line, and fitted with a ram and arrangements for discharging Whitehead torpedoes below the surface of the water, it was universally admitted that the new vessels would be an exceedingly serviceable class of ships for service on foreign stations, provided they proved to be good sailers. That this is the case may now be taken to have been demonstrated by actual experience.

H.M.S. 'Comus.'

The 'Comus,' the first of the so-called 'C' class of unarmoured

Figs. 280 and 281.

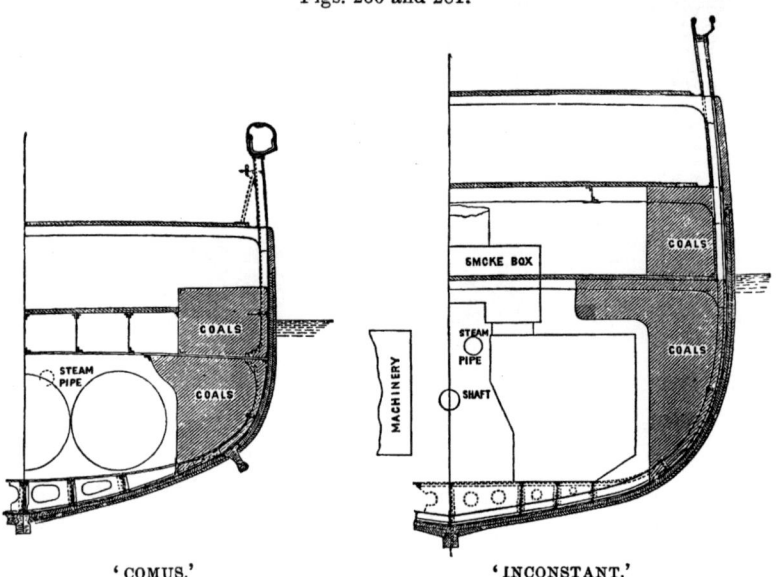

'COMUS.'   'INCONSTANT.'

corvettes commissioned for service on a foreign station, has recently made a good passage to the Cape, touching at Ascension and Tristan d'Acunha, and proved herself to be an excellent sailer.

At the official six hours' full-speed trial, the mean indicated horse-power was 2,460, being 100 horse-power in excess of the requirements of the contract. The maximum power obtained was 27,066·6, when the engines were making 100 revolutions per minute, the pressure of steam being 60 lbs., the vacuum 27 inches. During the whole time the engines worked in a satisfactory manner, and at the close of the trial the horse-power developed was considerably greater than at any other period. The 'Comus' was also tried on the measured mile off the Maplin Sands, when a mean speed of 13·8 knots was obtained. Coal bunkers are constructed at the sides of the ship, in order to afford protection to the engines and boilers. Each compartment is watertight. The stem below the bow forms a tremendous ram. The horse-power is 2,300, the speed thirteen knots, the length 225 feet. The engine-room and magazine are shell-proof.

The 'Carysfort' is another ship of the class. She was tried at the Maplin Sands in November 1879. This vessel is fitted with a patent screw, and the pitch was fixed at thirty feet. Four runs were made at half-boiler power, when the mean pressure of steam was 60·5 lbs.; vacuum, 25·7; revolutions per minute, 86·6; indicated horse-power, 2,447; speed, thirteen knots. Three runs were made with engines working at 66 revolutions per minute when the indicated horse-power was 1,075·5: speed, 9·97; pressure of steam, 62·2; vacuum, 26·8. The mean of three runs with engines working at 35 revolutions per minute gave the following result :—Pressure of steam, 61·8 lbs.; vacuum, 27; indicated horse-power, 564; speed, 7·98. The mean of the last series of runs obtained gave the following results :—Pressure of steam, 63 lbs.; vacuum, 27; revolutions, 35; indicated horse-power, 185; speed, 5·33. The draught of water forward was 15 ft. 2 in., and aft 18 ft. 3 in.

The 'gem class' of composite ships are of smaller size again. The 'gem class.' Though generally alike, there are some differences in the various individuals of the class, as will appear from the following details.

'The "Turquoise" was built at Messrs Earle and Co.'s ship- 'Turquoise.' building yard at Hull. She is one of the swift sailing vessels designed chiefly for service on foreign stations. She is constructed on the composite principle, the framing being of iron, covered with two thicknesses of teak planking. The principal dimensions are as follows:—Length between perpendiculars, 220 feet; extreme breadth, 40 ft. 1 in.; breadth moulded, 39 feet; depth in hold, 21 feet. A novelty in the design of this vessel is that the bow is built after the fashion of the American clippers, and has not the head-knees so commonly fitted to vessels of the Royal Navy. On the upper deck there are mounted twelve muzzle-loading rifled 64-pounder guns, on sliding platforms, which are so arranged that the fire of the guns can be concentrated on a point a comparatively short distance from the vessel. The bow and stern guns can either be concentrated with the other guns or fired ahead and astern respectively. The vessel will also carry two smaller guns for field or boat service, and the necessary apparatus for firing torpedoes. The internal arrangements have been designed so as to afford the greatest available amount of accommodation for the officers and men, the complement being 220.'

'The "Tourmaline" was built by Messrs. Dixon and Company, at Middlesborough. Her length is 250 feet, breadth 40 feet, and the engines, which are being constructed by Messrs. R. and W Hawthorn, of Newcastle-on-Tyne, are of 2,100 effective horse-power, horizontal compound, with six boilers. The keel and stem are formed of English oak and elm about two feet deep, with strong internal framing of iron. The sternposts are formed by two splendid trees of English oak, connected at the bottom by a massive casting of gun-metal weighing over six tons. The framework is all of iron, and the outside planking is composed of two thicknesses of East India teak, the inner being $3\frac{1}{2}$ inches, and the outer three inches in thickness. This is all secured to the iron framework by brass bolts through the inner plank-ing, the outer thickness being fastened by copper bolts through both planks, but not in contact with the framing of the vessel, so as to avoid any galvanic action between the iron and copper. The vessel is built with a beautiful clipper bow and female figure-head. She has a full forecastle and poop, both of which are so cut away at each side that her bow and stern guns may be trained in a direct line of fire right fore or aft. She has been heavily sparred as a full-rigged ship, and when not using her engines the propeller can be lifted up out of the water into an aperture prepared for it in her stern. The preparations for ventilation and fire extinction are most complete, and arrangements are made by which the magazines can be flooded from the sea in case of fire. The iron bulkheads, dividing the vessel into compartments, are all fitted with watertight doors, and the pumping gear is of unusual power. In addition to the pumps in connection with the engines, she is fitted with five of Downton's patent pumps, which are so arranged as to pump either from or into the various compartments of the vessel, and to act as fire-engines in case of fire. One pump is connected with a fresh-water service throughout the ship, and supplied by one of Normanby's patent distilling apparatus, capable of maintaining a large supply of fresh water sufficient for the full complement of 220 officers and men. The upper deck, in which the guns are placed, is of Dantzic crown oak four inches thick, and the lower and poop and forecastle decks of crown deals, being a class of timber specially used for Her Majesty's ships. The space between decks is entirely occupied by cabins for captains, officers, and men, with ward-room and sick bay. Below this deck are all the storerooms, and magazines, with the countless details that go to complete a man-of-war. The armament was originally intended to consist of fourteen 64-pounder guns on truck carriages, but it has since been decided that she shall have twelve 64-pounder rifled guns of the latest make, fitted upon slides.

'The "Opal" is another ship of the class. In January, 1876, this 'Opal.' vessel made her seventh trial on the Maplin Sands. On the former trials on the measured mile she made twelve knots an hour. The sea was very calm. The following is the result of the trial:—Average speed, 12·263 knots per hour the first six runs, 12·061 the second. Indicated horse-power the first six runs 1,667·443, second six runs, 1,655·006. She is constructed for 2,100 horse-power. The average steam-pressure during the trial was 56¼ lbs.; the draught of water, fore, 16 ft. 5½ in.; aft, 19 ft. 2 in.; and the average number of re-volutions 86·813 per minute.'

The following individuals belong to the newer 'composite sloop' class:—

'The "Phœnix," 6, composite sloop, was constructed at Devonport H.M.S. Dockyard. She is a sister ship to the "Dragon" and "Pegasus," 'Phœnix.' launched from the same yard, and to the "Miranda." They are all built upon the same moulds, with the exception that the "Phœnix" and the "Miranda" are fitted with raised poops, giving them better fighting qualities, and increasing the accommodation for officers. The "Phœnix" has a frame of iron with wood planking, is constructed to carry a ram, and will have a fore and aft fire. The length is 170 feet between perpendiculars, extreme breadth 36 feet, and depth of hold 16 ft. 9 in. The displacement, complete for sea, is 1,124 tons; the actual weight when launched was 565 tons. Messrs. Humphreys, Tennant and Co. have supplied the engines, which are of 900 horse-power, and she is expected to realise a speed of thirteen knots. The ordinary supply of coal is 100 tons, but space can be provided for 150 tons.'

The engines of one of the class, the 'Penguin, have been thus described :—

'The engines are on the simple expansion principle, supposed to be capable of developing the collective indicated power of at least 900 horses; the diameter of cylinders is 45 inches; length of stroke, 2 ft. 6 in.; and number of revolutions about 100 per minute. They have surface-condensers capable of being worked as common condensers; and there are circulating bilge, injection, feed, auxi-liary engine, and hand pumps. The boilers are cylindrical and three in number, and capable of carrying steam of 60 lbs. per square inch.'

The complement of this class is 140 officers and men. The

armament consists of two 7-in. 90-cwt. guns revolving, and four 64-pounder broadside guns.

The under-mentioned are types of the new 'composite gun-vessel' class :—

'Flamingo' class.
'The "Flamingo," 3, composite gun-vessel, was launched at Devonport Dockyard. This vessel is 150 feet long, has an extreme breadth of 29 feet, and draws eleven feet forward and thirteen feet aft. The engines are of 750 horse-power, and the estimated cost is 33,000*l.*'

'Rambler.'
The 'Rambler' has lately been launched at the building-yard of Messrs. John Elder and Co., of Glasgow. The dimensions are as follows: Length between perpendiculars, 157 feet; breadth, extreme, 29 ft. 6 in.; depth of hold, 14 ft. 5 in.; draught of water forward, 10 ft. 6 in., aft, 13 feet, mean, 11 ft. 9 in.; displacement, 774 tons. She will be armed with two 64-pounder muzzle-loading rifle guns, one of them being a bow and the other a stern chaser; and in addition she will have a 90-cwt. broadside gun. The vessel is constructed with a full poop and forecastle, a hull of iron framing and steel plating, the steel being from the works of the Steel Company of Scotland, planked with a double thickness of East India teak, three inches thick, fastened with yellow metal and copper bolts, and sheathed with copper to the water-line. The engines, which have

Figs. 282 and 283.

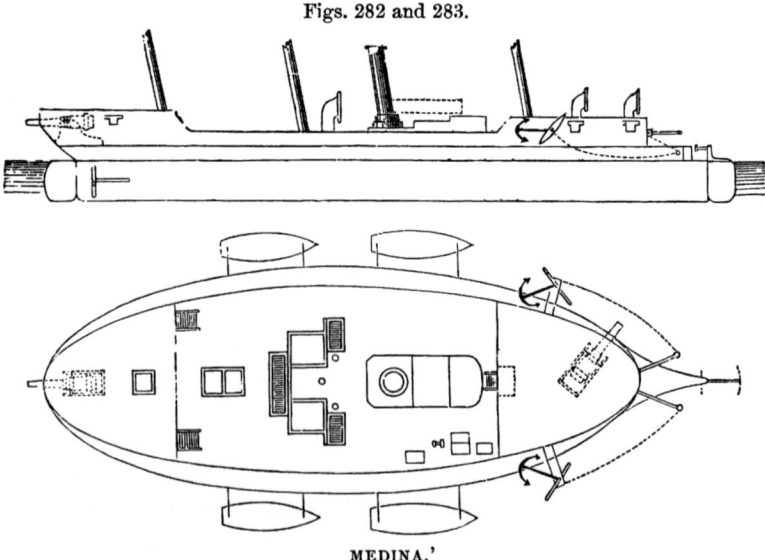

MEDINA.'

already been constructed by the firm, will indicate 750 horse-power. They are of the two-cylinder type, the diameters of the cylinders being 32 inches and 54 inches respectively for the high and low pressure, and the length of stroke is two feet.

The most recent class of gunboats is that represented by the 'Medina' and her consorts. This craft was built by Palmer's Shipbuilding and Iron Company at Jarrow-upon-Tyne. The hull is of iron, and the principal dimensions are : length, 110 feet; breadth, 34 feet; depth, 9 ft. 6 in.; indicated horse-power, 310; armament, three guns, 64-pdrs., and two Gatlings. She has a poop and topgallant forecastle, under the former of which one, and under the latter two, of her guns are mounted. She is propelled by twin two-bladed Griffiths' screws, and has a rudder at each end to obviate the necessity of turning round when employed on service in rivers. She has a fine entrance and a very flat bottom with a shallow keel. The sides tumble home in a remarkable manner and are very rounded. The arrangements for hoisting up her boats are such as to keep them well clear of the guns.

River gunboats.

Section II.—*French Unarmoured Vessels.*

It is only very lately that the unarmoured ship-building in France has attracted attention. Very important progress has however been made in the construction of fast cruisers within the last ten years. At the close of the war with Germany, when it was thought necessary to lay down a programme for the reconstruction of the French naval *matériel*, it was considered that cruisers of great speed were amongst the most urgent requirements of the fleet. The number of cruisers of the first and second classes was accordingly fixed at sixteen, and the number of the third class at eighteen. The rates of speed, which were at first intended to be 16·5 and 14·5 knots respectively, were soon afterwards raised to seventeen and sixteen knots. The displacements of 4,000 and 1,800 tons originally proposed were gradually increased to 5,400 and 3,200 tons. The cost advanced *pari passu* with the dimensions.

Previous to the introduction of the programme of reconstruction, the most important of the comparatively recent classes were represented by the 'Sané' and 'La-Clocheterie.' 'The "Sané,"' says M. Dislère, 'though her speed proved satisfactory, was not so completely successful as to seagoing qualities.' The 'La-Clocheterie' is one of the less recent second-class cruisers, and belongs to the same general class which includes the 'Infernet.' The 'La-Clocheterie' is a flush-decked corvette of the following dimensions :—

The 'La-Clocheterie.'

Length at load water-line   .   .   . 257 ft. 10 in
Breadth, extreme   .   .   .   . 35 ft. 9 in.
Depth to keel   .   .   .   . 21 ft. 9 in.
Load draught of water, forward   .   . 16 feet
      „   „   aft   .   . 18 ft. 7 in.
Load displacement   .   .   .   . 1,916 tons

The design of this vessel is peculiar. She has two sharp ends something after the fashion of a whale-boat. The armament is composed of ten 14 c/m. (5½-inch) breech-loading, non-armourpiercing guns, one of which is mounted *en barbette* on the forecastle and another on the poop. She is rigged with two masts with square sails, and a fore-and-aft rigged mizen-mast, having a total spread of canvas of 2,344 square yards. She is much more lightly sparred than our own vessels of the same class. She goes 10·5 knots under plain sail with the wind abaft the beam. The loss of canvas is compensated by additional coal-carrying capacity. She carries 300 tons of coal, calculated to suffice for thirty days' steaming at 8 knots, or for two months' steaming at five knots. The engines are of 450 nominal horsepower, with return connecting-rods,

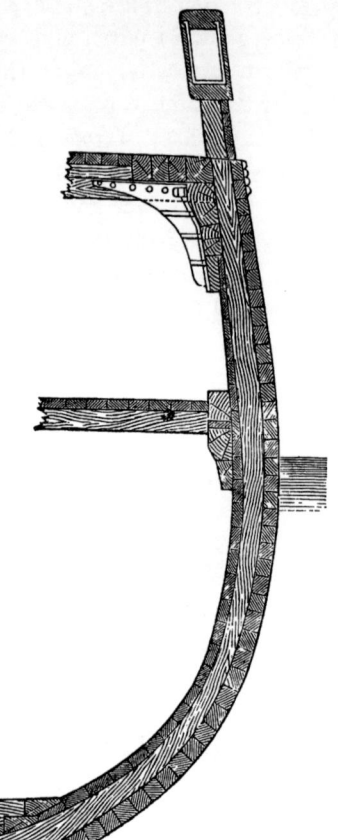

Fig. 284.

'LA-CLOCHETERIE' (MIDSHIP SECTION).

and are on the compound system. The interior diameter of the cylinders is 51 inches, and the length of stroke 2 ft. 5½ in. The highest horse-power indicated on the trial was 1,985, and the speed 13·73 knots.

The 'Chateau Renaud,' of the same class and date, was built by the firm of Normand et Cie., of Havre. The principal dimensions are :—

'Chateau Renaud.'

Length at water-line . . .	259 ft. 2 in.
Breadth, extreme	35 ft. 1 in.
Load displacement	1,829 tons
Indicated horse-power on trial trip .	1,500
Speed on trial trip	14·5 knots

The same firm also built the 'third-class cruiser' 'Talisman' of the following dimensions :—

'Talisman.'

Length at water-line . . .	224 ft. 4 in.
Breadth, extreme	33 ft. 6 in.
Displacement . . .	1,264 tons
Indicated horse-power on trial .	799
Mean speed	12·38 knots

The 'Talisman' appears on the list of the French navy as having six guns. Two 14 c/m. (5½-inch) guns are mounted upon high circular frameworks. They have an almost uninterrupted arc of fire of considerable extent over the low bulwarks ; these guns are not concealed by any screen whatever.

In settling the programme of 1872, the Minister of Marine, by the advice of his professional advisers, determined to order a number of cruisers of the first and second classes. It was thought, with reason, that cruisers of the larger dimensions, intended to keep the sea for a long time and in all weathers, would be better fighting and seagoing vessels if they had covered gun-decks, on which a part of their armament could be mounted. High speed and considerable dimensions were essential.

Un-armoured programme, 1872. First-class cruisers.

A competition having been opened, the designs of the 'Duquesne' and the 'Tourville,' models of which appeared in the Exhibition of 1878, were adopted. The displacement was carried to 5,400 tons, and has, in the case of the 'Tourville,' really reached 5,650 tons.

Thus designed, the first-class cruiser constitutes an uncommon type of which France and England have alone turned out examples necessarily few in number, on account of their enormous expense. With the high speed of seventeen knots—which has been realised within a tenth—the first-class cruiser was designed to prevent the escape of merchant vessels or mail steamers, however fast they may be. She may confidently reckon on being able to retreat from an armour-clad, while on the other hand her powerful armament mounted between decks will enable her to accept a combat with any hostile cruiser.

The design for the larger vessels having been settled in December, 1871, the programme was approved for the second-class

Second-class cruisers.

cruisers. These differed from the first-class cruisers in not having a 'tween deck battery, in having a speed of only sixteen knots, and an armament composed of four 16 c/m., or 5-ton, guns, pointed through sponson ports, as well as four 14 c/m., or 2½-ton, guns, mounted at ports of the usual pattern. The displacement was to be about 2,600 tons. The details of this programme were soon afterwards altered, and the weight of armament was materially increased. The model finally selected from several competitive designs for the 'Duguay-Trouin' class was shown in the Exhibition of 1878. In 1875, after the 'Duguay-Trouin' had been laid down, designs were approved for the second-class cruisers, the 'Villars' and 'Lapérouse.'

Tendency to reduced dimensions for un-armoured vessels.

The 'Duquesne' and 'Tourville' design has not been repeated. There is no sister ship to the 'Duguay-Trouin' on the stocks, whilst eight cruisers are in construction of the 'Villars' and 'Lapérouse' design. It seems, therefore, that, contrary to what has happened in the case of the seagoing 'squadron armourclads,' which exhibit a progressive increase in the displacement, a maximum was reached in the dimensions of the earliest of the large cruisers, and that the tendency has been towards a reduced displacement. The smaller cruisers, it may be remarked, are still sufficiently large to make long cruises, and strike heavy blows at the commercial marine of an enemy.

Third-class cruisers.

As cruisers of the third class, the list of the French fleet contains all the old first-class despatch vessels and two ships—the 'Rigault de Genouilly' and 'Eclaireur'—lately completed afloat, belonging to a new class, with much higher speed, and more heavily armed. The programme relating to their construction forms a sequel to the general programmes of the fleet as adopted in December, 1871. These vessels are to be considered as cruisers in European waters, and as look-out ships of squadrons. They may be employed, in time of peace, on foreign stations, and in time of war their speed of 15 knots will enable them to escape from a great majority of the cruisers which they are likely to encounter.

The new third-class cruisers of 1,650 tons displacement, heavily rigged, and with a good speed under steam, are perfectly fitted to carry on cruising warfare within a moderate distance from their base of operations.

The following is a more detailed account of the principal vessels included in the preceding summary.

The 'Tourville' was begun in August, 1873, launched in February, 1876, and handed over to the dockyard at Toulon in the month of June following. The frames, beams, decks, and side-plating are of iron. The iron-plating is cased with two thicknesses of teak as high as the upper deck, and the bottom is sheathed with copper. The stern-post and ram-stem are of metal. The hold is divided into watertight compartments by eight 'thwartship bulk-heads, carried up to the orlop deck ; the boilers occupy two of these compartments ; a ninth bulkhead isolates the ram forward. The principal dimensions from the plans are :—

Length extreme (measured from the axis of the rudder to the foremost end of the ram)	341 ft. 10 in.
Length at the water-line . . .	326 ft. 9 in.
Beam	50 feet
Depth	21 ft. 4 in.
Mean draught of water . . .	22 ft. 8 in.
Displacement . . .	5,436 tons
Immersed surface of midship section	796·75 sq. ft.
Spread of canvas . . .	20,451 sq. ft.

The rudder is of wood with metal braces.

The ordnance includes—on the main deck, fourteen 14 c/m., or 46-pdr., guns ; on the upper deck seven 19 c/m., or 7½-inch, guns, of which one is under the topgallant forecastle, and six are in half-turrets projecting beyond the ship's side. The coefficient of the weight of the armament amounts to ·055 of the displacement.

The engines are arranged in two distinct groups, each engine having two large and two small horizontal cylinders on the Woolf system. The single screw has four wide blades, with sabre-shaped curves. The boilers are of the high strengthened pattern officially approved for the Navy. The coal-supply is 660 tons, which can be increased to 800 tons, and which represents a distance under steam of 5,000 miles at ten knots. On the trial trip on January 4, 1878, the engines indicated 7,363 horse-power, with a mean draught of water of 20 ft. 10 in., the immersed surface of the midship section being 723·23 sq. ft. The speed was 16·9 knots. The coal-supply is sufficient for a distance of 5,000 miles.

In the turning trials the 'Tourville,' starting at a speed of fifteen knots, described a circle, 678 yards in diameter, in 6 min. 26 sec.

The 'Duquesne' is somewhat smaller, but closely resembles the last ship in design. The trials of this ship were finished in 1878. She was laid down in 1873 at a Government dockyard. The hull, which weighs 2,700 tons, is of steel with iron-plating ; it is covered with two thicknesses of wood, and coppered. The distinctive features of the 'Tourville,' as compared with the 'Duquesne,' are seen at a glance in the following table of dimensions.

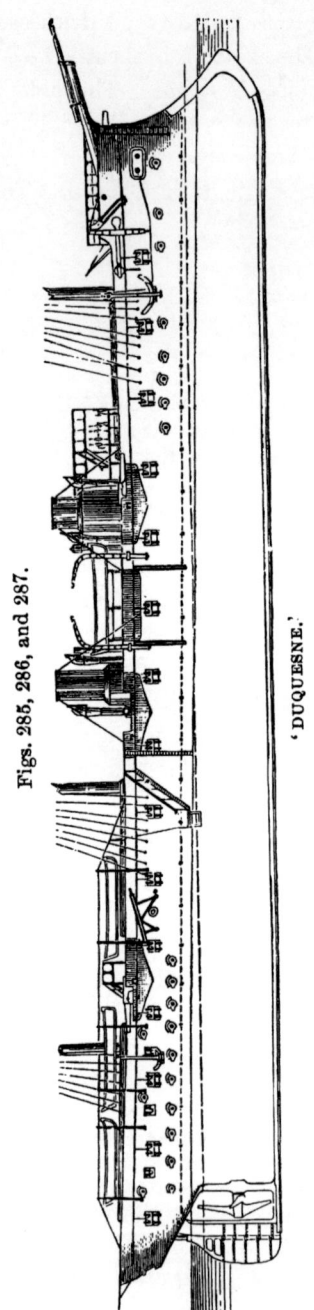

Figs. 285, 286, and 287.

'DUQUESNE.'

'DUQUESNE' (UPPER DECK).

1, 1, Skylights; 2, 2, Ladder-ways; 3, Standard compass; 4, Engine-room skylight; 5, Capstan; 6, Funnel.

Length at the water-line	.	.	326 feet
Breadth	.	.	50 feet
Draught of water (mean)	.	.	22 ft. 6 in.
Displacement	.	.	5,436 tons

The number and calibre of the guns carried are the same; and they are mounted in the same way in both ships. Like the 'Tourville,' the 'Duquesne' is a full-rigged ship. The engines are on the compound system, and have three large and three small horizontal cylinders. The 'Duquesne' is expected to prove as powerful and fast a ship, and as good a sea-boat as the 'Tourville'; but she is inferior in coal endurance. The supply amounts to 660 tons.

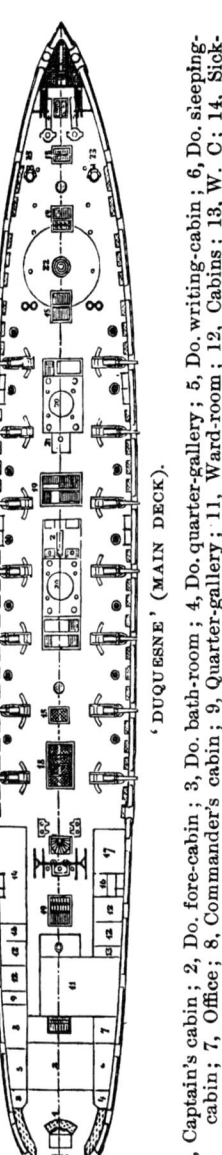

'DUQUESNE' (MAIN DECK).

1, Captain's cabin; 2, Do. fore-cabin; 3, Do. bath-room; 4, Do. quarter-gallery; 5, Do. writing-cabin; 6, Do. sleeping-cabin; 7, Office; 8, Commander's cabin; 9, Quarter-gallery; 11, Ward-room; 12, Cabins; 13, W. C; 14, Sick-bay; 16, Office; 17, Gun-room; 18, 18, Skylight's; 19, Ladders; 20, Funnels; 21, Galley; 22, Capstan; 23, Bitts.

The larger second-class cruiser, 'Duguay-Trouin,' was laid down in 1873 from the plans of M. Eynaud, and was launched in 1877. The hull is built in the same manner as those of the 'Duquesne' and the 'Tourville,' except that the orlop deck is laid with iron plating from the after bulkhead of the shellroom to the foremost bulkhead of the stokehole, and there is no 'tween-deck battery. The rudder is of wood, and the hold is divided into watertight compartments by eight bulkheads carried up to the gun deck, independently of that which closes the fore part, projecting forward in the shape of a ram.

The 'Duguay-Trouin.'

Principal dimensions from the plans:—

Length of hull at the water-line	290 feet
Beam	42 ft. 8 in.
Depth . . .	15 ft. 9 in.
Mean draught of water .	17 feet
Displacement . .	3,189 tons
Immersed surface of midship section . .	576 sq. ft.
Spread of canvas .	15,500 sq. ft.

The ordnance mounted on board consists of five 19 c/m., or 7½-inch, guns, of which one fires ahead and four are in unplated half-turrets or sponsons projecting beyond the ship's side, and of five 14 c/m., or 46-pounders, of which one can fire astern.

Figs. 288, 289, and 290.

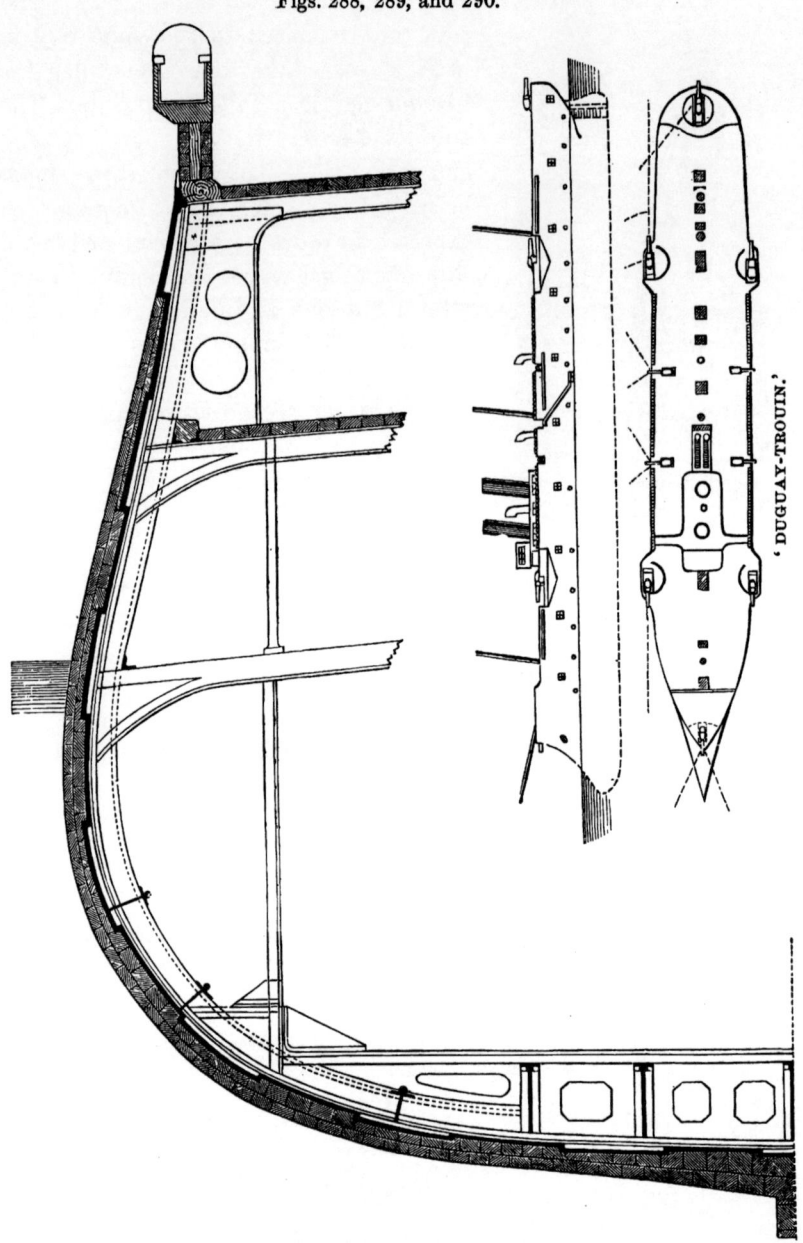

'DUGUAY-TROUIN' (MIDSHIP SECTION).

The engines, made at Indret, are on the compound system with three large and three small horizontal cylinders, working a single screw. The boilers are at a mean pressure of 32 lbs. The engines

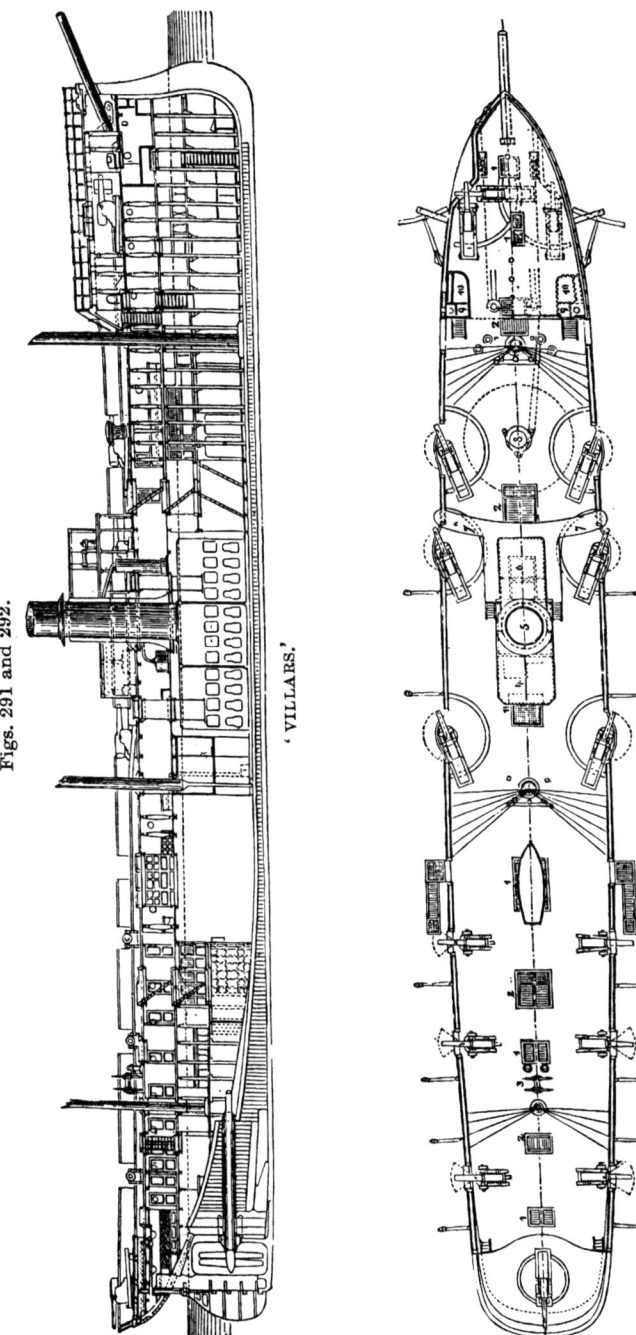

Figs. 291 and 292.

'VILLARS.'

'VILLARS' (UPPER DECK).

1, Skylights; 2, Ladders; 3, Wheel; 4, Galley; 5, Funnel; 6, Chart-room; 7, Bridge; 8, Capstan.

are to develop 3,740 horse-power, and the estimated speed is sixteen knots. The coal-supply is 430 tons.

The 'Villars' and second-class ships. Of smaller size, but belonging to the same class of second-class cruisers, are the 'Villars,' 'Forfait,' 'Magon,' and 'Roland.' The first-named was begun in 1875, and was designed by M. Sabattier. The hull is of wood, the weight being 1,000 tons. The beams and longitudinal girders are of iron. There is no continuous internal iron-plating, but only two flanged plates, to which the knees of the deck beams are secured. The planking is of wood. The rudder is also of wood, and the hold is divided into watertight compartments like that of the 'Duguay-Trouin.'

The principal dimensions and details as taken from the plans are :—

Length of hull at water-line . . .	249 ft. 4 in.
Beam	37 ft. 11 in.
Depth	15 ft. 2 in.
Mean draught of water . .	13 ft. 7 in.
Displacement	2,268 tons
Immersed surface of midship section .	448·6 sq. ft.
Spread of canvas . . .	13,993 sq. ft.

The armament is composed of six 16 c/m., or 100-pdr., guns, and nine 14 c/m., or 46-pounders., of which one is mounted on the topgallant forecastle and one on the stern gratings.

The engines, made at Indret, are to indicate 2,500 horse-power. The estimated speed is 15·5 knots; the coal-supply 400 tons.

The 'Lapérouse.' The 'Lapérouse,' laid down in 1875 from plans by M. Bienaymé, Naval Constructor, differs very slightly from the 'Villars,' as may be seen from the following principal dimensions :—

Length of hull at water-line . . .	262 ft. 5 in.
Beam	37 ft. 5 in.
Depth	15 ft. 1 in.
Mean draught of water . .	17 feet
Displacement . . .	2,236 tons
Immersed surface of midship section	433 9 sq. ft.

The build of the hull is exactly the same as that of the 'Villars,' except that in the bottom there are two strakes of iron and angle-irons. The armament, rig, horse-power, speed, and coal-supply are the same as those of the 'Villars.'

'Eclaireur' and 'Rigault de Genouilly.' The 'Eclaireur' and 'Rigault de Genouilly,' designed by the same Constructor as the 'Lapérouse,' are types of the third-class cruiser. The first-mentioned vessel was laid down in 1874. The hull is of wood and weighs 790 tons. The beams and longitudinals are of iron. The general system of construction is similar to that of the 'Villars' and 'Lapérouse.' The stem is specially constructed for ramming, and the bows are protected against a heavy sea by a topgallant forecastle. The rudder is of wood. The coefficient of weight of hull is ·48. The armament consists of eight 46-pounders, of which one is on the topgallant forecastle.

The principal details of the design are :—

Length of hull at water-line . . .	236 ft. 3 in.
Beam	35 ft. 5 in.
Depth in hold . . .	13 ft. 3 in.
Mean draught of water . .	14 ft. 9 in.
Displacement , . . .	1,643 tons
Under-water surface of midship section	366 sq. ft.
Spread of canvas . . .	13,519 sq. ft.

The vessel is a full-rigged barque.

The engines, manufactured at Indret, are on the compound

Figs. 293 and 294.

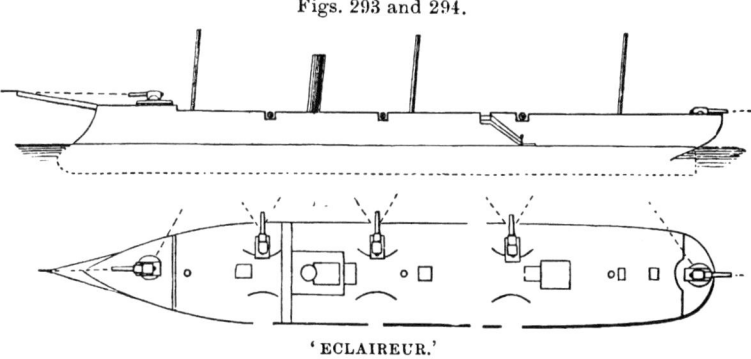

'ECLAIREUR.'

system with three large and three small cylinders. The boilers are cylindrical, and work at high pressure 59 lbs. The estimated speed is fifteen knots for 1,900 indicated horse-power. The coal supply is 210 tons.

The present gun-vessels of the French fleet answer to the ships which it was proposed in 1871–72 to call 'station gun-vessels.' They were thus defined :—Vessels fitted for carrying on warlike operations on the coast or great rivers and for service on foreign stations. The programme necessitated an armament including one powerful gun of 16 c/m., or 100-pdr., and some 14 c/m., or 46-pdr., guns. Gunvessels 'Lancier' class.

The name 'station gun-vessel' was not adopted, and, after several changes, the heavy 16 c/m., or 100-pdr., guns were given up. The ordnance now, therefore, comprises only 14 c/m., or 46-pdr., guns, like that of the third-class cruisers. . . . The 'Chasseur' was laid down in 1873, from designs by M. Sabattier, Director of

Material. The system of construction is similar to that of the 'Eclaireur,' a wooden hull with beams and braces of iron.

The principal dimensions of the plan are :—

Length of hull at water-line . . .	199 ft. 6 in.
Beam	28 ft. 5 in.
Depth	10 ft. 2 in.
Mean draught of water . .	11 feet
Displacement . .	794 tons
Immersed surface of midship section .	201·5 sq. ft.
Spread of canvas . . .	8,858 sq. ft.

The vessel is barque-rigged.

The armament is composed of four 14 c/m., or 46-pounder, guns, of which one is mounted on the topgallant forecastle.

The engine, made at Indret, is to indicate 700 horse-power; the boilers are to carry steam at an ordinary high pressure of 59 lbs. In the 'Bisson,' a vessel of the same class, on her trial trip, at a draught of water of 11 ft. 2 in., a speed of 12·18 knots was realised with 849 indicated horse-power. A circle 393 yards in diameter was described in 4 min. 19 sec. The coal-supply is 110 tons. The plan

Figs. 295 and 296.

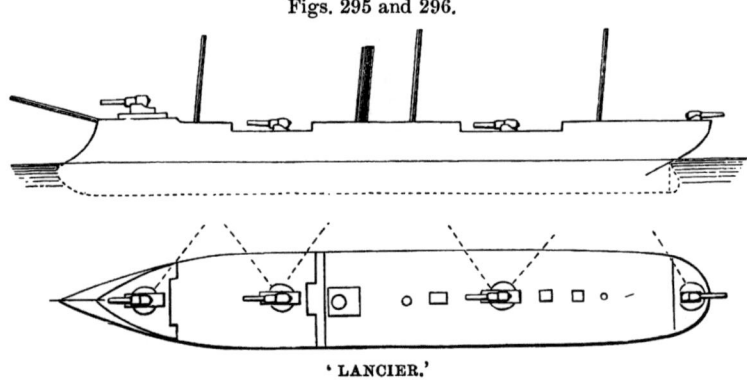

' LANCIER.'

of the 'Lancier' may be taken as a correct illustration of the principal features of the class of vessels we have under review.

The 'Crocodile' is a first-class gunboat, or perhaps more correctly gun-*vessel*, if we have regard to the distinction between the two designations in force in our own service. Like so many other vessels large and small, which have been recently added to the French Navy, she was begun in 1873. She is built on the composite system, and has the following dimensions :—

Length at the water-line . . .	141 ft. 8 in.
Beam	24 feet
Mean draught of water . .	8 ft. 3 in.
Displacement . . .	460 tons

The armament originally proposed for this vessel—which has apparently been lately changed—was one 7½-inch, or 19 c/m., gun, mounted on a slide amidships ; and two light 4-inch, or 10 c/m., guns, one forward and the other abaft. The vessel has three masts. The engines were made at the works of Claparéde and Co., at St. Denis, and have two cylinders on the Woolf system. The boilers are cylindrical, and have four furnaces. On the trial trip the horse-power indicated was 457, and the speed attained 9·7 knots. The 'Crocodile' can stow 50 tons of fuel.

Fig. 297.

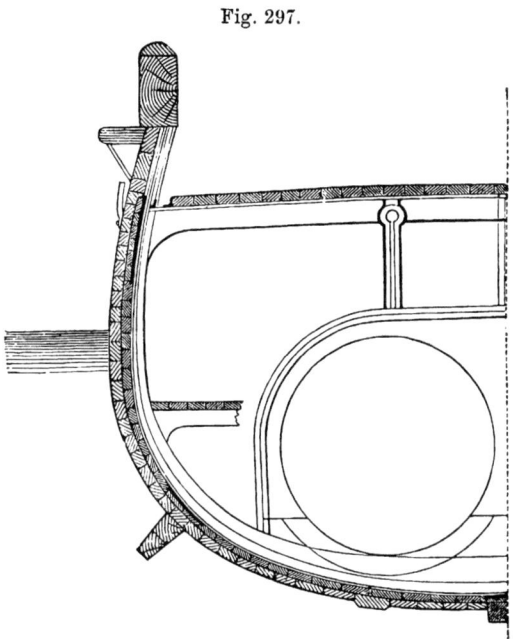

'CROCODILE' (MIDSHIP SECTION).

Section III.—*German, Italian, Austrian, Russian, and American Unarmoured Vessels.*

A. GERMAN.

The German Empire is proceeding with great energy in the construction of a modern cruising fleet. According to the programme of 1873, the navy of Germany was to possess twenty cruisers, to be completed in 1881.

The cruisers of the first class are represented by the 'Liepzig,' originally called the 'Thusnelda.' Taking into view the ever-increasing speed of foreign unarmoured ships and large Atlantic

The 'Leipzig.'

steamers, the Germans have found it necessary to secure a considerably higher speed than that contemplated in their original programme. It was accordingly laid down that the 'Leipzig, and her sister-ship, the 'Sedan,' should have a speed of fifteen knots at full boiler power. This involved a departure from the wooden construction, which had hitherto been adopted, as it could not be made rigid enough to stand the strain of such powerful machinery. But the necessity of protecting the bottom of the ship from fouling had been recognised as an essential condition of maintaining a high speed throughout a long commission. Hence, following the example of the designer of the 'Inconstant,' it was decided that iron should be employed to secure adequate strength in the hull, that a copper sheathing was essential, and that, to prevent galvanic action, the hull should be

Fig. 298.

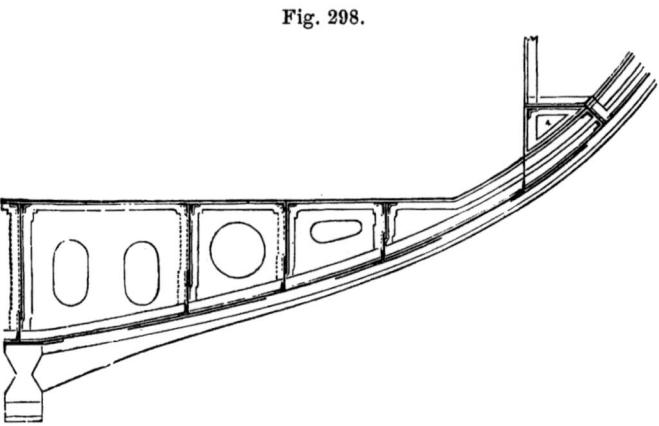

'LEIPZIG' (FLOORS BETWEEN KEELSON AND LONGITUDINALS).

covered with a double sheathing of wood. On this wood sheathing the sheets of copper were to be fastened. The great power of the machinery and the large supply of coal which it demands involve as a corollary considerable displacement, and a corresponding power of maintaining high speed. The ships of the 'Leipzig' class have a length of 282 ft. 2 in., a breadth of 45 ft. 11 in., a depth from the lower side of the upper deck to the upper edge of the keelson of 33 ft. 1 in., a draught of water when fully laden of 21 ft. 7 in., and a displacement of 3,925 tons.

The 'Leipzig' class.

The engines have three cylinders on the trunk principle; with surface condensers and superheaters to insure the most economical consumption of fuel. The indicated horse-power is 4,800; and six boilers with 28 furnaces supply steam to the engines. The armament consists of twelve of the new 17 c/m., 6¾-inch, or 6-ton guns, of which

ten are mounted on the main deck on the broadside, and two on
the upper deck. The latter command a direct fire both ahead and

Fig. 299.

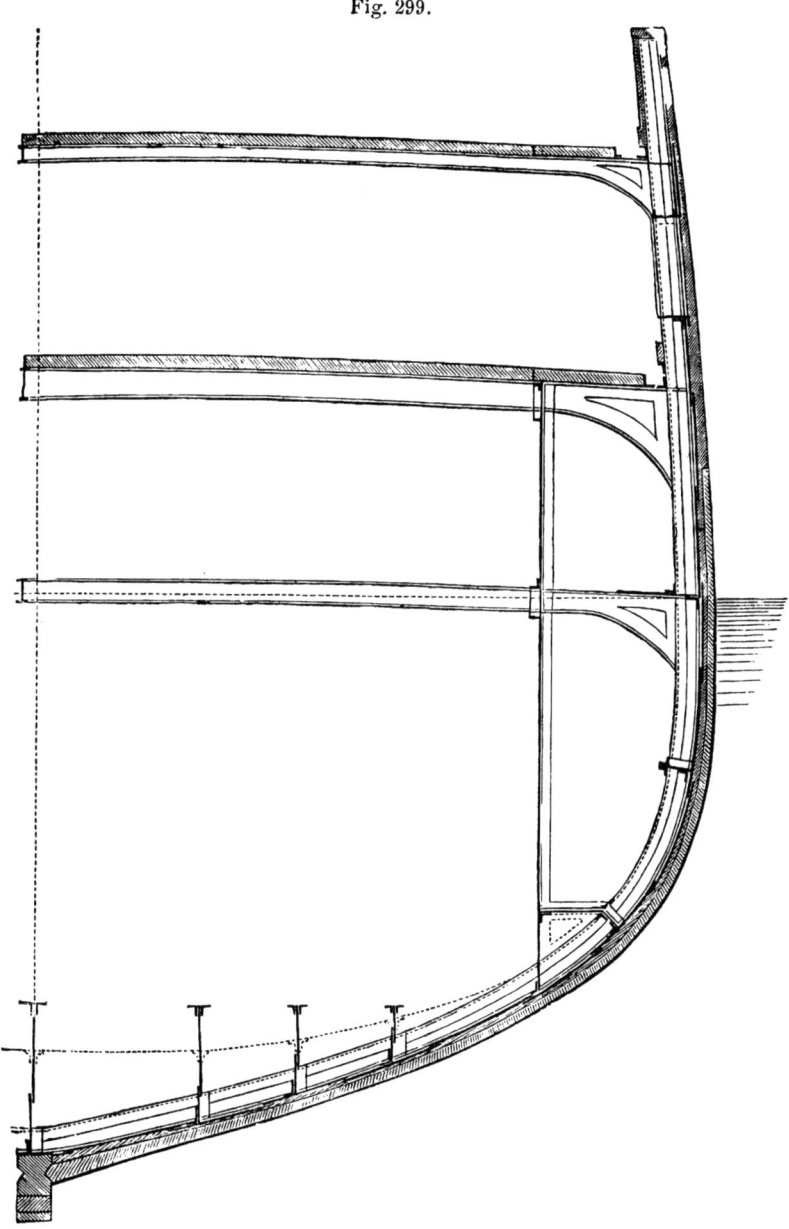

'LEIPZIG' (MIDSHIP SECTION).

astern. The foremost and aftermost guns will not be kept permanently in the bow or stern ports. They will generally be in

their proper ports on the broadside, nearest to the bow and the stern. The ship is heavily sparred, and is capable of cruising without the aid of steam. The lower masts are of iron, and the bowsprit can be housed. The funnel is fitted to be lowered, and the screw-propeller can be lifted. The complement consists of 425 officers and men. The stowage is sufficient for three months' provisions and for four weeks' water. A distilling apparatus has been provided. The plans and specifications for the 'Leipzig,' and her sister-ship, the 'Sedan,' were prepared at the Admiralty in Berlin. The contract for the construction was taken by the Vulcan Shipbuilding Company, of Stettin. The rigging, armament, and fitting, as well as the coppering of both ships, were carried out at the Imperial Dockyard at Kiel.

The 'Bismarck' class.

The German cruisers of the second class are represented by the 'Bismarck' type, of which five are built, and five others are building or ordered to be laid down. Their length is 244 ft. 4 in.; beam, 43 ft. 3 in.; depth, 31 ft. 6 in.; and displacement, 2,856 tons. Their armament consists of sixteen 15 c/m., 6-inch, or 4-ton guns, of which twelve are mounted on the main deck, and four on the upper deck. The engines are of 2,500 indicated horse-power, and the speed fifteen knots. The hull is of iron, and the sheathing zinc instead of copper.

The 'Gneisenau' is of nearly similar dimensions :—

Length between perpendiculars . .	. 245 feet
Beam, extreme . . .	. 45 feet
Draught of water, forward . .	. 17 ft. 10 in.
,, aft . . .	. 19 ft. 8 in.
Indicated horse-power . . .	. 2,500
Speed, estimated . . .	. 15 knots

The hull is divided into watertight compartments by seven bulkheads. The armament is sixteen 15 c/m, or 6-inch, guns, of which two on the forecastle can fire right ahead. The screw is fitted for raising.

A still unnamed corvette, at present designated 'F,' is on the stocks. The principal dimensions are :—

Length	. 227 feet
Beam	. 41 feet
Mean draught of water . .	. 18 feet
Displacement . . .	. 1,900 tons
Indicated horse-power . .	. 2,100
Speed, estimated . .	. 14·5 knots

The hull is of iron cased with four inches of teak and sheathed with zinc, and is divided into watertight compartments by seven bulkheads. She has six boilers of Siemens steel. The rig is that of a barque, and the screw is a lifting one. The coal-ssupply is 360 tons.

It is stated in the *Moniteur de la Flotte* that a new steel corvette has been recently commenced at Dantzig. The length is to be 227 feet, beam 41 feet, and draught of water about 22 feet. The estimated speed is from seventeen to eighteen knots.

The cruisers of the third class are of the 'Ariadne' type. The 'Ariadne,' 'Luise,' and their sister vessels have a length of 204 feet, a beam of 35 feet, a displacement of 1,692 tons, and an armament of six 15 c/m., 6-inch, or 4-ton guns, and two light 12 c/m., or 4¾-inch, guns, all on the upper deck. The engines are of 2,100 indicated horse-power, and the speed is given as thirteen knots. The 'Luise,' however, in a continuous six hours' trial with full boiler power attained a mean speed of fourteen knots. The hulls are of wood. *The 'Ariadne' class.*

The 'Freya' is of rather larger dimensions, the length being 259 feet, beam 36 ft. 1 in., draught of water nineteen feet, and displacement 1,985 tons. She is a wooden ship designed, like the 'Luise' and 'Ariadne,' at the Berlin Admiralty, and credited with a speed of 14½ knots. The 'Freya' is wholly built of wood, but the hull is materially strengthened by iron stringer-plates and deck-beams, and the greatest care has been taken in a ship of such fine lines to combine strength with lightness of construction. The armament is on the upper-deck, and consists of eight 15 c/m., or 6-inch, guns. The indicated horse-power of the engines is 2,400. The ship carries the spars of a full-rigged corvette, and has good speed under sail alone. At the trial trip she realised a speed of 15·2 knots, a result which exceeded the anticipations of her designers; the engines indicated 2,764 horse-power. The 'Freya' is intended to be employed in the pursuit of the light-armed vessels of an enemy, and to protect commerce. *The 'Freya.'*

In the German service we find two classes of cruising gun-vessels, and the 'Habicht' and 'Moeve' may almost be rated as a third class. The dimensions of these vessels, launched from the works of the Schikau Company at Elbing in May 1879, are: length 174 feet, beam 29 ft. 6 in., depth 11 ft. 5 in., displacement 848 tons, and horse-power 600 tons. The hulls are of iron cased with wood, and sheathed with zinc. The 'Albatross' type is rather smaller. They are 168 feet in length, 26 ft. 10 in. in breadth, with a depth of 10 ft. 10 in., and a displacement of 705 tons. The armament includes two 15 c/m., 6-inch, or 4-ton guns, and two 12 c/m., or 4¾-inch, guns. The horse-power is 600, and the speed 10·5 knots. The small class has a displacement of 350 to 500 tons, an armament *The 'Habicht' and 'Moeve.'* *The 'Albatross' class.*

of one 15 c/m., or 6-inch, gun, and two light pieces. The speed is from 8·4 to 9·8 knots.

B. ITALIAN.

The 'Garibaldi.'

Though the Italian Government have concentrated their efforts on their main object, that of providing the country with a squadron of armoured ships, the construction of non-armoured cruisers has received a fair share of attention. The 'Garibaldi' may be taken as a type of those recently constructed. This vessel, originally intended for a frigate, with a complement of 452, was altered to a corvette, with a complement of 350. Considerable alterations were made in the after body and in the screw-well. For twenty-eight guns on the main deck, and four on the upper deck, were substituted six 16 c/m., or 6-inch, Palliser-tubed rifled guns on the main, and two of the same calibre on the upper deck. Various considerations induced the authorities to refrain from making any alteration in the machinery. The displacement, as originally contemplated, was to have been 3,700 tons. It has been reduced to 3,440.

The 'Cristoforo Colombo.'

The 'Cristoforo Colombo' was constructed from designs by Commendatore B. Brin, Inspector of Naval Constructions. She was laid down in October 1872, and launched on September 17, 1875, at the Arsenal at Venice. The principal dimensions are the following :—

Length	248 ft. 5 in.
Beam	37 ft. 1 in.
Depth in hold . . .	16 ft. 1 in.
Displacement	2,354 tons
Immersed area of midship section .	488·25 sq. ft.

The system of construction is composite (*misto*). The hull, or rather the knuckle-timbers and planking, is of wood, chiefly oak from the forests of Romagna and Bastia. The beams of the orlop and upper decks are of iron. The hull is divided internally into eight compartments by seven transverse, iron, watertight bulkheads with doors of communication through each. The four central bulkheads are carried up to the upper deck. The remaining bulkheads are cut off at the orlop deck. The boilers are cylindrical, and eight in number. The engines are compound, and have three inverted vertical cylinders all of the same diameter, 1·57 m., or 61·8 inches, with a stroke of ·991 m., or 3 ft. 3 in., and capable of developing 4,000 horse-power. The coal-supply is 620 tons, or sufficient for 320 hours, at a speed of from 13 to 14 knots ; and for 98 hours for the full speed, calculated at between 17 and 18 knots. The 'Cristoforo Colombo' has three masts, square-rigged forward, and carries a 12 c/m., or 4¾-inch, Arm-

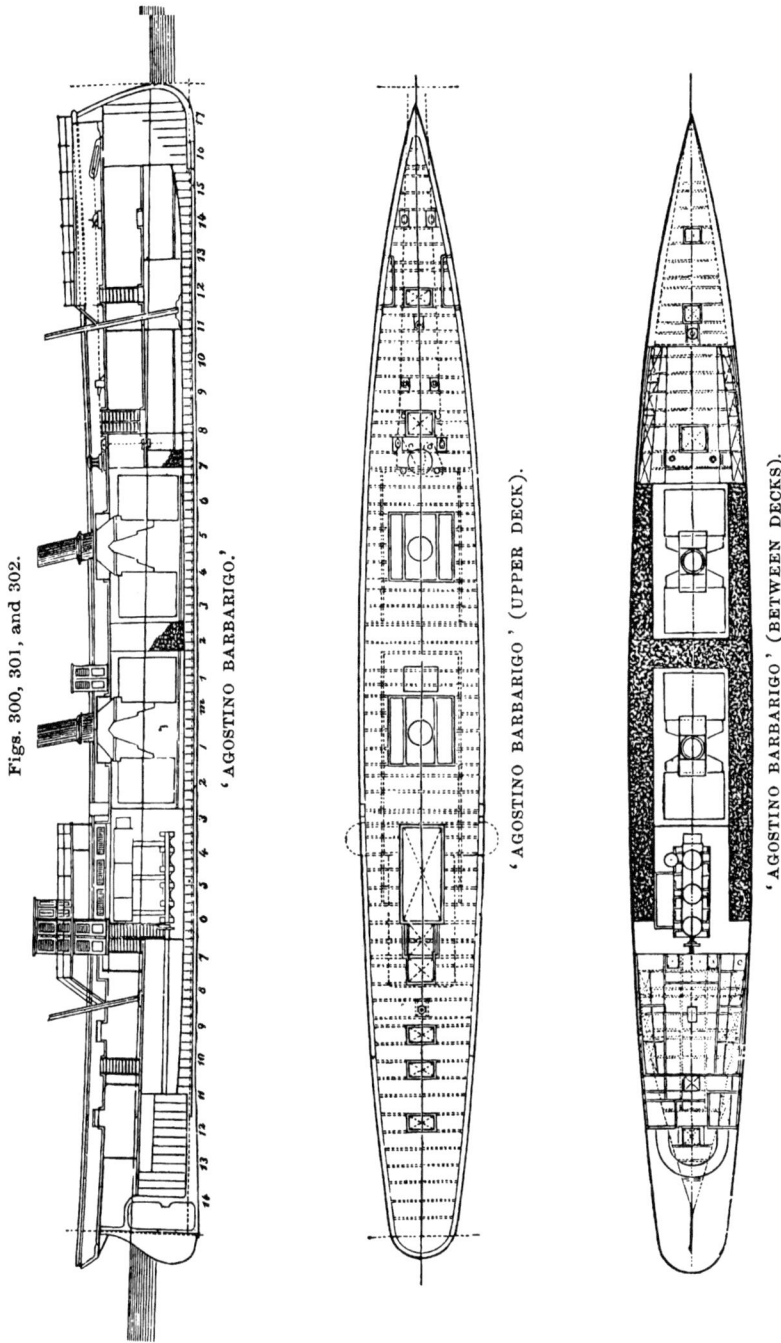

Figs. 300, 301, and 302.

'AGOSTINO BARBARIGO.'

'AGOSTINO BARBARIGO' (UPPER DECK).

'AGOSTINO BARBARIGO' (BETWEEN DECKS).

strong gun on the forecastle, and four others of the same size on the broadside on the upper deck. There are in addition two mitrailleuses.

The Italians have recently added two new dispatch-vessels to their fleet, the ' Staffeta ' and the ' Agostino Barbarigo.' The ' Staffeta ' is built of iron and is three-masted. Her dimensions are as follows: length on the water-line, 253 ft. 3 in.; breadth, 31 ft. 11 in.; mean draught of water, 14 ft. 4 in.; sail-surface, 8,541 square feet. The armament consists of five 4·7 inch guns. The engine, which was built in Italy, has developed 2,140 horse-power, and the speed has been recorded at 14½ knots an hour.

The ' Agostino Barbarigo ' is built of steel, and is intended for high speed. The principal dimensions are as follows: Length on the water-line, 216ft. 6 in.; breadth, 24 ft. 1 in.; mean draught of water, 10 ft. 9 in., sail-surface, 2,433 square feet. She is armed with three 4·7 inch guns. The engines were built in England and are expected to develop 1,676 horse-power. Another vessel similar to the ' Agostino Barbarigo,' the ' Marcantonio Colonna,' has been recently launched.

C. AUSTRIAN.

For the Austro-Hungarian Navy several cruisers have been built during the last few years. Those of the ' Radetzky ' type are 253 feet in length between the perpendiculars, and draw 23 ft. 7 in. of water. Their armament consists of 15 c/m., 6-inch, or 4-ton Krupp guns, and they have a speed of fourteen knots. The cruisers of the ' Donau ' class are 233 feet in length. They draw 19 ft. 7 in. They are armed with thirteen 15 c/m. (6-inch) Krupp guns, and their speed is twelve knots. The cruisers of the ' Zrinyi ' class, to which the ' Frundsberg ' belongs, are small. Their length is only 194 feet, and their draught of water 17 ft. 9 in. Their armament consists of four cast-iron 24-pdrs., and they have a speed of only eleven knots. The vessels of the ' Donau ' class are of wood; the others are built on the composite system.

D. RUSSIAN.

The most important class of unarmoured cruisers in the Russian Navy is represented by the ' Rasboynik ' and ' Nayesdnik.' These ships visited England at the end of 1879, and the following account of them is taken from descriptions published during their stay in this country :—

' These heavily-armed little craft, which are fully rigged and engined, and of which there are eight already built, form a new class of war vessel, and have been designed and constructed under the superintendence of Admiral Popoff. The " Rasboynik " is 240 feet in length, with a beam of 30 ft. 2 in., and her draught is 13 ft. 6 in. forward and 15 feet aft. Her displacement is 1,335 tons. She is built entirely of iron, and is cased with wood to the extent of six inches, like our own vessels of the " Volage " and " Boadicea " classes, to enable her to be copper- or zinc-bottomed. The " Nayesdnik," on the other hand, is a composite ship, having the frames only of iron, the hull itself being constructed of planking. In all other respects, however, they may be regarded as sister ships. The engines are by Baird, of St. Petersburg, and are of 250 nominal and 1,500 indicated horse-power, though they have developed 1,700 horses. They are of the horizontal return-action class, the piston crosshead working on a shoe-guide. The high-pressure cylinder is 50 inches, and the low-pressure cylinder 75 inches in diameter, and the stroke 2 ft. 9 in. The steam is supplied by four boilers arranged back to back across the ship, the stoking being performed at each end. The engines have been fitted with the Silver governor, to prevent racing when the screw is lifted out of the water, but, owing to a deficiency of steam area in the throttle valve, with which it is connected, a readjustment will have to be made. The bunkers hold sufficient coal to last fourteen days at half-boiler power and with a speed of from 8½ to 9 knots per hour. The propeller, which is of variable pitch, and made to lift upon deck when steam is not required, consists of a two-bladed screw, having a diameter of 13 ft. 4 in., and which with a pitch of sixteen feet has driven the ship at 13·25 knots. The armament of the corvette is varied and powerful. She carries three steel 6-inch pivot breechloading guns of the Krupp pattern, but manufactured at the Oboukoff Works in Russia, and four steel breechloading broadside guns of 10 c/m. calibre. These latter, which fire a shot of 22 lbs., are intended as torpedo guns and for saluting purposes. The heavy guns, which fire projectiles of 106 lbs., are arranged fore and aft along the middle line on the upper deck, and can be trained to fire across either beam or to give certain degrees of forward fire. This is a novel arrangement, but it possesses the great advantage of securing comparative steadiness of platform, and enables guns of heavier natures to be carried in small vessels. A couple of Palmkranz guns, which are substantially the same as the Nordenfelt machine-guns, are fitted on the bridge, and below these, on a platform outside the ship, are fittings for the fixing of a gun of a very novel character, which has not as yet been introduced into the English service. This is a steel breech-loading piece about three feet in length, and an inch and a half in calibre, manufactured by Engstroms, at Stafsjo, in Sweden. It is mounted upon a swivel, and a man

placed at the rear can sweep the horizon with it as readily as with a
rifle. It can discharge from eight to ten steel shells per minute,
and is fatal at 2,400 feet. The cartridge contains a percussion cap
like small-arm ammunition. The corvette also carries four Harvey
torpedoes, spar torpedoes, ground mines, and Whitehead torpedoes.
The Whiteheads are carried in four iron cases on the weather deck,
whence they are discharged. Two are 14 feet in length and
14 inches in diameter, the other two being of the exceptional length
of 19 feet, and 19 inches in diameter. The former have a speed of
22 knots for 600 feet, and the latter a speed of $20\frac{3}{4}$ knots for the same
distance. They are charged from the main deck by means of a small
air-pump, which was made by Mr. Whitehead at Fiume, and which is
capable of filling a reservoir of a capacity of eight cubic feet with 70
atmospheres in one hour and six minutes; and it is worth recording
that the reservoir and the fish torpedoes on deck are always kept
charged at their full power ready for instant use. The ground mines
already mentioned are for the protection of the ship while at anchor
in hostile waters. Forty-two mines are placed round the ship, each
being connected with firing keys fitted on the port bulwarks, so that
they can be exploded either from on board or automatically by the
concussion of an enemy's craft. There are also arrangements for
enabling the ship to drag buoyant torpedoes at the stern, and which
can be so regulated that they can be brought to cover the port and
starboard quarters. The " Rasboynik " is fitted with one of Siemens'
electric lights worked by an independent engine. She is three-
masted, the main and fore masts being provided with double topsail
yards; and all her boats are provided with Hill and Clark's hooks,
by means of which they can be lowered into the water while the ship
is under way. The corvette contains a complement of twenty officers
and 160 men.'

Whilst in English waters the ' Rasboynik' made some trial trips,
chiefly with a view to determine the most effective pitch of the screw
for vessels of her class. The pitch had been reduced to fourteen feet,
the finest yet tried. The result, however, showed that the pitch was
too small, and simply strained the engines to no purpose. Two runs
were made on the mile, with a mean result of 12·75 knots, the tide
and wind being in opposite directions, and thus serving to destroy
each other. The boiler pressure was 62 lbs., the vacuum 24 inches,
the revolutions 98 per minute, and the horse-power developed 1,758.
The power was thus far beyond the contract; but, owing to the fineness of the screw, it did little more than churn up the water. As yet,
a pitch of sixteen feet has been found to give the best speed. The

circle was turned in 5 min. 30 sec. with the helm hard over to star-board, and in 5 min. 20 sec. with the helm hard over to port, the diameter being respectively 532 and 442 yards. Subsequently the 'Rasboynik' made a final trial of her screw on the measured mile in Stokes Bay, and with the best results as regards speed which have been obtained since she was commissioned. The pitch was again reduced from eighteen feet to sixteen feet, and with 99 revolutions of the engines she averaged a mean speed of 13·115 knots an hour. The boiler pressure was 61 lbs., the vacuum 25·6 inches, and the power developed 1,818 horses. The slip was 15 per cent., and the trim of the ship on the occasion 12 ft. 8 in. forward and 14 ft. 6 in. aft.

The 'Plastoun' was laid down on September 1, 1877, and launched on May 9, 1879. The principal dimensions are as follows :—

Length between perpendiculars .	.	.	214 feet
„ at load water-line	.	.	.	207 ft. 6 in.
Beam to outside of wood-casing .	.	.	32 feet
„ not including wood-casing	.	.	31 feet
Draught of water, forward	.	.	.	13 ft. 6 in.
„ aft .	.	.	.	14 ft. 6 in.
Displacement .	.	.	.	.	1,334 tons

On the upper deck three 6-inch, or $15\frac{1}{4}$ c/m., rifled guns are mounted on turntables so as to fire in each beam : the armament also comprises four light bronze guns mounted on the broadside. The ship was built at St. Petersburg by a private company. The hull is of iron, sheathed with wood in two thicknesses, teak inside and larch outside. The bottom is coppered. The engines, made by the builders of the ship, are on the compound system, the indicated horse-power being 1,500. The 'Strelok' is of a similar type.

The Russian clipper 'Opritchnik,' has lately been added to the Russian Pacific Squadron : 1,000*l*. being spent by the authorities in tug hire and ice-cutting, to drag her through the ice to clear water, whence she was escorted by the steamers 'Neptune' and 'Freund' to Revel. The 'Opritchnik' was commenced in 1879, and her completion within a twelvemonth will appear extraordinarily rapid, when it is remembered that the ironclad 'Peter the Great' has afforded constant employment to the Russian dockyards since 1869. In style the clipper is very much like the two vessels 'Rasboynik' and 'Nayesdnik,' which visited Portsmouth on their way to the Pacific. She is about 214 feet long, 32 feet broad, and fourteen feet deep ; the displacement being 1,350 tons. The hull is built entirely of steel, and cost 594,350 roubles. The engines work up to 1,500 indicated horse-power. On the upper deck are four 6-inch guns, and two

9-pdrs. on either side. She carries Whitehead torpedoes and torpedo-boats, and six Hotchkiss cannon for repelling torpedo attacks. The speed is fourteen knots.

Mercan-
tile auxili-
aries. Numerically the most important additions to the cruising fleet of Russia within the last few years belong to the several classes of 'purchased cruisers,' the designation given to vessels originally built for mercantile steamers and bought by the Russian Government or patriotic societies from private owners in Russia, Germany, and the United States, and presented to the State. Many of these are ocean steamers of great size, high speed, and considerable coal-carrying capacity.

In 1878 the Russian Admiralty purchased three iron ocean steamers from the mercantile marine of the United States. The

Figs. 303 and 304

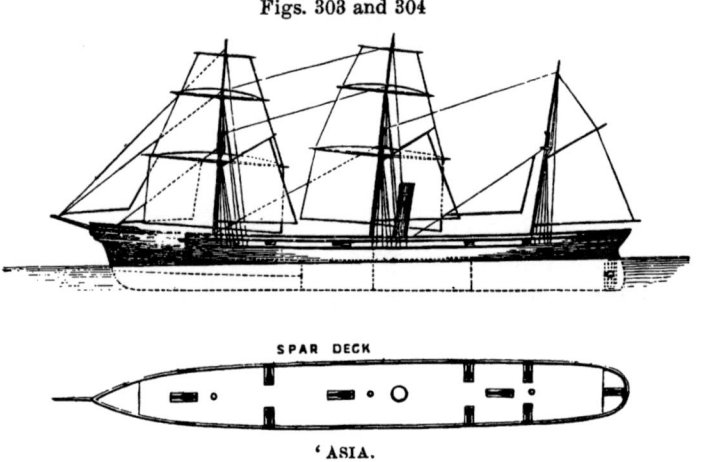

'ASIA.

names of these vessels were 'State of California,' 'Columbus,' and 'Saratoga.' The first two were constructed by Messrs. Wm. Cramp and Sons, and the third by Messrs. John Roach and Son. After the purchase had been completed, they were taken to Messrs. Cramp's iron shipbuilding yard at Philadelphia, converted into war-vessels, and renamed the 'Europe,' the 'Asia,' and the 'Africa.' Under these names they were completed, fitted, and equipped for service, the armament being placed on board in a European port.

Messrs. Cramp and Sons, in addition to fitting out these ships, constructed a fourth war-vessel, named the 'Zabiaca,' from designs prepared by the Russian Admiralty. The annexed drawings of the 'Asia' and the 'Zabiaca' will convey a general idea of the ships when they sailed from the Delaware for Copenhagen in the winter of 1878-79.

The principal advantages possessed by these cruisers are light draught of water, comparatively high speed, and considerable sail-area; the latter being 13,390 square feet, 12,902 square feet, and 11,393 square feet respectively, for the converted ships; while the 'Zabiaca' spreads 12,312 square feet of canvas, and realised a maximum speed on the Delaware of 15 knots per hour.

The hulls are divided into compartments by eleven watertight bulkheads, and the vertical engines, which are of the compound type and operate a single fixed screw-propeller, are protected above the water-line by armour. These ships are steered by steam-power as well as by hand, and have been fitted with the latest improvements and conveniences.

The motive machinery of the ' Zabiaca ' was tested in a continuous six hours' trial at sea off Cape Henlopen in April, 1879, with the

Figs. 305 and 306.

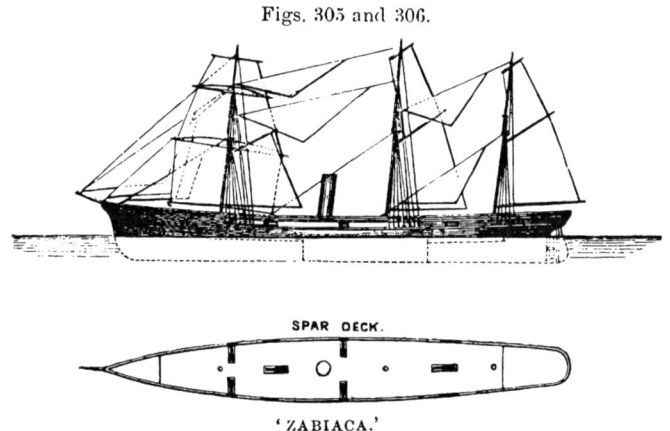

SPAR DECK.

' ZABIACA.'

following results, the means only of the four trials being given: Revolution of screw, 91·4 ; indicated horse-power, 1,464 ; coal consumed per horse-power, 2·35 lbs. ; displacement, 1,226 ; diameter of screw, 12 feet; pitch of screw, 17·5 feet ; pressure of steam, 81·1 lbs. ; speed, 14·41 knots per hour. With light draught and 832 tons displacement the ship has made 15½ knots per hour.

In addition to these American-built vessels, there is also attached to the Atlantic squadron the famous cruiser ' Cimbria,' which made such a sensation by her appearance in American waters at the time of the war with Turkey. She is a sister ship of the ' Moscow,' named hereafter in the Moscow cruiser fleet.

The following is a description which appeared in the *Times* of a large fast cruiser then being built in France :—

' The construction on the Clyde, at Messrs. John Elder and Co.'s yard, of a Popoff yacht for the Czar, which is at the same time a powerful fighting ship for shallow waters, is not the only sign of the activity of Russia in strengthening herself at sea. The Russian Volunteer Fleet, the patriotic organisation which procures ships with funds derived from public subscription, and has them manned and officered by the Imperial Navy, is having a fast cruiser built for it near Toulon under the supervision of the Imperial Government. The *Compagnie Nouvelle des Forges et Chantiers de la Méditerranée* now possesses the shipbuilding yard at La Seyne, at which 6,000 or 7,000 men have been employed at one time in turning out vessels of war for Spain, Russia, and other foreign countries. La Seyne is in a bay sheltered by the green headlands which enclose the roadstead of Toulon, and is half an hour's sail from the quay of Toulon town. At present the yards are comparatively slack, but one of the two large vessels building on the sequestered beach opposite the first naval arsenal of France is the new Russian cruiser—a fast and strong boat of steel and iron, armed with a beak, destined to carry tea and other high-freighted merchandise in time of peace, and in war to have her station wherever the merchantmen of the hostile Power congregate. The name of the as yet unfinished cruiser is the " Jaroslaw." The Russian Volunteer Fleet has four other vessels, named like this, after the place which has contributed the funds required to build or buy them. These are the " Moscow," the " Nijni Novgorod," the " Russia," and, lastly, the " St. Petersburg," formerly the "Thuringia" of the Hamburg-America Company, which is lying here now under repair immediately opposite the slip on which the " Jaroslaw" is being built. The " Jaroslaw" is sufficiently advanced to enable the visitor to form an idea of her size and general design. She is about 310 feet long, and her greatest width is 12·5 metres. The depth is 8·2 mètres, and the draught 6 mètres. The displacement is 3,150 tons. She is built with fine lines, and has an overhanging stern. She is strengthened with a double bottom, and her plates are $\frac{2}{3}$ inch thick. It is stated that she has eight bulkheads, but I was not able to check this number by observation. The engines are not yet in her. She will not, indeed, be launched for some time. When the engines arrive from Marseilles they are expected to indicate 3,000 horse-power, and to give the " Jaroslaw " a speed of from 15 knots to $15\frac{1}{2}$ knots an hour, which would be sufficient, if maintained, to enable her to overhaul our fastest mail boats, although the most recent of these have exceeded that rate on their trial trips. The armament will weigh 150 tons, and will consist of four cannon and two mortars. M. Lagarne is the engineer by whom she has been built. There are no very noticeable novelties in the design of the " Jaroslaw ": she is not from the point of view of naval science so remarkable as the " Amiral Duperré "—a great turret-ship for the French Government just launched from the La Seyne yard. It is as an instance of the determination of Russia to be in a position to cause annoyance to a maritime foe that she is worthy of observation, and the danger she exemplifies will probably best be met in England by the general adoption of the plan for strengthening and arming our mail steamers and merchant steamers.'

E. UNITED STATES.

The American Navy, which led the way in the construction of fast cruisers, has for some time remained in a stationary condition. The same remark indeed applies to the entire *matériel* of the fleet. The Congress of the United States in 1870 determined that the normal strength of the fleet should consist of ten ships of the first rate, which would be employed as flagships on foreign stations, and which were not to exceed 3,500 tons displacement. There were to be twenty ships of the second rate of 2,000 tons. Congress, however, was not prepared to vote the necessary sum for carrying out this programme, so that the fleet has been gradually declining, owing to the inevitable changes consequent on lapse of time and the breaking up of worn-out vessels. The Naval Department was absolutely compelled to supplement the insufficient appropriations of Congress by the sale of thirty small monitors, which were the least serviceable vessels of the type, and by disposing of some flush-decked corvettes of the 'Florida' (formerly ' Wampanoag ') class. At the trial in February, 1868, the latter ship maintained, during 37 hours, a mean speed of 16 knots, and for a short time attained the extraordinary speed of 17·7. The vibration, however, was so considerable that the form of the hull was sensibly changed. The consumption of coal was so great— 175 tons in 24 hours—that it was necessary to stow a certain quantity in the stoke-hole ; and the coal-endurance was reduced to 950 miles at full speed, and 2,600 miles at ten knots. In order to increase the limited accommodation in these ships, they were fitted with spar decks, four boilers were removed, and they were strengthened with stringer plates. The speed of the vessels after these alterations was from eleven to twelve knots. They carry 22 guns and increased supplies of provisions and coals. The individuals of this class, as originally designed, were to have a length of 342 feet, and a displacement of 4,000 tons. One of them, the ' Tennessee,' was flag-

The 'Wam panoag.'

ship in Chinese waters in 1878. An American newspaper reported, that 'under favourable circumstances she can steam eight knots an hour, but her consumption of coal to maintain that speed is as great, if not greater, than the ordinary simple engines would require.'

The 'Tren-ton.'

The most important cruising ship is the 'Trenton': illustrated by the longitudinal view and plans of spar and gun decks, showing the number and position of the guns. This vessel was designed by the late Isaiah Hanscom, Chief Constructor of the Navy, was built at the Brooklyn Navy Yard, by Naval Constructor Samuel H. Pook, and was launched January 1, 1876.

Figs. 307, 308, and 309.

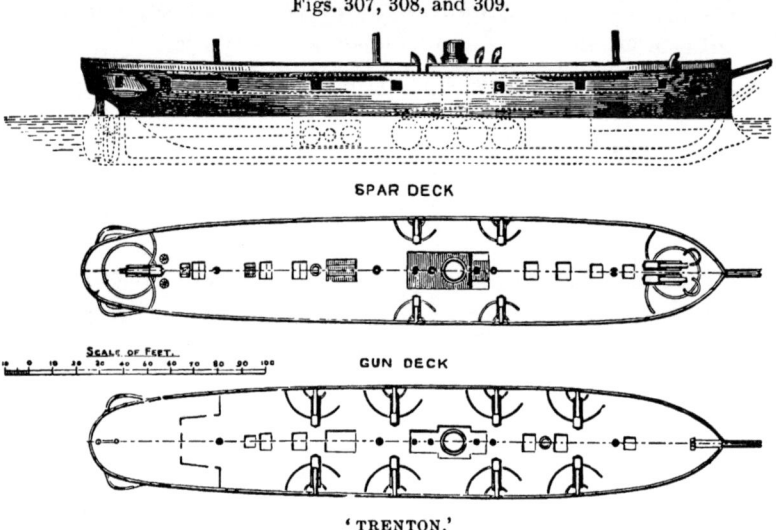

SPAR DECK

GUN DECK

SCALE OF FEET.

'TRENTON.'

The following is a general description, giving the principal dimensions :—

The hull is built of wood, has a ram bow, and is ship-rigged. The model is not sharp, and the dead rise amidships is scarcely perceptible ; but the keel increases in depth from 1 ft. 8 in. forward to 2 ft. 8 in. aft. She has large breadth of beam in proportion to her length, the ratio being 1 to 5·27. The greatest immersed transverse section is 137 ft. 10 in. from the stern-post, and the centre of buoyancy is 10 ft. 4 in. aft of this section. The forward bulkhead of the fire-room is watertight. The ram is constructed of wood and armed with a heavy composition casting. It is so designed that if broken off the ship would probably not leak much ; longitudinally it is strong, but laterally it is not. It projects eight feet forward of the stem, and its point is about nine feet below the water-line. The principal dimensions of the ship are as follows :—

Length of hull between perpendiculars . . .	253 feet
„ over all	271 ft. 6 in.
Breadth, extreme	48 feet
Depth of hold, from gun-deck	23 ft. 4 in.
Greatest immersed transverse section . .	780 sq. ft.
Area at load water-line	9,576 sq. ft.
Total sail-area of eleven principal sails . .	24,148 sq. ft.
Displacement	3,900 tons
Draught of water, forward	18 ft. 5 in.
„ aft	20 ft. 8 in.

This consists of a single four-bladed screw-propeller, operated by a three-cylinder compound engine, which is horizontal, back-acting, and has the high-pressure between the two low-pressure cylinders. The cylinders are designed to develop equal power. The low-pressure cranks are placed at a right-angle and the high-pressure crank bisects the angle between them. There are two tubular surface-condensers, which may be connected if desired. The main valves are common, double-ported slides, the high-pressure being fitted with the Mayer adjustable cut-off. The air, feed, and bilge pumps are worked from arms on the side-rods. There are two independent centrifugal circulating-pumps, with a capacity of about 2,500 gallons per minute when used on the bilge. The reversing gear is operated by a pair of oscillating engines, and the main engine is easily and rapidly managed.

Motive power and machinery.

There are eight cylindrical tubular boilers, having three furnaces each. They are arranged forward of the engine in a fore-and-aft fire-room, four on a side, and all connect with one smoke-pipe. The highest point of the boilers is about two feet below the water-line, and they are protected laterally by at least twelve feet of coal. The combined capacity of the steam bilge-pumps of the ship is about 3,200 gallons per minute. The ship is provided also with a steam windlass, a steering engine, two rotary steam winches, and a distilling apparatus. The following are the principal dimensions :—

Boilers.

Diameter of high-pressure cylinder . .	58½ inches
„ low-pressure cylinder . .	78 inches
Stroke of pistons	4 feet
Diameter of crank-shaft	18½ inches
„ screw-propeller . . .	19 ft. 6 in.
Pitch of screw-propeller, mean . . .	25 feet
Total condensing-surface	7,000 sq. ft.
Diameter of boilers	12 feet
Length of boilers	10 ft. 3 in.

Total grate-surface	.	.	.	.	498 sq. ft.
„ heating-surface	.	.	.	.	12,400 sq. ft.
Steam pressure in boilers		.	.	.	70 lbs.
Number of revolutions on trial at sea (maximum)				.	60
Indicated horse-power	„		„	.	3,100
Speed in knots, per hour	„		„	.	14

Arma-
ment.

The armament consists of eleven eight-inch muzzle-loading rifles, which were converted on the Palliser system from 11-inch cast-iron smooth-bores. There are four light guns for saluting purposes. Four of the rifles are mounted on each broadside of the gun-deck, two on the bow on the spar-deck, and one as a stern-chaser on the same deck. The particulars of the guns are as follows :—

Weight of each gun	.	.	.	7·7 tons
Total weight of guns, exclusive of carriages	.			85 tons
Weight of battering projectiles		.	.	179 lbs.
„ charge, maximum	.		.	35 lbs.
„ broadside, from six guns	.		.	1,074 lbs.
Range, at 3° elevation		.	.	1,880 yards
„ . at 5° elevation		.	.	2,850 yards
Muzzle velocity per second	.		.	1,450 feet

The
'Vandalia'
class.

After the 'Trenton' the cruising ships of the most value at present afloat are the 'Vandalia,' the 'Swatara,' the 'Marion,' the 'Quinnebaug,' and the 'Galena.' The 'Mohican' is on the blocks, but cannot as yet be counted in the list.

These ships were commenced in the navy yards in 1872–73; the 'Swatara' was completed and commissioned in 1874, the 'Vandalia' and the 'Marion' in 1875, and the others later. They are all wood-built and ship-rigged. The length of each vessel is 216 feet, breadth 38 feet, and displacement 1,900 tons, except the 'Vandalia,' which has more breadth and more displacement.

The conditions imposed in the design of the machinery were a maximum speed of twelve knots per hour, and the tops of the boilers were to be two feet below the load water-level. The engines are of the horizontal, back-acting type, being originally duplicates of those of the four vessels of the 'Alaska' class, but converted from simple into compound engines. They use steam at 80 lbs. pressure above the atmosphere.

The armament is carried on a single open deck between the fore-castle and poop, there being no stern-chaser or bow gun, except one light Parrott mounted above the forecastle.

It may be instructive, as a matter of comparison, to give the dimensions and particulars of the 'Vandalia' and one of the modern

British ships of the 'Garnet' class, described under the head of British unarmoured ships.

Comparison between the U.S.S. 'Vandalia' and H.B.M.S. ' Garnet.'

	'Vandalia'	'Garnet'
Length between perpendiculars . .	216 feet	220 feet
Breadth of beam, extreme . .	39 feet	40 feet
Immersed midship section . .	496 sq. ft.	486 sq. ft.
Depth of hold . . .	20 feet	21 feet
Draught, forward (load line) .	16 ft. 3 in.	15 ft. 6 in.
„ aft (load line) .	17 ft. 4½ in.	17 feet
Weight of hull . . .	—	1,110 tons
Displacement . . .	2,033 tons	2,120 tons [1]
Area of principal sails . .	14,792 sq. ft.	13,228 sq. ft.
Engines :—		
Type	compound	compound
Number of cylinders . .	2	2
Diameter of high-pressure cylinder	42 inches	57 inches
„ low-pressure cylinder	64 inches	90 inches
Stroke of piston . . .	3 ft. 6 in.	2 ft. 9 in.
Diameter of screw-propeller .	15 ft. 6 in.	15 feet
Pitch of screw-propeller .	21 feet	15 ft. 6 in.
Maximum revolutions of engines .	58	90
„ indicated horse-power .	1,200	2,000
„ speed per hour . .	12 knots	13 knots
Boilers :—		
Type	cylindrical, tubular	cylindrical, tubular
Number . . .	10	6
Diameter . . .	8 feet	10 feet
Length . . .	8 ft. 1 in.	9 feet
Total grate-surface . .	245 sq. ft.	245 sq. ft.
„ heating-surface .	5,982 sq. ft.	6,120 sq. ft.
Space occupied by machinery and coal	25,000 c. ft.	26,500 c. ft.
Armament :—		
Number and description of guns	one 8-in. rifle / six 9-in. smooth-bores / one 5·3-in. Parrott rifle	two 7-in. / ten 64-pr. / rifles.
Cost :—		
Hull, spars, boats, etc. . .	$344,312	$321,776
Machinery . . .	149,319	135,555
Total . .	$493,631 = £98,726	$457,331 = £91,466

The above comparison will serve as an example to show several important advantages possessed by British cruisers. Here are two

[1] The displacement of the 'Garnet' when building was registered in the Navy List as 1,865 tons, and the engine-power 2,100. It is now registered as recorded above.

modern vessels of very nearly the same tonnage, displacement, rig
and boiler-grate area, on which engine-power is based, but built of
different material and of quite different proportions. One is wood-
built and therefore subject to the usual decay and the cost resulting
therefrom. The other is built on the composite system, and as a
consequence has much greater strength to sustain engine-power, and
hence the line shafting, being on a rigid foundation, is not liable
to be forced out of alignment, while the frames, beams, bulkheads,
etc., being of iron and the planking of teak, which is equal to live
oak, far greater durability is secured. Again, the armament of the
' Garnet' is composed of modern rifled guns of long range and great
penetrating power, two guns being able to fire on a line with the
keel, one at the bow and the other at the stern. The ' Vandalia' is
armed with one converted rifle and six cast-iron smooth-bores, none of
which can be fired on a line with the keel. The ' Garnet' is provided
with a two-bladed lifting screw, while the ' Vandalia' is fitted with a
four-bladed propeller arranged to revolve when the ship is under
sail.

Both ships are engined on the compound system, and have the
same boiler-power as measured by the grate-area; but the engine
proportions differ very materially, owing principally to the difference
in the kind of coal used and the type of screw-propeller employed.
The quality of coal used by the English can be consumed at the rate
of 23 lbs. per hour on the square foot of grate, and the engines
are proportioned so as to work economically at this rate of combustion;
while the anthracite used in American war vessels can be consumed
only at the rate of $11\frac{1}{2}$ lbs. per hour on the square foot of grate,
without the aid of the steam blast in either case. The American
anthracite gives on an average from 12 to 20 per cent. of refuse,
while the best English coal produces only from six to twelve
per cent. It will thus be seen that the English possess a great
advantage in regard to motive power, the same boiler-grate area
requiring proportionally larger engines than are employed by the
Americans, and hence affording greater speed.

The large margin which exists between the engine-power of the
two ships and the maximum speed realised cannot be so readily
accounted for. The greatest speed reported on the trial of the
' Garnet' was thirteen knots, while the ' Vandalia' has realised only
twelve knots on the measured mile. Better results were achieved
by the ' Quinnebaug,' another ship of this class. The following is a
summary of a trial which took place on December 6, 1878; duration
of trial, $8\frac{1}{2}$ hours; steam-pressure on boilers, 80 lbs.; vacuum in con-

densers, 25·7 inches; revolutions per minute, mean 58, maximum 62·5; indicated horse-power, mean 937, maximum 1,096; mean speed for the whole run, 11·78 knots; maximum speed per hour, 13·2 knots; coal consumed per square foot of grate, 11 lbs.; kind of coal used, anthracite. From the foregoing figures it will be seen that with good bituminous coal the speed of this vessel will equal if not surpass any wooden war-vessel of her type and displacement afloat.

The record of the 'Vandalia' affords a good illustration of the efficiency of the type of machinery employed for her. This ship was first commissioned in 1875, and returned home, after a full three years' cruise, late in 1878, in good order, having steamed during her absence the very unusual distance of 26,230 knots. During the entire interval she was never detained a single day in port on account of repairs to the engines or boilers, or for work required in the engineer's department. A record equal to this can rarely be found on the logs of any other American ship of war. There can be no more convincing proof needed that the engines and boilers were properly designed and well built, and had excellent management and care during the cruise. The 'Quinnebaug' will doubtless prove as successful.

It should be mentioned that the boilers of the 'Galena' differ from those of the other vessels in having two furnaces in each instead of one, the shells being of the same dimensions. This arrangement possesses an advantage in some respects, but a disadvantage in view of the very contracted furnace and ash-pit.

The only other vessels in the cruising fleet of modern date are the 'Adams,' the 'Alliance,' the 'Essex,' the 'Enterprise,' and the 'Nipsic,' which are wood-built, and the 'Alert,' and the 'Ranger,' which are iron-built vessels. Smaller vessels.

The wood-built vessels are 185 feet between the perpendiculars, 35 feet extreme beam, have a mean draught of 12 ft. 9 in., and a displacement of 1,375 tons. They are engined on the compound system from the same drawings. The fixed single screw-propellers, 14 feet in diameter by 19 feet pitch, are operated by a pair of engines, having cylinders of 34 and 51 inches diameter respectively, and 42 inches stroke. The steam is furnished by eight boilers of the same type as those in the 'Vandalia' class, having one furnace each, with 192 square feet of grate surface. The boilers of this type have been tested by hydrostatic pressure up to 180 lbs. per square inch without any signs of yielding.

The 'Nipsic' of this class is exceptional in the fact that she has six boilers of larger diameter, with two furnaces to each ; but in this case the tops of the boilers are, at light draught, fourteen inches above the water-line, and at deep load draught, only six inches below the water-line.   This feature is objected to by commanding officers.

These vessels are barque-rigged, spread 1,769 square yards of canvas, and have an average maximum speed of about 10·5 knots.

The armament of all except the ' Nipsic ' consists of one 11-inch and four 9-inch smooth-bores, and one 60-pdr. rifle.   The ' Nipsic ' carries six 9-inch smooth-bores and one 8-inch and one 60-pdr. rifle.

The ' Alert,' and the ' Ranger '—iron-built vessels with unsheathed bottoms—are each 175 feet in length by 32 feet beam, with a mean load draught of 12 ft. 9 in., and a displacement of 1,020 tons.   They are propelled by a single fixed screw-propeller, operated by a pair of compound engines, having cylinders $28\frac{1}{4}$ and $42\frac{1}{2}$ inches in diameter respectively by 42 inches stroke, and a maximum indicated horse-power of 656, giving a speed of 10·5 knots.   The armament consists of one 11-inch and two 9-inch smooth-bores and one 60-pdr. rifle.

Figs. 310 and 311.

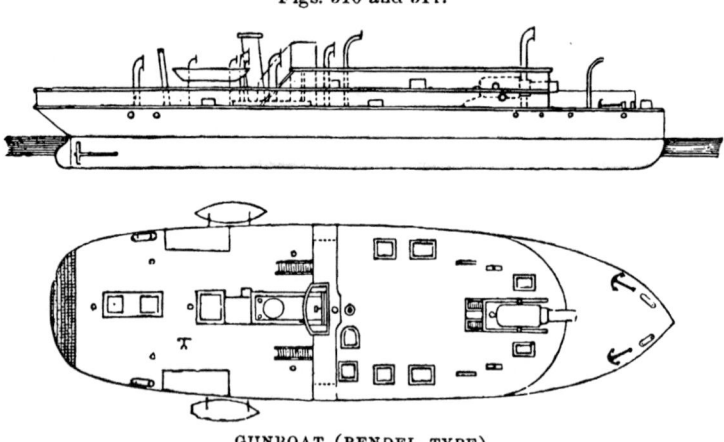

GUNBOAT (RENDEL TYPE).

Gunboats designed by Mr. Rendel.   The above engravings represent a type of gunboat which—with various dimensions and power of armament—is found in many navies. The design is attributed to Mr. G. Rendel, of Elswick.   The principle is that the gunboat should be practically a floating gun-carriage, with fair speed and great handiness.   The tonnage varies from 250 to twice that figure.   The gun carried in the earlier examples was of 12 tons, in the later British gunboats of the type it is of 18 tons, in other countries it is even heavier.

The newest gun-vessels built for the Chinese Government are described as follows in the *Times* of July 26, 1881 :—

'An important addition has just been made to the fleet of gun-vessels with which the Chinese navy has been supplied by Sir W. G. Armstrong and Co. during the last few years. Already 11 vessels have been sent out from time to time, differing in details, but uniting the peculiarity of extraordinary gun-power in diminutive craft. The two new vessels differ essentially from the preceding 11 in combining great speed with great gun-power. They resemble the others, however, in being wholly unarmoured. Their displacement is 1,350 tons. They are built of steel, and are propelled by twin screws driven by compound engines of, together, 2,600 indicated horse-power. They each carry two 26 ton 10-inch breech-loading guns, mounted upon centre pivots, one forward and one aft. Each of these heavy guns commands a nearly all-round fire. The charge of the gun is 180 lbs. of powder, and the weight of projectile 400 lbs.; the penetrative power equal to piercing 18 inches of solid, unbacked iron plate. They carry besides, in each, four 40-pdr. breech-loading guns, two 9-pdr. breech-loading guns, two Nordenfeldts, and four Gatlings, and furthermore two steam cutters fitted with spar torpedoes. The engines, boilers, magazines, and machinery are entirely below the water-line, and are further protected by a steel-plate under-water deck, the space between which and the main deck is divided into numerous watertight compartments, in which coal is stored, thus adding to the protection afforded by the deck. Hydraulic steering gear is provided and placed below the water-line, with alternative hand gear and tiller. The vessels are also armed with a formidable steel knife-edged spur or ram. The coal-bunkers take 300 tons of coal, and with that quantity the vessels can run continuously at a speed of about eight knots for four weeks together.

'On the 14th and 15th of July 1881, the new vessels went through a complete course of trials off the mouth of the Tyne, under Admiralty inspection. Their speed was tested over a course of $10\frac{3}{4}$ knots, and was shown to be, with all weights on board, on the average of two runs each, over 16 knots in one vessel, and 16 knots in the other. The guns were fired with battering charges abeam, ahead, and astern, and at different elevations up to the *maximum*. Not the slightest sign of weakness was exhibited in any part of their structure. The handiness of power of manœuvring was found remarkable. With engines stopped suddenly they were brought up in about $3\frac{1}{2}$ lengths. Reversing the engines brought them up in about $1\frac{1}{2}$ lengths. With one engine driving ahead and the other astern, they circled rapidly to port or to starboard in their own length. With the hydraulic gear, the rudder was put over from hard-a-port to hard-a-starboard in eight seconds. The vessels were kept easily circling round a drifting target at about 150 yards, while the target was being riddled by the machine-guns.

'Without claiming too much for these vessels, it should be remarked of them that the penetrative power and range of their guns, measured by the accepted official standard, exceed those of any gun yet afloat, except those of the English "Inflexible" and the Italian "Duilio." No unarmoured ship carries guns that can be compared for a moment with them, and no armoured ship equals the vessels in speed. The nearest is the "Duilio," of nine times their size. Thus their vastly superior gun-power would make them most formidable to the largest unarmoured vessels, and their superior speed and greater range and power of artillery would enable them to, in some measure, cope with an ironclad, since they could ordinarily choose their own distance, and from their diminutiveness would be very hard to hit ; nor would a single shot by any means disable them, owing to the under-water and other protection given to their vital parts. As skirmishers to open attack, or, as cavalry to harass a retreat, they would prove valuable adjuncts to a first-class navy, and they are not subject to the rapid depreciation which the progress of artillery imposes upon a costly and necessarily limited ironclad fleet.

'The vessels are being commissioned by Admiral Ting with officers and crews sent from China, and Admiral Ting will shortly call in at Portsmouth for the purpose of paying his respects and showing his vessels.'

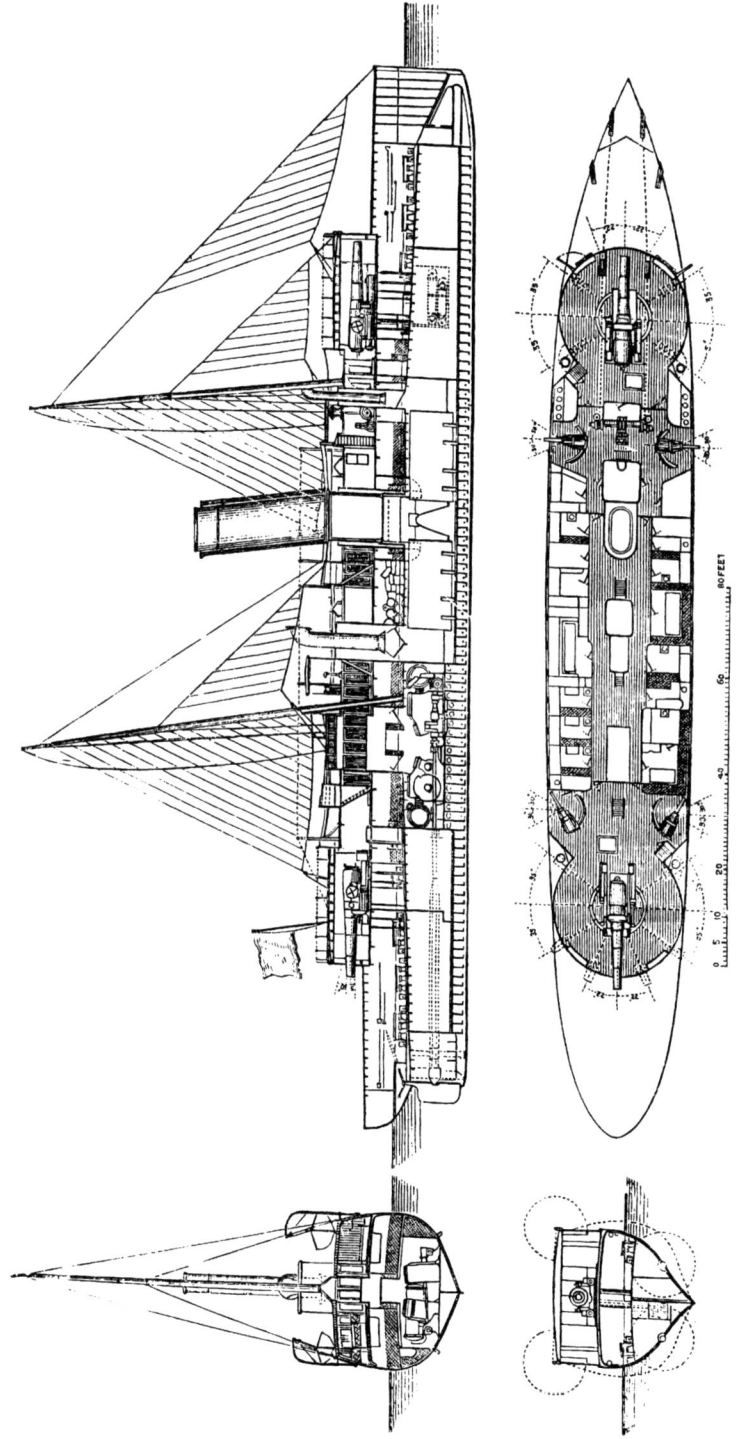

CHINESE GUN VESSEL.

TABLES OF SHIPS,

BRITISH AND FOREIGN.

ENGLAND.—*Armoured Ships*

Class	Name.	Displacement	Indicated Horse-power	Draught of Water	Length	Breadth	Where Built	Maker of Engines
		tons		ft. in	ft. in.	ft. in.		
Turret-ship	Ajax	8,490	6,000	24 0	280 0	66 0	Pembroke .	Penn. .
,,	Agamemnon . . .	8,490	6,000	24 0	280 0	66 0	Chatham .	Penn. .
Turret	Colossus . . .	9,150	6,000	26 3	325 0	68 0	Portsmouth	?
,,	Cyclops . . .	3,480	1,660	16 4	225 0	45 0	Blackwall .	Elder
,,	Devastation . .	9,330	6,650	27 6	285 0	62 3	Portsmouth	Penn.
,,	Dreadnought . .	10,820	8,200	26 9	320 0	63 10	Pembroke .	Humphreys
,,	Glatton . . .	4,910	2,870	19 0	245 0	54 0	Chatham .	Laird
,,	Gorgon . . .	3,480	1,650	16 4	225 0	45 0	Jarrow .	Ravenhill .
,,	Hecate	3,480	1,750	16 4	225 0	45 0	Poplar .	Ravenhill .
,,	Hydra	3,480	1,470	16 4	225 0	45 0	Glasgow .	Elder.
,,	Inflexible	11,400	8,000	25 5	320 0	75 0	Portsmouth	Elder.
,,	Majestic	9,150	6,000	26 3	325 0	68 0	Pembroke .	?
Masted turret-ship	Monarch	8,320	7,840	26 0	330 0	57 6	Chatham .	Humphreys
,,	Neptune	9,170	9,000	25 0	300 0	63 0	Poplar .	Penn. .
Turret-ship	Prince Albert . . .	3,880	2,130	20 4	240 0	48 1	Poplar .	Humphreys
Masted turret ship	Scorpion	2,750	1,450	16 11	224 6	42 4½	Birkenhead	Laird .
Turret-ship	Thunderer . . .	9,330	6,270	27 0	285 0	62 3	Pembroke .	Humphreys
Masted turret-ship	Wivern	2,750	1,450	16 8	224 6	42 4	Birkenhead	Laird .
Turret and ram	Conqueror . . .	6,200	4,500	24 0	270 0	58 0	Chatham .	?
,,	Hotspur	4,010	3,500	20 8	235 0	50 0	Glasgow .	Napier .
,,	Rupert	5,440	4,630	23 7	250 0	53 0	Chatham .	Napier .
Torpedo-ram	Polyphemus . . .	2,610	5,500	20 6	240 0	40 0	Chatham .	Humphreys
Turret-ships for Colonial defence	Abyssinia . .	2,900	950	14 6	225 0	42 0	Poplar .	Dudgeon .
	Cerberus . . .	3,340	1,370	15 3	225 0	45 0	Jarrow .	Maudslay .
	Magdala	3,340	1,440	15 3	225 0	45 0	Blackwall .	Ravenhill .

with Hulls of Iron or Steel.

Date of Completion	Cost		Armour			Backing	Armament	Speed
	Hull	Machinery	Side	Bulkhead	Turret			
	£	£	inches	inches	inches	inches		knots
Incomplete	350,000 Estimated	91,250 Estimated	18	16	16	15 to 6	4 12·5-in. 38-t. M.L.R.	? 13
Incomplete	350,000 Estimated	90,250 Estimated	18	16	16	15 to 6	4 12·5-in. 38-t. M.L.R.	? 13
Incomplete 1871	? 136,426	? 17,600	18 8 and 6	16½ 9 and 8 on breast-work	14 9 and 10	9 to 14 9 to 11	? 4 33-t. B.L.R. guns 4 10-in. 18-t. M.L.R.	? 14 11·03
1873 Complete	290,660 450,965 Estimated	63,188 107,000 Estimated	12 and 10 14, 13, 11, 10	— —	14 and 12 14	18 to 16 18 to 15	4 12-in. 35-t. M.L.R. 4 12·5-in. 38-t. M.L.R.	13·84 14·52
1872 1872	189,133 122,904	30,396 15,663	12 to 10 8 and 6	— 9 and 8 on breast-work	14 and 12 9 and 10	18 to 20 11 to 9	2 12-in. 25-t. M.L.R. 4 10-in. 18-t. M.L.R.	12·11 11·14
1872	124,906	15,687	8 and 6	9 and 8 on breast-work	9 and 10	11 to 9	4 10-in. 18-t. M.L.R.	10·90
1872	124,454	16,918	8 and 6	9 and 8 on breast-work	9 and 10	11 to 9	4 10-in. 18-t. M.L.R.	11·20
1881	458,100 Estimated	129,085 Estimated	24, 20, 16	22, 18, 14	16	17 to 25 on sides, 16 to 24 on bulk-heads, 18 on turrets	4 80-t. guns . .	? 14
Incomplete 1869	? 279,903	? 74,672	18 7 to 4	16½ —	14 10 and 8	9 to 4 12	? 4 43-t. B.L.R. guns 1 7-in. 6½-t. M.L.R. 2 9-in. 12-t. M.L.R. 4 12-in. 25-t. M.L.R.	? 14 14·94
—	Purchased	—	12 to 8	8	11 and 13	11 to 13 on sides, 15 to 13 on turrets	4 12·5-in. 38-t. M.L.R. 2 9-in. 12-t. M.L.R.	? 14·2
1866 1865	178,537 92,033	24,129 18,540	4½ 4½ and 3	— ?	5½ and 4½ 5	18 9	4 9-in. 12-t. M.L.R. 4 9-in. 12-t. M.L.R.	11·65 10·51
1877 1865	300,084 98,118	52,458 18,396	12 and 10 4½ and 3	— —	14 and 12 5	18 to 16 9	4 12·5-in. 38-t. M.L.R. 4 9-in. 12-t. M.L.R.	13·40 10·06
Incomplete	?	?	12 to 8½	11½ to 10½	12	10 to 13½ on sides, 9 on bulk-heads	? 2 43-t. B.L.R. guns	?
1871	135,067	36,461	11 and 8	—	8	15 to 12 on sides, 10 on turret	2 12-in. 25-t. M.L.R. 2 64-pdr. 71-cwt. M.L.R.	12·65
1874	193,171	39,506	12 to 9 & two thick-nesses of 8 and 6	—	8 and 4 in two thick-nesses	14 to 10 in two thick-nesses	2 10-in. 18-t. M.L.R. 2 64-pdr. 71-cwt. M.L.R.	13·59
Incomplete	80,000 Estimated	54,000 Estimated	3 & 2 on turtle-back, 3 on shields	—	—	None	(Machine-guns) .	? 17
1870	?	?	7 and 6	8 and 7 breast-work	10 and 8	11 to 9	4 10-in. 18-t. M.L.R.	9·59
1870	?	?	8 to 6	9 to 8 breast-work	10 and 9	11 to 9	4 10-in. 18-t. M.L.R.	9·75
1870	?	?	8 to 6	9 to 8 breastwork	10 and 9	11 to 9	4 10-in. 18-t. M.L.R.	10·67

ENGLAND.—*Armoured Ships with*

Class	Name	Displace-ment	Indicated Horse-power	Draught of Water	Length	Breadth	Where Built	Maker of Engines
		tons		ft. in.	ft. in.	ft. in.		
Broad ide	Achilles	9,820	5,720	27 3	380 0	58 3½	Chatham .	Penn. .
,,	Agincourt	10,690	6,870	27 9	400 0	59 5	Birkenhead	Maudslay .
,,	Alexandra	9,490	8,610	26 6	325 0	63 8	Chatham .	Humphreys
,,	Audacious	6,010	4,020	23 2	280 0	54 0	Glasgow .	Ravenhill .
,,	Belleisle	4,830	3,200	19 9	245 0	52 0	Poplar .	Maudslay .
,,	Bellerophon . . .	7,550	6,520	26 7	300 0	56 1	Chatham .	Penn. .
,,	Black Prince . . .	9,210	5,770	26 10	380 2	58 4	Glasgow .	Penn. .
,,	Defence	6,150	2,540	26 1	280 0	54 2	Jarrow .	Penn. .
,,	Hector	6,710	3,260	26 0	280 2	56 5	Glasgow .	Napier .
,,	Hercules	8,680	8,530	26 6	325 0	59 0½	Chatham .	Penn. .
,,	Invincible	6,010	4,830	22 9	280 0	54 0	Glasgow .	Napier .
,,	Iron Duke	6,010	4,270	22 7	280 0	54 0	Pembroke .	Ravenhill .
,,	Minotaur	10,690	6,700	27 5	400 0	59 4¾	Blackwall .	Penn. .
(Belted cruiser)	Nelson	7,320	6,000	24 8	280 0	60 0	Glasgow .	Elder .
,,	Northampton . . .	7,320	6,000	24 8	280 0	60 0	Glasgow .	Penn. .
Broadside	Northumberland . . .	10,580	6,560	27 9	400 4	59 5	Millwall .	Penn. .
,,	Orion	4,830	3,900	19 9	245 0	52 0	Poplar .	Maudslay .
,,	Penelope	4,470	4,700	17 6	260 0	50 0	Pembroke .	Maudslay .
,,	Resistance	6,150	2,430	26 10	280 0	54 1	Poplar .	Penn. .
(Belted cruiser)	Shannon	5,390	3,370	23 4	260 0	54 0	Pembroke .	Laird .
Broadside	Sultan	9,290	8,630	27 6	325 0	59 0½	Chatham .	Penn. .
,,	Superb	9,100	7,480	26 2	332 3	59 0	Blackwall .	?
,,	Swiftsure	6,640	4,910	26 0	280 0	55 0	Jarrow .	Maudslay .
(2 barbette towers)	Téméraire	8,540	7,700	27 2	285 0	62 0	Chatham .	Humphreys
Broadside	Triumph	6,640	4,890	26 2	280 0	55 0	Jarrow .	Maudslay .

Hulls of Iron or Steel—(continued.)

Date of Completion	Cost		Armour			Backing	Armament	Speed
	Hull	Machinery	Side	Bulkhead	Turret			
	£	£	inches	inches	inches	inches		knots
1864	375,429	69,117	4½	—	—	18	14 9-in. 12-t. M.L.R. / 2 7-in. 6½-t. M.L.R.	14·32
1868	381,700	83,777	5½	—	—	10	17 9-in. 12-t. M.L.R.	15·43
1877	394,263	120,061	12 to 6	—	—	12 and 10	10 10-in. 18-t. M.L.R. / 2 11-in. 25-t. M.L.R.	15·00
1869	193,863	52,619	8 to 6	—	—	10	10 9-in. 12-t. M.I.R. / 4 64-pdr. 71-cwt. M.L.R.	12·83
1878	Purchased	—	12, 10, 8, 4	9, 6, 5	—	16 and 9	4 12-in. 25-t. M.L.R.	12·20
1866	255,738	86,963	6	—	—	10	10 9-in. 12-t. M.L.R. / 5 7-in. 6½-t. M.L.R.	14·17
1862	283,154	74,482	4½	—	—	18	4 8-in. 9-t. M.L.R. / 24 7-in. 6½-t. M.L.R.	13·60
1862	197,879	34,357	4½	—	—	18	2 8-in. 9-t. M.L.R. / 14 7-in. 6½-t. M.L.R.	11·62
1864	237,438	45,764	4½	—	—	18	2 8-in. 9-t. M.L.R. / 16 7-in 6½-t. M.L.R.	12·36
1868	278,320	82,814	9 to 5	—	—	12 and 10	4 7-in. 6½-t. M.J..R. / 2 9-in. 12 t. M.L.R. / 8 10-in. 18-t. M.L.R.	14·69
1870	187,055	52,386	8 to 6	—	—	10	10 9-in. 12-t. M.L.R. / 4 64-pdr. 71-cwt. M.L.R.	14·09
1871	146,314	50,165	8 to 6	—	—	10	10 9-in. 12-t. M.L.R. / 4 64-pdr. 71-cwt. M.L.R.	13·64
1867	377,325	79,505	5½	—	—	10	17 9-in. 12-t. M.L.R.	14 41
—	259,652 Estimated	81,800 Estimated	9 and 6	9, 8, 6	—	13, 10, 11	4 10-in. 18-t. M.L.R. / 8 9-in. 12-t. M.L.R.	? 14·1
1878	277,138 Estimated	96,898 Estimated	9 and 6	9, 8, 6	—	13, 10, 11	4 10-in. 18-t. M.L.R. / 8 9-in. 12-t. M.L.R.	? 13·2
1868	391,481	79,871	5½	—	—	10	7 9-in. 12-t. M.L.R. / 20 8-in. 9-t. M.L.R.	14·13
Incomplete	Purchased	—	12, 10, 8, 6, 4	6 and 5	—	16 and 9	4 12-in. 25-t. M.L.R.	? 13
1868	145,993	40,855	6 and 5	—	—	10 and 11	8 8-in. 9-t. M.L.R. / 3 40-pdr. 35-cwt. M.L.R.	12·76
1862	208,250	33,765	4½	—	—	18	14 7-in. 6½-t. M.L.R. / 2 8-in. 9-t. M.L.R.	11·83
1877	230,673 Estimated	51,198 Estimated	9, 8, 6	—	—	10 and 12	7 9-in. 12-t. M.L.R. / 2 10-in. 18-t. M.L.R.	12·35
1871	281,373	76,042	9, 8, 6	—	—	12 and 10	4 9-in. 12-t. M.L.R. / 8 10-in. 18-t. M.L.R.	14·13
Incomplete	Purchased	Purchased	12, 10, 7	10, 7, 6, 5	8 on conning tower	12 to 12 in. armour, 11 to 7 in. armour, 10 in. to conning tower	16 10-in. 18-t. M.L.R.	13·8
1872	207,940	49,141	8 to 6	—	—	10 in.	10 9-in. 12-t. M.L.R. / 4 64-pdr. 71-cwt. M.L.R.	13·75
1877	352,015	102,954	11, 10, 9, 8	4, 3½, 1¼ on barbette tubes	10 fore 8 after	12 and 10 6 in. on barbette tubes	4 11-in. 25-t. M.L.R. / 4 10-in. 18-t. M.L.R.	14·5
1873	209,109	49,213	8 to 6	—	—	10	10 9-in. 12-t. M.L.R. / 4 64-pdr. 71-cwt. M.I.R.	14·07

ENGLAND.—*Armoured Ships with*

Class	Name	Displacement	Indicated Horse-power	Draught of Water	Length	Breadth	Where Built	Maker of Engines
		tons		ft. in.	ft. in.	ft. in.		
Broadside	Valiant	6,710	3,560	26 2	280 2	56 4	Poplar .	Maudslay .
(Armoured gunboat)	Viper	1,230	700	11 8	160 0	32 0	Poplar .	Maudslay .
,,	Vixen (iron and wood) .	1,250	740	11 8	160 0	32 5	Deptford Green .	Maudslay .
Broadside	Warrior	9,210	5,470	26 9	380 2	58 4	Blackwall .	Penn . .
(Armoured gunboat)	Waterwitch . . .	1,280	780	11 11	162 0	32 1	Blackwall .	Dudgeon .
Barbette ship	Collingwood . . .	9,150	7,000	—	325 0	68 9	Pembroke .	—
Armoured cruiser	Impérieuse	7,300	8,000	—	315 0	61 0	—	—
,,	Warspite	7,300	—	—	315 0	61 0	—	—

ENGLAND.—*Armoured Ships*

Class	Name	Displacement	Indicated Horse-power	Draught of Water	Length	Breadth	Where Built
		tons		ft. in.	ft. in.	ft. in.	
Broadside	Lord Warden	7,840	6,700	27 11	280 0	59 0½	Chatham .
,,	Pallas	3,790	3,580	24 3	225 0	50 0	Woolwich .
,,	Repulse	6,190	3,350	26 2	252 0	59 1½	Woolwich .
,,	Research	1,740	1,040	15 3	195 0	38 6	Pembroke .

ENGLAND.—

Class	Name	Displacement	Indicated Horse-power	Draught of Water	Length	Breadth	Where Built
		tons		ft. in.	ft. in.	ft. in.	
Frigate	Inconstant	5,780	7,360	25 6	337 4	50 3	Pembroke .
,,	Raleigh	5,200	6,160	24 7	298 0	49 0	Chatham .
,,	Shah	6,250	7,480	26 8	334 8	52 0	Portsmouth .

Hulls of Iron or Steel—(continued).

Date of Completion	Cost		Armour			Backing	Armament	Speed
	Hull	Machinery	Side	Bulkhead	Turret			
	£	£	inches	inches	inches	inches		knots
1865	271,964	48,324	4½	—	—	18	16 7-in. 6½-t. M.L.R. 2 8-in. 9-t. M.L.R.	12·65
1867	43,517	7,610	4½	—	—	10	2 7-in. 6½-t. M.L.R. 2 20-pdrs. 13-cwt. B.L.R.	9·59
1866	46,333	7,860	4½	—	—	10	2 7-in. 6½-t. M.L.R. 2 20-pdrs. 13-cwt. B.L.R.	8·89
1861	282,284	74,409	4½	—	—	18	28 7-in. 6½-t. M.L.R. 4 8-in. 9-t. M.L.R.	14·4
1867	44,253	14,5?2	4½	—	—	10	2 7-in. 6½-t. M.L.R. 2 20-pdrs. 13-cwt. B.L.R.	9·24
Building	—	—	—	—	—	—	? 4 43-t. B L.R. ? 6 6-in. B.L.R.	—
Building	400,000 Estimated		—	—	—	—	4 9·2-in. B.L.R. 6 6-in. B.L.R.	16
Building	400,000 Estimated		—	—	—	—	4 9·2-in. B.L.R. 6 6-in. B.L.R.	

with Hulls of Wood.

Maker of Engines	Date of Completion	Cost		Armour	Backing	Armament	Speed
		Hull	Machinery	Side			
		£	£	inches	inches		knots
Maudslay .	1867	247,009	68,582	4½ and 5½	31½	2 9-in. 12-t. M.L.R. 14 8-in. 9-t. M.L.R. 2 7-in. 6½-t. M.L.R.	13·50
Humphreys .	1866	143,164	39,806	4½	22	4 8-in. 9-t. M.L.R. 4 64-pdr. 64-cwt.	13·06
Penn . .	1870	156,246	27,394	6 and 4½	31	12 8-in. 9-t. M.L.R.	12·28
Watt . .	1864	55,093	10,150	4½	19½	4 7-in. 6½-t. M.L.R.	10·33

Unarmoured Ships.

When Built	Maker of Engines	Cost		Material of Hull	Armament	Speed
		Hull	Machinery			
		£	£			knots
1868	Penn	138,585	74,739	Iron sheathed with wood	10 9-in. R.M.L. ; 6 7-in. 6½-t. R.M.L.	16·51
1873	Humphreys	147,248	46,138	Iron sheathed with wood	2 9-in. 12-t. R.M.L. 14 7-in. 90 cwt. R.M.L. 6 64-pdrs.	15·50
1873	Ravenhill	177,912	57,333	Iron sheathed with wood	2 9-in. 12-t. R.M.L. 16 7-in. 6½-t. R.M.L. 8 64-pdrs.	16·45

ENGLAND.—*Unarmoured*

Class	Name	Displace-ment	Indicated Horse-power	Draught of Water	Length	Breadth	Where Built
		tons		ft. in.	ft. in.	ft. in.	
Corvette	Active	3,080	4,010	21 4	270 0	42 0	Thames Co., Blackwall .
,,	Amethyst	1,970	2,140	17 11	220 0	37 0	Devonport .
,,	Bacchante	4,130	5,250	23 5	280 0	45 6	Portsmouth .
,,	Blanche	1,760	2,160	16 5	212 0	36 0	Chatham .
,,	Boadicea	4,140	5,290	23 8	280 0	45 0	Portsmouth .
,,	Briton	1,860	2,150	17 1	210 0	36 0	Sheerness .
,,	Canada	2,380	2,300	18 6	225 0	44 6	Building, Portsmouth
,,	Carysfort	2,380	2,300	18 6	225 0	44 6	Glasgow, Elder & Co.
,,	Charybdis	2,250	1,360	20 2	200 0	40 4	Chatham .
,,	Cleopatra	2,380	2,300	18 10½	225 0	44 6	Glasgow, Elder & Co.
,,	Champion	2,380	2,300	18 10½	225 0	44 6	Glasgow, Elder & Co.
,,	Comus	2,380	2,300	18 10½	225 0	44 6	Glasgow, Elder & Co.
,,	Conquest	2,380	2,300	18 10½	225 0	44 6	Glasgow, Elder & Co.
,,	Constance	2,380	2,300	18 6	225 0	44 6	Chatham .
,,	Cordelia	2,380	2,300	18 6	225 0	44 6	Portsmouth
,,	Curacoa	2,380	2,300	18 10½	225 0	44 6	Glasgow, Elder & Co.
,,	Danäe	1,760	2,090	17 0	212 0	36 0	Portsmouth .
,,	Diamond	1,970	2,150	18 0	220 0	37 0	Sheerness .
,,	Dido	1,760	2,520	16 3½	212 0	36 0	Portsmouth .
,,	Druid	1,860	2,270	16 4½	220 0	36 0	Deptford .
,,	Eclipse	1,760	1,950	16 4	212 0	36 0	Sheerness .
,,	Emerald	2,120	2,170	19 0	220 0	40 0	Pembroke .
,,	Encounter	1,970	2,130	17 6	220 0	37 0	Sheerness .
,,	Euryalus	4,140	5,270	23 3	280 0	45 6	Chatham .
,,	Garnet	2,120	2,000	19 7	220 0	40 0	Chatham .
,,	Juno	2,240	1,380	18 6	200 0	40 4	Deptford .
,,	Modeste	1,970	2,180	17 10	220 0	37 0	Devonport .
,,	Opal	2,120	2,120	18 7	220 0	40 0	Sunderland, Doxford's
,,	Rover	3,460	4,960	22 11½	280 0	43 6	Blackwall, Thames Co.
,,	Ruby	2,120	1,830	18 8	220 0	40 0	Hull, Earle's Shipbuilding Co.
,,	Sapphire	1,970	2,360	18 1	220 0	37 0	Devonport .
,,	Sirius	1,760	2,330	16 4	212 0	36 0	Portsmouth .
,,	Spartan	1,760	1,990	16 9	212 0	36 0	Deptford .
,,	Tenedos	1,760	2,040	16 10	212 0	36 0	Devonport .
,,	Thalia	2,240	1,600	18 3	200 0	40 4	Woolwich .
,,	Thetis	1,860	2,270	17 6	220 0	36 0	Devonport .
,,	Tourmaline	2,120	1,970	18 8	220 0	40 0	Middlesbro', Dixon & Co.
,,	Turquoise	2,120	1,990	19 1	220 0	40 0	Hull, Earle's Shipbuilding Co.
,,	Volage	3,080	4,530	21 5	270 0	42 0	Blackwall, Thames Co.
,,	Wolverene	2,540	1,490	20 11	225 0	40 9	Woolwich .
Special screw despatch vessel	Iris	3,730	7,000 (twin screw)	22 0	300 0	46 0	Pembroke .

Ships—(continued).

When Built	Maker of Engines	Cost		Material of Hull	Armament	Speed
		Hull	Machinery			
		£	£			knots
1869	Humphreys	85,795	40,361	Iron cased with wood	18 64-pdr. R.M.L. .	14·97
1873	Rennie .	49,129	20,417	Wood	14 64-pdr. R.M.L. .	13·24
1876	Rennie .	152,454	76,954	Iron cased with wood	14 7-in. 90-cwt. R.M.L.	15·00
1867	Ravenhill .	42,769	22,420	Wood	12 64-pdr. R.M.L. .	13·63
1875	Rennie .	153,167	70,409	Iron cased with wood	14 7-in. 90-cwt. R.M.L. 2 64-pdrs.	14·89
1869	Rennie .	39,299	21,356	Wood	14 64-pdr. R.M.L. .	13·13
Building	Rennie .	78,000 Estimated	26,500 Estimated	Steel and iron cased with wood	? ?	13·00
1878	Elder & Co.	84,512	29,942	Steel and iron cased with wood	2 7-in. 90-cwt. R.M.L. 12 64-pdrs.	13·00
1859	Miller .	36,112	25,193	Wood	17 64-pdrs. . . .	13·40
1878	Humphreys	86,126	27,798	Steel and iron cased with wood	2 7-in. 90-cwt. R.M L. 12 64-pdrs.	13·00
1878	Elder & Co.	84,288	29,695	Steel and iron cased with wood	2 7-in. 90-cwt. R.M.L. 12 64-pdrs.	13·00
1878	Elder & Co.	84,497	29,477	Steel and iron cased with wood	2 7-in. 90-cwt. R.M.L. 2 64 pdrs.	13·00
1878	Humphreys	83,707	27,205	Steel and iron cased with wood	2 7-in. 90-cwt. R.M.L. 12 64-pdrs.	13·00 Est.
Building	Penn . .	78,000 Estimated	32,000 Estimated	Steel and iron cased with wood	? ?	13·00 Est.
Building	Rennie .	78,000 Estimated	26,500 Estimated	Steel and iron cased with wood	? ?	13·00 Est.
1878	Humphreys	85,833	27,098	Steel and iron cased with wood	2 7-in. 90-cwt. R.M.L. 12 64-pdrs.	13·00
1867	Napier .	43,513	21,207	Wood	12 64-pdrs. . . .	13·17
1874	Hawthorn .	50,607	26,189	Wood	14 64-pdrs. . . .	12·98
1869	Humphreys	36,417	19,574	Wood	12 64-pdrs. . . .	13·68
1869	Maudslay .	33,794	22,231	Wood	14 64-pdrs. . . .	13·07
1867	Napier .	39,242	24,084	Wood	12 64-pdrs. . . .	13·02
1876	Thomson .	72,312	26,130	Composite	12 64-pdrs. . . .	13·88
1873	Rennie .	43,271	19,827	Wood	14 64-pdrs. . . .	13·19
1877	Easton and Anderson	132,254	76,959	Iron cased with wood	2 7-in. 90-cwt. R.M.L.	14·72
1877	Hawthorn .	65,683	27,779	Composite	12 64-pdrs. . . .	13·21
1867	Humphreys	51,361	21,108	Wood	8 64-pdrs. . . .	10·87
1873	Napier .	49,518	22,094	Wood	14 64-pdrs. . . .	12·79
1875	Napier .	68,574	27,375	Composite	14 64-pdrs. . . .	13·13
1874	Ravenhill .	104,718	65,021	Iron cased with wood	2 7-in. 90 cwt. R.M.L. 16 64-pdrs.	14·53
1876	Earle's Shipbuilding Co.	66,113	27,003	Composite	12 64-pdrs. . . .	12·28
1874	Hawthorn .	51,986	26,311	Wood	14 64-pdrs. . . .	13·58
1868	Maudslay .	58,924	22,987	Wood	12 64-pdrs. . . .	13·09
1868	Rennie .	31,000	24,569	Wood	12 64-pdrs. . . .	13·16
1870	Elder .	39,226	20,121	Wood	12 64-pdrs. . . .	13·01
1869	Napier .	47,915	21,709	Wood	8 64-pdrs. . . .	11·14
1871	Rennie .	43,963	21,147	Wood	14 64-pdrs. . . .	13·39
1875	Hawthorn .	69,998	25,771	Composite	12 64-pdrs. . . .	12·62
1876	Earle's Shipbuilding Co.	68,089	27,458	Composite	12 64-pdrs. . . .	12·32
1869	Penn . .	84,775	41,378	Iron cased with wood	18 64-pdrs. . .	15·08
1863	Ravenhill .	61,593	23,308	Wood	17 64-pdrs. . . .	11·31
1877	Maudslay .	110,868	102,318	Steel	10 64-pdrs. . . .	18·00

ENGLAND.—*Unarmoured*

Class	Name	Displacement	Indicated Horsepower	Draught of Water	Length	Breadth	Where Built
		tons		ft. in.	ft. in.	ft. in.	
Special screw despatch vessels	Mercury	3,730	7,000 (twin screw)	22 0	300 0	46 0	Pembroke
	Leander	3,748	5,000	20 6	300 0	46 0	—
	Phaeton	3,748	5,000	20 6	300 0	46 0	—
	Arethusa	3,748	5,000	20 6	300 0	46 0	—
Sloop	Albatross	940	840	14 5	160 0	31 4	Chatham
,,	Alert	1,240	310	15 0	160 0	31 11	Pembroke
,,	Cormorant	1,130	950	15 3	170 0	36 0	Chatham
,,	Daring	940	920	14 1	160 0	31 4	Blackwall, Wigram
,,	Doterel	1,130	900	15 9	170 0	36 0	Chatham
,,	Dragon	1,140	1,010	15 9	170 0	36 0	Devonport)
,,	Dryad	1,620	1,570	17 1	187 0	36 0	Devonport
,,	Egeria	940	1,010	14 3	160 0	31 4	Pembroke
,,	Espiègle	1,137	900	15 9	170 0	36 0	Devonport
,,	Fantome	940	970	14 2	160 0	31 4	Pembroke
,,	Fawn	1,050	480	15 9	160 0	31 10	Deptford
,,	Flying Fish	940	840	14 2	160 0	31 4	Chatham
,,	Gannet	1,130	900	15 9	170 0	36 0	Sheerness
,,	Heroine	1,420	950	15 9	200 0	38 0	—
,,	Hyacinth	1,420	950	15 9	200 0	38 0	—
,,	Kingfisher	1,130	900	15 9	170 0	36 0	Sheerness
,,	Miranda	1,130	900	15 9	170 0	36 0	Devonport
,,	Mutine	1,137	900	15 9	170 0	36 0	Devonport
,,	Osprey	1,130	1,010	15 11	170 0	36 0	Sheerness
,,	Pegasus	1,130	970	15 9	170 0	36 0	Devonport
,,	Pelican	1,130	1,060	15 3	170 0	36 0	Devonport
,,	Penguin	1,130	760	16 1	170 0	36 0	Glasgow, Napier
,,	Phœnix	1,130	900	15 9	170 0	36 0	Devonport
,,	Satellite	1,420	950	15 9	200 0	38 0	Sheerness
,,	Rapid	910	460	14 6	160 0	30 4	Deptford
,,	Sappho	940	880	13 11	160 0	31 4	Blackwall, Wigram
,	Vestal	1,620	2,150	17 8	187 0	36 0	Pembroke
,,	Wild Swan	1,130	800	15 10	170 0	36 0	Glasgow, Napier
Paddle-wheel despatch vessel	Enchantress	1,000	1,320	11 1	220 0	28 2	Pembroke

Ships—(continued).

When Built	Maker of Engines	Cost (Hull)	Cost (Machinery)	Material of Hull	Armament	Speed
1878	Maudslay .	£ 103,807	£ 95,055	Steel	10 64-pdrs. . . .	knots 18·00
Building	—	—	—	Steel	10 6-in. R.B.L.	16
Building	—	—	—	Steel	10 6-in. R.B.L.	16
Building	—	—	—	Steel	10 6-in. R.B.L.	16
1873	Humphreys	28,729	9,697	Composite	2 7-in. 90-cwt. R.M.L. / 2 64-pdrs.	10·51
1856	Hawthorn	23,509	6,701	Wood	40 20-pdrs. . . .	7 68
1877	Humphreys	37,630	11,587	Composite	2 7-in. 90-cwt. R.M.L. / 4 64-pdrs.	11·31
1874	Penn. .	30,023	9,590	Composite	2 7-in. 90-cwt. R.M.L. / 2 64-pdrs.	10·64
1880	Maudslay .	39,750 Estimated	11,850 Estimated	Composite	2 7-in. 90-cwt. R.M.L. / 4 64-pdrs.	11·00
1878	Maudslay. .	36,427	13,069	Composite	2 7-in. 90-cwt. R.M.L. / 4 64-pdrs.	11·52
1866	Napier .	36,088	16,834	Wood	9 64-pdrs. . . .	11·87
1873	Humphreys	32,468	10,414	Composite	2 7-in. 90-cwt. R.M.L. / 2 64-pdrs.	11·30
Building	Making by Maudslay	37,000 Estimated	11,770 Estimated	Composite	2 7-in. 90-cwt. R.M.L. / 4 64-pdrs.	11·00
1873	Humphreys	30,343	10,197	Composite	2 7-in. 90-cwt. R.M.L. / 2 64-pdrs.	11·06
1856	Ravenhill .	21,746	6,591	Wood	4 20-pdrs. . . .	9·36
1873	Humphreys	29,444	10,001	Composite	2 7-in. 90-cwt. R.M.L. / 2 64-pdrs.	10·96
1878	Humphreys	39,581	12,889	Composite	2 7-in. 90-cwt. R.M.L. / 4 64-pdrs.	11·00
—	—	37,000 Estimated	—	Composite	—	11·00 Est.
—	—	37,000 Estimated	—	Composite	—	11·00 Est.
1879	Maudslay .	39,300 Estimated	11,850 Estimated	Composite	2 7-in. 90-cwt. R.M.L. / 4 64-pdrs.	11·00
1879	Napier .	37,000 Estimated	11,700 Estimated	Composite	2 7-in. 90-cwt. R.M.L. / 4 64-pdrs.	11·00
Building	Maudslay .	37,000 Estimated	11,770 Estimated	Composite	2 7-in. 90-cwt. R.M.L. / 4 64-pdrs.	11·00
1876	Humphreys	39,664	11,674	Composite	2 7-in. 90-cwt. R.M.L. / 4 64-pdrs.	11·64
1878	Laird	36,697	12,809	Composite	2 7 in. 90-cwt. R.M.L. / 4 64-pdrs.	11·47
1877	Humphreys	41,282	14,939	Composite	2 7-in. 90-cwt. R.M.L. / 4 64-pdrs.	12·24
1876	Hawthorn.	39,611	11,879	Composite	2 7-in. 90-cwt. R.M.L. / 4 64 pdrs.	11·00
1879	Humphreys	36,152	12,500	Composite	2 7 in. 90-cwt. R.M.L. / 4 64-pdrs.	11·00
—	—	39,300 Estimated	—	Composite	—	11·00
1860	Greenock Foundry Co.	21,132	7,367	Wood	1 7-in. 6½-t. R.M.L. / 2 40-pdrs.	9·12
1873	Humphreys	29,749	9,242	Composite	2 7-in. 90-cwt. R.M.L. / 2 64-pdrs.	10·59
1865	Maudslay .	40,482	20,208	Wood	9 64-pdr. R.M.L.	12·81
1876	Hawthorn.	39,643	11,853	Composite	2 7-in. 90-cwt. R.M.L. / 4 64-pdrs.	10·35
1862	Penn. .	30,114	14,045	Wood	—	14·02

ENGLAND.—*Unarmoured*

Class	Name	Displace-ment	Indicated Horse-power	Draught of Water		Length		Breadth		Where Built
		tons		ft.	in.	ft.	in.	ft.	in.	
Paddle-wheel despatch vessel	Helicon	1,000	1,610	10	5	220	0	28	2	Portsmouth .
,,	Lively	1,000	1,760	11	1	220	0	28	2	Sheerness .
,,	Salamis	1,000	1,440	11	2	220	0	28	2	Chatham .
,,	Vigilant	1,000	1,810	11	0	220	0	28	2	Devonport .
Torpedo vessel	Hecla	6,400	1,760	24	3	391	7½	38	9½	—
,,	Vesuvius	244	390 (twin screw)	8	6	90	0	22	0	Pembroke .
Gun-vessel	Bittern (1)	805	850 (twin screw)	10	1	170	0	29	0	Pembroke .
,,	Algerine (2)	774	750	13	0	157	0	29	6	Belfast, Harland and Wolf
,,	Arab (3)	720	660	14	0	150	0	28	6	Glasgow, Napier
,,	Avon (4)	603	530 (twin screw)	9	7	155	0	25	0	Portsmouth .

There are also (1) 12 gun-vessels of the 'Bittern' class, ranging from 805 to 865 tons displacement ; (2) 7 of the class, of from 573 tons to 610 tons. The number of gun-boats amounts to 69. There are also the troopships and

Ships—(continued).

When Built	Maker of Engines	Cost		Material of Hull	Armament	Speed
		Hull	Machinery			
1865	Ravenhill .	£ 32,326	£ 13,465	Wood	2 20-prd. R.B.L.	knots 14·50
1870	Penn. .	22,702	13,085	Wood	2 20-pdr. R.B.L.	15·24
1868	Ravenhill .	28,599	13,446	Wood	2 9-pdr. 8-cwt. R.M.L.	13·70
1871	Watt .	28,571	12,495	Wood	2 20-pdr. R.B.L.	14·79
1878	—	Purchased 126,190	Included in hull	Iron	5 64-prd. R.M.L. 1 40-pdr. R.B.L.	15·0
1874	Maudslay .	10,522	7,465	Iron	—	9·71
1869	Avonside Engine Co.	17,005	6,731	Composite	1 7-in. 6½-t. R.M.L. 2 40-pdr. R.B.L.	11·10
Build-ing	Laird .	21,750 Estimated	9,650 Estimated	Wood	1 7-in. 90-cwt. R.M.L. 2 64-pdr. R.M.L.	10·00
1874	Napier .	25,041	9,982	Composite	1 7-in. 90-cwt. R.M.L. 1 64-pdr. R.M.L.	10·39
1867	Maudslay .	16,547	5,797	Composite	1 7-in. 6½-t. R.M.L. . 1 64-pdr. R.M.L.	10·34

Algerine' class, from 774 to 780 tons ; (3) 4 of the ' Arab ' type, from 720 to 756 tons ; and (4) 22 of the ' Avon ' the Indian troopships, several small yachts, tugs, etc.

ARGENTINE REPUBLIC.—*Armoured Ships. Iron hulls.*

Class	Name	Displacement	Length	Beam	Depth in Hold	Armour Max.	Armour Min.	Backing	Draught of Water	Propeller	Indicated Horse-Power	Armament	Date of Launch	Builder	Speed	Coal Supply	Distance that can be steamed at 10 knots
		tons	ft. in.	ft. in.	ft. in.	inches	inches	in.	ft. in.						knots	tons	miles
Battery	Almirante Brown	4,200	240 0 (between perps.)	50 0	21 11	9	6	?	20 0	2	4,500	8 8-in. (11¼-t.) 6 40-pdr. Arm.	1880	Samuda	13·7	650	4,300
Monitor	Plata	1,535	180 0	43 0	—	6	4⅜	11⅞	10 6	2	750	11 9-in. Arm. (12½-t.) 2 light guns	1875	Laird	9·5	—	2,880 (full speed)
"	Andes	1,535	180 0	43 0	—	6	4⅜	11⅞	10 6	2	750	11 9-in. Arm. (12½-t.) 2 light guns	1874	Laird	9·5	—	2,880 (full speed)

ARGENTINE REPUBLIC.—*Unarmoured Ships. Iron hulls.*

Class	Name	Displacement	Length	Beam	Depth in Hold	Material of Hull	Draught of Water	Propeller	Indicated Horse-Power	Armament	Date of Launch	Builder	Speed	Coal Supply	Distance that can be steamed at 10 knots
		tons	ft. in.	ft. in.	ft. in.		ft. in.						knots	tons	miles
Gunboat	Parana	550	142 8	25 1	13 6	Iron	11 9	1	475	2 7-in. (6½-t.) 2 light guns	1874	Laird	11·0		
"	Uruguay	550	142 8	25 1	13 6	Iron	11 9	1	475	2 7-in. (6½-t.) 2 light guns	1874	Laird	11·0		
Gunboat, Rendel type	Constitucion	416	105 0	30 0	10 6	Iron	7 4½	2	420	1 11-in. Arm. (26½-t.)	1875	Laird	9·5		
"	Republica	416	105 0	30 0	10 6	Iron	7 4½	2	420	1 11-in. Arm. (26½-t.)	1876	Laird	9·5		
"	Bermejo	416	105 0	30 0	10 6	Iron	7 4½	2	420	1 11-in. Arm. (26½-t.)	1876	Rennie	9·5		
"	Picomayo	416	105 0	30 0	10 6	Iron	7 4½	2	420	1 11-in. Arm. (26½-t.)	1875	Rennie	9·5		

There are also 4 steamers with one screw, 2 paddle-wheel vessels of 200 Nom. H.-P., and 5 paddle-wheel vessels of 60 Nom. H.-P., all of older type.

AUSTRIA.—*Armoured Ships with Hulls of Iron.*

Class	Name	Displacement	Length	Beam	Depth in Hold	Armour Max.	Armour Min.	Backing	Draught of Water	Propeller	Indicated Horse-Power	Armament	Date of Launch	Cost	Speed	Coal Supply	Distance that can be steamed at 10 knots
		tons	ft. in.	ft. in.	ft. in.	inches	inches	in.	ft. in.					£	knots	tons	miles
Central battery	Tegetthoff .	7,450	286 11 (between perps.)	71 1	34 9	14½	1½	9¾	24 10	1	1,200 nom.	6 11-in. Krupp 8 light guns 6 Mitrail.	1878	247,378 (?)	14·0	670	3,300
,,	Custozza .	7,090	302 3 (between perps.)	58 0	31 2	11¾	1¼	8¼	24 7	1	4,820	8 10$\frac{3}{16}$-in. Krupp 8 light guns 4 Mitrail.	1872	414,400	14·0	584	1,624
Bow battery	Arch. Albert	6,020	285 2 (between perps.)	56 3	26 3	8	1¼	9½	22 0	1	4,060	8 9$\frac{7}{16}$-in. Krupp 8 light guns 4 Mitrail.	1872	357,600	13·5	453	1,472
,,	Don Juan of Austria	3,640	240 3	50 0	—	8	1¼	9¾	20 0	1	2,920	8 8¼-in. Krupp 6 light guns 4 Mitrail.	1875	—	13·6	380	2,000
,,	Kaiser Max .	3,640	240 3	50 0	—	8	1¼	9¾	20 0	1	2,890	8 8¼-in. Krupp 6 light guns 4 Mitrail.	1875	211,600	13·4	380	2,000
,,	Prince Eugene .	3,670	240 6	50 0	—	8	1¼	9¾	20 0	1	2,960	8 8¼-in. Krupp 6 light guns 4 Mitrail.	1877	—	13·5	380	2 000
Danube monitor	Maros . .	310	166 0	27 6	—	2½	?	7⅞	3 7	2	320	2 5⅞-in. W. 1 Mitrail.	1871	20,000	8·5		
,,	Leitha . .	310	166 0	27 6	—	2½	?	7⅞	3 7	2	320	2 5⅞-in. W. 1 Mitrail.	1871	20,000	8·5		

AUSTRIA.—*Armoured Ships with Hulls of Wood.*

Class	Name	Displacement	Length	Beam	Depth of Hold	Armour Max.	Armour Min.	Backing	Draught of Water	Propeller	Indicated Horse-Power	Armament	Date of Launch	Cost	Speed	Coal Supply	Distance that can be steamed at 10 knots
		tons	ft. in.	ft. in.	ft. in.	inches	inches	in.	ft. in.					£	knots	tons	miles
Central battery	Lissa . .	6,030	288 3 (between perps.)	56 9	—	$6\frac{1}{4}$	?	$29\frac{7}{8}$	25 3	1	4,100	12 $9\frac{7}{16}$-in. 6 light guns 4 Mitrail.	1869	412,800	13·3	489	1,420
„	Kaiser . .	5,840	254 0	58 3	—	$6\frac{1}{4}$	?	31	24 3	1	3,130	10 $9\frac{1}{16}$-in. Arm. 8 light guns	1871	337,200	12·7	—	1,519
Frigate	Arch. Ferd. Max.	5,170	262 0 (between perps.)	52 0	23 6	$4\frac{3}{4}$	?	$27\frac{7}{8}$	23 3	1	3,100	14 $7\frac{1}{16}$-in. Arm. 6 light guns 4 Mitrail.	1865	286,400	12·5		
„	Hapsburg .	5,170	262 0 (between perps.)	52 0	23 6	$4\frac{3}{4}$	?	$27\frac{7}{8}$	23 3	1	3,150	14 $7\frac{1}{16}$-in. Arm. 6 light guns 4 Mitrail.	1865	280,672	12·5		
„	Salamander .	3,040	205 9	46 0	—	$4\frac{5}{8}$	?	$22\frac{3}{4}$	20 8	1	2,060	10 $7\frac{1}{16}$-in. Arm. 6 light guns 4 Mitrail.	1861	164,800 (?)	11·4		

AUSTRIA.—*Unarmoured Ships.*

Class	Name	Displacement	Length	Beam	Depth of Hold	Material of Hull	Draught of Water	Propeller	Indicated Horse-Power	Armament	Date of Launch	Cost	Speed	Coal Supply	Distance that can be steamed at
		tons	ft. in.	ft. in.	ft. in.		ft. in.					£	knots	tons	miles
Frigate	Radetzky . .	3,140	253 0	47 0	—	Composite	20 8	1	600 nom.	15 $5\frac{7}{8}$-in. Krupp 2 light guns	1872	—	14·2		
„	Laudon . .	3,140	253 0	47 0	—	Composite	21 7	1	600 nom.	15 $5\frac{7}{8}$-in. Krupp 2 light guns	1873	—	13·6		
Spar-decked corvette	Donau . . .	2,510	233 0	41 0	—	Wood	19 8	1	400 nom.	11 $5\frac{7}{8}$-in. Krupp 1 light gun	1874	—	12·0		

,,	Saïda . . .	2,510	—	—	—	Wood	19 0	1	400 nom.	11 5⅞-in. Uchatius 1 light gun	1878	—	12·8		
,,	Dandolo . .	1,730	—	—	—	Wood	16 8½	1	230 nom.	14 5⅞-in. W. f. 1 light gun	1858	—	10·0		
,,	Arch. Frederic .	1,590	—	—	—	Wood	16 8	1	230 nom.	14 5⅞-in. W. f. 1 light gun	1857	—	9·3		
Corvette	Fasana . .	1,980	—	—	—	Wood	16 8	1	400 nom.	4 5⅞-in. Krupp 3 light guns	1870	—	12·3		
,,	Helgoland . .	1,830	—	—	—	Wood	16 8	1	400 nom.	5 5⅞-in. Krupp 1 light gun	1867	—	12·8		
,,	Zrinyi . . .	1,360	194 0	—	—	Composite	16 1	1	230 nom.	4 5⅞-in. W. f. 1 light gun	1871	—	11·7		
,,	Frundsberg . .	1,360	194 0	36 0	—	Composite	16 1	1	230 nom.	4 5⅞-in. W. f. 1 light gun	1873	—	11·8		
,,	Aurora. . .	1,360	194 0	—	—	Composite	16 1	1	230 nom.	4 5⅞-in. W. f. 1 light gun	1873	—	11·8		
Gun-vessel	Hum . . .	860	—	—		Wood	12 5	1	920	4 5⅞-in. W. f. 1 light gun	1861	—	13·0		
,,	Zara . . .	860	—	—	—	Steel	12 1	2	320 nom.	4 3½-in. Uchatius 1 light gun 2 Mitrail.	1879	—	?		
,,	Spalato . .	860	—	—	—	Steel	12 1	2	320 nom.	4 3½-in. Uchatius 1 light gun 2 Mitrail.	1879	—	?		
,,	N. N. (type Zara)	860	—	—	—	Steel	12 1	2	320 nom.	4 3½-in. Uchatius 1 light gun 2 Mitrail.	Building	—	?		
,,	Nautilus . .	580	—	—	—	Wood	11 1½	1	410	2 5⅞-in. W. f. 1 light gun	1873	—	9·7		
,,	Albatross . .	580	—	—	—	Wood	11 1½	1	580	2 5⅞-in. W. f. 1 light gun	1873	—	10·8		
,,	Kerka . . .	550	—	—	—	Wood	11 1½	1	300	2 5⅞-in. W. f. 1 light gun	1860	—	9·2		
,,	Narenta . .	550	—	—	—	Wood	11 1½	1	310	2 5⅞-in. W. f. 1 light gun	1860	—	9·2		
,,	Grille . . .	360	—	—	—	Wood	9 2½	1	320	2 5⅞-in. W. f. 1 light gun	1861	—	?		
,,	Sansego . .	360	—	—	—	Wood	9 2½	1	290	2 5⅞-in. W. f.	1861	—	9·4		
,,	Möve . . .	370	—	—	—	Wood	9 6½	1	140	2 5⅞-in. W. f. 1 light gun	1858	—	7·5		

There are also 7 paddle-wheel vessels of from 75 Nom. H.-P. to 300 Nom. H.-P., all of an old type, and each carrying 2 guns of the Uchatius pattern, of either 2¾-in. or 3½-in. bore.

BRAZIL.—*Armoured Ships with Hulls of Iron.*

Class	Name	Displacement	Length	Beam	Depth of Hold	Armour Max.	Armour Min.	Backing	Draught of Water	Propeller	Indicated Horse-Power	Armament	Date of Launch	Cost	Speed	Coal Supply	Distance that can be steamed at 10 knots
		tons	ft. in.	ft. in.	ft. in.	inches	inches	in.	ft. in.					£	knots	tons	miles
Turret	Solimoës .	3,700	240 0	58 0	13 9	12	5⅞	9¾	11 5	2	2,200	4 10-in. Whitworth	1875	—	11·2	200	
,,	Javari . .	3,700	240 0	58 0	13 9	12	5⅞	9¾	11 5	2	1,685	4 10-in. ,,	1875	—	10·4	200	
,,	Lima Barros.	1,350	180 0	36 0	—	4⅜	3	8¼	13 5	2	2,100	4 7-in. ,,	1866	—	12·0		
,,	Silvado. .	1,150	190 0	36 0	—	4⅜	3	9	10 6	2	947	4 70-pdr. ,,	1866	—	10·7		
,,	Bahia . .	1,000	178 0	35 0	11 0	4⅜	2⅞	10⅝	8 6	1	640	2 7-in. ,,	1865	—	10·5		
Central battery	Cabral . .	1,033	160 0	35 6	—	4⅜	2⅞	8¼	11 9	2	750	2 70-pdr. ,, 4 68-pdr. sm. br.	1866	—	10·5		
,,	Colombo .	1,033	160 0	35 6	—	4⅜	2⅞	8¼	12 1	2	750	4 7-in. Whitworth	1866	—	10·5		
,,	Herval . .	1,353	191 0	36 0	—	4⅜	2⅞	8⅝	9 6	2	600	4 7-in. ,,	1866	—	9·0		
,,	Mariz-é-Barros	1,444	198 10	31 0	—	4⅜	2⅞	8⅝	10 10	2	600	4 7-in. ,,	1866	—	9·0		
,,	Brazil . .	1,518	179 8	35 0	11 8	4⅜	2⅞	8⅝	12 5	1	975	4 7-in. ,, 4 68-pdr. sm. br.	1864	60,000	11·3		

BRAZIL.—*Armoured Ships with Hulls of Wood.*

Class	Name	Displacement	Length	Beam	Depth of Hold	Armour Max.	Armour Min.	Backing	Draught of Water	Propeller	Indicated Horse-Power	Armament	Date of Launch	Cost	Speed	Coal Supply	Distance that can be steamed at 10 knots
		tons	ft. in.	ft. in.	ft. in.	inches	inches	in.	ft. in.					£	knots	tons	miles
Central battery	Sete de Setembro	2,145	219 10	46 6		3⅞	?	?	15 1	2	2,000	4 9-in. Whitworth	1874	—	12·0		
,,	Tamandaré .	980	166 4	36 0	12 6	3⅞	2½	24¾	7 10	1	273	2 70-pdr. ,, 2 68-pdr. sm. br.	1865	—	8·5		
,,	Barroso . .	1,354	186 0	37 0	12 6	3⅞	2½	24¾	8 10	1	420	2 7-ir. Whitworth 3 32-pdr. ,, 2 68-pdr. sm. br.	1864	—	9·0		
River-Monitors	Alagoas .	340	120 0	28 0	5 11	4⅜	2	14½	4 10	2	75	1 70-pdr. Whitwth.	1864	—	7·5		
,,	Pará . .	340	120 0	28 0	5 11	4⅜	2	14½	4 10	2	75	1 70-pdr. ,,	1864	—	7 5		
,,	Rio Grande .	340	120 0	28 0	5 11	4⅜	2	14½	4 10	2	75	1 70-pdr. ,,	1864	—	7·5		
,,	S ta . atarina	340	120 0	28 0	5 11	4⅜	2	14½	4 10	2	75	1 70-pdr. ,,	1864	—	7·5		
,,	Clearà . .	340	120 0	28 0	5 11	4⅜	2	14½	4 10	2	75	1 7-in. ,,	1864	—	7·5		
,,	Piauhy . .	340	120 0	28 0	5 11	4⅜	2	14½	4 10	2	75	1 7-in. ,,	1864	—	7·5		

BRAZIL.—*Unarmoured Ships.*

Class	Name	Displacement	Length	Beam	Depth of Hold	Material of Hull	Draught of Water	Propeller	Indicated Horse-Power	Armament	Date of Launch	Cost	Speed	Coal Supply	Distance that can be travelled at 10 knots
		tons	ft. in.	ft. in.	ft. in.		ft. in.					£	knots	tons	miles
Corvette	Nictheroy	1,791	192 0	41 0	—	Wood	19 0	1	1,200	14 70-pdr. Whitworth / 2 7-in. „	1862	—	10·0	?	
,,	Guanabara	1,881	200 0	41 2	—	Wood	16 4	1	8,000	9 70-pdr. „	1877	—	?		
,,	Trajano	1,392	210 0	31 0	—	Wood	16 8	1	2,400	3 70-pdr. „	1873	—	14·5		
,,	Vital de Oliveira	1,402	203 5	34 2	—	Wood	13 9	1	?	4 70-pdr. „ / 2 32-pdr. / 2 68-pdr. smooth-bore	1867	—	?		
,,	Magé	791	181 0	26 11	—	Wood	11 10	1	400	2 70-pdr. Whitworth / 6 32-pdr. „	?	—	?		
,,	Belmonte	744	181 0	28 10	—	Wood	9 6	1	400	1 70-pdr. / 2 68-pdr. smooth-bore	?	—	?		

There are also some half-a-dozen screw gunboats of from 60 to 120 Nom. H.-P., and three paddle-wheel steamers of 250 Nom. H.-P.

CHILI.—*Armoured Ships with Hulls of Iron.*

Class	Name	Displacement	Length	Beam	Depth of Hold	Armour Max.	Armour Min.	Backing	Draught of Water	Propeller	Indicated Horse-Power	Armament	Date of Launch	Cost	Speed	Coal Supply	Distance that can be steamed at 10 knots
		tons	ft. in.	ft. in.	ft. in.	inches	inches	in.	ft. in.					£	knots	tons	miles
Central battery	Almirante Cochrane	3,500	210 0	45 9	21 8	9 + 1¼	4½	7¾	19 8	2	3,000	6 9-in. Armstrong / 2 light guns / 2 Mitrailleuse	1874	—	13·0	?300	
,,	Blanco Encalada	3,500	210 0	45 9	21 8	9 + 1¼	4½	7¾	19 8	2	3,000	6 9-in. Armstrong / 2 light guns / 2 Mitrailleuse	1875	—	12·0	? 00	
Turret	Huascar	2,032	200 0	35 0	20 0	4½	2½	14½	19 8	1	1,050	2 10-in. 12½-t. Armstrong guns / 2 40-pdrs.	1865	—	?18·0		

CHILI.—*Unarmoured Ships.*

Class	Name	Displacement (tons)	Length (ft. in.)	Beam (ft. in.)	Depth of Hold (ft. in.)	Material of Hull	Draught of Water (ft. in.)	Propeller	Indicated Horse-Power	Armament	Date of Launch	Cost (£)	Speed (knots)	Coal Supply (tons)	Distance that can be steamed at 10 knots (miles)
Corvette	O'Higgins .	1,101	218 6	33 4	—	Wood	17 4	1	1,200	3 8-in. Armstrong 4 40 pdr. „	1866	—	12·5		
„	Chacabuco .	1,101	218 6	33 4	—	Wood	17 4	1	1,200	3 8-in. „ 4 40-pdr. „	1866	—	12·5		
„	Magellanes .	775	190 0	28 0	—	Composite	14 9	1	1,230	1 8-in. „ 1 6-in. „ 2 light guns	1872	—	11·0		
„	Pilcomayo .	600	171 0	27 4	—	Wood	?	1	180 nom.	2 70-pdr. Armstrong 6 40-pdr. „	1874	—	?		

The war-vessels of this State have considerably altered of late, in consequence of the war between it and Peru.

CHINA.

Class	Name	Displacement (tons)	Length (ft. in.)	Beam (ft. in.)	Depth of Hold (ft. in.)	Material of Hull	Draught of Water (ft. in.)	Propeller	Indicated Horse-Power	Armament	Date of Launch	Cost (£)	Speed (knots)	Coal Supply (tons)	Distance that can be steamed at 10 knots (miles)
Gun-vessel	Wan-Niang-Tsing	1,450	222 0	30 2	17 4	Composite	13 1	—	—	1 9-t. 6 Vavasseur B.L.					
„	Foo-Poo . .	1,258	201 0	32 9	17 0	Composite	11 6	—	—	1 9-t. 6 Vavasseur B.L.					
„	Fei-Yune . .	1,258	—	—	—	Composite	—	—	—	1 9-t. 6 Vavasseur B.L.					
„	Che-An . .	—	—	—	—	Composite	—	—	—	1 9-t. 6 Vavasseur B.L.					
„	Wo-Kai . .	—	—	—	—	Composite	—	—	—	1 9-t. 6 Vavasseur B.L.					

Class	Name	Tons	Length ft. in.	Beam ft. in.	Draught ft. in.	Material			H.P.	Guns	Date		Speed
„	Teng-Ing-Chew	1,258	—	—	—	Composite	—	—	—	1 9-t. / 6 Vavasseur B.L.	—	—	—
„	Tei-An	1,258	—	—	—	Composite	—	—	—	1 9-t. / 6 Vavasseur B.L.	—	—	—
„	Wei-Juan	1,258	—	—	—	Composite	—	—	—	1 9-t. / 6 Vavasseur B.L.	—	—	—
„	Chung-Wo	—	—	—	—	Composite	—	—	—	1 9-t. / 6 Vavasseur B.L.	—	—	—
„	Mei-June	515	170 0	22 9	11 8	Composite	9	—	—	1 9-t. / 6 Vavasseur B.L.	—	—	—
„	Hok-Seng	—	—	—	—	Composite	—	—	—	1 7-t. / 5 Vavasseur B.L.	—	—	—
„	Tsing-Juen	572	—	—	—	Composite	—	—	—	1 7-t. / 5 Vavasseur B.L.	—	—	—
„	Ching-Woi	—	—	—	—	Composite	—	—	—	1 7-t. / 5 Vavasseur B.L.	—	—	—
„	Me-Sing	—	—	—	—	Composite	—	—	—	1 7-t. / 5 Vavasseur B.L.	—	—	—
„	Ting-Hai	—	—	—	—	Composite	—	—	—	1 7-t. / 5 Vavasseur B.L.	—	—	—
Gunboats at Tientsin	Alpha	400	120 0	30 0	10 0	Wood	7	2	310	1 38-t.	1876	—	9·2
	Beta	400	120 0	30 0	10 0	Wood	7	2	310	1 38-t.	1876	—	9·4
	Gamma	400	120 0	30 0	10 0	Wood	7	2	310	1 38-t.	1877	—	9·0
	Delta	400	120 0	30 0	10 0	Wood	10	2	310	1 38-t.	1877	—	9·0
	Epsilon	440	125 0	29 0	12 3	Steel	6	2	380	1 35-t. 11-in. Arm. / 2 12-pdr. B.L. Arm. / 2 Gatling	1879	—	10·0
Gunboat „	Zeta	440	125 0	29 0	12 3	Steel	6	2	380	1 35-t. 11-in. Arm. / 2 12-pdr. B.L. Arm. / 2 Gatling	1879	—	10·0
„	Eta	440	125 0	29 0	12 3	Steel	6	2	380	1 35-t. 11-in. Arm. / 2 12-pdr. B.L. Arm. / 2 Gatling	1879	—	10·0
„	Theta	440	125 0	29 0	12 3	Steel	6	2	380	1 35-t. 11-in. Arm. / 2 12-pdr. B.L. Arm. / 2 Gatling	1879	—	11·0
Gunboats of the Canton Squadron	Chento	—	—	—	—	Composite	—	—	Nom 80	7 guns	—	—	—
	Tching-Sing	—	—	—	—	Composite	—	—	70	6 guns	—	—	—
	Tching-Po	—	—	—	—	Composite	—	—	60	2 guns	—	—	—
	Tching-On	—	—	—	—	Composite	—	—	60	4 guns	—	—	—
	Quang-On	—	—	—	—	Composite	—	—	70	4 guns	—	—	—
	Sin-Tsing	—	—	—	—	Composite	—	—	75	3 guns	—	—	—
	Tsing-Po	—	—	—	—	Composite	—	—	—	—	—	—	—

CHINA.—(Continued).

Class	Name	Displacement (tons)	Length (ft. in.)	Beam (ft. in.)	Depth of Hold (ft. in.)	Material of Hull	Draught of Water (ft. in.)	Propeller	Indicated Horse-Power	Armament	Date of Launch	Cost (£)	Speed (knots)	Coal Supply (tons)	Distance that can be steamed at 10 knots (miles)
Gunboats for Customs duties at Canton	Chien-Jui	—	—	—	—	Composite	—	—	—	3 guns					
	Tchun-Tung	—	—	—	—	Composite	—	—	—	3 guns					
	Pang-Chao-Hai	—	194 0	22 0	—	Composite	—	—	—	4 guns					
	Shen-Chi	—	111 0	20 4	—	Composite	—	—	—	4 guns					
	Li-She	—	90 0	15 0	—	Composite	—	—	—	3 guns					
Gunboats for Customs duties at Amoy, Tientsin, and Shanghai	Ling-Feng	—	—	—	—	—	—	—	—	3 guns					
	Fei-Hoo	—	—	—	—	—	—	—	—	3 guns					
	Kiva-Shing	—	—	—	—	—	—	—	—	3 guns					
	Hai-Tung-Juen	200	—	—	—	Wood	—	—	—	3 guns					
	Chong-Sing (an old English gun-boat)	—	—	—	—	Wood	—	—	—	3 guns					
	Tong-Sing	—	—	—	—	Wood	—	—	40 nom.	1 18-t.					
	Ting-Hai	320	—	—	—	Wood	—	—	—	3 guns / 1 11-t. / 7 Vavasseur B.L. / 2 28-prd. brass howitzers					
	Yung-Woo	1,393	—	—	—	Composite	—	—	—	1 18-t.					
	Hong-Sing	—	—	—	—	Wood	—	1	—	1 18-t.					
Frigates stationed at Nankin	Hai-An	—	—	—	—	Wood	20 8	1	1,750	24 70-pdr. / 2 12-t.	1872		12·0		
	Yu-Yuen	—	—	—	—	Wood	20 8	1	1,750	24 70-pdr. / 2 12-t. / 5 Vavasseurs	1873		12·0		
	Chow-Kiang	—	—	—	—	Wood	—	—	—						
	Chih-Hai	—	—	—	—	Wood	—	—	—						
	Wai-Chiang	—	—	—	—	Wood	—	—	—						
	Poo-Too	—	—	—	—	Wood	—	—	—	3 guns 12-pdr. brass					

Also four torpedo-boats. The Chinese built at Shanghai in 1875 a small lightly-armoured river gun-boat.

DENMARK.—*Armoured Ships with Hulls of Iron.*

Class	Name	Displacement	Length	Beam	Depth of Hold	Armour Max.	Armour Min.	Backing	Draught of Water	Propeller	Indicated Horse-Power	Armament	Date of Launch	Cost	Speed	Coal Supply	Distance that can be steamed in 10 knots
		tons	ft. in.	ft. in.	ft. in.	inches	inches	in.	ft. in.					£	knots	tons	miles
Battery ship	Danmark .	4,747	270 0	49 6	30 0	5	$2\frac{7}{8}$	18	19 0	1	1,007	12 8-in. Arm. 12 6-in. Fins. 2 light guns	1864	—	8·1		
Monitor	Rolf Krake .	1,344	185 2	38 3	14 3	$4\frac{3}{8}$	2	9	10 6	1	750	2 8-in. Arm. 2 light guns	1863	—	7·8		
„	Lindormen .	2,076	210 0	39 5	—	$5\frac{1}{2}$	3	$9\frac{3}{4}$	13 9	2	1,560	2 9-in. Arm. 2 light guns	1868	—	12·0		
„	Gorm . .	2,344	231 0	49 0	—	7	$4\frac{3}{8}$	$9\frac{3}{4}$	13 9	1	1,670	2 10-in. Arm. 2 light guns	1870	104,000	12·2		
Central battery	Helgoland .	5,347	274 6	59 2	—	$12\frac{1}{4} + 1\frac{1}{2}$	6	$10\frac{1}{8}$	17 8	2	3,838	1 12-in. Krupp 4 $10\frac{3}{16}$-in. „ 5 $4\frac{11}{16}$-in. „	1878	264,000	13·0		
„	Odin . .	3,083	260 0	54 6	—	8	$4\frac{1}{2}$	$10\frac{1}{8}$	15 1	1	2,260	4 10-in. Arm. 6 light guns	1872	147,000	12·4		
Torpedo ship	Tordenskjold	2,400	215 0	42 0	—	—	—	—	—	—	2,500	1 $13\frac{3}{4}$-in. Krupp 1 $5\frac{7}{8}$-in. „ 6 light guns	1880	—	—		
Cruiser	Esbern Snare	527	150 0	26 0	—	2	2	$5\frac{7}{8}$	10 2	1	500	2 $5\frac{1}{2}$-in. Fins.	1862	—	11·0		
„	Absalon	527	150 0	26 0	—	2	2	$5\frac{7}{8}$	10 2	1		3 $5\frac{1}{2}$-in. Fins.	1862	—	11·0		

DENMARK.—*Armoured Ship with Hull of Wood.*

Class	Name	Displacement	Length	Beam	Depth of Hold	Armour Max.	Armour Min.	Backing	Draught of Water	Propeller	Indicated Horse-Power	Armament	Date of Launch	Cost	Speed	Coal Supply	Distance that can be steamed at 10 knots
		tons	ft. in.	ft. in.	ft. in.	inches	inches		ft. in.					£	knots	tons	miles
Battery ship	Peder Skram	3,373	220 0	48 0		5	$2\frac{7}{8}$		21 7	1	1,680	8 8-in. Arm. 8 6-in. Fins. 2 light guns	1864	—	11·7		

DENMARK.—*Unarmoured Ships.*

Class	Name	Displacement	Length	Beam	Depth of Hold	Material of Hull	Draught of Water	Propeller	Indicated Horse-Power	Armament	Date of Launch	Cost	Speed	Coal Supply	Distance that can be steamed in 10 knots
		tons	ft. in.	ft. in.	ft. in.		ft. in.					£	knots	tons	miles
Corvette	St. Thomas	1,572	217 0	32 0		Wood	17 0	1	1,870	1 8-in. Arm. 4 6-in Fins. 1 light gun	1871	—	13·6		
Schooner	Ingolf	870	186 3	27 0	13 10	Iron	12 5	1	670	3 5⅞-in. Krupp	1876	—	10·2		
Gun-vessel	Falster	3[illegible]6	108 0	28 0	—	Iron	7 6	1	510	1 10-in. Arm. 2 light guns	1873	—	9·8		
,,	Moën	356	108 0	28 0	—	Iron	7 6	1	523	1 10-in. Arm. 2 light guns	1875	—	9·8		
,,	Oresund	238	82 0	25 4	—	Iron	6 6	1	183	1 10-in. Arm. 2 light guns	1874	—	7·2		
,,	Storebelt	238	82 0	25 4	—	Iron	6 6	1	196	1 10-in. Arm. 2 light guns	1875	—	7·6		
,,	Littlebelt	238	82 0	25 4	—	Iron	6 6	1	187	1 10-in. Arm. 2 light guns	1875	—	7·2		
Gun-boat	Drogden (System Farcy)	11	52 3	13 8	—	Steel	3 7	2	40	1 9-in. Arm.	1872	—	6·0		

There are several old-fashioned frigates, corvettes, and gun-boats.

FRANCE.—*Armoured Ships with Hulls of Iron or Steel.*

Class	Name	Displacement	Length at Water-line	Beam	Depth of Hold	Armour Max.	Armour Min.	Backing	Draught of Water	Propeller	Indicated Horse-Power	Armament	Date of Launch	Cost	Speed	Coal Supply	Distance that can be steamed at 10 knots
		tons	ft. in.	ft. in.	ft. in.	inches	inches	in.	ft. in.					£	knots	tons	miles
Barbette-turret, & broadside	Amiral Baudin	11,441	319 4	68 3		21⅝	13¾	14⅛	26 2	2	?	3 100-t. 12 5½-in. 8 machine	?	Building	?		
,,	Amiral Duperré	10,486	319 9 (between perps.)	66 11	27 5	21⅝	9⅞	14⅛	26 9	2	?	4 13⅜-in.	1879	570,000	14·5	790	

Frigate	Couronne .	6,428	—		—		28	2	3⅞ 1½	3⅞ 1½	15	28	6	1	2,917	8 9⅜-in.	1861	—	12·66		
Central battery	Dévastation .	9,639	312	0	67	0	44	9	15	9⅜	12⅝	25	0	2	?	4 13⅜-in. 2 10⅝-in. 6 5½-in.	1879	—	?	610	2,800
Barbette-turret, & broadside	Formidable .	11,441	319	4	68	3			21⅝	13¾	14⅛	26	2	2	?	3 100-t. 12 5½-in. 8 machine	?	—	?		
Central battery	Foudroyant .	9,639	312	0	67	0	44	9	?	?	12⅝	25	0	2	?	?	?	—	?	506	2,800
„	Friedland .	8,916	317	0	58	0	34	10	7⅞ 1⅛	7 1⅛	15	29	11	1	4,428	8 10⅝-in. 8 5½-in.	1873	—	13·30		
Frigate	Heroïne .	6,007	262	5	56	0	29	3	5⅞	4⅜	26	27	5	1	3,318	8 9⅜-in. 3 7⅜-in. 2 5½-in.	1863	213,248	13·00		
?	Hoche . .	9,864	328	0	64	5	43	3	17¾	13¾	?	27	2	2	?	3 13⅜-in. 18 5½-in.	Bldg.	—	?		
?	Magenta .	9,864	328	0	64	5	43	3	17¾	13¾	?	27	2	2	?	3 13⅜-in. 18 5½-in.	?	—	?		
?	Marceau .	9,864	328	0	64	5	43	3	17¾	13¾	?	27	2	2	?	3 13⅜-in. 18 5½-in.	Bldg.	—	?		
?	Neptune .	9,861	328	0	64	5	43	3	17¾	13¾	?	27	0	2	?	3 13⅜-in. 18 5½-in.	Bldg.	—	?		
Central battery	Redoutable .	8,854	312	0	64	6	45	0	13¾	9	15	25	0	2	6,071	?	1876	—	14·66	510	2,800
„	Duguesclin .	5,869	266	0	57	0	25	4	9⅞	6⅜	15	25	3	?	?	4 9⅜-in. 6 5½-in. 1 7⅜-in.	In-comp.	—	?	300	
„	Vauban .	5,869	266	0	57	0	25	4	9⅞	6⅜	15	25	3	?	?	4 9⅜-in. 6 5½-in. 1 7⅜-in.	In-comp.	—	?	400	
Coast-service Vessels: Ram	Caïman .	7,239	278	3	59	0	24	7	19⅝	15¾	?	24	7	?	?	2 16½-in. 4 4-in.	?	—	?		
„	Fulminant .	5,584	248	0	57	9	23	0	13	11⅞	15¾	21	4	1	?	2 10⅝-in. 4 4-in.	1877	—	?		
„	Furieux .	5,695	247	10	59	0	23	3	19⅝	15¾	?	21	9	?	?	?	In-comp.	—	?		
„	Indomptable	7,184	279	10	59	0	24	7	19⅝	13	?	23	6	?	?	2 16½-in. 4 4-in. 2 Mitrailleuse	In-comp.	—	?		
„	Requin .	7,184	279	10	59	0	24	7	19⅝	11⅞ 4	?	23	6	?	?	2 16½-in. 4 4-in. 2 Mitrailleuse	In-comp.	—	?		

FRANCE.—*Armoured Ships with Hulls of Iron or Steel*—(continued).

Class	Name	Displacement	Length at Water line		Beam		Depth of Hold		Armour		Backing	Draught of Water		Propeller	Indicated Horse-Power	Armament	Date of Launch	Cost	Speed	Coal Supply	Distance that can be steamed at 10 knots
									Max.	Min.											
		tons	ft.	in.	ft.	in.	ft.	in.	inches	inches	in.	ft.	in.					£	knots	tons	miles
Coast-service Vessels: Ram	Terrible .	7,184	271	9	59	0	23	6	19⅝	13	?	23	6	?	?	2 16½-in. 4 4-in. 2 Mitrailleuse	In-comp.	—	?		
,,	Tonnerre .	5,584	241	9	57	9	20	7	13	11⅞	15¾	21	4	1	4,165	2 10⅝-in. 4 4-in.	1875	—	14·01		
1st class	Onondaga .	2,592							5⅛	?	11⅞	12	7	2	642	4 9⅜-in.	1863	196,600	6·46		
	Tempête .	4,523	241	6	57	9	16	9	13	11⅞	15¾	16	9	1		2 10⅝-in. 4 4-in.	1876	—	?		
	Tonnant .	4,523	241	6	57	9	16	9	17¾	13¾	15¾	16	9	?	?	2 13⅜-in.	?	—	?		
	Vengeur .	4,523	241	9	57	9	16	9	13	9⅜	15¾	16	9	?	?	2 13⅜-in.	1878	—	?		
Floating battery	Arrogante .	1,514	131	3	48	5			4⅝	4⅝	15¾	10	0	2	?	2 9⅜-in. 2 4-in. 3 5½-in. 2 6¼-in. 2 7⅜-in.	1864	46,000	5·92		
,,	Embuscade .	1,580	129	6	51	10	12	9	5½	5½	15¾	12	0	2	?	1 10⅝-in. 1 10⅝-in. 5 7⅜-in. 2 6¼-in. 3 5½-in. 2 4-in.	1865	67,200	8·51		
,,	Implacable .	1,434	131	3	48	5	10	5	4⅝	4⅝	15¾		7	2	?	1 10⅝-in. 1 7⅜-in. 4 6¼-in. 3 5½-in. 2 4-in.	1864	—	?		
,,	Imprenable .	1,615	129	6	51	10	12	9	5½	5½	15¾	11	3	2	?	2 4⅝-in. 2 6¼-in. 2 9⅜-in.	1867	—	5·51		
,,	Opiniâtre .	1,434	131	3	48	5	10	5	4⅝	4⅝	15¾	9	6	2	?	2 6¼-in. 4 7⅜-in. 2 4⅝-in.	1864	—	6·98		
,,	Protectrice .	1,580	129	6	51	10	12	9	5½	5½	15¾	12	0	2	?	4 7⅜-in. 2 4⅝-in.	1866				
,,	Refuge . .	1,449	129	6	51	10	12	9	5½	5½	15¾	10	6	2	?	4 7⅜-in. 2 4⅝-in.	1866				

FRANCE.—*Armoured Ships with Hulls of Wood.*

Class	Name	Displace-ment	Length at Water-line	Beam	Depth of Hold	Armour Max.	Armour Min.	Backing	Draught of Water	Propeller	Indicated Horse-Power	Armament	Date of Launch	Cost	Speed	Coal Supply	Distance that can be steamed at 10 knots
		tons	ft. in.	ft. in.	ft. in.	inches	inches	in.	ft. in.					£	knots	tons	miles
Central battery	Colbert .	8,617	317 9	56 6	25 4	$8\frac{5}{8}$	$7\frac{1}{16}$	$34\frac{5}{8}$	28 5	1	4,652	8 $10\frac{5}{8}$-in. 1 $9\frac{3}{8}$-in. 6 $5\frac{1}{2}$-in.	1875	—	14·47	700	
Frigate	Flandre .	5,964	295 3	56 6	27 10	$5\frac{7}{8}$	$5\frac{7}{8}$	26	27 6	1	3,536	8 $9\frac{3}{8}$-in. $\frac{3}{8}$-in.	1864	213,280	14·30		
,,	Gauloise .	5,916	295 3	56 6	27 10	$5\frac{7}{8}$	$5\frac{7}{8}$	26	27 7	1	7,635	8 $\frac{3}{8}$-in. 4 $7\frac{3}{8}$-in.	1865	—	13·80		
,,	Guyenne .	5,859	295 3	56 6	27 10	$5\frac{7}{8}$	$5\frac{7}{8}$	26	28 2	1	3,494	8 $9\frac{3}{8}$-in. 6 $7\frac{3}{8}$-in.	1865	—	13·70		
Central battery	Marengo .	7,172	282 6	56 10	25 10	$7\frac{7}{8}$	$7\frac{1}{16}$	$32\frac{1}{4}$	27 8	2		6 $10\frac{5}{8}$-in. 4 $13\frac{3}{8}$-in. 4 $4\frac{5}{8}$-in.	1869	280,000	13·5	650	
,,	Océan . .	7,749	282 6	56 10	25 10	$7\frac{7}{8}$	$7\frac{1}{16}$	$32\frac{1}{4}$	27 3	2	3,781	6 $10\frac{5}{8}$-in. 3 $13\frac{3}{8}$-in. 10 $4\frac{5}{8}$-in.	1868	—	13·70	650	
Frigate	Provence .	5,815	262 5	55 10	27 10	$5\frac{7}{8}$	$5\frac{7}{8}$	26	27 2	2	3,500	4 $10\frac{5}{8}$-in. 8 $9\frac{3}{8}$-in. 3 $7\frac{3}{8}$-in. 2 $5\frac{1}{2}$-in.	1863	217,600	13·90		
,,	Revanche .	5,790	262 5	55 10	27 10	$5\frac{7}{8}$	$5\frac{7}{8}$	26	27 1	2	3,187	8 $9\frac{3}{8}$-in. 3 $7\frac{3}{8}$-in. 2 $5\frac{1}{2}$-in.	1865	—	13·25		
,,	Savoie . .	5,896	262 5	55 10	27 10	$5\frac{7}{8}$	$5\frac{7}{8}$	26	28 0	1	3,050	8 $9\frac{3}{8}$-in. 3 $7\frac{3}{8}$-in. 2 $5\frac{1}{2}$-in.	1864	—	13·47		
,,	Solférino .	7,129	284 6	57 0	27 5	$4\frac{5}{8}$	$4\frac{5}{8}$	?	29 11	1	3,283	10 $9\frac{3}{8}$-in. 4 $7\frac{3}{8}$-in.	1861	237,200	12·70		
Central battery	Suffren . .	7,604	282 6	56 10	25 10	$7\frac{7}{8}$	$7\frac{1}{16}$	$32\frac{1}{4}$	29 10	1	4,181	4 $10\frac{5}{8}$-in. 4 $9\frac{3}{8}$-in. 5 $4\frac{5}{8}$-in.	1870	260,400	14·30	650	
Frigate	Surveillante .	6,220	262 5	56 4	27 10	$5\frac{7}{8}$	$5\frac{7}{8}$	26	29 1	1	3,254	8 $9\frac{3}{8}$-in. 4 $7\frac{3}{8}$-in.	1864	213,240	13·20		
Central battery	Trident .	8,814	317 9	56 4	25 4	$8\frac{5}{8}$	$7\frac{1}{16}$	$34\frac{5}{8}$	29 1	1	4,882	8 $10\frac{5}{8}$-in. 1 $9\frac{3}{8}$-in. 1 $5\frac{1}{2}$-in.	1875	—	14·17	630	

FRANCE.—*Armoured Ships with Hulls of Wood*—(continued).

Class	Name	Displacement	Length at Water-line	Beam	Depth of Hold	Armour Max.	Armour Min.	Backing	Draught of Water	Propeller	Indicated Horse-Power	Armament	Date of Launch	Cost	Speed	Coal Supply	Distance that can be steamed at 10 knots
		tons	ft. in.	ft. in.	ft in.	inches	inches	in.	ft. in.					£	knots	tons	miles
Frigate	Valeureuse	5,984	262 5	56 2	27 10	5⅞	5⅞	26	28 0	1	3,383	8 9⅜-in. 1 7⅜-in. 6 6¼-in.	1864	213,240	13·83		
Ironclad 2nd rate	Alma	3,788	229 10	46 6	22 10	5⅞	5⅞	26	23 11	1	1,896	6 7⅜-in. 4 4⅝-in.	1867	101,200	11·89		
,,	Armide	3,765	229 10	46 2	22 10	5⅞	5⅞	26	23 0	1	1,585	6 7⅜-in. 6 4⅝-in.	1867	—	11·56		
,,	Atalante	3,825	229 10	46 5	22 10	5⅞	5⅞	26	23 3	1	1,640	6 7⅜-in. 6 4⅝-in.	1868	—	11·83		
,,	Bayard (iron, steel, and wood)	5,881	265 9	57 2	23 4	9¾	6¼	15	24 11	2	?	5 7⅜-in. 4 8¼-in. 6 5½-in.	In-comp.	—	?		
,,	Belliqueuse	3,747	230 0	46 3	22 10	5⅞	5⅞	26	22 10	1	1,227	4 7⅜-in. 4 6¼-in. 4 5½-in.	1865	99,176	11·78		
,,	Jeanne d'Arc	3,675	230 3	46 1	19 10	5⅞	5⅞	26	22 10	1	1,884	6 7⅜-in. 4 4⅝-in.	1867	—	2·33		
,,	La Galissonnière	4,487	255 8	49 0	23 10	5⅞	5⅞	26	23 9	2	2,670	6 9⅜-in. 4 4⅝-in.	1872	—	13·08		
,,	Montcalm	3,889	230 3	46 1	22 10	5⅞	5⅞	26	23 7	1	1,830	6 7⅜-in. 4 4⅝-in.	1868	—	11·65		
,,	Reine-Blanche	3,845	230 3	46 2	22 10	5⅞	5⅞	26	23 8	1	1,860	6 7⅜-in. 4 4⅝-in.	1868	—	11·80		
,,	Thétis	3,621	230 3	46 2	22 10	5⅞	5⅞	26	20 10	1	1,676	6 7⅜-in. 4 4⅝-in.	1877	—	11·99		
,,	Triomphante	4,127	258 2	48 9	23 11	5⅞	5⅞	26	22 5	1	?	6 9⅜-in. 1 7⅜-in. 6 5½-in.	1877	—	?		
,,	Turenne	5,881	265 9	57 2	25 4	9¾	6¼	15	23 11	2	?	4 9⅜-in. 6 5½-in. 1 7⅜-in.	1879	—	?		
,,	Victorieuse	4,176	258 2	48 9	23 11	5⅞	5⅞	26	22 5	1	2,214	4 9⅜-in. 1 7⅜-in. 6 5½-in.	1875	—	12·75	300	
Coast service vessels, 2nd class	Bélier	3,589	196 10	53 0	17 7	8⅝	8⅝	31½	19 1	2	1,921	2 9⅜-in.	1870	—	12·37		
	Bouledogue	3,510	196 10	53 0	17 7	8⅝	8⅝	31½	18 2	?	1,827	2 9⅜-in.	1872	—	12·25		
	Cerbère	3,758	196 10	53 0	17 7	8⅝	8⅝	31½	19 7	2	1,560	2 9⅜-in.	1868	137,600	11·39		
	Taureau	2,718	194 9	47 3	16 6	5⅞	5⅞	26	17 9	2	1,793	1 9⅜-in.	1865	—	12·54		
		3,601	196 10	53 0	17 6	8⅝	8⅝	31½	17 8	2	1,880	2 9⅜-in.	1871	—	12·09		

FRANCE.—*Unarmoured Ships.*

Class	Name	Displacement	Length at Water-line	Beam	Depth of Hold	Material of Hull	Draught of Water	Propeller	Indicated Horse-Power	Armament	Date of Launch	Cost	Speed	Coal Supply	Distance that can be steamed at 10 knots
		tons	ft. in.	ft. in.	ft. in.		ft. in.					£	knots	tons	miles
Cruisers of 1st Class	Duquesne	5,522	329 4	51 0	35 10	Iron	?	1	?	14 5½-in. 7 7⅜-in.	1878	—	16·87	600	
,,	Iphigénie	3,192	240 2	46 6	24 4	Wood	22 4		?	10 4¼-in. 4 6¼-in.	?	—	13·5		
,,	Naïade Aréthuse	3,284	244 4	46 5	24 3	Wood	23 0	1	?	10 5½-in. 4 4¼-in.	?	—	15		
,,	Tourville	5,616	322 5	50 6	27 10	Iron	25 2	1	7,466	14 5½-in. 7 7⅜-in.	1876	—	16·89 ?	800	5,000
,,	Dubourdieu	3,355	253 7	45 4	31 5	Wood	22 10	1	?	20 5½-in. 4 6¼-in.	?	—	?		
,,	Capitaine Lucas	3,355	253 7	45 4	31 5	Wood	22 10	1	?	20 5½-in. 4 6¼-in.	?	—	?		
Cruisers of 2nd Class	Champlain	1,940	258 10	35 9	21 7	Wood	18 8	1	1,953	9 5½-in. 1 6¼-in.	1872	—	14·29		
,,	Château Renaud	1,830	259 2	35 1	—	—	—	—	1,500		—	—	14·5		
,,	D'Estaing	2,236	277 5	37 4	24 10	Wood	18 8	1	?	15 5½-in.	?	—	?		
,,	Duguay-Trouin	3,189	291 4	43 2	27 5	Iron	20 6	1	?	5 7⅜-in. 5 5½-in.	1877	—	?	430	
,,	Du-Petit-Thouars	1,962	262 0	35 9	21 7	Wood	18 8	1	2,018	10 5½-in.	1874	—	15·07		
,,	Fabert	2,060	260 5	36 0	21 7	Wood	19 1	1	1,107	8 5½-in.	1874	—	12·42		
,,	Forfait	2,268	249 4	38 0	22 10	Wood	18 0	1	?	15 5½-in.	?	—	?		
,,	Laclocheterie	1,994	262 0	35 8	21 7	Wood	18 9	1	1,918	10 5½-in.	1872	—	13·73	300	
,,	Infernet	1,961	262 0	35 8	21 7	Wood	18 8	1	1,918	1 6¼-in. 7 5½-in.	1872	—	13·73		
,,	Lapérouse	2,236	268 10	37 4	21 6	Wood	18 8	1	?	15 5½-in.	?	—	?		
,,	Magon	2,268	249 4	38 0	22 10	Wood	18 0	—	—	15 5½-in.	?	—	?		
,,	Monge	2,236	249 4	38 0	22 10	Wood	18 8	—	—	13 5½-in. 2 5½-in.	?	—	?		
,,	Sané	1,876	260 5	36 0	21 7	Wood	18 10	1	1,967	3 6¼-in.	1870	—	15·02		
,,	Nielly	2,236	249 4	38 0	22 10	Wood	18 8	—	—	15 5½-in.	?	—			
,,	Roland	2,268	249 4	38 0	22 10	Wood	17 2	—	—	15 5½-in.	?	—	?		
,,	Seignelay	1,943	260 5	36 0	21 7	Wood	18 1	1	1,967	8 5½-in.	1874	—	15·00		
,,	Villars	2,268	249 4	38 0	22 10	Wood	17 2	1	?	15 5½-in.	?	—	?		
Cruisers of 3rd Class	Beautemps-Beaupré	1,255	207 7	34 1	17 8	Wood	15 5	1	985	1 6¼-in. 5 5½-in.	1872	—	12·60		

FRANCE.—*Unarmoured Ships*—(continued).

Class	Name	Displacement (tons)	Length at Water-line (ft. in.)	Beam (ft. in.)	Depth of Hold (ft. in.)	Material of Hull	Draught of Water (ft. in.)	Propeller	Indicated Horse-Power	Armament	Date of Launch	Cost (£)	Speed (knots)	Coal Supply (tons)	Distance that can be steamed at 10 knots (miles)
Cruisers of 3rd Class	Duchauffaut	1,289	207 7	34 2	17 9	Wood	15 9	1	1,214	6 5½-in.	1872	—	12·72		
,,	Eclaireur	1,627	248 1	35 5	23 3	Wood	17 0	1	?	8 5½-in.	1877	—	?		
,,	Hugon	1,271	207 6	34 1	17 8	Wood	15 11	1	915	1 6¼-in., 5 5½-in.	1872	—	11·72		
,,	Talisman	1,264	224 4	33 6	—	Wood	17 0	1	?		?	—	?		
,,	Rigault-de-Genouilly	1,627	245 0	35 5	23 3	Wood		1	?	8 5½-in.	?	—	?		
,,	Vaudreuil	1,229	207 6	34 1	17 8	Wood	16 1	1	89	1 6¼-in., 4 5½-in., 1 4-in.	1870	—	10·77		
Gun-vessel	Crocodile	450	144 7	24 4	11 4	—	8 4	2	251	2 4-in.	1874	—	9·68		
,,	Lionne	460	143 7	23 11	12 0	Wood	9 7	1	?	2 4-in.	1874	—	?		
,,	Lutin	466	144 7	24 4	11 4	—	9 4	1	?	1 7⅜-in., 2 4-in.	1877	—	?		
,,	Lynx	471	144 7	24 4	11 8	Composite	9 4	?	427	2 5½-in., 2 4-in.	1878	—	?		
,,	Aspic	?	—	—	—	Composite	?	?	?	2 5½-in., 2 4-in.	?	—	?		
,,	Vipère	?	—	—	—	Composite	?	?	?	2 4-in.	?	—	?		
,,	Sagittaire	?	—	—	—	Composite	?	?	?	2 5½-in., 2 4-in.	?	—	?		
,,	Capricorne	?	—	—	—	Composite	?	1	?	2 5½-in., 2 4-in.	?	—	?		

There are also on the Navy List 10 Avisos, single screw, either building, or launched since 1870.
   ,,   7 Avisos de flotille, with single screw, either building, or launched since 1870.
   ,,   18 screw gunboats.
   ,,   several paddle-wheel vessels, mostly of an old type.
No vessel launched before 1870 has been counted, except it is a 'conversion.'

GERMANY—*Armoured Ships with Hulls of Iron or Steel.*

Class	Name	Displacement	Length between perpendiculars	Beam	Depth of Hold	Armour Max.	Armour Min.	Backing	Draught of Water	Propeller	Indicated Horse-Power	Armament	Date of Launch	Cost	Speed	Coal Supply	Distance that can be steamed at 10 knots
		tons	ft. in.	ft. in.	ft. in.	inches	inches	in.	ft. in.					£	knots	tons	miles
Central battery	König Wilhelm	9,757	355 0	60 0	25 5	$12+1\frac{1}{8}$	$4\frac{1}{3}+1\frac{1}{8}$	$9\frac{3}{4}$	26 $6\frac{1}{2}$	1	8,000	18 $9\frac{3}{8}$-in. Krupp	1868	498,400	14·7		
												5 $8\frac{1}{4}$-in. ,,					
,,	Friedrich Karl	6,007	300 0	54 6	22 4	5	3	$14\frac{7}{8}$	23 $10\frac{1}{2}$	1	3,500	16 $8\frac{1}{4}$-in. ,,	1867	318,800	13·6		
,,	Kronprinz	5,568	286 0	50 0	—	5	3	$16\frac{1}{8}$	24 3	1	4,800	16 $8\frac{1}{4}$-in. ,,	1867	302,242	14·3		
,,	Kaiser	7,676	280 0	62 4	24 6	$10+1\frac{1}{8}$	$5+1\frac{1}{8}$	$10\frac{1}{8}$	24 7	1	8,000	8 $10\frac{3}{16}$-in. ,,	1874	391,232	14·6	710	3,400
												1 $8\frac{1}{4}$-in. ,,					
												2 light guns					
,,	Deutschland	7,676	280 0	62 4	24 6	$10+1\frac{1}{8}$	$5+1\frac{1}{8}$	$10\frac{1}{8}$	24 7	1	8,000	8 $10\frac{3}{16}$-in. Krupp	1874	353,978	14·5	710	3,400
												1 $8\frac{1}{4}$-in. ,,					
												2 light guns					
Turret	Friedrich der Gross	6,770	307 0	53 6	23 9	$9\frac{1}{4}+1\frac{1}{8}$	$5+1\frac{1}{8}$	$8\frac{1}{4}$	24 7	1	5,400	4 $10\frac{3}{16}$-in. Krupp	1874	235,472	14·0	—	2,500
												2 $6\frac{11}{16}$-in. ,,					
,,	Preussen	6,770	308 6	53 6	23 9	$9\frac{1}{4}+1\frac{1}{8}$	$5+1\frac{1}{8}$	$8\frac{1}{4}$	24 7	1	5,400	4 $10\frac{3}{16}$-in. ,,	1873	253,931	14·0	—	2,500
												2 $6\frac{11}{16}$-in. ,,					
Corvette	Sachsen	7,400	298 0	60 0	27 3	$10+6+1\frac{1}{4}$		$7\frac{7}{8}$	19 8	2	5,600	6 $10\frac{3}{16}$-in. ,,	1877	304.646	14·0		
,,	Baiern	7,400	298 0	60 0	27 3	$10+6+1\frac{1}{4}$		$7\frac{7}{8}$	19 8	2	5,600	6 $10\frac{3}{16}$-in. ,,	1878	—	14·0		
,,	Würtemberg	7,400	298 0	60 0	27 3	$10+6+1\frac{1}{4}$		$7\frac{7}{8}$	19 8	2	5,600	6 $10\frac{3}{16}$-in. ,,	1878	—	14·0		
,,	Baden	7,400	298 0	60 0	27 3	$10+6+1\frac{1}{4}$		$7\frac{7}{8}$	19 8	2	5,600	6 $10\frac{3}{16}$-in. ,,	1880	—	14·0		
Monitor	Arminius	1,583	197 4	36 0	12 4	$4\frac{3}{8}$	3	9	13 $9\frac{1}{2}$	1	1,200	4 $8\frac{1}{4}$-in. ,,	1864	92,512	10·5		
Gun-vessel	Wespe	1,109	143 0	35 6	13 5	8	4	$7\frac{7}{8}$	10 2	2	700	1 12-in. ,,	1876	—	9·0	—	360 at 9 knots
,,	Viper	1,109	143 0	35 6	13 5	8	4	$7\frac{7}{8}$	10 2	2	700	1 12-in. ,,	1876	—	9·0	—	,,
,,	Biene	1,109	143 0	35 6	13 5	8	4	$7\frac{7}{8}$	10 2	2	700	1 12-in. ,,	1876	—	9·0	—	,,
,,	Mücke	1,109	143 0	35 6	13 5	8	4	$7\frac{7}{8}$	10 2	2	700	1 12-in. ,,	1877	—	9·0	—	,,
,,	Scorpion	1,109	143 0	35 6	13 5	8	4	$7\frac{7}{8}$	10 2	2	700	1 12-in. ,,	1877	—	9·0	—	,,
,,	Basilisk	1,109	143 0	35 6	13 5	8	4	$7\frac{7}{8}$	10 2	2	700	1 12-in. ,,	1878	—	9 0	—	,,
,,	Camaleon	1,109	143 0	35 6	13 5	8	4	$7\frac{7}{8}$	10 2	2	700	1 12-in. ,,	1878	—	9·0	—	,,
,,	Krokodil	1,109	143 0	35 6	13 5	8	4	$7\frac{7}{8}$	10 2	2	700	1 12-in. ,,	1879	—	9·0	—	,,
,,	Salamander	1,109	143 0	35 6	13 5	8	4	$7\frac{7}{8}$	10 2	2	700	1 12-in. ,,	1880	—	9·0	—	,,
,,	Natter	1,109	143 0	35 6	13 5	8	4	$7\frac{7}{8}$	10 2	2	700	1 12-in. ,,	1880	—	9·0	—	,,
,,	L. M. N.	1,109	143 0	35 6	13 5	8	4	$7\frac{7}{8}$	10 2	2	700	1 12-in. ,,	Bldg.	—	9·0	—	,,
Torpedo boat	Ziethen (iron)	975	226 0	25 0	18 6	—	—	—	11 $5\frac{1}{2}$	2	2,350	?	1876	—	16·3	—	
,,	Ulan (iron)	377	70 0	25 0	—	—	—	—	10 2	1	800	?	1876	—	12·5	—	

GERMANY.—*Armoured Ship with Hull of Wood.*

Class	Name	Displacement	Length between perpendiculars	Beam	Depth of Hold	Armour Max.	Armour Min.	Backing	Draught of Water	Propeller	Indicated Horse-Power	Armament	Date of Launch	Cost	Speed	Coal Supply	Distance that can be steamed at 10 knots
		tons	ft in.	ft. in.	ft. in.	inches	inches	in.	ft. in.					£	knots	tons	miles
Central battery	Hansa . .	3,610	235 2	45 0	19 6	$6\frac{1}{8}$	$4\frac{1}{8}$	$12\frac{1}{2}$	21 $7\frac{1}{2}$	1	3,000	8 $8\frac{1}{4}$-in. Krupp	1872	—	12·0		

GERMANY.—*Unarmoured Ships.*

Class	Name	Displacement	Length	Beam	Depth of Hold	Material of Hull	Draught of Water	Propeller	Indicated Horse-Power	Armament	Date of Launch	Cost	Speed	Coal Supply	Distance that can be steamed at 10 knots
		tons	ft. in.	ft. in.	ft. in.		ft. in.					£	knots	tons	miles
Spar-decked corvette	Leipsig . .	3,925	282 2	42 8	33 2	Iron and wood	21 7	1	4,800	12 $6\frac{11}{16}$-in. Krupp 4 light guns	—	—	16·0		
”	Prinn Adalbert .	3,925	282 2	42 8	33 2	Iron and wood	21 7	1	4,800	12 $6\frac{11}{16}$-in. Krupp 4 light guns	—	—	16·0		
”	Bismark . .	2,856	244 4	44 10	31 4	Iron and wood	19 8	1	2,500	16 $5\frac{7}{8}$-in. Krupp	—	—	13·5		
”	Blücher . .	2,856	244 4	44 10	31 4	Iron and wood	19 8	1	2,500	16 $5\frac{7}{8}$-in. ”	—	—	13·5		
”	Moltke . .	2,856	244 4	44 10	31 4	Iron and wood	19 8	1	2,500	16 $5\frac{7}{8}$-in. ”	—	—	13·5		
”	Stosch . . .	2,856	244 4	44 10	31 4	Iron and wood	19 8	1	2,500	16 $5\frac{7}{8}$-in. ”	—	—	13·5		
”	Gneisenau . .	2,856	244 4	44 10	31 4	Iron and wood	19 8	1	2,500	16 $5\frac{7}{8}$-in. ”	—	—	13·5		
”	Stein . . .	2,856	244 4	44 10	31 4	Iron and wood	19 8	1	2,500	16 $5\frac{7}{8}$-in. ”	—	—	13·5		
”	Elisabeth . .	2,508	216 10	41 7	13 2	Wood	19 $0\frac{1}{2}$	1	2,400	19 $5\frac{7}{8}$-in. ”	—	—	12·2		
”	Hertha . .	2,300	—	—	—	Wood	19 $0\frac{1}{2}$	1	1,500	19 $5\frac{7}{8}$-in. ”	—	—	10·7		

„	Vineta . . .	2,300	—		—		—		Wood	19	0½	1	1,500	19 $5\frac{7}{8}$-in. „	—	—	11·2
Flush-decked corvette	Freya . . .	1,985	259	0	36	1	14	0	Wood	18	4	1	2,764	8 $5\frac{7}{8}$-in. „	—	—	15·2
„	Ariadne . .	1,719	204	0	35	0	14	0	Wood	17	4	1	2,100	6 $5\frac{7}{8}$-in. „ 2 $4\frac{5}{8}$-in. „	—	—	12·9
„	Louise . . .	1,719	204	0	35	0	14	0	Wood	17	4	1	2,100	6 $5\frac{7}{8}$-in. „ 2 $4\frac{6}{8}$-in. „	—	—	14·1
„	Augusta . .	1,825	235	9	35	4	9	0	Wood	17	8	1	1,300	4 $5\frac{7}{8}$-in. „ 6 $4\frac{6}{8}$-in. „	1864	—	13·8
„	Victoria . .	1,825	235	9	35	4	9	0	Wood	17	8	1	1,300	4 $5\frac{7}{8}$-in. 6 $4\frac{5}{8}$-in. „	1864	—	13·9
„	E. F. . . .	2,169	227	0	41	0	23	9	Composite	18	4	1	2,100	?	Building	—	?
„	Ersatz. f. Vineta .	2,169	227	0	41	0	23	9	Composite	18	4	1	2,100	?	Building	—	?
„	Ersatz. f. Augusta	2,169	227	0	41	0	23	9	Composite	18	4	1	2,100	?	Building	—	?
„	G. Ers. f. Victoria	?	—		—		—		Steel	?		?	?	?	Building	—	?
Gun-vessel	Habicht . .	848	174	0	29	6	11	5	Composite	11	5	1	600	1 $5\frac{7}{8}$-in. Krupp 4 $4\frac{5}{8}$-in. „	1879	—	10·5
„	Möwe . . .	848	174	0	29	6	11	5	Composite	11	5	1	600	1 $5\frac{7}{8}$-in. „ 4 $4\frac{5}{8}$-in. „	1879	—	10·5
„	Albatross . .	716	168	0	26	10	10	10	Wood	10	6	1	600	2 $5\frac{7}{8}$-in. „ 2 $4\frac{5}{8}$-in. „	1871	—	10·5
„	Nautilus . .	716	168	0	26	10	10	10	Wood	10	6	1	600	2 $5\frac{7}{8}$-in. „ 2 $4\frac{5}{8}$-in. „	1871	—	10·5
„	Wolf . . .	489	139	8	25	1	13	8	Iron	9	10	1	340	2 $4\frac{7}{8}$-in. „ 4 light guns	1878	—	9·2
„	Hyäne . . .	489	139	8	25	1	13	8	Iron	9	10	1	340	2 $4\frac{7}{8}$-in. Krupp 4 light guns	1878	—	9·4
„	Iltis . . .	489	139	8	25	1	13	8	Iron	9	10	1	340	2 $4\frac{7}{8}$-in. Krupp 4 light guns	1878	—	9·0
„	Otter . . .	489	139	8	25	1	13	8	Iron	5	7	1	220	1 $4\frac{5}{8}$-in. Krupp	1877	—	8·0
„	Ersatz. f. Habicht	489	139	8	25	1	13	8	Iron	9	10	1	340	2 $4\frac{7}{8}$-in. „ 4 light guns	Building	—	9·0
„	Ersatz. f. Hai .	489	139	8	25	1	13	8	Iron	9	10	1	340	2 $4\frac{7}{8}$-in. Krupp 4 light guns	—	—	9·0
„	Ersatz. f. Hyäne .	489	139	8	25	1	13	8	Iron	9	10	1	340	2 $4\frac{7}{8}$-in. Krupp 4 light guns	—	—	9·0
„	Ersatz. f. Natter	489	139	8	25	1	13	8	Iron	9	10	1	340	2 $4\frac{7}{8}$-in. Krupp 4 light guns	Building	—	9·0
„	Cyclop . . .	412	125	0	23	0	12	0	Iron	8	2	1	250	2 $4\frac{5}{8}$-in. Krupp 2 light guns	1874	—	8·4

GERMANY.—Unarmoured Ships—(continued).

Class	Name	Displacement (tons)	Length (ft. in.)	Beam (ft. in.)	Depth of Hold (ft. in.)	Material of Hull	Draught of Water (ft. in.)	Propeller	Indicated Horse-Power	Armament	Date of Launch	Cost (£)	Speed (knots)	Coal Supply (tons)	Distance that can be steamed at 10 knots (knots)
Aviso-paddle	Hohenzollern	1,700	267 10	33 10	22 4	Iron	13 9	Pad.	3,000	—	1876	—	16·3	—	—
River gunboat	Rhein [1] (thin armour)	120	163 3	25 0	6 0	Iron	3 7	2	50 nom.	2 4⅝-in. Krupp	1874	—	6·0	—	—
„	Mosel (do.)	120	163 3	25 0	6 0	Iron	3 7	2	50 nom.	2 4⅝-in. „	1874	—	6·0	—	—

There are also several paddle-wheel vessels, but mostly of an old type ; also several gunboats of old build, etc, etc.

1 These thinly-armoured river craft resemble the Mississippi 'tin-clads' of the Secession War.

GREECE.—Armoured Ship with Hull of Iron.

Class	Name	Displacement (tons)	Length (ft. in.)	Beam (ft. in.)	Depth of Hold (ft. in.)	Armour Max. (inches)	Armour Min. (inches)	Backing (in.)	Draught of Water (ft. in.)	Propeller	Indicated Horse-Power	Armament	Date of Launch	Cost (£)	Speed (knots)	Coal Supply (tons)	Distance that can be steamed at 10 knots (knots)
Central battery	King Georgios	1,774	200 0	33 0	16 0	7	4⅜	9¾	16 1	2	2,400	2 9-in. Armstrong	1867	—	12·1	206	? 1200

GREECE.—Armoured Ship with Hull of Wood.

Class	Name	Displacement (tons)	Length (ft. in.)	Beam (ft. in.)	Depth of Hold (ft. in.)	Armour Max. (inches)	Armour Min. (inches)	Backing (in.)	Draught of Water (ft. in.)	Propeller	Indicated Horse-Power	Armament	Date of Launch	Cost (£)	Speed (knots)	Coal Suppl. (tons)	Distance that can be steamed at 10 knots (knots)
Central battery	Olga	2,354	—	—	—	5	2	2	15 5	1	1,950	2 9-in. Armstrong, 4 17-in. „, 2 6-in. „	1869	—	11·5		

GREECE.—*Unarmoured Ships.*

Class	Name	Displacement	Length	Beam	Depth of Hold	Material of Hull	Draught of Water	Propeller	Indicated Horse-Power	Armament	Date of Launch	Cost	Speed	Coal Supply	Distance that can be steamed at 10 knots
		tons	ft. in.	ft. in.	ft. in.		ft. in.					£	knots	tons	knots
Corvette	Miaulis . .	1,800	268 5	35 4	—	Iron and wood	18 0	1	2,200	4 small guns 2 Mitrailleuse 3 $6\frac{11}{16}$-in. Krupp 1 $5\frac{7}{8}$-in. ,,	1879	—	15·6		
,,	Themistocles .	?	—	—	—	?	?	1	?	? ?	?	—	11·5		
,,	Bobolina . .	1,950	—	—	—	Iron	?	1	1,800	6 $5\frac{7}{8}$-in. Krupp 4 Mitrailleuse	?	—	11·0		

There are also two gun-vessels of 200 indicated horse-power and four gun-vessels of 160 indicated horse-power; also three paddle-wheel vessels of 350 nominal horse-power.

Since the Greek Government has been making preparations against Turkey several torpedo-vessels have been ordered in England.

HOLLAND.—*Armoured Ships with Hulls of Iron.*

Class	Name	Displacement	Length	Beam	Depth of Hold	Armour Max.	Armour Min.	Backing	Draught of Water	Propeller	Indicated Horse-Power	Armament	Date of Launch	Cost	Speed	Coal Supply	Distance that can be steamed at 10 knots
		tons	ft. in.	ft. in.	ft. in.	inches	inches	in.	ft. in.					£	knots	tons	knots
Turret-ram	King of the Netherlands	5,400	268 0	49 10	32 6	8	$5\frac{7}{8}$	$11\frac{3}{4}$	19 8	2	4,500	4 Mitrailleuse 4 11-in. Arm. 4 $4\frac{5}{8}$-in. Krupp	1874	—	11·9		
,,	Prince Henry of the Netherlands	3,375	230 0	44 0	26 6	$4\frac{3}{8}$	$3\frac{7}{8}$	$9\frac{3}{4}$	18 0	2	2,400	4 $9\frac{1}{6}$-in. Arm. 4 $4\frac{5}{8}$-in. Krupp 4 Mitrailleuse	1866	—	12·1		
Ram	Stier . .	2,069	200 0	38 0	—	8 + 1	$3\frac{7}{8}$	$9\frac{3}{4}$	15 5	2	2,200	2 $9\frac{1}{16}$-in. Arm. 2 Mitrailleuse	1868	—	12·3	201	
,,	Schorpioen .	2,175	193 0	36 2	—	8	$3\frac{7}{8}$	$11\frac{3}{4}$	15 9	2	2,269	2 $9\frac{1}{16}$-in. Arm. 2 Mitrailleuse	1868	91,600	12·8	201	

HOLLAND.—Armoured Ships with Hulls of Iron—(continued).

Class	Name	Displacement (tons)	Length (ft. in.)	Beam (ft. in.)	Depth of Hold (ft. in.)	Armour Max. (inches)	Armour Min. (inches)	Backing (in.)	Draught of Water (ft. in.)	Propeller	Indicated Horse-Power	Armament	Date of Launch	Cost (£)	Speed (knots)	Coal Supply (tons)	Distance that can be steamed at 10 knots (knots)
Ram	Buffel	2,198	205 0	40 0	24 0	8	3 7/8	9 3/4	15 6	2	2,200	2 9 1/16-in. Arm. / 4 30-pdrs, sm. br. / 2 Mitrailleuse	1868	—	12·4		
"	Guinea	2,378	—	—	—	8	3 7/8	9 3/4	15 9	2	2,200	2 9 1/16-in. Arm. / 4 30-pdrs, sm. br. / 2 Mitrailleuse	1870	—	12·2		
Ram-monitor	Draak	2,156	—	—	—	8	5 7/8	11 3/4	10 9	2	800	2 11-in. Krupp / 2 Mitrailleuse	1877	—	?		
"	Matador	1,935	—	—	—	4 3/8	4 3/8	9 3/4	9 6	2	680	2 11-in. Krupp / 2 Mitrailleuse	1878	—	8·0		
"	Linpaard	1,525	—	—	—	4 3/8	4 3/8	9 3/4	8 6	2	680	1 11-in. Krupp / 2 Mitrailleuse	1876	—	8·0		
"	Hyaena	1,566	—	—	—	4 3/8	3	9 3/4	8 10	2	680	2 9 1/16-in. Arm. / 2 Mitrailleuse	1870	—	8·5		
"	Panter	1,566	—	—	—	4 3/8	3	9 3/4	8 10	2	680	2 9 1/16-in. Arm. / 2 Mitrailleuse	1870	—	8·5		
"	Haai	1,566	—	—	—	4 3/8	3	9 3/4	8 10	2	680	2 9 1/16-in. Arm. / 2 Mitrailleuse	1871	—	8·5		
"	Wesp	1,566	—	—	—	4 3/8	3	9 3/4	8 10	2	680	2 9 1/16-in. Arm. / 2 Mitrailleuse	1871	—	8·5		
"	Adder	1,566	—	—	—	4 3/8	3	9 3/4	8 10	2	680	2 9 1/16-in. Arm. / 2 Mitrailleuse	1871	—	8·5		
Monitor	Krokodil	1,530	180 0	44 0	11 6	5 3/8	4 3/8	9 3/4	9 6	2	630	2 9 1/16-in. Arm. / 1 Mitrailleuse	1868	—	8·5		
"	Heiligerlee	1,530	180 0	44 0	11 6	5 3/8	4 3/8	9 3/4	9 6	2	630	2 9 1/16-in. Arm. / 1 Mitrailleuse	1868	—	8·5		
"	Cerberus	1,530	180 0	44 0	11 6	5 3/8	4 3/8	9 3/4	9 7	2	630	2 9 1/16-in. Arm. / 1 Mitrailleuse	1869	—	8·5		
"	Bloodhound	1,530	180 0	44 0	11 6	5 3/8	4 3/8	9 3/4	9 6	2	680	2 9 1/16-in. Arm. / 1 Mitrailleuse	1869	—	8·5		
"	Tyger	1,414	—	—	—	4 3/8	4 3/8	9 3/4	8 10		680	2 9 1/16-io. Arm. / 1 Mitrailleuse	1868	—	8·5		
Gunboat	No. 1	400	—	—	—	4 3/8	2 7/8	10 5/8	7 6		360	2 60-pdrs., sm. br.	1863	—	9·0		
River-monitor	Vahalis	260	—	—	—	4 3/8	3 7/8	7	4 11	2	200	2 4 3/8-in. Krupp	1870	—	8·0		

,,	Isala .	367	151 0	18 4	4 3	5	$3\frac{7}{8}$	$5\frac{1}{8}$	4 3	2	320	2 $4\frac{5}{8}$-in. ,,	1876	—	8·0		
,,	Rhenus .	367	151 0	18 4	4 3	5	$3\frac{7}{8}$	$5\frac{1}{8}$	4 3	2	320	2 $4\frac{5}{8}$-in. ,,	1877	—	8·0		
,,	Mosa .	367	151 0	18 4	4 3	5	$3\frac{7}{8}$	$5\frac{1}{8}$	4 3	2	320	2 $4\frac{5}{8}$-in. ,,	1878	—	8·0		
,,	Merva .	367	151 0	18 4	4 3	5	$3\frac{7}{8}$	$5\frac{1}{8}$	4 3	2	320	2 $4\frac{5}{8}$-in. ,,	1879	—	8·0		

HOLLAND.—*Unarmoured Ships.*

Class	Name	Displacement	Length	Beam	Depth of Hold	Material of Hull	Draught of Water	Propeller	Indicated Horse-Power	Armament	Date of Launch	Cost	Speed	Coal Supply	Distance that can be steamed at 10 knots
		tons	ft. in.	ft. in.	ft. in.		ft. in.					£	knots	tons	knots
Corvette	Atjeh . . .	3,160	300 0	40 10	19 6	Iron and wood	20 0	1	2,750	6 $6\frac{11}{16}$-in. Krupp 4 $4\frac{5}{8}$-in. ,, 4 Mitrailleuse	1876	—	14·5	280	
,,	Tromp . . .	3,160	300 0	40 10	19 6	Iron and wood	20 0	1	2,750	6 $6\frac{11}{16}$-in. Krupp. 4 $4\frac{5}{8}$-in. ,, 4 Mitrailleuse	1877	—	14·5	280	
,,	Queen Emma .	3,160	300 0	40 10	19 6	Iron and wood	20 0	1	2,750	6 $6\frac{11}{16}$-in. Krupp 4 $4\frac{5}{8}$-in. ,, 4 Mitrailleuse	1879	—	14·5	280	
,,	De Ruyter . .	3,160	300 0	40 10	19 6	Iron and wood	20 0	1	3,000	6 $6\frac{11}{16}$-in. Krupp 8 $4\frac{5}{8}$-in. ,, 4 Mitrailleuse	1880	—	15·0	280	
,,	Van Galen . .	2,160	—	—	—	Wood	18 0	1	700	4 $7\frac{1}{16}$-in. H. 2 $6\frac{1}{4}$-in. ,, 4 Mitrailleuse	1872	—	8·2		
,,	Alkmaar .	1,010	—	—	—	Composite	14 9	1	600	1 $7\frac{1}{16}$-in. H. 2 $6\frac{1}{4}$-in. ,, 2 Mitrailleuse	1874	—	11·0		
,,	Suriname . .	850	—	—	—	—	11 5	1	350	1 $5\frac{7}{8}$-in. Krupp 3 $4\frac{5}{8}$-in. ,, 2 Mitrailleuse	1877	—	9·0		
,,	Bonnaire . .	850	—	—	—	—	11 5	1	350	1 $5\frac{7}{8}$-in. Krupp 3 $4\frac{5}{8}$-in. ,, 2 Mitrailleuse	1877	—	9·0		
,,	St. Eustatius .	850	—	—	—	—	11 5	1	350	1 $5\frac{7}{8}$-in. Krupp 3 $4\frac{5}{8}$-in. ,, 2 Mitrailleuse	1878	—	9·0		
,,	Aruba . . .	730	—	—	—	Composite	11 9	1	350	1 $7\frac{1}{16}$-in. H. 2 $4\frac{5}{8}$-in. Krupp	1873	—	9·0		

Several corvettes are down on the effective lists, but all built before 1870; and there are also some thirty gun-boats of the Rendel type, of 100 indicated horse-power, with an armament of either one Krupp gun of 11-inch and one Mitrailleuse, or of $9\frac{1}{16}$-in. Krupp; also twelve torpedo-boats.

HOLLAND.—East Indian Navy.—*Unarmoured Ships.*

Class	Name	Displacement	Length	Beam	Depth of Hold	Material of Hull	Draught of Water	Propeller	Indicated Horse-Power	Armament	Date of Launch	Cost	Speed	Coal Supply	Distance that can be steamed at 10 knots
		tons	ft. in.	ft. in.	ft. in.		ft. in.					£	knots	tons	knots
Corvette	Samarang . .	850	—	—	—	—	11 5	1	350	1 $7\frac{1}{6}$-in. Armstrong 2 $4\frac{5}{8}$-in. Krupp	1876	—	9·0		
,,	Batavia . .	850	—	—	—	—	11 5	1	350	1 $7\frac{1}{6}$-in. Armstrong 2 $4\frac{5}{8}$-in. Krupp	1876	—	9·0		
,,	Macasser . .	850	—	—	—	—	11 5	1	350	1 $7\frac{1}{6}$-in. Armstrong 2 $4\frac{5}{8}$-in. Krupp	1876	—	9·0		
,,	Padang . .	850	—	—	—	—	11 5	1	350	1 $5\frac{7}{8}$-in. ,, 3 $4\frac{5}{8}$-in. ,,	1878	—	9·0		
,,	Benkoelen . .	850	—	—	—	—	11 5	1	350	1 $5\frac{7}{8}$-in. ,, 3 $4\frac{5}{8}$-in. ,,	1880	—	9·0		
,,	Madura . .	850	—	—	—	—	11 5	1	350	1 $5\frac{7}{8}$-in. ,, 3 $4\frac{5}{8}$-in. ,,	1880	—	9·0		
,,	Sambas . .	750	—	—	—	Composite	11 5	1	350	1 $7\frac{1}{16}$-in. Armstrong 2 $4\frac{5}{8}$-in. Krupp	1874	—	9·5		
,,	Pontjanak . .	750	—	—	—	Composite	11 5	1	350	1 $7\frac{1}{16}$-in. Armstrong 2 $4\frac{5}{8}$-in. Krupp	1873	—	9·5		
,,	Bandjermassing .	750	—	—	—	Composite	11 5	1	350	1 $7\frac{1}{16}$-in. Armstrong 2 $4\frac{5}{8}$-in. Krupp	1874	—	9·5		
,,	Palembang . .	750	—	—	—	Composite	11 5	1	350	1 $6\frac{1}{4}$-in. H. 2 $4\frac{5}{8}$-in. Krupp	1874	—	9·5		
,,	Riouw . . .	730	—	—	—	Composite	11 5	1	340	1 $6\frac{1}{4}$-in. H. 2 $4\frac{5}{8}$-in. Krupp	1872	—	9·0		
,,	Banda . . .	730	—	—	—	Composite	11 5	1	340	1 $6\frac{1}{4}$-in. H. 2 $4\frac{5}{8}$-in. Krupp	1872	—	9·0		
,,	Amboina . .	730	—	—	—	Composite	11 5	1	340	1 $6\frac{1}{4}$-in. H. 2 $4\frac{5}{8}$-in. Krupp	1873	—	9·0		
,,	Deli . . .	730	—	—	—	Composite	11 5	1	340	1 $6\frac{1}{4}$-in. H. 2 $4\frac{5}{8}$-in. Krupp	1873	—	9·0		
Paddle-wheel vessel	Merapi . .	1,150	—	—	—	—	13 1	pad.	975	2 $6\frac{1}{4}$-in. H. 4 $4\frac{5}{8}$-in. Krupp	1874	—	?		
,,	Bromo . . .	1,150	—	—	—	—	13 1	pad.	975	2 $6\frac{1}{4}$-in. H. 4 $4\frac{5}{8}$-in. Krupp	1874	—	?		
,,	Oenarang . .	650	—	—	—	—	8 2	pad.	360	1 $6\frac{1}{4}$-in. H. 2 $4\frac{5}{8}$-in. Krupp	1875	—	?		

,,	Soembing . .	650	—	--	—	—	8 2	pad.	360	1 $6\frac{1}{4}$-in. H. 3 $4\frac{5}{8}$-n. Krupp	1878	—	?		
,,	Sindoro . .	650	—	—	—	—	8 2	pad.	360	1 $6\frac{1}{4}$-in. H. 3 $4\frac{5}{8}$-in. Krupp	1878	—	?		
,,	Salak . . .	200	—	—	—	—	6 6	pad.	290	1 $6\frac{1}{4}$-in. H. 2 $4\frac{5}{8}$-in. Krupp	1875	—	?		

There are also a few paddle-wheel vessels of old construction, but no vessels built before 1870 are counted as effective.

ITALY.—*Armoured Ships with Hulls of Iron or Steel.*

Class	Name	Displacement	Length	Beam	Depth of Hold	Armour Max.	Armour Min.	Backing	Draught of Water	Propeller	Indicated Horse-Power	Armament	Date of Launch	Cost	Speed	Coal Supply	Distance that can be steamed at 10 knots
		tons	ft. in.	ft. in.	ft. in.	inches	inches	in.	ft. in.					£	knots	tons	knots
Citadel ship	Dandolo .	10,434	340 11	64 9	21 11	$21\frac{5}{8}$	$13\frac{3}{4}$	$22\frac{3}{4}$	26 7	2	7,500	4 $17\frac{11}{16}$-in. Arm. 4 $4\frac{5}{8}$-in. ,,	1878	700,000	14·0	1,279	3,760
,,	Duilio . .	10,570	340 11	64 9	21 11	$21\frac{5}{8}$	$13\frac{3}{4}$	$22\frac{3}{4}$	26 9	2	7,500	4 $17\frac{11}{16}$-in. ,, 4 $4\frac{5}{8}$-in. ,,	1876	—	15·1	1,279	3,760
,,	Italia . .	13,851	400 6	72 9	21 0[1]	$33\frac{3}{8}$	16	$22\frac{3}{4}$	31 2	2	9,000	4 $17\frac{11}{16}$-in. ,, 18 $5\frac{7}{8}$-in. ,,	1880	766,908	16·0		
,,	Lepanto .	13,851	400 6	72 9	21 0[1]	$33\frac{3}{8}$	16	$22\frac{3}{4}$	31 2	2	9,000	—	—	—	16·0		
Turret ship	Affondatore .	4,070	290 0	40 0	—	5	$3\frac{1}{16}$	9	20 0	1	2,682	2 $8\frac{5}{8}$-in. ,,	1865	152,480	13·0		
Central battery	Ancona .	4,250	256 0	50 0	20 5	$4\frac{5}{8}$	$3\frac{1}{16}$	$13\frac{3}{4}$	21 11	1	2,548	2 $8\frac{5}{8}$-in. ,, 8 $7\frac{7}{8}$-in. ,,	1864	172,000	13·7		
,,	Castelfidardo	4,250	256 0	50 0	20 5	$4\frac{5}{8}$	$3\frac{1}{16}$	$13\frac{3}{4}$	21 11	1	2,'25	2 $8\frac{5}{8}$-in. ,, 8 $7\frac{7}{8}$-in. ,,	1863	—	12·0		
,,	Regina Maria Pia	4,250	256 0	50 0	20 5	$4\frac{5}{8}$	$3\frac{1}{16}$	$13\frac{3}{4}$	22 7	1	2,924	2 $8\frac{5}{8}$-in. ,, 8 $7\frac{7}{8}$-in. ,,	1863	—	13·0		
,,	San Martino	4,250	256 0	50 0	20 5	$4\frac{5}{8}$	$3\frac{1}{16}$	$13\frac{3}{4}$	22 7	1	2,924	2 $8\frac{5}{8}$-in. ,, 8 $7\frac{7}{8}$-in. ,,	1863	—	12·0		
,,	Terribile .	2,700	198 3	45 0	—	$4\frac{3}{8}$	$3\frac{1}{16}$	9	18 0	1	1,200	8 $7\frac{7}{8}$-in. ,,	1861	112,454	11·5		
,,	Formidabile .	2,700	198 3	45 0	—	$4\frac{3}{8}$	$3\frac{1}{16}$	9	18 0	1	1,200	8 $7\frac{7}{8}$-in. ,,	1861	118,000	11·5		
,,	Varese . .	2,000	198 3	42 4	—	$4\frac{3}{8}$	$3\frac{1}{16}$	9	15 9	1	993	4 $7\frac{7}{8}$-in. ,, 1 $6\frac{1}{4}$-in. Italian	1865	85,000	10·0		

[1] Under lower deck.

ITALY.—*Armoured Ships with Hulls of Wood.*

Class	Name	Displacement	Length	Beam	Depth of Hold	Armour		Backing	Draught of Water	Propeller	Indicated Horse-Power	Armament	Date of Launch	Cost	Speed	Coal Supply	Distance that can be steamed at 10 knots
						Max.	Min.										
		tons	ft. in.	ft. in.	ft. in	inches	inches	in.	ft. in.					£	knots	tons	knots
Battery	Palestro	6,161	265 0	57 10	—	$8\frac{5}{8}$	$5\frac{7}{8}$	$24\frac{1}{4}$	26 $10\frac{1}{2}$	1	3,496	1 11-in. Armstrong (25-t.) 6 $9\frac{13}{16}$-in. ,,	1871	247,780	13·0		
Central battery	Principe Amadeo	6,406	265 0	57 10	—	$8\frac{5}{8}$	$5\frac{7}{8}$	$24\frac{1}{4}$	27 $10\frac{1}{2}$	1	3,413	1 11-in. ,, (25-t.) 6 $9\frac{13}{16}$-in. ,,	1872	—	12·4		
,,	Venezia .	5,814	250 0	57 5	—	$5\frac{7}{8}$	$3\frac{7}{8}$	26	25 3	1	3,670	8 $9\frac{13}{16}$-in. ,, 1 $8\frac{5}{8}$-in. ,,	1869	231,007	13·6		
,,	Roma . .	5,700	250 0	57 5	—	$5\frac{7}{8}$	$3\frac{7}{8}$	26	25 3	1	3,738	9 $9\frac{13}{16}$-in. ,,	1865	—	13·1		

ITALY.—*Unarmoured Ships.*

Class	Name	Displacement	Length	Beam	Depth of Hold	Material of Hull	Draught of Water	Propeller	Indicated Horse-Power	Armament	Date of Launch	Cost	Speed	Coal Supply	Distance that can be steamed at 10 knots
		tons	ft. in.	ft. in.	ft. in.		ft. in.					£	knots	tons	knots
Frigate	Maria Adelaide. .	3,460	—	—	—	Wood	21 4	1	2,255	2 $4\frac{5}{8}$-in. Armstrong 1 $9\frac{13}{16}$-in. ,, 1 $8\frac{5}{8}$-in. ,, 2 $7\frac{7}{8}$-in. ,, 18 $6\frac{1}{4}$-in. H.	1859	—	12·0		
,,	Vittorio Emmanuele	3,460	—	—	—	Wood	22 3	1	1,488	4 $7\frac{7}{8}$-in. Armstrong 20 $6\frac{1}{4}$-in. Italian	1856	—	9·5		
Corvette	Garibaldi . .	3,440	—	—	—	Wood	22 3	1	1,079	8 $6\frac{1}{4}$-in. ,,	1860	—	9·5		
,,	Vettor Pisani .	1,700	213 6	38 9	—	Wood	18 0	1	956	14 $4\frac{5}{8}$-in. ,,	1869	—	9·6		
,,	Caracciolo . .	1,580	210 10	63 0	—	Wood	18 0	1	973	6 $6\frac{1}{4}$-in. ,,	1869	—	10·0		

Cruiser	Flavio Gioja	2,553	255 10	41 10	—	—	17 0	1	2,500	—	Building					
,,	Amerigo Vespucci	2,553	255 10	41 10	—	—	17 8	1	2,500	—	Building					
,,	Christoforo Colombo	2,290	248 5	37 1	16 1	Wood	17 0	1	3,782	5 4$\frac{5}{8}$-in. Armstrong	1875	—	16·3	620	? 4,000	
,,	Stafetta . .	1,510	253 3	31 11	—	Iron	15 5	1	2,140	5 2$\frac{15}{16}$-in. Italian	1876	—	15·1			
,,	Rapido . .	1,450	262 5	30 6		Iron	15 1	2	1,920	5 2$\frac{15}{16}$-in. ,,	1876	—	13·1			
,,	Agostin Barbarigo	660	216 6	24 1	15 0	—	12 5	1	1,750	2 4$\frac{5}{8}$-in. Armstrong	1879	45,000	15·9	200	4,300	
,,	Mercantonio Colonna	660	216 6	24 1	15 0	—	12 5	1	1,700	2 4$\frac{5}{8}$-in. ,,	1879	45,000	16·0	200	4,300	
	Vedetta . .	790	184 6	26 10	—	Iron	13 1	1	627	4 2$\frac{15}{16}$-in. Italian	1866	—	10·0			
Torpedo vessel	Pietro Micca .	520	203 0	19 6	—	Iron	11 9½	1	1,400	—	1876	—	14·5			
,,	Sebastian Verniero	520	—	—	—	Iron	11 9½	1	1,400	—	Building	—	17·0			
,,	Andrea Provana .	520	—	—	—	Iron	11 9½	1	1,400	—	Building	—	17·0			
Gun-vessel	Scilla . . .	1,050	178 4	28 7	—	Wood	14 1	1	823	1 6¼-in. Italian 3 4$\frac{5}{8}$-in. Armstrong	1874	—	10·9			
,,	Cariddi . .	1,050	178 4	28 7	—	Wood	14 1	1	973	1 6¼-in. Italian 3 4$\frac{5}{8}$-in. Armstrong	1875	—	10·5			
,,	Guardiano . .	265	—	—	—	Iron	6 6	2	231	1 8$\frac{5}{8}$-in. ,,	1874	—	8·7			
,,	Sentinella . .	265	—	—	—	Iron	6 6	2	260	1 8$\frac{5}{8}$-in. ,,	1874	—	9·2			

There are also 6 paddle-wheel vessels of 300 to 350 nominal horse-power, but all old-fashioned. And also 5 armed screw transport ships varying from 220 to 500 nominal horse-power.

JAPAN.—*Armoured Ship with Hull of Iron.*

Class	Name	Displacement	Length	Beam	Depth of Hold	Armour Max.	Armour Min.	Backing	Draught of Water	Propeller	Indicated Horse-Power	Armament	Date of Launch	Cost	Speed	Coal Supply	Distance that can be steamed at 10 knots
		tons	ft. in.	ft. in.	ft. in.	inches	inches	in.	ft. in.					£	knots	tons	knots
Central battery	Fu-So . .	3,718	220 0	48 0	20 4½	9	6	?	18 4	2	3,824	4 9$\frac{3}{8}$-in. Krupp 2 6$\frac{11}{16}$-in. ,,	1877	—	13·1	—	4,500

JAPAN.—*Armoured Ships with Hulls of Wood.*

Class	Name	Displacement	Length	Beam	Depth of Hold	Armour Max.	Armour Min.	Backing	Draught of Water	Propeller	Indicated Horse-Power	Armament	Date of Launch	Cost	Speed	Coal Supply	Distance that can be steamed at 10 knots
		tons	ft. in.	ft. in.	ft. in.	inches	inches	in.	ft. in.					£	knots	tons	knots
Belted cruiser	Kongo . .	2,200	231 0	40 9	—	$4\frac{3}{8}$	3	?	17 4	1	2,450	3 $6\frac{11}{16}$-in. Krupp 6 $5\frac{7}{8}$-in. "	1877	—	13·7	280	
"	Hiyei . .	2,200	231 0	40 9	—	$4\frac{3}{8}$	3	?	17 4	1	2,490	3 $6\frac{11}{16}$-in. " 6 $5\frac{7}{8}$-in. "	1878	—	14·4	280	
Belted ship	Rio-Jio . .	1,459	—	—	—	$6\frac{1}{4}$	$6\frac{1}{4}$	?	17 0	1	1,270	8 $5\frac{7}{8}$-in. (? Vavasseur) 2 $6\frac{1}{4}$-in. Armstrong	1864	—	10·0		
Ram	Adsuma .	700	—	—	—	$4\frac{3}{8}$	$2\frac{7}{8}$	?	13 1	1	1,300	1 $9\frac{1}{16}$-in. " 2 $6\frac{1}{4}$-in. "	1865	—	9·0		

JAPAN.—*Unarmoured Ships.*

Class	Name	Displacement	Length	Beam	Depth of Hold	Material of Hull	Draught of Water	Propeller	Indicated Horse-Power	Armament	Date of Launch	Cost	Speed	Coal Supply	Distance that can be steamed at 10 knots
		tons	ft. in.	ft. in.	ft. in.		ft. in.					£	knots	tons	knots
Corvette	Kaimu . . .	1,490	—	—	—	?	?	?	1,250	8 ?	Building	—	?		
"	Tenrio . . .	1,490	—	—	—	?	?	?	1,250	7 ?	Building	—	?		
Clipper	Seiki . . .	898	—	—	—	?	15 1	?	700	1 $5\frac{7}{8}$-in. Krupp 4 $4\frac{5}{8}$-in. "	1875.	—	11·5		
"	Iwaki . . .	600	—	—	—	?	?	?	650	3 ?	Building	—			

There are also several old-fashioned corvettes, clippers, and gun-vessels.

PORTUGAL.—Armoured Ship, Iron Hull.

Class	Name	Displacement (tons)	Length (ft. in.)	Beam (ft. in.)	Depth of Hold (ft. in.)	Armour Max. (inches)	Armour Min. (inches)	Backing	Indicated Horse-Power	Propeller	Draught of Water (ft. in.)	Armament	Date of Launch	Cost (£)	Speed (knots)	Coal Supply (tons)	Distance that can be steamed at 10 knots (knots)
Armoured cruiser	Vasco de Gama	2,479	216 0	40 0	25 0	10	6	1	3,625	2	19 0	2 10½-in. Krupp, 1 6-in. ", 3 light Arm.	1876	108,800	13½	? 50	

PORTUGAL.—Unarmoured Ships.

Class	Name	Displacement (tons)	Length (ft. in.)	Beam (ft. in.)	Depth of Hold (ft. in.)	Material of Hull	Draught of Water (ft. in.)	Propeller	Indicated Horse-Power	Armament	Date of Launch	Cost (£)	Speed (knots)	Coal Supply (tons)	Distance that can be steamed at 10 knots (knots)
Corvette	Rainha de Portugal	1,124	170 0	36 0	16 5	Composite	14 9	—	900	2 7-in. Armstrong, 6 40-pdr. "	1876	£	?		
"	Mindello	1,124	170 0	36 0	16 5	Composite	14 9	—	900	2 7-in. ", 6 40-pdr. "	1876	—	?		
Gun-vessel	Rio Lima	539	—	—	—	Composite	11 2	?	100	1 7-in. ", 6 40-pdr. "	1875	—	?		
"	Tamega	539	—	—	—	Composite	11 2	?	nom.	1 7-in. ", 4 40-pdr. "	1875	—	?		
"	Sado	539	—	—	—	Composite	11 2	?	100	1 7-in. ", 4 40-pdr. "	1875	—	?		
"	Douro	369	—	—	—	Composite	12 1	?	nom.	1 7-in. ", 4 40-pdr. "	1873	—	?		
"	Quanza	369	—	—	—	Composite	12 1	?	100	1 7-in. ", 2 40-pdr. "	1877	—	?		
"	Mondovi	339	123 0	23 10	11 4	Composite	9 6	?	nom.	1 7-in. ", 3 40-pdr. "	1879	—	?		
"	Bengo	339	123 0	23 10	11 4	Composite	9 6	?	90	1 7-in. ", 2 20-pdr. "	1879	—	?		
Paddle-wheel vessel	Faro	286	—	—	—	?	9 2	?	90	1 7-in. ", 2 20-pdr. "	Building	—	?		
"	Guadiana	161	—	—	—	?	8 10	—	40 nom.	1 7-in. ", 1 20-pdr. "	1879	—	?		
"	Guine	139	—	—	—	?	6 3	—	40 nom.	1 7-in. ", 1 20-pdr. "	1879	—	?		

There are also on the effective list 3 transports, several gunboats, paddle-wheel vessels, and other ships of old type.

RUSSIA.—*Armoured Ships with Hulls of Iron or Steel.*

Class	Name	Displace-ment	Length	Beam	Depth of Hold	Armour Max.	Armour Min.	Backing	Draught of Water	Propeller	Indicated Horse-Power	Armament	Date of Launch	Cost	Speed	Coal Supply	Distance that can be steamed at 10 knots
		tons	ft. in.	ft. in.	ft. in.	inches	inches	in.	ft. in.					£	knots	tons	knots
Battery ship	Knjaz Pozarski	4,809	280 0	49 0	23 6	$4\frac{3}{8}$	$2\frac{7}{8}$	$17\frac{5}{8}$	21 $11\frac{1}{2}$	1	2,835	8 8-in. Obukov 2 6-in. ,, 8 light guns	1867	—	10·6		
Belted cruiser	Gen. Admiral	4,603	285 9	48 2	22 10	$5\frac{7}{8}$	$3\frac{7}{8}$	$9\frac{3}{4}$	22 11	1	6,300	4 8-in. Obukov 2 6-in. ,, 4 light guns 2 Mitrail.	1873	—	13	1,000	5,900
,,	H. v. Edin-burgh	4,602	285 9	48 2	22 10	$5\frac{7}{8}$	$3\frac{7}{8}$	$9\frac{3}{4}$	22 11	1	6,300	4 8-in. Obukov 2 6-in. ,, 4 light guns 8 Mitrail.	1875	—	13	1,000	5,900
,,	Minin . .	5,740	289 3	49 0	—	$8 + 1\frac{1}{8}$	$5\frac{7}{8}$	?	23 7	1	5,729	4 8-in. Obukov 12 6-in. ,, 4 light guns 2 Mitrail.	1878	—	14·0		
Broad-side ship	Perwenee .	3,277	220 0	53 0	18 3	$4\frac{3}{8}$	$3\frac{7}{8}$	$9\frac{3}{4}$	14 5	1	900	10 8-in. Mörser O. 4 6-in. ,, 1 6-in ,,	1863	—	9·0		
,,	Netronjmenja	3,340	220 0	53 0	18 8	$4\frac{3}{8}$	$3\frac{7}{8}$	$12\frac{1}{8}$	15 1	1	1,632	16 8-in. Obukov 7 light guns	1864	—	8·0		
,,	Kreml . .	3,412	218 6	53 0	18 8	$5\frac{7}{8}$	$3\frac{7}{8}$	$17\frac{5}{8}$	15 1	1	1,121	16 8-in. Obukov 6 light guns	1864	—	8·5		
Turret	Peter the Great	9,665	330 0	64 0	25 10	$14 + 2\frac{7}{8}$	9	$9\frac{3}{4}$	24 7	2	8,000	4 12-in. Obukov 6 small guns 2 Mitrail.	1872	machinery only 156,016	13·2	1,200	3,700
,,	Adl. Lazareff	3,753	260 0	43 6	22 7	$4\frac{3}{8} + \frac{7}{8}$	$2\frac{7}{8}$	$17\frac{5}{8}$	20 0	1	2,004	3 11-in. Obukov 4 light guns 1 Mitrail.	1867	—	10·1		
,,	Adl. Greig .	3,841	260 0	43 6	21 10	$4\frac{3}{8} + \frac{7}{8}$	$2\frac{7}{8}$	$17\frac{5}{8}$	21 0	1	2,031	3 11-in. Obukov 4 light guns 1 Mitrail.	1868	—	10·3		
,,	Adl. Cicagoff	3,692	260 0	43 6	—	$5\frac{7}{8}$	$3\frac{7}{8}$	$17\frac{5}{8}$	18 4	1	2,060	2 11-in. Obukov 4 light guns 1 Mitrail.	1868	—	10·8		
,,	Adl. Spiridoff	3,744	260 0	43 6	—	$5\frac{7}{8}$	$3\frac{7}{8}$	$17\frac{5}{8}$	18 4	1	2,007	2 11-in. Obukov 4 light guns 1 Mitrail.	1868	—	10·8		
,,	Malakoff .	?	—	—	—	?	?	?	?	?	10,000	4 100-t.	Build-ing	—	?		

2-turret monitor	Tcharodjejka	1,881	210 0	42 0	12 5	$4\frac{3}{8}$	$3\frac{1}{4}$	$17\frac{5}{8}$	11 $1\frac{1}{2}$	2	786	4 9-in. Obukov 2 Mitrail.	1867	—	8 7		
,,	Russalka .	1,881	210 0	42 0	12 5	$4\frac{3}{8}$	$3\frac{1}{4}$	$17\frac{5}{8}$	11 $1\frac{1}{2}$	2	705	4 9-in. Obukov 2 Mitrail.	1867				
,,	Smerc . .	1,520	172 10	38 0	14 4	$4\frac{3}{8}$	$3\frac{7}{8}$	$7\frac{3}{4}$	12 1	2	700	2 9-in. Obukov 2 Mitrail.	1864	80,800	8·3		
1-turret monitor	Strjelec .	1,431	200 0	46 0	—	5 1-in. plates	—	39	11 6	1	444	2 9-in. Obukov 2 Mitrail.	1864	—	6·0		
,,	Jedinorog .	1,406	200 0	46 0	—	5 1-in. plates	—	39	11 6	1	460	2 9-in. Obukov 2 Mitrail.	1864	—	6·5		
,,	Latnik . .	1,515	200 0	46 0	—	5 1-in. plates	—	39	12 1	1	490	2 9-in. Obukov 2 Mitrail.	1864	—	6·5		
,,	Bronenosec .	1,381	200 0	46 0	11 10	5 1-in. plates	—	39	11 6	1	481	2 9-in. Obukov 2 Mitrail.	1864	—	7·7		
,,	Uragan .	1,415	200 0	46 0	—	5 1-in. plates	—	39	11 6	1	432	2 9-in. Obukov 1 Mitrail.	1864	—	7·0		
,,	Tifon . .	1,666	200 0	46 0	—	5 1-in. plates	—	39	12 1	1	430	2 9-in. Obukov 1 Mitrail.	1864	—	6·5		
,,	Lawa . .	1,591	200 0	46 0	—	5 1-in. plates	—	39	11 6	1	335	2 9-in. Obukov 2 Mitrail.	1864	—	7·2		
,,	Perm . .	1,549	200 0	46 0	—	5 1-in. plates	—	39	12 1	1	338	2 9-in. Obukov 2 Mitrail.	1864	—	6·5		
,,	Wjescun .	1,449	200 0	46 0	—	5 1-in. plates	—	39	11 6	1	529	2 9-in. Obukov 1 Mitrail.	1864	—	6·7		
,,	Koldun. .	1,666	200 0	46 0	—	5 1-in. plates	—	39	12 1	1	481	2 9-in. Obukov 1 Mitrail.	1864	—	8·3		

RUSSIA.—*Armoured Ships with Hulls of Wood.*

Class	Name	Displace-ment	Length	Beam	Depth of Hold	Armour Max.	Armour Min.	Backing	Draught of Water	Propeller	Indicated Horse-Power	Armament	Date of Launch	Cost	Speed	Coal Supply	Distance that can be steamed at 10 knots
		tons	ft. in.	ft. in.	ft. in.	inches	inches	in.	ft. in.					£	knots	tons	knots
Broad-side ship	Sewastopol	6,209	300 0	50 10	26 10	$4\frac{3}{8}$	$2\frac{7}{8}$	26	25 11	1	,088	16 8-in. Obukov 1 6-in. ,, 10 light guns 1 Mitrail.	1863	—	12·0		
,,	Petropaulski .	6,175	300 0	56 0	26 3	$4\frac{3}{8}$	$2\frac{7}{8}$	24	24 $11\frac{1}{2}$	1	2,808	21 8-in. Obukov 1 6-in. ,, 10 light guns	1865	—	11·0		

RUSSIA.—Unarmoured Ships.

Class	Name	Displacement (tons)	Length (ft. in.)	Beam (ft. in.)	Depth of Hold (ft. in.)	Material of Hull	Draught of Water (ft. in.)	Propeller	Indicated Horse-Power	Armament	Date of Launch	Cost (£)	Speed (knots)	Coal Supply (tons)	Distance that can be steamed at 10 knots (knots)
Clipper *	Kreuzer	1,334	213 10	32 10	—	Iron and wood	14 5	1	1,206	3 6-in. Obukov, 5 light guns, 1 Mitrail.	1875	—	12·4		6,000
,,	Djigit	1,334	213 10	32 10	—	,,	14 5	1	1,383		1875	—	12·4		
,,	Rasboynik	1,334	213 10	30 2	—	,,	14 4	1	1,500		1878	—	12·6		
,,	Najeadnik	1,334	213 10	32 10	—	,,	14 4	1	1,373		1878	—	13·2		
,,	Plastun	1,334	214 0	32 0	—	,,	14 4	1	1,466	3 6-in. Obukov, 4 light guns, 1 machine gun	1879	—	12·0		
,,	Strelok	1,334	213 10	32 10	—	,,	14 4	1	1,466		1879	—	12·5		
,,	Viestnik	1,334	213 10	32 10	—	,,	14 4	1	1,250		1879	—	13·5		
,,	Opritjnik	1,331	213 10	32 10	—	,,	14 4	1	1,250		Building	75,000	?		
,,	Zabijaka	1,200	—	—	—	Iron	11 10	1	1,300	2 6-in. Obukov, 4 light guns, 1 machine gun	,,	—	14·5		
Formerly merchant steamer	Europe	3,000	—	—	—	,,	18 4	1	1,800		1878	—	13·5		
,,	Asia	2,650	—	—	—	,,	17 4	1	1,050	3 6-in. Obukov, 6 9-pdr.	1878	—	12·5		
,,	Africa	2,580	—	—	—	,,	16 1	1	1,350	,,	1878	—	12·5		
,,	Rossja	3,098	—	—	26 10	Steel and iron	20 8	1	2,200	?	?	—	14·0		
,,	Jaroslaw	3,150	310 0	40 9	—	,,	19 8	1	3,000	?	1880	—	16·2		
,,	Rurik	1,575	—	—	—	Wood	15 9	Pad	—	2 6-in. Obukov, 4 light guns	1870	—	?		

There are also on the effective list 7 gunboats of the English 'Staunch' type, 12 other small gunboats, and several clippers of an old-fashioned type, also old frigates and corvettes.

* There are 8 clippers of this (the above) class of modern date.

RUSSIA:—Black Sea Fleet.—*Armoured Ships.*

Class	Name	Displacement (tons)	Length (ft. in.)	Beam (ft. in.)	Depth of Hold (ft. in.)	Armour Max. (inches)	Armour Min. (inches)	Backing (in.)	Draught of Water (ft. in.)	Propeller	Indicated Horse-Power	Armament	Date of Launch	Cost (£)	Speed (knots)	Coal Supply (tons)	Distance that can be steamed at 10 knots (knots)
Popoffka	V.-A. Popoff	3,590	121 0	121 0	14 0	8	8	15¾	13 5	4	2,230	4 light guns, 2 12-in. Obukov, 1 Mitrailleuse	1875	—	8·0		
„	Novgorod	2,705	101 0	101 0	13 0	9	8¼	9	13 0	6	3,300	2 light guns, 2 11-in. Obukov, 4 Mitrailleuse	1873	Machinery alone 43,150	6·5		
Gun-vessel	Nikopol	512	—	—	—	2⅞	2	9¾	5 3	2	320	—	1868	—	8·0		
„	Sistowo	512	—	—	—	2⅞	2	9¾	5 3	2	90	—	1868	—	8 0		

RUSSIA:—Black Sea.

Class	Name	Displacement (tons)	Length (ft. in.)	Beam (ft. in.)	Depth of Hold (ft. in.)	Material of Hull	Draught of Water (ft. in.)	Propeller	Indicated Horse-Power	Armament	Date of Launch	Cost (£)	Speed (knots)	Coal Supply (tons)	Distance that can be steamed at 10 knots (knots)
Yacht	Livadia	3,900	—	—	—	Iron	—	3	12 383	6 8-in. Obukov mortars, 4 6-in. „	1880	—	15·9		
Cruiser	Rossia	3,500	—	—	—	Iron	—	1	500	4 light guns, 6 Mitrailleuse	1873				
„	Opit	187	—	—	—	Iron	2	4 Pad.	60 nom.	2 light guns, 1 Mitrailleuse	1870				

In addition there are some 20 other steamers, but all of them built many years ago. There are also 16 schooners of about 250 indicated horse-power, mostly of old date. There are also 15 torpedo-boats, but this number is being largely increased.

RUSSIA:—SIBERIAN SQUADRON.

Class	Name	Displacement tons	Length ft. in.	Beam ft. in.	Depth of Hold ft. in.	Material of Hull	Draught of Water ft. in.	Propeller	Indicated Horse-Power	Armament	Date of Launch	Cost £	Speed knots	Coal Supply tons	Distance that can be steamed at 10 knots knots
Clipper	Abrek	1,069	—	—	—	Wood	13 1	1	1,109	3 6-in Obukov / 4 light guns	1860				
	Wostok	210	—	—	—	Iron	9 10	1	40 nom.	4 " "	1852				
Schooner	Jermak	706	—	—	—	Iron	11 1	1	60 nom.	4 " "	1870				
,,	Tungus	706	—	—	—	Iron	11 1	1	60 nom.	4 " "	1870				
Transport	Japonec	1,472	—	—	—	Wood	13 1	1	300 nom.	6 " "	1858				
,,	Maudyűr	1,187	—	—	—	Wood	12 1	1	150 nom.	—	1858				
,,	Morz	456	—	—	—	Wood	8 2	1	80 nom.	1 60-pdr. smooth-bore / 4 light guns	1860				
,,	Nerpa	379	—	—	—	Wood	7 10	1	60 nom.	1 6-in, Obukov / 4 light guns	1877				
,,	Siuris	79	—	—	—	Wood	7 10	1	60 nom.	1 6-in, Obukov / 4 light guns	Building 1863				
,,	Gornostaj	456	—	—	—	Wood	8 2	1	80 nom.	2 6-in. Obukov / 2 light guns	1863				
,,	Sokol	456	—	—	—	Wood	8 2	1	80 nom.	2 6-in. Obukov / 2 light guns	1856				
Steamer	Amerika	554	—	—	—	Iron	8 6	Pad.	140 nom.	—	1857				
,,	Amur	190	—	—	—	Iron	6 2	Pad.	100 nom.	—	1870				
,,	Sinfun	114	—	—	—	Iron	—	Pad.	20 nom.	—	1862				
,,	Buksir	48	—	—	—	Iron	5 7	Pad.	45 nom.	—	1862				
,,	Polga	48	—	—	—	Iron	5 7	Pad.	45 nom.	—	1862				
,,	Uspiech	48	—	—	—	Iron	5 7	Pad.	45 nom.	—					

SPAIN.—*Armoured Ships with Hulls of Iron.*

Class	Name	Displacement	Length between the perpendiculars	Beam	Depth of Hold	Armour Max.	Armour Min.	Backing	Draught of Water	Propeller	Indicated Horse-Power	Armament	Date of Launch	Cost	Speed	Coal Supply	Distance that can be steamed at 10 knots
		tons	ft. in.	ft. in.	ft. in.	inches	inches	in.	ft. in.					£	knots	tons	miles
Frigate	Vitoria .	7,100	316 6	57 0	35 1	$5\frac{3}{8}$	$3\frac{7}{8}$	$14\frac{1}{8}$	27 2	1	4,500	14 $6\frac{1}{4}$-in. Spanish 4 $9\frac{1}{16}$-in. Arm. 3 $7\frac{7}{8}$-in. "	1867	—	14·1		
"	Numancia .	7,200	313 7	56 11	28 11	5	$3\frac{7}{8}$	$11\frac{3}{4}$	26 7	1	3,700	8 $6\frac{1}{4}$-in. Spanish 3 $7\frac{7}{8}$-in. Arm. 6 $9\frac{1}{16}$-in. "	1864	315,600	12·9	740	

SPAIN.—*Armoured Ships with Hulls of Wood.*

Class	Name	Displacement	Length between the perpendiculars	Beam	Depth of Hold	Armour Max.	Armour Min.	Backing	Draught of Water	Propeller	Indicated Horse-Power	Armament	Date of Launch	Cost	Speed	Coal Supply	Distance that can be steamed at 10 knots
		tons	ft. in.	ft. in.	ft. in.	inches	inches	in.	ft. in.					£	knots	tons	miles
Frigate	Sagunto .	6,300	279 3	54 0	—	$5\frac{7}{8}$	$3\frac{7}{8}$	24	25 1	1	1,000 nom.	10 $8\frac{5}{8}$-in. Spanish 3 $7\frac{1}{16}$-in. "	1876	—	12·5		
"	Zaragoza .	5,400	270 7	54 1	—	$4\frac{5}{8}$	3	$25\frac{7}{8}$	24 1	1	800 nom.	6 $9\frac{1}{16}$-in. " 3 $7\frac{1}{16}$-in. " 8 $6\frac{1}{4}$-in. "	1867	—	10·9		
"	Mendez Nunez	3,250	—	—	—	$4\frac{3}{8}$	3	$20\frac{3}{8}$	22 0	1	500 nom.	4 $9\frac{1}{16}$-in. Arm.	1861	—	6·5	400	
River monitor	Puigcerdá .	520	131 3	29 7	—	$3\frac{7}{8}$	$2\frac{1}{4}$	9	6 6	2	328	1 $6\frac{1}{4}$-in. Spanish 2 $4\frac{5}{8}$-in. "	1875	—	8·2		
Battery	Duke of Tetuan	600	—	—	—	$3\frac{7}{8}$	$2\frac{7}{8}$	9	6 10	2	209	4 $4\frac{4}{8}$-in. " 1 $6\frac{1}{4}$-in. "	re-bldg	—	? 6·0		
"	Arapiles .	5,700	281 0	—	—	?	—	?	?	1	—	? ?	re-bldg	—	?		

SPAIN.—*Unarmoured Ships.*

Class	Name	Displacement	Length	Beam	Depth of Hold	Material of Hull	Draught of Water	Propeller	Nominal Horse-Power	Armament	Date of Launch	Cost	Speed	Coal Supply	Distance that can be steamed at 10 knots
		tons	ft. in.	ft. in.	ft. in.		ft. in.					£	knots	tons	miles
Cruiser	Castilla . .	?	242 9	42 7	29 6	Wood	?	?	400	? ?	Bldg.	—	15		
,,	Aragon . .	?	242 9	42 7	29 6	Wood	?	?	400	? ?	1879	—	15		
,,	Navarra . .	?	242 9	42 7	29 6	Wood	?	?	400	? ?	Bldg.	—	15		
,,	Maria de Molina	?				?	?	?	300	? ?	1877	—	?		
,,	Jorge Juan . .	920	203 5	29 7	11 8	Iron	12 3	?	250	? ?	1876	—	12·1	130	
,,	Sanches Barcáiz-tequi	920	203 5	29 7	11 8	Iron	12 3	?	250	? ?	1876	—	12·1	130	
,,	Diana . . .	?				?	?	?	160	? ?	1871	—	?		
Despatch vessel	Fernando el Cató-lice	500	157 5	23 6	7 10	Iron	8 6	?	137	? ?	1875	—	?		
,,	Marqués del Duero	500	157 5	23 6	7 10	Iron	8 6	?	137	? ?	1875	—	?		

A large number of old-fashioned vessels, frigates, corvettes and gunboats, still remains on the Effective List.

SWEDEN AND NORWAY:—SWEDEN.—*Armoured Ships with Hulls of Iron.*

Class	Name	Displacement	Length	Beam	Depth of Hold	Armour: Turret	Armour: Water-line	Backing	Draught of Water	Propeller	Indicated Horse-Power	Armament	Date of Launch	Cost	Speed	Coal Supply	Distance that can be steamed at 10 knots
		tons	ft. in.	ft. in.	ft. in.	inches	inches	in.	ft. in.					£	knots	tons	miles
Monitor	John Ericsson	1,522	197 0	46 10	—	10⅝	4⅞	31½	11 5	1	380	2 15-in. Rod.	1865	—	7·0	?65	
,,	Thordön .	1,522	197 0	46 10	—	10⅝	4⅞	25⅞	11 5	1	380	2 9·448-in. Fins.	1866	—	7·5		
,,	Tirfing . .	1,522	197 0	46 10	—	10⅝	4⅞	25⅞	11 5	1	380	2 9·448-in. ,,	1866	—	7·5		
,,	Loke . .	1,620	205 3	45 4	—	17⅝	4⅞	40	12 1	1	460	2 9·448-in. ,,	1871	—	8·0		
Armour gunboat	Gerda . .	461	131 0	22 3	8 3	16⅝	2½	33⅞	8 2	2	133	1 9·448-in. ,,	1871	—	8·0		
,,	Hildur . .	461	131 0	22 3	8 3	16⅝	2½	33⅞	8 2	2	133	1 9·448-in. ,,	1871	—	8·0		
,,	Ulf . .	461	131 0	22 3	8 3	16½	2½	33⅞	8 2	2	155	1 9·448-in. ,,	1873	18,800	8·0	20	
,,	Björn . .	461	131 0	22 3	8 3	16⅝	2½	33⅞	8 2	2	155	1 9·448 in. ,,	1873	—	8·0		

SWEDEN AND NORWAY:—SWEDEN.—*Unarmoured Ships.*

Class	Name	Displacement	Length	Beam	Depth of Hold	Material of Hull	Draught of Water	Propeller	Indicated Horse-Power	Armament	Date of Launch	Cost	Speed	Coal Supply	Distance that can be steamed at 10 knots
		tons	ft. in.	ft. in.	ft. in.		ft. in.					£	knots	tons	miles
Frigate	Vanadis . . .	2,130				Wood	—	1	1,400	8 $6\frac{1}{4}$-in. Finspong 8 $7\frac{3}{8}$-in. smooth-bore	1870	—	11·5		
Corvette	Balder . . .	1,900	224 6	37 7	15 2	Wood	—	1	1,380	6 $6\frac{1}{4}$-in. ,, 2 30-pdr. ,,	1871	—	12·4	? 350	940
,,	Gefle . . .	1,298			—	Wood	—	1	900	2 $6\frac{1}{4}$-in. Finspong 6 $4\frac{5}{8}$-in. ,,	?	—	9·0		
,,	Saga . . .	1,549	200 7	38 5	—	Wood	—	1	900	1 $6\frac{1}{4}$-in. ,, 6 $4\frac{5}{8}$-in. ,,	1878	—	13·0		
,,	Thor . . .	1,085	—		—	Wood	—	1	640	4 24-pdr. smooth-bore 1 $8\frac{1}{4}$-in. ,,	?	—	9·8		
Gunboat	Blenda . . .	532	171 10	26 4	—	Iron	9 4	2	398	1 $10\frac{5}{8}$-in. Finspong 1 $4\frac{5}{8}$-in. ,,	1875	—	13·2		
,,	Disa . . .	532	171 10	26 4	—	Iron	9 4	2	570	1 $10\frac{5}{8}$-in. ,, 1 $4\frac{5}{8}$-in. ,,	1875	—	13·2		
,,	Urd . . .	550	175 10	26 6	—	Iron	9 7	2	804	1 $10\frac{5}{8}$-in. ,, 1 $4\frac{5}{8}$-in. ,,	1877	—	13·5		
,,	Verdande . .	550	175 10	26 6	—	Iron	9 7	2	780	1 $10\frac{5}{8}$-in. ,, 1 $4\frac{5}{8}$-in. ,,	1878	—	13·5		
,,	Skuld . . .	550	175 10	26 6	—	Iron	9 7	2	780	1 $10\frac{5}{8}$-in. ,, 1 $4\frac{5}{8}$-in. ,,	1879	—	13·5		
,,	Rota . . .	550	175 10	26 6	—	Iron	9 7	2	780	1 $10\frac{5}{8}$-in. ,, 1 $4\frac{5}{8}$-in. ,,	1878	—	13·5		
,,	Skagul . . .	550	175 10	26 6	—	Iron	9 7	2	780	1 $10\frac{5}{8}$-in. ,, 1 $4\frac{5}{8}$-in. ,,	1878	—	13·5		
,,	Skäggald . .	550	175 10	26 6	—	Iron	9 7	2	780	1 $10\frac{5}{8}$-in. ,, 1 $4\frac{5}{8}$-in. ,,	1879	—	13·5		
,,	Edda . . .	640	—	—	—	Iron	—	2	960	1 10-in. Armstrong 1 6-in. ,,	1880	—	14·5		
Torpedo	Ran . . .	630	188 4	26 3	—	Iron	—	2	960	1 $4\frac{5}{8}$-in. Finspong 2 Mitrailleuse	1877	—	13·4	—	1,000

Also ten smaller gunboats of 60 nominal horse-power, each carrying one 4·72-inch Finspong.

SWEDEN AND NORWAY:—NORWAY.—*Armoured Ships.*

Class	Name	Displacement	Length	Beam	Depth of Hold	Armour Max.	Armour Min.	Backing	Draught of Water	Propeller	Indicated Horse-Power	Armament	Date of Launch	Cost	Speed	Coal Supply	Distance that can be steamed at 10 knots
		tons	ft. in.	ft. in.	ft. in.	inches	inches	in.	ft. in.					£	knots	tons	miles
Monitor	Thor	2,003	176 6	46 0	12 0	$14\frac{3}{8}$	$6\frac{7}{8}$	37	13 9	1	600	2 11-in. Arm.	1872	—	8·3	138	138
,,	Trudvang	1,515	168 6	45 2	12 0	$12\frac{1}{8}$	$4\frac{7}{8}$	$38\frac{1}{8}$	11 9	1	500	2 11-in. ,,	1869	66,800	8·5	138	138
,,	Miölner	1,515	168 6	45 2	12 0	$12\frac{1}{8}$	$4\frac{7}{8}$	$38\frac{1}{8}$	11 9	1	450	2 11-in. ,,	1868	—	8·0	138	138
,,	Scorpionen	1,447	164 0	43 11	12 0	$12\frac{1}{8}$	$4\frac{7}{8}$	$38\frac{1}{8}$	11 5	1	350	2 11-in. ,,	1866	—	6·0	138	138

SWEDEN AND NORWAY:—NORWAY.—*Unarmoured Ships.*

Class	Name	Displacement	Length	Beam	Depth of Hold	Material of Hull	Draught of Water	Propeller	Indicated Horse-Power	Armament	Date of Launch	Cost	Speed	Coal Supply
		tons	ft. in.	ft. in.	ft. in.		ft. in.					£	knots	tons
Gun-vessel	Sleipner	580	165 0	32 5	—	Iron	—	2	800	1 $10\frac{5}{16}$-in. Krupp	1877	—	12·0	—
,,	Ellida	580	165 0	32 5	—	Iron	—	2	800	1 $5\frac{7}{8}$-in. ,, 1 $10\frac{3}{16}$-in. ,,	1880	—	?	—
,,	N.N.N.	255	—	—	—	Iron	—	2	210	1 $5\frac{7}{8}$-in. 1 $10\frac{5}{8}$-in. Arm.	Building	—	8·0	—
,,	Vale	238	—	—	—	Iron	—	2	210	1 $10\frac{5}{8}$-in. ,,	1874	—	8·0	—
,,	Uller	238	—	—	—	Iron	—	2	210	1 $10\frac{5}{8}$-in. ,,	1876	—	8·0	—

In addition to the above there is a large number of gunboats, but all of an old build. There are also a few frigates and corvettes of an old-fashioned type.

TURKEY.—Armoured Ships with Hulls of Iron.

Class	Name	Displacement (tons)	Length (ft. in.)	Beam (ft. in.)	Depth of Hold (ft. in.)	Armour Max. (inches)	Armour Min. (inches)	Backing (in.)	Draught of Water (ft. in.)	Propeller	Indicated Horse-Power	Armament	Date of Launch	Cost (£)	Speed (knots)	Coal Supply (tons)	Distance that can be steamed at 10 knots (miles)
Central battery	Messudijé	8,950	332 0	59 0	25 0	12 + 1 1/2	7	9 7/8	25 11	1	7,910	12 9 13/16-in. Arm.; 3 7 1/2-in. „	1875	—	13·1		
„	Nussratije	7,920	292 3	—	—	12 + 1 1/4	5 7/8	18	24 6	1	6,800	10 9 1/16-in. „; 2 7 1/16-in. „	Building 1868	—	?	400	
„	Assar-i-Tefvik	5,687	275 4	50 0	—	8	5 3/4	9	21 0	1	3,100	6 9 3/16-in. „; 2 7 7/8-in. „	1868	—	13·5		
Broadside frigate	Azizié	6,400	293 0	56 0	—	4 1/4	3	9	24 11	1	900 nom.	14 7 7/8-in. „; 1 9 1/16-in. „; 10 36-pdr. smooth-bore	1864	—	12·0		
„	Orchanié	6,400	293 0	56 0	—	4 1/4	3	9	24 11	1	900 nom.	14 7 1/16-in. Arm.; 1 9 1/16-in. „; 10 36-pdr. smooth-bore	1864	—	12·0		
„	Mahmudié	6,400	293 0	56 0	—	4 1/4	3	9	24 11	1	900 nom.	14 7 1/16-in. Arm.; 1 9 1/16-in. „; 10 36-pdr. smooth-bore	1864	—	12·0		
„	Osmanie	6,400	293 0	56 0	—	4 1/4	3	9	24 11	1	900 nom.	14 7 1/16-in. Arm.; 1 9 1/16-in. „; 10 36-pdr. smooth-bore	1864	—	12·0		
Corvette	Mukademme-i-Haïr	2,760	235 0	43 0	19 8	9	4 3/8	9 7/8	18 4	1	2,700	4 9 1/16-in. Arm.	1869	—	12·5		
„	Feth-i-Bulend	2,760	235 0	43 0	19 0	9	4 3/8	9 7/8	18 4	1	3,250	4 9 1/16-in. „	1869	—	13·5		
„	Idschlalié	2,228	219 0	41 0	26 6	5 3/4	3 7/8	13	17 0 1/2	1	300 nom.	4 9 1/16-in. „; 1 7 1/16-in. „	1870	—	11·0		
„	Assar-i-Schefket	2,046	210 0	40 0	25 4	5 3/8	3	9	17 0	2	350 nom.	5 9 1/16-in. „	1869	—	11·3		
„	Neaschum-i-Schefket	2,046	210 0	40 0	—	5 3/8	3	9	17 0	2	350 nom.	5 9 1/16-in. „	1868	—	11·3		
„	Avni Illah	2,380	230 0	35 6	—	6	4 7/8	9 7/8	16 0	2	400 nom.	5 9 1/16-in. „	1868	—	12·5		
„	Muni-i-Zafer	2,380	230 0	36 0	—	6	4 5/8	9 7/8	16 0	2	400 nom.	4 9 1/16-in. „	1868	—	12·5		

TURKEY.—Armoured Ships with Hulls of Iron—(continued).

Class	Name	Displacement (tons)	Length (ft. in.)	Beam (ft. in.)	Depth of Hold (ft. in.)	Armour Max. (inches)	Armour Min. (inches)	Backing (in.)	Draught of Water (ft. in.)	Propeller	Indicated Horse-Power	Armament	Date of Launch	Cost (£)	Speed (knots)	Coal Supply (tons)	Distance that can be steamed at 10 knots (miles)
Turret	Hütz-i-Rahman	2,500	204 0	43 2	16 6	$5\frac{3}{8}$	$4\frac{3}{8}$	$9\frac{3}{4}$	19 0	1	200 nom.	2 $9\frac{7}{16}$-in. Arm. 2 $7\frac{1}{16}$-in. ,, 1 $4\frac{7}{8}$-in. ,,	1868	—	12·0		
Monitor	Hezber .	652	—	24 9	—	3	3	$5\frac{3}{8}$	5 3	2	404	2 $4\frac{7}{8}$-in. Krupp	1875	—	7·0		
River gunboat	Feth-i-Islam .	511	100 0	24 9	—	3	2	$9\frac{5}{8}$	5 6	1	290	2 $4\frac{7}{8}$-in. Arm.	1864	—	8·0		
,,	Semendire .	511	100 0	24 9	—	3	2	$9\frac{5}{8}$	5 6	1	290	2 $4\frac{7}{8}$-in. ,,	1864	—	8·0		

On the List of the Turkish Navy there is also a large number of old-fashioned frigates, corvettes, sloops, and gunboats.

UNITED STATES.—Armoured Ships with Hulls of Iron or Steel.

Class	Name	Displacement (tons)	Length between the perpendiculars (ft. in.)	Beam (ft. in.)	Depth of Hold (ft. in.)	Armour Max. (inches)	Armour Min. (inches)	Backing (in.)	Draught of Water (ft. in.)	Propeller	Indicated Horse-Power	Armament	Date of Launch	Cost (£)	Speed (knots)	Coal Supply (tons)	Distance that can be steamed at 10 knots (miles)
Two-turret Monitor	Miantonomoh	3,825	250 0	55 6	16 6	7	3	$\frac{7}{8}$	14 0	2	1,600	4 10-in. American B.L.R.	Re-building	272,000	12·0	331	
,,	Monadnoc .	3,815	250 0	55 6	16 6	7	3	$7\frac{7}{8}$	14 0	2	1,600	4 10-in. American B.L.R.	—	272,000	8·0	331	
,,	Terror .	3,815	250 0	55 6	16 6	7	3	$7\frac{7}{8}$	14 0	2	1,600	4 10-in. American B.L.R.	—	206,800	12·0	331	
One-turret Monitor	Ajax .	2,100	225 0	43 8	—	$6\frac{1}{2}$	5	—	13 5	2	400 nom.	2 15-in. Rodman	1864	—	6·8		
,,	Canonicus .	2,100	225 0	43 8	—	$6\frac{1}{2}$	5	—	13 5	2	400 nom.	2 15-in. ,,	1864	—	8·0		
,,	Mahopac .	2,100	225 0	43 8	—	$6\frac{1}{2}$	5	—	—	2	400 nom.	2 15-in. ,,	1865	—	8·0		

Class	Name	Displacement (tons)	Length between the perpendiculars (ft. in.)	Beam (ft. in.)	Depth of Hold (ft. in.)	Armour Max (inches)	Armour Min (inches)	Backing (in.)	Draught of Water (ft. in.)	Propeller	Indicated Horse-Power	Armament	Cost (£)	Date of Launch	Speed (knots)	Coal Supply (tons)	Distance that can be steamed at 10 knots (miles)
„	Manhattan	2,100	225 0	43 8	—	6½	5	—	13 5	2	400 nom.	2 15-in. „	—	1865	8·0		
„	Sangus	2,100	225 0	43 8	—	6½	5	—	13 5	2	400 nom.	2 15-in. „	—	1864	8·0		
„	Wyandotte	2,100	225 0	43 8	—	6⅛	5	—	13 5	2	400 nom.	2 15-in. „	—	1865	8·0		
„	Comanche	1,875	200 0	46 0	—	5	—	—	11 5	2	200 nom.	11 11-in. D.	—	1863	8·0		
„	Catskill	1,875	200 0	46 0	—	5	—	—	11 5	2	200 nom.	11 11-in. „	—	1863	8·0		
„	Jason	1,875	200 0	46 0	—	5	—	—	11 5	2	200 nom.	11 11-in. „	—	1864	8·0		
„	Lehigh	1,875	200 0	46 0	—	5	—	—	11 5	2	200 nom.	11 11-in. „	—	1864	8·0		
„	Montank	1,875	200 0	46 0	—	5	—	—	11 5	2	200 nom.	11 11-in. „	—	1864	8·0		
„	Nahant	1,875	200 0	46 0	—	5	—	—	11 5	2	200 nom.	11 11-in. „	—	1864	8·0		
„	Nantucket	1,875	200 0	46 0	—	5	—	—	11 5	2	200 nom.	11 11-in. „	—	1863	8·0		
„	Passaic	1,875	200 0	46 0	—	5	—	—	11 5	2	200 nom.	11 11-in. „	—	1863	8·0		
Torpedo-vessel	Intrepid	1,123	167 3	35 0	—	5	—	13⅛	11 9	2	800 nom.	—	—	1874	9·5		
„	Alarm	700	173 0	28 0	—	3⅞	—	15¾	11 1	1	800	1 10-in. H. American	—	1873	15·0		

UNITED STATES.—Armoured Ships with Hulls of Wood.

Class	Name	Displacement (tons)	Length between the perpendiculars (ft. in.)	Beam (ft. in.)	Depth of Hold (ft. in.)	Armour Max (inches)	Armour Min (inches)	Backing (in.)	Draught of Water (ft. in.)	Propeller	Indicated Horse-Power	Armament	Cost (£)	Date of Launch	Speed (knots)	Coal Supply (tons)	Distance that can be steamed at 10 knots (miles)
Two-turret Monitor	Puritan	6,200	280 0	60 0	—	10	3⅞	21	16 8	2	3,500	4 10-in. H. B.L.R American	—	Re-building —	13·0		
„	Amphitrite	3,825	250 0	55 6	—	7	3	7⅞	14 1	2	1	4 10-in. H. B.L.R. American	201,600	—	13·0		

UNITED STATES.—*Armoured Ships with Hulls of Wood*—(continued).

Class	Name	Displacement (tons)	Length between the perpendiculars (ft. in.)	Beam (ft. in.)	Depth of Hold (ft. in.)	Armour Max. (inches)	Armour Min. (inches)	Backing (in.)	Draught of Water (ft. in.)	Propeller	Indicated Horse-Power	Armament	Date of Launch	Cost (£)	Speed (knots)	Coal Supply (tons)	Distance that can be steamed at 10 knots (miles)
Two-turret Monitor	Colossus	6,000	322 7	52 10	18 10	8	6⅛	7⅞	—	—	—	4 10-in. American B.L.R. 6 7-in. Parrot	—	—	12·0	—	—
,,	Massachusetts	6,000	322 7	52 10	18 10	8	6⅛	7⅞	—	—	—	4 10-in. American B.L.R.	—	—	12·0	—	—
One turret Monitor	Oregon	6,000	322 7	52 10	18 10	8	6⅛	7⅞	—	—	—	4 10-in. American B.L.R.	—	—	12·0	—	—
,,	Dictator	4,500	312 0	50 0	—	8	6⅛	—	21 0	—	—	2 15-in. Rodman	—	—	14·0	—	—

UNITED STATES.—*Unarmoured Ships.*

Class	Name	Displacement (tons)	Length (ft. in.)	Beam (ft. in.)	Depth of Hold (ft. in.)	Material of Hull	Draught of Water (ft. in.)	Propeller	Indicated Horse-Power	Armament	Date of Launch	Cost (£)	Speed (knots)	Coal Supply (tons)	Distance that can be steamed at 10 knots (miles)
Corvette	? New York	4,070	—	—	—	Wood	18 8	1	—	—	Building 1876	—	—	—	—
,,	Trenton	3,900	253 0	48 0	28 0	Wood	21 7	1	—	11 8-in. Amer. 2 light guns	—	—	13·0	—	—
,,	Vandalia	2,180	220 3	38 0	19 0	Wood	17 0	1	—	1 11-in. Amer. 1 60-pdr. ,, 6 9-in. smooth-bore	1874	—	12·5	—	—
,,	Quinnebaug	1,900	216 0	30 0	—	Wood	17 8	1	—	2 light guns 1 8-in. Amer. 1 60-pdr. ,, 6 9-in. smooth-bore	1875	—	11·5	—	—

Name						Material				Armament			
Swatara	„	1,900	216 0	—	30 0	Wood	18 0	1	—	1 11-in. Amer.; 1 60-pdr. „	1873	—	1·5
Galena	„	1,900	216 0	—	30 0	Wood	18 0	1	—	6 9-in. smooth-bore; 1 8-in.	1871	—	12·5
Marion	„	1,900	—	—	—	Wood	18 0	1	—	1 60-pdr. Amer.; 6 9-in. smooth-bore; 1 8-in.	1873	—	12·5
Mohican	„	1,900	216 0	—	30 0	Wood	18 0	1	—	1 60-pdr. Amer.; 6 9-in. smooth-bore; 1 8-in.	Building	—	12·5
Adams	„	1,375	185	—	35 0	Wood	16 4	1	—	1 60-pdr. Amer.; 6 9-in. smooth-bore; 2 8-in.	1874	—	11·5
Alliance	„	1,375	185	—	35 0	Wood	16 1	1	—	1 60-pdr. Amer.; 4 9-in. smooth-bore; 2 8-in.	1875	—	11·5
Essex	„	1,375	185	—	35 0	Wood	16 4	1	—	1 60-pdr. Amer.; 4 9-in. smooth-bore; 2 8-in.	1874	—	10·5
Enterprise	„	1,375	185	—	35 0	Wood	16 1	1	—	1 60-pdr. Amer.; 4 9-in. smooth-bore; 2 8-in.	1874	—	11·5
Nipsic	„	1,375	185	—	35 0	Wood	16 1	1	—	1 60-pdr. Amer.; 4 9-in. smooth-bore; 2 8-in.	1878	—	11·5
Alert	„	1,020	175	—	28 0	Wood	13 9	1	—	1 60-pdr. Amer.; 4 9-in. smooth-bore; 1 11-in.	1874	—	10·6
Ranger	„	1,020	175	—	28 0	Wood	13 9	1	—	1 60-pdr. Amer.; 2 9-in. smooth-bore; 1 11-in.	1874	—	9·5
Yantic	„	900	180	—	30 0	Wood	13 1	1	—	1 60-pdr. Amer.; 2 9-in. smooth-bore; 3 8-in.; 1 60-pdr. „	1878	—	9·5

INDEX.

ABR

A BREK, Russian clipper, 596
Absalon, Danish cruiser, 571
Abyssinia, British turret ship, 18, 108, 174, 550
Achilles, British broadside ship, 7, 8, 68–71, 80, 89, 552
Active, British unarmoured corvette, 479, 491, 556
Adams, American unarmoured corvette, 545, 546, 605
Adder, Dutch ram-monitor, 152, 584
Admirals Greig, Lazareff, Spiridoff, Tchitchachoff, Russian turret ships, 159, 592
Adsuma, Japanese ram, 590
Affondatore, Italian turret ship, 147, 587
Africa (ex Saratoga), Russian unarmoured ship, 536, 594
Agamemnon, British turret ship, 28, 242, 251 n., 430–437, 550
Agincourt, British broadside ship, 7, 61, 63, 68–69, 80, 552 ; trial of, with Devastation, 350–354
Agostino Barbarigo, Italian unarmoured cruiser, 532, 589
Ahmed Pasha, designs of, 183
Ajax, British turret ship, 28, 242, 251 n., 430–437, 550
— American 1-turret monitor, 131, 602
Alabama, Confederate ship, cruise of the, 477
Alagoas, Brazilian river monitor, 566
Alarm, American torpedo-vessel, 603
Albatross, British unarmoured sloop, 558
— Austrian unarmoured gun-vessel, 565
— German unarmoured gun-vessel, 529
Albert, experimental boat built on the Ruthven principle, 94
Alert, British unarmoured sloop, 558
— American unarmoured corvette, 545, 546, 605
Alexandra (ex Superb), British broadside ship, 10, 273–283, 402, 454, 552 ; compared with Téméraire, 287

ARE

Algerine, British unarmoured gun-vessel, 560
Alkmaar, Dutch unarmoured corvette, 585
Allen's propulsion patent, 93
Alliance, American unarmoured corvette, 545, 546, 605
Alma, French second-rate, 23, 49–50, 219
Almirante Brown, Argentine battery ship, 323, 562
Almirante Cochrane, Chilian central battery ship, 252–255, 321, 567
Alpha, Chinese gunboat, 569
Amboina, Dutch E.I unarmoured corvette, 586
America, war of secession in, 477–478. See United States
Amerigo Vespucci Italian unarmoured cruiser, 589
Amerika, Russian steamer, 596
Amethyst, British unarmoured corvette, 556 ; action of, with the Huascar, 412
Amiral Baudin, French barbette-turret and broadside ship, 30, 315–316, 572
Amiral Duperré, French barbette-turret and broadside ship, 29, 308–315, 454, 572
Amphitrite, American 2-turret monitor, 136, 142–143, 603
Amur, Russian steamer, 596
Ancona, Italian central battery ship, 126
Andrea Provana, Italian unarmoured torpedo-vessel, 588
Arab, unarmoured gun-vessel, 560
Aragon, Spanish unarmoured cruiser, 598
Arapiles, Spanish battery ship, 597
Archduke Albert, Austrian bow-battery ship, 268–272, 563
Archduke Ferdinand Maximilian, Austrian converted frigate, 116–118, 260, 564
Archduke Frederic, Austrian unarmoured spar-decked corvette, 565
Arçon, Chevalier d', floating batteries of, at siege of Gibraltar, 4
Arethusa, British steel despatch vessel, 505–506

ARE

Aréthuse, French unarmoured cruiser, 577

Argentine Republic, armoured ship-building of the, 207–209, 323–325; tables of ships, 562

Ariadne, German unarmoured flush-decked corvette, 529, 581

Armide, French second-rate, 25, 576

Arminius, German monitor, 32, 147, 579

Armour, steel, 450

— side, abandonment of, 462, 468

— 'sandwich' system of, 395

Armour-plates, thickness of, 5, 6, 7, 8, 11, 12, 395, 437; curvature of, 320–321; composite, or steel-faced, 323, 397, 436

Armstrong, Sir W., artillery of, 71

Arrogante, French floating battery, 31, 44, 167–168, 574

Aruba, Dutch unarmoured corvette, 585

Asia (ex Columbus), Russian unarmoured ship, 536, 594

Aspic, French unarmoured gun-vessel, 578

Assar-i-schefket, Turkish corvette, 113–114, 601

Assar-i-tefvik, Turkish central battery ship, 115–116, 601

Atahualpa, Peruvian turret ship, 154

Atalante, French second-rate, 25, 576

Atjeh, Dutch unarmoured corvette, 585

Audacious, British broadside ship, 10, 100–108, 552

Audenet, M., designs of, 5

Augusta, German unarmoured flush-decked corvette, 581

— Ersatz für, German unarmoured flush-decked corvette, 581

Aurora, Austrian corvette, 565

Austria, shipbuilding in: armoured, 111, 116–118, 217, 258–260, 268–272, 316–323; unarmoured, 532; tables of ships, 563–565

Avni-illah, Turkish corvette, 113, 601

Avon, British unarmoured gun-vessel, 560

Azizieh, Turkish broadside frigate, 601

BACCHANTE, British unarmoured corvette, 486–491, 556

Baden, German corvette, 31, 459, 579

Bahia, Brazilian turret ship, 154–155, 566

Baiern, German corvette, 31, 455, 459, 579

Balder, Swedish unarmoured corvette, 599

Ballast-keel of Polyphemus, 475

Baltic coast, defence of the, 32

Banda, Bandjermassing, Dutch E.I. un-armoured corvettes, 586

Barbette system of the French navy, 23–25

— ships, mastless, 455–476

— turrets, 11, 283; disappearing arma-ment in, 284, 293

BLA

Barnaby. Mr., designs of, 22, 26, 27, 387

— quoted or referred to: on the cost of the Warrior, 60; Hercules, 98; Auda-cious class, 103–104; British ironclads compared, 105; Sultan, 108–109; Glatton and Cyclops compared, 179–180; Russian popoffkas, 188; Shannon design, 233; Nelson type, 247–250; Alexandra and Téméraire compared, 288; Devastation and Thunderer, 342–344; Dreadnought, 374–375; Inflexible, 388–395, 408, 409, 426, 441; Italia and Lepanto, 468; on the question of pro-portions, 402

Barroso, Brazilian central battery ship, 566

Basilisk, German gun-vessel, 579

Batavia, Dutch E.I. unarmoured cor-vette, 586

Batteries démontables, 44

— floating, at the siege of Gibraltar, 4; in the Crimean war, 5, 43

Battery, bow, 267–272, 274

— central, 11, 273–325; preferable to the turret system in seagoing ships, 328

— overhanging, 113

— projecting midship, 321

Bayard, French second-rate, 30, 222, 576

Beautemps-Beaupré, French unarmoured cruiser, 577

Bélier, French coast-service vessel, 32, 165–167, 172, 576

Belleisle (ex Paykisherreef), British broad-side ship, 11, 182–184, 552

Bellerophon, British broadside ship, 9, 28, 77, 80, 83–89, 248–250, 454

Belliqueuse, French second-rate, 23, 48–49, 218, 576

Bellona. See Lima Barros

Belmonte, Brazilian unarmoured cor-vette, 567

Belt and battery system, 85

Belted cruisers, 226–229

Bengo, Portuguese unarmoured gun-vessel, 591

Benkoelen, Dutch E.I. unarmoured cor-vette, 586

Benton, American armoured paddle-steamer, 131

Bermejo, Argentine unarmoured gun-boat, 562

Berserk, Swedish armour gunboat, 599

Beta, Chinese gunboat, 569

Bienaymé, M., designs of, 522

Biene, German gun-vessel, 217, 579

Bismarck, German unarmoured spar-decked corvette, 528, 580

Bisson, French unarmoured cruiser, 524

Bittern, British unarmoured gun-vessel, 560

Björn, Swedish armour gunboat, 598

Black Prince, British broadside ship, 6, 59–61, 63, 64, 80, 89, 552

Black Sea, defence of, 184–185; Russian fleet in the, 595

BLA

Blanche, British unarmoured corvette, 556

Blanco Encalada (*ex* Valparaiso), Chilian central battery ship, 252–255, 321, 567

Blenda, Swedish unarmoured gunboat, 599

Bloedhond, Dutch monitor, 584

Blonde. *See* Shah

Blücher, German unarmoured spar decked corvette, 580

Boadicea, British unarmoured corvette, 486–488, 556

Bobolina, Greek unarmoured corvette, 583

Bonnaire, Dutch unarmoured corvette, 585

Bouledogue, French coast-service vessel, 32, 165, 172, 576

Bow, U form of, 83

Bow-battery system, 267–272

Bow fire in central battery ships, 9–11, 86

Boys, Admiral, *quoted*, on the Inflexible, 413–414

Bracket-frame system of construction, 82

Brazil, armoured shipbuilding of, 152–157, 204–207; tables of ships, 566–567

Brazil, Brazilian central battery ship, 155–156, 566

Brin, Commendatore, designs of, 530–531

Briton, British unarmoured corvette, 556

Bromo, Dutch E.I. paddle-wheel vessel, 586

Bronenosec, Russian 1-turret monitor, 593

Brun, M., his improvements in batteries démontables, 45

Buffel, Dutch ram, 151, 584

Buksir, Russian steamer, 596

Bussy, M. de, designs of, 13, 169, 172, 300, 301

CABRAL, Brazilian central battery ship, 156, 566

Caïman, French ram, 21, 172, 173 *n.*, 573

Caledonia, British broadside ship, 7, 76, 80, 89

Camäleon, German gun-vessel, 579

Canada, British unarmoured corvette, 556

Canonicus, American 1-turret monitor, 131, 602

Capitaine Lucas, French unarmoured cruiser, 577

Capricorne, French unarmoured gun-vessel, 578

Captain, British turret ship, 16, 105, 327, 345–346

Caracciolo, Italian unarmoured corvette, 588

Cariddi, Italian unarmoured gun-vessel, 589

Carysfort, British unarmoured corvette, 509, 556.

CON

Casemate ships, the term, 40

Castelfidardo, Italian central battery ship, 126

Castilla, Spanish unarmoured cruiser, 598

Catskill, American 1-turret monitor, 131, 603

Cerbère, French coast-service vessel, 32, 165, 172, 576

Cerberus, British turret ship, 18, 108, 174, 550

— Dutch turret ship, 151–152

Chacabuco, Chilian unarmoured corvette, 568

Challenger, British unarmoured corvette, 507

Champion, British unarmoured corvette, 556

Champlain, French unarmoured cruiser, 577

Charybdis, British unarmoured corvette, 556

Chasseur, French unarmoured cruiser, 523–524

Château Renaud, French unarmoured cruiser, 514–515, 577

Che-an, Chinese gun-vessel, 568

Chento, Chinese gunboat, 569

Chien-jui, Chinese gunboat, 570

Chih-hai, Chinese frigate, 570

Chili, armoured shipbuilding of, 252–254; tables of ships, 567–568

China, unarmoured shipbuilding of, 547–548; table of ships, 568–570

Ching-wo, Chinese gun-vessel, 569

Chong-sing, Chinese gunboat, 570

Chow-kiang, Chinese frigate, 570

Chung-wo, Chinese gun-vessel, 569

Cimbria, Russian unarmoured cruiser, 537

Circular vessels. *See* Popoffkas

Cleará, Brazilian river monitor, 566

Cleopatra, British unarmoured corvette, 556

Coal, American, 544

Colbert, French central battery ship, 12, 55–56, 104, 575

Coles, Captain Cowper, designs of, 16, 148, 152, 158, 160, 163, 226, 326

Collingwood, British barbette ship, 469–472, 554

Colomb, Captain, on our naval requirements, 33

Colombo, Brazilian central battery ship, 156, 566

Colossus, British steel turret ship, 28, 433, 438–445, 550

— American 2-turret monitor, 140, 604

Columbus. *See* Asia

Comanche, American 1-turret monitor, 131, 603

Commerce, protection of, 34

Comus, British unarmoured corvette, 263, 507, 508, 556

Conqueror, British turret ram, 28, 433, 438–439, 445–448, 550

Conquest, Constance, British unarmoured corvettes, 556

CON

Constitucion, Argentine unarmoured gun-boat, 562
Conte Verde, Italian corvette, 126
Cordelia, British unarmoured corvette, 556
Cork chambers, 393, 394, 458, 463
Cormorant, British unarmoured sloop, 558
Corvette, the term, 40
Corvettes, C class of, 507; 'Gem' class, 257, 258, 509
Coupette, Herr, his improvements in marine engineering, 334
Couronne, French frigate, 5, 6, 48, 81, 573
Crimean war, floating batteries in the, 4
Cristoforo Colombo, Italian unarmoured cruiser, 530, 589
Crocodile, French unarmoured gun-vessel, 524–525, 578
Cruisers, armoured, 218–266; belted, 226–229; unarmoured, 477–546
Curaçoa, unarmoured corvette, 556
Custozza, Austrian central battery ship, 268–272, 316–317, 563
Cyclop, German unarmoured gun-vessel, 581
Cyclops, British turret ship, 18, 179–181, 550

Danae, British unarmoured corvette, 556
Dandolo, Austrian unarmoured spar-decked corvette, 565
— Italian citadel ship, 27, 395, 448, 453–454, 587; compared with Amiral Duperré, 314–315
Danmark, Danish battery ship, 571
Daring, British unarmoured sloop, 558
Dawson, Captain, on the Gorgon class, 180
Defence, British broadside ship, 6, 63–64, 80, 89, 90, 105, 106, 552
Deli, Dutch paddle-wheel vessel, 586
Delta, Chinese gunboat, 569
Denmark, armoured shipbuilding in, 111, 146, 210–211, 469; tables of ships, 571–572
De Ruyter, Dutch unarmoured corvette, 585
Designs, committee on, 19, 346
D'Estaing, French unarmoured cruiser, 577
Deutschland, German central battery ship, 10, 14, 273, 295–298, 321, 414, 579
Devastation, British turret ship, 19, 20, 28, 209, 264, 335–336, 342–359, 385, 386, 395, 550; compared with Peter the Great, 361–363; with Dreadnought, 374, 379
Dévastation, French central battery ship, 5, 14, 304–308, 573
Diamond, British unarmoured corvette, 556
Diana, Spanish unarmoured cruiser, 598

EAD

Dictator, American monitor, 133–135, 604
Dido, British unarmoured corvette, 556
Disa, Swedish unarmoured gunboat, 599
Dislère, M., quoted or referred to: on armoured ship construction in France, 48; on the Hansa, 219; Victorieuse type, 221–222; armoured second-rates of the French navy, 224; Shannon, 235–236; Nelson type, 246; turrets, 284; Téméraire, 288; armaments of French ships, 302, 308; Custozza and Tegetthoff, 316–319; German turret ships, 334; Neptune, 339; Devastation, 355–356; Dreadnought, 386; Inflexible, 428; Italia, 466–467; Sané, 513
Djigit, Russian unarmoured clipper, 594
Donau, Austrian unarmoured spar-decked corvette, 532, 564
Don Juan, Austrian bow-battery ship, 258, 563
Doterel, British unarmoured sloop, 558
Douglas, Sir Howard, on our naval requirements, 34
Douro, Portuguese unarmoured gun-vessel, 571
Draak, Dutch ram-monitor, 152, 584
Dragon, British unarmoured sloop, 511, 558
Draught fore and aft, 83
Dreadnought (ex Fury), British turret ship, 21, 28, 373–387, 395, 402, 550; compared with Alexandra and Téméraire, 292; with Peter the Great, 362, 374; with Devastation and Thunderer, 374
Drogden, Danish unarmoured gunboat, 572
Druid, British unarmoured corvette, 556
Dryad, British unarmoured sloop, 558
Dubourdieu, French unarmoured cruiser, 577
Duchauffaut, French unarmoured cruiser, 578
Duguay-Trouin, French unarmoured cruiser, 516, 519–522, 577
Duguesclin, French central battery ship, 30, 222–224, 573
Duilio, Italian citadel ship, 27, 448–453, 454, 587
Duke of Edinburgh, Russian belted cruiser, 226, 228, 592
Duke of Tetuan, Spanish battery ship, 597
Dunderberg, American ironclad. See Rochambeau
Du-Petit-Thouars, French unarmoured cruiser, 577
Dupuy de Lôme, M., designs of, 5, 46, 48, 50, 51, 53, 165
Duquesne, French unarmoured cruiser, 515, 517–519, 577

Eads, Captain, river-service ironclads of, 131–133; his method of raising and lowering guns, 293

ECL

Eclaireur, French unarmoured cruiser, 516, 522–524, 578

Eclipse, British unarmoured corvette, 556

Edda, Swedish unarmoured gunboat, 599

Egeria, British unarmoured sloop, 558

Elder, Messrs., design for a circular ship by, 185

Electricity, guns fired by, 373

Electric lamps, 355, 475

Elgar, Mr., *quoted* or *referred to* : on the Warrior, 60 ; on Sir E. Reed's improvements, 85 ; on the designs for the Captain, 327

Elisabeth, German unarmoured spardecked corvette, 580

Ellida, Norwegian unarmoured gunvessel, 600

Elliott, Admiral Sir G., on the essentials of a ship of war, 41

Emerald, British unarmoured corvette, 556

Embuscade, French floating battery, 31, 44, 574

Enchantress, British despatch vessel, 558

Encounter, British unarmoured corvette, 556

Engines, water-jet, 92–93

— compound, 90

— inverted or 'hammer,' 403

— of wrought iron, steel, and brass, 289

England, progress of shipbuilding in armoured, 5–32, 58–111, 173–184, 229–252, 263–266, 263–266, 273–295, 299–300, 326–329, 335–359, 364–448, 469–476 ; unarmoured, 477–513 ; tables of ships, 550–561

Enterprise, British converted corvette, 9, 23, 80, 85–86

— American unarmoured corvette, 545, 546, 605

Epsilon, Chinese gunboat, 569

Erebus, British floating battery, 5, 43

Ericsson, designs of, for monitor vessels, 128–130, 133

Esbern Snare, Danish cruiser, 571

Espiegle, British unarmoured sloop, 558

Essex, American unarmoured corvette, 545, 546, 605

Eta, Chinese gunboat, 569

Europe (*ex* State of California), Russian unarmoured ship, 536, 594

Euryalus, British unarmoured corvette, 486, 491

Eynaud, M., designs of, 519

FABERT, French unarmoured cruiser, 577

Falster, Danish unarmoured gun-vessel, 572

Fantome, British unarmoured sloop, 558

Faro, Portuguese paddle-wheel vessel, 591

Fasana, Austrian unarmoured corvette, 565

Favourite, British frigate, 80, 86

Fawn, British unarmoured sloop, 558

GAR

Fei-yune, Chinese gun-vessel, 568

Fenris, Swedish armour gunboat, 599

Ferdinand Max, Austrian converted frigate. *See* Archduke Ferdinand Maximilian

Fernando el Catolico, Spanish despatchvessel, 598

Feth-i-bulend, Turkish corvette, 114–115, 601

Feth-i-Islam, Turkish river gunboat, 602

Flamingo, British unarmoured composite gun-vessel, 512

Flandre, French frigate, 8, 48, 50, 104, 575

Flavio Gioja, Italian unarmoured cruiser, 589

Florida, American unarmoured flushdecked corvette, 539

Flying Fish, British unarmoured sloop, 558

Folke, Swedish armour gunboat, 599

Foo-poo, Chinese gun-vessel, 568

Foo-so, Japanese central battery ship, 255–258, 589

Forfait, French unarmoured cruiser, 522, 577

Formidabile, Italian central battery ship, 126, 587

Formidable, French barbette-turret and broadside ship, 30, 315–316, 573

Foudroyant, French central battery ship, 14, 304–308, 573

Fowler's steering propeller, 94

France, progress of shipbuilding in : armoured 4–32, 43–57, 111, 165–173, 219–225, 300–316 ; unarmoured, 513–525 ; tables of ships, 572–578

Franco-Italian war, 44–45

Freeboard, 327, 339, 342

French Navy, compared with English, 80–81, 100, 103–105

Freya, German unarmoured flush-decked corvette, 529, 581

Friedland, French central battery ship, 8, 55–56, 100, 104

Friedmann's projector, 233

Friedrich Carl, German central battery ship, 12, 118–119, 579

Friedrich der Grosse, German masted turret ship, 22, 329–335, 579

Frigate, the term, 40

Froude, Mr., investigations of, 402, 441

Frundsberg, Austrian corvette, 532, 565

Fulminant, French ram, 21, 168, 172, 573

Furieux, French ram, 21, 168, 172, 573

Fury. *See* Dreadnought

GALENA, American unarmoured corvette, 542, 545, 605

Gamma, Chinese gunboat, 569

Gannet, British unarmoured sloop, 558

Garibaldi, Italian unarmoured corvette, 530, 588

Garmer, Swedish armour gunboat, 599

Garnet, British unarmoured corvette, 556 ;

GAU

compared with U.S.S. Vandalia, 543–544. *See* 'Gem' Class

Gauloise, French frigate, 8, 575

Geffe, Swedish unarmoured corvette, 599

'Gem' class, British unarmoured corvettes, 257, 258, 509–511

General Admiral, Russian belted cruiser, 26, 226, 228, 592

Gerda, Swedish armour gunboat, 598

German coast, defence of, 213

Germany, progress of shipbuilding in: armoured, 12, 14, 22, 30, 118–121, 147, 211–217, 218, 395–398, 329–335, 455–459; unarmoured, 525–530; tables of ships, 579–582

Gibraltar, siege of, 4

Glatton, British turret ship, 18, 32, 176, 550. *See* Hotspur

Gloire, La (*ex* Napoléon), the first ironclad frigate, 5, 46, 80

Gneisenau, German unarmoured spar-decked corvette, 528, 580

Gorgon, British turret ship, 18, 179, 180, 550

Gorm, Danish monitor, 210–211, 571

Gornostaj, Russian transport, 596

Goulaeff, Captain, his description of the Popoffkas, 184–186; of the Czar's yacht Livadia, 194, 196

Gravière, Admiral de la, on the duty of a navy, 33

Great Eastern steamship, 454

Greece, armoured shipbuilding of, 262; tables of ships, 582–583

Grille, Austrian unarmoured gun-vessel, 568

— Prussian gunboat, 25

Grivel, Baron, *quoted* or *referred to* : on barbette guns, 24; the Monitor, 129; the single screw for rams, 167

Grosser Kurfürst, German masted turret ship, 22, 329

Guadiana, Portuguese paddle-wheel vessel, 591

Guanabara, Brazilian unarmoured corvette, 567

Guardiano, Italian unarmoured gun-vessel, 589

Guine, Portuguese paddle-wheel vessel, 591

Guinea, Dutch ram, 584

Gunboats, Rendel type of, 546; river, latest, 513

Gun-carriages, disappearing, 284, 293; working of, 367–368

Gun-vessels, French, 523

Gunnery. *See* Shoeburyness

Guns, invention of shell-firing from, 3; heavy breech-loading, introduced into the French Navy, 50; worked by hydraulic machinery, 368–370; simultaneous firing of, by electrical machinery, 373; progressive increase in the weight and power of, 437; height of axis of, in certain ships, 454
25-ton, 328

HUA

Guns, 35-ton, 357

— 38-ton, calibre of, 366

— 43-ton, breech-loading, 446

— 80-ton, 389; mounting of, 400

— 100-ton, 315, 409, 466

Guyenne, French frigate, 8, 575

HAAI, Dutch ram monitor, 152, 584

Habicht, German unarmoured gun-vessel, 529, 581

— Ersatz für, German unarmoured gun-vessel, 581

Habsburg, Austrian converted frigate, 116–118, 260, 564

Haï, Ersatz für, German unarmoured gun-vessel, 581

Hai-an, Chinese frigate, 570

Haï-tung-juen, Chinese gunboat, 570

Hamidieh, Turkish central battery ship, 273

Hansa, German central battery ship, 30, 218–219, 580

Hanscom, Mr. I., designs of, 540

Hastings, Captain Abney, his early advocacy of shells in naval warfare, 3

Haye, Commander, on the seaworthiness of the Cyclops and Glatton classes, 181

Hecate, British turret ship, 18, 179, 550

Hecla, British torpedo vessel, 560

Hector, British broadside ship, 7, 65, 80, 89, 552

Heiligerlee, Dutch monitor, 151–152, 584

Helgoland, Austrian unarmoured corvette, 565

— Danish central battery ship, 469, 571

Helicon, British despatch vessel, 560

Hercules, British broadside ship, 9, 10, 28, 94–100, 105, 552

Heriz, Señor, his narrative of American shipbuilding, 130; on the essential qualities of war ships, 42

Heroine, British unarmoured sloop, 558

Héroïne, French frigate, 8, 573

Hertha, German unarmoured spar-decked corvette, 580

Herval, Brazilian central battery ship, 157, 566

Hezba, Turkish monitor, 602

Hildur, Swedish armour gunboat, 598

Hi-yei, Japanese belted cruiser, 255–258, 590

Hoche, new French ship, 30 *n.*, 316, 573

Hohenzollern, German aviso paddle-vessel, 582

Hok-seng, Chinese gun-vessel, 569

Holland, armoured ship-building in, 111, 148–152; tables of ships, 583–587

Hong sing, Chinese gunboat, 570

Hood, Admiral, on the rig of the Inflexible, 407

Hotspur, British turret ram, 18, 174, 184, 550; experiment with, upon the Glatton, 177–179

Huascar, Chilian (formerly Peruvian) turret ship, 153–154; action of, with Shah and Amethyst, 412

HUF

Hüfz-i-rahman, Turkish turret ship, 112, 602

Hugon, French unarmoured cruiser, 578

Huin, M., designs of, 316

Hum, Austrian unarmoured gun-vessel, 565

Hunt, Mr. Ward, on the Polyphemus, 472–476

Hyacinth, British unarmoured sloop, 558

Hyæna, Dutch ram monitor, 152, 584

Hyäne, German unarmoured gun-vessel, 581

— Ersatz für, German unarmoured gun-vessel, 581

Hydra, British turret ship, 18, 179, 550

IDAHO, Federal American cruiser, 477

Idschlalijé, Turkish corvette, 113–114, 601

Iltis, German unarmoured gun-vessel, 581

Imim-i-zafer, Turkish corvette, 113, 601

Impérieuse, British armoured cruiser, 265, 554

Implacable, French floating battery, 31, 167, 574

Imprenable, French floating battery, 31, 574

Inconstant, British unarmoured frigate, 478–479, 554

Independencia, Brazilian ship. See Neptune

— Peruvian central battery ship, 154

Indomptable, French ram, 21, 172, 573

Infernet, French unarmoured cruiser, 577

Inflexible, British turret ship, 23, 27–28, 233, 387–430, 441–442, 550

Inglefield, Admiral, on the Devastation, 354

Inglis, Colonel, on the relative resistance of armour plates, 395

Ingolf, Danish unarmoured schooner, 572

Intrepid, American torpedo-vessel, 603

Invincible, British broadside ship, 102, 552

— French frigate, 5, 48

Iphigénie, French unarmoured cruiser, 577

Iris, British steel despatch vessel, 491–499, 556

Ironclads, the first, 5; nomenclature of, 40; cost of the first English sea-going, 60; bad sea-going qualities of, 270; slow progress in constructing, 434

Iron Duke, British broadside ship, 102, 105, 106, 250, 552

Isala, Dutch river monitor, 585

Italia, Italian citadel ship, 410, 459–469, 587

Italy, progress of shipbuilding in: armoured, 27, 111, 125–126, 147, 448–454, 459–469; unarmoured, 530–532; tables of ships, 587–589

Iwaki, Japanese unarmoured clipper, 590

KOL

JAPAN, armoured shipbuilding of, 255–258; tables of ships, 589–590

Japonec, Russian transport, 596

Jaroslaw, Russian unarmoured ship, 538–539, 594

Jason, American 1-turret monitor, 131, 603

Javari, Brazilian turret ship, 207, 566

Jeanne d'Arc, French second-rate, 25, 576

Jedinorog, Russian 1-turret monitor, 593

Jermak, Russian schooner, 596

John Ericsson, Swedish monitor, 598

Jorge Juan, Spanish unarmoured cruiser, 598

Juels, Lieutenant, his descriptions of Russian monitors, 157, 158

Juno, British unarmoured corvette, 556

KAIMU, Japanese unarmoured corvette, 590

Kaiser, Austrian converted central battery ship, 118, 564

— German central battery ship, 9, 14, 273, 295–298, 321, 414, 579

Kaiser Max, Austrian bow-battery ship, 258, 563

Kalamazoo, American wooden monitor, 136

Keel, ballast, 475

Kerka, Austrian unarmoured gun-vessel, 565

Key, Admiral, particular service squadron of, 181

Kinburn, bombardment of, 5, 43–44

King of the Netherlands, Dutch turret ram, 148–149, 583

King George, Greek central battery ship, 262–263, 277, 582

King, Chief Engineer, quoted or referred to: on the Hercules, 95–96; designs for the Audacious class, 102–103; armament of the Tonnerre, 170; Russian circular vessels, 189–192; Shannon, 231; Nelson and Northampton, 237–240; Alexandra, 278–281; Téméraire, 283–284; Kaiser and Deutschland, 295–298; Amiral Duperré compared with the Dandolo, 309–315; Neptune, 339; Devastation, 344–354, 357; Peter the Great, performances of, 363; Thunderer, 364–373; Dreadnought, 375–380, 384–386; Inflexible, 387; controversy respecting this ship, 410–411; Conqueror, 445; Sachsen, 455–458; Italia and Lepanto, 459–466

— Captain, gun-carriage of, 293

Kingfisher, British unarmoured sloop, 558

Kiva-shing, Chinese gunboat, 570

Knjaz-Pojarski, Russian battery ship, 124, 592

Koch, Herr, designs of, 329

Koldun, Russian 1-turret monitor, 593

KON

Kon-go, Japanese belted cruiser, 255–258, 590
König Wilhelm, German central battery ship, 12, 119–121, 579
Kreml, Russian broadside ship, 124, 592
Kreuzer, Russian unarmoured clipper, 594
Krokodil, Dutch monitor, 151–152, 584
— German gun-vessel, 579
Kron Prinz, German central battery ship, 12, 119, 579
Kronenfels, Captain von, on the armament of the Redoutable, 303
Krupp, steel guns of, 50

LA CLOCHETERIE, French unarmoured cruiser, 513–514, 577
La Galissonnière, French second-rate, 26, 221, 576
Lancier, French gun-vessel, 524
Lapérouse, French unarmoured cruiser 516, 522, 577
La Plata, Argentine monitor, 207–209
La Seyne, shipbuilding yard at, 538
Latnik, Russian 1-turret monitor, 593
Laudon, Austrian unarmoured frigate, 564
Lave, French ironclad, 5
Lawa, Russian 1-turret monitor, 593
Leander, British steel despatch vessel, 263, 505–506, 558
Lebelin de Dionne, M., his defence of the Tonnerre, 171 ; designs of, 222
Lehigh, American 1-turret monitor, 131, 603
Leipzig (ex Thusneld), German unarmoured spar-decked corvette, 40, 525–528, 580
Leitha, Austrian monitor, 217, 563
Lemoine, M., designs of, 31
Lepanto, Italian citadel ship, 410, 459–469, 587
Lima Barros (ex Bellona), Brazilian turret ship, 155, 566
Lindormen, Danish monitor, 210, 571
Ling-feng, Chinese gunboat, 570
Lionne, French unarmoured gun-vessel, 578
Li-she, Chinese gunboat, 570
Lissa, Austrian converted central battery ship, 117–118, 564
Lissa, battle of, 267
Littlebelt, Danish unarmoured gun-vessel, 572
Livadia, Russian imperial yacht, 194–204, 595
Lively, British despatch vessel, 560
Loke, Swedish monitor, 598
Lord Clyde, British frigate, 77, 79, 80
Lord Warden, British broadside frigate, 77, 78–79, 80
Los Andes, Argentine monitor, 207, 562
Luft-i-dschelil, Turkish ironclad, 112
Luipard, Dutch ram monitor, 152, 584

MER

Luise, German unarmoured flush-decked corvette, 529, 581
Lutin, Lynx, French unarmoured gun-vessels, 578

MACASSAR, Dutch E. I. unarmoured corvette, 586
Mackrow, Mr., design of, 262
Madura, Dutch E. I. unarmoured corvette, 586
Magdala, British turret ship, 18, 108, 174, 550
Magé, Brazilian unarmoured corvette, 567
Magellanes, Chilian unarmoured corvette, 568
Magenta, French ironclad ram, 7, 48, 49, 271, 316
— new French ship, 30 n., 316, 573
Magnanime, French ironclad, 8
Magon, French unarmoured cruiser, 522, 577
Mahmoudieh, Turkish broadside frigate, 112, 601
Mahopac, American 1-turret monitor, 131, 602
Majestic, British turret ship, 28, 434, 438–439, 550
Malakoff, Russian turret ship, 592
Manhattan, American 1-turret monitor, 131, 603
Marcantonio Colonna, Italian unarmoured cruiser, 532, 589
Marceau, new French ship, 30 n., 316, 573
Marchal, M., quoted or referred to : on the Hotspur, 175 ; Glatton, 177 ; Victorieuse and La Galissonnière compared, 221 ; Austrian bow-battery ships, 270, 271
Marengo, French central battery ship, 8, 50, 53, 103, 104, 575
Maria Adelaide, Italian unarmoured frigate, 588
Maria de Molina, Spanish unarmoured cruiser, 598
Marion, American unarmoured corvette, 542, 605
Mariz-e-Barros, Brazilian central battery ship, 157, 566
Maros, Austrian monitor, 217, 563
Marqués del Duero, Spanish despatch vessel, 598
Massachusetts, American 2-turret monitor, 140, 604
Masts, hollow, 279–280 ; steel, 407–408
Matador, Dutch ram-monitor, 152, 584
Maudyür, Russian transport, 596
Medina, British unarmoured gunboat, 513
Mei-june, Chinese gun-vessel, 569
Memdouhyeh. See Superb
Mendez Nuñez, Spanish frigate, 122, 597
Merapi, Dutch E.I. paddle-wheel vessel, 586

MER

Mercury, British steel despatch vessel, 500–505, 558

Merrimac, American Confederate iron-clad, 128 ; action of, with the Monitor, 16

Merva, Dutch river monitor, 585

Me-sing, Chinese gun-vessel, 569

Messudieh (sister ship to H.M.S. Superb), Turkish central battery ship, 116, 273, 601

Miantonomoh, American 2-turret monitor, 136–140, 158, 343, 602

Miaulis, Greek unarmoured corvette, 583

Milwaukee class, American gunboats, 193

Mindello, Portuguese unarmoured corvette, 591

Mines, ground, 534

Minin, Russian belted cruiser, 226–228, 592

Minotaur, British broadside ship, 7, 9, 28, 61, 63, 66, 71–75, 80, 98, 105, 343, 552

Miölner, Swedish monitor, 600

Miranda, British unarmoured sloop, 511, 558

Modeste, British unarmoured corvette, 556

Moen, Danish unarmoured gun-vessel, 572

Moeve, Austrian unarmoured gun-vessel, 565

— German unarmoured gun-vessel, 529, 581

Mohican, American unarmoured corvette, 542, 605

Moltke, German unarmoured spar-decked corvette, 580

Monadnock, American 2-turret monitor, 136, 140, 343, 602

Monarch, British masted turret ship, 16, 105, 326–329, 454, 550 ; compared with Devastation, 343

Moncrieff, Major, his method of raising and lowering guns, 293–294

Mondovi, Portuguese unarmoured gun-vessel, 591

Monge, French unarmoured cruiser, 577

Monitor, American Federal ironclad, 128–130. See Merrimac

Monitors, American, two-gun single-turreted, 131 ; large seagoing, 134

— Russian, 157

Montauk, American 1-turret monitor, 131, 603

Montcalm, French second-rate, 25, 576

Morz, Russian transport ship, 596

Mosa, Dutch river monitor, 585

Moscow, Russian unarmoured cruiser, 538

Mosel, German unarmoured river gun-boat, 217, 582

Möve. See Moeve.

Mücke, German gun-vessel, 217, 579

Mukademme-i-haïr, Turkish corvette, 114–115, 601

Mutine, British unarmoured sloop, 558

Muzzle-pivoting, 368

OEN

NAHANT, American 1-turret monitor, 131, 603

Naïade, French unarmoured cruiser, 577

Nantucket, American monitor, 131

Napoléon. See Gloire

Napoleon III., floating batteries of, 4 ; suggests the construction of batteries démontables, 45

Narenta, Austrian unarmoured gun-vessel, 565

Natter, German gun-vessel, 579

— Ersatz für, German unarmoured gun-vessel, 581

Nautilus, experimental boat built on the Ruthven principle, 94

— Austrian unarmoured gun-vessel, 565

— German unarmoured gun-vessel, 581

Navarra, Spanish unarmoured cruiser, 598

Navy, British, functions of the, 33 ; state of, in 1862, 76

Nayesdnik, Russian unarmoured clipper, 532–534, 594

Nedschm-i-schefket, Turkish corvette, 113–114, 601

Nelson, British belted cruiser, 26, 237–252, 454, 552

Neptune (ex Independencia), British masted turret-ship, 22, 288, 335–341, 402, 414, 550

— new French ship, 30 n., 316, 573

Nerpa, Russian transport, 596

Netronmenja, Russian broadside ship, 124, 592

New York, American unarmoured corvette, 604

Nictheroy, Brazilian unarmoured corvette, 567

Nielly, French unarmoured cruiser, 577

Nijni-Novgorod, Russian unarmoured ship, 538

Nikopol, Russian gun-vessel, 595

Nipsic, American unarmoured corvette, 545–546, 605

Noel, Commander, on the Shannon, 235

Normandie, French frigate, 5, 48

Northampton, British belted cruiser, 26, 237–251, 552

North Sea coast, defence of the, 32

Northumberland, English broadside ship, 7, 61, 63, 66–68, 80, 552

Norway. See Sweden

Novgorod, Russian popoffka, 185–193, 595

Numancia, Spanish frigate, 121, 597

Nussratieh, Turkish central battery ship, 273, 601

OCEAN, British converted frigate, 7, 76–78, 80

Océan, French central battery ship, 8, 24, 50, 53, 103, 104, 454, 575

Odin, Danish central battery ship, 211, 571

Oenarang, Dutch E.I. paddle-wheel vessel, 586

OHI

O'Higgins, Chilian unarmoured corvette, 568
Olga, Greek central battery ship, 582
Onondaga, French (formerly American) coast-service vessel, 143, 574
Opal, British unarmoured corvette, 511, 556
Opiniâtre, French floating battery, 31, 167, 574
Opit, Russian cruiser, 595
Opritchnik, Russian unarmoured clipper, 535, 594
Oregon, American monitor, 140, 604
Oresund, Danish unarmoured gun-vessel, 572
Orion, English broadside ship, 11, 182–184, 202, 552
Orkanieh, Osmanieh, Turkish broadside frigates, 112, 601
Osprey, British unarmoured sloop, 558
Otter, German unarmoured gun-vessel, 581

PADANG, Dutch E.I. unarmoured corvette, 586
Paget, Lord Clarence, on the strength of the navy in 1862, 76, 80
Paixhans, General, his invention of shell-firing from guns, 3
Palembang, Dutch E.I. unarmoured corvette, 586
Palestro, French floating battery, 31, 44
— Italian battery ship, 588
Pallas, British broadside ship, 9, 23, 77, 80, 83, 89–91, 554
Palliser shot, 97, 397–398
Pang-chao-hai, Chinese gunboat, 570
Panter, Dutch ram-monitor, 152, 584
Pará, Brazilian river monitor, 566
Paraguay, war of, with Brazil, 155–157
Parana, Argentine unarmoured gunboat, 562
Paris, Admiral, on the qualities of the Dunderberg and Onondaga, 143–144
Passaic, American 1-turret monitor, 131, 603
Paykisherreef, Turkish corvette. See Belleisle
Peder Scram, Danish battery ship, 571
Pegasus, British unarmoured sloop, 511, 558
Pelican, British unarmoured sloop, 558
Penelope, English broadside ship, 9, 91, 202, 552
Penguin, British unarmoured sloop, 511, 558
Perm, Russian 1-turret monitor, 593
Peru, armoured shipbuilding of, 152–154
Pervenec, Russian broadside ship, 124, 592
Peter the Great, Russian turret ship, 360–364, 374, 395, 592
Petropaulski, Russian broadside ship, 122–124, 593
Phaeton, British steel despatch vessel, 505–506, 568

RAM

Phœnix, British unarmoured sloop, 511, 558
Piauhy, Brazilian river monitor, 566
Pietro Micco, Italian unarmoured torpedo-vessel, 589
Pilcomayo, Argentine unarmoured gunboat, 562
— Chilian unarmoured corvette, 568
Plastoun, Russian unarmoured clipper, 535, 594
Plata, Argentine monitor, 562
Polga, Russian steamer, 596
Polyphemus, torpedo-ram, 472–476
Pontjanak, Dutch E.I. unarmoured corvette, 586
Poo-too, Chinese frigate, 570
Popoffkas, Russian circular batteries, 184–194
Ports, indented, 9; recessed, 275
Portugal, armoured shipbuilding of, 260–262; tables of ships, 591
Pothuau, Admiral, his statement concerning the Caïman, 173 n
Preussen, German masted turret ship, 22, 329–335, 579
Prince Albert, British turret ship, 16, 80, 160, 163–164
— German monitor, 32
Prince Consort, British converted ship, 7, 76, 77, 80
Prince Eugene, Austrian bow-battery ship, 258, 563
Prince Henry of the Netherlands, Dutch turret ram, 148, 583
Principe Amadeo, Italian central battery ship, 125, 588
Prinz Adalbert, German unarmoured spar-decked corvette, 580
Prinz Hendrik, Dutch turret ship, 16
Protectrice, French floating battery, 31, 574
Provence, French frigate, 8, 48, 50, 575
Puigcerdá, Spanish river monitor, 597
Puritan, American 2-turret monitor, 133–135, 141, 603

QUANG-ON, Chinese gunboat, 569
Quanza, Portuguese unarmoured gun-vessel, 591
Queen Emma, Dutch unarmoured corvette, 585
Quinnebaug, American unarmoured corvette, 542, 544, 545, 604

RADETZKY, Austrian unarmoured frigate, 40, 532, 564
Rainha de Portugal, Portuguese unarmoured corvette, 59
Raleigh, British unarmoured frigate, 479, 482–485, 554
Ram, importance of the, 267; arrangement of the, 302
Rambler, British unarmoured composite gun-vessel, 512

RAN

Ran, Swedish unarmoured torpedo vessel, 599

Ranger, American unarmoured corvette, 545, 546, 605

Rapido, Italian unarmoured cruiser, 589

Rasboynik, Russian unarmoured clipper, 532–535, 594

Redoutable, French central battery ship, 13, 288, 300–303, 573

Reed, Sir E. J., improvements of, 8–10, 14, 185; system of, 82–110; ships built from his designs, 173, 183, 252, 255, 273, 295, 335; his designs for unarmoured cruisers, 478, 479

quoted or *referred to*: on the progress of improvements in ironclads, 63; armour plating of Hercules, 96 *n.*; the Russian circular vessels, 188; Livadia, 200–204; Tegetthoff, 319–323; Devastation, alterations of, 356; Duilio and Dandolo, 410; Inflexible, 411–428; Italia and Lepanto, 468

Refuge, French floating battery, 31, 574

Regina Maria Pia, Italian central battery ship, 126, 587

Reine Blanche, French second-rate, 25, 576

Rendel, Mr., his hydraulic system of working guns, 294, 368, 398, 466; gunboat design of, 546

Republica, Argentine unarmoured gunboat, 562

Repulse, British broadside ship, 76, 79–80, 554

Requin, French ram, 21, 172, 573

Research, British broadside ship, 80, 86, 554

Resistance, British broadside ship, 6, 63–64, 80, 105, 106, 552

Revanche, French frigate, 8, 575

Rhein, German unarmoured river gunboat, 217, 581

Rhenus, Dutch river monitor, 585

Richelieu, French turret ship, 12, 53–55, 100, 104

Rigault de Genouilly, French unarmoured cruiser, 516, 522, 578

Rio Grande, Brazilian river monitor, 566

Rio-jio, Japanese belted ship, 590

Rio Lima, Portuguese unarmoured gun-vessel, 591

Riouw, Dutch E.I. unarmoured corvette, 586

Roanoke, American converted ship, 130

Robinson, Admiral Sir Spencer, improvements due to, 84

quoted or *referred to*: on the Hercules type, 94–95; Hercules, Achilles, and French ironclads compared, 100; Audacious class compared with French ships, 104–105; in praise of the Audacious class, 106; Nelson class, 250–252; Monarch, performances of, 328; Devastation, 344

Rochambeau, French ironclad (*ex* Dunderberg, American), 143–146

SAL

Roland, French unarmoured cruiser, 522, 577

Rolf Krake, Danish monitor, 16, 146, 153, 571

Roma, Italian central battery ship, 125, 588

Romako, Herr, designs of, 116–117, 259, 268, 317

Rossja, Russian unarmoured ship, 538, 594

— Russian Black Sea cruiser, 595

Rota, Swedish unarmoured gunboat, 599

Roussalka, Russian monitor, 158, 136

Rover, British unarmoured corvette, 506, 556

Royal Alfred, British converted frigate, 7, 76, 77, 80

Royal Oak, British converted frigate, 69, 76, 77, 80

Royal Sovereign, British turret ship, 16, 80, 160–163

Ruby, British unarmoured corvette, 556

Rudder, Stanhope, 88

Rumsey, James, his experiment in propulsion, 93

Rupert, British turret ram, 18, 181–182, 184, 438, 550

Rurik, Russian unarmoured ship, 594

Russalka, Russian 2-turret monitor, 593

Russell, Mr. Scott, on the construction of the Warrior, 60; on converted ships, 77; his table of dimensions of the earlier types of monitors, 134

Russia, progress of shipbuilding in: armoured, 26, 111, 122–125, 157–160, 184–204, 226–229, 360; unarmoured, 532–539; tables of ships, 592–596

Ruthven, Mr., system of propulsion of, 93–94

Ryder, Admiral, on the Audacious, 107; on the seaworthiness of the Gorgon class, 180

Sabattier, M., designs of, 55, 173, 219, 310, 522, 523

Sachsen, German corvette, 30, 455–459, 579

Sado, Portuguese unarmoured gun-vessel, 591

Saga, Swedish unarmoured corvette, 599

Sagittaire, French unarmoured gun-vessel, 578

Sagunto, Spanish frigate, 122, 597

Saïda, Austrian unarmoured spar-decked corvette, 565

St. Eustatius, Dutch unarmoured corvette, 585

St. Petersburg (*ex* Thuringia), Russian unarmoured ship, 538

St. Thomas, Danish unarmoured corvette, 572

Salak, Dutch E.I. paddle-wheel vessel, 587

Salamander, Austrian converted frigate, 118, 260, 564

— German gun-vessel, 579

SAL

Salamis, British despatch-vessel, 560
Samarang, Dutch E.I. unarmoured corvette, 586
Sambas, Dutch E.I. unarmoured corvette, 586
Sanches Barcaiztequi, Spanish unarmoured cruiser, 598
'Sandwich' system of arm ur, 395
Sané, French unarmoured cruiser, 513, 577
San Martino, Italian central battery ship, 126, 587
Sansego, Austrian unarmoured gunvessel, 565
Santa Catarina, Brazilian river monitor, 566
Sapphire, British unarmoured corvette, 556
Sappho, British unarmoured sloop, 558
Saratoga. See Africa
Sartorius, Sir George, 472
Satellite, British unarmoured sloop, 558
Saugus, American 1-turret monitor, 131, 603
Savoie, French frigate, 8, 575
Schleswig-Holstein, coast defence of, 32
Schorpioen, Dutch ram, 149–150, 583
Scilla, Italian unarmoured gun-vessel, 589
Scorpion, British masted turret ship, 16, 80, 89, 146
— German gun-vessel, 217, 579
Scorpionen, Swedish monitor, 600
Scott, Admiral, quoted or referred to : on the Minotaur alterations, 71, 74 ; armaments of Bellerophon, 89; of Audacious class, 106 ; and of Nelson and Northampton, 246 n.; Sultan, 109 ; Inconstant's gun arrangement, 479
— Captain, his system of working guns, 368
Screw, two-bladed, 88
Screws, twin, adoption of, in the British Navy, 19, 280; utility of, 403
Sebastian Verniero, Italian unarmoured torpedo-vessel, 589
Seignelay, French unarmoured cruiser, 577
Seiki, Japanese unarmoured clipper, 590
Sells, Mr., his duplex valve, 497
Semendire, Turkish river gunboat, 602
Sentinella, Italian unarmoured gunvessel, 589
Sete de Setembro, Brazilian central battery ship, 566
Sevastopol, Russian broadside ship, 122–124, 593
Shah (ex Blonde), British unarmoured frigate, 233, 479–482 ; action of, with the Huascar, 412, 554
Shannon, British belted cruiser, 26, 229–236, 245, 552
Shells, destructive power of, against wooden ships first shown, 3
Shen-chi, Chinese gunboat, 570
Shields, rifle, 74

STA

Shipbuilding, cellular system of, 9 ; bracket-frame system of, 12
Shipping, British, 35, 36
Ships, war, classification of, 37–41 ; qualities necessary in, 41–42 ; proportions of, 28, 402, 441; freeboard of, 17, 180, 342
— armoured, historical sketch of improvements in, 3–32 ; detailed descriptions of, 43–476. See under respective countries
— unarmoured, 477–548
— barbette, mastless, 455–476
— bow-battery, 267–272
— central-battery, 273–325
— circular, 184–194
— coast-service, requirements of, 15 ; progress in constructing, 128–217
— converted, 76–80
— cruising, armoured, 218–266 ; unarmoured, 477–546
— turret, masted, 326–341 ; mastless, 342–454
Shoeburyness, experiments at, with Warrior target, 71; Hercules target, 96–98 ; Inflexible target, 397–398
Siberian squadron, 596
Silvado, Brazilian turret ship, 157, 566
Sindoro, Dutch E.I. paddle-wheel vessel, 587
Sinfun, Russian steamer, 596
Sinope, destruction of the Turkish fleet at, 3
Sin-tsing, Chinese gunboat, 569
Sirius, British unarmoured corvette, 556
Sistowo, Russian gun-vessel, 595
Siuris, Russian transport, 596
Skagul, Skäggald, Swedish unarmoured gunboats, 599
Sköld, Swedish armour gunboat, 599
Skuld, Swedish unarmoured gunboat, 599
Sleipner, Norwegian unarmoured gunvessel, 600
Sloops, composite, 511
Smerc, Russian 2-turret monitor, 158, 160, 593
Soembing, Dutch E.I. paddle-wheel vessel, 587
Sokol, Russian transport, 596
Solférino, French frigate, 7, 48, 49, 575
Solimões, Brazilian turret ship, 204–207, 566
Sölve, Swedish armour gunboat, 599
Spain, armoured ship uilding in. 111, 121–122; tables of ships, 597–598
Spalato, Austrian unarmoured steel-hull gun-vessel, 565
Spartan, British unarmoured corvette, 556
Spezzia, experiments at, 395
Staffeta, Italian unarmoured cruiser, 532, 589
Stanhope rudder, 88
Starting gear, steam, 484
State of California. See Europe

STE

Steel, resistance of, 436, 439
Steering-gear, protection of, 61 ; steam, 292
Steering-propeller, Fowler's, 94
Stein, German unarmoured spar-decked corvette, 580
Stewart, Sir W. Houston, *quoted*, on the designs of the Nelson type, 245–246 ; on the Inflexible, 414
Stier, Dutch ram, 150, 583
Storebelt, Danish unarmoured gun-vessel, 572
Stosch, German unarmoured spar-decked corvette, 580
Strelok, Russian unarmoured clipper, 535, 594
Strjelec, Russian 1-turret monitor, 593
Suffren, French central battery ship, 8, 50–53, 575
Sultan, British broadside ship, 10, 62, 100, 108, 402, 552 ; Admiral Scott's suggested improvements for, 107, 109–110 ; trial of, with the Devastation, 350–335
Sumter, cruise of the, 477
Superb (*ex* Memdouhyeh), British broadside ship, 11, 299–300, 552
— Turkish sister ship of. *See* Messudieh
— (late). *See* Alexandra
Superstructures, 20, 21, 180
Surinam, Dutch unarmoured corvette, 585
Surveillante, French frigate, 8, 104, 575
Swatara, American unarmoured corvette, 542, 605
Sweden and Norway, tables of ships belonging to, 598–600
Swiftsure, British broadside ship, 28, 102, 108, 552

TALISMAN, French unarmoured cruiser, 515, 578
Tamandare, Brazilian central battery ship, 566
Tamega, Portuguese unarmoured gun-vessel, 591
Taureau, French coast-service vessel, 18, 31, 165, 166, 172, 576
Tcharodjejka, Russian monitor, 158, 160, 593
Tching-on, Tching-po, Tching-sing, Chinese gunboats, 569
Tchun-tung, Chinese gunboat, 570
Tegetthof, Austrian central battery ship. 273, 316–323, 563
Tei-an, Chinese gun-vessel, 569
Téméraire, British central battery ship, 11, 273, 283–288, 552 ; compared with Alexandra, 287
Tempête, French coast-service vessel, 21, 168, 172, 574
Tenedos, unarmoured corvette, 556
Teng-ing-chew, Chinese gun vessel, 569
Tennessee, American unarmoured corvette, 539

TRI

Tenrio, Japanese unarmoured corvette, 590
Terribile, Italian central battery ship, 126, 587
Terrible, French ram, 21, 173, 574
Terror, British floating battery, 5, 43
— American 2-turret monitor, 136, 140. 142–143, 602
Thalia, British unarmoured corvette, 556
Themistocles, Greek unarmoured corvette, 583
Theta, Chinese gunboat, 569
Thétis, French second-rate, 25, 576
Thomson, Sir William, sounding machine of, 245
Thor, Norwegian monitor, 600
— Swedish unarmoured corvette, 599
Tho·dön, Swedish monitor, 598
Thunderbolt, British floating battery, 5, 43
Thunderer, British turret ship, 21, 265, 342, 364–373, 384, 385, 395, 407, 432 ; compared with Peter the Great, 362 ; with Dreadnought, 374, 378–382
Thuringia. *See* St. Petersburg
Thusnelda. *See* Leipzig
Tifon, Russian 1-turret monitor, 593
Tigre, French ram, 32, 165, 172
Tijger, Dutch monitor, 151–152, 584
Ting hai, Chinese gun-vessel, 569
— Chinese gunboat, 570
Tirfing, Swedish monitor, 598
Tong-sing, Chinese gunboat, 570
Tonnant, French coast-service vessel, 21, 168, 172, 574
Tonnante, French (Crimean) floating battery, 5
Tonnerre, French coast-service vessel, 21, 168–172, 574
Toogood's propulsion patent, 93
Tordenskjold, Danish torpedo ship, 571
Torpedoes, experiments with, on board the Glatton, 179
— towing, of the French navy, 225
— Whitehead, apparatus for launching, 428–430
Torpedo boats, defence against, 181
Torpedo ram ship, 472–476
Tourmaline, British unarmoured corvette, 510, 556
Tourville, French unarmoured cruiser, 515–519, 577
Towers, as distinguished from turrets, 283 *n*., 312 *n*.
Trade, British maritime, extent of, 34–36
Trajano, Brazilian unarmoured corvette, 567
Trenton, American unarmoured corvette, 540, 604
Trevelyan, Mr., on our new armoured cruisers, 263–264
Trident, French central battery ship, 12, 55–56, 104, 575
Triomphante, French second-rate, 26, 219, 576

TRI

Triumph, British broadside ship, 102, 107, 108, 552

Tromp, Dutch unarmoured corvette, 585

Tromp, Lieutenant, his work on armoured ships, 3

Trudvang, Norwegian monitor, 600

Tsing-juen, Tsing-po, Chinese gun-vessels, 569

Tungus, Russian schooner, 596

Turenne, French second-rate, 30, 222, 576

Turkey, armoured shipbuilding in, 111–116; table of ships, 601–602

Turquoise, British unarmoured corvette, 509, 556

Turrets, as distinguished from towers, 283 n., 312 n.; armour of, 396, 431

— barbette, 23

— fixed, of the Téméraire, 283

— revolving, antipathy of the French to, 173 n., 284; method of rotating, 399

— projecting bow, 312

— echeloned, 396

Turret ships, introduction of, into the British Navy, 160; abandonment of masts in, 17, 19

UHLAN, German torpedo-boat, 579

Ulf, Swedish armour gunboat, 598

Uller, Norwegian unarmoured gun-vessel, 600

United States, progress of shipbuilding in : armoured, 111, 128–146, 477; unarmoured, 539–546; tables of ships, 602–605

Uragan, Russian 1-turret monitor, 593

Urd, Swedish unarmoured gunboat, 599

Uruguay, Argentine unarmoured gunboat, 562

Uspiech, Russian steamer, 596

VAHALIS, Dutch river monitor, 584

Vale, Norwegian unarmoured gun-vessel, 600

Valeureuse, French frigate, 8, 104, 576

Valiant, British broadside ship, 7, 64–65, 80, 554

Valparaiso. See Blanco-Encalada

Vandalia, American unarmoured corvette, 542–545, 604

Van Galen, Dutch unarmoured corvette, 585

Vanguard, British broadside ship, 102–106

Varese, Italian central battery ship, 126, 587

Vasco de Gama, Portuguese armoured cruiser, 260–262, 591

Vauban, French central battery ship, 30, 222, 454, 573

Vaudreuil, French unarmoured cruiser, 578

Vedetta, Italian unarmoured cruiser, 589

Venezia, Italian central battery ship, 125, 588

WOK

Vengeur, French coast-service vessel, 21, 168, 172, 574

Verdande, Swedish unarmoured gunboat, 599

Vestal, British unarmoured sloop, 558

Vesuvius, British torpedo-vessel, 560

Vettor Pisani, Italian unarmoured corvette, 588

Vice-Admiral Popoff, Russian popoffka, 185–194, 595

Victoria, German unarmoured flush-decked corvette, 581

— G. Ersatz für, German unarmoured flush-decked corvette, 581

Victorieuse, French second-rate, 25, 219–222, 576

Viestnik, Russian unarmoured clipper, 594

Vigilant, British despatch vessel, 560

Villars, French unarmoured cruiser, 516, 521–522, 577

Vineta, German unarmoured spar-decked corvette, 581

— Ersatz für, German unarmoured flush-decked corvette, 581

Viper, British gunboat, 80, 92, 554

— German gun-vessel, 217, 579

Vipère, French unarmoured gun-vessel, 578

Vital de Oliveira, Brazilian unarmoured corvette, 567

Vitoria, Spanish frigate, 121–122, 597

Vittorio Emmanuele, Italian unarmoured frigate, 588

Vixen, British gunboat, 80, 92, 554

Volage, British unarmoured corvette, 479, 491, 556

WAI-CHIANG, Chinese frigate, 570

Wampanoag, Federal American cruiser, 477–478

Wan-niang-tsing, Chinese gun-vessel, 568

Warrior, broadside ship, the first ironclad English frigate, 6, 59–64, 80–81, 89, 105

Warspite, new British armoured cruiser, 265, 554

Water-jet engine, 92

Waterwitch, British gunboat, 80, 92

Wei-juan, Chinese gun-vessel, 569

Wesp, Dutch ram-monitor, 152, 584

Wespe, German gun-vessel, 32, 211–217, 579

White, Mr., on the Russian circular vessels, 188

Whitehead torpedo. See Torpedoes

Wild Swan, British unarmoured sloop, 558

Wilson, Mr. George, his compound armour-plate, 397

Wivern, British masted turret ship, 16, 80, 89, 146, 550

Wjescun, Russian 1-turret monitor, 593

Wo-kai, Chinese gun-vessel, 568

Wolf, German unarmoured gun-vessel, 581

Wolverene, British unarmoured corvette, 556

Wostok, Russian clipper, 596

Würtemberg, German corvette, 31, 455, 579

Wyandotte, American 1-turret monitor, 131, 603

YANTIC, American unarmoured corvette, 605

Yung-woo, Chinese gunboat, 570

Yu-yuen, Chinese frigate, 570

ZABIACA, Russian unarmoured clipper, 536–537, 594

Zara, Austrian unarmoured steel-hull gun-vessel, 565

Zaragoza, Spanish frigate, 122, 597

Zealous, British converted ship, 76, 80

Zeta, Chinese gunboat, 569

Ziethen, German torpedo-boat, 579

Zinc sheathing, 506

Zrinyi, Austrian unarmoured corvette, 532, 565

LONDON : PRINTED BY
SPOTTISWOODE AND CO., NEW-STREET SQUARE
AND PARLIAMENT STREET

Warrior.

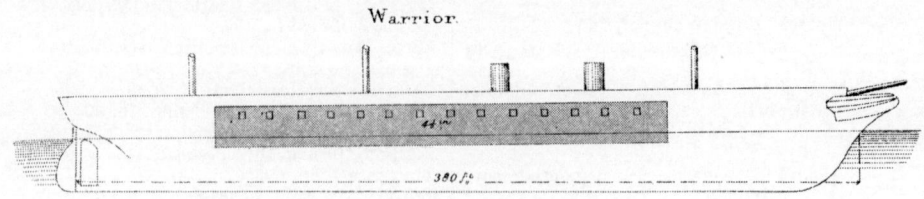

44″

380 ft.

"Minotaur" Class.

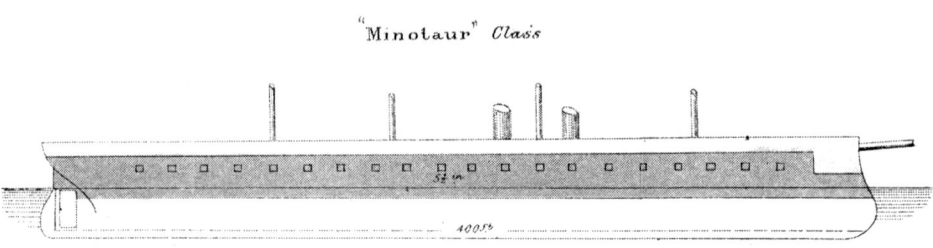

42 in

400 ft

Bellerophon.

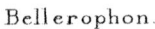

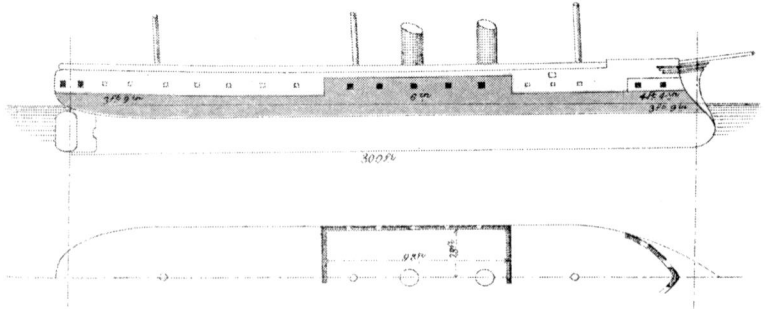

6 in

300 ft

9 in

Pl. 1

Hercules

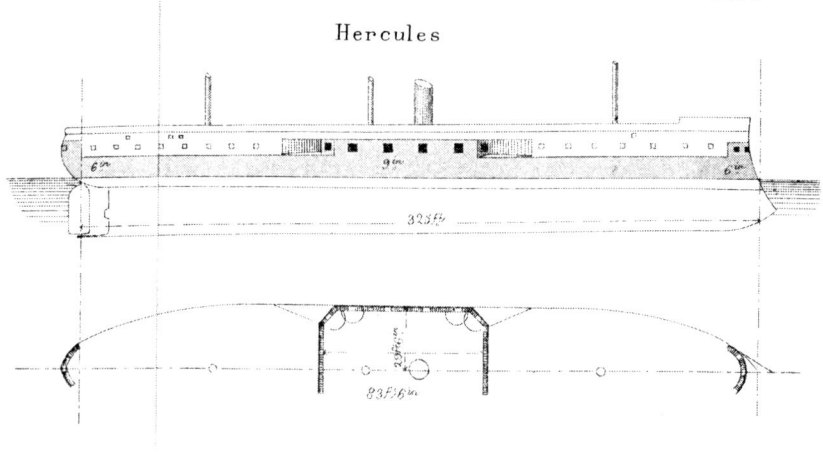

Penelope

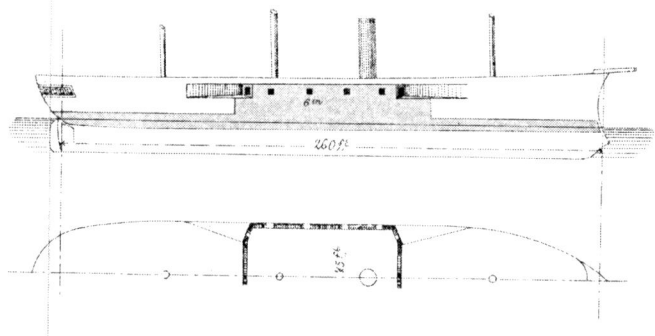

Enterprise

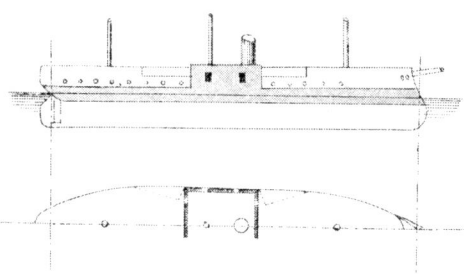

Sultan.

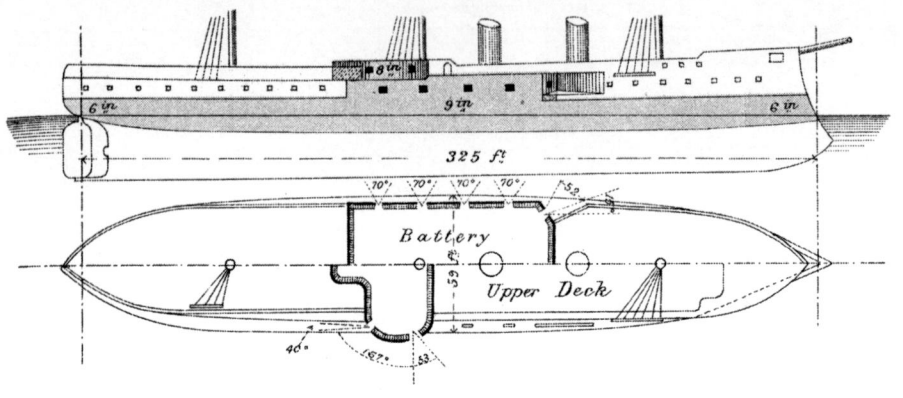

325 ft.

Battery

Upper Deck

Superb.

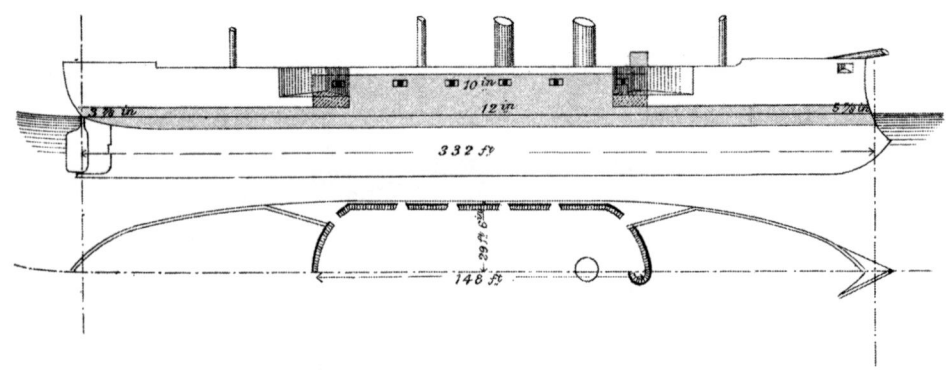

332 ft.

148 ft.

Pl. II

Alexandra.

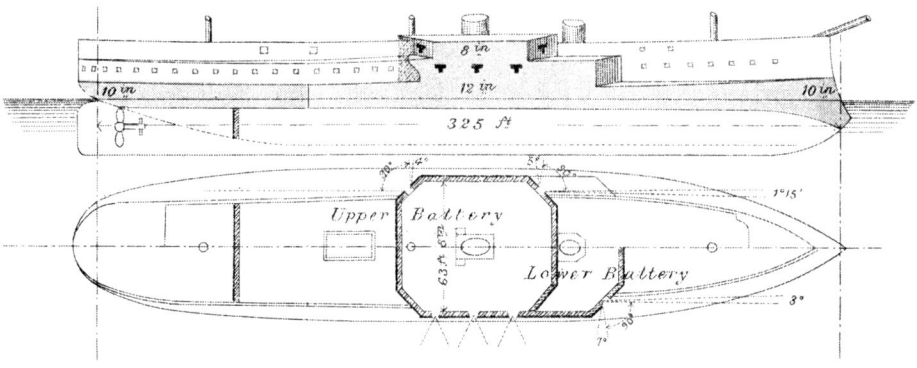

Temeraire

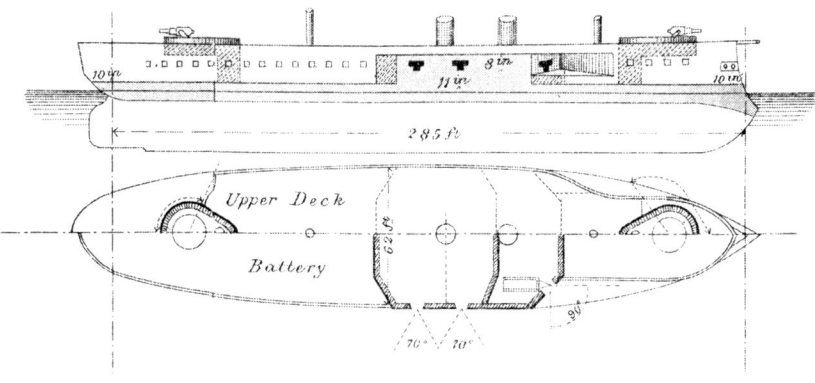

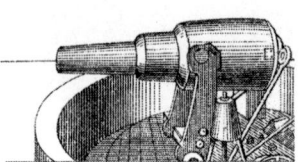

Téméraire's Gun,
loading position.

Téméraire's (
firing position

"Audacious" *Class.*

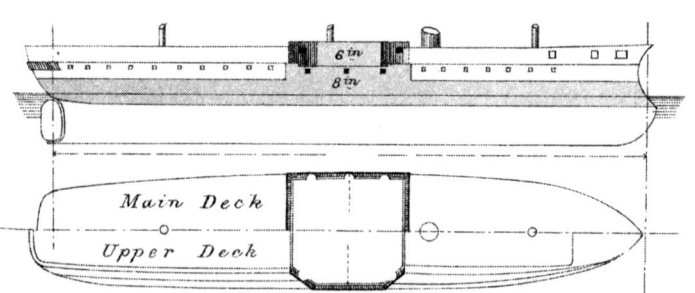

Main Deck

Upper Deck

Upper an
Batte
"Audaciou

Pl. III.

Shannon.

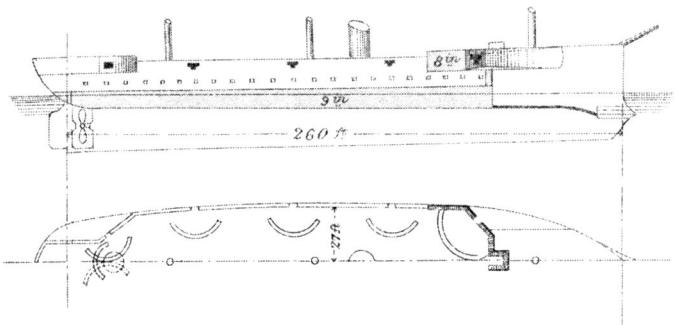

Nelson.

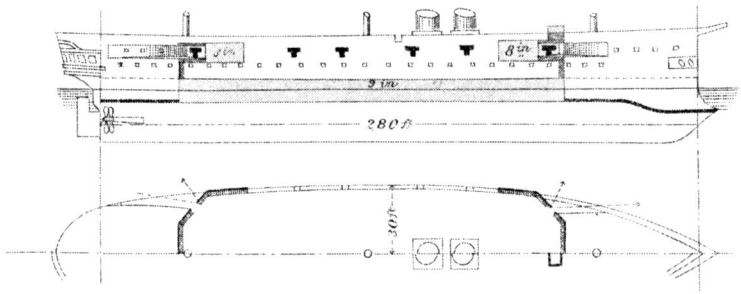

Captain.

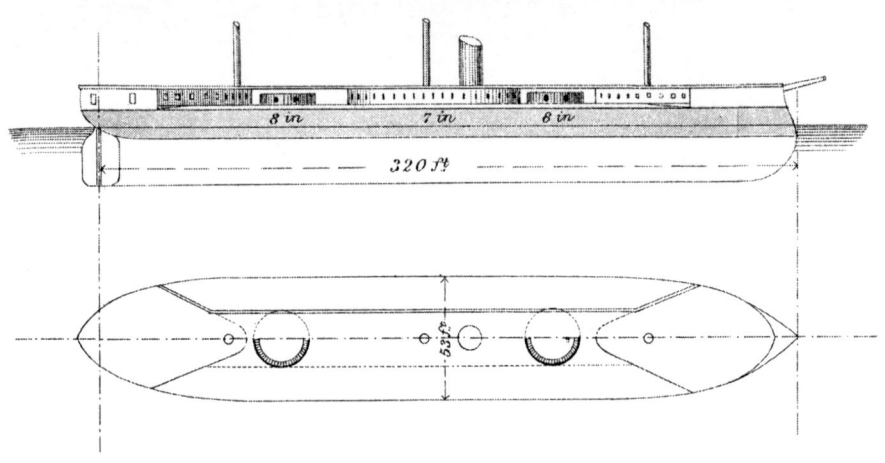

8 in   7 in   6 in

320 ft.

53 ft.

Monarch

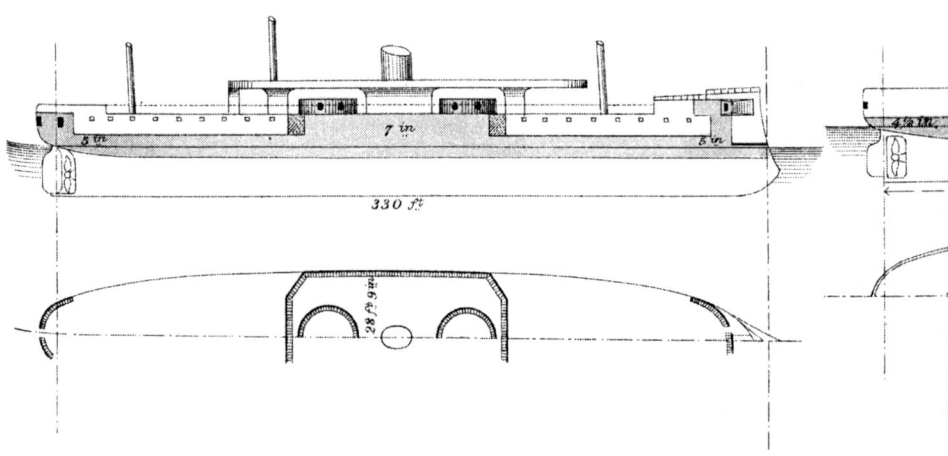

8 in   7 in   8 in

330 ft.

28 ft 9 in.

Pl. IV.

Neptune.

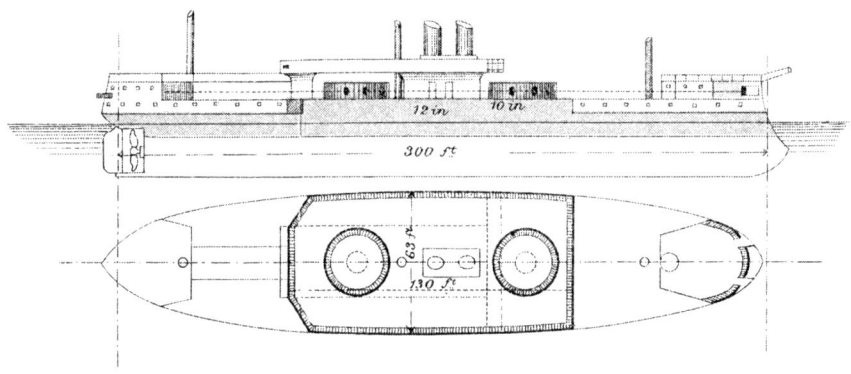

"Preussen" Class.

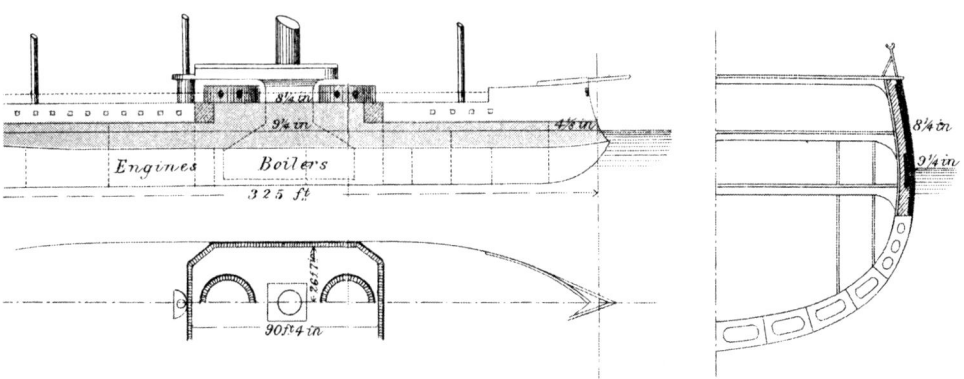

"Devastation" Class

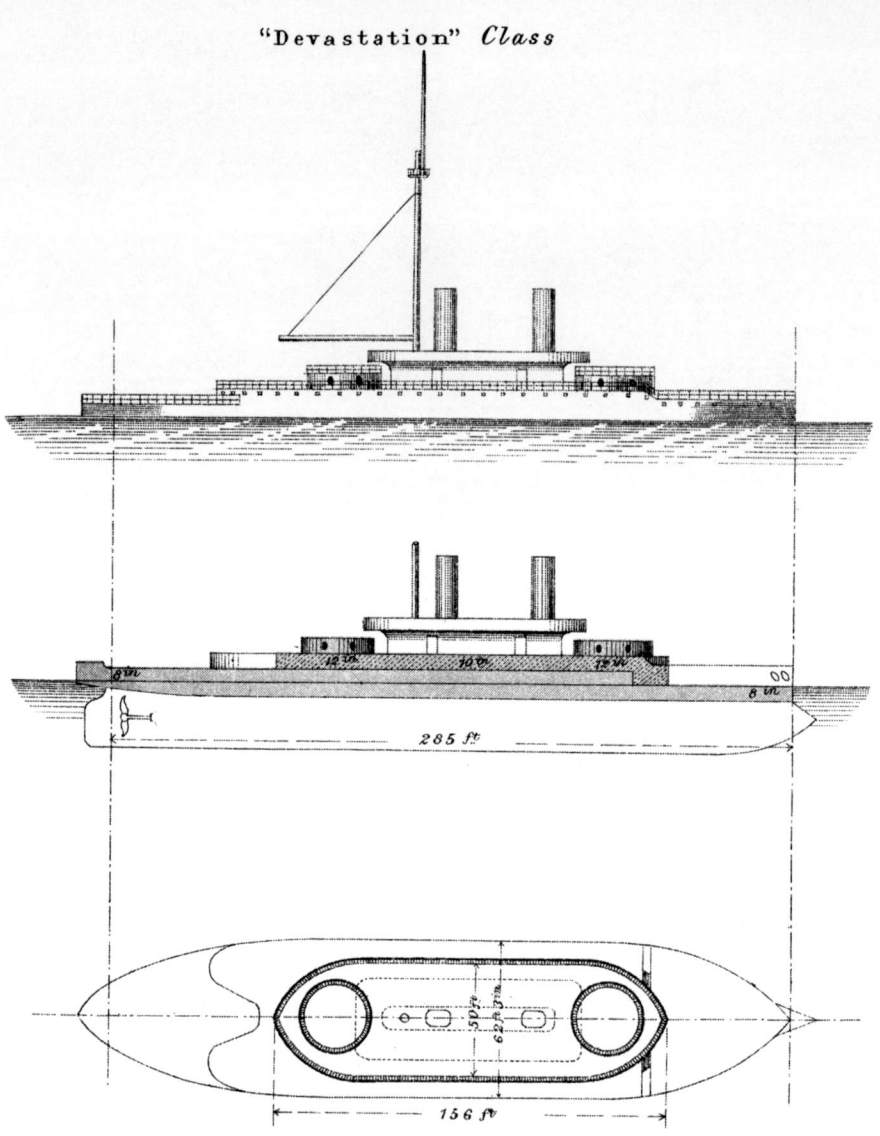

Pl. V.

Dreadnought.

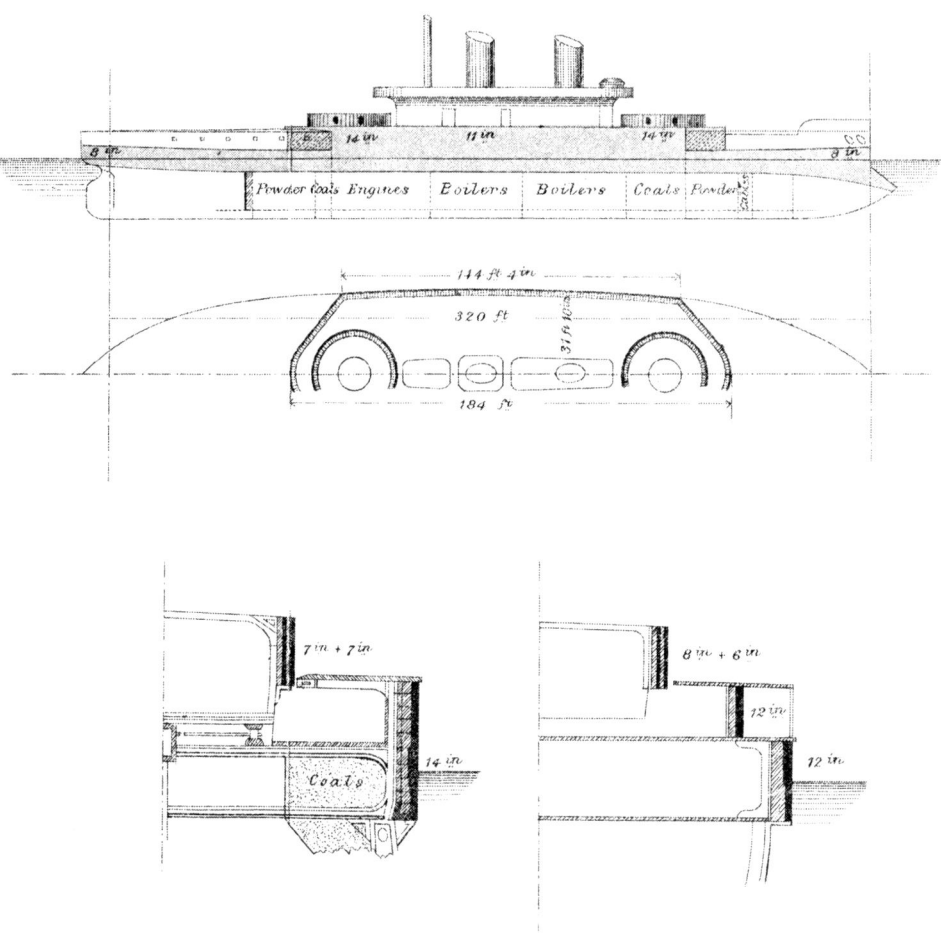

"Cyclops" Class.

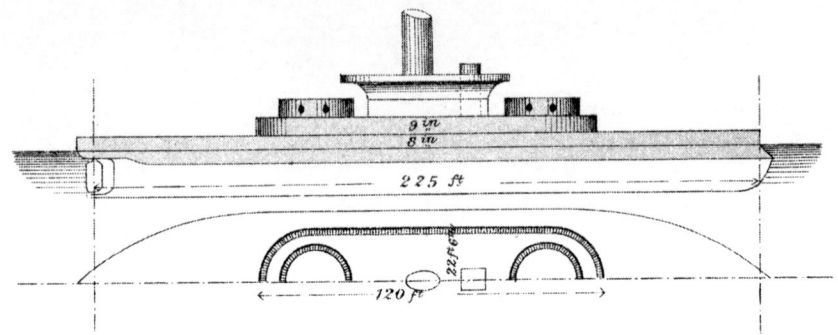

Glatton.

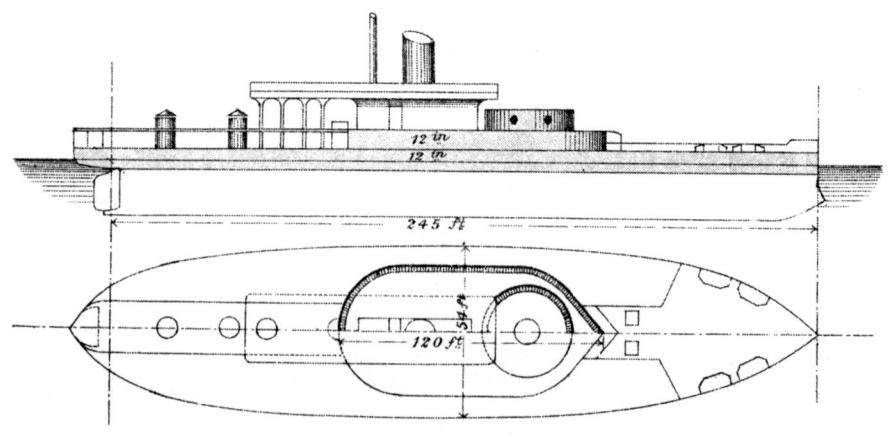

Pl. VI.

Hotspur.

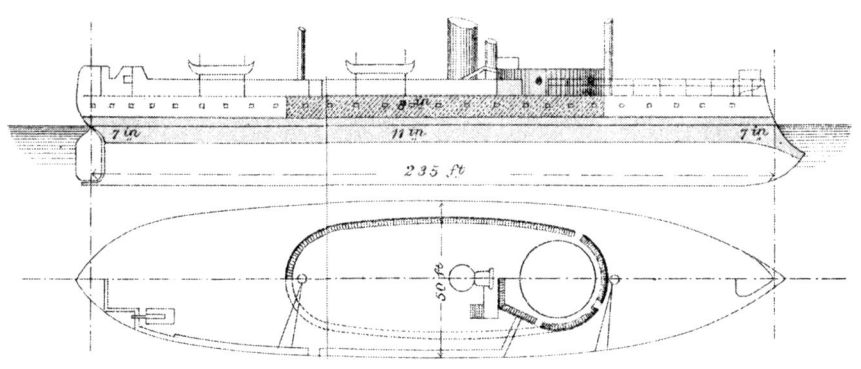

Rupert.

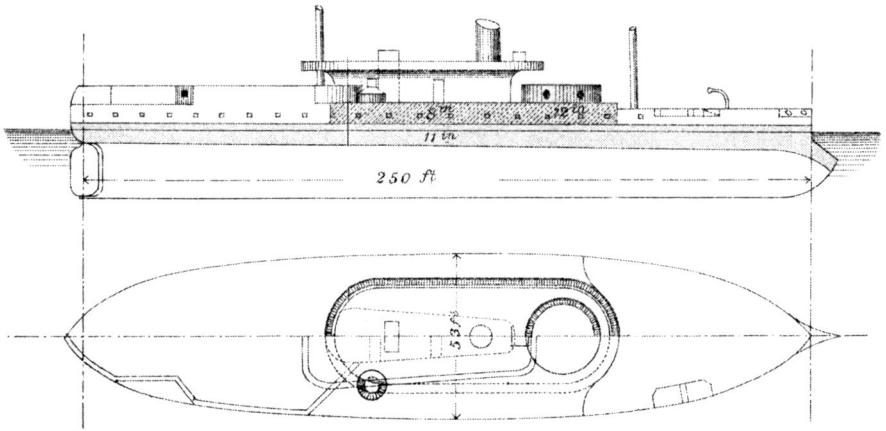

Inflexible

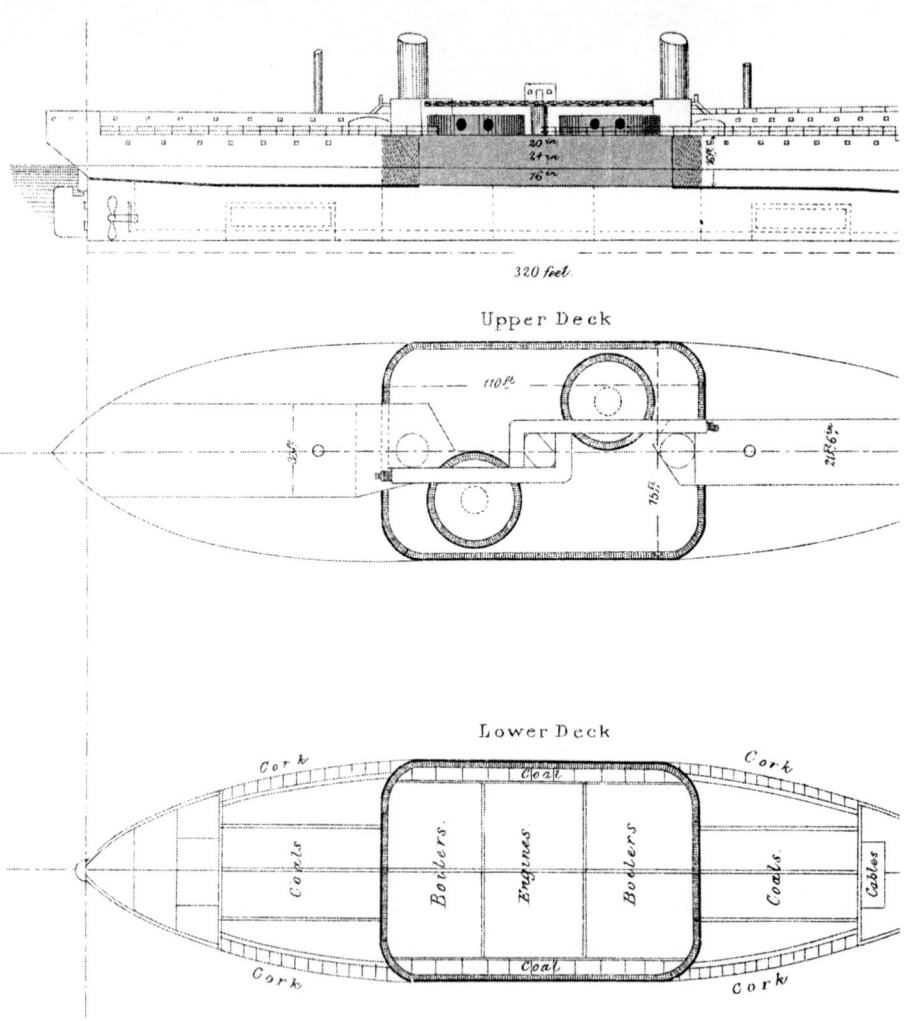

320 feet.

Upper Deck

Lower Deck

Pl. VII.

Inflexible _ after Turret.

Gloire

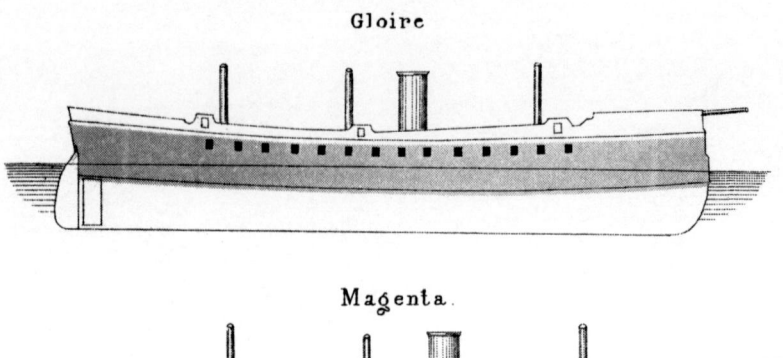

Magenta.

Alma.

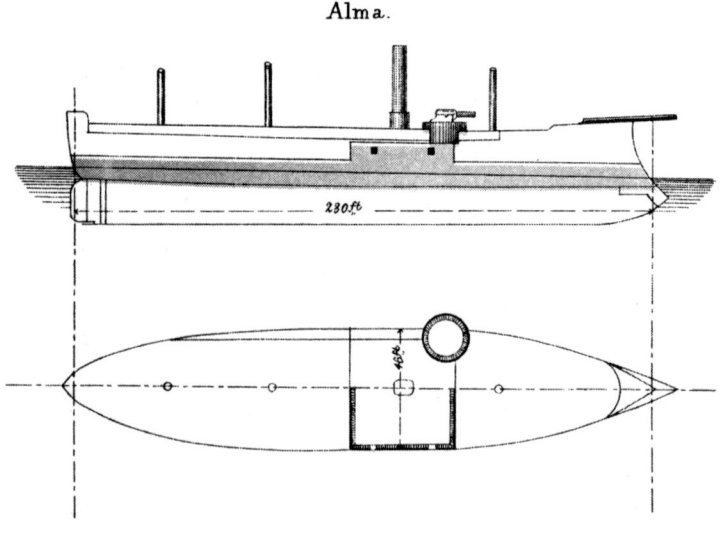

230 ft.

Richelieu.

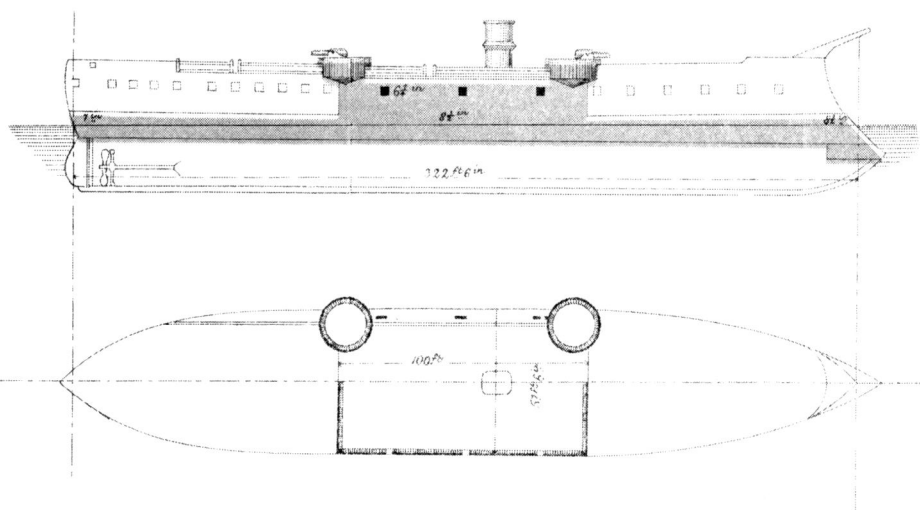

"Ocean" Class.

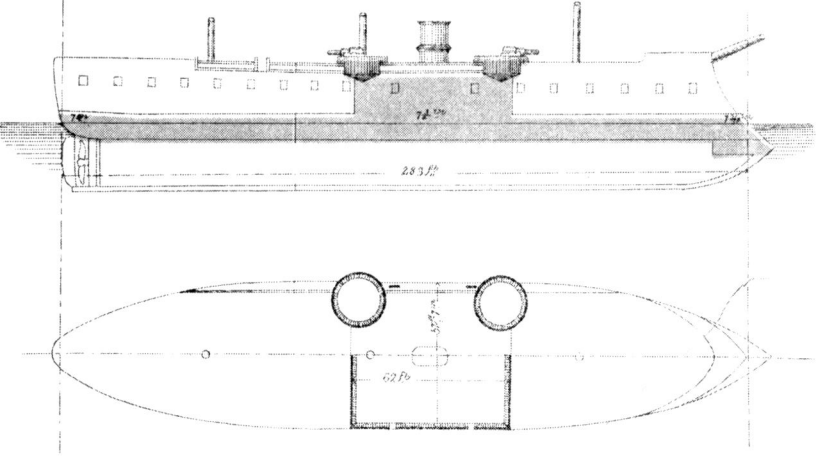

French
Dévastation.

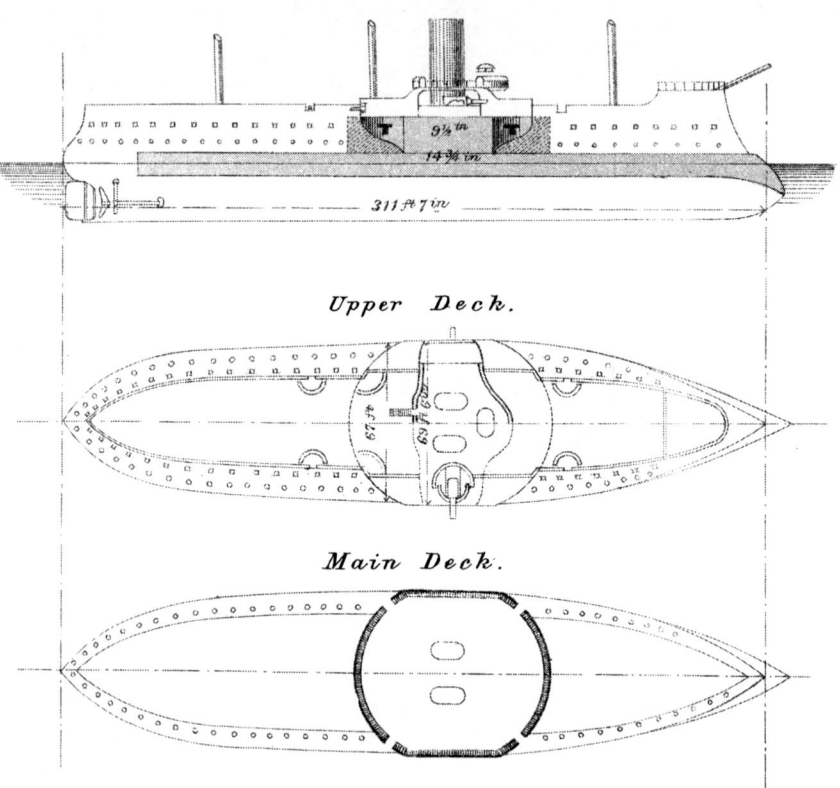

311 ft 7 in.

9½ in.
14¾ in.

Upper Deck.

Main Deck.

Pl. IX.

Amiral Duperrè.

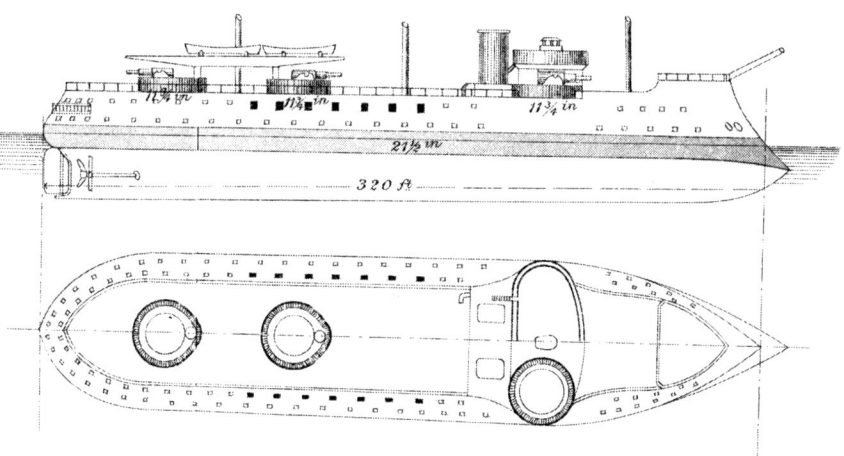

Duguesclin.

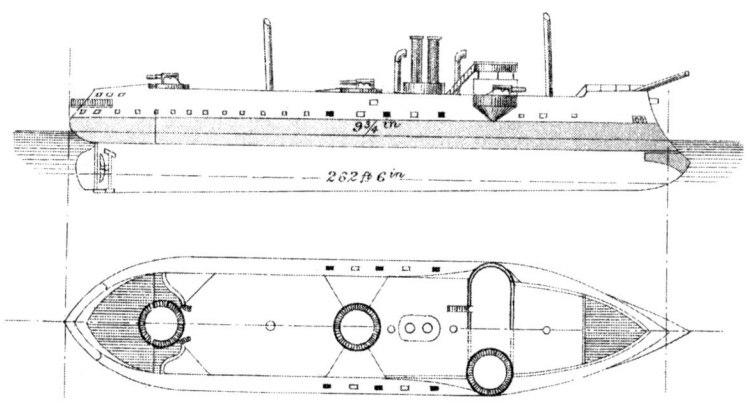

Cerbère

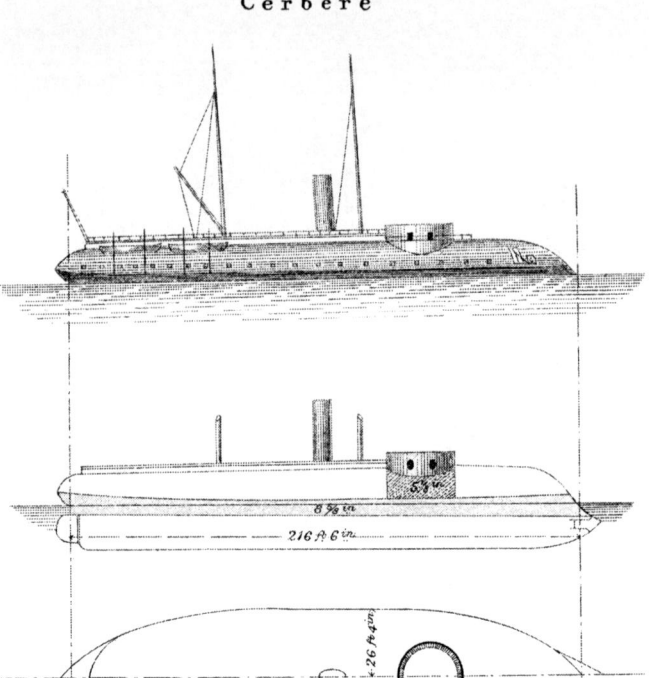

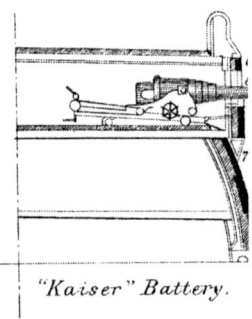

"Kaiser" Battery.

Pl. X.

König Wilhelm.

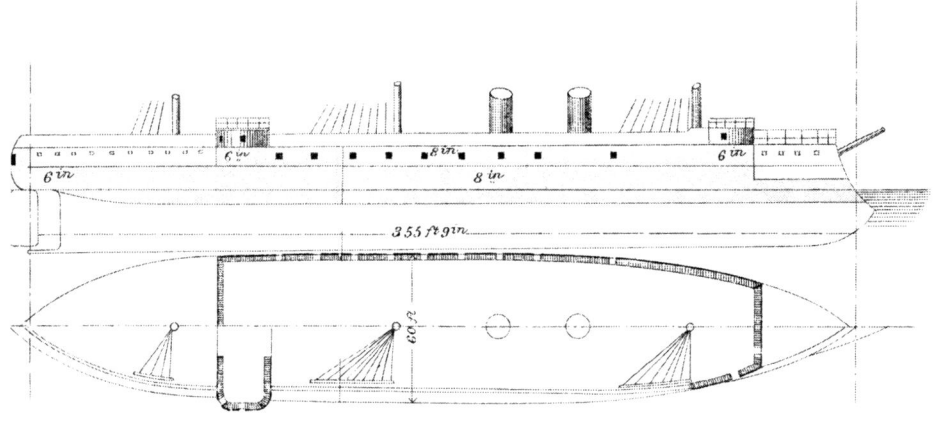

"Kaiser" Class.

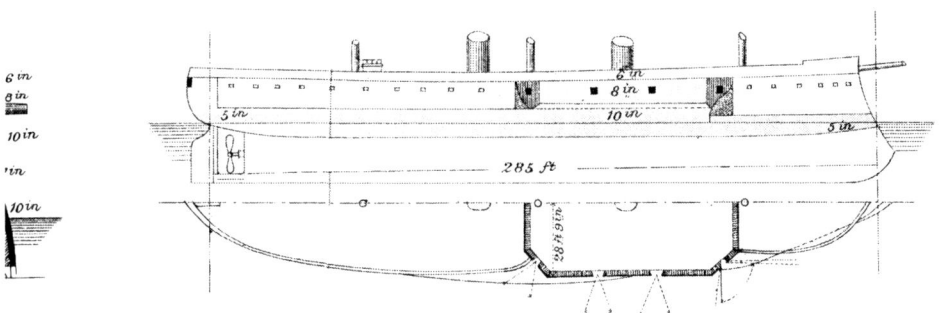

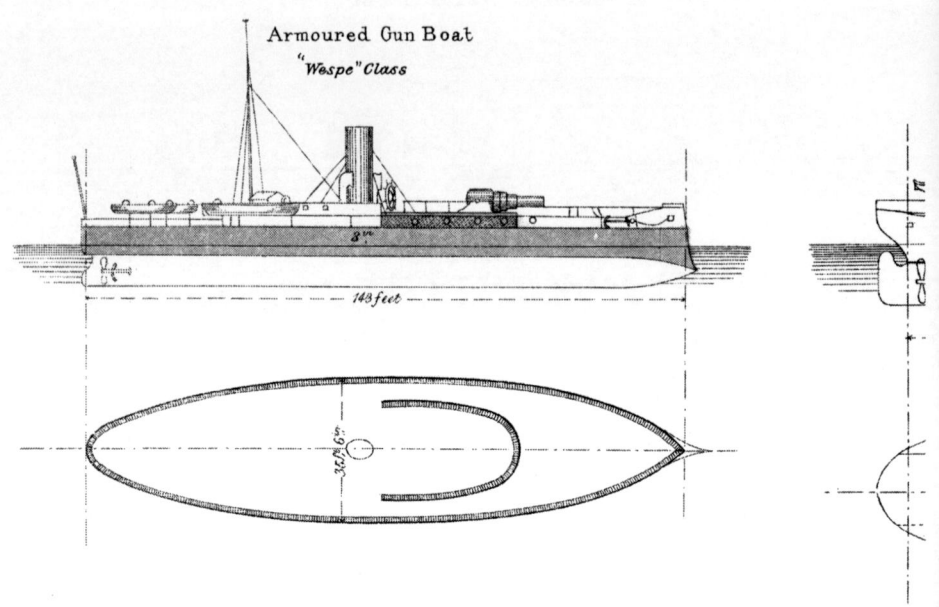

Armoured Gun Boat
"Wespe" Class

143 feet

35ft 6in

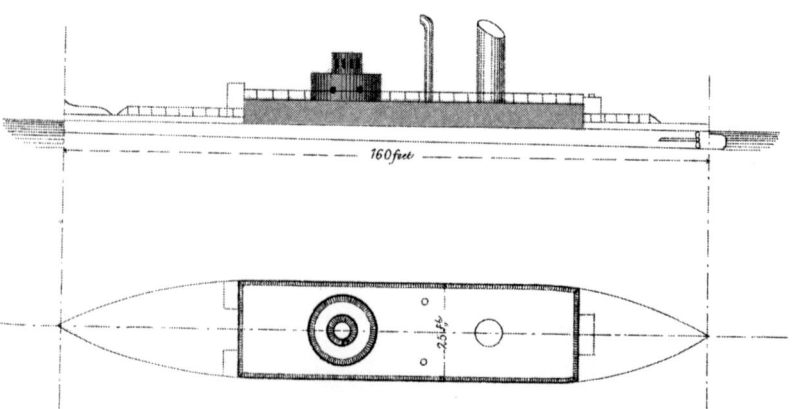

Armoured River Gun Boat
"Rhein" Class

160 feet

25ft

Pl. XI

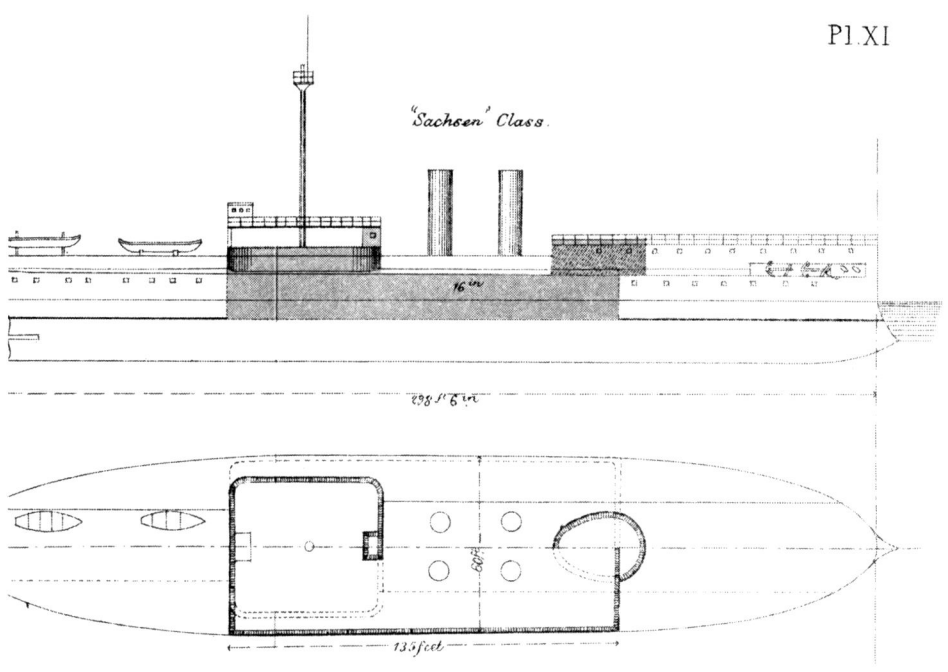

"Sachsen" Class.

16 in

135 feet

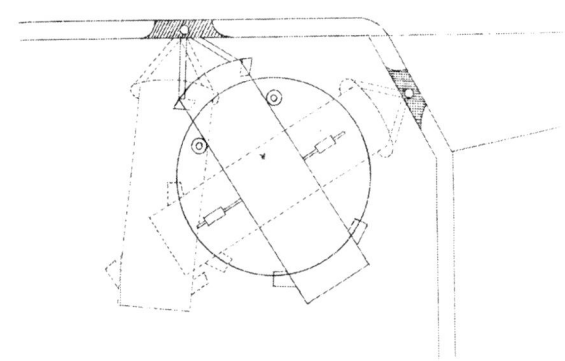

Angle Port of H.M.S. Hercules

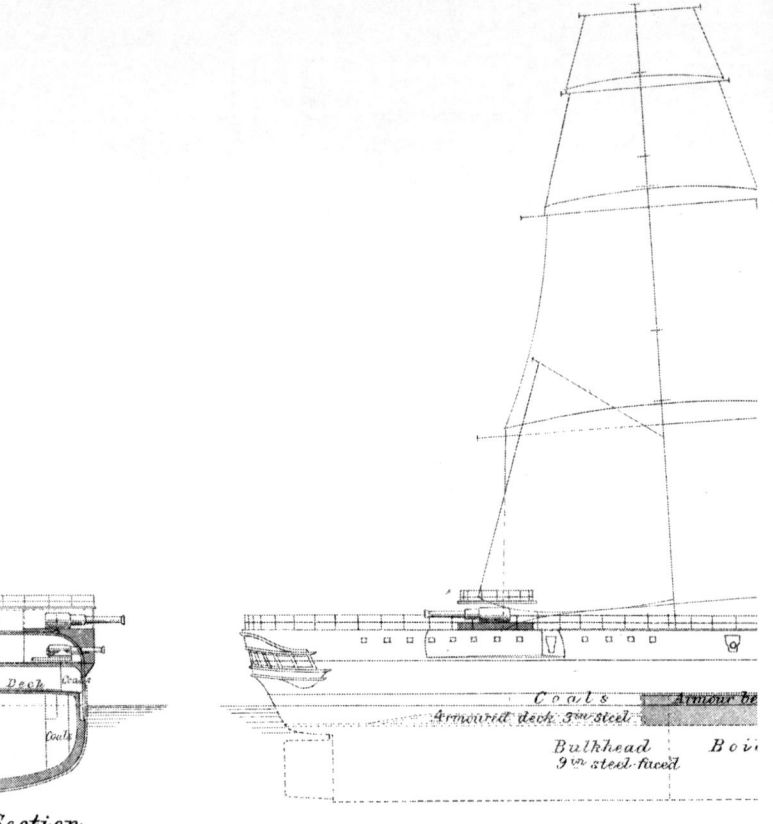

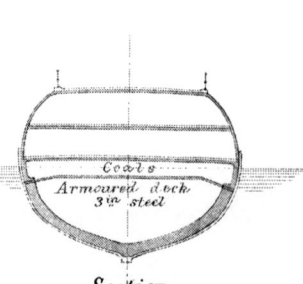

Midship Section.

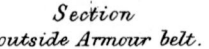

*Section
outside Armour belt.*

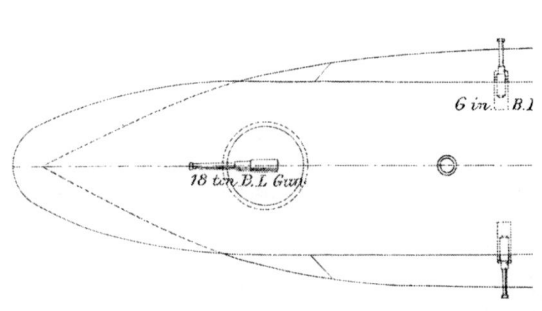

Pl. XII.

oured Cruisers

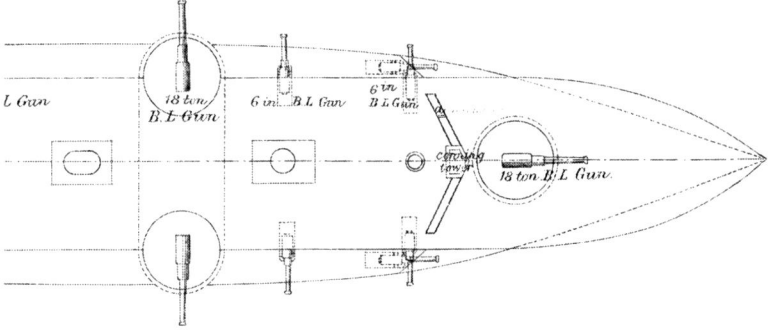

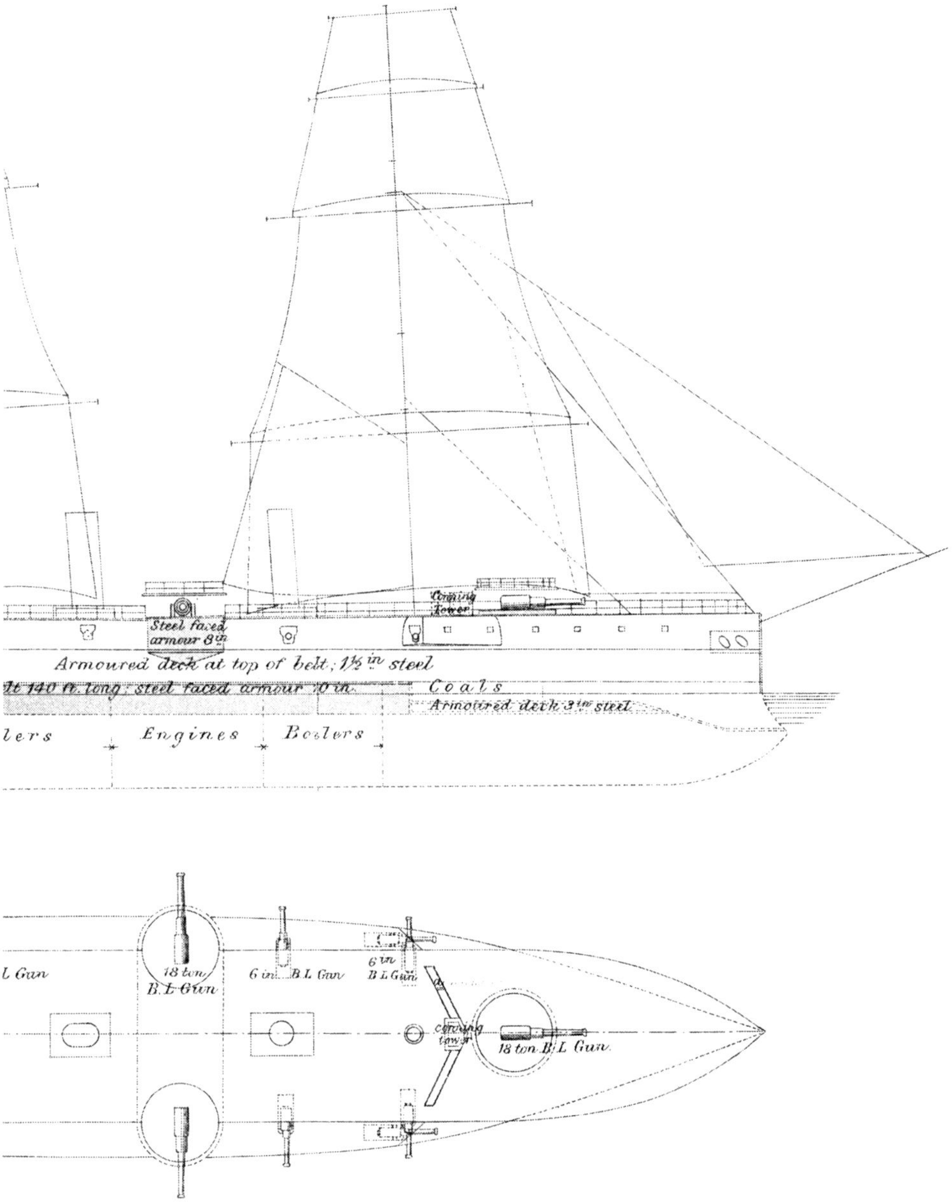

Steel faced
armour 8in

Armoured deck at top of belt ; 1½in steel

It 140 ft. long ; steel faced armour 10 in.   Coals

Armoured deck 3in steel

lers   Engines   Boilers

L Gun   18 ton   6 in   B L Gun   6 in
            B L Gun   B L Gun

                          conning
                           tower   18 ton B L Gun

Pl. XIII.

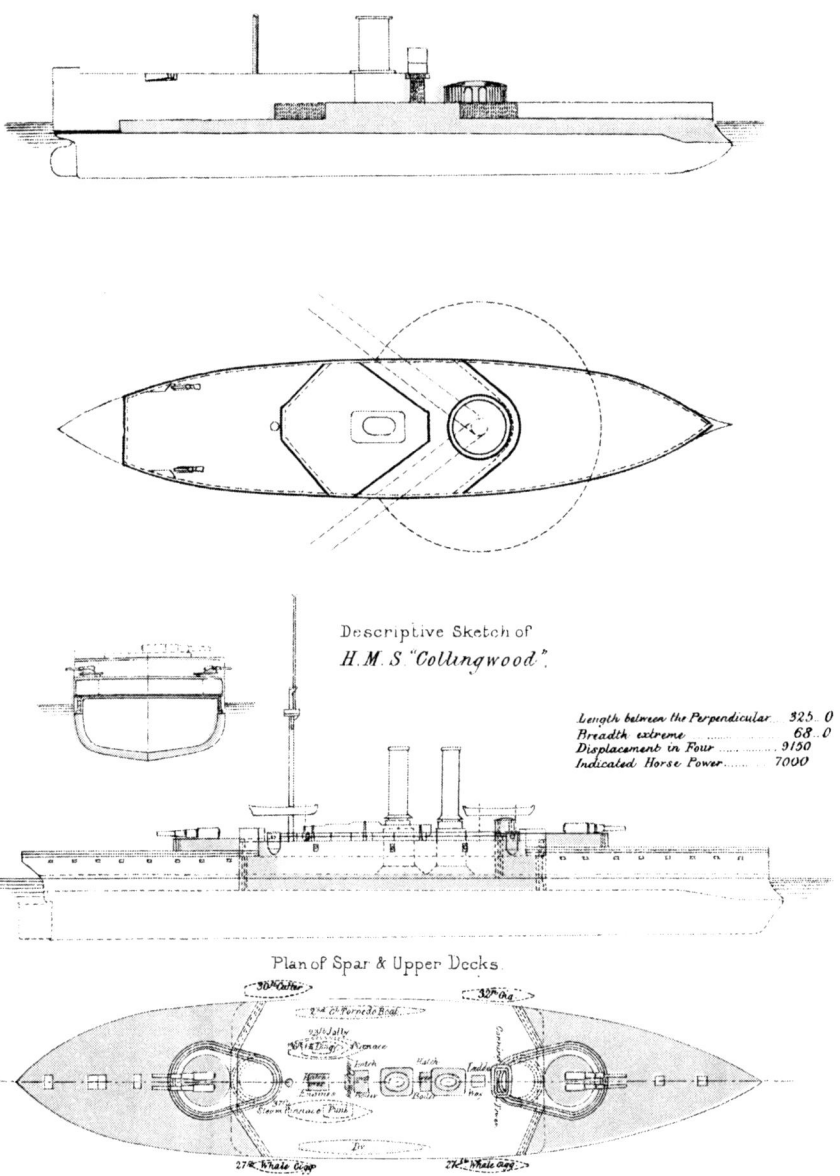

The Conqueror.
(Modified Rupert.)

Descriptive Sketch of
H.M.S "Collingwood".

Length between the Perpendicular ... 325. 0
Breadth extreme .... 68..0
Displacement in Four 9150
Indicated Horse Power 7000

Plan of Spar & Upper Decks.

Hanhart lith.

Italia and Lepanto

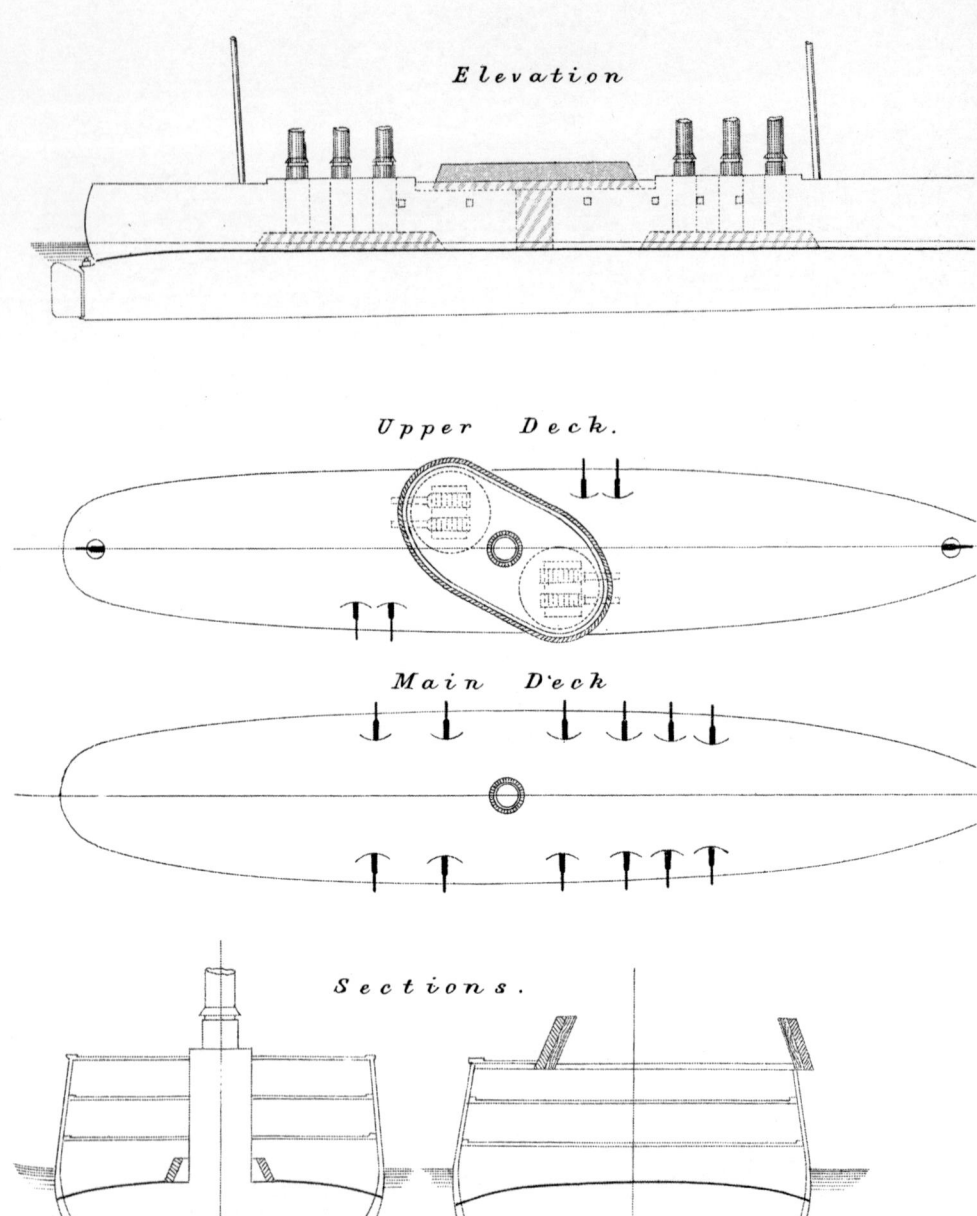

Elevation

Upper Deck.

Main Deck

Sections.

Pl. XIV.

Duilio and Dandolo.

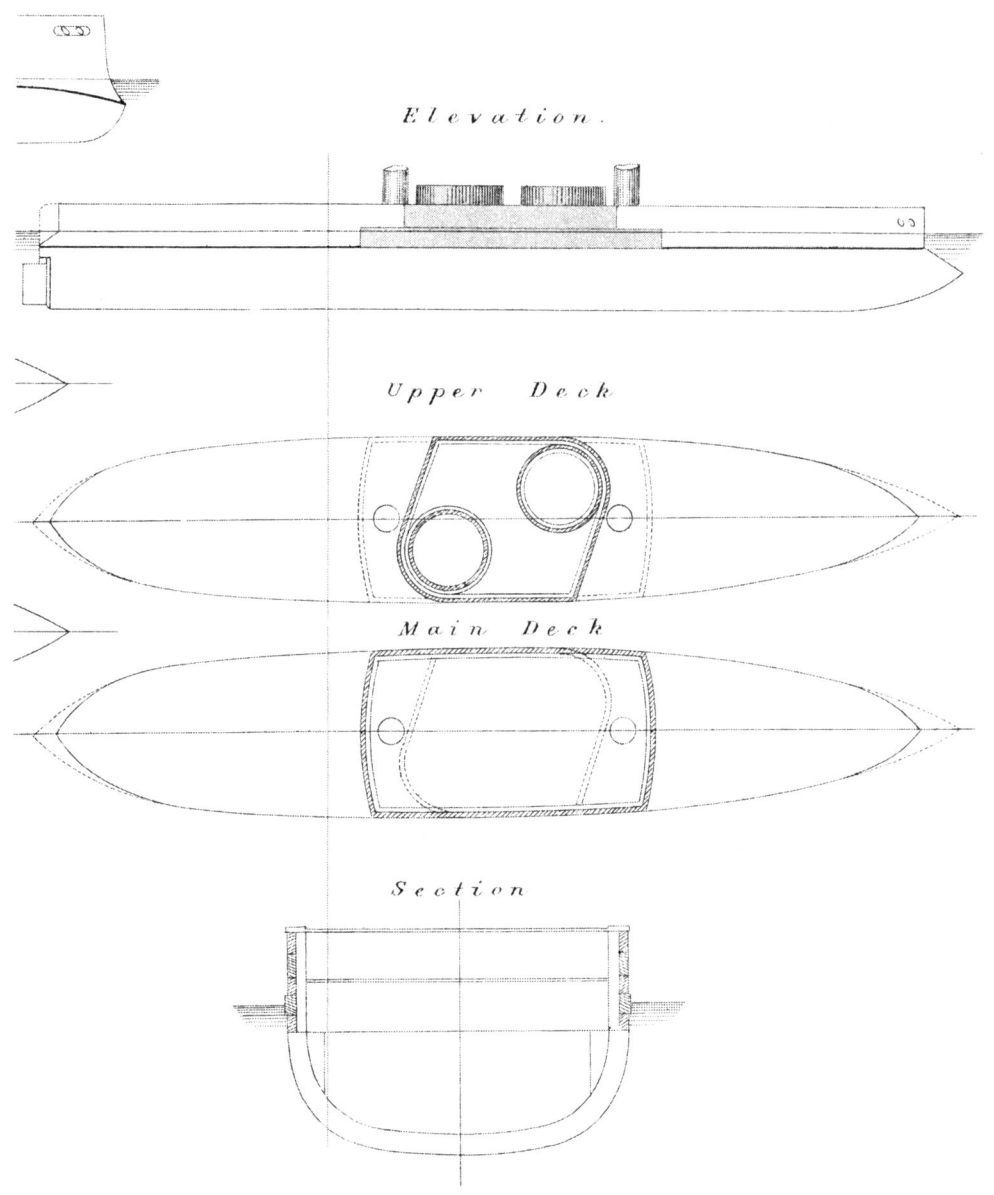

Elevation.

Upper Deck

Main Deck

Section

Lightning Source UK Ltd.
Milton Keynes UK
30 November 2010

163709UK00001B/98/P